COOK'S

ILLUSTRATED

～ 2012 ～

$35.00

Published by
America's Test Kitchen
17 Station Street
Brookline, MA 02445

ISBN-13: 978-1-936493-33-3
ISBN-10: 1-936493-33-0
ISSN: 1933-639X

To get home delivery of *Cook's Illustrated* magazine, call 800-526-8442 inside the U.S., or 515-247-7571 if calling from outside the U.S., or subscribe online at www.cooksillustrated.com.

In addition to *Cook's Illustrated* Annual Hardbound Editions available from each year of publication (1993–2012), America's Test Kitchen offers the following cookbooks and DVD sets:

THE COOK'S ILLUSTRATED COOKBOOK SERIES
The Cook's Illustrated Cookbook
The Science of Good Cooking
The America's Test Kitchen Menu Cookbook
Soups, Stews & Chilis
The Best Skillet Recipes
The Best Slow & Easy Recipes
The Best Chicken Recipes
The Best International Recipe
The Best Make-Ahead Recipe
The Best 30-Minute Recipe
The Best Light Recipe
The Cook's Illustrated Guide to Grilling and Barbecue
Best American Side Dishes
The Best Cover & Bake Recipes
The New Best Recipe
Steaks, Chops, Roasts, and Ribs
Baking Illustrated
Perfect Vegetables
Italian Classics
The Best American Classics
The Best One-Dish Suppers
The America's Test Kitchen Menu Cookbook

AMERICA'S TEST KITCHEN ANNUALS
The Best of America's Test Kitchen (2007–2013 Editions)
Cooking for Two (2009–2012 Editions)
Light & Healthy (2010–2012 Editions)

THE AMERICA'S TEST KITCHEN SERIES DVD SETS
(featuring each season's episodes from our hit public television series)
The *America's Test Kitchen* 4-DVD Set (2002–2012 Seasons)
The *America's Test Kitchen* 2-DVD Set (2001 Season)

THE AMERICA'S TEST KITCHEN SERIES COMPANION COOKBOOKS
America's Test Kitchen: The TV Companion Cookbook (2012)
America's Test Kitchen: The TV Companion Cookbook (2011)
The Complete America's Test Kitchen TV Show Cookbook (2010)
America's Test Kitchen: The TV Companion Cookbook (2009)
Behind the Scenes with America's Test Kitchen (2008)
Test Kitchen Favorites (2007)
Cooking at Home with America's Test Kitchen (2006)
America's Test Kitchen Live! (2005)
Inside America's Test Kitchen (2004)
Here in America's Test Kitchen (2003)
The America's Test Kitchen Cookbook (2002)

THE AMERICA'S TEST KITCHEN LIBRARY SERIES
The America's Test Kitchen Do-It-Yourself Cookbook
Slow Cooker Revolution
Simple Weeknight Favorites
The Best Simple Recipes
Best Grilling Recipes
Best Potluck Recipes
Blue Ribbon Desserts
From Our Grandmothers' Kitchens

ADDITIONAL BOOKS FROM AMERICA'S TEST KITCHEN
The America's Test Kitchen Quick Family Cookbook
The America's Test Kitchen Healthy Family Cookbook
The America's Test Kitchen Family Cookbook
The America's Test Kitchen Family Baking Book
The Best Simple Recipes
Slow Cooker Revolution
The Complete Cook's Country TV Show Cookbook
Cook's Country Annual Hardbound (2005–2012 Editions)
1993–2012 Cook's Illustrated Master Index

Visit our online bookstore at www.cooksillustrated.com to order any of our cookbooks and DVDs listed above. You can also order subscriptions, gift subscriptions, and any of our cookbooks and DVDs by calling 800-611-0759 inside the U.S., or at 515-246-6911 if calling from outside the U.S.

BC = Back Cover

NUMBER 114

JANUARY & FEBRUARY 2012

COOK'S
ILLUSTRATED

Reinventing
Beef Stew
Forget the Rules

Great Home Fries
And Plenty of Them

Easy Homemade
Chocolate Truffles
Better Than Store-Bought

Hearty Vegetable Tart
Perfect Free-Form Crust

Braised Pork Chops
New Route to Maximum Flavor

Tasting Spaghetti
Italian Imports vs. American-Made

Testing All-Purpose Cleaners
Perfect Croissants
Quicker Fish Chowder
A Guide to Sweeteners
Chicken Marbella Updated

www.CooksIllustrated.com
$5.95 U.S./$6.95 CANADA

CONTENTS
January & February 2012

COOK'S ILLUSTRATED

Founder and Editor Christopher Kimball
Editorial Director Jack Bishop
Executive Editor, Magazines John Willoughby
Executive Editor Amanda Agee
Test Kitchen Director Erin McMurrer
Managing Editor Rebecca Hays
Senior Editors Keith Dresser
Lisa McManus
Bryan Roof
Associate Features Editors Elizabeth Bomze
Danette St. Onge
Copy Editors Nell Beram
Megan Chromik
Associate Editors Andrea Geary
Amy Graves
Andrew Janjigian
Dan Souza
Test Cook Lan Lam
Assistant Editors Hannah Crowley
Shannon Friedmann Hatch
Taizeth Sierra
Assistant Test Cook Celeste Rogers
Executive Assistant Christine Gordon
Assistant Test Kitchen Director Gina Nistico
Senior Kitchen Assistants Meryl MacCormack
Leah Rovner
Kitchen Assistants Maria Elena Delgado
Ena Gudiel
Andrew Straaberg Finfrock
Executive Producer Melissa Baldino
Associate Producer Stephanie Stender
Contributing Editors Matthew Card
Dawn Yanagihara
Consulting Editor Scott Brueggeman
Science Editor Guy Crosby, Ph.D.

Online Managing Editor David Tytell
Online Editor Kate Mason
Online Assistant Editors Eric Grzymkowski
Mari Levine
Video Operations Manager Peter Tannenbaum
Media Producer Alexandra Pournaras
Associate Editor/Camera Operator Nick Dakoulas
Assistant Editor/Camera Operator Jesse Prent

Design Director Amy Klee
Art Director, Magazines Julie Bozzo
Deputy Art Director Susan Levin
Designer Lindsey Timko
Art Director, Marketing/Web Christine Vo
Associate Art Directors, Marketing/Web Erica Lee

Designers, Marketing/Web Elaina Natario
Mariah Tarvainen
Staff Photographer Daniel J. van Ackere
Online Photo Editor Steve Klise

Vice President, Marketing David Mack
Circulation Director Doug Wicinski
Circulation & Fulfillment Manager Carrie Fethe
Partnership Marketing Manager Pamela Putprush
Marketing Assistant Lauren Perkins
Customer Service Manager Jacqueline Valerio
Customer Service Representatives Jessica Amato
Morgan Ryan

Director of Sponsorship Sales Anne Traficante
Retail Sales & Marketing Manager Emily Logan
Client Service Manager, Sponsorship Bailey Snyder

Production Director Guy Rochford
Senior Project Manager Alice Carpenter
Production & Traffic Coordinator Kate Hux
Asset & Workflow Manager Andrew Mannone
Production & Imaging Specialists Judy Blomquist
Heather Dube
Lauren Pettapiece

Technology Director Rocco Lombardo
Systems Administrator Marcus Walser
Development Manager Robert Martinez
Software Project Manager Michelle Rushin
Business Analyst Wendy Tseng
Web Developers Chris Candelora
Cameron MacKensie

VP New Media Product Development Barry Kelly
Social Media Manager Steph Yiu

Chief Financial Officer Sharyn Chabot
Human Resources Director Adele Shapiro
Publicity Deborah Broide

PRINTED IN THE USA

LIMES Oval, thin-skinned Persian limes are the most commonly available variety in the U.S. Smaller, Ping-Pong-ball-size Key limes are less bracing; their zest and juice are whisked together with egg yolks and sweetened condensed milk to make the filling for Key lime pie. The elliptically shaped limequat, a cross between a lime and a kumquat, leans more toward sour than sweet and is typically candied. Unlike other lime varieties, its skin and pith are edible. Round, yellow-skinned sweet limes are hardly tart and can be peeled and eaten out of hand like any other low-acid citrus. Kaffir limes are aggressively sour and distinguishable by their thick, wrinkled rind. Finger limes are no bigger than a pinky. They vary from murky green to reddish-orange, and the exterior hints at the color of the rounded vesicles within. Crimson blood limes, found in Australia, are a hybrid of red finger limes and mandarin oranges. Their juice is sharp, crisp, and clean.
COVER (Mushrooms): Robert Papp; BACK COVER (Limes): John Burgoyne

America's TEST KITCHEN

RECIPES THAT WORK

America's Test Kitchen is a very real 2,500-square-foot kitchen located just outside of Boston. It is the home of *Cook's Illustrated* and *Cook's Country* magazines and is the workday destination of more than three dozen test cooks, editors, and cookware specialists. Our mission is to test recipes over and over again until we understand how and why they work and until we arrive at the best version. We also test kitchen equipment and supermarket ingredients in search of brands that offer the best value and performance. You can watch us work by tuning in to *America's Test Kitchen* (www.AmericasTestKitchenTV.com) on public television.

THE GOLDEN RULE

Ed Perry is a former marine biologist who studied sponges; they are easy to photograph underwater since, as he says with a grin, they don't swim around much. He now works full-time building black powder rifles, old-fashioned flintlocks, the same type of gun used in the American Revolution. A few weekends ago, I stopped by to pick up a double-barrel 20-gauge shotgun; it was heavy, exquisitely crafted, and also a reminder that during the American Revolution, actually hitting the intended target was rare, especially on rainy days when the saying "Keep your powder dry" was good advice. A wet day in 1776 was likely to be a day off or a marching day if you were, say, one of the Ethan Allen boys from Vermont.

Just as I was about to leave, Ed drew a line on a piece of paper and said, "If you had to cut this line into two parts while maintaining a sense of both unity and diversity, how would you do it?" Cutting it in half wouldn't work since there would be no diversity, but some random spot—say, cutting the line near one end—didn't help with the idea of unity. The answer was to cut the line at the "golden ratio," so that the ratio of the large part of the line to the small was equal to the ratio of the entire line to the large part. (Specifically, this works out to be about 5 to 3 or, to be exact, 1.618 . . .) This is also the basis for the famous Fibonacci series, in which the next number in a sequence is the sum of the last two numbers (1 + 1 = 2, 1 + 2 = 3, 3 + 2 = 5, 5 + 3 = 8 . . .). As this series progresses, it approaches

the golden ratio of 1.618. And as Ed pointed out, with a bit of transposing, these Fibonacci numbers were also the figures used in the da Vinci code. He went on to show me that this ratio was used in all the parts of an 18th century rifle, barrel to stock, rifle length to barrel. And as any architect knows, the same ratio was used for centuries in building design.

In Vermont, most of us live in small towns. Ours has a firehouse, two churches (each uses the services of the same minister), and a country store, Sherman's, that sells pretty good coffee, miscellaneous hardware, jarred pig's knuckles, beer, and nickel candy but no gas (for years, to discourage business the sign on the pump read "$8.21/gallon"). We also have a small library with Saturday night movies, a surplus of sap houses, a veterinarian, a lawyer, and two large farms. If you make the time to talk to the locals, you'll find out that Doug's last deer was shot at 84 yards using a long-barreled pistol with a scope and that Nancy knows more about what to do on a horse than many cowboys. Axel is always ready with a fish story, and just when you wonder if even half of it is true, he takes out a few color prints that prove him no liar. And there is no dearth of expertise in town about bread baking, logging, farming, hunting, Shakespeare, training dogs, history, playing the blues, construction, big

Christopher Kimball

equipment, and auto repair.

It isn't easy to scratch the surface of a Vermonter, but once you see the pattern you'll see it in everyone you meet. The larger part is self-reliance, the knowledge that on a cold wintry night you can head down into the dirt-floor basement and restart the furnace, find the horses that broke through the fence overnight, or tell the difference between sugar and red maple. The smaller part is an intimate sense of place, to know who lived in Beattie Hollow a generation ago, the last time the Sheldon store was still open for business, or who was buried standing straight up in his grave. As in the golden ratio, the two things are intimately related, and together they form a constant, a thread that runs all the way from the town line by Hebron to the end of Chambers Hollow, where if you look closely enough, you'll also come across the haunted chimney.

We often measure life by the number of new experiences we accumulate; Vermonters measure what remains steady. There are good years and bad years in sap production or the number of deer weighed in at Sherman's store, but each of us is expected to measure up in the eyes of our neighbors. That's the golden rule in country living, a sense of self and place in service of others, a formula that can be calculated right down to the last decimal place.

COOK'S ILLUSTRATED MAGAZINE
Cook's Illustrated magazine (ISSN 1068-2821), number 114, is published bimonthly by Boston Common Press Limited Partnership, 17 Station St., Brookline, MA 02445. Copyright 2012 Boston Common Press Limited Partnership. Periodicals postage paid at Boston, Mass., and additional mailing offices USPS #012487. Publications Mail Agreement No. 40020778. Return undeliverable Canadian addresses to P.O. Box 875, Station A, Windsor, ON N9A 6P2. POSTMASTER: Send address changes to *Cook's Illustrated*, P.O. Box 6018, Harlan, IA 51593-1518. For subscription and gift subscription orders, subscription inquiries, or change-of-address notices, visit us at www.AmericasTestKitchen.com/customerservice or write us at *Cook's Illustrated*, P.O. Box 6018, Harlan, IA 51593-1518.

FOR LIST RENTAL INFORMATION, CONTACT Specialists Marketing Services, Inc., 777 Terrace Ave., 4th Floor, Hasbrouck Heights, NJ 07604; 201-865-5800.
EDITORIAL OFFICE 17 Station St., Brookline, MA 02445; 617-232-1000; fax 617-232-1572. Subscription inquiries, visit www.AmericasTestKitchen.com/customerservice or call 800-526-8442.
POSTMASTER Send all new orders, subscription inquiries, and change-of-address notices to *Cook's Illustrated*, P.O. Box 6018, Harlan, IA 51593-1518.

ILLUSTRATION: RANDY GLASS

A Winning Kombu-nation

I've heard about putting a strip of seaweed in the pot when cooking dried beans. What purpose does it serve?

JAMES MACLEAN
TAMPA, FLA.

➢ Some sources claim that dried *kombu* (a kelp used extensively in Japanese cuisine, primarily for making *dashi* stock) neutralizes difficult-to-digest small carbohydrates in beans—not a theory we planned on evaluating in the test kitchen! But we hazarded a guess that the seaweed could also act as a flavor enhancer. Kombu, after all, is one of the richest sources of glutamates and nucleotides, which together produce an amplified umami taste. Our taste tests showed that kombu not only boosts bean flavor but also improves texture: Pinto beans soaked and then cooked in water with a strip of kombu had soft skins and smooth interiors; soaked beans cooked in water alone were more grainy and tough.

Our favorite bean-cooking method calls for overnight brining; the sodium in the salt solution replaces some of the calcium and magnesium in the bean skins, making them more permeable and resulting in more tender beans inside and out. Kombu works in a similar fashion, its sodium and potassium ions trading places with minerals in the beans to create a smoother, creamier consistency. But we also found that kombu eliminates the need for the overnight soak; dried beans that went directly into the pot with the seaweed were nearly as tender as those that had been soaked in plain water or even brined.

We still prefer brining beans because we always have salt on hand, but if you're the last-minute type, you might consider stocking dried kombu (available at Asian markets and natural foods stores) in your pantry. In 4 quarts of water, simmer 1 pound of beans, 1 tablespoon of salt (for seasoning), and one 3 by 5-inch strip of kombu until the beans are tender.

BRINY FIX FOR GRAINY BEANS
A little *kombu* (a form of seaweed) added to the pot with dried beans eliminates the need for soaking.

SEND US YOUR QUESTIONS We will provide a complimentary one-year subscription for each letter we print. Send your inquiry, name, address, and daytime telephone number to Notes from Readers, *Cook's Illustrated*, P.O. Box 470589, Brookline, MA 02447, or to NotesFromReaders@AmericasTestKitchen.com.

Cardamom Conundrum

On a recent visit to a spice shop, I was surprised to see three different kinds of cardamom pods for sale: white, green, and black. How do they differ?

JESSICA BRADWELL
SAGINAW, MICH.

➢ The delicate complexity of cardamom makes it a popular spice in several cuisines, most notably Middle Eastern, Indian, and Scandinavian. Green cardamom is the most commonly found variety in the United States, and white cardamom is simply green cardamom that has been bleached so as not to discolor light-colored baked goods and other foods. Black cardamom (also called large cardamom) is not true cardamom but a relative.

To test for flavor differences, we removed the seeds from the inedible green, white, and black cardamom pods, ground the seeds in a coffee grinder, and used the spice to flavor sugar cookies. We also crushed all three kinds of pods and steeped them in the rice cooking water for separate batches of our Chicken Biryani.

All three forms of cardamom boasted similar flavors—pine-y, sweet, and floral, with a peppery, warm finish—but intensity levels varied. In both applications, the green cardamom was the most vibrant and balanced. Not surprisingly, the flavor of the bleached pods paled in comparison to the green, and—since they cost almost twice as much—we won't purchase them again. Black cardamom offered hints of eucalyptus, and as it is generally dried over fire, it boasted smoky nuances that we appreciated in savory biryani but not in cookies. For an all-purpose choice, we'll be going green when it comes to cardamom.

| BLACK: | GREEN: | WHITE: |
| SMOKY | ALL-PURPOSE | BLAND |

Ready-to-Use Quinoa

I love quinoa but it's a pain to rinse before cooking. Is there an easier way?

LAUREN BUCKLAND
OAKLAND, CALIF.

➢ Thoroughly washing quinoa before cooking removes all traces of its bitter saponin coating, nature's way of making the high-protein seeds unattractive to birds and other seedeaters. In addition to being unpalatable, saponin is mildly toxic, causing low-level gastrointestinal distress in some people.

But cleaning quinoa is a chore because the tiny seeds (often mistakenly called grains) can easily slip through a fine-mesh strainer and down the drain.

Many brands of quinoa available in supermarkets today are prewashed and require no rinsing. We tested one prewashed brand against traditional quinoa to see if anything besides the bitterness was lost. We found that the traditional quinoa offered no flavor or textural advantages.

Prewashed quinoa costs a few cents more per ounce, but we think the convenience is worth it.

Quick Fix for Corked Wine?

It doesn't happen often, but every now and then I find myself with a corked bottle of wine. Is there anything I can do with it—besides pour it down the drain?

VIG KRISHNAMURTHY
CAMBRIDGE, MASS.

➢ The chemical culprit responsible for a "corked," or tainted, bottle of wine—which will have an unmistakable musty smell and acrid taste—is TCA (2,4,6-trichloroanisole). TCA is produced when fungi naturally present in the cork encounter chlorophenols—ironically a product of the chlorine bleaching process used to sterilize cork. While TCA is harmless to health, it renders wine undrinkable.

It never occurred to us that there might be a way to salvage the wine, but with a little digging, we actually found a quirky recommendation: Submerge a ball of plastic wrap in the wine and let it sit for a while. As odd as it sounds, the theory behind the suggestion makes sense: The polyethylene material attracts the TCA, effectively removing it from the wine.

With nothing to lose, we tracked down four corked bottles, poured half of each into a jar with a loose wad of plastic wrap, sealed the lids, and soaked them for 10 minutes, shaking each sample occasionally. When we sipped the treated wines, we found that the nasty "dirty-socks" odor and bitterness from the TCA were indeed greatly reduced. But we also noticed that the plastic had absorbed many of the desirable aromatic compounds, leaving the wines tasting flat and muted—and still unfit for drinking or cooking. Your best bet: Return the tainted wine for a refund.

THE PULL OF PLASTIC
Submerging plastic wrap in tainted wine removes bitter taste—but also pulls out desirable flavor compounds in the process.

Pickling Salt

I've noticed that many pickle recipes call for pickling salt. What is this ingredient? And is there a substitute?

JOSEPHINE MORE
WARREN, R.I.

➤ Pickling salt is pure sodium chloride that's free of the anticaking agents and other additives found in table salt. This means that it dissolves completely in brine, leaving the liquid perfectly clear. Table salt, on the other hand, includes a small amount of calcium silicate or silico-aluminate, which keeps the small crystals from clumping during storage. These additives are not water-soluble (if they were, they could not perform their intended function), so they can make a brine cloudy.

To find a substitute, we singled out another salt that we know doesn't include additives: kosher salt.

IN A PICKLE
Free of anticaking agents, pickling salt dissolves clearly.

Except for a larger crystal size, it is otherwise identical to pickling salt. Because of the size difference (and because kosher salt crystal size varies from brand to brand), the salts cannot be directly substituted. For every teaspoon of pickling salt, you'll need 2 teaspoons of Diamond Crystal Kosher Salt or 1½ teaspoons of Morton's Kosher Salt.

Aluminum Cookware Controversy

I've heard conflicting reports that cooking in aluminum pots and pans is risky because aluminum can leach into the food. Should I avoid using aluminum cookware?

DENISE TING
CAMBRIDGE, MASS.

➤ Lightweight aluminum is an excellent heat conductor, but it's also highly reactive with acidic foods such as tomatoes, vinegar, and citrus. Cooking these in aluminum can alter the food's flavor and appearance and leave the pan with a pitted surface. In our tests, we detected an unpleasant metallic taste in tomato sauce and lemon curd cooked in aluminum pots.

The amount of aluminum that leaches into food, however, is minimal. In lab tests, tomato sauce that we cooked in an aluminum pot for two hours and then stored in the same pot overnight was found to contain only .0024 milligrams of aluminum per cup. (A single antacid tablet may contain more than 200 milligrams of aluminum.) Our science editor reports that the consensus in the medical community is that using aluminum cookware poses no health threat.

In short: While untreated aluminum is not unsafe, it should not be used with acidic foods, which may ruin both the food and the cookware. Also note that aluminum cookware that has been anodized (hardened through a process that renders it nonreactive) or clad in a nonreactive material, such as stainless steel or a nonstick coating, does not leach into or react with foods.

WHAT IS IT?

I came across this gadget at a roadside antique shop. Do you have any idea what it is?

ROBERTA DALY
FRAMINGHAM, MASS.

Your item is a Squeezo Strainer, which dates back to 1907, when an Italian immigrant, Anthony Berarducci, brought sketches of the hand-cranked milling machine to America. Twelve years later, he began manufacturing the tool himself. The device quickly prepares fresh or steamed fruits and vegetables for sauces and purees. Whole produce is placed in the 2½-quart hopper, and with gentle pressure from the plunger and a few turns of the handle, juice and pulp flow down the ramp into a bowl. Unlike a food mill, which collects skins and seeds in its hopper that must be cleaned between batches, the Squeezo conveniently expels waste into a separate container. Squeezos are still being manufactured today and are available for around $200.

SQUEEZE PLAY
The Squeezo Strainer works just as advertised, effortlessly pureeing fruit and leaving the skin and seeds behind.

Muffin Pan Myth

I've always been told that if you're making a half batch of muffins or cupcakes and thus don't fill all the cups in the pan with batter, you should fill the empty cups with water. Is this really necessary?

GAIL JENSEN
CINCINNATI, OHIO

➤ Proponents of this practice contend that filling empty cups with water serves two functions: preventing the pan from warping and acting as a "heat sink" to ensure that muffins next to empty cups heat evenly (avoiding stunted growth or spotty browning).

We tested this theory by baking one muffin pan completely filled with batter, one pan in which only half of the 12 cups were filled with batter and the remaining six with water, and one pan in which six of the cups were filled with batter and the other six left empty. The results? All muffins had the same height, texture, and color, and none of the tins warped.

On reflection, the results made sense: In a full 12-cup muffin pan, all but the two center muffins are directly exposed to the oven's heat on at least one side to no ill effect. Furthermore, if your muffin pan warps, that's a sign that you need to find a better quality pan.

A PAN HALF FULL
A shortage of batter won't cause short muffins.

Black Rice

I've recently started seeing black rice at my supermarket. Can you tell me more about it?

KEN SIMPSON
GENEVA, N.Y.

➤ Like brown rice, black rice is unpolished, meaning that the hull of the grain—a rich source of insoluble fiber—is still intact. But only black rice contains anthocyanins, the same antioxidant compounds that make blueberries and blackberries such valuable additions to our diets. These compounds are what turn the rice a deep purple as it cooks.

Many varieties and brands of black rice are available; we cooked up Forbidden Rice by Lotus Foods, adding 3½ cups of water and 1 teaspoon of salt to 2 cups of rice and cooking it covered over low heat. The grains were tender in just 30 minutes (about half the time it takes to cook brown rice). The cooked grains remained distinct and firm to the bite, with tasters describing the flavor as pleasantly nutty and slightly sweet. As an even more nutritious, quicker cooking alternative to brown rice, what's not to like?

IS BLACK THE NEW BROWN?
Like brown rice, black rice is highly nutritious, plus it cooks in about half the time.

ILLUSTRATION: JOHN BURGOYNE

Quick Tips

⤛ COMPILED BY SHANNON FRIEDMANN HATCH ⤜

Cooking with Computers

Len Schiff of Little Neck, N.Y., often refers to recipes on his tablet computer while cooking, but he doesn't want to touch the screen mid-prep with hands covered in oil, flour, or raw chicken juices. Instead of having to repeatedly wash his hands, he picks up a baby carrot to use as a stylus for scrolling. When he's done cooking, he simply throws the carrot away.

Less-Mess Nut Chopping

No matter how carefully Harrison Ranson of Novato, Calif., chopped nuts with his chef's knife, they inevitably flew across the cutting board and countertop. He now uses his apple cutter: Pressing the tool straight down chops the nuts into pieces while keeping them in place.

Tidier Cake Frosting

After cutting out a circle of parchment paper to line her cake pan, Kelly Herold of Newport Beach, Calif., would always discard the remainder of the sheet. Then she discovered that the leftover paper makes the perfect "bib" for protecting her cake plate when she frosts the baked layers.

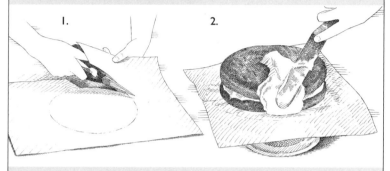

1. Use the bottom of a cake pan to trace a circle on a piece of parchment paper. Cut out the circle, use it to line the cake pan, and reserve the rest of the parchment sheet.
2. When the cake is ready to frost, place it on a cake plate and arrange the reserved parchment around it like a bib. Discard the parchment after frosting.

Taming Curled Parchment Paper

Guild Nichols of Boston, Mass., was tired of the way that the parchment paper he uses to line a baking sheet inevitably curls toward the center as he's trying to portion out cookie or biscuit dough. He found a solution: He places a small magnet at each corner of the sheet to hold down the paper. After he's done portioning, he removes the magnets and places the baking sheet in the oven.

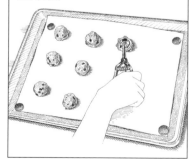

Keeping Dry Goods Dry

David Shaw of Somerville, Mass., has found a way to beat the humidity that can turn opened dry goods in his pantry stale. He fills empty paper tea bags (or small pouches of cheesecloth) with rice and places them inside the storage containers before reclosing. The rice absorbs any extra moisture and can easily be replaced as it becomes necessary.

Storing Baking Stones

A baking stone helps create crisp, evenly browned pizza, calzones, and bread, but the rough edges and long, heavy profile of rectangular models can scrape cabinet linings. Kay Stringari of Truckee, Calif., has a solution.

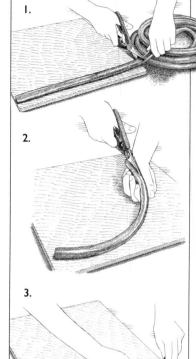

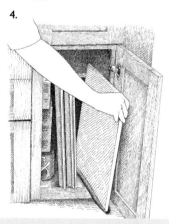

1. Cut a piece of rubber hose (standard irrigation hose will work) to the length of a baking stone's short edge.
2. Slit the tube open along one side.
3. Insert the stone into the slit, creating a cover for the rough edge.
4. To store, slide the stone into the cabinet with the covered edge on the bottom. Remove the hose before using the stone.

ILLUSTRATION: JOHN BURGOYNE

SEND US YOUR TIPS We will provide a complimentary one-year subscription for each tip we print. Send your tip, name, and address to Quick Tips, *Cook's Illustrated*, P.O. Box 470589, Brookline, MA 02447, or to QuickTips@AmericasTestKitchen.com.

Quicker Tofu Prep

Pressing tofu dry prior to cooking improves its texture and allows for better browning, but it's a time-consuming process. Kelsey Glennon and Jonah Choiniere of New York, N.Y., use this shortcut.

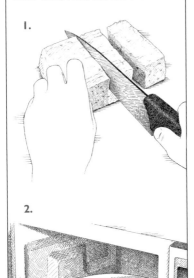

I. Drain the tofu and cut it into pieces of the desired size.
2. Place the tofu on a coffee filter set on a plate; microwave on medium power for 4 to 6 minutes or until the coffee filter is damp.

Cleaner Batter Pouring

Beth Chupp of Syracuse, Ind., has found a way to prevent the gunky buildup around the lip of the liquid measuring cup that she uses to portion pancake, muffin, and cupcake batter: She spritzes vegetable oil spray along the cup's edge. Batter slides cleanly out over the slippery layer.

A Foiled Plan

Rather than cutting and wrapping strips of aluminum foil around her pie's edges to safeguard against burnt crusts, Sharon Lehman of Newton, Kan., uses this simpler method.

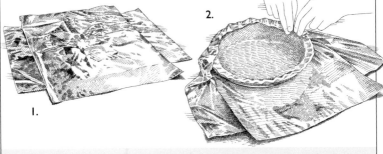

I. Arrange two 18-inch sheets of aluminum foil so they are perpendicular to each other.
2. Set the unbaked pie crust in the center and fold all four ends of foil up and over the edges of the crust to form a shield; bake as directed.

Rolling Pin Stand-In

When her rolling pin was nowhere to be found, Pearl Frank of Rego Park, N.Y., improvised by filling a plastic 2-liter bottle with water and freezing it. The ice in the bottle had a twofold benefit: It provided leverage for even rolling and also kept the dough cool, which prevents sticking.

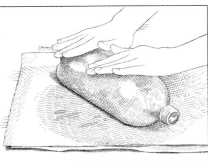

Simpler Straining

Rather than dirtying a colander to rinse and drain canned goods like beans and olives, Jesus Sanchez of Davis, Calif., uses the following method.

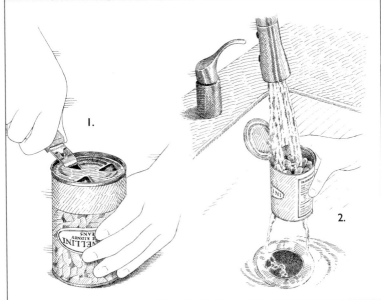

I. Hold the can upside down over the sink and make 3 small holes at the bottom with a church key or can opener.
2. Turn the can right side up, set it over the clean drain in the sink, and then open the top with a can opener. Liquid from the can will drain through the holes in the bottom. You can then rinse the contents directly in the can.

Watching Your Dough

Baking suppliers sell special buckets that protect rising dough from drafts and have markings to show when dough has doubled in size, but these products can be expensive and difficult to find. Deborah Tarentino of Pittsburgh, Pa., uses a clean, food-safe 5-quart clear plastic paint bucket from her local hardware store. It, too, has markings on the side so that she can easily track the dough's rise—and it's a fraction of the cost of a baker's bucket.

Securing Slippery Cutting Boards

To keep her favorite plastic cutting board from sliding around the counter as she chops, Mary DeCamp of Chattanooga, Tenn., wraps a thick rubber band around each end, creating a stable nonskid surface for safe chopping.

Shrewd Sheath

Instead of investing in knife guards for seldom-used cutlery like cleavers, Pearl Fok of Winnipeg, Manitoba, reuses the plastic binding spines from old vinyl report covers. She simply cuts them to the correct length and slides them onto the blades.

Rethinking Beef Stew

When we took a closer look at the way Spanish cooks make beef stew, we found a whole new approach to one of our favorite winter dishes.

⇒ BY BRYAN ROOF ⇐

Few cuisines can rival the complexity of Spanish food, with its influences from ancient Greece and Rome, North Africa, and even the Americas. This multilayering of flavors and textures is particularly apparent in the meat stews from the country's easternmost region of Catalonia. Almost all begin with a slow-cooked jam of onions and tomatoes known as *sofrito* and end with the stirring in of *picada*, a pesto-like paste that includes fried bread, herbs, and ground nuts, and which gives the stew body and even more dimension. Cinnamon and smoked paprika are also common, along with a sherry-like fortified wine known as *vi ranci*. Though stews made from game, boar, or sausage are most typical in Catalonia, I was intent on investigating beef stew. When a search turned up only a handful of recipes, I consulted the renowned Spanish chef José Andrés, whose restaurants include Jaleo in Washington, D.C. Andrés explained the scarcity: Because Catalonia has little pastureland, beef stews are a special indulgence.

I love beef, so there was no question that any Catalan-style stew I came up with would feature it. After jotting down a few pointers from Andrés, I set out to build my own recipe.

Flavor Foundation

While most American beef stews are made with chuck roast, Spanish cooks employ a variety of cuts, including flank or skirt steak, blade steak, or short ribs. I tested all of these, comparing each one to chuck. The long, fibrous muscles of flank and skirt steak led to stringy results, and blade steak was flavorful but tended to dry out due to its lower fat content. I settled on boneless beef short ribs. Not only were these easier to butcher than a chuck roast, which is full of intramuscular fat and sinew, but they boasted outstanding beef flavor and became supremely tender and moist after a long, slow simmer. I seared chunks of short ribs in batches in a Dutch oven and then transferred them to a plate so I could prepare the foundation of my stew: the sofrito.

This flavor base is the cornerstone of not only Catalan cooking but also much of Spanish cuisine, lending remarkable depth to countless recipes. A traditional sofrito consists of finely chopped onions

Spanish beef stew is characterized by a thick, intensely flavored sauce.

browned slowly over low heat and brightened with tomatoes (and sometimes herbs, spices, and aromatics). We've discovered that a small amount of salt and sugar added to onions helps draw out their moisture, both hastening and deepening the level of caramelization, so I sprinkled a smidge of each onto two minced onions as they cooked over the traditional very low heat in olive oil. Once the onions were soft and dark brown (this took 30 to 40 minutes), I added tomatoes.

I experimented with canned and fresh tomatoes, preferring the latter for their greater acidity and brightness. I found, however, that fresh tomatoes had to be peeled, lest the skins make the stew stringy. Our standard method of blanching tomatoes before peeling seemed too fussy, particularly since I was using only two plum tomatoes. I decided to try a simpler method I'd seen in a Spanish cookbook: scraping the pulpy flesh of the tomatoes over the large holes of a box grater and then discarding the leathery skin. This worked beautifully. Along with the tomatoes, I stirred a bay leaf and a teaspoon of heady smoked paprika into the onions.

After 10 more minutes of cooking, the sweet and savory flavors of the sofrito had fully melded and its texture was sticky and jamlike. But nearly 45 minutes had passed, and I couldn't help but wonder if I could cut back on some of the cooking time. When I sampled sofritos cooked for 15 and 30 minutes alongside a 45-minute flavor base, I had my answer. The long-cooked sample had a significantly richer, more developed taste—the shorter versions simply didn't have enough time to thoroughly caramelize. There would be no shortcuts taken here.

I nestled several batches of seared short-rib chunks atop the slow-cooked sofrito and poured in cooking liquids, experimenting with various combinations of chicken broth, beef broth, and water. Surprisingly, the broths actually detracted from the flavor of the beef and sofrito. Tasters preferred the cleanness of a stew made with water alone, which allowed more of the beef, onion, and tomato flavors to dominate.

As for the sherry that is typically added, the sofrito was already providing mild sweetness, and tasters thought that vi ranci (as well as American-made sherries) rendered the sauce too cloying. Instead, I turned to wine. I remembered a tip from Andrés that besides sherry, less-assertive white wine is often preferred to red wine in stew as it complements, rather than overpowers, the flavor of the meat. I selected a dry Spanish white (Albariño), which my tasters agreed worked far better in the stew than red wine did. In the end, I simmered the beef in just 1½ cups each of water and wine. To capture the warm spice flavor typical of Catalan stew, I also stirred a touch of cinnamon along with a sprig of fresh thyme into the pot.

Uncovering Searing Secrets

My stew was coming along nicely, but after searing the short ribs and cooking the sofrito, I was an hour into my recipe, and I hadn't even started simmering the beef. I wondered whether searing the meat (a process that took about 15 minutes total) was absolutely necessary. Spanish stews are usually simmered covered, but I had an idea.

In our recipe for Hungarian Beef Stew, we were able to do away with searing since the meat was cooked on a bed of onions with no added liquid.

PHOTOGRAPHY: CARL TREMBLAY

Shaking Up Stew Standards

To achieve the supremely beefy and complex flavor profile of Spanish beef stew, we learned a few new tricks—and gave up some long-held notions.

START WITH SOFRITO
A slow-cooked mixture of onions, tomatoes, spices, and herbs—known as *sofrito* in Spain—forms a flavor-packed base for the stew.

GO FOR WHITE WINE
We typically use red wine in beef stew. Here, we agreed with Spanish cooks that red wine competes with beefy flavor, so we reached for white instead.

SWAP THE ROAST FOR RIBS
Most stew recipes (including many of ours) call for chuck-eye roast. Boneless beef short ribs are even beefier-tasting and are easier to break down.

SKIP THE SEAR
By cooking the stew in the oven and leaving the pot uncovered, any part of the beef not submerged in liquid can brown, making searing unnecessary.

END WITH PICADA
A mixture of ground toasted bread, almonds, garlic, and parsley—the *picada*—stirred in before serving brightens the stew's flavor and thickens the broth.

Any portion of meat sitting above the liquid released by the onions was exposed to the heat of the oven and browned nearly as well as if it were seared, developing thousands of new flavor compounds. To see if I could eliminate searing in this recipe, I set the oven to a moderate 300 degrees and prepared a comparison of stews made with seared and unseared meat, leaving the unseared batch uncovered to fully expose it to the heat of the oven. When the stews emerged from the oven 2½ to 3 hours later, they tasted remarkably similar. I concluded that I could eliminate searing. An added benefit of this move was that the gentle, ambient heat of a low oven provided more reliable results than the stove, which runs the risk of scorching the meat on the bottom of the pot.

Having achieved tender, intensely flavored beef, it was time for the critical final flourish: the picada. Some experts wager that this bracing mixture of fried bread, nuts (most often almonds or hazelnuts), garlic, olive oil, and herbs (typically parsley) ground together has been used in Catalan cooking since the 13th and 14th centuries. In stews, the nuts and bread bulk up the braising liquid, and the garlic and parsley add flavor and freshness.

Opting for blanched almonds, which, unlike hazelnuts, require no fussy skinning, I sautéed ¼ cup of nuts with chunks of bread and a couple of cloves of minced garlic in olive oil before processing the whole lot with the parsley in a food processor. Stirred into the finished stew, the picada gave the dish a jolt of bright flavor, but I wondered if it would be even better if I left the garlic raw. Sure enough, a subsequent batch with raw garlic imparted a pungency to the stew that tasters loved. And although a food processor proved faster and more convenient than a mortar and pestle, its whizzing blade muddied the grassy flavor of the parsley, so I minced it with a knife before combining it with the ground ingredients.

Thus far, my stew contained no vegetables, and although I didn't plan on loading it up with carrots, peas, and potatoes like a typical American stew, some additional element seemed appropriate. It only made sense to feature a popular Catalan ingredient: oyster mushrooms. Rather than cook them directly in the stew, which spoiled their delicate flavor and texture, I sautéed them separately. The mushrooms went into the finished stew along with the picada and a shot of sherry vinegar. Here was a beef stew—rich and fragrant with the flavors of Catalonia—that included classic Spanish techniques, plus a few of my own.

CATALAN-STYLE BEEF STEW WITH MUSHROOMS
SERVES 4 TO 6

Remove the woody base of the oyster mushroom stem before cooking. An equal amount of quartered button mushrooms may be substituted for the oyster mushrooms. Serve the stew with boiled or mashed potatoes or rice.

Stew
- 2 tablespoons olive oil
- 2 large onions, chopped fine
- ½ teaspoon sugar
  Kosher salt and pepper
- 2 plum tomatoes, halved lengthwise, pulp grated on large holes of box grater, and skins discarded
- 1 teaspoon smoked paprika
- 1 bay leaf
- 1½ cups dry white wine
- 1½ cups water
- 1 large sprig fresh thyme
- ¼ teaspoon ground cinnamon
- 2½ pounds boneless beef short ribs, trimmed and cut into 2-inch cubes

Picada
- ¼ cup whole blanched almonds
- 2 tablespoons olive oil
- 1 slice hearty white sandwich bread, crust removed, torn into 1-inch pieces
- 2 garlic cloves, peeled
- 3 tablespoons minced fresh parsley

- ½ pound oyster mushrooms, trimmed
- 1 teaspoon sherry vinegar

1. FOR THE STEW: Adjust oven rack to middle position and heat oven to 300 degrees. Heat oil in Dutch oven over medium-low heat until shimmering. Add onions, sugar, and ½ teaspoon salt; cook, stirring often, until onions are deeply caramelized, 30 to 40 minutes. Add tomatoes, smoked paprika, and bay leaf; cook, stirring often, until darkened and thick, 5 to 10 minutes.

2. Add wine, water, thyme, and cinnamon to pot, scraping up any browned bits. Season beef with 1½ teaspoons salt and ½ teaspoon pepper and add to pot. Increase heat to high and bring to simmer. Transfer to oven and cook, uncovered. After 1 hour stir stew to redistribute meat, return to oven, and continue to cook uncovered until meat is tender, 1½ to 2 hours longer.

3. FOR THE PICADA: While stew is in oven, heat almonds and 1 tablespoon oil in 10-inch skillet over medium heat; cook, stirring often, until almonds are golden brown, 3 to 6 minutes. Using slotted spoon, transfer almonds to food processor. Return now-empty skillet to medium heat, add bread, and cook, stirring often, until toasted, 2 to 4 minutes; transfer to food processor with almonds. Add garlic and process until mixture is finely ground, about 20 seconds, scraping bowl as needed. Transfer mixture to bowl, stir in parsley, and set aside.

4. Return now-empty skillet to medium heat. Heat remaining 1 tablespoon oil until shimmering. Add mushrooms and ½ teaspoon salt; cook, stirring often, until tender, 5 to 7 minutes. Transfer to bowl and set aside.

5. Remove bay leaf. Stir picada, mushrooms, and vinegar into stew. Season with salt and pepper. Serve.

TO MAKE AHEAD: Follow recipe through step 2 and refrigerate for up to 3 days. To serve, add 1 cup water and reheat over medium heat. Proceed with step 3.

See the Tricks of the Stew
Video available FREE for 4 months at
www.CooksIllustrated.com/feb12

Really Good Vegetable Tart

We knew we wanted the ease of a free-form tart, but the typical delicate butter pastry just wouldn't do. And how could we avoid a soggy vegetable filling?

> BY ANDREW JANJIGIAN <

Compared with more formal tarts baked in fluted pans, a free-form tart's beauty lies in its rustic simplicity. You roll out the dough, add the filling, and then draw in its edges to form a pleated packet. This method requires far less effort than precisely fitting pastry into a molded pan, and it looks just as attractive.

But when it comes to savory applications, free-form tarts can have their flaws. Many recipes simply borrow a standard pastry dough intended for fruit and swap in vegetables. After trying a few such versions, I realized that for vegetables, not just any old crust would do. Vegetables have far less of the pectin that holds on to moisture and binds a fruit filling together, so they are particularly prone to leaking liquid into the crust or falling apart when the tart is sliced. What's more, vegetables don't pack the concentrated, bright flavors of fruit. To make up for these deficits, I needed a crust that was extra-sturdy and boasted a complex flavor of its own. I also wanted a robust-tasting filling with enough sticking power to hold together when cut.

Structural Analysis

I started by putting together a basic all-butter pie dough, trading half of the white flour for the whole-wheat kind. The earthy flavor of whole-wheat flour, I hoped, would complement the savory filling, and its coarser consistency would turn out a pleasantly hearty crumb. I pulsed the dry ingredients and butter in the food processor a few times, then dumped the mixture into a bowl, added a little water, and stirred it until thoroughly combined. To ensure that the butter stayed firm enough to leave air pockets when it melted in the oven, creating flakiness, I chilled the dough for about an hour before rolling it out.

The good news: The butter and all of that whole-wheat flour added up to a great-tasting crust. The bad news: It had none of the flaky yet sturdy texture that I'd been looking for. Instead, it was crumbly and dense. And I was pretty sure I knew why.

All doughs, pastry or otherwise, get their structure from gluten, the network of proteins that forms when flour is mixed with water. The challenge when working with whole-wheat flour is that it contains

We borrowed a puff pastry trick to make a flaky yet sturdy dough.

the bran and germ. (These fibrous outer layers of the wheat berry are stripped away in white flour, leaving only the inner core, or endosperm.) Since the bran and germ contain none of the gluten-forming proteins found in the endosperm, the more whole-wheat flour in a dough, the heavier and more prone it will be to falling apart.

To strengthen the dough, I'd obviously need to cut back on the whole-wheat flour, but 25 percent was as low as I could go before I lost too much of the whole wheat's nice nutty taste. And there was another problem: As the proportion of white flour, and therefore gluten, increased, the dough became tough. I didn't think I was overworking the dough—a typical cause. Then it occurred to me that the problem might be water. Because the bran and germ need more water than the endosperm to become fully hydrated, I'd added a little more to the dough than I would have in an all-white-flour dough. I realized that the extra liquid was being taken up by the white flour's gluten-forming proteins, thus creating more gluten and making the

dough more susceptible to overworking. To reduce toughness, then, I'd need to either cut back on the water or find an even gentler way to handle the dough.

Liquid Assets

Our previous solution to tough pastry—replacing some of the water with vodka—creates a dough too soft to work as a free-form crust. I knew that acids can weaken the bonds that form between gluten strands, so I decided to try adding vinegar. I found that a teaspoon—the most I could add before the dough tasted too vinegary—did tenderize it a little, but not enough.

What if I took a hands-off approach to mixing and let the flour absorb the water on its own? I hoped that partially mixing the dough so that not all of the flour was mixed in and then letting it rest before rolling it out might allow the water to migrate to drier parts and produce pastry that was workable—but not overworked.

I gave it a shot, just barely mixing the dry and wet ingredients together and then chilling the dough briefly. When I pulled the dough out an hour or so later, it was clear that I was on to something: Without any effort on my part, most of the dry flour had disappeared; even better, the dough was remarkably supple but not floppy. I gently nudged it together and then rolled it out and baked it at 375 degrees. The result: a tender, moist, and decently flaky crust without the least bit of toughness. But the perfectionist in me wouldn't settle for decently flaky. I wanted a crust with the long, striated layers in puff pastry; such large horizontal sheets would also make the crust more resistant to splitting when sliced. But the hundreds of layers in puff pastry are created through the painstaking process of rolling and folding the dough many times and chilling it in between. Curious to see what

Don't Doubt Your Dough

Barely mixing the dough and then resting it in the refrigerator hydrates the flour while minimizing gluten development, for a more tender crust. Don't worry if the dough looks loose and shaggy—it's supposed to.

SHAGGY DOUGH

PHOTOGRAPHY: CARL TREMBLAY

would happen if I mimicked this approach in a more modest way, I dumped the rested shaggy mass onto the countertop, rolled it into a rectangle, and folded it into thirds, like a business letter. I repeated the process just twice more. The results were even better than I'd hoped: The increase in layers rendered the crust wonderfully flaky and less apt to shatter when cut.

Fill 'er Up

Working with a sturdy crust, however, didn't mean that I could throw in the vegetables—shiitake mushrooms and leeks—raw: They'd still leach far too much moisture and render the crust soggy. Fortunately, sautéing the leeks only took a few minutes and also helped concentrate their flavor. And I hastened the evaporation process by heating the mushrooms in the microwave. To introduce rich, complex flavor and not too much moisture, I worked in a hefty dollop of crème fraîche and some Dijon mustard and layered a few handfuls of crumbled Gorgonzola between the vegetables just before baking.

A hearty filling bound by a buttery crust, this rustic tart amounted to a perfect cold-weather meal—one so good I'd be tempted to make it year-round.

MUSHROOM AND LEEK GALETTE WITH GORGONZOLA
SERVES 6

Cutting a few small holes in the dough prevents it from lifting off the pan as it bakes. A pizza stone helps to crisp the crust but is not essential. For our free recipes for Butternut Squash Galette with Gruyère and Potato and Shallot Galette with Goat Cheese, go to www.CooksIllustrated.com/feb12.

Dough
- 1¼ cups (6¼ ounces) all-purpose flour
- ½ cup (2¾ ounces) whole-wheat flour
- 1 tablespoon sugar
- ¾ teaspoon salt
- 10 tablespoons unsalted butter, cut into ½-inch pieces and chilled
- 7 tablespoons ice water
- 1 teaspoon white vinegar

Filling
- 1¼ pounds shiitake mushrooms, stemmed and sliced thin
- 5 teaspoons olive oil
- 1 pound leeks, white and light green parts only, sliced ½ inch thick and washed thoroughly (3 cups)
- 1 teaspoon minced fresh thyme
- 2 tablespoons crème fraîche
- 1 tablespoon Dijon mustard
  Salt and pepper
- 3 ounces Gorgonzola cheese, crumbled (¾ cup)

- 1 large egg, lightly beaten
  Kosher salt
- 2 tablespoons minced fresh parsley

ILLUSTRATION: JOHN BURGOYNE

KEYS TO MAKING A FLAVOR–PACKED, STURDY VEGETABLE TART

MAKE A WHOLE-WHEAT CRUST Whole-wheat flour contributes earthy flavor that complements the savory filling. Its coarser consistency makes for a hearty crumb.

PRECOOK THE VEGETABLES Removing moisture from the vegetables is crucial to concentrating flavor and preventing a soggy crust. We microwave and drain the mushrooms and combine them with browned leeks.

ADD BOLD-FLAVORED BINDERS To help the vegetables stay neatly bound and add complexity to the filling, we worked in a rich, three-part binder: crème fraîche, Dijon mustard, and crumbled Gorgonzola.

1. FOR THE DOUGH: Process flours, sugar, and salt in food processor until combined, 2 to 3 pulses. Add butter and pulse until it forms pea-size pieces, about 10 pulses. Transfer mixture to medium bowl.

2. Sprinkle water and vinegar over mixture. With rubber spatula, use folding motion to mix until loose, shaggy mass forms with some dry flour remaining (do not overwork). Transfer mixture to center of large sheet of plastic wrap, press gently into rough 4-inch square, and wrap tightly. Refrigerate for at least 45 minutes.

3. Transfer dough to lightly floured work surface. Roll into 11 by 8-inch rectangle with short side of rectangle parallel to edge of work surface. Using bench scraper, bring bottom third of dough up, then fold upper third over it, folding like business letter into 8 by 4-inch rectangle. Turn dough 90 degrees counterclockwise. Roll out dough again into 11 by 8-inch rectangle and fold into thirds again. Turn dough 90 degrees counterclockwise and repeat rolling and folding into thirds. After last fold, fold dough in half to create 4-inch square. Press top of dough gently to seal. Wrap in plastic wrap and refrigerate for at least 45 minutes or up to 2 days.

4. FOR THE FILLING: Cover mushrooms in bowl and microwave until just tender, 3 to 5 minutes. Transfer to colander to drain and return to bowl. Meanwhile, heat 1 tablespoon oil in 12-inch skillet over medium heat until shimmering. Add leeks and thyme, cover, and cook, stirring occasionally, until leeks are tender and beginning to brown, 5 to 7 minutes. Transfer to bowl with mushrooms. Stir in crème fraîche and mustard. Season with salt and pepper to taste. Set aside.

5. Adjust oven rack to lower middle position, place pizza stone on oven rack, and heat oven to 400 degrees. Remove dough from refrigerator and let stand at room temperature for 15 to 20 minutes. Roll out on generously floured (up to ¼ cup) work surface to 14-inch circle about ⅛ inch thick. (Trim edges as needed to form rough circle.) Transfer dough to parchment paper–lined rimmed baking sheet. With tip of paring knife, cut five ¼-inch circles in dough (one at center and four evenly spaced midway from center to edge of dough). Brush top of dough with 1 teaspoon oil.

6. Spread half of filling evenly over dough, leaving 2-inch border around edge. Sprinkle with half of Gorgonzola, cover with remaining filling, and top with remaining Gorgonzola. Drizzle remaining 1 teaspoon oil over filling. Grasp 1 edge of dough and fold up outer 2 inches over filling. Repeat around circumference of tart, overlapping dough every 2 to 3 inches; gently pinch pleated dough to secure but do not press dough into filling. Brush dough with egg and sprinkle evenly with kosher salt.

7. Lower oven temperature to 375 degrees. Bake until crust is deep golden brown and filling is beginning to brown, 35 to 45 minutes. Cool tart on baking sheet on wire rack for 10 minutes. Using offset or wide metal spatula, loosen tart from parchment and carefully slide tart off parchment onto cutting board. Sprinkle with parsley, cut into wedges, and serve.

TECHNIQUE | PLEATING A FREE–FORM TART

It's surprisingly simple to create pleated edges around free-form tarts.

1. Gently grasp 1 edge of dough and make 2-inch-wide fold over filling.

2. Lift and fold another segment of dough over first fold to form pleat. Repeat every 2 to 3 inches.

Updating Chicken Marbella

More than 25 years ago, this dinner-party mainstay put *The Silver Palate Cookbook* on the map. Could we retool the recipe for today's tastes?

⇒ BY DAN SOUZA ⇐

In 1977, a gourmet shop called the Silver Palate opened in Manhattan's Upper West Side and introduced New Yorkers to their first bite of chicken Marbella. Inspired by the Moroccan tagines and Spanish braises that owners Julee Rosso and Sheila Lukins had sampled while traveling abroad in the 1960s, the shop's signature dish offered Americans a taste of then-exotic flavors: briny capers and bold Spanish olives baked with chicken and tender prunes in a sweet-and-tangy sauce. The shop closed in 1993, but the dish lives on in kitchens throughout America.

The original recipe starts with four whole chickens that are quartered into split breasts and legs and marinated overnight in olive oil, red wine vinegar, garlic, olives, prunes, capers (including their juice), oregano, bay leaves, and plenty of salt and pepper. Everything is then transferred to shallow baking dishes, moistened with white wine, topped with a cup of brown sugar, and baked (with frequent basting) in a 350-degree oven for about an hour.

When I made this modern classic in the test kitchen, it was easy to see why its unique balance of flavors has made it such an enduring hit. But there were also a number of problems. While the chicken was juicy, its flavor was very subtle despite the overnight soak. The skin remained pale and flabby, and the sauce, though well seasoned, was quite sweet, lacking the pungency that its ingredient list would suggest. In the enterprising spirit of Rosso and Lukins, I set out to create an updated version of this classic dinner-party favorite.

Goodbye, Marinade

To make the dish more feasible as a weeknight supper, I first scaled it down to four to six servings (the original recipe serves 16 to 24). I also saved myself the trouble of butchering by switching from whole chickens to split breasts and leg quarters.

Next to go: the overnight marinade. Years of test-

We kept Marbella's signature ingredients—capers, olives, and prunes—but developed a new technique for crispier skin and more balanced flavor.

ing have taught us that marinades aren't miracle cure-alls for bland, dry meat, as was once believed. We've found that regardless of how long a marinade remains in contact with meat, its flavor never penetrates more than a few millimeters into the flesh. What's more, an excess of acidic marinade ingredients (such as lemon juice, vinegar, and wine) can actually overtenderize meat, making its surface mushy. And forget about crisp skin: The lengthy soak waterlogs poultry skin, which in turn inhibits rendering and browning. For these reasons, we generally reserve marinades for thin steaks or boneless, skinless chicken breasts and cap marinating time at about an hour.

There is one element of a marinade that does live up to the hype, however: salt. As in a brine, salt in a marinade penetrates into the muscle fibers, seasoning meat and helping it hold on to its juices. To confirm that the salt was the only real player, I ran a side-by-side test pitting chicken pieces treated with the original marinade against a batch that was simply salted (both sat overnight in the fridge). Sure enough, both samples emerged equally succulent. In fact, tasters preferred the salted chicken, noting that the

vinegar had turned the marinated chicken mealy. So I ditched the marinade entirely and decided to focus only on salting or brining to increase juiciness and tenderness.

Unfortunately, time turned out to be the other key factor. Salting, as I had just proved, did a good job, but it took at least six hours to have an impact (with better results after 24 hours). Brining was faster but—just like the marinade—left me with limp, waterlogged chicken skin that resisted browning and diluted the sauce during baking. Reluctantly, I scratched these pretreatments off of my list and turned my attention to the cooking method, hoping to find an alternative path to moist, flavorful meat.

A Change of Vessel

With liquid-based pretreatments like marinating and brining out of the picture, I now had to find other ways to build flavor: I could sear the chicken to jump-start browning and build a sauce from the fond. I seasoned two split breasts and two leg quarters with salt and pepper and placed them, skin side down, in a smoking-hot 12-inch skillet. Once the skin turned golden, I flipped the parts over and transferred them to a shallow baking dish. After pouring off most of the rendered fat from the skillet, I set about building the sauce. I stirred in the oil, vinegar, olives, capers, and other ingredients and cooked them for a minute. I deglazed the skillet with white wine, poured the sauce around the chicken, and transferred everything to a 400-degree oven (the liquid came about halfway up the chicken pieces, leaving the skin exposed to the direct heat of the oven). In the hope of allowing the skin to continue rendering, I scrapped the brown

Silver Classics

PHOTOGRAPHY: CARL TREMBLAY

sugar coating (relying on the prunes for sweetness) and didn't baste, since moist skin can't climb above a paltry 212 degrees (the boiling point of water) and thus doesn't render or brown much.

The good news was that the sauce was more flavorful, albeit still a little thin. But despite my intentions, the skin hadn't rendered or colored much more than it had after the initial browning. I realized the problem: The straight sides of the baking dish were trapping moisture. I'd already dirtied a skillet. Could I take further advantage of its shallow walls and cook the chicken through in the pan? I gave it a shot, returning the seared chicken to the skillet after building my sauce and then placing the skillet in the oven to finish cooking in the more-even heat. Sure enough, the skillet's low, flared sides allowed more steam to escape, resulting in well-browned skin and a more concentrated sauce. Finally I was getting somewhere.

But there was still more work to do. Tasters complained that the dish didn't seem cohesive. Specifically, none of the sauce's flavor had transferred to the chicken.

A Sticky Situation

Perhaps a more concentrated sauce was the answer. I ramped up the amount of olives, capers, prunes, and garlic, and to boost meatiness and complexity, I started exploring other seasonings, including onions, anchovies, and red pepper flakes. Onions didn't impress tasters, but minced anchovies (which added a rich depth without tasting fishy) and a pinch of pepper flakes earned rave reviews. The sauce finally came together with the addition of ¾ cup of chicken broth. The chicken, however, was still bland.

Desperate for a fix, I lifted my self-imposed ban on basting and moistened the chicken with the sauce as it cooked, but the technique proved both inconvenient and ineffective. Even with frequent basting, the sauce merely dripped back into the pan and I ran into the same old problem of soggy, unrendered skin. While mulling over how I could get the flavor to "stick" to the chicken, I hit on the solution: I'd make a paste that would literally adhere to the skin.

I prepped another batch, pureeing some of the prunes, olives, and capers with garlic, anchovies, oregano, pepper flakes, and olive oil. After searing the chicken, I spread an even layer of paste on each piece before transferring the skillet to the oven. Things looked promising during the first half of cooking, as the paste started to develop a rich, dark patina. But it continued to darken, and by the time the meat was cooked through, the surface was charred. The paste had also prevented the skin from rendering fully. The only upside was that the chicken tasted juicier than it had in previous batches. The paste's thick consistency—essentially a mixture of fat and dense fiber—must have halted evaporative moisture loss. Could I keep this benefit without suffering the shortcomings of the paste? For the next test, I waited until the chicken was about half-cooked and the skin well rendered and browned before adding the paste.

The original chicken Marbella featured chicken parts marinated overnight and then baked.

PROBLEM Pale, flabby skin
SOLUTIONS Ditch the marinade since it turns skin soggy (and never permeates the flesh anyway). Sear the chicken to crisp the skin before adding liquid.

PROBLEM Bland meat
SOLUTION Smear a potent paste of capers, garlic, anchovies, olives, prunes, oregano, and red pepper flakes onto the chicken after it is seared.

PROBLEM Overly sweet, lackluster sauce
SOLUTIONS Eliminate brown sugar and use the flavorful fond from searing the chicken (plus more caper-prune-olive paste) to form the base of the sauce. Balance the flavors with butter, vinegar, and parsley.

After another 10 minutes in the oven, the paste had caramelized and the flavors had bloomed, making this the best-tasting chicken yet.

Wondering if I could use the paste to deepen the flavor of the sauce as well, I caramelized some of the paste in the skillet after browning the chicken, spreading the remainder on the parts themselves. Just as I had hoped, the sauce was deeply flavorful and possessed a velvety texture thanks to the pureed prunes. A last-minute knob of butter, a teaspoon of red wine vinegar, and a sprinkle of fresh parsley pulled everything into balance.

With these changes, my colleagues agreed I'd made a good dish even better—and a version that might live on for another 25 years.

CHICKEN MARBELLA
SERVES 4 TO 6

Any combination of split breasts and leg quarters can be used in this recipe.

Paste
⅓	cup pitted green olives, rinsed
⅓	cup pitted prunes
3	tablespoons extra-virgin olive oil
4	garlic cloves, peeled
2	tablespoons capers, rinsed
3	anchovy fillets, rinsed
½	teaspoon dried oregano
½	teaspoon pepper
¼	teaspoon kosher salt
	Pinch red pepper flakes

Chicken
2½–3	pounds bone-in, skin-on split chicken breasts and/or leg quarters, trimmed
	Kosher salt and pepper
2	teaspoons olive oil
¾	cup low-sodium chicken broth
⅓	cup white wine
⅓	cup pitted green olives, rinsed and halved
1	tablespoon capers, rinsed
2	bay leaves
⅓	cup pitted prunes, chopped coarse
1	tablespoon unsalted butter
1	teaspoon red wine vinegar
2	tablespoons minced fresh parsley

1. FOR THE PASTE: Adjust oven rack to middle position and heat oven to 400 degrees. Pulse all ingredients in food processor until finely chopped, about ten 1-second pulses. Scrape down bowl and continue to process until mostly smooth, 1 to 2 minutes. Transfer to bowl. (Paste can be refrigerated for up to 24 hours.)

2. FOR THE CHICKEN: Pat chicken dry with paper towels. Sprinkle chicken pieces with 1½ teaspoons salt and season with pepper.

3. Heat oil in 12-inch skillet over medium-high heat until just smoking. Add chicken, skin side down, and cook without moving it until well browned, 5 to 8 minutes. Transfer chicken to large plate. Drain off all but 1 teaspoon fat from skillet and return to medium-low heat.

4. Add ⅓ cup paste to skillet and cook, stirring constantly, until fragrant and fond forms on pan bottom, 1 to 2 minutes. Stir in broth, wine, olives, capers, and bay leaves, scraping up any browned bits. Return chicken to pan, skin side up (skin should be above surface of liquid), and roast, uncovered, for 15 minutes.

5. Remove skillet from oven and use back of spoon to spread remaining paste over chicken pieces; sprinkle prunes around chicken. Continue to roast until paste begins to brown, breasts register 160 degrees, and leg quarters register 175 degrees, 7 to 12 minutes longer.

6. Transfer chicken to serving platter and tent loosely with aluminum foil. Remove bay leaves from sauce and whisk in butter, vinegar, and 1 tablespoon parsley; season with salt and pepper to taste. Pour sauce around chicken, sprinkle with remaining 1 tablespoon parsley, and serve.

Great Home Fries for a Crowd

Could the key to really good, genuinely crisp home fries be really bad boiled potatoes?

⇒ BY ANDREA GEARY ⇐

Despite the cozy image conjured by the name, few people actually make home fries at home. That's probably because producing the perfect article—a mound of golden-brown potato chunks with crisp exteriors and moist, fluffy insides dotted with savory onions and herbs—calls for more time, elbow grease, and stovetop space than most cooks care to devote to the project. First of all, when you start with raw potatoes, achieving that ideal crisp, well-browned exterior requires frequently turning them in the pan for the better part of an hour. Then there's the matter of the yield: Even a roomy 12-inch skillet barely holds enough potatoes to serve two people. But since the prospect of juggling multiple sizzling skillets is enough to give even the most confident cook pause, making home fries for a larger gathering is out of the question. No wonder most of us eat our home fries at diners or buffet tables, where large-scale production and lengthy holding times often result in potatoes that are limp and greasy.

I wanted to find a way out of this sorry situation. My goal: nicely crisped home fries with tender interiors that would serve six hungry people—and wouldn't chain the cook to the stove for an hour.

Boiling Point

Since time was a priority, I decided to rule out any recipes that began with raw spuds and look for those that called for some form of parcooking. Even though it would dirty more dishes, parcooking would dramatically cut down on frying time. Our science editor also pointed out that using a moist heat method like boiling would actually aid in my goal of a crisp exterior. This is because when the starch granules in potatoes absorb water, they swell and release the water-soluble starch amylose. Once the amylose on the surface of the potato dries out, it hardens, creating a crisp shell. Parboiling it would be.

Roasting the parboiled potatoes on a preheated baking sheet produces extra-crisp crusts.

I wasn't sure which type of potato would work best, so I tested the three main kinds: waxy, low-starch red-skinned spuds; all-purpose, medium-starch Yukon Golds; and floury, high-starch russets. I peeled and diced the potatoes into rough ¾-inch chunks, covered them with cold salted water, and boiled them until just cooked through. After draining the diced potatoes, I let them cool and dry slightly while I heated three cast-iron skillets. While I was frying the potatoes in the skillets with some vegetable oil for about four minutes per side, frantically flipping, I added another goal to my list: only one cooking vessel at a time.

Tasters almost universally rejected the texture of the red-skinned potatoes as too waxy for home fries. Though some praised the creaminess of the Yukon Golds, the majority preferred the earthy flavor of russets. I also knew that the higher starch content of russets would make for a crustier exterior. But as it did with the other potatoes, precooking caused the russets to become more porous, so they absorbed

almost all of the oil in the pan before they'd been turned even once. The upshot was that only the first side of each cube came out golden brown while the other sides stuck to the pan, leaving their browned crusts behind. The simple fix was to boil the potatoes just until their outsides were softened but their insides were still firm. This meant that only the outermost, fully cooked layer of potato absorbed oil, leaving more oil in the pan to prevent sticking and promote even browning.

With browning under control, it was time to turn to the next pressing issue: batch size. Since I'd vowed not to repeat the stressful experience of multiple skillets, I tried successive batches in a single skillet, holding each completed batch in a warm oven until all of the potatoes were fried. Not only was this approach too time-consuming, but the potatoes waiting in the oven grew soft outside and dry in the middle as moisture migrated from their cores to their surfaces.

Home-Roasted Potatoes?

I couldn't ignore the fact that the oven was ideal for large batches, so I decided to try high-temperature roasting. I was heartened to find plenty of Internet recipes purporting to make "oven home fries" without any parboiling at all. While many of these recipes produced evenly browned potatoes, they sadly did not deliver the crucial crisp texture of the real deal, plus they required nearly an hour of roasting time.

Undaunted, I decided to see if parcooking the potatoes, which at least encouraged a crisp exterior, would help. (It would also cut down on roasting time.) As before, I parboiled my potatoes for five minutes until they were nearly (but not completely) cooked through. I tossed them with butter (for flavor) and then transferred them to an oiled, rimmed baking sheet that I had preheated in a 500-degree oven to mimic the surface of a hot skillet. After 40 minutes of roasting (and occasional turning), the exteriors were perfectly brown and crisp—but the insides were dry and overcooked. Cutting the roasting time to 25 minutes left the insides moist and creamy but the outsides pale and soft.

Given that a baking sheet had the potential to yield three times as many servings as a skillet, I had to find a way to make the oven work.

PHOTOGRAPHY: CARL TREMBLAY

HOW MUSHY BOILED POTATOES LEAD TO CRISP HOME FRIES

USE RUSSETS We like the earthy flavor that russets bring to home fries, plus their high starch content helps create a substantial golden-brown crust.

PARBOIL Adding potatoes to boiling (not cold) water cooks them more on the outside than on the inside—just the uneven effect we want.

ADD BAKING SODA Baking soda accentuates the uneven cooking by quickly breaking down the exteriors, leaving the insides nearly raw.

TOSS WITH SALT Salt roughs up the drained potatoes, so their moisture evaporates more readily, leading to better crisping in the oven.

ROAST Pretreated potatoes achieve a "fried" texture after oven roasting. This technique yields three times as many servings as frying in a skillet.

The World's Worst Boiled Potatoes

What I needed to do was somehow alter the boiling step to exaggerate the difference in doneness between the exterior and the interior of the potatoes before I roasted them. I wanted a thin outer layer of blown-out, starchy potato that would brown thoroughly in the oven but a raw middle that would stay moist during the time that it took to brown the outside. In short, I needed a method for making really bad boiled potatoes.

I remembered a test kitchen potato salad recipe in which we'd discovered that adding a bit of vinegar to the boiling water keeps potatoes firm during cooking. The acid slows the breakdown of the pectin that holds the potato cells together, resulting in boiled potatoes that stay firm and intact. If a bit of acid in the water produced the best boiled potatoes, would adding its opposite—an alkaline substance—produce the worst?

I put 3½ pounds of peeled, chunked potatoes in a saucepan and covered them with 10 cups of cold water plus 2 teaspoons of alkaline baking soda, which I hoped would speed up the breakdown of pectin on the outside of the potato and turn it mushy. But after five minutes of boiling, the potatoes were blown out through and through. Undeterred, I cut back on the baking soda. After experimenting, I found that just ½ teaspoon produced the desired effect: floury outsides and uncooked insides. But could I take things even further? Since starting potatoes in cold water helps ensure even cooking and my goal was uneven cooking, why not chuck the spuds into boiling water? This not only made the outsides even pastier and left the insides totally raw but also reduced the parcooking to one minute. Perfect.

I had one more trick to try. I was already tossing the drained parcooked chunks with butter before placing them on the baking sheet, but I tossed them with kosher salt as well. In the past we've found that the coarse salt roughs up the surface of the potatoes so that moisture evaporates faster, leading to better browning. This worked beautifully to create nicely browned home fries with just the crisp, fried texture that I'd been seeking—and I'd only had to turn the potatoes twice in the oven.

My recipe still lacked onions, so I searched for a way to incorporate them without compromising the now-perfect texture of the potatoes. Mixing chopped onions with the spuds before they went into the oven left the onions burnt on the outside and raw in the middle; mixing them in halfway through roasting had a similar effect. In the end, I found that placing oiled and salted onions in the center of the baking sheet 15 minutes into roasting the potatoes (at which point I also turned the potatoes) allowed them to soften a bit. After another 15 minutes, I mixed the onions and potatoes together and cooked them about five minutes longer. A pinch of cayenne tossed with the salted potatoes gave them kick, and a sprinkling of chives at the end enhanced the onion flavor.

I could now make great home fries for a group without working myself into a tizzy. And I didn't even need to haul out the skillet.

HOME FRIES
SERVES 6 TO 8

Don't skip the baking soda in this recipe. It's critical for home fries with just the right crisp texture.

3½   pounds russet potatoes, peeled and cut into ¾-inch dice
½   teaspoon baking soda
3   tablespoons unsalted butter, cut into 12 pieces
    Kosher salt and pepper
    Pinch cayenne pepper
3   tablespoons vegetable oil
2   onions, cut into ½-inch dice
3   tablespoons minced chives

1. Adjust oven rack to lowest position, place rimmed baking sheet on rack, and heat oven to 500 degrees.

2. Bring 10 cups water to boil in Dutch oven over high heat. Add potatoes and baking soda. Return to boil and cook for 1 minute. Drain potatoes. Return potatoes to Dutch oven and place over low heat. Cook, shaking pot occasionally, until any surface moisture has evaporated, about 2 minutes. Remove from heat. Add butter, 1½ teaspoons salt, and cayenne; mix with rubber spatula until potatoes are coated with thick, starchy paste, about 30 seconds.

3. Remove baking sheet from oven and drizzle with 2 tablespoons oil. Transfer potatoes to baking sheet and spread into even layer. Roast for 15 minutes. While potatoes roast, combine onions, remaining 1 tablespoon oil, and ½ teaspoon salt in bowl.

4. Remove baking sheet from oven. Using thin, sharp metal spatula, scrape and turn potatoes. Clear about 8 by 5-inch space in center of baking sheet and add onion mixture. Roast for 15 minutes.

5. Scrape and turn again, mixing onions into potatoes. Continue to roast until potatoes are well browned and onions are softened and beginning to brown, 5 to 10 minutes. Stir in chives and season with salt and pepper to taste. Serve immediately.

SCIENCE Potato Chain Reaction

While developing a potato salad recipe not too long ago, we discovered that adding vinegar to the cooking water creates an acidic environment that slows the breakdown of the pectin that holds potato cells together, resulting in a firm, intact texture. So when our home fries required a thin outer layer of mush that would brown thoroughly in the oven, we took the opposite approach: We created an alkaline environment by adding a little bit of baking soda to the water. After just one minute in the pot, the exteriors of the potatoes became so soft that they were mushy—but the interiors remained raw. This lead to potatoes that more readily crisped on the outside but didn't dry out on the inside.

How could just ½ teaspoon of baking soda added to 10 cups of water be so powerful? It's because alkaline baking soda triggers a chain reaction that literally unzips the backbone of the pectin molecules and causes them to fall apart. This requires only enough alkali to raise the pH of the water high enough to start the reaction, after which it becomes self-sustaining.

BOILED WITH BAKING SODA (pH 3)

BOILED WITH VINEGAR (pH 8.1)

Perfect Braised Pork Chops

To get juicy, tender meat and a rich, silky sauce, we first had to pick the right chop for the job. Then it was a matter of divide and conquer.

⇒ BY LAN LAM ⇐

When I think of pork chops, I think of a simple, no-frills cut that I can just slap into a hot skillet and have on the table in minutes. But lately I've been hearing people talk about braised pork chops. The more I considered this option, the better it seemed. Not only did the slow, gentle approach of braising promise flavorful, tender chops, but it also meant that I'd end up with a rich, glossy sauce. This, I thought, would take pork chops to a whole new level. I was also attracted to the idea of braising smaller cuts like chops in place of the more typical roast—I wouldn't have to trim intramuscular fat and/or tough silverskin from the roast and retie it with twine before it went into the pan, nor would there be any carving to do after cooking. Sounded good to me.

That said, when I went into the test kitchen to try out a few recipes, none lived up to their promise. The meat was dry and bland, swimming in liquid that lacked both complexity and the silky body of a long, gently simmered sauce. Clearly I had some work to do.

A Cut Above

Before I started fiddling with the cooking method, I had an important decision to make at the supermarket: exactly which chops to buy. Most of the recipes I tried called simply for loin chops, which I took to mean center-cut chops, which are some of the most widely available pork chops in the butcher case. I wondered if that choice could be part of the problem. A whole pork loin is an oblong cut that runs from the shoulder of the pig all the way down to its hip, and from that roast butchers cut four different chops: blade, rib, center cut, and sirloin. Calling for a "loin chop," then, was about as specific as calling for a "steak."

I knew that the muscle and fat makeup of the four chops varies considerably (see "Chop Shop(ping),"

We didn't even have to sear the chops to give this braise great flavor.

page 30) and that the only way to find the best cut for the job would be to test them all in a basic braise. I brined each set of chops (a pretreatment that I knew would help ensure seasoning and juiciness), patted them dry, and seared them in a Dutch oven just long enough to develop some flavorful browning on the meat and the fond on the bottom of the pot—a crucial step for creating a richly flavored sauce. Then I browned the aromatics and deglazed the pot with red wine, which I hoped would temper the meaty richness of the chops. Finally, I poured in some chicken broth, covered the pot, and pushed it into a low (275-degree) oven to simmer gently for about 90 minutes.

When I sliced the meat and called my tasters, the results were unanimous: All but one of the chops had cooked up stringy and bland, officially disqualifying the center-cut, rib, and sirloin contenders from the running. But the blade chops were promising; they contained a good bit of marbling and connective tissue, both of which were breaking down during cooking, lending the meat flavor and also helping preserve its juiciness. The drawback was that the chops buckled considerably during searing and, as

a result, didn't take on much browning or supply much fond to the bottom of the pot. Without that foundation of flavor, the sauce was lackluster and thin, and the wine's contribution one-dimensional and a bit harsh. Blade chops were also a little harder to find in the store, but I decided they were worth seeking out. All in all, this was a good start.

Chop Chop

I retested the searing step to get a closer look at the buckling problem and watched as the dense rim of connective tissues on the side opposite the bone began to contract like a rubber band as soon as the chop came in contact with the hot surface. In fact, the chops contorted so dramatically that I found myself forcing the meat flat with tongs and a spatula. It was awkward to say the least, not to mention ineffective. The lack of fond on the bottom of the vessel also explained why the sauce tasted so anemic. For the sake of both aesthetics and flavor, I had to figure out a way to keep the chops flat. What would happen, I wondered, if I trimmed away the offending portion of connective tissue before searing?

After making a few quick cuts, I placed a new batch of chops in the hot Dutch oven, where they

Trim Your Chops

The band of fatty connective tissue and shoulder meat along the outer edge of blade chops contributes body and flavor to the braise—but it also causes the chops to buckle. To cut out the structural issues without sacrificing flavor, we trim away the band, chop it up, and save the pieces for searing.

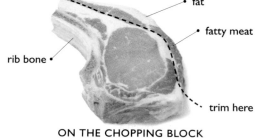

ON THE CHOPPING BLOCK
Trim off the swath of fatty meat and any cartilage running along the edge of the chop. Cut the scraps into 1-inch pieces.

PHOTOGRAPHY: CARL TREMBLAY

stayed flat and took on an even layer of color. This was great news, I thought, until I took a peek at the bottom of the pot. Where I expected to find a thick, crusty layer of fond I found a few faint patches of browning—hardly the makings of a flavorful sauce. Where had all the fond gone? I glanced over to the cutting board and realized the real ingredient for fond was that pile of fatty scraps I was about to pitch into the trash.

That gave me an idea: Rather than toss the fatty trimmings, I chopped them into 1-inch pieces and seared them to generate fond. In less than 10 minutes, I had the most substantial layer of browning yet, thanks to the increased surface area of the smaller pieces. In fact, the fond was so impressive that I wondered if I needed to sear the chops themselves. One side-by-side test gave me my answer: The braise made with unseared chops was every bit as meaty as the seared batch. To take full advantage of their flavor, I left the chunks in the pot during braising, knowing that their rich fat would only add to the porky flavor and unctuousness of the sauce.

Getting a Raise

Even more intriguing, the chopped-up scraps seemed to serve a structural function as well. After searing the trimmings, sautéing the aromatics, deglazing the pan, and adding the broth, I nestled the chops on top of the chunks, where they rested well above the liquid line. When I pulled this batch out of the oven roughly 90 minutes later, not only was the sauce richer and more flavorful, but the chops were noticeably juicier than they had been when they'd cooked more thoroughly submerged in the liquid.

When I mentioned this textural improvement to our science editor, he reminded me of two key facts: First, air conducts heat much less efficiently than liquid. Second, the secret to braising is ensuring that the temperature of the meat hovers for as long as possible in a particular sweet spot—that is, between 160 and 180 degrees. In that range, the meat's collagen converts into gelatin, which holds on to the meat's juices. Too little heat and the meat won't produce enough gelatin; too much and its muscle fibers will wring out moisture before the gelatin can soak it up. The bottom line in this case: The combination of air and liquid was holding the less-submerged chops at a temperature that allowed them to produce a good bit of gelatin and retain their moisture. And just to ensure that they held on to every bit of their flavorful juice, I borrowed a common meat cookery trick: resting the braised chops for 30 minutes before slicing into them, which gives the meat juices ample time to redistribute throughout the meat.

SEAR TRIMMINGS
The trimmed scraps from blade chops contain lots of fat and (in some cases) cartilage. Searing them builds so much flavorful browning that searing the chops themselves isn't necessary.

BROWN ONIONS
To build complex flavor, sauté the onions in the rendered pork fat until golden brown with garlic, thyme, bay leaves, ginger, and allspice.

DEGLAZE
To add acidity, sweetness, and complexity to the braising liquid, deglaze the pot with a combination of red wine, ruby port, and red wine vinegar.

USE TRIMMINGS
Laying the chops on top of the trimmings raises them well above the liquid, where they will cook more gently and retain their flavorful juices.

Final Flourishes

Thanks to the trimmings and staple aromatics like garlic, thyme, and bay leaves, the braising liquid now had decent flavor, but a few tasters remarked that it lacked body, depth, and even some brightness. Fixing the first problem was easy; I simply strained and defatted the liquid and reduced it for about five minutes. A pat of butter whisked in off heat added silkiness and a bit more viscosity.

As for the latter critiques, I tried finishing the pot with a splash of wine, but everyone agreed that only furthered the harshness we'd detected early on. To take the edge off, I went in search of something sweeter in the pantry and came across a bottle of ruby port. Replacing some of the red wine with the fortified stuff went a long way but also flattened the flavor a bit. I wasn't crazy about upping the booziness, so instead I added a touch of red wine vinegar along with the wines, the bright acidity of which brought the sweet-tart balance into equilibrium. I also tossed in a knob of crushed fresh ginger and a dash of allspice, both of which lent this latest batch a rich, spicy aroma.

Just before serving, I added a final splash of vinegar and a handful of chopped parsley, spooned the liquid over the tender, juicy chops, and knew I had finally done right by this classic technique.

RED WINE–BRAISED PORK CHOPS
SERVES 4

Look for chops with a small eye and a large amount of marbling, as these are the best suited to braising. The pork scraps can be removed when straining the sauce in step 4 and served alongside the chops. (They taste great.)

> Salt and pepper
> 4 (10- to 12-ounce) bone-in pork blade chops, 1 inch thick
> 2 teaspoons vegetable oil
> 2 onions, halved and sliced thin
> 5 sprigs fresh thyme plus ¼ teaspoon minced

> 2 garlic cloves, peeled
> 2 bay leaves
> 1 (½-inch) piece ginger, peeled and crushed
> ⅛ teaspoon ground allspice
> ½ cup red wine
> ¼ cup ruby port
> 2 tablespoons plus ½ teaspoon red wine vinegar
> 1 cup low-sodium chicken broth
> 2 tablespoons unsalted butter
> 1 tablespoon minced fresh parsley

1. Dissolve 3 tablespoons salt in 1½ quarts cold water in large container. Submerge chops in brine, cover, and refrigerate for 30 minutes to 1 hour.

2. Adjust oven rack to lower-middle position and heat oven to 275 degrees. Remove chops from brine and pat dry with paper towels. Trim off meat cap and any fat and cartilage opposite rib bones. Cut trimmings into 1-inch pieces. Heat oil in Dutch oven over medium-high heat until shimmering. Add trimmings and brown on all sides, 6 to 9 minutes.

3. Reduce heat to medium and add onions, thyme sprigs, garlic, bay leaves, ginger, and allspice. Cook, stirring occasionally, until onions are golden brown, 5 to 10 minutes. Stir in wine, port, and 2 tablespoons vinegar and cook until reduced to thin syrup, 5 to 7 minutes. Add chicken broth, spread onions and pork scraps into even layer, and bring to simmer. Arrange pork chops on top of pork scraps and onions.

4. Cover, transfer to oven, and cook until meat is tender, 1¼ to 1½ hours. Remove from oven and let chops rest in pot, covered, 30 minutes. Transfer chops to serving platter and tent with aluminum foil. Pour braising liquid through fine-mesh strainer set over large bowl; discard solids. Transfer braising liquid to fat separator and let stand for 5 minutes.

5. Wipe out now-empty pot with wad of paper towels. Return defatted braising liquid to pot and cook over medium-high heat until reduced to 1 cup, 3 to 7 minutes. Off heat, whisk in butter, minced thyme, and remaining ½ teaspoon vinegar. Season with salt and pepper to taste. Pour sauce over chops, sprinkle with parsley, and serve.

A Guide to Everyday Sweeteners

Not just for desserts, these kitchen essentials play a crucial role in browning, tenderizing, adding structure to baked goods, and even enhancing savory dishes. BY DANETTE ST. ONGE

SWEETENERS

Granulated Sugar

The relatively fine crystals and neutral flavor of granulated sugar, highly refined from sugarcane or sugar beets, make it the most versatile sweetener we know. Superfine sugar is simply granulated sugar processed into tinier crystals.

➤ **How We Use It:** We almost always turn to granulated sugar in cakes, singling out the superfine kind when a delicate, grit-free texture is desired (e.g., in sponge cake, shortbread, and meringues). Superfine sugar is also ideal in drinks, where it dissolves almost instantly.

➤ **Make Your Own Superfine Sugar:** Process 1 cup plus 2 teaspoons of granulated sugar in a food processor for 15 to 30 seconds. Yield: 1 cup

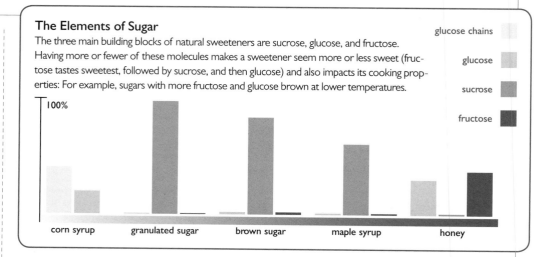

The Elements of Sugar

The three main building blocks of natural sweeteners are sucrose, glucose, and fructose. Having more or fewer of these molecules makes a sweetener seem more or less sweet (fructose tastes sweetest, followed by sucrose, and then glucose) and also impacts its cooking properties: For example, sugars with more fructose and glucose brown at lower temperatures.

Legend: glucose chains, glucose, sucrose, fructose

Chart (100%): corn syrup, granulated sugar, brown sugar, maple syrup, honey

Brown Sugar

Whether light or dark, brown sugar is refined cane sugar that has molasses added back in, contributing flavor and moisture. Dark brown sugar is 6.5 percent molasses; light brown is 3.5 percent.

➤ **How We Use It:** We like how the caramel notes of brown sugar add dimension to sauces, glazes, and baked goods. These sugars can also add chewiness to cookies because they attract and absorb moisture from the surrounding air.

➤ **Make Your Own:** Mix 1 tablespoon of molasses into 1 cup of granulated sugar. (For dark brown sugar, use 2 tablespoons of molasses.) Yield: 1 cup

➤ **Swapping Light for Dark:** In taste tests, we found it hard to distinguish between light and dark brown sugars. In baked goods, if a recipe calls for less than ¼ cup, you're safe using the two interchangeably. Anything more than that and the difference in moisture levels between the sugars can begin to affect the texture.

➤ **Properly Packed:** We're fans of weighing dry ingredients to eliminate any discrepancies in measuring. Whether light or dark, 1 cup of brown sugar that's densely packed should weigh the same as 1 cup of granulated sugar: 7 ounces.

Confectioners' Sugar

Confectioners' sugar is granulated sugar processed 10 times to an ultra-fine powder, with cornstarch added to prevent clumping.

➤ **How We Use It:** Ideal for dusting finished desserts, this sugar's ability to dissolve easily also makes it a good choice for icings, glazes, and candy.

➤ **Make Your Own:** Process 1 cup of granulated sugar and 1 teaspoon of cornstarch in a blender or spice grinder for three minutes. Strain through a mesh strainer to remove any remaining large particles. Yield: 1 cup

Turbinado and Demerara Sugar

Also referred to as "raw" sugar. The coarse amber grains of these products are the residue left after sugarcane has been partially processed to remove some of its molasses. They have a similar texture and delicate molasses taste, but turbinado sugar has been steam-washed and spun in a turbine.

➤ **How We Use It:** The large crystals of these sugars do not readily dissolve—a reason to avoid them in dough. Instead, we like to sprinkle them on muffin tops to create crunch or to form the caramel crust on crème brûlée.

Honey

Honey varies considerably depending on the type of nectar from which it's made. Color generally indicates depth of flavor: Lighter shades will be more mellow and darker shades richer and even slightly bitter.

➤ **How We Use It:** In baking applications, we prefer milder honeys such as orange blossom and clover, which won't compete with other flavors.

Maple Syrup

Maple syrup is from the boiled-down sap of the sugar maple tree. It comes in four grades that reflect when the sap was harvested: grade A light, medium amber, and dark amber; and grade B.

➤ **How We Use It:** For most cooking applications, we prefer the darker, more assertive flavor of grade B. Grade A dark amber is a close second for cooking and our preference for topping pancakes.

➤ **Test Kitchen Favorite:** Maple Grove Farms Pure Maple Syrup

Molasses

A byproduct of the sugar-refining process, molasses boasts a naturally earthy, sweet, smoky flavor. With the exception of ultra-bitter blackstrap molasses, we find that all styles—mild, unsulfured, and robust—are equally acceptable in baking.

➤ **How We Use It:** Molasses isn't just for gingerbread or baked beans. We like adding 2 teaspoons of molasses to chili to give it more dimension.

➤ **Test Kitchen Favorite:** Brer Rabbit All Natural Unsulphured Molasses Mild Flavor

Corn Syrup

Unlike cloyingly sweet high-fructose corn syrup used in processed foods, ordinary corn syrup is only about 65 percent as sweet as sugar. It comes in two forms—light and dark—but we've found that flavor differences are very subtle.

➤ **How We Use It:** Because corn syrup won't crystallize, it's particularly valuable in ice cream, candy, and frosting—even in sauces and glazes.

SUGAR: A MULTITASKER IN BAKING AND COOKING

The sucrose, glucose, and fructose in real sugars contribute much more to baking and cooking than just sweetness.

BROWNING

During cooking and baking, some sucrose breaks down into glucose and fructose, which brown at lower temperatures, providing flavor and color in baked goods.

LEAVENING

Sugar is a prime contributor to the rise of cakes, cookies, and quick breads because it helps incorporate air bubbles into the batter during creaming.

TENDERIZING

Sugar is a major tenderizer. It inhibits gluten formation by preventing some of the water in the dough from hydrating flour proteins.

ON THE SAVORY SIDE

A dash of sugar in savory dishes has a complex, indirect impact on flavor, amping up tastes that might otherwise fade into the background. It can also bring balance to sour, salty, spicy, or bitter ingredients. What's more, sprinkling sugar over the surface of vegetables, fish, or raw meat or adding it to a brine can enhance browning.

UNCOMMON USES FOR SUGAR

Odor Eliminator

To get rid of onion or garlic smell on your hands, wet your hands with warm water, sprinkle with a tablespoon of granulated sugar, rub for a minute, and then rinse off. The sugar crystals act like porous sponges to absorb some of the odor molecules.

Chewiness Preserver

Because sugar absorbs moisture from the air, storing soft or chewy cookies in a closed container with a few cubes of sugar keeps them from drying out. In tests, cookies stored this way retained a just-baked texture for two days.

Pain Reliever

Next time you burn your tongue on a hot drink, try pressing your tongue directly against a spoonful of sugar. The crystals will immediately begin to dissolve—a process that pulls heat from the tongue, dulling the pain.

LOW-CALORIE SWEETENERS

There are plenty of sugar substitutes on the market. However, we tested six types and have yet to find one that's a universal stand-in for the white stuff.

SWEETENER	PERFORMANCE
AGAVE SYRUP Natural sweetener made from the evaporated sap of the Mexican agave plant. **Brand name:** Madhava Agave Nectar	About 1.5 times sweeter than sugar. Ideal for sweetening beverages, as it dissolves easily and has a relatively neutral taste. Not good for baking: Cookies were bready; cakes had a chewy layer of agave stuck in the pan.
ERYTHRITOL Crystallized form of the sugar alcohol erythritol. **Brand name:** Organic Zero	Terrific in beverages. Baking was another story: Sugar cookies turned out crumbly; cakes and muffins were chewy.
GRANULATED SUCRALOSE Sweetener derived from sucrose plus chlorine. **Brand name:** Splenda	Perfectly acceptable in drinks, cobbler, and fruit-pie filling. But sugar cookies were overly soft and cakey and lacked sweetness.
GRANULATED SUCRALOSE BLEND Mix of granulated sucralose and granulated sugar. **Brand name:** Splenda	Drinks, cobbler, and fruit-pie filling all tasted fine. Sugar cookies had surprisingly decent texture but exhibited slight "artificial" aftertaste.
"LITE" CORN SYRUP Blend of glucose and sucralose. **Brand name:** Karo	Sugar cookies and pecan bars had decent texture but unpleasant aftertaste. Frosting was downright rubbery.
SACCHARIN Sweetener derived from petroleum. **Brand name:** Sweet'N Low	Harsh, metallic aftertaste in drinks and baked goods. Sugar cookies were crumbly, and cakes and muffins were chewy. One upside: The metallic taste was less noticeable in fruit-pie fillings.
STEVIA Natural, calorie-free sweetener extracted from the leaves of the stevia plant (a sunflower cousin). **Brand name:** Truvia	Mouth-puckering bitterness in beverages as well as in baked goods. Produced sugar cookies that were dry and crumbly rather than soft and chewy.

STORAGE AND HANDLING

Keeping Brown Sugar Soft

Placing a soaked shard of terra cotta in a sealed container with brown sugar will keep it moist indefinitely.

Quick Fix for the Hard Stuff

Some sources recommend microwaving hardened brown sugar, but we find that this method can leave solid spots. A better way: Place the sugar in a pie plate and bake it in a preheated 250-degree oven for several minutes.

Easy Spooning

Place metal measuring spoons under hot water before dipping them in syrupy sweeteners like honey and maple syrup, and the sticky stuff will slide right off.

Making Honey Crystal Clear

Honey never spoils, but it can crystallize and harden. To return honey to a clear, fluid state, heat it: Microwave it in 10-second increments until the crystals dissolve, or place the glass jar in a pan of hot water.

Busting Up Clumps

Even when stored in an airtight container, granulated sugar can form large, solid lumps. A few strokes with a potato masher will return it to a pourable state.

Quicker Fish Chowder

Searching for a route to fresher, cleaner flavors, we got a bonus: shorter cooking time.

≥ BY BRYAN ROOF ≤

New England fish chowder got its start on the fishing vessels that plied the Newfoundland coast in the 18th century. Sailors would throw a piece of their catch (typically cod or haddock) into a pot with water, salt pork, and bulky crackers known as ship's biscuits or hardtack, which helped thicken the stock. When chowder hit the New England mainland at the turn of the 19th century, cooks took to bulking up the broth with potatoes instead of crackers, and milk—especially canned evaporated milk—became a regular addition. Today, the richness quotient has been upped even further, with chowders often featuring a base consisting almost entirely of cream.

The trouble is, many modern chowders are so rich that they mask the flavor of the fish altogether. I wanted to honor the soup's simple roots by showcasing moist, tender morsels of fish in a delicate, clean-tasting broth.

Meaty cod was not only the most traditional choice, it was also easy to find. As for the broth, I ruled out fussy, from-scratch stock from the get-go, turning instead to store-bought clam juice and chicken broth. I made two batches of chowder, first rendering diced salt pork and then gently sweating onions, thyme, salt, and a bay leaf in its fat. I then added 7 cups of either clam juice or chicken broth to each pot, along with peeled and diced Yukon Gold potatoes (chosen for their subtle buttery flavor). When the potatoes were just tender, I stirred in chunks of cod and simmered the chowders 10 minutes longer. Both were flops: The salty clam juice was too potent (even in a subsequent batch cut with water) and chicken broth was, well, too chicken-y. That left me with plain water.

When I cooked up a water-based chowder, I was encouraged to find that the broth had a clean, light flavor. But the fish itself got mixed reviews: After just 10 minutes of cooking, some pieces were moist and tender while others were dry and overdone. And the potatoes hadn't absorbed any of the fish's flavor. Fortunately, I had a simple idea that I hoped would solve both problems: I would use the cod to make an ultra-quick fish stock and then simmer the potatoes in the stock. I slipped cod fillets into the water flavored with salt pork, onion, and seasonings;

covered the pot; turned off the heat; and let the fish poach for five minutes. I then transferred the fillets to a bowl and set them aside. Tasting my speedy stock, I was happy to discover that it had developed a significant amount of flavor in just five minutes. Plus, this gentle approach eliminated any chance of overcooking the fragile fillets.

Next I added the potatoes to the broth and simmered them until tender. Finally, I returned the fillets to the pot, stirring to separate them into chunks. Great news: Every bite of fish was perfectly tender, and the potatoes, having soaked up the savory broth, now tasted fabulous.

On to the dairy. For tradition's sake, I experimented with replacing 2 cups of the water with evaporated milk, added in once the potatoes were tender. The resulting chowder was panned for its sweetness, as was one made with equal parts evaporated and regular milk. Half-and-half was too rich: It masked the delicate flavors that I was working hard to protect. In the end, tasters applauded the light, fresh taste of chowder made with whole milk. A tablespoon of cornstarch whisked into the milk before adding it to the pot coated its proteins, preventing it from curdling as the soup simmered.

TASTING Oyster Crackers

A good oyster cracker should not only keep its crunch in soup but also serve as an out-of-the-box snack. We sampled four national brands. OTC crackers, the most traditional, were unleavened balls the size and consistency of "jawbreakers" that tasters found "bland." We much preferred the crackers from Sunshine, which were smaller, lighter, and crispier, making them easier to eat in soup and better suited for snacking. For complete tasting results, go to www.CooksIllustrated.com/feb12. –Sarah Seitz

CAPTAIN OF CRUNCH
Sunshine Krispy
Soup & Oyster Crackers
Price: $3.49 for 11 oz
Comments: Even in soup, these "light," "crisp" crackers boasted addictively "toasty" flavor and crunch.

DOUGH BOY
OTC Oyster Crackers
Price: $2.88 for 10 oz
Comments: "Giant," "too hard," and "raw"-tasting, these traditional crackers prompted comparisons to "jawbreakers" and "dog biscuits."

Tasters requested one last refinement, complaining that the salt pork flavor was overbearing. Instead of dicing the salt pork, I left it in two large chunks that didn't produce as much browning and used butter to sweat the onions. Sure enough, the broth now had a milder pork flavor that allowed the fish to shine.

At last, here was an updated chowder that paid homage to its New England pedigree.

NEW ENGLAND FISH CHOWDER
SERVES 6 TO 8

Haddock, or other flaky white fish, may be substituted for cod. Garnish the chowder with minced fresh chives, crisp bacon bits, or oyster crackers.

- 2 tablespoons unsalted butter
- 2 onions, cut into ½-inch dice
- 4 ounces salt pork, rind removed, rinsed, and cut into 2 pieces
- 1½ teaspoons minced fresh thyme
  Salt and pepper
- 1 bay leaf
- 5 cups water
- 2 pounds skinless cod fillets, sliced crosswise into 6 equal pieces
- 1½ pounds Yukon Gold potatoes, peeled and cut into ½-inch dice
- 2 cups whole milk
- 1 tablespoon cornstarch

1. Melt butter in Dutch oven over medium heat. Add onions, salt pork, thyme, ¾ teaspoon salt, and bay leaf; cook, stirring occasionally, until onions are softened but not browned, 3 to 5 minutes. Add water and bring to simmer. Remove pot from heat, gently place cod fillets in water, cover, and let fish stand until opaque and nearly cooked through, about 5 minutes. Using metal spatula, transfer cod to bowl.

2. Return pot to medium-high heat, add potatoes, and bring to simmer. Cook until potatoes are tender and beginning to break apart, about 20 minutes.

3. Meanwhile, whisk milk, cornstarch, and ½ teaspoon pepper together in bowl. Stir milk mixture into chowder and return to simmer. Return fish and any accumulated juices to pot. Remove pot from heat, cover, and let stand for 5 minutes. Remove and discard salt pork and bay leaf. Stir gently with wooden spoon to break fish into large pieces. Season with salt and pepper to taste. Serve immediately.

Watch It Become Chowder
Video available FREE for 4 months at
www.CooksIllustrated.com/feb12

Real Croissants at Home

Croissants can be a culinary triumph—or a waste of time. Our recipe guarantees success.

≥ BY ANDREA GEARY ≤

I can think of two reasons why almost nobody makes croissants. First, most folks buy them from a bakery, or even a coffee shop or supermarket. Second, the process is long and daunting. It pairs the challenge of preparing a laminated pastry (one composed of many layers of fat and dough) with the potential unpredictability of a yeasted item. Even if you follow a recipe to the letter, the results don't always bake up as they should: a deep golden brown, shatteringly crisp surface that gives way to delicate layers of buttery, rich-yet-light pastry within.

I can also think of two reasons why making your own croissants is absolutely worth the effort. For starters, most commercial croissants are squat, dense, or just plain bland. Plus, there's nothing quite as satisfying as pulling off this feat yourself—from folding and shaping the dough, to filling your kitchen with the scent of warm pastry, to watching your brunch guests swoon.

That said, achieving consistent results is difficult. Sometimes the croissants collapse during baking and turn dense, losing their signature layers; other times the butter leaks out onto the baking sheet, yielding thick-crusted specimens that have essentially fried in their own fat. And then there's the sheer force required to muscle the gluten-heavy dough into submission. It would be a challenge, but I decided to get into the kitchen and learn where I was veering off course.

Tiers of Joy

Before homing in on specific problems, I reviewed the basics of laminated pastry. Flour, milk, yeast, a bit of melted butter, sugar, and salt are mixed together, rested briefly, rolled into a rectangle, and refrigerated. The dough is then rolled into a larger rectangle and wrapped around a large block of cold butter, and the dough-butter package (known as a plaque) is rolled into a long rectangle. This is where the trademark layering happens: The plaque is folded into thirds, yielding layers of dough separated by layers of butter. This rolling and folding process (called a "turn") is repeated up to five times, tripling the number of layers with each turn. Finally, the plaque is rolled again, cut into triangles, shaped into crescents, left to rise, brushed with egg wash, and baked.

To get started, I rounded up several recipes and found that the techniques—specifically the number of turns—varied widely: anywhere from two (which

A carefully orchestrated process yields astonishingly flaky, delicate croissants.

makes nine layers of dough) to a bicep-punishing five (which theoretically produces 243 layers). Figuring out the ideal number of turns would be an important first step, as the turning process has a twofold effect: It not only creates layers in the dough but also develops gluten (the elastic protein that is formed when the flour is moistened), which causes the dough to stubbornly bounce back and resist rolling. Strong dough is no problem for bakeshops, which use machines called sheeters (similar to huge pasta machines) to roll out the plaque. But for my at-home recipe, I'd need a dough that I could manage with just my hands.

To my great relief, too many turns ended up being detrimental. As the layers of fat became thinner, they were more easily absorbed into the dough, eventually yielding a pastry more akin to brioche—rich and tender, but with a homogeneous, bready crumb. Three turns seemed to be the magic number for producing the most distinct layers.

But rolling and folding the dough three times was still hard. Knowing that the protein content of the flour was directly affecting the gluten development, I made three new batches with different types (and brands) of flour: one with moderate-protein (10.5 percent) Gold Medal all-purpose flour; another with higher-protein (11.7 percent) all-purpose flour

from King Arthur; and a final sample with high-protein (14 percent) bread flour. As I expected, the higher the protein, the more gluten developed, and the more difficult the plaque was to roll out. Still, the test was informative. The bread-flour croissants were the best I'd ever made: tall, crisp, and filled with airy spirals of buttery pastry.

It turns out that gluten doesn't just make a dough more elastic; it also makes it more resistant to tearing during rolling, rising, and baking (when it expands), and strong enough to maintain the thin sheets necessary for distinct layering. But since my hands were blistered from rolling out this sturdy bread-flour dough, I decided to compromise with the higher-protein all-purpose flour, hoping that I could find another way to make the dough more compliant.

Fat of the Land

That left me with the butter. From the start I'd defaulted to Land O'Lakes (about 81 percent butterfat), but some recipes called for European-style butter, the butterfat content of which typically starts at around 83 percent and goes up as high as 86 percent. Another point I noted: Recipes using standard butter called for kneading it with a bit of flour before shaping it into a block, while those that specified European-style butter added no flour to the block. Not sure what effect the flour or the extra fat might have, I made three batches of croissants using European-style butter, standard butter mixed with flour, and unadulterated standard butter, respectively.

The differences were remarkable. When I tried shaping the unfloured standard butter, it broke into pieces, and the resulting dough baked up heavy. Flouring the standard butter helped, and the croissants were nicely layered—but didn't compare with those made with European-style butter. The higher-fat dough not only proved easier to work with but also boasted superior layering and ultra-rich flavor.

I did some homework and learned two reasons why more butterfat made such a difference. First, butter with less fat contains more water. Butter with 81 percent fat, for example, contains about

PHOTOGRAPHY: CARL TREMBLAY

15 percent water, while butter with 83 percent fat has about 13 percent. This variance may sound small, but in fact the lower-fat butter has roughly 15 percent more water than the higher-fat butter—a difference significant enough that the extra water in the regular-butter dough was gluing the layers together, leading to a dense crumb. It also explained the purpose of adding flour to the standard butter: It soaked up the extra moisture.

Second, higher-fat butter remains solid over a wider temperature range, meaning that it's more pliable when cold and also holds its shape better as it warms up. This is advantageous since the butter for laminated dough must be firm to function as a barrier between distinct layers of dough and, therefore, must remain solid as the dough is handled.

Stay Cool

I'd made great progress but had one more problem to iron out. For consistently tall, flaky results, I needed the butter and dough to be at exactly the same degree of malleability during rolling. I had been refrigerating the plaque between turns, but this resulted in butter that was firmer than the dough and therefore prone to breaking (and sticking where the butter was absent). Conversely, if I left the plaque at room temperature, the butter became softer than the dough and leaked out during rolling. The secret would be ensuring that these two markedly different components had the same putty-like texture. But how?

It wasn't until I contacted a local baker, Christy Timon of Clear Flour Bread, in Brookline, Massachusetts, that I came upon the solution: freezing the dough. As Timon demonstrated, super-chilling the butter-dough square for 30 minutes before rolling firmed the dough to the consistency of the butter without appreciably altering the texture of the butter. Together with the higher-protein all-purpose flour and the European-style butter, this freezer technique added up to a hat trick of discoveries that led to layering so distinct that it was visible even in the raw dough.

Confident that I had finally mastered croissants, I prepared a final batch. When I removed the bronzed beauties from the oven, the layers that had been subtly suggested in the raw dough had bloomed into crisp, delicate tiers. My colleagues declared them a triumph, regretting only that the testing had come to an end.

Three Tricks Guarantee Flaky Croissants

USE HIGH-PROTEIN FLOUR
High-protein all-purpose flour such as King Arthur develops more gluten and is more resistant to tearing.

USE EUROPEAN-STYLE BUTTER
Higher-fat European-style butter contains less water than domestic butter, thereby creating flakier layers.

FREEZE THE DOUGH
To ensure that the butter and the dough surrounding it are equally malleable, briefly freeze the packet.

CROISSANTS
MAKES 22 CROISSANTS

Twelve croissants are baked first; the remaining 10 can be frozen. The croissants take at least 10 hours to make from start to finish, but the process can be spread over two days. We strongly encourage using high-protein all-purpose flour, such as King Arthur, and European-style butter (we like Plugrá). If the dough retracts or softens at any point, fold it into thirds, wrap it in plastic, and freeze it for 15 minutes. Do not make these in a room that is warmer than 80 degrees.

- 3 tablespoons unsalted butter plus 24 tablespoons (3 sticks) unsalted European-style butter, very cold
- 1¾ cups whole milk
- 4 teaspoons instant or rapid-rise yeast
- 4¼ cups (21¼ ounces) all-purpose flour
- ¼ cup (1¾ ounces) sugar
-    Salt
- 1 large egg
- 1 teaspoon cold water

1. Melt 3 tablespoons butter in medium saucepan over low heat. Remove from heat and immediately stir in milk (temperature should be lower than 90 degrees). Whisk in yeast; transfer milk mixture to bowl of stand mixer. Add flour, sugar, and 2 teaspoons salt. Using dough hook, knead on low speed until cohesive dough forms, 2 to 3 minutes. Increase speed to medium-low and knead for 1 minute. Remove bowl from mixer and cover with plastic wrap. Let dough rest at room temperature 30 minutes.

2. Transfer dough to parchment paper–lined baking sheet and shape into 10 by 7-inch rectangle about 1 inch thick. Wrap tightly with plastic and refrigerate for 2 hours.

3. BUTTER BLOCK: While dough chills, fold 24-inch length of parchment in half to create 12-inch rectangle. Fold over 3 open sides of rectangle to form 8-inch square with enclosed sides. Crease folds firmly. Place 24 tablespoons cold butter directly on counter and beat with rolling pin for about 60 seconds until butter is just pliable but not warm, then fold butter in on itself using bench scraper. Beat into rough 6-inch square. Unfold parchment envelope. Using bench scraper, transfer butter to center of parchment, refolding at creases to enclose. Turn packet over so that flaps are underneath and gently roll until butter fills parchment square, taking care to achieve even thickness. Refrigerate at least 45 minutes.

4. LAMINATE: Transfer dough to freezer. After 30 minutes, transfer to lightly floured counter and roll into 17 by 8-inch rectangle with long side parallel to edge of counter. Unwrap butter and place in center of dough. Fold sides of dough over butter so they meet in center. Press seam together with fingertips. With rolling pin, press firmly on each open end of packet. Roll out lengthwise into 24 by 8-inch rectangle. Starting at bottom of dough, fold into thirds like business letter into 8-inch square. Turn dough 90 degrees counterclockwise. Roll out lengthwise again into 24 by 8-inch rectangle and fold into thirds. Place dough on sheet, wrap tightly with plastic, and return to freezer for 30 minutes.

5. Transfer dough to lightly floured counter so that top flap opens on right. Roll out dough lengthwise into 24 by 8-inch rectangle and fold into thirds. Place dough on sheet, wrap tightly with plastic, and refrigerate for 2 hours or up to 24 hours.

6. SHAPE: Transfer dough to freezer. After 30 minutes, transfer to lightly floured counter and roll into 18 by 16-inch rectangle with long side of rectangle parallel to edge of counter. Fold upper half of dough over lower half. Using ruler, mark dough at 3-inch intervals along bottom edge with bench scraper (you should have 5 marks). Move ruler to top edge of dough, measure in 1½ inches from left, then use this mark to measure out 3-inch intervals (you should have 6 marks). Starting at lower left corner, use sharp pizza wheel or knife to cut dough from mark to mark. You will have 12 triangles and 5 diamonds; discard scraps. Unfold diamonds and cut into 10 triangles (making 22 equal-size triangles in total).

7. Position 1 triangle on counter. (Keep remaining triangles covered with plastic.) Cut ½-inch slit in center of short side of triangle. Grasp triangle by 2 corners on either side of slit and stretch gently, then stretch bottom point. Place triangle on counter so point is facing you. Fold down both sides of slit. Roll top of triangle partway toward point. Gently grasp point with 1 hand and stretch again. Resume rolling, tucking point underneath. Curve ends gently toward each other to create crescent. Repeat with remaining triangles.

8. Place 12 croissants on 2 parchment-lined sheets at least 2½ inches apart. Lightly wrap with plastic. Let stand at room temperature until nearly doubled in size, 2½ to 3 hours. (Shaped croissants can be refrigerated for up to 18 hours. Remove from refrigerator to rise and add at least 30 minutes to rising time.)

9. After croissants have been rising for 2 hours, adjust oven racks to upper-middle and lower-middle positions and heat oven to 425 degrees. In small bowl, whisk together egg, water, and pinch salt. Brush croissants with egg wash. Place croissants in oven and reduce temperature to 400 degrees. Bake for 12 minutes, then switch and rotate baking sheets. Continue to bake until deep golden brown, 8 to 12 minutes longer. Transfer to wire rack and cool about 15 minutes. Serve warm or at room temperature.

TO MAKE AHEAD: After shaping, place 10 croissants 1 inch apart on parchment-lined sheet. Wrap with plastic and freeze until solid, about 2 hours. Transfer to zipper-lock bag and freeze for up to 2 months. Bake frozen croissants as directed from step 8, increasing rising time by 1 to 2 hours.

MAKE THE BUTTER BLOCK

1. Fold 24-inch length of parchment in half to create 12-inch rectangle. Fold over 3 open sides to form 8-inch square.

2. Using rolling pin, beat cold butter until just pliable.

3. Fold butter in on itself using bench scraper. Beat into rough 6-inch square.

4. Unfold parchment envelope and, using bench scraper, transfer butter to parchment, refolding at creases to enclose.

5. Turn packet over, and gently roll out so butter fills parchment, taking care to achieve even thickness. Refrigerate.

LAMINATE THE DOUGH

1. After freezing dough for 30 minutes, roll into 17 by 8-inch rectangle. Place unwrapped butter in center of dough.

2. Fold sides of dough over butter so they meet in center. Press seam together with fingertips.

3. With rolling pin, press firmly on each open end of packet. Roll out dough lengthwise into 24 by 8-inch rectangle.

4. Starting at bottom of dough, fold into thirds like business letter. Turn dough 90 degrees. Roll and fold into thirds again.

5. Place dough on sheet, wrap with plastic, and return to freezer for 30 minutes. Roll and fold into thirds, then rewrap and refrigerate for 2 hours.

SHAPE THE CROISSANTS

1. After freezing dough for 30 minutes, roll into 18 by 16-inch rectangle. Fold upper half of dough over lower half.

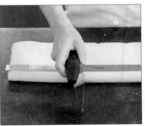

2. Using ruler, mark dough at 3-inch intervals along bottom edge. Move ruler to top edge of dough, measure in 1½ inches from left, then use this mark to measure out 3-inch intervals.

3. Using pizza wheel or knife, cut dough from mark to mark. You should have 12 triangles and 5 diamonds; discard scraps.

4. Unfold diamonds and cut into 10 triangles (making 22 equal-size triangles in total).

5. Cut ½-inch slit in center of short side of each triangle.

6. Grasp triangle by 2 corners on either side of slit and stretch gently, then stretch bottom point.

7. Place triangle on counter so point is facing you. Fold down both sides of slit.

8. Roll top of triangle partway toward point.

9. Gently grasp point and stretch again. Resume rolling, tucking point underneath.

10. Curve ends gently toward each other to create crescent.

Chocolate Truffles Made Simple

Turning out dense, creamy, professional-quality chocolate truffles at home was easy—once we found a cure for the grainy texture.

⇒ BY RAQUEL PELZEL ⇐

Chocolate truffles are inherently simple confections. These rich, dense balls of ganache often contain nothing more than good-quality bar chocolate and heavy cream. Yet they're surprisingly difficult to get right. The chocolate-to-cream ratio must be spot-on; otherwise, the truffle will be either overly dense or too soft to hold its shape. Creating a smooth, shiny coating is even more finicky—and then you've got to contend with the mess of dipping the truffle into it. Finally, there's shaping. The pros use a pastry bag, but it takes practice to produce perfectly symmetrical pieces.

My goal was clear: come up with an approach that would produce flawless results for anyone, regardless of their candy-making experience. Ditching the tempered chocolate coating was one way I could abridge the process; I'd go for the more rustic approach of rolling the truffles in cocoa. Beyond that, I'd have to do some experimenting.

Against the Grain

I threw together a basic ganache: 4 ounces of warm cream poured over 12 ounces of chopped chocolate and blended in a food processor until smooth. Then I chilled the mixture, piped it into balls, firmed the pieces in the fridge, and rolled them in cocoa. What I wanted was fudgy, silky ganache. What I got, unfortunately, was dry and gritty.

I needed a way to loosen up and smooth out the texture of the ganache without pushing it into the realm of chocolate sauce, so I tried an obvious quick fix: upping the cream. This made for a ganache that was creamier, but rolling the more-fluid mixture was nearly impossible.

Paging through my research recipes for ideas, I noticed that some called for adding butter to the ganache to make it more silky. Others also incorporated a little corn syrup, which makes the ganache feel smoother by reducing the size of the chocolate's sugar

Refrigerated in an airtight container, these truffles keep for up to a week.

crystals; when they're too large, they can be detected as grainy. Adding a little of each helped, but even then the truffles weren't as satiny-textured as I wanted.

Clearing the Air

I'd taken the ingredient list as far as it could go, so I approached the graininess problem from another angle: the mixing method. The food processor, immersion blender, and stand mixer all produced truffles that weren't as smooth as I'd hoped. Mechanical intervention was apparently not the way to go.

Our science editor quickly fingered the problem: air. Instead of smoothing out the ganache, the high-speed mixing was incorporating too much air, causing the emulsion to break. More specifically, the droplets of fat were coating the surface of the air bubbles instead of the cocoa particles; as a result, the cocoa particles absorbed water and stuck together in larger clumps that we were detecting as graininess.

That meant I needed to do everything I could to decrease the air in the ganache. I tried hand-whisking the chocolate and warm cream, but the method still required a good bit of stirring just to melt the chocolate. I was better off premelting the chocolate in the microwave until it was almost completely fluid. (While I was at it, I microwaved the cream, too.) Then I stirred the corn syrup (plus vanilla extract and salt) into the cream and poured the liquid over the mostly melted chocolate. Instead of a whisk—specifically designed to incorporate air—I grabbed a wooden spoon, gradually working in the butter before piping and chilling the ganache. The improvement was startling. The grit wasn't gone, but it was markedly reduced.

A Different Kind of Cool-Down

It was time to try a technique that I'd come across in my research but had pushed to the back of my mind: Instead of chilling the ganache immediately after mixing it, some chocolatiers allow it to sit at room temperature overnight, claiming that the

Truffle Trials We Overcame

Truffles may be nothing more than chocolate ganache rolled in a coating, but they're full of potential pitfalls.

DULL EXTERIOR •
Tempering chocolate for the coating gives it a glossy sheen—but unless you're a professional chocolatier, it's a tricky business. One wrong move and the results can easily turn matte and look smudged.

DRIPPY MESS •
Chocolate-dipped truffles must be drained—and tend to drip all over the counter.

• **GRAINY INTERIOR**
Even if the ganache looks creamy and smooth when warm, it can turn gritty and grainy as it cools.

• **LOPSIDED LOOKS**
Piping perfectly round truffles takes a practiced, steady hand. Otherwise, the results will be lopsided.

PHOTOGRAPHY: CARL TREMBLAY

HOW TO GET SILKY-SMOOTH TRUFFLES

START WITH MELTED CHOCOLATE Microwaving the chocolate before mixing it with the cream allows us to stir—rather than whisk—them together, reducing the air that can cause grittiness.

ADD CORN SYRUP, THEN BUTTER Corn syrup smooths over the gritty texture of granulated sugar. Small pieces of softened butter add silkiness.

COOL IT DOWN GRADUALLY Allowing the mixture to cool at room temperature for two hours before chilling prevents the formation of grainy crystals.

gradual cooling makes for a creamier product. It was worth a shot. I mixed up another batch of ganache and let it cool on the counter for eight hours before shaping the truffles. The change was astonishing—the texture of the ganache was silky smooth, without a trace of grittiness. Our science editor explained: When melted chocolate cools and resolidifies, the crystalline structure of its cocoa butter is reorganized. Chilling the ganache in the refrigerator produced a more stable crystalline structure that melts at higher than body temperature, leading to a perception of graininess. The slower cool-down led to a different, more desirable set of crystals that literally melt in the mouth, for a sensation of ultra-smoothness. But did I really have to leave the ganache overnight? I wondered if I could get this same effect with a shorter rest at room temperature, to keep truffle making a same-day project. To my delight, I found that a two-hour cool-down produced the same marvelously creamy texture. The only issue was that without any refrigeration, the ganache was too soft to work with. I solved this by chilling the ganache for two hours after cooling it on the counter—a step that didn't add back any graininess.

The only remaining glitch: shaping. I wanted to avoid a pastry bag, since perfect results take practice. But forming the truffles with a mini ice-cream scoop, a melon baller, or a measuring spoon didn't work; I ended up scraping the ganache out of the utensils with my fingers. I finally came across a promising solution from chocolatier Alice Medrich: Cool the ganache in a baking dish and then unmold the mostly solid block, cut it into squares, and roll them into rounds. This worked perfectly, the chocolate slabs just soft enough to roll without cracking.

The last step before chilling, rolling the truffles in cocoa powder, was easy—provided I could keep my warm hands from smearing the chocolate. I handled the pieces as little as possible, until I realized that I could use the cocoa to my advantage. Before rolling, I lightly dusted my palms with the dry powder, which kept the melting problem in check. And once I cut the cocoa powder with a little confectioners'

sugar to reduce bitterness and chalkiness, several tasters noted that they preferred this rustic, more distinct contrast to the tempered chocolate shell.

Firm, velvety smooth, and round, these truffles are plenty simple for beginners yet handsome enough to please even the most discriminating chocolatier.

CHOCOLATE TRUFFLES
MAKES 64 TRUFFLES

In step 5, running your knife under hot water and wiping it dry makes cutting the chocolate easier. We recommend using Callebaut Intense Dark L-60-40NV or Ghirardelli Bittersweet Chocolate Baking Bar. If giving the truffles as a gift, set them in 1½-inch candy cup liners in a gift box and keep them chilled. For our free recipe for Chocolate Chai Masala Truffles, go to www.CooksIllustrated.com/feb12.

Ganache

- 2 cups (12 ounces) bittersweet chocolate, roughly chopped
- ½ cup heavy cream
- 2 tablespoons light corn syrup
- ½ teaspoon vanilla extract
  Pinch salt
- 1½ tablespoons unsalted butter, cut into 8 pieces and softened

Coating

- 1 cup (3 ounces) Dutch-processed cocoa
- ¼ cup (1 ounce) confectioners' sugar

1. FOR THE GANACHE: Lightly coat 8-inch baking dish with vegetable oil spray. Make parchment sling by folding 2 long sheets of parchment so that they are as wide as baking pan. Lay sheets of parchment in pan perpendicular to each other, with extra hanging over edges of pan. Push parchment into corners and up sides of pan, smoothing flush to pan.

2. Microwave chocolate in medium bowl at 50 percent power, stirring occasionally, until mostly melted and few small chocolate pieces remain, 2 to 3 minutes; set aside. Microwave cream in measuring

cup until warm to touch, about 30 seconds. Stir corn syrup, vanilla, and salt into cream and pour mixture over chocolate. Cover bowl with plastic wrap, set aside for 3 minutes, and then stir with wooden spoon to combine. Stir in butter, one piece at a time, until fully incorporated.

3. Using rubber spatula, transfer ganache to prepared pan and set aside at room temperature for 2 hours. Cover pan and transfer to refrigerator; chill for at least 2 hours. (Ganache can be stored, refrigerated, for up to 2 days.)

4. FOR THE COATING: Sift cocoa and sugar through fine-mesh strainer into large bowl. Sift again into large cake pan and set aside.

5. Gripping overhanging parchment, lift ganache from pan. Cut ganache into sixty-four 1-inch squares (8 rows by 8 rows). (If ganache cracks during slicing, let sit at room temperature for 5 to 10 minutes and then proceed.) Dust hands lightly with cocoa mixture to prevent ganache from sticking and roll each square into ball. Transfer balls to cake pan with cocoa mixture and roll to evenly coat. Lightly shake truffles in hand over pan to remove excess coating. Transfer coated truffles to airtight container and repeat until all ganache squares are rolled and coated. Cover container and refrigerate for at least 2 hours or up to 1 week. Let truffles sit at room temperature for 5 to 10 minutes before serving.

HAZELNUT-MOCHA TRUFFLES

Substitute 2 tablespoons Frangelico (hazelnut-flavored liqueur) and 1 tablespoon espresso powder for vanilla. For coating, omit confectioners' sugar and use enough cocoa to coat hands while shaping truffles. Roll shaped truffles in 1½ cups finely chopped toasted hazelnuts.

EQUIPMENT TESTING Moka Pots

Often referred to as poor man's espresso machines, Italian moka pots are small, inexpensive (less than $100) coffee makers that use steam pressure to force hot water up through coffee grounds. That pressure isn't high enough for true espresso extraction, but the coffee that moka pots make is stronger and more complex than anything brewed in a drip machine. Of the eight pots we tested—three 3-cup stovetop designs and five 6-cup electric models—the electric mokas were universally disappointing, as they failed to deliver enough power and produced flat, characterless coffee. Conversely, two of the three stovetop devices brewed rich, full-bodied coffee—once we had mastered subtle techniques like tamping the grinds and immediately removing the pot from the heat. For complete testing results and tips for brewing moka pot coffee, go to www.CooksIllustrated.com/feb12. –Taizeth Sierra

TOP POT
The classically designed Bialetti Moka Express ($24.95) quickly brewed rich, strong coffee.

Pesto Sauces for Cheese Ravioli

Packaged ravioli are super convenient.
But choose the wrong sauce and dinner will be a washout.

⇒ BY DAVID PAZMIÑO ⇐

Packaged cheese ravioli seem like a no-brainer for weeknight cooks: Just top them with a quick-simmered red sauce (or even reach for a jarred one) and dinner is served. But this approach ignores an unfortunate reality of premade ravioli: Inevitably, excess water trapped inside the ravioli during boiling leaks out when you cut into them, waterlogging the dish. Tomato sauce just doesn't have enough body or concentrated flavor to stand up to the extra liquid. Simple sauces based on browned butter, olive oil, or cream aren't a great choice either: Lacking the sharpness required to provide a contrast with the typical ricotta filling, they make for a heavy, cloying dish.

The ideal sauce, I reasoned, would be a thick, concentrated mixture—one that the excess water would loosen and dilute to the proper consistency and flavor. It occurred to me that pesto might be just the thing. In addition to boasting robust flavor and substantial texture, it would match the convenience of store-bought ravioli since it takes mere minutes to whip up in the food processor.

There's nothing wrong with Genovese basil and pine-nut pesto, but I wanted to branch out. Recalling a wonderfully bold red pepper spread that I had tasted on crostini, I wondered if I could translate its smoky tang into a pesto sauce, so I tried replacing the basil in a traditional pesto recipe with jarred roasted red peppers. It was a good start, but the slightly bitter edge of the pine nuts clashed with the peppers' sharpness. Replacing the pine nuts with sweeter pistachios improved matters, but the result lacked complexity. The solution: adding some basil back into the mix. Then there was the garlic. I had been using three cloves, which tasters thought overwhelmed the other flavors. Even two cloves were too harsh, so I borrowed a test kitchen trick, blanching them in the boiling pasta water to mellow their bite. Problem solved.

With that template in place, I moved on to variations, pairing an assertive central ingredient with Parmesan cheese, blanched garlic, and complementary herbs and toasted nuts or seeds. Because the water content varied with each batch, I tailored the fat level in each to obtain the right consistency.

There was one last consideration: how best to cook store-bought ravioli. Because the texture and moisture level of the pastas differed widely from brand to brand, and because the package instructions universally overestimated cooking time, I came up with my own indicator: Once the corners of the ravioli were slightly tender—but not mushy—I took them off the heat.

I now had a repertoire of fresh, easy, intensely flavorful sauces that elevated a convenience food to something worth making anytime.

ROASTED RED PEPPER AND PISTACHIO PESTO FOR CHEESE RAVIOLI
MAKES ABOUT 1½ CUPS

Fresh or frozen ravioli may be used. For our free recipe for Fennel and Tarragon Pesto for Cheese Ravioli, go to www.CooksIllustrated.com/feb12.

- 2 garlic cloves, unpeeled
- 1¼–1¾ pounds cheese ravioli
  Salt and pepper
- 1½ cups jarred roasted red peppers, rinsed and patted dry
- 1 cup fresh basil
- 1½ ounces Parmesan cheese, grated (¾ cup)
- ½ cup raw shelled pistachios, toasted
- ¼ cup extra-virgin olive oil

1. Bring 4 quarts water to boil in large pot. Add garlic to water and cook for 1 minute. Using slotted spoon, transfer garlic to bowl and rinse under cold water to stop cooking. Peel and mince garlic.

2. Add ravioli and 1 tablespoon salt to boiling water and cook, stirring often, until al dente. Reserve ½ cup cooking water, then drain ravioli and return to pot.

3. Pulse garlic, red peppers, basil, Parmesan, and pistachios in food processor until finely ground, 20 to 30 pulses, scraping down bowl as needed. With processor running, slowly add oil until incorporated. Season with salt and pepper to taste.

4. Add 1 cup pesto to ravioli and gently toss to combine, adding 1 tablespoon cooking water at a time, as needed, to adjust consistency. Serve, passing remaining pesto separately.

SAGE, WALNUT, AND BROWNED BUTTER PESTO FOR CHEESE RAVIOLI

Heat 6 tablespoons butter in 10-inch skillet over medium-high heat, swirling constantly until golden brown and butter has nutty aroma, 2 to 4 minutes. Remove skillet from heat and add ¾ cup chopped fresh sage to butter. Set aside to cool, about 10 minutes. Proceed with recipe, substituting butter mixture for roasted red peppers, fresh parsley for basil, and toasted walnuts for pistachios, and omitting olive oil.

GREEN OLIVE, ALMOND, AND ORANGE PESTO FOR CHEESE RAVIOLI

Substitute ½ cup pitted green olives for roasted red peppers, 1½ cups fresh parsley for basil, and toasted slivered almonds for pistachios. Add ½ teaspoon grated orange zest and 2 tablespoons orange juice to food processor in step 3 and increase amount of olive oil to ½ cup.

KALE AND SUNFLOWER SEED PESTO FOR CHEESE RAVIOLI

Substitute 2 cups chopped kale leaves for roasted red peppers and toasted sunflower seeds for pistachios. Add ½ teaspoon red pepper flakes to food processor in step 3 and increase amount of olive oil to ½ cup.

Tasting Supermarket Cheese Ravioli

Store-bought cheese ravioli offer convenience, but are any worth the time savings? We tasted five nationally available brands of cheese ravioli and found that the best had maximum cheese per square (or round), with at least 1 gram of filling for every 2 grams of pasta. But the filling had to taste, well, cheesy—it needed some Parmesan or Romano along with the usual ricotta, not fillers of cracker meal or a heavy hand with spices and herbs. One of the most recognizable brands, Buitoni, lost points for a filling that was too sparse, a fault mitigated by pasta "with good bite" that wasn't "hard or chewy." Our favorite, Rosetto Cheese Ravioli, was "like a burst of creamy cheese in your mouth," with a "perfect dough-to-filling ratio" and a "nice, springy" texture to the pasta. For complete tasting results, go to www.CooksIllustrated.com/feb12.
—Amy Graves

CHEESE PLATE
Rosetto Cheese Ravioli bursts with creamy ricotta, Parmesan, and Romano. Its pasta wrapping is thick enough to stay intact during boiling.

Rating All-Purpose Spray Cleaners

For cutting through grease, grime, and food splatters on counters, stoves, and cabinets, which household cleaning spray is best?

⇒ BY LISA McMANUS & TAIZETH SIERRA ⇐

When it's time to clean grease, grime, and food splatters from your kitchen, a spray cleaner is a great solution. But which to choose? Store shelves teem with options, including all-purpose and kitchen-specific sprays, antibacterial products promising to wipe out food-borne bacteria, and scented cleaners that vow to leave the kitchen free of odors. Then there's the growing category of "green" cleaning sprays claiming to offer a nontoxic, more "natural," environmentally friendly choice. We wanted a spray that first and foremost works fast, cleaning thoroughly without leaving a sticky residue or damaging surfaces. Next, we'd consider whether we would insist that it also kill germs or be environmentally friendly. Frankly, "green" cleaners have always seemed pretty wimpy, and they cost more, too. Would newer products make that trade-off a thing of the past?

We chose nine cleaning sprays, all top-selling brands. Five were antibacterial; four billed themselves as green or natural. To mimic the most common kitchen use of these cleaners, we tested them on countertops made from a range of materials (including porous butcher-block wood and nonporous Corian and stainless steel) that we dirtied up by spraying them with vegetable oil. We then squirted the cleaners on finished-wood kitchen cabinets that we also coated in oil. Next we tackled the tougher jobs, attacking greasy stovetops, tomato sauce–splattered microwave interiors, and the grime on stainless steel range hoods. Finally, in a separate blind test with 23 America's Test Kitchen staff members, we gathered opinions on the cleaners' fragrances, giving preference to those whose scents were most appealing to the majority.

Wipeout

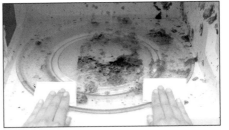

Some cleaners, like Method (left), cut through splattered tomato sauce; others, like Mr. Clean (right), smeared it.

Lift and Separate

Household spray cleaners may promise unique cleaning powers, but when you decipher the alphabet soup on their ingredient labels, they're mostly composed the same way. According to Jim Hammer, president of Mix Solutions, a product-formulation consulting firm in Uxbridge, Massachusetts, all spray cleaners have three main elements: surfactants, solvents, and a buffering system. Surfactants alter the surface tension of liquids, so water and solvents (the cleaning ingredients) can penetrate and dissolve soils. Buffering agents help by raising or lowering the product's acidity to let it bond with (and fight) different types of soils.

The main difference between antibacterial and other cleaners is that antibacterial products also contain ingredients aimed at killing specific sets of germs. The Environmental Protection Agency classifies these as pesticides—which is why there are no green antibacterial cleaners (though these products can also be effective at killing the same types of bacteria; see "Do You Need an Antibacterial Cleaner?" on page 26). The antibacterial cleaners in our lineup use either bleach or powerful quaternary ammonium compounds ("quats") derived from petroleum that work as both surfactant and disinfectant. Bleach and quats are toxic to not only bacteria but also humans. Cleaners containing them include warnings to rinse surfaces after use and to avoid contact with skin and eyes.

The active ingredients in some green cleaners, however, may not be quite as environmentally friendly or as natural as their labels would have you believe. (In fact, there are no government regulations controlling the use of "green" or "natural" on the labels of these products. The Federal Trade Commission has merely issued voluntary guidelines.) One such cleaner in our lineup, Simple Green, uses surfactants known as alcohol ethoxylates. While these compounds are far more biodegradable than the quats in antibacterial cleaners, the way they are manufactured is still a concern for environmental watchdogs, Hammer told us. The three so-called natural cleaners in our lineup use surfactants known as alkyl polyglucosides. Though processed from plant sources including coconut and corn, these agents are arguably no more natural than compounds derived from petroleum—also a natural source. However, they come from renewable sources and can claim to be more benign: None of the cleaners containing them cited warnings or required rinsing. "[Alkyl

We wanted a cleaner that didn't just clean—it had to have a scent that wouldn't make us flinch or gag.

polyglucosides] have low toxicity and excellent biodegradability," Hammer said. "On top of that, they just work very well. [These] products have really come a long way, just in the past few years."

Down in the Dirt

We couldn't take Hammer's word for that, so we headed into the kitchen. The most common use of multipurpose sprays is cleaning countertops after prepping food and cooking. As a challenge, we spritzed Corian counters and finished-wood cabinets with vegetable oil and left it to sit and get sticky over a weekend before bringing out the battery of spray cleaners. We repeated this test with freshly sprayed oil on nonporous Corian and stainless steel, as well as on porous butcher-block wood, comparing the results. Each time, we noticed that some cleaners took much more spraying and wiping to get surfaces grease- and streak-free (making the products less cost-effective, too). Porous wood absorbed strong fragrances from some sprays, so we needed to rinse them off, adding steps to our cleaning. Bleach in one product seemed harsh for everyday use; it discolored

Watch Lisa Clean

Video available FREE for 4 months at www.CooksIllustrated.com/feb12

the wood where we'd scrubbed. Several cleaners left traces of oil that took multiple rounds to remove, while one or two stood out for making it possible to clean quickly and thoroughly with minimal swipes. And the green and natural cleaners? A mixed bag. Some did very well, others left streaks and took extra wiping, but all were gentle on wood. We observed very similar results in further tests in which we cleaned smears of lasagna from stainless steel worktops and oil from finished-wood cabinets.

For a really tough job, we tackled greasy stovetops and the stainless steel hoods over our test kitchen ranges. All of the cleaners cut grease in both locations—eventually. On the stove, the best (including one particularly effective natural cleaner) took as few as eight sprays, the worst (an antibacterial product) up to 14—nearly 75 percent more. A handful of offenders left streaks on stainless steel, despite our best scrubbing efforts.

Cleaning food-splattered microwave ovens is a job nobody likes. We took it to extremes, heating an uncovered bowl of tomato sauce until it erupted on every surface; we even cooked the mess for an extra minute and let it cool and harden. This test really separated the powerful from the weak: Some cleaners cut right through the sticky globs of sauce; others merely smeared it around.

This test highlighted another problem: the impact of overpowering scents in a confined space. Several sprays were too potent to leave in the microwave without rinsing them out, and antibacterial cleaners carry warnings about breathing fumes. Fragrance is a big deal: Companies work hard to conjure up fields of flowers, pine forests, and other signals that your kitchen is fresh. Familiar scents also build brand loyalty. In our blind smell test, participants described memories, both pleasant ("reminds me of Mom's house") and not ("smells like the stuff they used after a kid threw up in school"). Only one antibacterial cleaner made it into the top three most appealing scents; generally, testers were put off by their chemical smell. ("Quats are pretty stinky," Hammer agreed.) Attempts to hide overpowering chemical odors with strong fragrances usually backfired. In our smell test, natural cleaners took three of the top spots—including an unscented spray (though a few testers wanted a scent, just to prove that they'd cleaned).

Streaking to the Finish

By the conclusion of our testing, we had found our favorite. The top spot went to a natural, green product, Method All-Purpose Natural Surface Cleaner (French Lavender). It packed plenty of cleaning power into each spray and cost just 14 cents per ounce, which turned out to be the average price among the nine top-selling brands in our lineup. It cut through grease and food splatters quickly and efficiently and didn't leave a cloying smell, streaks, or residue, saving effort, time, and money. We'd be happy to use it in our kitchen—and we won't feel we're sacrificing cleaning performance for an environment-friendly choice or paying more for it.

Do You Need an Antibacterial Cleaner?

Classified by law as pesticides, antibacterial cleaners are registered with the Environmental Protection Agency (EPA), which requires substantial proof of any germ-killing claims. Those claims are very specific and limited. In fact, some (including two cleaners in our lineup) don't even claim to kill E. coli, one of the most commonly feared food-borne bacteria. It's worth noting that the products' germ-killing ingredients aren't so good for humans or the kitchen, either: Labels include warnings about fumes and contact with skin or eyes, the importance of rinsing food-contact surfaces after use, and potential damage to common materials.

Kills Salmonella enterica, Escherichia coli O157:H7, Pseudomonas aeruginosa, Staphylococcus aureus, Avian Influenza A H1N1 Virus and Herpes Simplex Virus 1 & 2.

Use this product to clean:
• Counters • Sinks • Stovetops • Cabinets • Appliance Exteriors

DIRECTIONS FOR USE:
It is a violation of Federal law to use this product in a manner inconsistent with its labeling. To Operate: Turn nozzle counter clockwise to preferred usage. To Refill: Remove trigger sprayer. [...] ur in product from refill container and replace trigger. To Clean: Apply to surface until thoroughly wet. [...] e with a clean cloth or sponge. No rinsing required. To Sanitize: Leave for 30 seconds before wiping. To Disinfect: Leave f[...] es before wiping. Rinse all food contact surfaces with water after use. Does not harm most kitchen surfa[...] nted surfaces, test a small inconspicuous area first. Do not use on eating/cooking utensils, glasses/dish[...] re, unfinished, oiled or waxed wood floors. This product is not recommended for use on marble, brass, [...] or finished wood surfaces. Rinse all food contact surfaces with potable water.

TIONARY STATEMENTS: Hazards to Humans and Domestic Animals G: Causes substantial but temporary eye injury. Do not get in eyes, on skin or on clothing. Wash thorough[...] after handling and before eating, drinking, chewing gum or using tobacco. Prolonged or frequently repea[...] y cause allergic reacti[...]

Follow the fine print: The antibacterial sprays we tested require waiting anywhere from 30 seconds to 10 minutes before wiping in order to kill germs.

To see if you really need antibacterial sprays to kill germs, we sent one antibacterial spray, Lysol, and the four nonantibacterial sprays in our lineup to an independent laboratory. We also sent a bottle of ordinary white vinegar. The lab inoculated glass slides with measured quantities of E. coli or salmonella and then sprayed them with each of the cleaning products as well as with the undiluted vinegar. After 30 seconds (a time frame specified for sanitizing on the Lysol label), the lab counted the remaining microorganisms without wiping or rinsing (so that any reduction in bacteria would result from the cleaning product alone). This test was repeated a second time and the results were averaged. While we wouldn't want to stake a brand's reputation on the results of just two tests, they provided an interesting snapshot.

The surprise: All the cleaners reduced both types of bacteria by more than 99 percent, with the best performers (including Lysol) knocking out more than 99.9 percent of the germs and the "worst" performers coming in closer to 99.8 percent—a reduction that still sounded pretty good to us. But was it?

"[99.8 percent] is a good reduction but not enough to really do the job," said product-formulation consultant Jim Hammer. He noted that the EPA usually requires at least a 99.9 percent reduction. Our winning cleaner, Method All-Purpose Natural Surface Cleaner, eliminated 99.9 percent of the salmonella and 99.8 percent of the E. coli. (Vinegar killed 99.9 percent of both types of bacteria. Too bad it left behind a streaky residue and a pungent smell.)

Why would cleaners without antibacterial agents kill germs? Their surfactants (compounds that break into the surface of liquids) disrupt the organism's cell wall, creating a bactericidal effect—basically, they make the bacteria explode and die. "It's not as strong as a quaternary ammonium compound [the predominant cleaning and germ-killing agents used in antibacterial sprays], but it does kill off some of the bacteria," Hammer explained.

That said, even antibacterial sprays don't work as advertised unless you follow label instructions to the letter, including, as a few products recommend, precleaning, spraying, waiting 10 minutes, wiping thoroughly, and rinsing with water. Essentially, if you choose an antibacterial spray and don't use it correctly, it's not doing the work you expect. Alternatively, if you choose a spray with no antibacterial claims, it's still doing some germ killing. We'll leave the final choice to you. –L.M.

The Chemistry of Cleaners

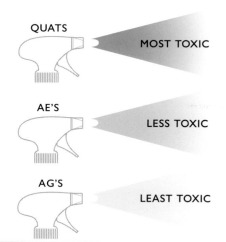

QUATS — **MOST TOXIC**

Antibacterial cleaners rely on harsh chemicals like bleach or quaternary ammonium compounds ("quats") that are harmful to bacteria as well as to humans.
Cleaners with "quats" (or bleach):
Lysol, Fantastik, Formula 409, Clorox Clean-Up, Mr. Clean

AE'S — **LESS TOXIC**

Other cleaners use alcohol ethoxylates ("AEs") that are more biodegradable and less toxic than quats but are a concern to environmental watchdogs.
Cleaners with "AEs": Simple Green

AG'S — **LEAST TOXIC**

So-called natural cleaners are manufactured from plant-derived alkyl polyglucosides ("AGs") that are harmless to humans.
Cleaners with "AGs":
Method, Seventh Generation, Clorox Green Works

TESTING ALL-PURPOSE CLEANERS

We tested nine national top-selling brands of all-purpose or kitchen spray cleaners drawn from data compiled by the Chicago-based market research firm SymphonyIRI Group. In final rankings, we weighted cleaning performance more heavily than scent preferences. Information about ingredients, antibacterial claims, and product warnings (which may be excerpts of longer lists) are from product labels and manufacturers' websites. We purchased products in Boston-area supermarkets. They are listed below in order of preference.

CLEANING PERFORMANCE:

We cleaned counters (Corian, wood, and stainless steel), wood cabinets, and stovetops that we made sticky with vegetable oil; microwave interiors splattered with cooked-on tomato sauce; and stainless steel range hoods encrusted with the grime of a day's worth of cooking. We assessed how much scrubbing and additional spraying were needed to eliminate the food and grease. Cleaning performance was weighted most heavily in the rankings.

STREAKING: Sprays that left few or no streaks after cleaning received higher scores.

SPRAYS TO CLEAN STOVETOP: We sprayed a stovetop with a measured amount of vegetable oil; turned all burners to high for one minute; allowed the stovetop to cool for two minutes; and used each cleaner, wiping with paper towels and keeping track of the number of sprays required.

SCENT: We rated each product's scent in a blind test with 23 staffers. We weighted scent less heavily than cleaning ability in our rankings.

	CRITERIA		TESTERS' COMMENTS

HIGHLY RECOMMENDED

METHOD All-Purpose Natural Surface Cleaner (French Lavender)
Price: $3.79 for 28 oz (cost per oz: 14 cents)

Cleaning performance	★★★
Streaking	★★★
Sprays to clean stovetop	8
Scent	★★★

This spray embodies the winning combination of being pleasant to use and cleaning thoroughly and effectively with a minimum number of squirts. It cut grease, lifted stuck-on messes, and left surfaces shining.

RECOMMENDED

LYSOL Antibacterial Kitchen Cleaner (Citrus Scent)
Price: $2.99 for 22 oz (cost per oz: 14 cents)
Antibacterial claims: Kills 99.9% of *E. coli* and *Salmonella enterica*
Warnings: Rinse food contact surfaces after use. Do not get in eyes, on skin, or on clothing. Wash thoroughly after handling.

Cleaning performance	★★★
Streaking	★★★
Sprays to clean stovetop	8
Scent	★★

Three stars for completely cleaning grease off the range hood in one swipe—and for leaving no streaks. It did fairly well with the splattered microwave, but we needed to rinse with water afterward, adding steps to an already messy job. It cut grease on countertops and its smell was not bad, though it reminded some testers of Nair chemical hair remover.

RECOMMENDED WITH RESERVATIONS

SEVENTH GENERATION Natural All Purpose Cleaner, Free & Clear
Price: $5.49 for 32 oz (cost per oz: 17 cents)

Cleaning performance	★★
Streaking	★★
Sprays to clean stovetop	10
Scent	★★★

Some testers appreciated this product as the only unscented cleaner in the lineup; others preferred some scent, if only as an indicator that cleaning was going on. Its cleaning power was fair but left some streaks.

FANTASTIK Antibacterial All Purpose Cleaner Heavy Duty
Price: $2.99 for 32 oz (cost per oz: 9 cents)
Antibacterial claims: Kills 99.9% of *E. coli* and *Salmonella choleraesuis*
Warnings: Rinse all food-contact surfaces after use. Avoid contact with eyes, skin, or clothing.

Cleaning performance	★★
Streaking	★★
Sprays to clean stovetop	9
Scent	★

This product claims to kill household bacteria in as few as 10 seconds, and its spraying action has particularly good coverage. Unfortunately, it smells terrible, reminding one tester of Raid insect spray (both products are made by SC Johnson). It cut through stuck-on microwave splatters but left streaks on other surfaces.

FORMULA 409 Antibacterial Kitchen All-Purpose Cleaner (Lemon Fresh)
Price: $3.49 for 22 oz (cost per oz: 16 cents)
Antibacterial claims: Kills *Salmonella choleraesuis*
Warnings: Rinse food-contact surfaces with water. Avoid contact with eyes, skin, or clothing.

Cleaning performance	★★
Streaking	★★
Sprays to clean stovetop	14
Scent	★★

Despite being antibacterial, this spray doesn't claim to kill *E. coli*, and it must stand for 10 minutes to kill any germs. It required extra sprays to clean the splattered microwave and greasy stovetop, and left streaks on stainless steel, although it did an adequate cleaning job.

CLOROX Green Works 97% Naturally Derived All-Purpose Cleaner
Price: $3.29 for 32 oz (cost per oz: 10 cents)

Cleaning performance	★★
Streaking	★½
Sprays to clean stovetop	12
Scent	★★

A decent performer when it came to cleaning the countertops, greasy range hood, and stovetop, but it required extra sprays and wiping and left streaks. It also struggled to cut through splatters in the microwave.

NOT RECOMMENDED

MR. CLEAN with Febreze Freshness Antibacterial Spray (Citrus & Light)
Price: $2.99 for 32 oz (cost per oz: 9 cents)
Antibacterial claims: Kills 99.9% of *E. coli*
Warnings: Rinse all food-contact surfaces after use. Avoid contact with eyes or clothing.

Cleaning performance	★
Streaking	★
Sprays to clean stovetop	10
Scent	★

Its cleaning power was only so-so, it does not claim to kill salmonella, and it left plenty of streaks. In other words, this orange-tinted spray was a bust. Its scent was sickeningly sweet and chemical-y. About halfway through testing, we began flinching when it was Mr. Clean's turn.

SIMPLE GREEN All-Purpose Cleaner, Concentrated
Price: $4.99 for 22 oz (cost per oz, used full strength: 23 cents)
Warnings: Use in well-ventilated areas. Do not use on leather, suede, or unfinished wood. If eye contact occurs, flush well with water.

Cleaning performance	★
Streaking	★
Sprays to clean stovetop	10
Scent	★

The first problem: This product comes in a full 22-ounce spray bottle yet is described as "concentrate." (Are we supposed to dump it out, dilute it, put some back, and store the rest elsewhere?) Worse, even full strength, its cleaning performance was weak. Its scent reminded some of Porta-Johns.

CLOROX Clean-Up Cleaner with Bleach
Price: $4.19 for 32 oz (cost per oz: 13 cents)
Antibacterial claims: Kills *Salmonella enterica*
Warnings: Not recommended for use by persons with heart conditions or chronic respiratory problems.

Cleaning performance	★
Streaking	★
Sprays to clean stovetop	11
Scent	★

Between a long list of scary warnings, the harsh vapors, the powerful bleach scent, and the weak cleaning performance (and streaky residue), this cleaner is not recommended. Does not claim to kill *E. coli*.

The Best Brand of Spaghetti

Our tests proved that once pasta is topped with sauce, flavor differences from brand to brand are very subtle. But texture is a whole different story.

> BY AMY GRAVES <

Given its impressive sales figures, you'd never guess that spaghetti (and all dried semolina pasta) was once an obscure ingredient made almost exclusively in Italy. Last year Americans spent $1.5 billion on these strands, using them as a quick base for everything from hearty ragu, to grassy pesto, to plain old butter and cheese. Besides convenience, the other draw of dried spaghetti is that it's inexpensive—or at least it used to be. When we recently browsed the options at the supermarket, we discovered that while you can still pick up a 1-pound package for as little as a dollar and change, you can also spend more than three times that amount. For a product that typically lists just durum semolina (coarsely ground durum wheat, the universal choice for dried pasta) and maybe added vitamins, the difference in price is astonishing. How much better could a pound of pasta costing more than $4 really be?

To answer that question, we rounded up eight nationally available brands ranging in price from $1.39 to $4.17 per pound. Two were domestically made bestsellers, and the remaining six were Italian imports. (New World Pasta, the producer of one of the domestic samples, is a conglomerate that

Cloudy with a Chance of Mushiness

Cloudy pasta water isn't necessarily an indication that you've overcooked the noodles. It can be a visual cue that the strands have weak structure and break down too much as they boil, resulting in mushy texture. Even though we kept a close eye on both pots, our favorite spaghetti, from De Cecco, cooked up firm and springy in relatively clear water (left), while the low-ranking Montebello noodles, boiled for the same amount of time, swam in cloudy, starchy water (right) and were soft.

CLEARER WATER = FIRM PASTA

CLOUDIER WATER = WEAK PASTA

also bought out several other regional American brands, and it uses the same formula to make them all.) We cooked the strands until al dente and tasted them two ways: glossed with mild-flavored olive oil and coated with a simple tomato sauce. We knew what we were looking for: Good pasta tastes clean, wheaty, and faintly nutty and boasts a firm, springy chew, with nary a hint of starchiness or gumminess.

The Spaghetti Breakdown

We'll level with you. When it came to taste, there wasn't a truly bad noodle in the bunch. With a few exceptions, the oil-dressed samples tasted pretty darn similar, garnering at least a few compliments like "buttery," "nutty," or "toasty." Flavor differences were even harder to tease out once the tomato sauce came into play, and all of the spaghettis grasped the marinara relatively well.

Texture, however, was another matter. We cooked the spaghetti according to the times suggested on their packages (8 to 13 minutes, depending on the strands' thickness) and removed them from the boiling water early if they tasted "done." None of the samples were unacceptable, but regardless of how vigilantly we tracked their doneness, some noodles cooked up sticky and gummy, while the best spaghettis were springy and firm.

Just to weed out any possibility of operator error, we sent a package of each spaghetti to an independent lab, Northern Crops Institute, at North Dakota State University. The lab cooked and then evaluated the samples based on three criteria: the finished weight of the cooked noodles (a measure of how much water the noodles absorb during cooking), "cook loss" (how much dissolved starch the noodles release into the cooking water), and firmness (how much force it takes to cut through a strand of cooked pasta). The lab's findings confirmed our own: Our favorite spaghetti had a relatively low cooked weight, the least starchy water by a large margin, and the firmest texture after boiling. Now we just needed to figure out why.

Since the ingredient lists don't vary much, we were skeptical that we'd find many answers on the package labels, but we gave them closer scrutiny anyway. No surprise: Semolina was the primary ingredient in every sample. Besides being distinguished by its tawny golden color, this coarsely milled durum wheat is high in protein, which ensures a particularly strong gluten network that helps the noodles maintain their springy, resilient texture as they boil.

The more significant discovery was that both of the American-made spaghettis, from Barilla and Ronzoni, also contain durum flour. According to Mehmet Tulbek, technical director at Northern Crops Institute, durum flour contains the same high level of protein as semolina, but it's a finer, cheaper grind that some manufacturers blend into the dough to help contain costs. The trade-off, according to Tulbek, is that the finer particles of durum flour tend to break down more easily, so the noodles leach more starch and turn mushy more easily. Cutting corners with durum flour might account for why some tasters found the texture of these two brands "gummy" and "mealy," particularly when sampled with nothing more than olive oil to cover their flaws.

But that still didn't explain the mushy texture we detected in some of the pastas made with 100 percent semolina. Could the way the dough was processed also affect the texture?

Pressing Matters

To cut pasta into shapes, most dough is passed through the holes of a die. All dies were originally made with bronze blocks, which give the noodles' surface a rough-hewn, almost dusty appearance that some manufacturers still prefer; they claim that sauce clings better to the coarse, craggy exterior. Meanwhile, other pasta producers, including both American brands in our lineup, have switched to Teflon-coated dies, mostly for cosmetic reasons. Because it's nonstick, Teflon reduces the surface tension of the dough extrusion and, as a result, produces smoother, shinier noodles. We found that sauce clung equally well to noodles made by both types of dies—but could bronze dies be responsible for producing the firmer texture we noticed in some of the spaghettis? As it turned out, no. While our favorite pasta was produced by bronze dies, so were our two least favorite brands, assailed for having "mushy," "soft" texture "with no spring in the bite."

According to Tulbek, the more important distinction is not the material of the die; it's a question of how well the extruder and the die have been maintained. Whether bronze or Teflon, dies don't last forever; the heat, friction, and pressure applied to the dough wear down and loosen the extruder parts over time. When this happens, the machine is no longer able to press the dough with enough force to make perfectly compact strands of spaghetti, and the texture of the noodles suffers. Based on our results, we could only assume that some extruders were in better shape than others.

TASTING SPAGHETTI

Twenty-one *Cook's Illustrated* staff members tasted eight brands of dried spaghetti selected from a list of top-selling brands compiled by the Chicago-based market research firm SymphonyIRI Group. We boiled each sample until al dente and tasted them tossed with olive oil as well as sauced with a simple marinara. An independent laboratory analyzed their gluten strength (as measured by the starch lost in cooking). Information on drying temperatures was provided by the pasta companies. Prices were paid in Boston-area supermarkets and online, and brands appear below in order of preference.

RECOMMENDED

DE CECCO Spaghetti No. 12
Source: Italy
Price: $1.39 for 1 lb
Ingredients: Durum wheat semolina, niacin, ferrous lactate, thiamine mononitrate, riboflavin, folic acid
Processing method: Pressed through bronze dies; dried at 158°
Starch in cooking water: 4.88%
Comments: This Italian import boasted "clean wheat flavor" and a "firm, ropy quality"; in fact, the lab confirmed these strands as the strongest of all the samples, with the lowest percentage of "cook loss." The texture was just as good when we added sauce—"firm," with "good chew."

RUSTICHELLA D'ABRUZZO Pasta Abruzzese di Semola di Grano Duro
Source: Italy
Price: $4.56 for 17.5 oz ($4.17 for 1 lb)
Ingredients: Durum wheat semolina
Processing method: Pressed through bronze dies; dried at 95°
Starch in cooking water: 5.78%
Comments: Even though these noodles were dried at a low 95 degrees (higher drying temperatures can produce stronger strands), they retained a delightfully "firm" bite and chew that tasters raved about. We also appreciated this pricey Italian brand's "nutty," "toasty" taste, which came through even under a coating of marinara.

GAROFALO Spaghetti
Source: Italy
Price: $2.49 for 1 lb
Ingredients: Durum wheat semolina, niacin, iron lactate, thiamine mononitrate, riboflavin, folic acid
Processing method: Pressed through bronze dies; dried at 176°
Starch in cooking water: 5.42%
Comments: Tossed with olive oil, this Italian pasta ranked highest for flavor that was "buttery" and "rich-tasting" and had a "roughness" to the exterior that numerous tasters appreciated. However, that pleasant coarseness was obscured by the sauce, under which the noodles became slightly "gummy."

DELALLO Spaghetti No. 4
Source: Italy
Price: $2.81 for 1 lb
Ingredients: Semolina, ferrous lactate (iron), niacin, thiamine mononitrate, riboflavin, folic acid
Processing method: Pressed through bronze dies; dried at 167°
Starch in cooking water: 6.32%
Comments: In general, tasters found this spaghetti to be "middle-of-the-road." It didn't stand out for having major flaws, and it didn't elicit rave compliments. Its taste was "light" but still "wheaty," while its texture was deemed "fine," with "nice elasticity" and "fair chew."

RONZONI Spaghetti
Source: USA
Price: $1.39 for 1 lb
Ingredients: Semolina (wheat), durum flour, niacin, iron (ferrous sulfate), thiamine mononitrate, riboflavin, folic acid
Processing method: Pressed through Teflon-coated dies; dried at 190°
Starch in cooking water: 5.68%
Comments: Overall, this brand passed muster. But perhaps due in part to ultra-high-temperature drying, which cooks out flavor, some tasters thought this mass-market American spaghetti "lacked nuttiness." The inclusion of fine-ground durum flour may have accounted for why some tasters found the texture "mealy."

BARILLA Spaghetti
Source: USA
Price: $1.67 for 1 lb
Ingredients: Semolina (wheat), durum flour, niacin, iron (ferrous sulfate), thiamine mononitrate, riboflavin, folic acid
Processing method: Pressed through Teflon-coated dies; dried at ultra-high temperature (company would not provide exact data)
Starch in cooking water: 5.62%
Comments: "There is something a little flat about the flavor of this," said one taster about this American bestseller, which we speculated must have been dried at a temperature high enough to make it taste less wheaty than some. Others agreed, some also noting the noodles' "gummy" consistency. Overall, though, tasters found the strands "OK" but "unremarkable."

RECOMMENDED WITH RESERVATIONS

MONTEBELLO Organic Spaghetti
Source: Italy
Price: $2.99 for 1 lb
Ingredients: Organic durum wheat semolina
Processing method: Pressed through bronze dies; dried at 130–150°
Starch in cooking water: 7.56%
Comments: It wasn't flavor criticisms that sank this imported spaghetti to the lower rungs of the chart; most tasters praised the "clean," "bright," "almost nutty" taste. These strands lost the most starch during cooking, for a "mushy," "crumbly" texture.

BIONATURAE Organic 100% Durum Semolina Spaghetti
Source: Italy
Price: $3.59 for 1 lb
Ingredients: Organic durum wheat semolina
Processing method: Pressed through bronze dies; dried at 95–100°
Starch in cooking water: 5.70%
Comments: This Italian brand was "sticky" and "soft" and offered "no spring in the bite," possibly due to a weaker gluten structure resulting from a low drying temperature. But the low temperature didn't seem to preserve a good wheaty taste; most tasters homed in on one particular adjective: "bland."

Degrees of Difference

The other major processing step is drying the noodles. Drying times and temperatures range widely among brands: Some companies dry their pasta low (95 to 100 degrees) and slow (over many hours, or even days) in drying rooms, claiming that it preserves flavor. Others, including Barilla and Ronzoni, place the noodles in special ultra-high-temperature (UHT) ovens and crank the heat to 190 degrees or higher, which gets the job done faster. According to Tulbek, the high heat cross-links some of the gluten strands and can strengthen the pasta. But UHT drying has a downside: It tends to cook out some of the pasta's flavor, an effect we noticed in the duller taste of these two UHT-dried brands.

Ultimately, we liked six of the eight samples enough to recommend them. But one pasta, De Cecco, stood out for particularly good texture—the result, we could only assume, of balancing all the variables most successfully. It contains no durum flour, is likely extruded through well-maintained dies, and dries for 18 hours at a moderately high 158 degrees. That combination of factors made for rich, nutty, wheaty-tasting strands that retained their al dente bite better than other brands—including the priciest samples. In fact, at $1.39 a pound, De Cecco was one of the two least expensive spaghettis we tasted. The priciest sample in the lineup, from Rustichella d'Abruzzo ($4.56 a pound), came in at a close second. But we won't ever feel a need to reach for it as long as there's a box of De Cecco on the shelf.

CONTENTS

March & April 2012

COOK'S
ILLUSTRATED

Founder and Editor Christopher Kimball
Editorial Director Jack Bishop
Executive Editor, Magazines John Willoughby
Executive Editor Amanda Agee
Test Kitchen Director Erin McMurrer
Managing Editor Rebecca Hays
Senior Editors Keith Dresser
Lisa McManus
Associate Features Editors Elizabeth Bomze
Danette St. Onge
Copy Editors Nell Beram
Megan Chromik
Associate Editors Andrea Geary
Amy Graves
Andrew Janjigian
Dan Souza
Test Cook Lan Lam
Assistant Editors Hannah Crowley
Shannon Friedmann Hatch
Taizeth Sierra
Assistant Test Cook Celeste Rogers
Executive Assistant Christine Gordon
Assistant Test Kitchen Director Gina Nistico
Senior Kitchen Assistants Meryl MacCormack
Leah Rovner
Kitchen Assistants Maria Elena Delgado
Ena Gudiel
Andrew Straaberg Finfrock
Executive Producer Melissa Baldino
Associate Producer Stephanie Stender
Contributing Editors Matthew Card
Dawn Yanagihara
Consulting Editor Scott Brueggeman
Science Editor Guy Crosby, Ph.D.
Online Managing Editor David Tytell
Online Editor Kate Mason
Online Assistant Editors Eric Grzymkowski
Mari Levine
Associate Editor, Video Nick Dakoulas

Design Director Amy Klee
Art Director, Magazines Julie Cote
Deputy Art Director Susan Levin
Designer Lindsey Timko
Associate Art Director, Marketing/Web Erica Lee
Designers, Marketing/Web Elaina Natario
Mariah Tarvainen
Staff Photographer Daniel J. van Ackere
Online Photo Editor Steve Klise

Vice President, Marketing David Mack
Circulation Director Doug Wicinski
Circulation & Fulfillment Manager Carrie Fethe
Partnership Marketing Manager Pamela Putprush
Marketing Assistant Lauren Perkins
Customer Service Manager Jacqueline Valerio
Customer Service Representatives Jessica Amato
Morgan Ryan

Chief Operations Officer David Dinnage
Production Director Guy Rochford
Senior Project Manager Alice Carpenter
Production & Traffic Coordinator Kate Hux
Asset & Workflow Manager Andrew Mannone
Production & Imaging Specialists Judy Blomquist
Heather Dube
Lauren Pettapiece
Technology Director Rocco Lombardo
Systems Administrator Marcus Walser
Development Manager Robert Martinez
Software Project Manager Michelle Rushin
Business Analyst Wendy Tseng
Web Developers Chris Candelora
Cameron MacKensie
Human Resources Director Adele Shapiro

VP New Media Product Development Barry Kelly
Social Media Manager Steph Yiu

Chief Financial Officer Sharyn Chabot
Director of Sponsorship Sales Anne Traficante
Retail Sales & Marketing Manager Emily Logan
Client Service Manager, Sponsorship Bailey Snyder
Publicity Deborah Broide

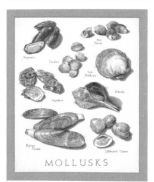

MOLLUSKS

MOLLUSKS dwell in aquatic or damp environments, often inside hard shells that
protect their soft bodies. Bivalves, such as littleneck clams and mussels, have two closed
hinged shells when raw. When cooked, the shells open, revealing the meat inside.
Oysters are often served raw; their shells must be pried open with an oyster knife. Also
bivalves, scallops are most often sold shucked. They range from the pencil-eraser-size
bay variety to larger half-dollar-size sea scallops. Cockles are distinguished by their ribbed,
heart-shaped shells and can also be served raw. Razor clams should be cooked: Atlantic
varieties have a long, slender silhouette, while those from the West Coast are more
round. Whelks, which are related to the conch, have tan or gray shells streaked with
white or brown. Italian Americans call them *scungilli* and serve them chilled in salad or
simmered in marinara sauce. Edible sea snails, such as the periwinkle, are typically boiled
with seaweed. COVER *(Melon):* Robert Papp; BACK COVER *(Mollusks):* John Burgoyne

America's
TEST KITCHEN

RECIPES THAT WORK

America's Test Kitchen is a very real 2,500-square-foot kitchen located just outside of Boston. It is the home of *Cook's Illustrated* and
Cook's Country magazines and is the workday destination of more than three dozen test cooks, editors, and cookware specialists.
Our mission is to test recipes over and over again until we understand how and why they work and until we arrive at the best ver-
sion. We also test kitchen equipment and supermarket ingredients in search of brands that offer the best value and performance.
You can watch us work by tuning in to *America's Test Kitchen* (www.AmericasTestKitchen.com) on public television.

PRINTED IN THE USA

TASTING SPAGHETTI

Twenty-one *Cook's Illustrated* staff members tasted eight brands of dried spaghetti selected from a list of top-selling brands compiled by the Chicago-based market research firm SymphonyIRI Group. We boiled each sample until al dente and tasted them tossed with olive oil as well as sauced with a simple marinara. An independent laboratory analyzed their gluten strength (as measured by the starch lost in cooking). Information on drying temperatures was provided by the pasta companies. Prices were paid in Boston-area supermarkets and online, and brands appear below in order of preference.

RECOMMENDED

DE CECCO Spaghetti No. 12
Source: Italy
Price: $1.39 for 1 lb
Ingredients: Durum wheat semolina, niacin, ferrous lactate, thiamine mononitrate, riboflavin, folic acid
Processing method: Pressed through bronze dies; dried at 158°
Starch in cooking water: 4.88%
Comments: This Italian import boasted "clean wheat flavor" and a "firm, ropy quality"; in fact, the lab confirmed these strands as the strongest of all the samples, with the lowest percentage of "cook loss." The texture was just as good when we added sauce—"firm," with "good chew."

RUSTICHELLA D'ABRUZZO Pasta Abruzzese di Semola di Grano Duro
Source: Italy
Price: $4.56 for 17.5 oz ($4.17 for 1 lb)
Ingredients: Durum wheat semolina
Processing method: Pressed through bronze dies; dried at 95°
Starch in cooking water: 5.78%
Comments: Even though these noodles were dried at a low 95 degrees (higher drying temperatures can produce stronger strands), they retained a delightfully "firm" bite and chew that tasters raved about. We also appreciated this pricey Italian brand's "nutty," "toasty" taste, which came through even under a coating of marinara.

GAROFALO Spaghetti

Source: Italy
Price: $2.49 for 1 lb
Ingredients: Durum wheat semolina, niacin, iron lactate, thiamine mononitrate, riboflavin, folic acid
Processing method: Pressed through bronze dies; dried at 176°
Starch in cooking water: 5.42%
Comments: Tossed with olive oil, this Italian pasta ranked highest for flavor that was "buttery" and "rich-tasting" and had a "roughness" to the exterior that numerous tasters appreciated. However, that pleasant coarseness was obscured by the sauce, under which the noodles became slightly "gummy."

DELALLO Spaghetti No. 4
Source: Italy
Price: $2.81 for 1 lb
Ingredients: Semolina, ferrous lactate (iron), niacin, thiamine mononitrate, riboflavin, folic acid
Processing method: Pressed through bronze dies; dried at 167°
Starch in cooking water: 6.32%
Comments: In general, tasters found this spaghetti to be "middle-of-the-road." It didn't stand out for having major flaws, and it didn't elicit rave compliments. Its taste was "light" but still "wheaty," while its texture was deemed "fine," with "nice elasticity" and "fair chew."

RONZONI Spaghetti
Source: USA
Price: $1.39 for 1 lb
Ingredients: Semolina (wheat), durum flour, niacin, iron (ferrous sulfate), thiamine mononitrate, riboflavin, folic acid
Processing method: Pressed through Teflon-coated dies; dried at 190°
Starch in cooking water: 5.68%
Comments: Overall, this brand passed muster. But perhaps due in part to ultra-high-temperature drying, which cooks out flavor, some tasters thought this mass-market American spaghetti "lacked nuttiness." The inclusion of fine-ground durum flour may have accounted for why some tasters found the texture "mealy."

BARILLA Spaghetti
Source: USA
Price: $1.67 for 1 lb
Ingredients: Semolina (wheat), durum flour, niacin, iron (ferrous sulfate), thiamine mononitrate, riboflavin, folic acid
Processing method: Pressed through Teflon-coated dies; dried at ultra-high temperature (company would not provide exact data)
Starch in cooking water: 5.62%
Comments: "There is something a little flat about the flavor of this," said one taster about this American bestseller, which we speculated must have been dried at a temperature high enough to make it taste less wheaty than some. Others agreed, some also noting the noodles' "gummy" consistency. Overall, though, tasters found the strands "OK" but "unremarkable."

RECOMMENDED WITH RESERVATIONS

MONTEBELLO Organic Spaghetti
Source: Italy
Price: $2.99 for 1 lb
Ingredients: Organic durum wheat semolina
Processing method: Pressed through bronze dies; dried at 130–150°
Starch in cooking water: 7.56%
Comments: It wasn't flavor criticisms that sank this imported spaghetti to the lower rungs of the chart; most tasters praised the "clean," "bright," "almost nutty" taste. These strands lost the most starch during cooking, for a "mushy," "crumbly" texture.

BIONATURAE Organic 100% Durum Semolina Spaghetti
Source: Italy
Price: $3.59 for 1 lb
Ingredients: Organic durum wheat semolina
Processing method: Pressed through bronze dies; dried at 95–100°
Starch in cooking water: 5.70%
Comments: This Italian brand was "sticky" and "soft" and offered "no spring in the bite," possibly due to a weaker gluten structure resulting from a low drying temperature. But the low temperature didn't seem to preserve a good wheaty taste; most tasters homed in on one particular adjective: "bland."

Degrees of Difference

The other major processing step is drying the noodles. Drying times and temperatures range widely among brands: Some companies dry their pasta low (95 to 100 degrees) and slow (over many hours, or even days) in drying rooms, claiming that it preserves flavor. Others, including Barilla and Ronzoni, place the noodles in special ultra-high-temperature (UHT) ovens and crank the heat to 190 degrees or higher, which gets the job done faster. According to Tulbek, the high heat cross-links some of the gluten strands and can strengthen the pasta. But UHT drying has a downside: It tends to cook out some of the pasta's flavor, an effect we noticed in the duller taste of these two UHT-dried brands.

Ultimately, we liked six of the eight samples enough to recommend them. But one pasta, De Cecco, stood out for particularly good texture—the result, we could only assume, of balancing all the variables most successfully. It contains no durum flour, is likely extruded through well-maintained dies, and dries for 18 hours at a moderately high 158 degrees. That combination of factors made for rich, nutty, wheaty-tasting strands that retained their al dente bite better than other brands—including the priciest samples. In fact, at $1.39 a pound, De Cecco was one of the two least expensive spaghettis we tasted. The priciest sample in the lineup, from Rustichella d'Abruzzo ($4.56 a pound), came in at a close second. But we won't ever feel a need to reach for it as long as there's a box of De Cecco on the shelf.

CONTENTS

March & April 2012

MOLLUSKS

MOLLUSKS dwell in aquatic or damp environments, often inside hard shells that protect their soft bodies. Bivalves, such as littleneck clams and mussels, have two closed hinged shells when raw. When cooked, the shells open, revealing the meat inside. Oysters are often served raw; their shells must be pried open with an oyster knife. Also bivalves, scallops are most often sold shucked. They range from the pencil-eraser-size bay variety to larger half-dollar-size sea scallops. Cockles are distinguished by their ribbed, heart-shaped shells and can also be served raw. Razor clams should be cooked: Atlantic varieties have a long, slender silhouette, while those from the West Coast are more round. Whelks, which are related to the conch, have tan or gray shells streaked with white or brown. Italian Americans call them *scungilli* and serve them chilled in salad or simmered in marinara sauce. Edible sea snails, such as the periwinkle, are typically boiled with seaweed. COVER *(Melon)*: Robert Papp; BACK COVER *(Mollusks)*: John Burgoyne

RECIPES THAT WORK

America's Test Kitchen is a very real 2,500-square-foot kitchen located just outside of Boston. It is the home of *Cook's Illustrated* and *Cook's Country* magazines and is the workday destination of more than three dozen test cooks, editors, and cookware specialists. Our mission is to test recipes over and over again until we understand how and why they work and until we arrive at the best version. We also test kitchen equipment and supermarket ingredients in search of brands that offer the best value and performance. You can watch us work by tuning in to *America's Test Kitchen* (www.AmericasTestKitchenTV.com) on public television.

COOK'S
ILLUSTRATED

Founder and Editor	Christopher Kimball
Editorial Director	Jack Bishop
Executive Editor, Magazines	John Willoughby
Executive Editor	Amanda Agee
Test Kitchen Director	Erin McMurrer
Managing Editor	Rebecca Hays
Senior Editors	Keith Dresser
	Lisa McManus
Associate Features Editors	Elizabeth Bomze
	Danette St. Onge
Copy Editors	Nell Beram
	Megan Chromik
Associate Editors	Andrea Geary
	Amy Graves
	Andrew Janjigian
	Dan Souza
Test Cook	Lan Lam
Assistant Editors	Hannah Crowley
	Shannon Friedmann Hatch
	Taizeth Sierra
Assistant Test Cook	Celeste Rogers
Executive Assistant	Christine Gordon
Assistant Test Kitchen Director	Gina Nistico
Senior Kitchen Assistants	Meryl MacCormack
	Leah Rovner
Kitchen Assistants	Maria Elena Delgado
	Ena Gudiel
	Andrew Straaberg Finfrock
Executive Producer	Melissa Baldino
Associate Producer	Stephanie Stender
Contributing Editors	Matthew Card
	Dawn Yanagihara
Consulting Editor	Scott Brueggeman
Science Editor	Guy Crosby, Ph.D.
Online Managing Editor	David Tytell
Online Editor	Kate Mason
Online Assistant Editors	Eric Grzymkowski
	Mari Levine
Associate Editor, Video	Nick Dakoulas
Design Director	Amy Klee
Art Director, Magazines	Julie Cote
Deputy Art Director	Susan Levin
Designer	Lindsey Timko
Associate Art Director, Marketing/Web	Erica Lee
Designers, Marketing/Web	Elaina Natario
	Mariah Tarvainen
Staff Photographer	Daniel J. van Ackere
Online Photo Editor	Steve Klise
Vice President, Marketing	David Mack
Circulation Director	Doug Wicinski
Circulation & Fulfillment Manager	Carrie Fethe
Partnership Marketing Manager	Pamela Putprush
Marketing Assistant	Lauren Perkins
Customer Service Manager	Jacqueline Valerio
Customer Service Representatives	Jessica Amato
	Morgan Ryan
Chief Operations Officer	David Dinnage
Production Director	Guy Rochford
Senior Project Manager	Alice Carpenter
Production & Traffic Coordinator	Kate Hux
Asset & Workflow Manager	Andrew Mannone
Production & Imaging Specialists	Judy Blomquist
	Heather Dube
	Lauren Pettapiece
Technology Director	Rocco Lombardo
Systems Administrator	Marcus Walser
Development Manager	Robert Martinez
Software Project Manager	Michelle Rushin
Business Analyst	Wendy Tseng
Web Developers	Chris Candelora
	Cameron MacKensie
Human Resources Director	Adele Shapiro
VP New Media Product Development	Barry Kelly
Social Media Manager	Steph Yiu
Chief Financial Officer	Sharyn Chabot
Director of Sponsorship Sales	Anne Traficante
Retail Sales & Marketing Manager	Emily Logan
Client Service Manager, Sponsorship	Bailey Snyder
Publicity	Deborah Broide

PRINTED IN THE USA

VERMONT CREED II

Since my first Vermont Creed was published in 2009, I have received a drawerful of suggestions from friends and neighbors about missing tenets. Here is the rest of the list.

Silence Is Golden: Verbal proliferation will only lead to trouble, as any horse trader will tell you. Calvin Coolidge once told Governor Canning Cox of Massachusetts, who was complaining about having to speak with so many constituents, "Canning, the trouble is, you talk back."

Walk, Don't Run: I have never seen a Vermonter run after anything, including a spooked beefer or a good deal down at Walmart. If you take your time, you will find that the journey is almost always more interesting than the destination. As Vermonters are apt to say, "I wouldn't run uphill after it."

Never Judge a Vermonter by His Overalls: Don't confuse appearances with intelligence. Some of the scruffiest, most unlikely characters I have ever met are a lot smarter than I am. They may be knee-deep in manure and drive a pickup so rusted that the cab and the bed travel in different directions, but the joke will be on you if you take them for granted.

Never Back Down: When Tom first came to Vermont, he was hunting on the property of John Kurasinksi, a neighbor who disliked trespassers. Tom was sitting under an oak during deer season, and John walked up and in a loud voice asked him what the heck he thought he was doing. Tom replied, "Well, I'm trying to shoot a deer, but it's kind of tough with you making all of that noise!" John just broke out laughing and they became fast friends.

He's His Own Toad!: One of my favorite Vermont stories involves two kids, a stick, and a toad. A city kid up for the summer was spied poking a large toad with a stick. A local boy told him to quit poking the toad. The city kid responded, "Well, it's my toad, ain't it?" The Vermonter stared him down and replied, "Well, in Vermont, he's his own toad." Yup.

Don't Panic: Vermonters always remain calm, even in the worst circumstances. Silas came across a hat sitting in the middle of a muddy road. Using a hoe, he lifted up the hat and found his neighbor, Heber, up to his ears in mud. "Heber," Silas observed, "you're really in it." "I'm OK," Heber replied, "but the team's in pretty deep."

An Ounce of Prevention Pays Off: Split and stack your wood in August. Check your snow tires in September. Clean the treads on your excavator before winter so they don't freeze. Clean your flues before the snow flies. Pump out your septic tank every two years. Sight in your rifle long before the season opens. Don't get ready after you have to be ready.

A Penny Saved Is a Penny Earned: A disagreeable Vermont farmer was married to a woman of Scottish heritage, and after 20 years, he reluctantly took his wife on a vacation. They were staying at an inn, and on the second morning she awoke looking forward to her breakfast of a boiled egg and coffee. When she noticed that her husband had died during the night, she rushed downstairs to the kitchen and yelled, "Only boil one egg!" It's easier to save money than it is to make it.

Christopher Kimball

Don't Shoot the Dog: This was a piece of advice given to me by Tom, president of the Old Rabbit Hunters Association. Put another way: It's a good thing to keep your eye on the ball, but don't forget the big picture. You could end up with a dead dog—or worse.

Old Is Better than New: A new truck or tractor is not something to be wished for. They cost money, they are unfamiliar, and it takes years to get to know the old equipment—just like an old friend. Vermonters don't need new friends or new equipment: It takes too long to break them in.

Vermont Ain't New Hampshire: It isn't New York or Maine either. It's not that those other states are so terrible; it's just that they aren't Vermont. If you don't know where you are from, how do you know where you are going?

None of Your Business: Vermonters don't mind a bit of gossip—there isn't much else to do in winter—but on your land you are king. You can bury junk cars, keep your house covered in tar paper so your taxes stay low, and walk around naked from dawn to dusk and nobody is going to call you on it. Just remember that if you do something really stupid, that's none of their business either; you'll have to dig yourself out.

Park Your Truck Facing Home: When in the woods, always park your pickup facing the way you came. That way, if you are injured in a hunting or logging accident, you have a better chance of making it out alive. The worst-case scenario is bound to happen, and a bit of forethought will save your life.

FOR INQUIRIES, ORDERS, OR MORE INFORMATION

www.CooksIllustrated.com
At www.CooksIllustrated.com, you can order books and subscriptions, sign up for our free e-newsletter, or renew your magazine subscription. Join the website and gain access to 19 years of Cook's Illustrated recipes, equipment tests, and ingredient tastings, as well as companion videos for every recipe in this issue.

COOKBOOKS
We sell more than 50 cookbooks by the editors of Cook's Illustrated. To order, visit our bookstore at www.CooksIllustrated.com.

COOK'S ILLUSTRATED MAGAZINE
Cook's Illustrated magazine (ISSN 1068-2821), number 115, is published bimonthly by Boston Common Press Limited partnership, 17 Station St., Brookline, MA 02445. Copyright 2012 Boston Common Press Limited Partnership. Periodicals postage paid at Boston, Mass., and additional mailing offices, USPS #012487. Publications Mail Agreement No. 40020778. Return undeliverable Canadian addresses to P.O. Box 875, Station A, Windsor, ON N9A 6P2. POSTMASTER: Send address changes to Cook's Illustrated, P.O. Box 6018, Harlan, IA 51593-1518. For subscription and gift subscription orders, subscription inquiries, or change-of-address notices, visit us at www.AmericasTestKitchen.com/customerservice or write us at Cook's Illustrated, P.O. 6018, Harlan, IA 51593-1518.

FOR LIST RENTAL INFORMATION Contact Specialists Marketing Services, Inc., 777 Terrace Ave., 4th Floor, Hasbrouck Heights, NJ 07604; 201-865-5800.
EDITORIAL OFFICE 17 Station St., Brookline, MA 02445; 617-232-1000; fax 617-232-1572. Subscription inquiries, visit www.AmericasTestKitchen.com/customerservice or call 800-526-8442.
POSTMASTER Send all new orders, subscription inquiries, and change-of-address notices to Cook's Illustrated, P.O. Box 6018, Harlan, IA 51593-1518.

Mango Varieties

I often see two different kinds of mangos in the produce aisle: one that's big, round, and reddish green and another that's small, golden, and kidney-shaped. Do they taste the same?

MARJORIE DUNLOP
LEXINGTON, KY.

➤ There are hundreds of varieties of mangos, but most American supermarkets carry just one or two kinds. The large red fruit you describe is likely the Tommy Atkins variety, typically sourced from Mexico, Guatemala, and Brazil, whereas the smaller yellow fruit is probably the Ataulfo variety, which usually comes from Mexico. We commonly see the Champagne brand of the Ataulfo mango in our supermarkets in the Boston area.

We chose fully ripe samples of each type, looking for flesh that was yielding when we pressed it but not mushy, similar to the ideal texture of a peach. As we prepared the mangos for tasting, we noticed that the Tommy Atkins fruit had a larger pit than the more petite Ataulfo, in keeping with its larger size. Both types were juicy and soft, but the texture of the Ataulfo won out for being especially silky and tender. The flavor of the Ataulfo was also more complex, offering floral notes along with sweetness and tang. The pleasant piney flavor often associated with mangos was more present in the Tommy Atkins variety.

So, which to buy? Since the Tommy Atkins is usually less expensive and perfectly acceptable, we'll stick with it for most uses, but we're likely to splurge on the more luxurious Ataulfo type when mangos are the focal point of the dish.

TOMMY ATKINS
Juicy and piney.

ATAULFO
Silkier, sweeter, and floral.

Soy Milk Substitute, Revisited

Is soy milk an acceptable substitute for whole milk in cooking and baking?

ALEXANDER YATES
BEVERLY HILLS, CALIF.

➤ When we first tested subbing soy milk for regular whole milk in 2006, we determined that the sweetened kind that was most available at the time was fine for baking and desserts but created a cloying sweetness in savory applications like béchamel. Now that most brands of soy milk offer an unsweetened version of their product, we decided it was time to reevaluate.

We used unsweetened soy milk in yellow cake and vanilla cream pie filling as well as in fish chowder and béchamel. Tasters reported that the cake and pie filling were slightly less rich than the dairy versions in flavor and texture (not surprising, considering that sweetened or unsweetened soy milk contains half the fat of whole milk) but were still acceptable. As for béchamel, tasters declared it bland, watery, and unappealing, noting that there was little to distract from the soy flavor and the lack of dairy richness. In the more complex chowder, the soy flavor was less noticeable, but we needed to add twice as much thickener to achieve a consistency that was comparable to that of the sample made with regular milk. Also, soy milk can curdle if it gets too hot. To prevent this, add it off heat and then warm the soup gently just to serving temperature.

Our advice: Go ahead and use both sweetened and unsweetened soy milk in desserts. Unsweetened soy milk will work in savory dishes, as long as there is enough richness and complexity in the recipe to make up for its thin flavor and consistency.

Canned Food's Real Shelf Life

I recently used a can of chicken broth from my pantry and later noticed that it had a "best by" date that was several years past. But it tasted completely fine, and no one got sick. So what's the deal with "best by" dates?

LIZA WEISSTUCH
BOSTON, MASS.

➤ The "best by" date printed on some canned foods is not a hard-and-fast "expiration" date: It refers strictly to the manufacturer's recommendation for peak quality, not safety concerns. In theory, as long as cans are in good shape and have been stored under the right conditions (in a dry place between 40 and 70 degrees), their contents should remain safe to use indefinitely.

That said, natural chemicals in foods continually react with the metal in cans, and over time, canned food's taste, texture, and nutritional value will gradually deteriorate. The question is when. Manufacturers have an incentive to cite a "best by" date that is a conservative estimate of when the food may lose quality. But it's possible that some canned foods will last for decades without any dip in taste or nutrition. In a shelf-life study conducted by the National Food Processors Association and cited in *FDA Consumer*, even 100-year-old canned food was found to be remarkably well preserved, with a drop in some nutrients but not others.

Dates aside, cans with a compromised seal (punctured, rusted through, or deeply dented along any seam) should never be used. And discard immediately any cans that are bulging or that spurt liquid when opened: These are warning signs of the presence of the rare but dangerous botulism bacteria, *Clostridium botulinum.*

Gluten–Free Flour

There's a new gluten-free flour available called C4C that supposedly can be subbed "cup for cup" for wheat flour in recipes. Does it really work?

CHRIS HANNIGAN MORRISON
HARVARD, MASS.

GLUTEN-FREE FLOUR
C4C can be successfully swapped for wheat flour in most baking recipes.

➤ This proprietary mix of gluten-free starches and flours (mostly cornstarch, plus tapioca flour and white and brown rice flours augmented with milk powder and xanthan gum) was developed by Lena Kwak, research chef to Thomas Keller, creator of the French Laundry in Napa Valley and Per Se in New York City. Eager to put this product to the test, we subbed C4C for all-purpose flour in sugar cookies, drop biscuits, pie crust, a quick chocolate cake, and, because of a testimonial on the C4C website, brioche.

The cookies made with C4C were chewy in the middle, crisp at the edges, and perfectly shaped—nearly indistinguishable from those made with wheat flour—and the biscuits and chocolate cake were also remarkably similar to their gluten-containing counterparts. The pie crust, which we sampled without filling, was a bit flat-tasting and brittle in comparison with the flaky conventional crust, but tasters agreed that these defects would be less noticeable in an actual pie. The C4C brioche, however, was a dense, dry disappointment.

Though it can't be substituted for wheat flour in bread dough without tweaking the recipe, C4C is the closest thing to a universally applicable gluten-free substitute we've tested to date. The only drawbacks: It's currently only available at Williams-Sonoma retail outlets and Keller's Bouchon Bakery chain (or through mail order from either company) and will set you back a whopping $19.95 for a 3-pound bag.

Errata

➤ The pH values in the captions for the science sidebar in our home fries story (January/February 2012) were transposed. The correct values are: Boiled with Baking Soda (pH 8.1) and Boiled with Vinegar (pH 3).

Frosting Failure

I've attempted your Lemon Layer Cake (March/April 2007) a few times. The fluffy white icing always looks thick and stable going onto the cake, but after a short while it turns soft and runs down the sides. What am I doing wrong?

CAROLYN OTTO
FOND DU LAC, WIS.

➤ The frosting for this cake is a variation on the classic seven-minute icing. Egg whites, sugar, lemon juice, and corn syrup are mixed together and then warmed gently over simmering water. The mixture is then whipped to stiff peaks before being applied to the cake, where it should remain stable for a full three days.

We wondered if your problem might stem from underheating the egg white mixture before whipping it. We created two batches of icing, heating the egg white mixture in one to the 160 degrees specified in the recipe and the other to just 140 degrees. An hour after whipping both batches, the 140-degree icing was a soupy mess, while the 160-degree sample was picture-perfect.

Here's why: As egg whites and sugar are agitated, the tightly coiled egg proteins temporarily unravel and cross-link with each other, allowing air to be trapped inside the matrix. Heating the egg whites before whipping causes the proteins to permanently unwind and cross-link, so the icing holds its shape—but only if the eggs are heated to a high-enough temperature of 160 degrees. If the mixture has not been sufficiently heated, the network isn't as stable and will eventually break down, turning the icing runny.

To ensure that your icing lasts as long as the cake, make sure to stick your thermometer deep into the center of the egg white mixture. Verify the temperature by stirring the mixture and taking a second reading.

PROPERLY HEATED
Cooking egg whites to 160 degrees ensures that they hold their shape in icing.

UNDERHEATED
Undercooked egg whites will eventually soften and turn runny.

The Fruit and Vegetable Blues

I recently used red onions in a frittata and was surprised to see that they turned bluish green during cooking. What happened?

TED HANSEN
RICHMOND, VA.

➤ Red onions—as well as other red produce, including cabbage and cherries—are rich in pigments called anthocyanins. When they're cooked with acid, their color intensifies, but when combined with an alkaline component, they can turn a startling bluish-green color. Since eggs—specifically egg whites—are basic, ranging from 7.6 to 9.5 on the pH scale, they are most likely responsible for the blue color in your frittata.

FULL STEAM AHEAD
This cooker steams as well today as it did more than a century ago.

Just for fun, we decided to see if we could reverse the color change once a fruit or vegetable with anthocyanin turns blue. We sautéed red cabbage and then added a pinch of baking soda to turn it blue. We found that a splash of vinegar brought its red color right back. This trick may not have a practical application, but it might impress your friends.

Pasta Pronto?

I've recently started seeing three-minute pasta at my supermarket. Is it any good?

CAROLYN MONTGOMERY
BUFFALO, N.Y.

➤ Ronzoni offers three-minute pasta in elbows, rotini, and penne. It is simply much thinner than conventional versions of these pasta shapes, so it hydrates more quickly. When we compared Quick Cook 3-Minute Elbows with traditional elbows from our favorite brand for this type of pasta, Barilla (following the cooking directions on each box), the traditional noodles were unanimously preferred. The Quick Cook Elbows disappointed with a mushy, gummy texture that seemed flimsy and insubstantial alongside the nice chew of the regular pasta.

We're all for speeding up dinner prep, but considering that quick-cook pasta saves mere minutes, we see no point in cutting this particular corner.

FAST BUT FLIMSY
Quick-cooking pasta is not worth the shortcut.

I found this item at an antique shop in New York. Can you tell me what it's used for?

JESSICA PUGLIESE
OAKLAND, CALIF.

This tin and copper "Mrs. Kinney's Steam Cooker," patented in 1895 by Clara and Simon Kinney, originally sold for $5. It consists of a water chamber topped with three perforated food compartments. A 1900 advertisement for the tool promised "a great saving in fuel," as an entire meal could be prepared on a single burner of a gas or wood stove. It also assured housewives that food would not burn or stick, so that "dish washing ceases to be a bugbear."

We gave it a whirl, using the device to cook chicken, cabbage, apples, and puddings. Despite its considerable age, the steamer worked admirably. A spout in the bottom chamber made it easy to monitor and adjust the water level, and the hinged door gave us easy access to each compartment to check for doneness and to remove or add items without having to dismantle the cooker (unlike a stacking Chinese steamer).

Freezing Avocados

I occasionally have trouble using up avocados before they get overripe. Can I freeze them?

EMILY HOFFMAN
LOS ANGELES, CALIF.

➤ To find out, we froze the ripe fruit two ways: whole unpeeled samples and avocados that we halved, pitted, peeled, and then coated in lemon juice (to prevent oxidation) before sealing in zipper-lock bags. After a couple of weeks, we defrosted the samples and tasted them sliced and mashed into guacamole.

The good news is that none of the fruit turned brown. But whether we froze them whole with the skin on or in peeled slices, freezing destroyed the avocado's signature creamy texture, making it watery and mushy. It turns out that in addition to having a high fat content, avocados also contain lots of water. When the sharp ice crystals that form during freezing slash the fruit's cells, they burst, leaking water and creating mushiness when the avocado is defrosted.

One application where the avocado's compromised texture wasn't noticeable? Pureed into salad dressing. So unless you're a big fan of avocado-based dressing, freezing the fruit won't do you much good.

SEND US YOUR QUESTIONS We will provide a complimentary one-year subscription for each letter we print. Send your inquiry, name, address, and daytime telephone number to Notes from Readers, *Cook's Illustrated*, P.O. Box 470589, Brookline, MA 02447, or to NotesFromReaders@AmericasTestKitchen.com.

Quick Tips

⋙ COMPILED BY SHANNON FRIEDMANN HATCH ⋘

The Great Caper Strainer

Rather than use a large colander to drain brine-packed capers, Sandy Finkel of Encino, Calif., turns to her tea strainer. The tool, which fits inside a teacup, is ideal for an ingredient usually measured out in small quantities, and its tight-knit weave prevents the tiny capers from falling through.

Printed Recipe Hang-Up

Jeff Kwong of Los Angeles, Calif., prefers to print recipes that he's found on the Internet rather than referring to them on his computer screen. But the printed pages take up valuable counter space and can be awkward to read on a flat surface. As a fix, he props a baking sheet or cookie sheet against the wall and hangs the recipe on it with binder clips. (If your baking sheet is magnetic, you can use magnets to attach the printout.)

Homemade Knife Block

To keep an assortment of knives on the countertop for easy access and to shield them when not in use, Billie Dionne of Hooksett, N.H., uses this knife block stand-in: a tall plastic container filled with rice. (Dried beans also work.) The rice creates a "slotless" universal system that accommodates a range of different-size knives.

No-Clean Panini Press

Panini presses make it easy to whip up Italian-style grilled sandwiches, but scrubbing away grease and melted-on cheese after each use can be a chore. Peter Walker of Bellingham, Wash., wraps his sandwiches in parchment paper before placing them in the press. The parchment can take the heat and catches spills, eliminating the need for cleanup.

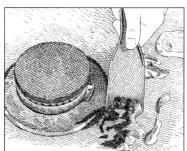

A Gentler Way to Clean Tough Spots

Removing stubborn caked-on food from stovetops or countertops often requires scrubbing with steel wool or harsh cleaners, both of which can scratch delicate kitchen surfaces. Instead, Lon Ponschock of Appleton, Wis., employs a plastic putty knife. Its flexible edge gives him just enough leverage to pry off the stuck-on food without damaging the surface underneath.

Keeping Tabs on Dish Duty

Tired of guessing whether or not the dishwasher has been run, John Herrmann of Corvallis, Ore., erases all doubt by attaching a light-colored clothespin or bag clip to one of the wire racks and writing an X on it with a nontoxic dry-erase marker prior to running the appliance. The cycle washes away the mark—a quick visual indicator of a clean load.

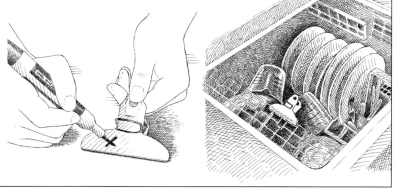

SEND US YOUR TIPS We will provide a complimentary one-year subscription for each tip we print. Send your tip, name, and address to Quick Tips, *Cook's Illustrated*, P.O. Box 470589, Brookline, MA 02447, or to QuickTips@AmericasTestKitchen.com.

Removing Produce Stickers

It's easy to puncture thin-skinned produce like plums and tomatoes when peeling away the produce sticker. Sonia Crowley of Bellingham, Wash., gently pries the sticker away with a vegetable peeler—the blade catches the paper's edge and lifts it off without damaging the skin.

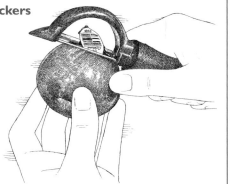

Clear Proof

Naomi Portugaise of Bloomfield Hills, Mich., knows that in order for dough to be properly proofed, it must double in size. However, it's hard to gauge the dough's progress when it is hidden under a hand towel. To solve this dilemma, she covers her loaf pans with a clear plastic top from her prewashed greens containers.

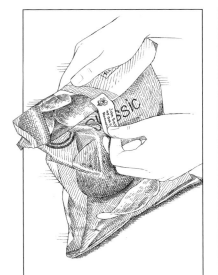

Label Conscious

When she's not sticking them on outgoing envelopes and packages, Alice Smith of Putnam, Conn., puts the free address labels she receives in the mail to use in her kitchen. The easy-peel strips seal opened chip and cereal bags and retain their sticking power until the bags are empty.

Pour Some Sugar

Tired of spilling dry ingredients like baking soda and sugar when measuring small amounts from the box or jar, Margot Hovley of Centerville, Utah, uses a tip she found on the Internet: She transfers them to canning jars—and adds a spout.

1. Using a sharp knife or razor, cut the top off an empty salt container with a built-in spout.

2. Fill an empty widemouthed canning jar with the desired ingredient, place the salt-carton top on the rim, and screw on the jar band to secure it.

A Cleaner Press for Frozen Spinach

Removing excess water from thawed frozen spinach by pressing it against a colander or squeezing it by hand or in a towel inevitably leaves little green bits everywhere. Loretta Ferraro of Bridgton, Maine, has a neater approach: She punctures the bag a few times with a fork and sets it inside a bowl to defrost. Once the spinach has thawed, she squeezes the bag; water drains out through the holes without mess or waste.

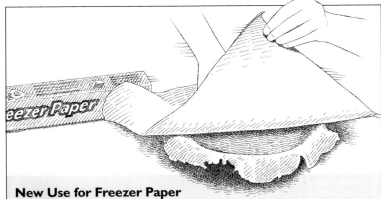

New Use for Freezer Paper

Instead of rolling out pastry or pie dough on parchment paper or plastic wrap, Melissa Andre of San Francisco, Calif., uses plastic-coated freezer paper. Its stiff plastic surface makes it easy to peel away the rolled dough and transfer it to the pie pan.

Creating Order in the Cabinet

Rather than installing custom cabinet dividers, Laurence Marshall of Camden, Maine, devised this low-cost solution for storing cookware lids: He placed a metal file sorter inside the cabinet and loaded the lids into each compartment. Now, instead of searching through a disorganized heap for the right top to his pot, he can quickly grab exactly what he needs.

Introducing Chicken Adobo

Filipino Adobo is a quick-cooking, pantry-ready braise with bold, tangy flavors and tender meat. To adapt it for the American kitchen, we borrowed a regional ingredient and a French technique.

⇒ BY BRYAN ROOF ⇐

Adobo may be considered the national dish of the Philippines, but thanks to the country's melting pot ancestry, the formula for making it is remarkably varied. The core concept is meat marinated and braised in vinegar and soy sauce, with lots of garlic, bay leaves, and black pepper. Everything from that point on, however, is open to interpretation. Chicken is the usual choice, but pork is also found. In the Philippines, coconut-sap vinegar is preferred, but when that isn't available, rice vinegar is a popular substitute. Plenty of recipes also call for cider or plain old distilled vinegar. Some versions go heavy on the soy sauce, rendering the dish a distant relative of Japanese teriyaki, while others use the soy more sparingly and stir in rich coconut milk for a result that is more currylike.

What most Filipino recipes do seem to agree on: This dish is simple and easy to prepare; the ingredients are few and mostly pantry staples; and the finished product—tender meat napped in a reduction of the tangy braising liquid—boasts bold, well-developed flavors.

I armed myself with Filipino cookbooks and tried a bunch of recipes based on my protein of choice: chicken. The common starting point couldn't have

All you need for this Filipino classic is one skillet and about an hour.

been easier: Combine all the ingredients—vinegar, soy sauce, garlic, bay leaves, pepper, and chicken—in a large bowl. Marinating times, however, were all over the place: as brief as 30 minutes to as long as 24 hours. The results were predictably varied, but unfortunately all were problematic, with aggressively tart and salty flavors and sauce that was too runny to cling to the meat. Most troubling of all was the meat, which more often than not sported a tough, mealy outer layer. With the goal of bringing more balance and body to the dish, and producing meat that was juicy and tender, I started to work up my own take on adobo.

The Joy of Soy

Using the best elements of my research recipes, I built a working formula around bone-in, skin-on chicken thighs. With more fat and collagen than breasts and more meat on the bone than drumsticks, thighs are rich, flavorful, and particularly well suited to braising. Plus, the meat's skin would give the sauce something to cling to.

I went with cider vinegar for its round, fruity flavor; tested marinating times from one end of

the spectrum to the other; braised each batch in its respective soaking liquid for about 40 minutes; removed the meat to rest; reduced the liquid until it had thickened slightly; and then recombined the two components. I wasn't surprised when my tasters panned all of the adobos as too tart; I'd worry about evening out the flavors later. It was the tough, mealy texture of the meat that was more troubling. If anything, I expected that the chicken would be mushy, as we've always found that to be the effect of acidic marinades on meat. Puzzled, I relayed the result to our science editor, who offered an explanation: While it is well-known that soaking meat in moderately acidic marinades causes its surface to become mushy, particularly acidic mixtures like this one can cause surface proteins to bind and squeeze out moisture, drying out and toughening the meat's exterior. And it doesn't take long; tasters reported that even the 30-minute samples felt the effects.

I tried skipping the marinade altogether, but that knee-jerk reaction was too drastic. While I'd done away with the meat's tough chew, I'd also inadvertently wiped out its flavor, and tasters complained that the chicken and sauce now tasted like separate entities. Extending the braising time might have infused more salty-sour punch in the meat but not without delaying what I hoped would be a quick-to-prepare dinner. Instead, I reviewed our previous research on marinades and came up with my next test: marinating in only soy sauce. In past tests, we've discovered that while there are very few marinade ingredients that actually make their way beyond the surface of the meat, salt is one of them; in fact, it's the most important one, as it both seasons and tenderizes the meat. Sure enough, when I repeated the marinade test using only soy sauce, the flavor and tenderness of the meat improved radically. And as a boon to my plan for making this a weeknight dinner, tasters assured me that there was no appreciable difference in flavor or texture between the thighs marinated for 30 to 60 minutes and those that I'd left in the soy bath for much longer. But I was far from finished. The tartness of the sauce was still way off base, and even after reducing, it lacked enough body to cling to the meat.

Going Coconuts

Diluting the braising liquid with water was one option to tame the tartness, but the testing was a bust; rather than balancing out the acidity, the water merely dulled the overall flavor of the dish.

PHOTOGRAPHY: CARL TREMBLAY

As I found myself at an impasse, I also happened to have plans to be in New York City, and a colleague suggested that I stop into Filipino chef Romy Dorotan's acclaimed Purple Yam restaurant in Brooklyn to try his adobo. His version was terrific, and when I inquired about the recipe, Dorotan revealed that he added coconut milk to the braising liquid, which he told me is customary in adobos native to southern Luzon, the largest of the Philippine islands. I'd shied away from the super-rich milk in my earlier tests, fearing that it would muddy the flavor of the braise. But his version convinced me otherwise, as it perfectly tempered the salt and acidity while still allowing for plenty of tanginess. The effect wasn't unlike the way that oil tames the acid in a French vinaigrette.

I returned to the test kitchen and whisked a can of coconut milk into the braising liquid of my next batch. Tasters praised the balanced flavors and declared this my best adobo yet, save for one objection: The double dose of fat from the chicken skin and the coconut milk had rendered the sauce a little greasy. I also had a related demand of my own: This being a braise, I wasn't banking on crackly crisp skin, but thus far it had been downright soggy. Discarding the skin altogether might have been one option, but I was counting on its craggy exterior to grip the sauce.

Cold Case

Fortunately, the explanation behind both problems was obvious: My one-step cooking method wasn't exposing the chicken to any high, dry heat, so there was no opportunity to render any of the skin's gummy fat layer and crisp its surface. Easy fix, right? Just throw the thighs skin side down into a ripping hot skillet for a few minutes before moving them into the braising liquid. Wrong. Sure, the skin looked crispy and nicely browned, but slicing below the surface revealed that the thick fat pad was still there. Leaving the thighs in the hot pan for several more minutes to render the fat wasn't a better idea; by the time the skin had shed most of its fat, it was also literally burnt to a crisp.

The problem got me thinking about other types of poultry with a thick fat cap and my mind turned to duck breasts. When I worked in French bistros, I learned a standard method for melting down the dense white layer in duck: Place the meat skin side down in a "cold" (read: room-temperature) pan and then turn up the heat. As the pan gradually gets hotter, the fat under the skin has enough time to melt away before the exterior burns. Figuring the technique would translate to chicken, I placed the marinated thighs skin side down in a 12-inch nonstick skillet and then turned the heat to medium-high. Sure enough, after about 10 minutes the skin was not only sheer but also gorgeously browned. Even better, when I briefly removed the thighs from the pan before adding the braising liquid, I dumped out nearly ⅓ cup of fat. Greasiness problem solved. And although I knew that the skin wouldn't stay super-crisp, I did employ one last deliberate trick to keep as much of its crackly texture as possible. When I returned the chicken thighs to the skillet with the

Balancing Act

The two core components of Filipino adobo—vinegar and soy sauce—add up to a predictably sharp, salty braising liquid. To even out the acidity and salt, we took a cue from a regional variation and added a can of coconut milk. The thick, rich milk mellows those harsher flavors while still allowing for plenty of tanginess. It also adds welcome body to the sauce.

SALTY AND SOUR
Soy sauce and vinegar are staples in Filipino adobo.

THICK AND CREAMY
We add coconut milk for body and richness.

braising liquid, I started them skin side down and then flipped them halfway through so that the skin finished face up, hence it could dry out a little before serving.

I'd been at the stove for less than an hour when I removed the chicken from the pan and briefly reduced the cooking liquid until it thickened up a bit. I poured the tangy, coconut milk–enriched sauce over the tender pieces of chicken, sprinkled on a handful of sliced scallion for color and freshness, and dug in, admiring how nicely these bold flavors had melded together—and how I'd finally created a version of adobo that I could proudly call my own.

FILIPINO CHICKEN ADOBO
SERVES 4

Light coconut milk can be substituted for regular coconut milk. Serve this dish over rice.

- 8 (5- to 7-ounce) bone-in chicken thighs, trimmed
- ⅓ cup soy sauce
- 1 (13½-ounce) can coconut milk
- ¾ cup cider vinegar
- 8 garlic cloves, peeled
- 4 bay leaves
- 2 teaspoons pepper
- 1 scallion, sliced thin

1. Toss chicken with soy sauce in large bowl. Refrigerate for at least 30 minutes and up to 1 hour.

2. Remove chicken from soy sauce, allowing excess to drip back into bowl. Transfer chicken, skin side down, to 12-inch nonstick skillet; set aside soy sauce.

3. Place skillet over medium-high heat and cook until chicken skin is browned, 7 to 10 minutes. While chicken is browning, whisk coconut milk, vinegar, garlic, bay leaves, and pepper into soy sauce.

4. Transfer chicken to plate and discard fat in skillet. Return chicken to skillet skin side down, add coconut milk mixture, and bring to boil. Reduce heat to medium-low and simmer, uncovered, for 20 minutes. Flip chicken skin side up and continue to cook, uncovered, until chicken registers 175 degrees, about 15 minutes. Transfer chicken to platter and tent loosely with aluminum foil.

5. Remove bay leaves and skim any fat off surface of sauce. Return skillet to medium-high heat and cook until sauce is thickened, 5 to 7 minutes. Pour sauce over chicken, sprinkle with scallion, and serve.

Look: It Becomes Adobo
Video available FREE for 4 months at
www.CooksIllustrated.com/apr12

Super-Chunky Granola

We've had it with the overpriced (and underwhelming) store-bought stuff. For homemade granola with real bite, what you need is some bark.

> BY ADAM RIED <

Whether paired with milk, fresh fruit, or yogurt—or eaten by the fistful as a snack—granola is a must-have in my kitchen. Too bad the commercially prepared kind is such a let-down. Whether dry and dusty, overly sweet, infuriatingly expensive ($10 for a 12-ounce bag?), or all of the above, it's so universally disappointing that I recently vowed never to purchase another bag.

Of course, that meant that if I wanted to enjoy granola, I had to make my own. I expected a homemade version to dramatically improve matters, but it only partially helped. Sure, do-it-yourself granola afforded me the opportunity to choose exactly which nuts and dried fruit I wanted to include, as well as how much. But there was a downside: The slow baking and frequent stirring that most recipes recommend results in a loose, granular texture. I wanted something altogether different: substantial clumps of toasty oats and nuts. My ideal clusters would be markedly crisp yet tender enough to shatter easily when bitten—I definitely didn't want the density or tooth-chipping crunch of a hard granola bar.

Starting from square one, I laid out my plan of attack: I would nail down particulars about the oats and nuts first and then set my sights on achieving substantial chunks.

Starting with the Basics

I got down to business and set up my own little granola factory, baking test batches using instant, quick, steel-cut, and old-fashioned whole rolled oat varieties. It was no surprise that instant and quick oats baked up unsubstantial and powdery. Steel-cut oats suffered the opposite problem: Chewing them was like munching gravel. Whole rolled oats were essential for a hearty, crisp texture.

Nuts, on the other hand, offered much more flexibility. Almost any type—I chose almonds for my working recipe—did just fine, contributing rich,

To produce distinct clusters, allow the granola to cool on the baking sheet for an hour before breaking it apart.

toasty flavor that developed as the cereal roasted in the oven, along with plenty of crunch. While many recipes advocate adding them whole, I preferred chopping them first for more even distribution.

As for other potential dry add-ins, more unusual grains (such as quinoa or amaranth) and seeds (sunflower, flax, pumpkin, and so on) are terrific choices, but since I planned on making granola often, I wanted to keep things simple, with ingredients that I routinely stock in my pantry.

With two of the primary players settled, I mixed up a batch using 5 cups of rolled oats and 2 cups of chopped almonds coated with my placeholder liquids: honey and vegetable oil (plus a touch of salt). I used a rubber spatula to spread the sticky concoction onto a baking sheet that I'd first lined with parchment for easier cleanup. I deliberated over what oven temperature to choose, and I settled on a relatively moderate 375 degrees to ward off

scorching and allow the ingredients to brown slowly and evenly. I stirred the mixture every 10 minutes or so until it was evenly golden, which took about 30 minutes. The granola boasted a fantastic toasty scent coming out of the oven, but just as I had feared, there were no hearty chunks.

Temporarily setting the textural issue aside, I considered the other ingredients, starting with the sweetener. Honey and maple syrup are the most common choices, but even in small amounts, the honey struck many tasters as too distinct. Maple syrup was preferred for its milder character, especially when I balanced it with the subtle molasses notes offered by light brown sugar. One-third cup of each for 7 cups of nuts and oats gave the granola just the right degree of sweetness.

The other major component in most granola recipes is fat. But because fat-free commercial versions are so popular and I didn't want to leave any stone unturned, I whipped up a batch in which I left the oil out of the recipe completely. No dice: The fat-free cereal was so dry and powdery that no amount of milk or yogurt could rescue it. I eventually determined that ½ cup was the right amount of oil for a super crisp—but not greasy—texture. Our science editor explained that fat is essential for a substantial crisp texture versus a parched, delicate one: Fat and liquid sweeteners form a fluid emulsion that thoroughly coats ingredients, creating crunch as the granola bakes. Without any fat, the texture is bound to be dry and fragile (see "For Better Granola, Add Fat"). I did two final fat experiments, swapping butter for the oil in the first, only to find that it was prone to burning. In a subsequent trial, extra-virgin olive oil gave the cereal a savory slant that divided tasters, so I stuck with my original choice: neutral-tasting vegetable oil.

Granola Gone Wrong

Most store-bought granola is so bad (and so overpriced), we're surprised anyone ever buys it.

- Without oil to provide moisture, fat-free versions contain dry, dusty oats.
- Baked with the other ingredients, dried fruit turns tough and leathery.
- Loose oats, versus chunks, too readily absorb the milk or yogurt and turn soggy.

PHOTOGRAPHY: CARL TREMBLAY

KEYS TO CHUNKIER GRANOLA

PRESS DOWN
Spread oat mixture onto parchment-lined baking sheet. Press it firmly with spatula to create compact layer.

BAKE BUT DON'T STIR
Bake granola at 325 degrees for 40 to 45 minutes. Rotate pan halfway through baking but don't stir.

BREAK UP
Break cooled granola "bark" into pieces as large as you'd like.

Putting the Pressure On

My granola now possessed well-balanced flavor and perfectly crisp oats and nuts, but I still had to deal with the issue of how to create big clumps. As I paged through cookbooks looking for a magic bullet, I uncovered a lot of interesting suggestions, including adding dry milk powder, egg whites, and sweet, sticky liquids like apple juice or cider to the mix. Sadly, none produced the clusters of my dreams.

If an additional ingredient couldn't help create the substantial chunks I sought, how about adjusting my technique? I'd been reaching into the oven to repeatedly stir the granola as it baked, so I decided to try skipping this step. To make sure that the cereal wouldn't burn in the absence of stirring, I dropped the oven temperature to 325 degrees and extended the cooking time to 45 minutes. Sure enough, some olive-size pieces did form in a no-stir sample—but I wanted more (and larger) chunks. For my next try, I used a spatula to press the hot granola firmly into the pan as soon as it emerged from the oven so that the cooling syrup would bind the solids together as it hardened. This worked, but only to a point. Could I take this idea to the next level?

Since the raw granola mixture was so sticky with syrup and oil, I wondered if muscling it into a tight, compact layer in the pan before baking would yield larger nuggets. I gave it a try, happily finding that when I pulled the cereal from the oven, it remained in a single sheet as it cooled. Now the end product was more of a granola "bark," which was ideal, since I could break it into clumps of any size. Not only had I finally achieved hefty—yet still readily breakable—chunks, but as an added boon, this granola was now hands-off, aside from my having to rotate the pan halfway through baking.

Finishing with Fruit

All that my chunky granola needed now was sweet bits of dried fruit. I tested a variety of choices—raisins, apple, mango, pineapple, cranberries, and pear—finding that they all either burned or turned leathery when baked with the other ingredients. To rectify this, I tried plumping the fruit in water or coating it with oil to help prevent moisture loss.

And yet time and time again, it emerged from the oven overcooked. It eventually became clear that the best way to incorporate the fruit was to keep it away from heat altogether, only stirring it in once the granola was cool.

My simple recipe was nearly complete, but I wanted to create a tiny bit more depth. After some tinkering, I found that a healthy dose of vanilla extract (I used a whopping 4 teaspoons) was just the ticket, accenting the maple, nut, and fruit flavors without overwhelming them.

Finally, I developed a few twists on my basic formula by switching up the fruit-and-nut pairings and accenting them with flavor boosters like coconut, citrus zest, and warm spices.

Forget the store-bought stuff. Home is where you'll find the holy grail of granola: big, satisfying clusters and moist, chewy fruit.

ALMOND GRANOLA WITH DRIED FRUIT
MAKES ABOUT 9 CUPS

Chopping the almonds by hand is the first choice for superior texture and crunch. If you prefer not to hand chop, substitute an equal quantity of slivered or sliced almonds. (A food processor does a lousy job of chopping whole nuts evenly.) Use a single type of your favorite dried fruit or a combination. Do not use quick oats.

- ⅓ cup maple syrup
- ⅓ cup packed (2⅓ ounces) light brown sugar
- 4 teaspoons vanilla extract
- ½ teaspoon salt
- ½ cup vegetable oil
- 5 cups old-fashioned rolled oats
- 2 cups (10 ounces) raw almonds, chopped coarse
- 2 cups raisins or other dried fruit, chopped

1. Adjust oven rack to upper-middle position and heat oven to 325 degrees. Line rimmed baking sheet with parchment paper.

2. Whisk maple syrup, brown sugar, vanilla, and salt in large bowl. Whisk in oil. Fold in oats and almonds until thoroughly coated.

3. Transfer oat mixture to prepared baking sheet and spread across sheet into thin, even layer (about ⅜ inch thick). Using stiff metal spatula, compress oat mixture until very compact. Bake until lightly browned, 40 to 45 minutes, rotating pan once halfway through baking. Remove granola from oven and cool on wire rack to room temperature, about 1 hour. Break cooled granola into pieces of desired size. Stir in dried fruit. (Granola can be stored in airtight container for up to 2 weeks.)

PECAN-ORANGE GRANOLA WITH DRIED CRANBERRIES

Add 2 tablespoons finely grated orange zest and 2½ teaspoons ground cinnamon to maple syrup mixture in step 2. Substitute coarsely chopped pecans for almonds. After granola is broken into pieces, stir in 2 cups dried cranberries.

SPICED WALNUT GRANOLA WITH DRIED APPLE

Add 2 teaspoons ground cinnamon, 1½ teaspoons ground ginger, ¾ teaspoon ground allspice, ½ teaspoon freshly grated nutmeg, and ½ teaspoon black pepper to maple syrup mixture in step 2. Substitute coarsely chopped walnuts for almonds. After granola is broken into pieces, stir in 2 cups chopped dried apples.

TROPICAL GRANOLA WITH DRIED MANGO

Reduce vanilla extract to 2 teaspoons and add 1½ teaspoons ground ginger and ¾ teaspoon freshly grated nutmeg to maple syrup mixture in step 2. Substitute coarsely chopped macadamias for almonds and 1½ cups unsweetened shredded coconut for 1 cup oats. After granola is broken into pieces, stir in 2 cups chopped dried mango or pineapple.

HAZELNUT GRANOLA WITH DRIED PEAR

Substitute coarsely chopped, skinned hazelnuts for almonds. After granola is broken into pieces, stir in 2 cups chopped dried pears.

For Better Granola, Add Fat

When we mixed up a batch of granola in which we left out the oil, the resulting cereal was a real flop, the oats having taken on a crisp but overly dry consistency. It turns out that fat is essential for creating a likable crispness.

Here's why: When the water in a viscous liquid sweetener (like the maple syrup in our recipe) evaporates in the heat of the oven, the sugars left behind develop into a thin coating on the oats and nuts. But without any fat, the sugar coating will become brittle and dry. Only oil can provide a pleasantly crisp coating with a sense of moistness.

Sichuan Stir-Fried Pork in Garlic Sauce

When it comes to replicating this classic Chinese stir-fry at home, the biggest issue is vexingly familiar: how to cook tender, juicy pork.

> BY ANDREW JANJIGIAN <

I remember stir-fried pork in garlic sauce, but not fondly. When I was growing up, this was the dish of wormy pork strips swimming in a generic "brown sauce" that my parents ordered as kid-friendly (read: not spicy) fare to follow up the egg rolls. I liked it well enough then, but my appreciation for this Cantonese American mainstay nose-dived sharply over the years, and with it went any expectation I had that a pork dish featuring garlic sauce would be something other than gloppy, greasy, and boring.

Fast-forward decades later to my introduction to *yu xiang* pork. With thin-cut strips of pork, a soy-based sauce, and plenty of garlic, this Sichuan staple looks similar to the Cantonese version, but its punched-up flavors make it seem anything but related. Yu xiang translates literally as "fish-fragrant," but the sauce isn't the least bit fishy. (The name refers to its origins as a condiment for seafood.) Rather, it's a mix of salty, sweet, hot, and—thanks to a healthy splash of Chinese black vinegar—sour flavors that, when prepared well, balance out into a bold-tasting, silky sauce that coats the super-tender meat and accompanying vegetables. These usually feature a crunchy element like celery, bamboo shoots, or water chestnuts, plus dark, wrinkly wood ear mushrooms.

That's what it tastes like in a restaurant, anyway. But since I'd found plenty of recipes for yu xiang pork in Chinese cookbooks, I figured I'd make it myself. The method looked easy enough: Gently parcook the meat in oil, drain it, and set it aside; turn up the heat and add aromatics and Asian broad-bean chili paste, followed by the vegetables; return the meat to the pan along with the sauce ingredients and simmer until thickened.

But my attempts were all disappointments. None achieved the requisite balance of yu xiang; one tasted cloyingly sweet, while another overdid it on the vinegar and left tasters puckering. Some were thin and

Our version of this hot, sour, salty, and sweet Chinese stir-fry calls for an unlikely cut of pork.

watery, others slick and greasy. The biggest problem of all, however, was the pork itself. In most cases, its texture was dry, chewy, and stringy, and the sauce wasn't sufficiently camouflaging those flaws.

International Velvet

Figuring I'd tackle the meat itself first, I spread my test recipes out in front of me and discovered the common problem: Almost all of them called for pork loin, a lean, notoriously unforgiving cut that tends to cook up dry and fibrous. Switching to another cut was an obvious move, so I surveyed the butcher case and came back with two fattier cuts that promised more flavor and tenderness— namely, pork shoulder and country-style spareribs. Both cuts tasted markedly richer and juicier, but shoulder meat came with its own set of challenges. Not only was it hard to find in quantities small enough for stir-fry purposes (I only needed about 12 ounces) but it required

quite a bit of knife work to trim out the excess fat and pare it down to matchstick-size pieces. Country-style ribs, cut from the shoulder end of the loin, were a lot easier to butcher, so I went with them.

Now that I was using a fattier cut, I wondered if the low-temperature fat bath was actually necessary. It seemed to me that the only purpose of that step was to ensure that the lean tenderloin emerged moist and silky. But when I tried to eliminate the step, even this more marbled cut didn't cook up as supple as the best yu xiang pork I've eaten in restaurants. If I wanted supremely tender, juicy pork without the mess of all that oil, I'd have to look for another way.

Fortunately, there's a far simpler technique from Chinese cookery that tackles the problem of meat drying out in a stir-fry: velveting. This approach involves coating the meat in a cornstarch slurry to provide an insulating barrier that shields the meat from the pan's high temperatures. I gave it a whirl, mixing 2 teaspoons of cornstarch with an equal amount of rice wine and tossing it with the pork before proceeding with the recipe. Though a definite improvement, the leaner pieces of sparerib meat were still less tender and juicy than I wanted. For the results that I was after, I needed a technique that offered more than just a starch overcoat; it would have to actually tenderize the meat, too.

Soda Solution

As it happens, we learned an interesting fact about meat texture during a recent tasting: Tenderness, especially in pork, is highly dependent on the pH of the meat; the higher the pH the more tender it will

PHOTOGRAPHY: CARL TREMBLAY

be. If I could find a way to artificially boost the pH of the meat, it might just soften up a bit. And I had just the ingredient in mind to help: alkaline baking soda.

My plan was to soak the pork in a solution of baking soda (1 tablespoon) and water (½ cup) for an hour or so and then proceed with velveting. And the results were promising; even the leaner strips of meat were considerably more tender. Too tender, in fact, and also soapy-tasting. I'd overcompensated a bit, so in the next batch I cut back to 1 teaspoon of baking soda and soaked the meat for just 15 minutes. I also rinsed the pork afterward, to remove any residual soda. This time the pork was perfect: marvelously juicy and supple. Even better, I didn't need much more than 2 tablespoons of oil to cook the meat.

Balancing Game

Meanwhile, the other half of the equation—the sauce—needed adjusting to achieve just the right balance of salty, sour, sweet, and spicy flavors. Starting with a base of equal parts soy sauce and rice wine, plus 4 teaspoons of tangy Chinese black vinegar and a tablespoon of sesame oil, I diluted the mixture with enough chicken broth to amply coat the meat and vegetables and stirred in 2 teaspoons of cornstarch for thickening. Then I fried up some minced garlic and scallion whites and a few teaspoons of broad-bean chili paste in a nonstick skillet, poured in the sauce mixture, and simmered it until it turned glossy. Not bad, tasters said, but they wanted more—particularly more sweetness and more savory depth.

The first request was easy to fulfill with a couple of tablespoons of sugar. It was boosting the savoriness of the dish that was more challenging. I spent more than 30 subsequent tests tinkering with the ratios of sesame oil, vinegar, garlic, and bean paste, but each batch still lacked a certain full-bodied depth that I remembered in the restaurant versions I'd tried. Two likely reasons: Many restaurants build the sauce from a base of homemade stock (instead of canned chicken broth), and some also add monosodium glutamate to punch up the savoriness. Neither of those ingredients would be in my recipe, so I started rooting through my pantry for ingredients that I thought might do the trick and came away with two successful (albeit untraditional) additions: fish sauce and ketchup, both of which are naturally packed with flavor-enhancing glutamates. Just 2 teaspoons of each rounded out the savory flavor we were looking

Pork loin, the usual stir-fry choice, is lean and dry. Instead, we use boneless country-style spareribs, which are fattier (they're cut from the blade end of the loin) and more tender.

COUNTRY-STYLE RIBS
These well-marbled slabs contain flavorful dark meat.

for. As an added bonus, the ketchup also contributed to the smooth viscosity of the sauce.

A few last substitutions: Instead of hard-to-find wood ear mushrooms, I went with shiitakes. I also settled on readily available celery over water chestnuts for a contrasting crunch. Though Chinese black vinegar and Asian broad-bean chili paste are popping up in more and more supermarkets, I found that equal parts balsamic and rice vinegars provided a fine alternative to the former and either Asian chili-garlic paste or Sriracha sauce made a good sub for the latter (but in smaller amounts).

At last, I had a version of yu xiang pork as good as anything I'd order in a Sichuan restaurant.

SICHUAN STIR-FRIED PORK IN GARLIC SAUCE
SERVES 4 TO 6

If Chinese black vinegar is unavailable, substitute 2 teaspoons of balsamic vinegar and 2 teaspoons of rice vinegar. If Asian broad-bean chili paste is unavailable, substitute 2 teaspoons of Asian chili-garlic paste or Sriracha sauce. Serve with steamed white rice.

Sauce
- ½ cup low-sodium chicken broth
- 2 tablespoons sugar
- 2 tablespoons soy sauce
- 4 teaspoons Chinese black vinegar
- 1 tablespoon toasted sesame oil
- 1 tablespoon Chinese rice wine or dry sherry
- 2 teaspoons ketchup
- 2 teaspoons fish sauce
- 2 teaspoons cornstarch

Pork
- 12 ounces boneless country-style pork ribs, trimmed
- 1 teaspoon baking soda
- ½ cup cold water
- 2 teaspoons Chinese rice wine or dry sherry
- 2 teaspoons cornstarch

Stir-Fry
- 4 garlic cloves, minced
- 2 scallions, white parts minced, green parts sliced thin
- 2 tablespoons Asian broad-bean chili paste
- 4 tablespoons vegetable oil
- 6 ounces shiitake mushrooms, stemmed and sliced thin
- 2 celery ribs, cut on bias into ¼-inch slices

1. FOR THE SAUCE: Whisk all ingredients together in bowl; set aside.

2. FOR THE PORK: Cut pork into 2-inch lengths, then cut each length into ¼-inch matchsticks. Combine pork with baking soda and water in bowl. Let sit at room temperature for 15 minutes.

3. Rinse pork in cold water. Drain well and pat dry with paper towels. Whisk rice wine and cornstarch in bowl. Add pork and toss to coat.

4. FOR THE STIR-FRY: Combine garlic, scallion whites, and chili paste in bowl.

5. Heat 1 tablespoon oil in 12-inch nonstick skillet over high heat until just smoking. Add mushrooms and cook, stirring frequently, until tender, 2 to 4 minutes. Add celery and continue to cook until celery is crisp-tender, 2 to 4 minutes. Transfer vegetables to separate bowl.

6. Add remaining 3 tablespoons oil to now-empty skillet and place over medium-low heat. Add garlic-scallion mixture and cook, stirring frequently, until fragrant, about 30 seconds. Transfer 1 tablespoon garlic-scallion oil to small bowl and set aside. Add pork to skillet and cook, stirring frequently, until no longer pink, 3 to 5 minutes. Whisk sauce mixture to recombine and add to skillet. Increase heat to high and cook, stirring constantly, until sauce is thickened and pork is cooked through, 1 to 2 minutes. Return vegetables to skillet and toss to combine. Transfer to serving platter, sprinkle with scallion greens and reserved garlic-scallion oil, and serve.

A Better Way to Poach Fish

Restaurants have an unusual technique for turning out supremely moist, tender fillets of fish. But adapting it for the home cook required an even more unlikely trick.

> BY DAN SOUZA

If your experience with poached fish is limited to the lean, bland preparation you might be served at a wedding or a weight-loss spa, a technique popular at high-end restaurants will permanently change your perception—and serve as a reminder as to why poaching became a classic approach to cooking fish in the first place. The key perk: Submerging fish in liquid and gently cooking it at below-simmer temperatures—anywhere from 130 to 180 degrees—renders the delicate flesh silky and supple. In this case, however, there is one major amendment to the technique that elevates it above any poached fish I'd ever tasted: Rather than the usual lean bath of water, wine, broth, or some combination thereof, the poaching liquid is olive oil.

I had to admit: On paper, cooking delicate fish fillets in a pot of fat sounds like a greasy recipe for disaster, but the results were stunning—lighter, moister, and more fragrant than any traditionally poached fish I'd ever tasted—and they explained why this technique has become so popular in top restaurants. Another plus: The flavor-infused poaching oil can be whirred into a rich, glossy emulsion and drizzled over the fish as a sauce. The dish, I realized, would make elegant fare, provided I could get around one obvious challenge: the cost—and mess—of heating up a large amount of olive oil for just one meal. I would have to figure out how to scale the oil way back.

Oil Embargo

My first decision was to go with skinless fillets since the oil would never get hot enough to crisp the skin. I settled on cod for its firm, meaty flesh and clean flavor. As for the amount of oil, I reasoned that the smaller the surface area of the cooking vessel, the deeper the liquid would pool, so I reached past my trusty 12-inch nonstick skillet for its 10-inch sibling. Unfortunately, this setup still demanded about 1½ cups of oil to cover the four 6-ounce fillets. My only other idea was

An onion placed in the middle of the fillets allows us to shallow-poach them in just ¾ cup of oil.

to displace some of the oil by placing half an onion in the skillet and arranging the fillets around it—a trick that worked but got me down only another ¼ cup. Clearly, I needed a more drastic solution.

That's when I started to wonder if completely immersing the fillets in oil was necessary. The alternative—pouring enough oil into the pan to come roughly halfway up the sides of the fish (about ¾ cup)—would mean flipping the fish partway through poaching to ensure that it cooked through. But that seemed a small price to pay for significantly cutting my oil dependence. I gave it a shot, basting the exposed half of each fillet with a few spoonfuls of oil (to prevent evaporation), popping a lid on the pan, and placing the skillet over the lowest burner setting. The good news was that the method worked; the fillets were supremely moist and tender—considerably more so than any water-poached fish and not at all oily (see "Why Poach in Oil?").

The bad news was that it was fussy. With relatively little oil in the pan, the temperature spiked quickly and required that I constantly fiddle with the burner knob to keep the oil in my target range (140 to 150 degrees), which would slowly bring my fish to an ideal internal temperature of 130 degrees, with

little risk of going over. Placing a homemade heat diffuser fashioned from a ring of aluminum foil over the burner didn't reliably tame the flame. What I needed was a steadier, less-direct heat source, and for that I turned to the oven.

I figured that I could simply bring the oil to 140 degrees on the stovetop, slip in the fish, and then transfer the skillet into a low oven. But it wasn't quite that easy; the oil temperature immediately plummeted when I added the still-cold fillets, and the temperature recovery time in the oven was slow. But I had an idea: I'd heat the oil on the stovetop to well above my target temperature and then rely on the oven's more-even heat to keep it in the poaching sweet spot.

After a slew of tests, I hit upon a winning combination: Heat the oil to 180 degrees, nestle in the fillets (each sprinkled with kosher salt), and set the pan in a 250-degree oven. The oil temperature recovered within 15 minutes, by which point the lower half of the fish was cooked. I flipped the fillets, replaced the lid, and returned them to the oven. This batch emerged incredibly moist and velvety, and thanks to my oven method, the process was now largely hands-off. What I had was good—but I wanted to make it even better.

Crunch Time

We often salt meat and allow it to rest before cooking, both to enhance juiciness and to bring seasoning deep into the interior. Why not try this with fish? For my next round of testing, I salted the fillets about 20 minutes before cooking. This technique worked beautifully: Moisture beaded on the surface of the fish, where it dissolved the salt and created a concentrated brine that was eventually absorbed back into the flesh to bolster flavor.

I also wanted something that could serve as a textural contrast to the silky fish. Restaurants often garnish their oil-poached fillets with lightly fried vegetables and fresh herbs, and I reasoned that I could approximate that by crisping something in the oil before cooking the fish. Fried artichoke hearts have always been a favorite of mine, so I defrosted a bag of them, patted them dry, and halved them lengthwise before tossing them with cornstarch (for extra crunch) and dropping them into the shimmering oil with some minced garlic.

Tasters loved the crisp garnish, but after cranking up the heat to fry, I then had to wait more than 10 minutes for the oil to cool to my target of 180 degrees before the pan went into the oven. The

PHOTOGRAPHY: CARL TREMBLAY

POACHING FISH OUT OF WATER

Oil poaching is not only a foolproof technique for cooking delicate fish but also a seamless way to create a crispy garnish and elegant sauce from the same oil.

FRY GARNISH Frying artichoke hearts and garlic in oil yields a crisp garnish that provides a nice contrast to the fish.

COOL HOT OIL Pouring ¼ cup of fresh oil into the strained frying oil helps cool it to a gentle poaching temperature.

DISPLACE OIL Adding an onion half displaces the oil, so it comes up higher in the pan—and we can use less of it.

TRANSFER TO OVEN Poaching in a low oven (rather than on the stove) guarantees more even cooking.

MAKE VINAIGRETTE Using the flavorful poaching oil to create a simple vinaigrette adds brightness.

---

solution proved easy: Rather than dump in all the oil at once, I'd fry the garnishes in ½ cup of oil, strain it, and add the remaining ¼ cup of room temperature oil to the pan to speed the cooling. The tweak made all the difference; about five minutes after frying, the oil was cool enough for poaching.

Dressed to Impress

Frying up a garnish had also left me with an added bonus: flavor-infused oil to use for a sauce. I poured ½ cup into the blender and whirred it with whole cherry tomatoes (for bright sweetness), half a shallot, sherry vinegar, and salt and pepper. After a quick spin on high speed and a pass through a fine-mesh strainer, I had a silky-smooth vinaigrette.

Dressed up with the sauce, the crispy artichoke garnish, a few slices of fresh cherry tomato, and a fistful of chopped parsley, my elegant plate was complete—not to mention plenty simple to pull off at home.

SCIENCE ## Why Poach in Oil?

Poaching in oil allows fish to retain more of its juices than poaching in wine or broth, leading to remarkably moist, velvety results. This is because cooking in oil is inherently more gentle than cooking in water (see "Why Food Cooks Slower in Oil than in Water," page 30). And while you might expect that fish poached in fat would be greasy, it actually absorbs very little oil. Why? In order for oil to penetrate the fish, moisture must exit first. But because oil and water repel each other, it's very difficult for moisture inside the fish to readily enter the oil. Hence, more of the juices stay in the fish. In fact, in our tests, oil-poached fish lost just 14 percent of its weight during cooking, while water-poached fillets lost 24 percent.

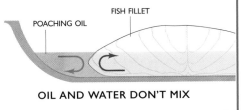

POACHING OIL   FISH FILLET

OIL AND WATER DON'T MIX

POACHED FISH FILLETS WITH SHERRY-TOMATO VINAIGRETTE
SERVES 4

Fillets of meaty white fish like cod, halibut, sea bass, or snapper work best in this recipe. Just make sure the fillets are at least 1 inch thick. A neutral oil such as canola can be substituted for the pure olive oil. The onion half in step 3 is used to displace the oil; a 4-ounce porcelain ramekin may be used instead. Serve with couscous or steamed white rice. For our free recipe for Poached Fish Fillets with Cilantro and Jalapeño Vinaigrette, go to www.CooksIllustrated.com/apr12.

Fish
- 4 (6-ounce) skinless white fish fillets, 1 inch thick
  Kosher salt
- 4 ounces frozen artichoke hearts, thawed, patted dry, and sliced in half lengthwise
- 1 tablespoon cornstarch
- ¾ cup olive oil
- 3 garlic cloves, minced
- ½ onion, peeled

Vinaigrette
- 4 ounces cherry tomatoes
- ½ small shallot, peeled
- 4 teaspoons sherry vinegar
  Kosher salt
- ½ teaspoon pepper

- 1 tablespoon chopped fresh parsley
- 2 ounces cherry tomatoes, cut into ⅛-inch-thick rounds

1. FOR THE FISH: Adjust oven racks to middle and lower-middle positions and heat oven to 250 degrees. Pat fish dry with paper towels and season each fillet with ¼ teaspoon salt. Let sit at room temperature for 20 minutes.

2. Meanwhile, toss artichokes and cornstarch in bowl to coat. Heat ½ cup oil in 10-inch nonstick skillet over medium heat until shimmering. Shake excess cornstarch from artichokes and add to skillet;

cook, stirring occasionally, until crisp and golden, 2 to 4 minutes. Add garlic and continue to cook until garlic is golden, 30 to 60 seconds. Strain oil through fine-mesh strainer into bowl. Transfer artichokes and garlic to ovenproof paper towel–lined plate and season with salt. Do not wash strainer.

3. Return strained oil to skillet and add remaining ¼ cup oil. Place onion half in center of pan. Let oil cool until it registers about 180 degrees, 5 to 8 minutes. Arrange fish fillets, skinned side up, around onion (oil should come roughly halfway up fillets). Spoon a little oil over each fillet, cover skillet, transfer to middle rack, and cook for 15 minutes.

4. Remove skillet from oven. Using 2 spatulas, carefully flip fillets. Cover skillet, return to middle rack, and place plate with artichokes and garlic on lower-middle rack. Continue to cook fish until it registers 130 to 135 degrees, 9 to 14 minutes longer. Gently transfer fish to serving platter, reserving ½ cup oil, and tent fish loosely with aluminum foil. Turn off oven, leaving plate of artichokes in oven.

5. FOR THE VINAIGRETTE: Process whole cherry tomatoes, shallot, vinegar, ¾ teaspoon salt, and pepper with reserved ½ cup fish cooking oil in blender until smooth, 1 to 2 minutes. Add any accumulated fish juice from platter, season with salt to taste, and blend for 10 seconds. Strain sauce through fine-mesh strainer, pressing on solids to extract as much liquid as possible (discard solids).

6. To serve, pour vinaigrette around fish. Garnish each fillet with warmed crisped artichokes and garlic, parsley, and tomato rounds. Serve immediately.

POACHED FISH FILLETS WITH MISO-GINGER VINAIGRETTE

For fish, substitute 8 scallion whites, sliced ¼ inch thick, for artichoke hearts; omit garlic; and reduce amount of cornstarch to 2 teaspoons. For vinaigrette, process 6 scallion greens, 8 teaspoons lime juice, 2 tablespoons mirin, 4 teaspoons white miso paste, 2 teaspoons minced ginger, and ½ teaspoon sugar with ½ cup fish cooking oil as directed in step 5. Garnish fish with 2 thinly sliced scallion greens and 2 halved and thinly sliced radishes.

Spaghetti al Vino Bianco

We'd heard about pasta cooked in red wine, but its tannic flavor and gray color left us cold. Could white wine come to the rescue?

> BY ANDREA GEARY <

A plate of pasta and a glass of wine are a natural pairing. But I'd long heard references to a dish called *spaghetti al vino rosso* that exploits their affinity: You actually cook the pasta in wine instead of water and then top it off with olive oil, a bit of butter, and a sprinkling of cheese. The concept is not without precedent. We know that stirring rice in a wine-spiked broth as it cooks transforms it from a blank slate into a complex and wonderful risotto. I figured the same could be true of pasta if I could just pin down a reliable recipe.

Easier said than done. Recipes were hard to track down, and the ones I found were all over the map. One called for boiling the spaghetti in a 50/50 mix of water and red wine that was then (wastefully) poured down the drain. In another, a whole bottle of wine was reduced to a glaze (eliminating all of its pleasant booziness) and used to coat spaghetti cooked separately in water. A third approach resembled risotto-making and seemed the most promising: parcooking the pasta in water and then transferring it to a skillet where about 2 cups of wine were added in increments so that the pasta could absorb the wine as it finished cooking.

Made this way, the dish wasn't perfect. While tasters liked the pasta's lively wine kick, they also found that the dish tasted tannic. The deal breaker, though, was its unappetizing purple-gray color.

My research indicated that this was a dish almost always made with red wine. Nevertheless, I couldn't help but wonder what would happen if I swapped the red wine for white, which would at least get rid of the hideous mauve color. I tried it and found that the switch also solved the tannin problem, since such flavors come from the grape skins, which are removed early in the process of making white wine. But now I had a new issue: The spaghetti wasn't as robustly flavored when made with white wine.

I thought back to the method that reduced a full bottle of wine in a skillet. I experimented with reducing about a third of a bottle of white wine to a glaze while the spaghetti parcooked in water. Then I introduced the partially cooked spaghetti to the glaze and added the remainder of the bottle gradually, stirring as the spaghetti finished cooking. The glaze provided a subtle complexity that the dish had previously lacked, but we agreed that this spaghetti was going to need more than just olive oil, butter, and grated Pecorino Romano to be anything other than an Italian *primo*, or first course.

Garlic and red pepper flakes were natural additions, and they were easily incorporated into the glaze. Crisp, salty pancetta sprinkled over the pasta before serving was also a shoo-in. Casting about for a green that wouldn't require parcooking, I landed on arugula. Its peppery notes complemented the other flavors perfectly. Pine nuts added textural dimension.

My spaghetti was almost complete, but it seemed a tad dry. I had been stirring in some cold butter along with reserved pasta water at the end, but the resulting sauce was too insubstantial. A little bit of cream was just the thing to bulk it up. Admittedly, I'd taken liberties by using white wine, but I was willing to bet that no one who tasted my recipe would complain.

SPAGHETTI AL VINO BIANCO
SERVES 4

For this dish, you should use a good-quality dry white wine but avoid a heavily oaked white such as Chardonnay. If the wine reduction is too sharp in step 2, season to taste with up to 1 tablespoon of sugar, adding it in 1-teaspoon increments.

1	tablespoon extra-virgin olive oil
4	ounces pancetta, cut into ¼-inch pieces
2	garlic cloves, minced
	Pinch red pepper flakes
1	bottle (750 ml) dry white wine
	Salt and pepper
	Sugar
1	pound spaghetti
5	ounces (5 cups) baby arugula
⅓	cup heavy cream
1	ounce Pecorino Romano, grated (½ cup), plus extra for serving
¼	cup pine nuts, toasted and chopped coarse

1. Heat oil and pancetta in 12-inch skillet over medium-high heat; cook until pancetta is browned and crisp, 4 to 5 minutes. Using slotted spoon, transfer pancetta to paper towel–lined plate. Pour off and discard all but 2 tablespoons rendered fat from skillet.

2. Return skillet to medium-low heat and add garlic and pepper flakes. Cook, stirring frequently, until garlic begins to turn golden, 1 to 2 minutes. Carefully add 1½ cups wine and increase heat to medium-high. Cook until wine is reduced to ½ cup, 8 to 10 minutes. Add ½ teaspoon salt. Taste and season with up to 1 tablespoon sugar if needed.

3. Bring 4 quarts water to boil in large pot. Add

pasta and 1 tablespoon salt and cook, stirring often, until pasta is flexible but not fully cooked, about 4 minutes. Reserve 2 cups pasta water, then drain pasta.

4. Transfer pasta to skillet with reduced white wine. Place skillet over medium heat; add ½ cup unreduced wine and cook, tossing constantly until wine is fully absorbed. Continue to add remaining wine, ½ cup at a time, tossing constantly, until pasta is al dente, about 8 minutes. (If wine is absorbed before spaghetti is fully cooked, add ½ cup reserved pasta water at a time to skillet and continue to cook.)

5. Remove skillet from heat. Place arugula on top of spaghetti; pour ¼ cup reserved pasta water over arugula, cover, and let stand for 1 minute. Add cream and ¼ cup Pecorino Romano; toss until sauce lightly coats pasta and arugula is evenly distributed. Season with salt and pepper to taste. Transfer to serving platter and sprinkle with pancetta, remaining ¼ cup Pecorino Romano, and pine nuts. Serve immediately, passing extra Pecorino Romano separately.

Philly Cheesesteaks at Home

We set out to reproduce this classic sandwich without the pricey rib eye, a deli slicer, or a flattop griddle.

≳ BY ANDREW JANJIGIAN ≲

You can get a steak sub just about anywhere, but a real cheesesteak comes from only one place: Philadelphia. Fancy steakhouse interpretations aside, the meat is always sliced paper-thin and presented in one of two forms: cooked as is so that the wide swaths wrinkle from the griddle's heat or chopped with the edge of a metal spatula as it sizzles on the flattop, producing fine bits that fry and crisp in their own rendered fat. Either way, the meat is generously heaped into a soft-crumbed, crisp-crusted torpedo roll along with your cheese of choice: provolone, American, or, most famously, a ladle of "Whiz." It's an unapologetically decadent, classically American behemoth of a sandwich.

I'm a fan of the hashed style myself, in which the well-browned bits are especially savory and the cheese is folded in with the meat, acting just as much like a velvety binder as like a rich, salty flavor booster. Unfortunately, I don't get to Philly as often as I'd like, and my craving for the sandwich made me so bold as to wonder if I couldn't pull off a close replica in my own kitchen.

Admittedly, it was a tall order—particularly the texture of the meat, which relied on two kitchen appliances that I (and most other home cooks) don't own: a meat slicer to shave the steak super-thin and a griddle to cook it in a single layer and maximize browning. What's more, many steak shops use rib eye—beautifully marbled and flavorful but, for most of us, prohibitively expensive ($15 to $20 per pound) as sandwich meat. I'd need substitutes for all three.

I thought about asking a butcher to slice the meat for me but soon realized that would be a dead end; even if he or she were willing to indulge my odd request, the raw meat would first have to be frozen overnight to make this even possible. My other supermarket shortcut idea was to buy thin-sliced deli roast beef and fry it, but this, too, was a bust. Even when it was cooked in a generous amount of fat, the lean, bland roast tasted unmistakably like lunchmeat. I had no choice: I'd have to slice the meat myself.

Without a meat slicer, I had three options available: a mandoline, a food processor, or a steady hand and a sharp knife. Using fat-streaked blade steaks as a placeholder, I ran the meat through both appliances but had little luck with either. Though the mandoline produced properly thin sheets, it was slow-going—not to mention knuckle-jeopardizing—work. The food processor seemed like a better, faster alternative at first but not once the chunks of

meat got caught between the slicing blade and the lid, turning swiftly to paste. We'd have to go with hand slicing.

But shaving 2 pounds of meat by hand would require more than a steady hand and a sharp knife. I also needed the right cut of meat, one that was marbled, tender, and reasonably priced as well as a cut that I could easily slice against the grain, so that it would readily break apart into chewy-tender bits as it cooked. Blade steaks were one option, as were top round, flap meat (known as sirloin tips), boneless short ribs, and skirt steak. I cut each into 3-inch-wide strips and then, before slicing, froze the pieces for about an hour. It's a preslicing trick we frequently turn to in the test kitchen; firming up the meat makes it easier to slice cleanly.

The options dwindled quickly: Short ribs, though well marbled like rib eye, developed an unpleasant liver-y flavor, while top round and blade steak were both difficult to slice across the grain and chewy and tough when cooked. Flap meat and skirt steak, meanwhile, boasted big beefy flavor, not to mention a long grain that made them easy to slice thinly. Of the two, skirt steak was the clear winner: In addition to being easily sliceable, its extremely loose grain helped it break down. Then, to further mimic the way cheesesteak slingers hash the meat with the edges of metal spatulas, I coarsely chopped it before cooking.

That left just one more substitution: finding a viable alternative to the griddle. The advantage of the roomy flattop is that moisture evaporates almost instantly, allowing the meat to crisp up nicely. Unfortunately, it was impossible to brown 2 pounds of meat in the confines of a 12-inch nonstick skillet; with so little surface area and 2-inch walls, the meat stewed in its own juices. But the fix wasn't a hard one: I simply cooked the meat in two stages, letting each batch drain in a colander before returning it to the pan to mix with the cheese.

But the cheese was a dilemma of its own. While tasters liked the smoky tang of provolone, they decided the gooey, melty quality of American was essential. (Cheez Whiz appealed to no one.) My nontraditional solution: Sharpening up the flavor of the smooth-melting American stuff with a little grated Parmesan.

Topped with traditional fixin's like pickled hot peppers and sautéed onions, this sandwich was as close to the real deal as I'd ever had, plus it didn't require a trip to Philly.

Shrimp 101

How to buy, prep, and cook juicy, tender shrimp. BY SHANNON FRIEDMANN HATCH

BUYING BASICS

Ensuring tender, briny-tasting shrimp starts at the seafood counter, where many of the rules that apply to buying fish don't hold true for shrimp.

Go for White
Increasingly, seafood markets and gourmet shops sell a range of different shrimp species. We compared the three most commonly available types (pink, white, and black tiger) and found that white shrimp had the firmest flesh and the sweetest taste.

Don't Be Fooled by "Fresh"
Just because shrimp is raw doesn't mean it's fresh. Since only 10 percent of the shrimp sold in this country comes from U.S. sources (in recent years, the majority has come from Thailand, followed by Indonesia and Ecuador), chances are the shrimp has been previously frozen. Unless you live near a coastal area, "fresh" shrimp likely means defrosted shrimp.

Don't Buy Defrosted
Once shrimp are defrosted for the seafood case, the quality declines with each passing day. Unless you ask, there's no telling how long they have been on display—and in our tests, defrosted shrimp tasted noticeably less fresh even after a day of storage. But if you must buy defrosted, look for unblemished and firm shrimp that fill the shell and smell of the sea.

Buy Individually Quick-Frozen
In general, IQF stands for "individually quick-frozen": Shrimp are spread on a conveyor belt and frozen at sea, locking in quality and freshness. All bagged frozen shrimp fall into this category; however, it's not always on the label. Shrimp are also sometimes frozen at sea with water in 5-pound blocks packed in boxes. We prefer bagged individually quick-frozen shrimp, as you can thaw exactly what you need.

Check the Ingredient List
"Shrimp" should be the only ingredient listed on the bag or box. In effort to prevent darkening or water loss during thawing, some manufacturers add salt or STPP (sodium tripolyphosphate). Our tasters found an unpleasant texture in salt-treated and STPP-enhanced shrimp; the latter also had a chemical taste.

Buy Wild
We've found that wild shrimp have a sweeter flavor and firmer texture than farm-raised, making their higher price worth it. (In this country, 75 percent of the wild shrimp sold comes from the U.S. Gulf of Mexico.) Unless you can purchase them right off the boat, only buy wild shrimp frozen. Because fresh wild shrimp are minimally processed, they are usually shipped with the heads on. The head contains digestive enzymes that break down muscle proteins rapidly after death, resulting in mushy meat. Freezing halts this activity.

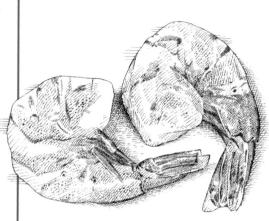

MAGIC NUMBER: 21/25 — Extra-large shrimp (21/25) are our go-to when we want a browned exterior. This count is the most widely available in stores, and the shrimp's meaty size allows them to stay on the heat longer before turning rubbery.

It's the Count That Counts
There's no industry standard for labeling shrimp sizes, so one vendor's large may be another's extra-large. Instead of size, focus on count per pound, which always appears on the bag. The letter *U* stands for "under" (e.g., U/10 means under 10 shrimp per pound). Two numbers separated by a slash indicates a range. Most important: The smaller the number per pound, the larger the shrimp. Here are the most widely available sizes.

TEST KITCHEN NAME	COUNT PER POUND
Jumbo	16/20
Extra-Large	21/25
Large	26/30
Medium	41/50
Small	51/60

PREP WORK

The Right Way to Thaw
Frozen shrimp should be fully thawed before cooking—but how you defrost the shrimp affects its final flavor and texture. In tests, we got the firmest, juiciest results by defrosting the shrimp overnight in the refrigerator. For faster defrosting, place the bag under cold running water until the shrimp are fully thawed.

Peeling Made Easy
Remove the telson, the small pointed section at the top of the tail. Holding the shrimp in one hand, move the thumb of your opposite hand up from the legs and around the shrimp, removing most of the shell. Pull gently on the tail to remove the remainder of the shell.

Quick Deveining
For aesthetic reasons, we like to remove the thick, dark line that runs along the shrimp's back. Holding the shelled shrimp between your thumb and forefinger, use a sharp paring knife to make a shallow cut along the back, exposing the veinlike digestive tract. Lift it out with the knife's tip.

Pan Searing

A blazing-hot skillet produces nice browning but can quickly turn delicate shrimp tough. Our approach guarantees juicy shrimp—and a golden crust.

ADD SUGAR
Tossing the shrimp with a little sugar speeds up browning so they need less time over heat.

FLIP OFF HEAT
Removing the pan from the heat before flipping shrimp prevents them from overcooking.

1. Heat 1 tablespoon oil in 12-inch skillet over high heat until smoking. Meanwhile, toss 1½ pounds extra-large (21/25) shrimp, ¼ teaspoon salt, ¼ teaspoon pepper, and ¼ teaspoon sugar in medium bowl.

2. Add half of shrimp to pan in single layer and cook until spotty brown and edges turn pink, about 1 minute.

3. Remove pan from heat; using tongs, flip each shrimp and let stand until all but very center is opaque, about 30 seconds. Transfer shrimp to large plate.

4. Repeat with second tablespoon oil and remaining shrimp; after second batch has stood off heat, return first batch to skillet and toss to combine. Cover skillet and let stand until shrimp are cooked through, 1 to 2 minutes. Serve immediately.

Grilling

A modified two-level fire gives us a hot zone for cooking the shrimp and a cool side where we keep sauce at the ready. For the sauce, try our Spicy Lemon-Garlic Sauce for shrimp skewers (available free at www.CooksIllustrated.com/apr12).

PACK TIGHTLY
Threading shrimp front to back helps them cook more slowly, ensuring that they don't dry out.

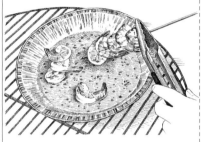

FINISH IN SAUCE
Sliding the almost-cooked shrimp into a flavorful sauce cooks them at a gentler pace.

1. Thread 1½ pounds extra-large (21/25) shrimp head to tail onto 3 metal skewers. Brush both sides with oil and season with salt and pepper; sprinkle 1 side with pinch sugar.

2. Arrange 6 quarts burning coals over one-half of grill; leave other half empty. Cover grill and heat until hot. Heat sauce in disposable aluminum pan on hot side of grill; transfer to cooler side. Place skewers sugared sides down on hot side of grill; grill uncovered until lightly charred, 4 to 5 minutes. Flip and grill until second side is pink, 1 to 2 minutes longer.

3. Using tongs, slide shrimp off skewers into sauce and toss. Transfer to hot side of grill and cook, stirring, until shrimp are opaque, 30 seconds. Serve immediately.

Poaching

We eschew the typical method for poaching shrimp destined for shrimp cocktail or salad—plunging them into hot water—for a far gentler approach.

1. Combine 1 pound extra-large (21/25) shrimp, ¼ cup lemon juice, spent lemon halves, 5 parsley sprigs, 3 tarragon sprigs, 1 teaspoon whole peppercorns, 1 tablespoon sugar, and 1 teaspoon salt with 2 cups cold water in medium saucepan.

2. Place saucepan over medium heat and cook shrimp, stirring frequently, until pink and centers are no longer translucent, 8 to 10 minutes (water should register 165 degrees and should just bubble around pan edges).

3. Remove pan from heat, cover, and let shrimp sit in broth for 2 minutes. Meanwhile, fill medium bowl with ice water.

4. Drain shrimp and discard lemon halves, herbs, and spices. Transfer shrimp to ice water to stop cooking, about 3 minutes. Remove shrimp and pat dry with paper towels.

START COLD
Starting in cold water means the inside and outside of the shrimp cook more evenly.

FINISH OFF HEAT
Allowing shrimp to finish cooking off heat guarantees juicy results.

Stir-Frying

Most stir-fries sear the vegetables and protein together, which is guaranteed to turn shrimp chewy. We have a better way. For the sauce, see our Stir-Fried Shrimp with Snow Peas and Red Bell Pepper in Hot and Sour Sauce (available free at www.CooksIllustrated.com/apr12).

1. Marinate 1 pound extra-large (21/25) shrimp, 1 minced garlic clove, 1 tablespoon minced ginger, and ½ teaspoon salt in 1 tablespoon vegetable oil for 30 minutes.

2. Stir-fry ¾ pound chopped vegetables in 1 tablespoon oil over high heat until browned. Transfer to bowl; add 1 tablespoon oil to pan and stir-fry 1 sliced garlic clove and 1 sliced shallot.

3. Add shrimp, reduce heat to medium-low, and stir-fry until light pink, 1 to 1½ minutes. Add sauce; return to high heat and cook, stirring constantly, until shrimp are cooked through, 1 to 2 minutes. Return vegetables to skillet, toss to combine, and serve immediately.

MARINATE FIRST
Stir-fry sauces never really penetrate shrimp. For super-flavorful results, marinate them first.

REDUCE HEAT
To prevent shrimp from overcooking, first stir-fry veggies over high heat and then add shrimp and lower flame.

Italian Wedding Soup

A super-flavorful soup enriched with meatballs and tender greens? Sounds like a match made in heaven—but we didn't want to spend all day creating it.

> BY MATTHEW CARD

I've never been to a wedding banquet in Milan, Venice, or Palermo, but I'd hazard a guess that Italian wedding soup would not have been on the menu. Its Italian name, *minestra maritata* ("married soup"), refers not to actual nuptials but to the marriage of hearty greens to a savory mixture of meats against the backdrop of a rich broth. The Italian-American rendition takes this pairing even further by transforming the meats into tender miniature meatballs and adding bits of wheaty pasta.

But over the years, Italian wedding soup has lost touch with its roots, sliding into the dodgy territory of convenience food. Most recipes seem to call for nothing more than simmering a few cans of broth, adding some ersatz "meatballs" in the form of dollops of Italian sausage, dumping in a bag of greens, and dusting it all with grated Parmesan before slapping the soup on the table. I didn't want a project that took an entire afternoon at the stove, but surely there was a middle ground that would bring back the deeper, more complex flavors of the old-fashioned version.

Building the Broth

Traditionally, Italian wedding soup is built from a base of meaty *brodo*, brewed from cured meats and the bits, bobs, and bones of animals both hoofed and winged, for a broth that doesn't taste strongly of any one particular kind of meat. Beyond gathering the requisite odd parts and specialty meats, cooks must spend hours simmering traditional brodo to fully develop its flavor—not to mention the constant skimming to remove foam and the tedious work of separating out the fat. Overall, this is more time and attention than most of us want to devote to a soup. But I hoped that with the right collection of meats, aromatics, and flavorings I could render store-bought broth into something resembling a classic brodo in the 30-odd minutes it would take to prepare meatballs.

Witness the Marriage

Video available FREE for 4 months at www.CooksIllustrated.com/apr12

We cook the signature ingredient—tender miniature meatballs—in the broth, which skips the messy step of browning them first.

Since I wanted a base with a well-rounded meaty taste, it made sense to use both chicken and beef broths. After a bit of experimentation, I found that a 2:1 ratio of chicken broth to beef broth, cut with a little water, tasted the most balanced. Some basic aromatics, like sautéed onion and a few smashed cloves of garlic, nudged the broth in the right direction, especially with a sharpening splash of dry white wine. To further enrich the broth, I tried adding carrots and celery but found the sweetness of the former too cloying while the metallic taste of the latter came on too strong. A fennel bulb turned out to be a better choice, lending a pleasant anise note and mild warmth.

With convenience in mind, I eschewed the gnarly cuts used in traditional brodo in favor of easy-to-find, bone-in pieces. I tried out chicken wings, country-style pork ribs, and beef short ribs. They all contributed terrific flavor but made the broth too fatty, and my half-hour time frame was not enough to extract maximum flavor from the bones. Then it occurred to me: Since I would be using ground meat to make the meatballs, why not enlist some of it to lend flavor to the broth as well? After the meat had contributed its richness to the broth, I could strain out the nubbly bits—an easy enough step. I took a few ounces

of the ground beef and pork that I'd bought to make the meatballs and lightly browned them along with the aromatics before adding the broth. The ground meats cooked quickly and the broth's meatiness was clearly amplified—another step in the right direction. But my soup base still tasted too thin, lacking the full-throated savor of a long-simmered stock.

Several traditional recipes that I'd consulted called for the leftover bone and scraps from a leg of prosciutto. Ever looked for a prosciutto bone? It's easier to find hens' teeth. Chopped and blended in with the ground meats, a few thin slices of the salt-cured pork, which is packed with the glutamates that contribute savory richness to food, did help matters. But I couldn't tolerate discarding $10 worth of top-shelf charcuterie when I strained the broth. I tried out a few other Italianate flavor enhancers, both traditional and non. A Parmesan rind proved that it's easy to be too cheesy, sun-dried tomatoes tasted too sour and dyed the stock a ruddy color, and anchovies took the broth into overly salty territory.

Continuing my search for flavor-boosting ingredients, I borrowed an idea from our recipe for Farmhouse Vegetable and Barley Soup (November/December 2011): the combo of dried porcini mushrooms and soy sauce. I loved the deep earthiness that the mushrooms provided, but soy sauce in the amount necessary to detect any real difference made the broth too salty. I experimented with—and quickly ruled out—other *umami* boosters, including fish sauce and miso. They all added flavor but also muddied the primal meatiness that my brodo required. Then I remembered a condiment that tends to get pushed to the back of my pantry:

WHIP IT GOOD

Beating the ground pork distributes fat and moisture evenly for meatballs with a springy bite.

Worcestershire sauce. This dark, old-fashioned liquid was bringing a jolt of savory flavor to meats and Bloody Marys long before umami became a household word. I added a dash of the stuff and noted that the broth's flavor was now somewhat deeper. A full tablespoon galvanized that flavor, highlighting the beef and pork alike. With just 30 minutes and a well-edited handful of ingredients, I now had a full afternoon's worth of flavor in my pot.

Meatball Matters

Italian meatballs are often rolled from a blend of ground beef, pork, and veal and bound with a panade, a mixture of bread and dairy (and sometimes eggs) that moisturizes the meats and prevents their proteins from binding too tightly and growing tough. Why the blend of meats? Each brings something to the party: Beef packs big flavor; pork adds sweetness and richness; and veal's high concentration of gelatin gives the meatballs body while keeping them tender and light. Ground veal, though, can be hard to find. What happens if you simply skip it? My veal-less meatballs were a bit chewy and bland.

I wondered if I needed a substitute for veal, or if a cooking method could compensate for its missing attributes. Drawing on test kitchen experience, I ended up turning to both approaches. When we tackled Swedish meatballs (another meatball typically made from a beef-pork-veal blend), we found success using ground beef and pork alone by adding a secret ingredient: baking powder. Just 1 teaspoon ensured that the meatballs remained light once cooked. We'd also borrowed a technique from sausage making, whipping the ground pork in a stand mixer until it formed a smooth emulsion before adding the panade, seasonings, and ground beef. This step evenly distributes the pork's fat and moisture and traps them both within the meat's protein structure so that the meatballs remain juicy and pleasingly supple. (Pork has a lower proportion of muscle fibers than beef and can be whipped without risk of toughening.) Both of these tricks brought the same great results to my mini meatballs.

Some Italian wedding soup recipes instruct you to pan-fry the meatballs before adding them to the brodo, but my tasters disliked the crisp exterior of browned meatballs in soup, plus the extra step was a hassle. But when I cooked the meatballs directly in the broth, the egg in the panade made the meatballs turn out rubbery (the proteins in eggs and meat bind to form an elastic structure, which grows more resilient when cooked in liquid). Out went the egg—with no ill effect. I also learned that batches with a high ratio of panade to meat produced lighter, almost dumpling-like meatballs that paired really well with the tender greens and pasta.

With the texture of the meatballs perfected, I just needed to fine-tune their flavor. Finely grated onion was a must, and a little Parmesan, blended into the panade, brought a subtle nuttiness. Dried herbs added little, but fresh oregano tied everything together and tempered the meatballs' richness.

Going Green

All manner of greens find their way into this soup. I started my testing with spinach, a popular choice, but was disappointed by the way it quickly turned limp and slimy. Sturdier chard, cabbage, escarole, and kale were more successful, with kale's meaty texture and assertive flavor trumping the rest. Thinly sliced into a chiffonade, kale strands wove themselves into an unwieldy clump; chopped bits worked better. The small pieces kept to themselves, fit tidily on a spoon, and softened in the time it took the pasta to cook.

And what about that pasta? Tiny bite-size shapes, like ditalini, worked best. To avoid mushy pasta, I added it at the last minute, testing it frequently. In just less than an hour in the kitchen, I had an elegant, satisfying soup tasting of far more work than I had invested—a successful compromise between tradition and convenience.

ITALIAN WEDDING SOUP
SERVES 6 TO 8

Use a rasp-style grater to process the onion and garlic for the meatballs. Tubettini or orzo can be used in place of the ditalini.

Broth

- 1 onion, chopped
- 1 fennel bulb, stalks discarded, bulb halved, cored, and chopped
- 4 garlic cloves, peeled and smashed
- ¼ ounce dried porcini mushrooms, rinsed
- 4 ounces ground pork
- 4 ounces 85 percent lean ground beef
- 1 bay leaf
- ½ cup dry white wine
- 1 tablespoon Worcestershire sauce
- 4 cups low-sodium chicken broth
- 2 cups beef broth
- 2 cups water

Meatballs

- 1 slice hearty white sandwich bread, crusts removed, torn into 1-inch pieces
- 5 tablespoons heavy cream
- ¼ cup grated Parmesan cheese
- 4 teaspoons finely grated onion
- ½ teaspoon finely grated garlic
  Salt and pepper
- 6 ounces ground pork
- 1 teaspoon baking powder
- 6 ounces 85 percent lean ground beef
- 2 teaspoons minced fresh oregano

- 1 cup ditalini pasta
- 12 ounces kale, stemmed and cut into ½-inch pieces (6 cups)

1. FOR THE BROTH: Heat onion, fennel, garlic, porcini, pork, beef, and bay leaf in Dutch oven over medium-high heat; cook, stirring frequently,

Flavorful Soup Stock on the Fly

Skipping the fuss of a typical brodo doesn't have to mean sacrificing flavor. By doctoring commercial chicken broth, we got comparably rich-tasting results in under an hour.

ATYPICAL AROMATIC	TWO MEATS

We rejected the standard carrots and celery for the anise notes of fennel. Onion and garlic, though, were musts.	No need to seek out meat scraps and bones for depth. A broth simmered with ground pork and beef is plenty savory.
TWO BROTHS	UMAMI BOOSTERS

In addition to chicken broth, we use beef broth to mimic the flavor of traditional brodo.	*Umami*-packed porcini mushrooms and Worcestershire sauce amp up the broth's meaty flavor.

until meats are no longer pink, about 5 minutes. Add wine and Worcestershire; cook for 1 minute. Add chicken broth, beef broth, and water; bring to simmer. Reduce heat to low, cover, and simmer for 30 minutes.

2. FOR THE MEATBALLS: While broth simmers, combine bread, cream, Parmesan, onion, garlic, and pepper to taste in bowl; using fork, mash mixture to uniform paste. Using stand mixer fitted with paddle, beat pork, baking powder, and ½ teaspoon salt on high speed until smooth and pale, 1 to 2 minutes, scraping down bowl as needed. Add bread mixture, beef, and oregano; mix on medium-low speed until just incorporated, 1 to 2 minutes, scraping down bowl as needed. Using moistened hands, form heaping teaspoons of meat mixture into smooth, round meatballs; you should have 30 to 35 meatballs. Cover and refrigerate for up to 1 day.

3. Strain broth through fine-mesh strainer set over large bowl or container, pressing on solids to extract as much liquid as possible. Wipe out Dutch oven and return broth to pot. (Broth can be refrigerated for up to 3 days. Skim off fat before reheating.)

4. Return broth to simmer over medium-high heat. Add pasta and kale; cook, stirring occasionally, for 5 minutes. Add meatballs; return to simmer and cook, stirring occasionally, until meatballs are cooked through and pasta is tender, 3 to 5 minutes. Season with salt and pepper to taste, and serve.

Hearty French Potato Casserole

In the old days, this rich dish got its deep flavor and silky texture from meat drippings. Could we get the same luxurious results without a roast?

> BY BRYAN ROOF ≤

In the French dish known as *pommes de terre boulangère*, or "baker's potatoes," incredibly tender potatoes nestle in a rich, meaty sauce beneath a delicately browned crust. The name dates to a time when villagers used the residual heat of the baker's oven to cook dinner at the end of the day. Chicken, pork, or beef would roast on an upper oven shelf while this casserole of thinly sliced potatoes and onions bubbled away underneath, seasoned by the savory fat and juices dripping from above.

Today French chefs no longer cook pommes de terre boulangère beneath a blistering roast, but they impart the same unctuous flavor, deep-brown color, and supreme tenderness using hearty meat stock and a well-calibrated oven. While I could spend hours making stock from scratch, that was too much time and effort for a side dish. I wanted a potato casserole with deep flavor and a super-tender texture—after a reasonable amount of work.

Since I was seeking a creamy consistency, only one potato variety would do: the moderately starchy, buttery-tasting Yukon Gold. A mandoline was an ideal tool for slicing the peeled spuds since I wanted them to be wafer-thin (about ⅛ inch)—any thicker and the casserole would be too chunky, losing its refined nature. I added a thinly sliced onion to the Yukons, packed the mixture into a greased baking dish, poured in 3 cups of store-bought beef broth, and slid the casserole into a 350-degree oven. It was no surprise when this test batch revealed two big flaws. First, the sauce was bland and tasted . . . well, canned. And second, its consistency was soupy, lacking the requisite creaminess.

I tackled the flavor issue first. To temper the beef broth's undesirable qualities, I diluted it with an equal amount of commercial chicken broth. This mellowed the flavor of both, for a blend that didn't taste processed. But that doesn't mean it tasted meaty. Since potatoes boulangère was sometimes roasted beneath poultry, I experimented with scattering chicken wings atop the potatoes before baking, hoping that the wings would infuse the slices with rich flavor. But this was only effective if I first browned the chicken on both sides—an extra step that I wasn't willing to incorporate.

Next, I turned to flavor-packed pork options like ham hocks, pancetta, and bacon. I simmered a hock briefly in the broth, expecting it to impart smokiness, but the effect was negligible. (I could have cooked it longer but I wanted a quick fix.) For the pancetta and bacon, I simply rendered them until crisp and then tossed the pieces with the potatoes and onion. Both were much more effective at boosting meatiness than the ham hock was, but in the end, tasters preferred the smoky bacon.

Next up: the onion. I found inspiration from another French classic: onion soup, in which onions are deeply caramelized to concentrate their flavor. Cooking the sliced onion to a deep molasses-y brown made it too sweet for this dish, but sautéing it in some of the leftover bacon fat until golden brown was enough to bring out remarkable complexity.

A scattering of fresh thyme, sprinkles of salt and pepper, plus a few pats of butter—the flavor of my potatoes was in really good shape. But I still needed to improve the too-thin sauce and somehow make the overall texture silkier and more luscious.

My first attempt to remedy the consistency of the sauce was twofold: I decreased the amount of broth to 2½ cups and increased the oven temperature to 425 degrees so that more liquid would evaporate during baking. When I started to see improvement, I took things one step further by bringing the broth to a simmer in the pot used to cook the onion, giving it a jump start on reducing in the oven. As a bonus, this deglazing step captured all of the flavorful fond left behind by the bacon and caramelized onion.

The broth had now cooked down, but it was still neither thick nor creamy. Then it dawned on me. I had been submerging my sliced potatoes in water to keep them from discoloring while I prepped the remaining ingredients—a common practice, but one that also washes away most of the spuds' starch. Without enough starch, my sauce couldn't thicken up. I tried again with unsoaked potatoes and witnessed a striking difference. The sauce now glazed the potatoes and onion in a velvety cloak. As a final measure, I made sure to allow the casserole to rest for a good 20 minutes before serving it. This went a long way toward developing a silky, creamy texture, since the starch granules in the potatoes continued to absorb moisture and swell as they cooled.

With a few modifications, I had been able to achieve a satisfying version of pommes de terre boulangère within a reasonable time frame, making this once-obscure dish now popular fare in my house.

POTATO CASSEROLE WITH BACON AND CARAMELIZED ONION
SERVES 6 TO 8 AS A SIDE DISH

Do not rinse or soak the potatoes, as this will wash away their starch, which is essential to the dish. A mandoline makes slicing the potatoes much easier. For the proper texture, make sure to let the casserole stand 20 minutes before serving.

3	slices thick-cut bacon, cut into ½-inch pieces
1	large onion, halved and sliced thin
1¼	teaspoons salt
2	teaspoons chopped fresh thyme
½	teaspoon pepper
1¼	cups low-sodium chicken broth
1¼	cups beef broth
3	pounds Yukon Gold potatoes, peeled
2	tablespoons unsalted butter, cut into 4 pieces

1. Adjust oven rack to lower-middle position and heat oven to 425 degrees. Grease 13 by 9-inch baking dish.

2. Cook bacon in medium saucepan over medium-low heat until crisp, 10 to 13 minutes. Using slotted spoon, transfer bacon to paper towel–lined plate. Remove and discard all but 1 tablespoon fat from pot. Return pot to medium heat and add onion and ¼ teaspoon salt; cook, stirring frequently, until onion is soft and golden brown, about 25 minutes, adjusting heat and adding water 1 tablespoon at a time if onion or bottom of pot becomes too dark. Transfer onion to large bowl; add bacon, thyme, remaining 1 teaspoon salt, and pepper. Add broths to now-empty saucepan and bring to simmer over medium-high heat, scraping bottom of pan to loosen any browned bits.

3. Slice potatoes ⅛ inch thick. Transfer to bowl with onion mixture and toss to combine. Transfer to prepared baking dish. Firmly press down on mixture to compress into even layer. Carefully pour hot broth over top of potatoes. Dot surface evenly with butter.

4. Bake, uncovered, until potatoes are tender and golden brown on edges and most of liquid has been absorbed, 45 to 55 minutes. Transfer to wire rack and let stand for 20 minutes to fully absorb broth before cutting and serving.

The Best Cinnamon Swirl Bread

To rid this bread of its dense crumb, leaking filling, and huge gaps, we had to engineer a lofty dough and a sticky filling—and then find the right shaping method.

> BY DAN SOUZA

Cinnamon swirl bread always sounds terrifically appealing in theory, but until recently, I've ended up being disappointed every time I've tried it. My ideal is a fluffy, delicate crumb that's studded with plump raisins and laced with a substantial swirl of gooey cinnamon sugar. But most versions I've sampled are either austere white sandwich loaves rolled up with a bare sprinkle of cinnamon and sugar or overly sweet breads ruined by gobs of filling oozing from the cracks.

When I finally stumbled upon cinnamon bread nirvana, it was in the unlikeliest of places: Tokyo's Narita Airport. A bit groggy from a long flight, I took a mindless bite of a lightly toasted slice of swirl bread that I'd bought at a bakery kiosk and realized I'd found it. Beneath the lightly crisp exterior, the crumb was so springy, moist, and feathery it could be pulled into cotton candy–like strands. This style of wispy, milky-sweet Japanese white sandwich bread, called *shokupan*, proved the perfect foil for a sweet, viscous spiral, which, in this case, was red-bean paste. I vowed to figure out a cinnamon swirl version with raisins once I was back home.

Turning Japanese

I decided to focus first on the bread and worry about incorporating the swirl and the raisins down the line. But when recipes for shokupan written in English proved hard to come by, I sought out an expert: Takeo Sakan, head baker at Boston's acclaimed Japonaise Bakery & Café. To help me better understand how shokupan is made, we compared it with American sandwich bread. The two styles share a number of the same ingredients: flour, yeast, salt, water, milk, sugar, and butter. Shokupan, however, boasts considerably more fat (roughly twice as much butter, plus an egg) and more sugar, which accounts for its particularly tender crumb. Another major difference: Shokupan contains more gluten—the network of proteins that builds structure and allows bread to rise high and retain its springy crumb. To achieve that result, Sakan relies on a combination of thorough kneading and specialty high-gluten flour, which contains even more of the structure-building proteins than the bread flour used in most American

Our makeover of this classic loaf bakes up tall, springy, moist, and swirled with plenty of gooey cinnamon sugar.

sandwich breads. It's that marriage of particularly strong gluten and tenderizers like fat and sugar that produces shokupan's airy-yet-sturdy crumb.

I took careful notes throughout my morning with Sakan and returned to the test kitchen emboldened to mix up my own version. There was one change to Sakan's recipe I'd make immediately, however: Since the high-gluten flour he used requires mail-ordering, I'd have to stick with bread flour and worry about making up for the lack of gluten later. Otherwise, I followed his lead: I mixed the flour with yeast, sugar, and nonfat dry milk powder; added water (1½ cups) plus an egg and 8 tablespoons of softened butter for richness; and kneaded the mixture in a stand mixer for a few minutes until it formed a cohesive mass. After letting the dough rest for about 20 minutes, I added the salt and then let the mixer knead the dough for a longer stretch—about 10 minutes, by which time the dough was smoother and more workable. I mixed in a generous handful of

golden raisins (which are more plump and moist than dark raisins) and left the dough to proof in a turned-off oven. Because warm, humid air stimulates yeast activity and speeds rise time, I'd placed a loaf pan of boiling water on the oven floor, simulating the proof boxes used by professional bakers. Forty-five minutes later, I patted the dough into a rectangle, sprinkled a placeholder cinnamon sugar filling over the surface, rolled it into a spiral, fitted it into a loaf pan, and let it proof for another 45 minutes, when the dough had doubled in size. I brushed the dough with an egg wash for shine and baked it until the crust was dark brown.

But while the color of the bread was handsome, the crumb itself was far from ideal. Among other problems, I couldn't replicate the bread's hallmark lift and airy texture. In fact, I could tell something had gone wrong as soon as I'd mixed up the dough. Unlike the springy, elastic mass that Sakan had made, mine was slack and easily extensible. The reason, no doubt, had a lot to do with the lower-protein bread flour.

On the Rise

I had one solution in mind to strengthen the dough: Work in more air. While you might think of oxygen as merely providing lift to baked goods, it's also the driving force behind gluten development, enabling the proteins in flour to

A Better Base for Cinnamon Swirl Bread

The usual base for cinnamon swirl bread is American sandwich bread, but we looked to a different source: shokupan, Japan's version of the same loaf. Shokupan relies on of lots of fat, high-protein flour, and thorough kneading to create a crumb that's feathery light yet still strong enough to support a gooey cinnamon filling.

JAPANESE SHOKUPAN

Anatomy of a Failed Loaf

Cinnamon swirl bread's inherent predicament: The dough and the filling don't mix. But the problems don't stop there.

• **BREAD GAPS**
Because the dough and filling don't readily bind, air and steam get trapped in the spiral, compressing the bread and creating significant gaps.

• **FILLING RUNS**
The typical filling made with granulated sugar has no sticking power and puddles at the bottom of the bread.

• **LOAF SPRINGS A LEAK**
Thanks to the gaps and the weight of the filling, the seam of the loaf is compromised, so the filling spills out.

cross-link and form a tightly bonded network. The more oxygen the dough gets, the tighter the bonds will be, and the stronger the gluten network. In fact, professional bakers often add natural or chemical oxidizers to doughs for this very reason. But since I didn't have access to these products, I decided to try more organic alternatives. My first test: introducing two sets of "folds" into the process. By deflating the dough and folding it back onto itself several times, I incorporated more air into it, thereby encouraging the bread to expand and rise more. I also increased the kneading time to about 15 minutes, rendering it even more elastic and better able to trap gas for a taller rise. This bread baked up noticeably higher, but still not as tall as the shokupan loaves I'd tasted.

Leaving the technique alone for the moment, I scanned my ingredient list for other ways to boost the bread's height. When I got to the butter, I paused. I knew that incorporating it into the dough at the outset was coating the flour proteins with fat, preventing them from bonding and inhibiting gluten formation. A better method, I reasoned, would be to knead the dough almost completely to develop gluten and then work in some softened butter during the final minutes of kneading. The idea worked, save for the soft butter pieces smearing into the dough and not incorporating evenly. My quick fix: tossing the pieces with a tablespoon of flour before letting them soften, which helped the dough grip the butter and pull it into the dough. The resulting loaf was gorgeously lofty—by far the best bread yet. It would serve as the perfect counterpoint for my next challenge: a gooey cinnamon sugar swirl.

Mind the Gap

In all honesty, I thought perfecting a thick cinnamon swirl would be the easy part of making this bread—until my first attempt at incorporating it. The bread rose beautifully tall during the first half of baking and then sprung a leak and spewed molten cinnamon sugar from its crevices. After letting this disaster of a loaf cool for a bit, I sliced it open, discovering a mangled mix of dense bread, huge gaps, and puddles of cinnamon filling. I would soon come to learn that all three flaws were the perennial problems with swirled breads.

Our science editor explained: All of these issues boil down to the fact that the sugary filling and bread don't readily bind. During proofing, the gas produced by the yeast leaks from the dough into the spiral, and because it has no place to go, the gas pushes apart the layers of dough. This separation becomes more distinct during baking, when steam also fills the gaps. At the same time, all that pressure compresses the dough, further widening the trails for the cinnamon sugar filling to flow to the bottom of the bread and eventually burst through its seam.

What I needed, then, was a way to encourage binding between the swirl and the dough. I added a slew of different ingredients to the filling to see if any would help it adhere: flour, eggs, pectin, corn syrup, pureed raisins, cooked caramel, crushed cinnamon cereal, and ground-up nuts. Most of the loaves still baked up with comically large gaps. In desperation, I even went so far as to make a second dough spiked with cinnamon and roll that up with the regular dough. That took care of the gapping problem but also did away with the gooey filling.

That's when I realized that adding extra ingredients to the swirl might not be as effective as examining the ingredients I already had in it. Up to this point, the filling consisted of ½ cup of granulated sugar and 1 tablespoon of ground cinnamon per loaf. I baked more loaves, this time trading the granulated stuff for confectioners' sugar as well as tripling the cinnamon. The loaves showed significant improvement, and the answer turned out to be simple. First, when powdery confectioners' sugar absorbs water from the dough, it immediately dissolves, forming a sticky paste. This paste is thickened by the cornstarch in the confectioners' sugar along with the abundance of carbohydrates in the amped-up amount of cinnamon. The thickened paste doesn't pool at the bottom of the bread as readily and is sticky enough to help hold the layers together as the bread expands during proofing.

This was by far the best loaf I had made to date, but unfortunately, I couldn't always replicate it; I still got the occasional spewing leak or gaping hole. Lightly spraying the dough with water before and after dusting on the filling helped the paste form even more quickly, but it wasn't enough.

From Russia with Loaves

Having already fiddled with the filling ingredients, I got to thinking about the swirl itself. A spiral was attractive (and certainly traditional) but impractical, and it made me wonder if there wasn't anything I could do during shaping to help the situation. Since gas trapped between the layers of dough was the trigger for the gapping, perhaps what I needed was to provide a way for it to escape. I tested a multitude of different shaping techniques that created crevices in the dough that would allow gas to escape, including monkey bread and braids. The easiest of these shaping methods, which cut down on gapping and leaking considerably, was an attractive weave called a Russian braid. To make it, I first sprinkled filling over the dough, rolled it into a cylinder just as before, and then halved it lengthwise to reveal the striations of dough and filling. I then stretched these two halves slightly and twisted them together (keeping the cut surfaces facing up to expose the nice-looking striations) to form a tight loaf. This way, any gas that would have been trapped between the layers was able to escape, and the bread baked up tightly seamed and beautifully marbled. One last

Making a Sticky Filling That Sticks

The cinnamon sugar swirl isn't just for flavor; it needs to function as an adhesive between the pieces of dough. Here's how we altered the typical formula.

POWDERED SUGAR
Confectioners' sugar contains cornstarch that thickens up the filling and makes it less runny.

LOTS OF CINNAMON
Cinnamon contains starches that thicken the filling and help it form a sticky paste.

SPRITZ OF WATER
Lightly misting the dough before and after adding the filling creates extra adhesiveness.

TECHNIQUE | WEAVING A TIGHT CINNAMON SWIRL BREAD, RUSSIAN–STYLE

The benefit of a Russian braid—other than good looks—is that it solves the gapping that plagues swirl breads. The twisted shape tightly seals the pieces of dough together while providing plenty of escape routes for the excess air that would otherwise compress the dough and create tunnels in the loaf.

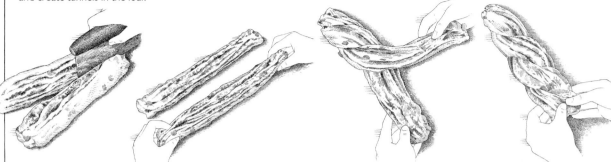

CUT LENGTHWISE
Using bench scraper or sharp chef's knife, cut filled dough in half lengthwise. Turn halves so cut sides are facing up.

STRETCH
With cut sides up, stretch each half into 14-inch length.

FOLD LEFT OVER RIGHT
Pinch 2 ends of strips together. To braid, take left strip of dough and lay it over right strip of dough.

REPEAT AND PINCH
Repeat braiding, keeping cut sides face up, until pieces are tightly twisted. Pinch ends together.

---

tweak: To prevent any risk of burning the raisins or the bread's sugary surface, I pushed the exposed pieces of fruit into the braid and tented the loaves with aluminum foil halfway through baking.

Thanks to research, trial and error, and my happenstance breakfast at Narita Airport, I'd come up with the bread I'd always envisioned: a burnished crust encasing springy, airy, slightly sweet bread streaked with thick lines of gooey cinnamon filling.

CINNAMON SWIRL BREAD
MAKES 2 LOAVES

To achieve the proper dough consistency, make sure to weigh your ingredients. The dough will appear very wet and sticky until the final few minutes of kneading; do not be tempted to add supplemental flour.

Dough

8	tablespoons unsalted butter
3¾	cups (20⅔ ounces) bread flour, plus extra for work surface
¾	cup (2¾ ounces) nonfat dry milk powder
⅓	cup (2⅓ ounces) granulated sugar
1	tablespoon instant or rapid-rise yeast
1½	cups (12 ounces) warm water (110 degrees)
1	large egg, lightly beaten
1½	teaspoons salt
1½	cups (7½ ounces) golden raisins

Filling

1	cup (4 ounces) confectioners' sugar
3	tablespoons cinnamon
1	teaspoon vanilla extract
½	teaspoon salt
1	large egg, lightly beaten with pinch of salt

1. FOR THE DOUGH: Cut butter into 32 pieces and toss with 1 tablespoon flour; set aside to soften while mixing dough. Whisk remaining flour, milk powder, sugar, and yeast together in bowl of stand mixer. Using stand mixer fitted with dough hook, add water and egg and mix on medium-low speed until cohesive mass forms, about 2 minutes, scraping down bowl if necessary. Cover mixing bowl with plastic wrap and let stand for 20 minutes.

2. Adjust oven rack to middle position and place loaf or cake pan on bottom of oven. Remove plastic from mixer bowl, add salt, and mix on medium-low speed until dough is smooth and elastic and clears sides of bowl, 7 to 15 minutes. With mixer running, add butter, few pieces at a time, and continue to knead until butter is fully incorporated and dough is smooth and elastic and clears sides of bowl, 3 to 5 minutes longer. Add raisins and mix until incorporated, 30 to 60 seconds. Transfer dough to large greased bowl and, using bowl scraper or rubber spatula, fold dough over itself by gently lifting and folding edge of dough toward middle. Turn bowl 90 degrees; fold again. Turn bowl and fold dough 6 more times (total of 8 folds). Cover tightly with plastic and transfer to middle rack of oven. Pour 3 cups boiling water into loaf pan in oven, close oven door, and allow dough to rise for 45 minutes.

3. Remove bowl from oven and gently press down on center of dough to deflate. Repeat folding step (making total of 8 folds), re-cover, and return to oven until doubled in volume, about 45 minutes.

4. FOR THE FILLING: Whisk filling ingredients together until well combined; set aside.

5. Grease two 8½ by 4½-inch loaf pans. Transfer dough to lightly floured counter and divide into 2 pieces. Working with 1 piece of dough, pat into rough 6 by 11-inch rectangle. With short side fac-

ing you, fold long sides in like business letter to form 3 by 11-inch rectangle. Roll dough away from you into ball. Dust ball with flour and flatten with rolling pin into 7 by 18-inch rectangle with even ¼-inch thickness. Using spray bottle, spray dough lightly with water. Sprinkle half of filling mixture evenly over dough, leaving ¼-inch border on sides and ¾-inch border on top and bottom; spray filling lightly with water. (Filling should be speckled with water over entire surface.) With short side facing you, roll dough away from you into firm cylinder. Turn loaf seam side up and pinch closed; pinch ends closed. Dust loaf lightly on all sides with flour and let rest for 10 minutes. Repeat with second ball of dough and remaining filling.

6. Working with 1 loaf at a time, use bench scraper to cut loaf in half lengthwise; turn halves so cut sides are facing up. Gently stretch each half into 14-inch length. Line up pieces of dough and pinch 2 ends of strips together. Take piece on left and lay over piece on right. Repeat, keeping cut side up, until pieces of dough are tightly twisted. Pinch ends together. Transfer loaf, cut side up, to prepared loaf pan; push any exposed raisins into seams of braid. Repeat with second loaf. Cover loaves loosely with plastic, return to oven, and allow to rise for 45 minutes. Remove loaves and water pan from oven; heat oven to 350 degrees. Allow loaves to rise at room temperature until almost doubled in size, about 45 minutes longer (top of loaves should rise about 1 inch over lip of pan).

7. Brush loaves with egg mixture. Bake until crust is well browned, about 25 minutes. Reduce oven temperature to 325 degrees, tent loaves with aluminum foil, and continue to bake until internal temperature registers 200 degrees, 15 to 25 minutes longer.

8. Transfer pans to wire rack and let cool for 5 minutes. Remove loaves from pans, return to rack, and cool to room temperature before slicing, about 2 hours.

TO MAKE AHEAD: Baked and cooled loaves can be wrapped in double layer of plastic and stored at room temperature for 2 days. To freeze bread for up to 1 month, wrap it with additional layer of foil.

Watch It Take Shape
Video available FREE for 4 months at www.CooksIllustrated.com/apr12

Peanut Butter Sandwich Cookies

We wanted a cookie so packed with peanut flavor that it needed no crosshatch to identify it.

⇒ BY ANDREA GEARY ⇐

Being a peanut butter cookie is a lot like being a lady: If you have to announce that you are, you aren't. I admit to taking liberties with Margaret Thatcher's famous line (she drew a parallel between being powerful and being a lady), but to a peanut butter obsessive like me, that distinguishing crosshatch on top of a traditional peanut butter cookie feels like a cheat. A cookie shouldn't have to rely on a homey hieroglyph to proclaim its identity. Great flavor speaks for itself.

Their looks aside, I've always had another issue with peanut butter cookies: The raw dough tastes better than the baked treats. This is because in the presence of heat, the starch granules in flour soak up peanut flavor molecules like a sponge, reducing their aroma and limiting their ability to interact with our tastebuds. The upshot is that a traditional peanut butter cookie becomes flavor challenged as soon as it hits the oven. As I mulled over the facts, it occurred to me that a sandwich cookie—that is, two peanut butter cookies enclosing a filling made primarily with uncooked (read: full-flavored) peanut butter—might be the ideal delivery system for the strong flavor that I craved.

The cookies themselves would have to be quite thin and flat (so you could comfortably eat two of them sandwiched with filling) as well as crunchy, to contrast with the creamy center. As for that smooth filling, it had to be substantial enough that it wouldn't squish out the sides of the cookies with each bite. I also wanted my cookies to have the simplicity of a drop cookie: no chilling of the dough, no slicing, no rolling, and no cutting.

Starting in the Middle

Because a good sandwich cookie is all about balanced flavors and textures, I knew that the filling would influence my cookie and vice versa. I chose to start with the simpler filling. Most recipes call for blending

A carefully calibrated dough guarantees thin, flat, crispy cookies.

peanut butter and confectioners' sugar (granulated sugar remains too gritty and doesn't provide much thickening power) with a creamy element, such as butter, cream cheese, heavy cream, or even marshmallow crème. I settled on butter, which provided the silkiest consistency and allowed for the purest peanut butter flavor. I softened 3 tablespoons of butter with ¾ cup of creamy peanut butter in the microwave and then, to keep the peanut flavor in the forefront, stirred in a modest ½ cup of confectioners' sugar.

This low-sugar filling tasted great, but it was far too soft, squirting out from my placeholder cookies as soon as I pressed them together. To thicken things up, I ultimately found that I had to double the sugar amount, for a filling that was very sweet. For a perfectly balanced whole, I would have to counter with a significantly less sweet cookie frame.

Crunch Time

Setting the filling aside, I put together a dough with 3 tablespoons of butter, ½ cup of peanut butter, two eggs, 1 cup of sugar, 2 cups of flour, and ½ teaspoon each of baking soda and salt. After portioning the dough and baking it at 350 degrees for about 12 minutes, I had cookies that weren't bad for a first try, offering just the right degree of sweetness to complement the sugary filling. But they were too thick and soft. I wanted more spread, more crunch, and—if I could pack it in—more peanut flavor.

My first change was to scrap one of the eggs (they contribute protein that traps air and makes baked goods cakey), replacing it with 3 tablespoons of milk. I knew that other factors influence how much cookie dough will spread in the oven: sugar (more sugar equals more spread) and moisture level (more moisture leads to a looser dough that spreads more readily). I'd already established that I couldn't make the dough any sweeter, so my only option was to increase the moisture level by cutting back on flour. Since my goal was also a super-nutty-tasting cookie, I decided to replace a full cup of flour with finely chopped peanuts, which would absorb far less moisture as well as add welcome crunch and peanut flavor. These changes helped, but the cookies still weren't spreading enough.

What would happen if I actually took out

What's with Those Flourless Peanut Butter Cookies?

Since we knew that the starch granules in flour mute the flavor of peanut butter, we briefly turned our attention to an Internet sensation: flourless peanut butter cookies, made with just peanut butter, sugar, egg, and sometimes a bit of baking soda. Indeed, when we tried a sample batch of our cookies sans flour, they tasted super peanut-y and baked up looking much like traditional peanut butter cookies. Why didn't these flourless cookies melt right off of the cookie sheet? Because peanut butter contains approximately 20 percent carbohydrates and 25 percent protein, components that absorb moisture and harden into a stable network in the heat of the oven. But without the sturdier structure that only starch from wheat flour can provide, these cookies fell apart in our hands before we could even take a bite. –A.G.

PHOTOGRAPHY: CARL TREMBLAY

FILLING COOKIES EVENLY

SCOOP IT WARM
Using a #60 scoop or a table-spoon measure, portion warm filling onto the bottom cookies (turned upside down).

SQUISH IT GENTLY
Rather than smearing the filling with a knife or offset spatula, top it with a second cookie and press gently until it spreads to the edges.

all of the flour? The idea wasn't without precedent. Flourless peanut butter cookie recipes abound on the Internet, and I'd always been curious about them. (See "What's with Those Flourless Peanut Butter Cookies?") I eliminated the flour and, to my surprise, found that the resulting cookies were not that much thinner or flatter, though they tasted great. They were also far too crumbly. I added flour back incrementally, finding that a ratio of ¾ cup flour to the ½ cup of peanut butter created relatively thin, nutty-tasting cookies that were still sturdy enough to serve as a shell for the filling. Finally, to get them thinner, I relied on brute force: After portioning the dough on the baking sheet, I used my wet hand to squash it into even 2-inch rounds.

I was almost there, but I had one final trick up my sleeve: tinkering with the baking soda. In other cookie recipes, we have found that adding extra soda causes the bubbles within dough to inflate so rapidly that they burst before the cookies set, leaving the cookies flatter than they would be with less soda. A mere ¼ teaspoon of baking soda would be sufficient to leaven the ¾ cup of flour in my recipe; when I quadrupled that amount to a full teaspoon, the cookies quickly puffed up in the oven and then deflated. Voilà: greater spread, just as I had hoped. In addition, these cookies boasted a coarser, more open crumb, which provided extra routes through which moisture could escape. This left the cookies even drier and crunchier—a better foil for the creamy filling.

Spread 'Em
With my creamy, peanut-y filling and ultra-crunchy cookies ready to go, it was time to put the two components together. But on my first few maddening attempts, the cookies shattered into pieces as I tried to spread the firm filling. I resisted the urge to loosen the filling with more butter, lest it squish out from between the cookies, making the package impossible to eat with any degree of decorum. Then I realized that it was a matter of timing: If I prepared the filling right before assembly, it could be easily scooped and squished between the cookies while it was still warm from the microwave—no painstaking spreading

necessary—after which it would cool and set to an ideal firm texture.

At last, I had a cookie with a simple, understated appearance that delivered the powerful peanut wallop promised (but rarely provided) by those pretenders sporting the traditional fork marks. Acknowledging that not everyone is as fanatical about peanut butter as I am, I developed a couple of fillings that tempered the intensity of the peanut butter with ingredients like honey, cinnamon, and milk chocolate. Even with these additions, these cookies are unmistakably of the peanut butter variety, no crisscrosses required.

PEANUT BUTTER SANDWICH COOKIES
MAKES 24 COOKIES

Do not use unsalted peanut butter for this recipe.

Cookies
1¼	cups (6¼ ounces) raw peanuts, toasted and cooled
¾	cup (3¾ ounces) all-purpose flour
1	teaspoon baking soda
½	teaspoon salt
3	tablespoons unsalted butter, melted
½	cup creamy peanut butter
½	cup (3½ ounces) granulated sugar
½	cup packed (3½ ounces) light brown sugar
3	tablespoons whole milk
1	large egg

Filling
¾	cup creamy peanut butter
3	tablespoons unsalted butter
1	cup (4 ounces) confectioners' sugar

1. FOR THE COOKIES: Adjust oven racks to upper-middle and lower-middle positions and heat oven to 350 degrees. Line 2 baking sheets with

parchment paper. Pulse peanuts in food processor until finely chopped, about 8 pulses. Whisk flour, baking soda, and salt together in bowl. Whisk butter, peanut butter, granulated sugar, brown sugar, milk, and egg together in second bowl. Stir flour mixture into peanut butter mixture with rubber spatula until combined. Stir in peanuts until evenly distributed.

2. Using #60 scoop or tablespoon measure, place 12 mounds, evenly spaced, on each prepared baking sheet. Using damp hand, flatten mounds until 2 inches in diameter.

3. Bake until deep golden brown and firm to touch, 15 to 18 minutes, switching and rotating sheets halfway through baking. Let cookies cool on sheets for 5 minutes. Transfer cookies to wire rack and let cool completely, about 30 minutes. Repeat portioning and baking remaining dough.

4. FOR THE FILLING: Microwave peanut butter and butter until butter is melted and warm, about 40 seconds. Using rubber spatula, stir in confectioners' sugar until combined.

5. TO ASSEMBLE: Place 24 cookies upside down on work surface. Place 1 level tablespoon (or #60 scoop) warm filling in center of each cookie. Place second cookie on top of filling, right side up, pressing gently until filling spreads to edges. Allow filling to set for 1 hour before serving. Assembled cookies can be stored in airtight container for up to 3 days.

PEANUT BUTTER SANDWICH COOKIES WITH HONEY-CINNAMON FILLING

Omit butter from filling. Stir 5 tablespoons honey and ½ teaspoon ground cinnamon into warm peanut butter before adding confectioners' sugar.

PEANUT BUTTER SANDWICH COOKIES WITH MILK CHOCOLATE FILLING

Reduce peanut butter to ½ cup and omit butter from filling. Stir 6 ounces finely chopped milk chocolate into warm peanut butter until melted, microwaving for 10 seconds at a time if necessary, before adding confectioners' sugar.

Perfecting the Peanut Butter Sandwich Cookie

Many recipes for peanut butter sandwich cookies disappoint with soft, dull-tasting cookies and overly sweet fillings. Here's how we improved the concept.

- **Super-Crunchy Cookies** Fewer eggs and more baking soda add up to thin, flat, extra-crisp cookies.

- **A Smooth—but Not Runny—Filling** Creaminess was crucial, but so was a filling that didn't squish out the sides. Our formula: peanut butter, butter, and enough confectioners' sugar to firm up the texture.

- **Big Peanut Flavor** Replacing some of the flour with chopped toasted peanuts made the cookies extra nutty.

Scrutinizing Sauté Pans

These big, straight-sided vessels have their uses, but how much should you pay for a pan you don't pull out every day?

> BY LISA McMANUS ≼

We don't reach for sauté pans very often in the test kitchen. Despite their name, these wide, flat-bottomed pans with relatively high, L-shaped sides are not the best choice for searing. For that task, we prefer skillets with low, sloping walls that encourage evaporation and browning. Nor are sauté pans our go-to for deep frying or stewing—tasks best done in a tall Dutch oven.

That said, these mid-height, mid-weight, lidded vessels are ideal for cooking down heaps of greens, and their straight sides—high enough to corral splatters but low enough to easily reach into with tongs—are great for shallow frying. It's also our preferred pan for braising recipes that require browning and then adding liquid. The walls prevent spills as you stir, pour off oil, or transfer the pan from stove to oven.

Like all cookware, a sauté pan needs to do one thing particularly well: heat evenly. Other than that, we wanted a model that felt balanced and comfortable to maneuver—stove-to-oven transfers need to be steady, not shaky—and that came with a tight-fitting lid to keep food and heat well contained.

With those criteria in mind, we bought nine models ranging from $64 to $224.95, all built according to our preferred cookware construction: aluminum (an excellent heat conductor but highly reactive with acidic foods) surrounded by layers of stainless steel (nonreactive and less conductive, so it modulates heat distribution). Of those, six were fully clad tri-ply (translation: the entire pan consisted of three layers), and one pan boasted seven layers from top to bottom. The other two were single-layer constructions sporting aluminum and steel disks attached to the bottom that made just their bases tri-ply. We skipped over nonstick and anodized pans; none of the tasks best suited to sauté pans require a nonstick coating, and the light color of traditional surfaces makes it easier to monitor the browned bits of fond that develop and form the basis of flavorful pan sauces. The task list—fried chicken, braised cabbage, Mexican rice, Swedish meatballs, and crêpes (to gauge even browning)—would single out a pan that truly deserved a place in our cookware arsenal.

Surface Tension

Capacities varied (3 quarts and up), but the pans came in two distinct shapes: low and wide or tall and narrow. This meant that the diameter of their cooking surfaces ranged considerably—from 9 to 11¼ inches. We figured the wider pans would fare better, since their greater surface area would mean less batch cooking.

To some extent, that was true. We could fit only four or five pieces of chicken in the 9-inch pans, forcing us to fry in two batches. Even then, the pieces were crammed together, making it tricky to flip them. Meatballs were also a little crowded and harder to turn in smaller pans. On the other hand, there was such a thing as too much surface area. When we poured oil into the 11- and 11¼-inch pans, it spread too thinly across the surface, requiring us to add a lot more oil than the recipe specified. Wider models also heated unevenly: Chicken and meatballs emerged with dark and light patches, indicating hot spots.

To get a more detailed picture of the pans' browning patterns, we poured crêpe batter over each model's surface. The results mirrored the chicken and meatball tests: While the seven smaller sauté pans turned out evenly golden pancakes, the two larger models produced spottily browned crêpes—an indication that the broad cooking surfaces struggled to maintain even heat from edge to edge. That test narrowed down our preferences to the midsize (9½- to 10-inch) pans.

Two other major factors determined steady heating: the thickness of the cooking surface and the weight of the pan. Here again, moderation proved to be key. The pans with the thinnest bottoms (1.78 and 2.32 millimeters thick, respectively) overheated within minutes of hitting the burner, and the lightest pan, which clocked in at a scrawny 2.9 pounds without its lid (the heaviest weighed nearly 2 pounds more), couldn't braise the cabbage without burning it. Meanwhile, the two chunky disk-bottom pans, which were nearly four times thicker, started off heating at a slow, steady clip and then quickly got hotter, forcing us to constantly lower the flame to avoid scorching. Moderately thick, moderately heavy models were substantial enough to modulate heat but not so bulky that they retained too much of it.

Ease of use boiled down to a handful of features. How much the pan weighed factored into its ability to heat evenly, but the distribution of that weight singled out sauté pans that felt safe and comfortable to handle versus those that were unwieldy.

Then there was the problem of handles that were either slippery or, worse, that heated up during cooking. Grips with some traction or edge were pluses—a discovery that we made when a few rounded handles slid precariously in our potholder-protected hands as we poured off hot oil. Stay-cool handles were also beneficial, and "helper" loops opposite the main handle eased lifting when the pans were full.

Finally, there was the lid. We knew that we were looking for weighty, ovensafe models that tightly locked in the food. Tempered glass tops didn't prove as handy as they seemed; if they steamed up, they obscured any view of the cooking progress.

The Pan to Pick

There's no getting around it: We loved the Viking Stainless 7-Ply 3-Quart Sauté Pan ($219.95). Yes, its price is steep, but it offered a stellar heating performance, a roomy cooking surface (a good 10½ inches—a more generous expanse than the cooking surface of our favorite Dutch oven, as well as of our recommended skillet), a stay-cool handle, a helper loop, and a snug-fitting lid. But if you can't bring yourself to spend more than $200 on a pan that you won't use every day, and you can do with less cooking surface and a slight drop in quality, the Cuisinart MultiClad Pro Triple-Ply 3½-Quart Sauté Pan ($79.95) is a good bargain bet.

What Can a Sauté Pan Do Better than a Skillet?

SHALLOW-FRY The taller walls of a good sauté pan are better at corralling greasy splatters than the low, sloping sides of a skillet.

BROWN 'N' BRAISE The broad, flat bottom boasts ample surface area for browning foods like meatballs, and the deeper design offers room for added liquid. The helper handle takes the worry out of lifting a full, heavy pan.

If you want to add a sauté pan to your arsenal, our winner, from Viking, is an excellent pan that will last a lifetime.

TESTING SAUTÉ PANS

We tested nine sauté pans. Pans are listed in order of preference; sources for the winning pans are on page 32.

PERFORMANCE:
We made crêpes to observe heat distribution; Swedish meatballs to assess the shape and size of the cooking surface; and Mexican rice to evaluate sautéing and steaming, the fit of a lid, and a pan's ability to withstand oven heat. We also shallow-fried chicken pieces to assess capacity and ability to maintain consistent temperatures. Braising cabbage in cream tested capacity, the fit of the lid, and the ability to braise without scorching.

EASE OF USE:
We considered how the pan's weight, balance, and handle shape (and presence of a helper handle, if any) contributed to maneuverability and whether its capacity, the height of its sides, and the width of its cooking surface made it easy to use for a variety of recipes. Pans lost points for hot handles.

DIMENSIONS:
The diameter of the cooking surface (measured inside the pan, across the flat portion of the bottom), the height of the sides, and the thickness of the cooking surface.

	CRITERIA		TESTERS' COMMENTS

HIGHLY RECOMMENDED

VIKING Stainless 7-Ply 3-Quart Sauté Pan 
Model: VSC0303 Price: $219.95
Weight (without lid): 4.6 lb
Dimensions: 10½ in by 2¼ in; 3.88 mm thick
Material: Stainless with aluminum core; metal lid
Ovensafe Temperature: 600°F

Performance ★★★
Ease of Use ★★★

This midsize pan's heft was a boon to steady heating and even browning, and it's so well proportioned that the weight didn't bother us. The handle sported a ridge for a secure grip and stayed cool on the stove; the heavy, sturdy lid fit securely.

ALL-CLAD Stainless 3-Quart Tri-Ply Sauté Pan 
Model: 16711 Price: $224.95
Weight (without lid): 3.1 lb
Dimensions: 9¾ in by 2 in; 2.8 mm thick
Material: Stainless with aluminum core; metal lid
Ovensafe Temperature: 500°F

Performance ★★★
Ease of Use ★★★

Our previous favorite is back in an updated induction-compatible version. The price hike is disappointing, but it cooks steadily, browns evenly, has a stay-cool handle, and is well balanced and relatively lightweight.

RECOMMENDED

CUISINART MultiClad Pro Triple-Ply 3½-Quart Sauté Pan with Lid
Model: MCP33-24H Price: $79.95
Weight (without lid): 3.4 lb
Dimensions: 9 in by 3 in; 3.7 mm thick
Material: Stainless with aluminum core; metal lid
Ovensafe Temperature: 550°F

Performance ★★★
Ease of Use ★★½

Although its cooking surface is narrow, causing some crowding, this pan browned food evenly. Its well-balanced body made for easy lifting and pouring, and its handle stayed cool on the stove.

CALPHALON Tri-Ply Stainless 3-Quart Sauté Pan 
Model: 1767729 Price: $124.95
Weight (without lid): 3.2 lb
Dimensions: 9½ in by 2¼ in; 3.43 mm thick
Material: Stainless with aluminum core; glass lid
Ovensafe Temperature: 450°F

Performance ★★½
Ease of Use ★★★

Even though this model fried chicken and braised meatballs just as well as our Best Buy—and offered slightly more surface area—it dropped a notch for costing roughly 50 percent more. It's light enough to lift easily, and the handle stayed cool.

RECOMMENDED WITH RESERVATIONS

LE CREUSET Tri-Ply Stainless 3-Quart Sauté Pan 
Model: SSC5100-24 Price: $154.95
Weight (without lid): 2.9 lb
Dimensions: 9 in by 2¼ in; 2.32 mm thick
Material: Stainless with aluminum core; metal lid
Ovensafe Temperature: 425°F

Performance ★★
Ease of Use ★★½

This was the lightest pan and also one of the thinnest; it ran hot, scorching braising cabbage. Its narrow surface accommodated only half a batch of chicken. The good news: Its light body and stay-cool handle made it comfortable to maneuver.

TRAMONTINA Tri-Ply Clad 12-Inch Stainless Steel Jumbo Cooker with Lid 
Model: 80116/510 Price: $64
Weight (without lid): 4.7 lb
Dimensions: 11¼ in by 2⅝ in; 3.71 mm thick
Material: Stainless with aluminum core; metal lid
Ovensafe Temperature: 450°F

Performance ★★
Ease of Use ★★

A lot of bang for your buck when it comes to surface area. However, its extra-broad surface browned unevenly and required extra cooking oil. It was also one of the heaviest pans in the lineup, requiring two hands to lift. Fortunately, it features a helper handle.

AMERICAN KITCHEN by Regal Ware Tri-Ply Stainless Steel Covered 12-Inch Sauté Pan 
Model: AK712-FP Price: $129.95
Weight (without lid): 4.2 lb
Dimensions: 11 in by 3 in; 1.78 mm thick
Material: Stainless with aluminum core; metal lid
Ovensafe Temperature: 500°F

Performance ★★
Ease of Use ★★

Roomy, cleanly designed, and fitted with a sturdy lid, this pan looked like a winner until we discovered its most notable feature: an ultra-thin base, which accounted for its hot spots and uneven browning. It was also quite heavy when full, and its breadth required extra cooking oil.

NOT RECOMMENDED

FISSLER Original Pro Collection Sauté Pan with Lid 
Model: 84 376 24 Price: $225.99
Weight (without lid): 4.7 lb
Dimensions: 9 in by 2⅝ in; 7.25 mm thick
Material: Stainless and aluminum disk bottom; metal lid
Ovensafe Temperature: 425°F

Performance ★★
Ease of Use ★

For $226, we expected stellar performance. Instead, this narrow, heavy model was fitted with a bulky disk bottom that accumulated heat and responded sluggishly. Its round, slippery handle gets very hot. Perfectly vertical sides made stirring and whisking difficult.

BERNDES Cucinare Tri-Ply 11-Inch Sauté Pan with Lid
Model: 063668 Price: $119.95
Weight (without lid): 4 lb
Dimensions: 9¾ in by 2 in; 7.64 mm thick
Material: Stainless and aluminum disk bottom; glass lid
Ovensafe Temperature: 320°F

Performance ★½
Ease of Use ★

This tinny pan with a very thick disk bottom felt chintzy and awkward. Heat accumulated in the disk (and the handle), forcing us to lower the flame multiple times to avoid scorching. The real deal breaker: Plastic fittings in the lid limit its ovensafe temperature to only 320 degrees.

The Best Canned Whole Tomatoes

When it comes to the best canned tomatoes, is Italian pedigree the determining factor, or do the sweetest, brightest-tasting specimens come from this side of the Atlantic?

≥ BY HANNAH CROWLEY ≤

If you believe all the hype from Italian chefs and cookbooks, then San Marzano tomatoes are the best tomatoes in the world. Promoters of the prized crop claim that the climate and fertile soil in the eponymous southern region of Italy where they grow are behind the fruit's meaty texture, juiciness, and exceptional flavor. Only tomatoes grown in the region from seeds dating back to the original cultivar and according to strict standards may receive the elite Denominazione d'Origine Protetta (DOP) label. In the past, San Marzanos were hard to come by in the United States, but that never deterred loyalists, who sought out cans from gourmet markets and online retailers. In recent years, however, San Marzano tomatoes have become easier to find, showing up in regular supermarkets and under different brand names. That's partly because not all brands labeled "San Marzano" are DOP-certified. These days, some of the tomatoes are even grown in the United States from San Marzano seeds.

Regardless of where they're from, the wider availability of San Marzanos renewed our general interest in canned whole tomatoes—a product that we frequently prefer to diced or crushed. (Oftentimes, the latter two are selected from fruit that's been damaged during harvesting and have been more thoroughly treated with firming agents to prevent them from breaking down.) We decided to hold a taste-off: San Marzanos versus everything else. After collecting 10 different brands—three labeled San Marzano, the other seven a mix of Italian, Canadian, and American products—we sampled them straight out of the can as well as simmered in both quick- and long-cooked tomato sauces.

Our questions: Are San Marzanos really the ultimate canned whole tomatoes—that is, bright, sweet, and tangy, with meat that's plush and soft enough to melt into a sauce but without completely dissolving? More important, would they taste noticeably better than regular tomatoes once they'd been cooked down in a sauce with aromatics and wine?

Surprisingly, the answer to both questions was a definitive "no."

Though each of the three San Marzano samples elicited a few lukewarm compliments here and there—"agreeable flavor"; "nice blank-slate tomatoes"—none of them delivered the bold, deeply fruity taste that we were expecting, nor did they hold their shape well. In fact, these tomatoes scored well below several of the domestic samples, the best of which were deemed "bright," "complex," "meaty," and—as one taster noted in amazement—like "real" tomatoes.

Also remarkable: Whether or not the tomato was a true San Marzano didn't matter. The DOP-certified brand was actually our least favorite of the three, which debunked the hype over the San Marzano pedigree once and for all. But now we had a more challenging question to answer: What made the other samples taste good?

Sweet and Sour

For starters, sweetness. Scientists gauge this particular quality in tomatoes according to the Brix scale—a measurement of the sugar (per 100 grams) in liquid. Generally, the higher the Brix of tomatoes, the greater the perception of good, ripe tomato flavor.

When we had an independent lab measure the Brix of each brand's tomato solids, the results were conclusive: Our three least favorite brands (including the DOP-certified San Marzanos) were the least sweet, with tasters panning their "weak," "washed out" flavor, whether cooked or eaten straight from the can. Conversely, tasters praised the "fruity," "real summer" sweetness of our two favorite tomatoes, whose sweetness levels were relatively high. However, the sweetest samples of all—which happened to be the other two San Marzanos—landed in the middle of the pack, proving that when it comes to optimal tomato flavor, sweetness is not the only dynamic in play.

The other half of good tomato flavor is acidity—and lots of it. Bright tanginess balances out the sweetness and (like salt) enhances other pleasing flavors by masking bitterness. Sure enough, when we had the lab measure the pH of all the samples, we discovered that the tomatoes with the lowest pH (i.e., the most acidic tomatoes) almost invariably scored the highest, earning tasters' approval for their "fresh," "fruity" flavors, while the least acidic tomatoes tanked. The lone exception was bottom-ranked Tuttorosso, which boasted a good level of acidity but not much sweetness—a combination that gave it an "unbalanced" flavor that tasters assailed for being "nothing like a summer tomato."

Salt played only a relatively minor role in our overall preferences. The American samples contained a lot more sodium than did imported brands (at least 20 times more, in some cases), and in the plain tasting some tasters preferred them for it. But sodium levels didn't influence our preferences in either of the cooked applications, and since canned tomatoes are rarely eaten uncooked, we didn't factor salt content into our rankings.

In the Flesh

Good balance was the key to optimal tomato flavor, and it was a quality that tasters looked for in the fruits' texture, too. Overly firm specimens lost points for their "rubbery" bite, while tomatoes that broke down completely were docked for "mushiness." Our three top-ranking brands boasted a firm but tender bite, even after a lengthy simmer. But what accounted for the differences in texture?

For one thing, calcium chloride. All five American products were treated with this salt, which manufacturers add to maintain the tomatoes' firmness, whereas the imported brands were not. We figured that for better or for worse, the widespread use of this additive in domestic canned tomatoes couldn't help but drive our American tasters' preference for tomatoes that retain a little structure.

While we liked the tomatoes to be somewhat firm, we didn't like their flesh to be overly thick. In the 1960s, mechanical harvesting replaced handpicking

Engineering the Ideal Canned Tomato

Farmed for Flavor
The best tomatoes are cultivated to be both highly acidic and very sweet. The walls of their flesh shouldn't be too thick, allowing for an abundance of jelly and seeds—the most flavorful part of the tomato.

FRESH

Processed for Firmness
Italian cooks might feel just the opposite, but our American tasters preferred brands that included calcium chloride, which helps ensure that the tomatoes won't turn mushy during cooking—an issue with the additive-free imports.

CANNED
Our winner, Muir Glen, holds up better than the rest.

TASTING CANNED WHOLE TOMATOES

Twenty-one *Cook's Illustrated* staff members sampled 10 nationally available brands of supermarket canned whole tomatoes in three blind tastings—plain and simmered in quick- and long-cooked tomato sauces—rating the samples on tomato flavor, texture, and overall appeal. An independent laboratory also measured the Brix (sugar levels) and pH (acidity) of all the samples; a higher Brix means more sweetness, while a lower pH corresponds to greater acidity. Brands were selected from top-selling supermarket tomatoes, as compiled by SymphonyIRI Group, a market research firm based in Chicago, Illinois. Tasting scores were averaged, and brands appear below in order of preference.

RECOMMENDED

MUIR GLEN Organic Whole Peeled Tomatoes
Price: $2.99 for 28 oz
Origin: USA **Calcium Chloride:** Yes
pH: 3.91 (high acidity) **Brix:** 6 (high sweetness)
Comments: "Reminds me of a real summer tomato," said one taster about our favorite sample. No wonder: Its strong acidity and high level of sweetness made for flavor that was "vibrant" and "sweet in a natural way." The addition of calcium chloride gave the tomatoes a "nice firm texture" that held up even after hours of simmering.

HUNT'S Whole Plum Tomatoes
Price: $1.95 for 28 oz
Origin: USA **Calcium Chloride:** Yes
pH: 4.16 (moderately high acidity) **Brix:** 5.5 (moderate sweetness)
Comments: Even after two hours of simmering in our long-cooked sauce, these calcium chloride–treated tomatoes were "meaty," with "distinct shape." A relatively high Brix value and low pH—an ideal combination for tomatoes—explained their "fruity," "bright" flavors.

RECOMMENDED WITH RESERVATIONS

RED GOLD Whole Peeled Tomatoes
Price: $1.36 for 14.5 oz
Origin: USA **Calcium Chloride:** Yes
pH: 3.91 (high acidity) **Brix:** 4.7 (low sweetness)
Comments: These nicely "firm," globe-shaped tomatoes shared the same low pH (i.e., strong acidity) as our favorite brand, but they lacked its sweetness. As a result, several tasters found them "a bit sharp," even in the long-cooked sauce. Others liked the big acid punch, praising their "bright" flavor.

CENTO San Marzano Certified Peeled Tomatoes
Price: $3.79 for 28 oz
Origin: Italy **Calcium Chloride:** No
pH: 4.25 (moderate acidity) **Brix:** 7 (high sweetness)
Comments: Although these non–DOP certified San Marzano tomatoes scored highest for sweetness, they lacked acidity, and tasters found their flavor merely "average"—even "untomatoey." That said, they fared best of all the Italian brands, particularly because their texture "held up" relatively well in sauce.

BIONATURAE Organic Whole Peeled Tomatoes
Price: $3.39 for 28.2 oz
Origin: Italy **Calcium Chloride:** No
pH: 4.28 (moderate acidity) **Brix:** 5.6 (moderate sweetness)
Comments: Without calcium chloride, these Italian tomatoes were so "mushy" that they "tasted like sauce" before we had even cooked them. Their "sweet" flavor redeemed them for some tasters, but with only moderate acidity, they also tasted "flat."

RECOMMENDED WITH RESERVATIONS, CONTINUED

SAN MARZANO Whole Peeled Tomatoes
Price: $3.99 for 28 oz
Origin: USA **Calcium Chloride:** Yes
pH: 4.26 (moderate acidity) **Brix:** 6.4 (high sweetness)
Comments: What's in a name? In this case, not much. These impostor "San Marzano" tomatoes were grown domestically with seeds from Italy's famous varietal. Some tasters picked up on their high level of sweetness and complimented them for it, but without equally high acidity, the tomatoes' flavor was also "muted."

RIENZI Selected Italian Plum Tomatoes
Price: $1.95 for 28 oz
Origin: Italy **Calcium Chloride:** No
pH: 4.22 (moderate acidity) **Brix:** 5.4 (moderate sweetness)
Comments: Tasters noticed this sample's lack of calcium chloride in all three applications, describing the tomatoes as "mushy" and "borderline soupy." Thanks to low acid and moderate sweetness, their flavor was middle-of-the-road: "fruity" and "light" but also "uninspired."

EDEN Organic Whole Roma Tomatoes
Price: $3.79 for 28 oz
Origin: Canada **Calcium Chloride:** No
pH: 4.31 (moderately low acidity) **Brix:** 4.2 (low sweetness)
Comments: With the least amount of sweetness, not much acidity, and no added salt, these tomatoes didn't "pack much punch." Some tasters considered that effect pleasantly "clean" and "light," whereas others complained that they offered "no real tomato flavor at all," particularly in the long-simmered sauce.

PASTENE San Marzano Tomatoes of Sarnese Nocerino Area D.O.P.
Price: $4.53 for 28 oz
Origin: Italy **Calcium Chloride:** No
pH: 4.32 (moderately low acidity) **Brix:** 4.6 (low sweetness)
Comments: We had high expectations for these pricey DOP-certified San Marzano tomatoes but came away disappointed. Because of low sweetness and acidity, their flavor translated as "weak" and "thin"—at best "clean" and "straightforward." Like the other calcium chloride–free samples, they broke down easily.

NOT RECOMMENDED

TUTTOROSSO Peeled Plum Shaped Tomatoes
Price: $1.79 for 28 oz
Origin: USA **Calcium Chloride:** Yes
pH: 4.14 (moderately high acidity) **Brix:** 4.5 (low sweetness)
Comments: We like a bit of firmness to our tomatoes, but thanks to their particularly thick flesh, these samples were "tough," "chewy," and "fibrous." Worse, their low sweetness and acidity made them taste "muted," "unbalanced," and "nothing like summer tomatoes."

---

in this country, speeding up the process. Growers then had to breed a tomato sturdy enough to withstand the rigors of machine harvesting, which meant they needed a fruit with thicker walls (known as pericarp). The trade-off was less flavor. The reason? Tomato flesh isn't where most of the flavor is; it's in the "jelly" that surrounds the seeds in the fruit's hollow spaces. When the flesh got thicker, those cavities got smaller, leaving less room for the jelly.

To see if this trend lined up with our results, we took a sample from each can, measured the thickness of its pericarp with a caliper, and scooped out and weighed its jelly. Indeed, our least favorite tomatoes had the thickest pericarp, with tasters describing them as "tough," "chewy," and "bland." The tomatoes we liked best had thinner, tender-firm walls, and their cavities were the largest and most full of flavorful jelly.

American Beauties
As it turned out, the San Marzano hype was all for naught. We didn't even prefer Italian-grown tomatoes. Rather, we most enjoyed the bold acidity, high sugar content, and firm bite of all-American Muir Glen Organic Whole Peeled Tomatoes. Hunt's Whole Plum Tomatoes finished a close second, with tasters particularly admiring their firm texture and pleasing acidity. We'll be stocking up on both.

Why Food Cooks Slower in Oil than in Water

EGG IN WATER
After 6 minutes at 165 degrees, this egg is well on its way to being poached.

EGG IN OIL
After 6 minutes at the same temperature, this egg is still raw.

One of the niftiest things we learned from our Poached Fish Fillets recipe (page 13) is that the fish cooks more gently (and slowly) in oil than in water—even when both liquids are exactly the same temperature. This is true, it turns out, not just for fish but for any other food, including eggs (see photos at left). But how can this be? Isn't temperature what determines speed of cooking? As it happens, equally critical is the liquid's thermal capacity, or how much energy is needed to change its temperature by 1 degree centigrade. Oil has roughly half the thermal capacity of water, which means it requires half the amount of energy to reach the same temperature as an equal volume of water. This, in turn, means it has less energy to transfer to food and will cook it more slowly.

While we understood the concept, it seemed to defy common sense. So we decided to check it out using our own senses. We heated equal amounts of water and oil to 135 degrees and then asked test cooks to stick a finger in each liquid simultaneously. Testers immediately snatched their fingers out of the water, which felt very hot, but left them in the oil, which felt merely warm. Point proved.

Salt Your Egg Wash

An egg wash consists of a beaten egg thinned with a little water or milk, and it's used to develop shine and golden-brown color on the surface of breads, pastries, and pie crusts. Some recipes specify adding salt to the wash, claiming that it creates a better shine, but that didn't prove true in our experiments. We did find, however, that in addition to flavoring the wash, salt helps denature the proteins in the egg, making it more fluid and therefore much easier to brush evenly and gently over delicate doughs. We'll be adding a pinch of salt to our egg washes from now on.

A Better Brine?

We've always been big advocates of brining (soaking meat in a saltwater solution). As salt is drawn into meat, the protein structure of the meat changes, reducing its overall toughness and increasing its capacity to hold on to water and stay juicy during cooking. A brine also thoroughly seasons meat all the way to its interior.

We generally recommend brining in a solution that's roughly 9 percent salt by weight (9 grams of salt for every 100 grams of water). Several scientific studies, however, have shown that meat absorbs the most moisture at a salt concentration of about 6 percent.

When we compared chicken breasts brined in 6 percent and 9 percent salt concentrations, the 6 percent sample indeed soaked up slightly more salt water. But overall, tasters still preferred the chicken brined in a 9 percent solution because they liked its somewhat saltier taste. Our conclusion: A 9 percent solution might be slightly less than optimal in terms of saltwater absorption, but it still provides the best balance among a brine's threefold effects, producing meat that's tender, juicy, and well seasoned.

When Fresh-Squeezed Isn't Best

LET IT AGE
Lemon and lime juices taste better when allowed to rest a few hours after squeezing.

When more than one bartender friend told us that lemon and lime juices that are several hours old taste better than the just-squeezed stuff, we decided to see for ourselves. We pressed several fresh lemons and limes and refrigerated their juices, covered, for four hours. We then used the samples in batches of lemonade and limeade, comparing them with versions made with just-squeezed juice. Sure enough, tasters preferred the aged-juice drinks, noting that they had a more mellow yet complex flavor.

It turns out that terpenes, aromatic compounds in lime and lemon oil, start to oxidize when the juice rests. In this case, oxidation is a good thing: A chemist in the juice industry explained that oxidized terpenes consistently present a truer, more preferred citrus flavor than unoxidized terpenes.

So if you've got the time, letting juice rest for a few hours before mixing your drinks can make for better-tasting citrus ades and cocktails. Any longer than six hours, though, and the juice may start to lose its potency and develop off-flavors. (Note: This aged-is-better phenomenon is not true of oranges, since they contain a compound called LARL that can make their juice turn bitter when exposed to air.)

TECHNIQUE | SPIRAL-CUT PINEAPPLE

Removing the prickly "eyes" from pineapple typically either involves wasting a lot of the fruit or creating unsightly gouges. The spiral-cut technique popular in Asian countries preserves more of the best part of the fruit while sculpting it into an attractive shape.

1. With sharp knife, slice off crown and bottom of pineapple.

2. Holding pineapple upright, pare off rind from top to bottom as thin as possible. Lay fruit on 1 side.

3. Working around pineapple, cut shallow, diagonal V-shaped grooves just deep enough to remove eyes, following their natural spiral pattern. Slice pineapple as desired.

Crisp-fried herbs such as parsley, sage, mint, and basil make appealing garnishes, but frying them can be a messy process that uses a lot of oil. Our easier microwave method calls for just a few teaspoons of oil.

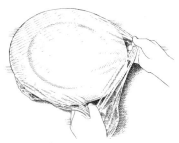   

1. Stretch plastic wrap tightly over plate with slightly raised rim to create flat surface. Cut 2 equal circles of parchment paper (both slightly smaller than diameter of plate) and lay 1 on taut plastic.

2. Dip herb leaves in vegetable oil so that both sides are evenly coated (gently shaking off any excess), then arrange in single layer on parchment on plate.

3. Cover oiled herbs with second piece of parchment, followed by more plastic, pulled as tight as possible to help keep leaves flat.

4. Poke several vent holes in plastic, then microwave for 3 to 4 minutes. Gently blot cooled leaves between paper towels before using.

Ice Cubes That Last Twice as Long

Why is it that the ice served by restaurants and bars can be sparkling clear—but the cubes you make at home are cloudy? The cloudiness in ice comes from dissolved gases and minerals. In an ice cube tray or home ice maker, water freezes from the outside in, pushing these impurities into the still-liquid center of each cube, where they eventually freeze, leaving an opaque, bubble-ridden core.

Commercial ice machines first purify water with a built-in filtration system and then rapidly freeze it in progressive layers of ultra-thin sheets, a process that prevents air bubbles from becoming trapped in the cubes. The resulting translucent ice isn't just for show: Its crystals are more tightly bound, so it melts more slowly, preventing waterlogged beverages.

You can make almost perfectly clear ice at home if you eliminate as many impurities as possible from the start. Use distilled water (which, unlike tap water, contains no minerals) and boil it for a few minutes to drive off dissolved gases before freezing it (there's no need to cool down the water first). In our tests, the super-clear ice lasted about twice as long as regular cubes.

Fizzier Pop

When we recently evaluated home seltzer makers, we noticed that the instructions for all of the models recommend starting with cold water rather than room temperature or warm water. Curious about this guideline, we tried carbonating water at 32 degrees, 68 degrees, and 140 degrees. The results surprised us. The 32-degree water turned out incredibly effervescent, with small, long-lasting bubbles, while the 140-degree water was barely carbonated. The 68-degree sample sat right in the middle of these two extremes. A review of some scientific literature confirmed our observations: Water at 32 degrees can hold five times more carbon dioxide than water at 140 degrees.

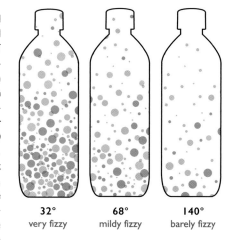

32°	68°	140°
very fizzy	mildy fizzy	barely fizzy

Why the drastic difference? Unlike solids, which become more soluble as the temperature of a liquid increases (for example, it's much easier to dissolve sugar in hot liquids than in cold), gas is harder to incorporate into warmer liquids. That's because when gas gets warm it expands and dissipates, so there is less of it available to be dissolved in liquid. So for the fizziest homemade sodas and seltzer, always use ice-cold water.

No More Stringy Drumsticks

What's not to like about chicken drumsticks, which boast juicy, flavorful dark meat and are so easy to pick up from the plate? We can think of one thing: They're full of stringy tendons. We figured out a clever way to remove the tendons before cooking.

 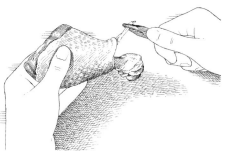

1. Holding a paring knife just above the ankle and perpendicular to the bone, slice around the circumference all the way to the bone. This will expose the ends of about six thin white tendons.

2. Using a clean pair of pliers, grip the end of each tendon and pull firmly to remove it. Repeat until there are no more visible tendons.

Faster Brown Rice

Since brown rice can take 45 minutes to an hour to cook, we wondered if soaking it ahead of time could speed up the cooking (just as it does with dried beans). We're pleased to report success: After soaking in room temperature water for at least six hours, brown rice cooked in only 30 minutes. The simplest approach is to place the rice and premeasured cooking water (use 1½ cups of water per cup of rice) directly into a pot or rice cooker (before leaving for work, for example) and let it soak. Then it's merely a question of adding salt and turning on the heat when you're ready to cook. Besides the abbreviated cooking time, there's an added benefit: The long soak softens the hard outer bran layer much better than simmering alone does, resulting in rice that's far more tender and fluffy. (Just don't soak rice for longer than 24 hours: It can start to sprout or ferment.)

SOAKED FOR SPEED
Soaking brown rice speeds up cooking.

EQUIPMENT CORNER

⇒ BY HANNAH CROWLEY, AMY GRAVES, LISA McMANUS & TAIZETH SIERRA ⇐

EQUIPMENT TESTING Manual Espresso Maker

When we tested hand-powered espresso makers in 2008, we recommended an inexpensive portable device called the AeroPress ($29.95). While the machine is easy to use, the espresso that it produces falls just short of the ideal deep, rich coffeehouse brew. Would the latest manual model, the Presso Espresso Machine, be worth the higher price tag

($150, which is still far lower than that of electric machines)? Like the AeroPress, the Presso is designed for simplicity. The 11-inch tool consists of two long, curved levers attached to a wishbone-shaped body, a clear hot-water chamber with markings for single and double shots, and a portafilter for grounds. Also included are a measuring scoop that doubles

EASY ESPRESSO
The Presso requires no barista skills to produce great espresso.

as a tamper, an adapter for making two single shots simultaneously, and a syringe-like milk foamer (you simply stick it into milk and pump the plunger to froth). The instructions were clear, and the superb result—rich, full-bodied espresso topped with a nice *crema*—had test cooks lining up for shots.

EQUIPMENT TESTING Pie Lattice Tools

The time and finesse required to cut and weave strips of fragile dough scare off many people from attempting a lattice pie crust. Bakeware companies have stepped in with a variety of tools to help. We tried out four such gadgets, using them to shape the top crusts on peach pies. For comparison, we also used our tried-

A LOT OF DOUGH
The Paderno cutter effortlessly slices dough strips, but for $125, it ought to bake the pie, too.

and-true method of measuring strips with a ruler and then cutting them out with a pizza wheel. Most of the specialty tools were flops: Dough got stuck around the wheels of a small roller-style device, ruining the pattern. One stamp-style cutter gave us a crude-looking lattice. Another had a delicate pattern but the blades didn't cut all the way through the dough. The priciest, a multiwheel cutter from Paderno World Cuisine ($125) that can be adjusted to different widths, glided effortlessly over the rolled-out dough, cutting perfect strips that we then wove into a lattice. However, our ruler-and-pizza-wheel method works just as well, minus the hefty price.

EQUIPMENT TESTING Induction Interface Disks

Does switching to an induction range mean saying goodbye to your favorite pots and pans? Because induction cookers use electromagnetic energy to generate heat, they work only with cookware made of iron or magnetic gauges of steel. (If a magnet sticks to its base, your pan will work on an induction stove.) For nonmagnetic cookware, the answer might be an induction interface disk, a Ping-Pong paddle–shaped device that sits under your incompatible pot and acts as a converter, transferring heat by conduction. We tested three models priced from $48.95 to $99.95, using them to boil water and make pancakes under non-induction-ready

pans. One small carbon steel disk never managed to bring the 2 quarts of water to a boil or fully cook a pancake, and its metal feet scratched our cooktop's glossy surface. We had more success with the other two models, made of

MAKING THE TRANSFER
The Max Burton tool transfers heat evenly and reliably but adds time to cooking.

smooth 18/10 stainless steel. These models reliably boiled water and cooked pancakes—albeit in twice the time it would take using straight induction and a compatible pan (or about the same time it would take on a gas burner). We strongly favored the Max Burton Induction Interface Disk, which has an aluminum core for speedy heat distribution and a comfortable, heatproof rubber handle. At $48.95, it costs less than a new induction-ready saucepan.

NEW PRODUCT Collapsible Mini Colander

When all you need to rinse is a handful of berries, the last thing you want to do is unearth (and later clean) a big colander. The Collapsible Mini Colander from Progressive International ($6.13) holds 3½ cups and folds down to a height of just 1 inch. Unfolded, this 8-inch-long silicone colander is sturdy, and its oval shape made it easy to tip rinsed food into a container with no spills. But the best part is its plastic base, which pops on to seal the colander's holes so you can flood the contents before draining or set it on a counter without drips. It's dishwasher-safe but hand washes in a flash (it has no crevices to trap dirt) and after weeks of use showed nary a sign of wear. It's our new go-to gadget for washing small quantities of fruit and vegetables.

MIGHTY MINI
The sturdy, easy-to-use Progressive colander is just the right size for washing a pint of berries.

NEW PRODUCT Recipe Holder

Not all recipes come from magazines and cookbooks, and a sheet of paper— whether it's a printout from an online resource or a hand-written index card—can easily get lost in the countertop shuffle. The Recipe Rock from Architec ($9.99) offers a clever way to hold recipes upright. This small, weighty plastic holder sits solidly

ROCK SOLID
The Recipe Rock from Architec keeps your recipes in easy view while you cook.

on a flat surface while its concave front cradles pages at a perfect angle for comfortable viewing. The pages are held in place by a metal ball and an embedded magnet so strong it gripped 10 sheets of 8½ by 11-inch paper. Its compact 2-inch size takes up very little counter space, and it tucks away neatly in a drawer. The smooth surface wipes clean easily. We'll use it to make sure we don't get fouled up while following a recipe.

For complete testing results, go to www.CooksIllustrated.com/apr12.

Sources Prices were current at press time and do not include shipping. Contact companies to confirm information or visit www.CooksIllustrated.com for updates.

PAGE 7: RICE COOKER
• Progressive International Microwave Rice Cooker: $8.99, item #SPM2030051201, Sears (800-349-4358, **www.sears.com**).

PAGE 11: GARLIC GADGETS
• MIU Stainless Steel Garlic & Truffle Slicer: $4.95, item #616653, Cooking.com (800-663-8810, **www.cooking.com**).
• Amco Rub-A-Way Bar: $6.95, item #B000FOJUJY, Amazon (866-216-1072, **www.amazon.com**).
• Chef'n GarlicZoom XL: $14.99, item #003848501191, Chef Central (**www.chefcentral.com**).

PAGE 14: PASTA FORK
• OXO Nylon Spaghetti Server: $6.99, item #1190900, OXO (800-545-4411, **www.oxo.com**).

PAGE 27: SAUTÉ PANS
• Viking Stainless 7-Ply 3-Quart Sauté Pan: $219.95, item #VK-VSC0303, MetroKitchen (888-892-9911, **www.metrokitchen.com**).
• Cuisinart MultiClad Pro Triple-Ply 3½-Quart Sauté Pan: $79.95, item #2201, Chef's Catalog (800-338-3232, **www.chefscatalog.com**).

PAGE 32: ESPRESSO MAKER
• Presso Espresso Machine: $150, Presso USA (810-643-1800, **www.presso.us**).

PAGE 32: INDUCTION INTERFACE DISK
• Max Burton Induction Interface Disk: $48.95, item #07-1949, Chef Tools (206-933-0700, **www.cheftools.com**).

PAGE 32: MINI COLANDER
• Progressive International Collapsible Mini Colander: $6.13, item #CC-6G, Amazon.

PAGE 32: RECIPE HOLDER
• Recipe Rock by Architec: $9.99, item #832277011546, Kitchen & Company (800-458-2616, **www.thekitchenstore.com**).

INDEX
March & April 2012

Filipino Chicken Adobo, 7

French Potato Casserole, 20

Cinnamon Swirl Bread, 23

Spaghetti al Vino Bianco, 14

Italian Wedding Soup, 19

Poached Fish with Sherry-Tomato Vinaigrette, 13

Peanut Butter Sandwich Cookies, 25

Sichuan Stir-Fried Pork in Garlic Sauce, 11

Almond Granola with Dried Fruit, 9

Philly Cheesesteaks, 15

AMERICA'S TEST KITCHEN
Public television's most popular cooking show

Join the millions of home cooks who watch our show,
America's Test Kitchen, on public television every week.
For more information, including recipes and program
times, visit www.AmericasTestKitchenTV.com.

AMERICA'S TEST KITCHEN RADIO

Tune in to our new radio program featuring answers
to listener call-in questions, ingredient taste test and
equipment review segments, and in-depth reporting
on a variety of topics. To listen to episodes, visit
www.AmericasTestKitchen.com/Radio.

DOWNLOAD OUR FREE
Cook's Illustrated iPhone App

Features a collection of our top recipes, along with
tastings, videos, and useful timer and shopping list features.
CooksIllustrated.com members can access 19 years of
recipes, videos, tastings, and more. Go to
www.CooksIllustrated.com/iPhone.

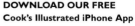

PHOTOGRAPHY: CARL TREMBLAY; STYLING: MARIE PIRAINO, CATRINE KELTY

Mussels

Sea Snails

Cockles

Sea Scallop

Oysters

Whelk

Razor Clams

Littleneck Clams

MOLLUSKS

NUMBER 116

MAY & JUNE 2012

COOK'S
ILLUSTRATED

Spice-Rubbed Grilled Steaks
This Rub Stays on the Steak

Our Favorite Quick Tips

Spicy Pork Tacos
Bold Flavors, Tender Pork

Perfect Chicken Salad
Most Tender Chicken Ever?

Rating Hot Sauces
More than Just Heat

Carrot Layer Cake
Old Favorite Gets Dressed Up

Italian-Style Ratatouille
Testing Box Graters
Homemade Fresh Pasta
Great Crab Cakes
Chinese Chicken Wraps
Easy Indian Flatbread

www.CooksIllustrated.com
$5.95 U.S./$6.95 CANADA

0 74470 62805 7

0 6>

CONTENTS

May & June 2012

COOK'S ILLUSTRATED

Founder and Editor **Christopher Kimball**
Editorial Director **Jack Bishop**
Executive Editor, Magazines **John Willoughby**
Executive Editor **Amanda Agee**
Test Kitchen Director **Erin McMurrer**
Managing Editor **Rebecca Hays**
Senior Editors **Keith Dresser**
Lisa McManus
Associate Features Editors **Elizabeth Bomze**
Danette St. Onge
Copy Editors **Nell Beram**
Megan Chromik
Associate Editors **Andrea Geary**
Amy Graves
Andrew Janjigian
Dan Souza
Test Cook **Lan Lam**
Assistant Editors **Hannah Crowley**
Shannon Friedmann Hatch
Taizeth Sierra
Assistant Test Cook **Celeste Rogers**
Executive Assistant **Christine Gordon**
Assistant Test Kitchen Director **Gina Nistico**
Test Kitchen Manager **Leah Rovner**
Senior Kitchen Assistant **Meryl MacCormack**
Kitchen Assistants **Maria Elena Delgado**
Ena Gudiel
Andrew Straaberg Finfrock
Executive Producer **Melissa Baldino**
Associate Producer **Stephanie Stender**
Production Assistant **Kaitlin Hammond**
Contributing Editors **Matthew Card**
Dawn Yanagihara
Consulting Editor **Scott Brueggeman**
Science Editor **Guy Crosby, Ph.D.**
Managing Editor, Web **Christine Liu**
Online Associate Editors **Eric Grzymkowski**
Mari Levine
Senior Video Editor **Nick Dakoulas**

Design Director **Amy Klee**
Art Director **Julie Cote**
Deputy Art Director **Susan Levin**
Associate Art Director **Lindsey Timko**
Deputy Art Director, Marketing/Web **Erica Lee**
Designers, Marketing/Web **Elaina Natario**
Mariah Tarvainen
Staff Photographer **Daniel J. van Ackere**
Online Photo Editor **Steve Klise**

Vice President, Marketing **David Mack**
Circulation Director **Doug Wicinski**
Circulation & Fulfillment Manager **Carrie Fethe**
Partnership Marketing Manager **Pamela Putprush**
Marketing Assistant **Lauren Perkins**
Customer Service Manager **Jacqueline Valerio**
Customer Service Representatives **Jessica Amato**
Morgan Ryan

Chief Operations Officer **David Dinnage**
Production Director **Guy Rochford**
Senior Project Manager **Alice Carpenter**
Project Manager **Kate Hux**
Asset & Workflow Manager **Andrew Mannone**
Production & Imaging Specialists **Judy Blomquist**
Heather Dube
Lauren Pettapiece
Technology Director **Rocco Lombardo**
Systems Administrator **Marcus Walser**
Development Manager **Robert Martinez**
Software Project Manager **Michelle Rushin**
Business Analyst **Wendy Tseng**
Web Developers **Chris Candelora**
Cameron MacKensie
Human Resources Director **Adele Shapiro**

VP New Media Product Development **Barry Kelly**
Social Media Manager **Steph Yiu**

Chief Financial Officer **Sharyn Chabot**
Director of Sponsorship Sales **Anne Traficante**
Retail Sales & Marketing Director **Emily Logan**
Client Services Manager **Bailey Snyder**
Publicity **Deborah Broide**

BANANAS Of the hundreds of cultivars of banana, the Cavendish variety is the type most commonly found in American supermarkets. Finger-size bananas, labeled baby, mini, or *niño*, look like shrunken Cavendishes with deep yellow flesh, thin skin, and, when ripe, a floral sweetness. The stocky burro—also referred to as Orinoco—is best eaten when the skin is golden with brown speckles. Expect lemon undertones and a creamy texture. Manzanos and red bananas also offer prominent fruity aftertastes—apple and raspberry, respectively—and are best when very ripe. Thai *nam wah* bananas can be eaten out of hand, but their firmer flesh also withstands cooking. They are traditionally battered and fried, or simmered in coconut milk. Plantains are typically fried, baked, or boiled and can be prepared at all stages of ripeness. When still green, their flesh is dense and starchy; as the fruit ripens, it turns softer and sweeter.

COVER (Lettuce): Robert Papp; BACK COVER (Bananas): John Burgoyne

RECIPES THAT WORK®

America's Test Kitchen is a very real 2,500-square-foot kitchen located just outside of Boston. It is the home of *Cook's Illustrated* and *Cook's Country* magazines and is the workday destination of more than three dozen test cooks, editors, and cookware specialists. Our mission is to test recipes over and over again until we understand how and why they work and until we arrive at the best version. We also test kitchen equipment and supermarket ingredients in search of brands that offer the best value and performance. You can watch us work by tuning in to *America's Test Kitchen* (www.AmericasTestKitchenTV.com) on public television.

CHILDISH THINGS

I am a preachy type and so, for years, I have occasionally acted as lay minister at our small Methodist church. The steepled white clapboard building is located next to Green River Farm, our family's former homestead where we raised pigs and Angus. I wasn't sure why my mother (she was our farmer in chief) chose to pair those two animals until the day that she cooked a hamburger made from half Angus and half pork sausage. I saw the light.

Midweek before my annual sermon, I grabbed a Bible and the Methodist hymnbook and tried to fashion a narrative, one that would make sense to a group of locals as well as flatlanders. A few phrases kept reappearing in my sermons, including this famous line from 1 Corinthians: "When I became a man, I put away childish things."

Despite my homilies, I never did put away childish things. As a towheaded youngster, I spent summers walking the woods of our town, from Minister to Swearing Hill, from Red to Egg Mountain, and from the cave up in Beartown to the one just off of Bentley Road that you could have driven a truck through, if you could only figure out how to get it in there in the first place. I usually carried a 22 because Vermonters never walk the woods without a rifle and so I took potshots at crows, grouse, and woodchucks, mostly in vain. Most of all, my expeditions were much like those of Tom Sawyer: rummaging around old cellar holes; pocketing handmade 20 penny nails found in abandoned barns; and exploring post-WWII Chevys, finding mattress springs tattered and naked in the back seat and rabbits living under the hood.

My sister, Kate, and I had our own private Narnia, an unexplored map of swamps, hollows, peaks, and high pastures, with Woodards, Bentleys, Skidmores, Hurds, and Woodcocks printed on mailboxes and with sheep fencing and barbed wire high up off the valleys, where dense stands of poplar, birch, oak, and maple had taken back the pastures of an older generation. To the remaining local farmers, it may have been a hard life but it was a child's world in the woods where one might peek out from the undergrowth and see a doe with an hours-old fawn learning to stand; a red fox, tail straight back, trotting briskly across a horse pasture; or a helix of humming bees two stories high, floating slowly above the long grasses of August on their way to a new home in the distant woods.

The beauty of childhood is that there is eternal mystery in the undiscovered. Kate and I could stumble into a new universe by standing in a small, cold brook, scooping up a salamander-length crayfish; by exploring abandoned tar-paper hunting shacks with Ball jars of ancient specimens; by watching a roly-poly porcupine waddling through a pine forest; or by surprising a brindled bobcat standing tall in the middle of the dirt road just past one of the best fishing holes in the Green River.

Perhaps Paul, who was a prolific author and endless font of advice for early Christian communities, meant something different by "childish things" in his missive to the Corinthians. Nobody is suggesting that we abandon the usual hallmarks of adult behavior, including the notions of personal responsibility, the benefits of long-term thinking, and one's debt to society.

A few lucky adults, however, are able to figure out which bits of childhood are worth keeping and which to discard. These are folks who have open,

Christopher Kimball

youthful faces, who are quick to laugh at themselves, and who are happy to stand up to life's iniquities with good humor and resolve. They are also able to see transcendence through the gauzy curtain of everyday life, whether in the crazed yipping of coyotes on a moonless night or when standing in midtown Manhattan, watching the ebb and flow.

Years ago I wrote about a neighbor whom I had interviewed a few weeks before her death. It was a cool Sunday afternoon in early May. We sat on her deck overlooking the garden with tumbles of large rocks, each of which had a particular history. Farther afield was a small orchard, the apple blossoms pink with ripe buds. I remember small things from that day: attaching a small black microphone to her sweater, the sound of the scruffy wind in the earphones, and the weathered gray of the old barn that had been turned into a sauna a generation before—the place where many of the town's long-standing couples first met. And, most of all, the light in her eyes, the upward turn at the corners of her mouth, and a pixie childishness as she was turning life's last corner.

These two things together—light and dark—can be seen clearly only by those with a child's imagination. It reminds me of an old rock-and-roll lyric: "Your eyes looked through your mother's face." On that spring Sunday years ago, I saw the eyes of a child peering through the face of someone on the edge of death. Putting away childish things is good advice, I suppose, but to walk through the woods, or life, with the eyes of a child is the ultimate blessing.

FOR INQUIRIES, ORDERS, OR MORE INFORMATION

www.CooksIllustrated.com
At www.CooksIllustrated.com, you can order books and subscriptions, sign up for our free e-newsletter, or renew your magazine subscription. Join the website and gain access to 19 years of *Cook's Illustrated* recipes, equipment tests, and ingredient tastings, as well as companion videos for every recipe in this issue.

COOKBOOKS
We sell more than 50 cookbooks by the editors of *Cook's Illustrated*. To order, visit our bookstore at www.CooksIllustrated.com.

COOK'S ILLUSTRATED MAGAZINE
Cook's Illustrated magazine (ISSN 1068-2821), number 116, is published bimonthly by Boston Common Press Limited partnership, 17 Station St., Brookline, MA 02445. Copyright 2012 Boston Common Press Limited Partnership. Periodicals postage paid at Boston, Mass., and additional mailing offices, USPS #012487. Publications Mail Agreement No. 40020778. Return undeliverable Canadian addresses to P.O. Box 875, Station A, Windsor, ON N9A 6P2. POSTMASTER: Send address changes to *Cook's Illustrated*, P.O. Box 6018, Harlan, IA 51593-1518. For subscription and gift subscription orders, subscription inquiries, or change-of-address notices, visit us at www.AmericasTestKitchen.com/customerservice, call us at 800-526-8442 or write us at *Cook's Illustrated*, P.O. 6018, Harlan, IA 51593-1518.

FOR LIST RENTAL INFORMATION Contact Specialists Marketing Services, Inc., 777 Terrace Ave., 4th Floor, Hasbrouck Heights, NJ 07604; 201-865-5800.
EDITORIAL OFFICE 17 Station St., Brookline, MA 02445; 617-232-1000; fax 617-232-1572. Subscription inquiries, visit www.AmericasTestKitchen.com/customerservice or call 800-526-8442.
POSTMASTER Send all new orders, subscription inquiries, and change-of-address notices to *Cook's Illustrated*, P.O. Box 6018, Harlan, IA 51593-1518.

≽ BY ANDREA GEARY & DAN SOUZA ≼

Troubleshooting Boiled Eggs

My hard-cooked eggs are sometimes underdone in the center of the yolk even when I use your "foolproof" recipe (March/April 2003). Where could I be going wrong?

KATE CHUPREVICH
BROOKLYN, N.Y.

☛After boiling hundreds of eggs, we stand behind our method: Place eggs (large, extra-large, or jumbo) in a single layer in a saucepan, cover with cold water so that the water level measures 1 inch above the tops of the eggs, and bring to a boil over high heat. Remove the pan from the heat, cover, and let it sit for 10 minutes. Transfer the eggs to an ice bath for five minutes and then peel.

Because the eggs cook via residual heat—an extremely gentle method—the whites should emerge fully set but still tender with yolks that are uniformly opaque but not chalky and without green rings around their edges (a sign of overcooking). This is because the eggs are exposed to the greatest heat for a short time at the beginning of the process when overcooking is not a danger. As time passes, the temperature of the water gradually drops and the cooking process slows and eventually halts after 10 minutes, when the water is too cool to cook the eggs any further. (The ice bath doesn't stop the cooking; it simply chills the eggs for easier peeling.)

If your eggs turn out underdone, it is either because the saucepan and its contents are not getting hot enough initially or they are not retaining sufficient heat. To reach the proper starting temperature, make sure the water has come to an actual boil (large bubbles rapidly breaking the surface) before removing the saucepan from the heat and covering it. To properly retain heat, be sure to use a saucepan with a snug-fitting lid so the water will not cool too quickly, and use the proper amount of water—too little and the temperature will drop too quickly (leaving your eggs undercooked); too much and the temperature will not drop quickly enough (overcooking the eggs). Finally, it is important that the water be cold initially. Warm water won't take as long to boil, which will shorten the time that your eggs are exposed to heat.

Learn Online at Our Cooking School

Want to master egg cookery with the help of a test kitchen expert? Our staff is offering personalized instruction in more than 100 subjects, including classic French omelets and Italian frittatas. Learn how to poach, fry, scramble, and more. Visit **www.TestKitchenSchool.com.**

Old-School Ice Cream

I'm always curious when I see old-fashioned ice and rock salt ice-cream makers for sale. How do they measure up to today's modern machines?

HAYFORD PIERCE
TUCSON, ARIZ.

☛We compared two old-fashioned makers (one hand-cranked model, one motorized) with our favorite automatic machines (the Whynter SNÖ Professional Ice Cream Maker and the Cuisinart Automatic Frozen Yogurt–Ice Cream & Sorbet Maker). We churned vanilla ice cream in each and tasted for density and iciness.

All four batches exhibited similar levels of iciness, but density, which depends on how much air is incorporated into the ice cream base, was a different story. Because the motorized rock salt machine turned the mixing paddle faster than the other machines, it whipped in more air and produced a relatively light, fluffy batch of ice cream. The manual machine was difficult to churn at an even clip for 30 minutes; as a result, its ice cream tended to be more dense than the motorized version's. However, since both old-fashioned models required adding ice and rock salt multiple

RETRO ICE CREAM?
Old-fashioned electric models produce a lighter, fluffier ice cream than modern machines.

times during the churning process, we're sticking with the automatic machines, which produced consistently dense results with no tinkering.

Any Port in a Storm?

I often stock tawny port in my liquor cabinet because I like to drink it. Can I substitute tawny port for the ruby variety in a recipe?

JAMIE HARVEY
GREENVILLE, S.C.

☛The difference between tawny and ruby port lies in the aging process. Before it is bottled, tawny port spends at least two years (and as many as 40 years) in wooden barrels, where it picks up a caramel color and toasty, nutty flavors. Ruby port, on the other hand, is typically aged for only two years and spends little or no time in wood, so it retains a vibrant red color and possesses a more straightforward, fruity character. Ruby port is generally used in cooking for two reasons: First, it tends to be less expensive than tawny, and second, its brilliant red hue is thought to add visual appeal. When we sampled each kind of port on its own, the differences were apparent, but would they be so obvious when each wine was used in a recipe?

In caramelized onions, a pan sauce, and raspberry sorbet, we found that the nuances of flavor we had noted in the tawny port were pretty much lost in cooking or—in the case of the sorbet—obscured by the assertive berry flavor. And the color difference ended up not making such a difference after all; each of the finished dishes boasted a lovely rosy color.

The bottom line: If you don't mind sacrificing some of your expensive tipple, go ahead and use tawny port instead of ruby.

Garlic Safety

You've noted in previous issues that because of the risk of botulism, garlic can't be safely stored in oil for more than 24 hours. What about vinaigrettes made with garlic?

JULIE OTIS
BELLEVILLE, ONTARIO

☛To answer your question, we consulted Dr. Linda Harris, associate director of the U.C. Davis Western Institute for Food Safety and Security. According to Dr. Harris, homemade vinaigrettes that contain garlic don't present a botulism poisoning risk because the acid in vinegar inhibits bacterial growth, particularly if the oil and vinegar separate so that the garlic is sitting in vinegar alone. For added safety, said Harris, the dressing can be stored refrigerated. The same advice holds true for vinaigrettes made with other flavoring ingredients that can potentially harbor botulism spores, like shallots and fresh herbs.

Quality, though, is a different issue. We found that a simple vinaigrette made with ⅓ cup of vinegar, 1 cup of oil, and 1 teaspoon of minced garlic only lasted for 24 hours in the refrigerator before the garlic started to taste "pickled."

IN A PICKLE
Botulism isn't a concern when garlic is an ingredient in vinaigrette.

Papaya Puzzle

Is the crunchy fruit used to make Thai green papaya salad a different fruit from the soft orange papaya you find at the supermarket?

KELLY JACKSON
GRAND RAPIDS, MICH.

➤ Though very different in taste, texture, and appearance, green and orange papaya are actually the same fruit picked at different stages of development. The tender, creamy, orange-fleshed papaya is harvested when fully mature (though the exterior may still be green). Tasters described it as "sweet," "melon-y," and even somewhat "cheesy." Because it is very low in acid, it is often spritzed with lime juice to provide balance.

Immature green papaya has crisp white flesh with very little flavor. It is prized mostly for its crunch and used primarily as a base for salads, most notably in the Thai classic *som tam*, where it serves as a bland backdrop for the powerful flavors of chile, lime, garlic, and fish sauce. Tasters characterized green papaya as "clean-tasting" and "like cucumber or jícama"; in fact, jícama and seeded cucumber make good substitutes if green papaya is unavailable.

GREEN PAPAYA
The firm white flesh of green papaya comes from the same fruit as orange papaya—it just hasn't ripened.

Freezing Gnocchi

I love your recipe for Potato Gnocchi (September/October 2011). Can the gnocchi be frozen for a quick weeknight meal?

STEPHANIE B. LINDSAY
NEW YORK, N.Y.

➤ When we froze a batch of gnocchi as soon as they were formed, the frozen dumplings feathered apart in boiling water. We tried again, air-drying the dumplings until a thin skin formed on their surfaces and then freezing. That did the trick: The strengthened gnocchi held their shape beautifully and cooked as well as fresh ones.

To freeze gnocchi, place them on a heavily floured parchment-lined baking sheet and let them air-dry at room temperature for at least one hour and up to four hours. Transfer the baking sheet to the freezer; freeze the gnocchi until solid, about 45 minutes; and then place the frozen pieces in a zipper-lock bag and store in the freezer for up to one month. Cook the frozen gnocchi straight from the freezer as directed in the recipe (they will take slightly longer to float—indicating that they are done cooking—than fresh).

ILLUSTRATION: JOHN BURGOYNE

WHAT IS IT?

I found this medieval-looking tool in the kitchen drawer of an old house. Do you know what it is?

ZAK DAY
OCEANSIDE, CALIF.

HOLDING STEADY
This vintage roast holder is our new favorite carving tool.

Your item is a roast holder made by Carvel Hall Cutlery. The chrome-plated tool, which was invented in 1947, was designed to aid in carving large cuts of meat, such as ham, turkey, and, of course, roasts. As the device's patent states, the four ½-inch spikes stabilize the meat, thus preventing it from "slipping or twisting or oscillating" during slicing, and the tines at the front help with serving the slices. We tested it on a 15-pound country ham and were impressed: Typically we steady meat with a carving fork or tongs during slicing, but it still wobbles slightly with each cut. The roast holder's wide base did a better job of securely locking the ham in place, and the handle was comfortable to grasp.

Temperature Shock on Beer

Unless I know I'm going to have room to refrigerate it, I never buy chilled beer because I've heard that temperature changes can cause it to develop the off-flavors and aromas associated with "skunked" beer. Is this true?

MIKAELA BLOOMBERG
SAN FRANCISCO, CALIF.

➤ We knew from our beer storage experiment (July/August 2011) that buying and keeping beer cold helps preserve its fresh taste, but we were also curious to see if so-called temperature abuse can produce off-flavors. To find out, we purchased a case of chilled beer (in cans to avoid any issues of light exposure) and divided the contents into two groups. Half of the cans went into the refrigerator as a control, while we subjected the others to significant temperature fluctuations: three hours in an 85-degree water bath, followed by an overnight chill. After repeating the "shock" process three times, we tasted both batches of beer side by side.

As it turned out, no one noticed a skunk flavor in either sample. We also spoke with David Grinnel, vice president of brewing quality at Boston Beer Company, who confirmed that skunked beer flavors and aromas are the result of light exposure, not temperature fluctuations. So buy your beer in cans or dark bottles and don't be afraid to buy it chilled, even if you won't be able to keep it cold once you get it home.

DID YOU KNOW? All products reviewed by America's Test Kitchen, home of *Cook's Illustrated* and *Cook's Country* magazines, are independently chosen, researched, and reviewed by our editors. We buy products for testing at retail locations and do not accept unsolicited samples for testing. We do not accept or receive payment or consideration from product manufacturers or retailers. Manufacturers and retailers are not told in advance of publication which products we have recommended. We list suggested sources for recommended products as a convenience to our readers but do not endorse specific retailers.

Fro Yo

Can leftover yogurt be successfully frozen?

GINGER IRVINE
PORT ALSWORTH, ALASKA

➤ To find out, we froze plain yogurt—whole milk, low-fat, and nonfat—for two nights, after which we defrosted it in the refrigerator. We used the thawed yogurt in plain muffins and uncooked yogurt sauce and compared them with samples prepared with never-frozen yogurt. All of the muffins were identical in appearance, taste, and texture, but the previously frozen yogurt produced sauces that were markedly runny and slightly broken in appearance.

Here's why: When milk is heated to make yogurt, its proteins coagulate to form a weak gel that traps the water and fat. But as ice crystals form during freezing, water is drawn away from the protein network, causing the gel to weaken or even collapse. Once thawed, the protein network does not re-form, explaining our thin, separated results.

Some brands of commercial yogurt contain added stabilizers such as pectin that reinforce the protein network and, as a result, may fare better when frozen. But to avoid any problems, we recommend that you use thawed yogurt only for baking applications.

CURDLED YOGURT
Freezing breaks down yogurt, making it unusable in uncooked applications like this sauce. (It's fine for baking.)

SEND US YOUR QUESTIONS We will provide a complimentary one-year subscription for each letter we print. Send your inquiry, name, address, and daytime telephone number to Notes from Readers, *Cook's Illustrated*, P.O. Box 470589, Brookline, MA 02447, or to NotesFromReaders@AmericasTestKitchen.com.

Quick Tips

≥ COMPILED BY SHANNON FRIEDMANN HATCH ≤

Slow-Flow Oil

A drizzle of highly flavored oil like truffle oil or toasted sesame oil can add character and complexity to a dish, but if too much accidentally gushes from the bottle, it can also ruin it. To prevent this, Ning Zhou of Brooklyn, N.Y., holds a chopstick across the bottle opening with its tip pointed toward the food as she pours—the oil travels along the length of the chopstick in a thin stream, making it easier to control the flow.

Cabinet Pot Rack

Wall- or ceiling-mounted racks and railings are a great storage solution for pots and pans, but not every kitchen can accommodate them. Smiley Nesbitt of Vancouver, British Columbia, converted a corner cabinet into a catchall for her cookware by removing the shelves and attaching hooks to the underside of the cabinet's top. Lids stack neatly beneath the hanging pots and pans.

A Safer Way to Pit Avocados

A popular trick for pitting an avocado calls for inserting a chef's knife into the stone of the halved fruit and twisting the avocado's base to remove the tough core. Wary of the knife's sharp blade, Stephen Quandt of New York, N.Y., instead turns to his waiter's corkscrew. The tool securely (and safely) hooks into the pit and can then be easily pulled out.

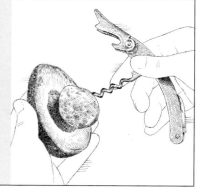

Giving Sauces the Squeeze

Dispensing condiments like sour cream at a party can get messy—globs end up on the tabletop and serving spoons inevitably travel from one bowl to another. Holly Devine of New York, N.Y., sets out toppings in clear plastic squeeze bottles, simplifying serving and cleanup.

Cleaning Bottleneck Containers

Narrow-mouthed bottleneck containers require a long, slim brush to reach the bottom and clean the interior. In lieu of purchasing a specialized tool, Johnny Bootlace of Seattle, Wash., adds a handful of uncooked rice, water, and dish soap to the bottle, covers the top, and shakes vigorously. The grains' friction against the sides loosens any grime and offers a nearly scrub-free solution.

A Better Way to Grease the Grill

Finding himself out of paper towels one day, Duane Hellums of Louisville, Ky., used some standard coffee filters to oil his grill grate. He found that the sturdy filter paper was less apt to tear or leave behind fuzz, and—since it's less absorbent than paper towels—he can get the job done using less oil.

SEND US YOUR TIPS We will provide a complimentary one-year subscription for each tip we print. Send your tip, name, and address to Quick Tips, *Cook's Illustrated*, P.O. Box 470589, Brookline, MA 02447, or to QuickTips@AmericasTestKitchen.com.

ILLUSTRATION: JOHN BURGOYNE

A Hard Nut to Crack

Mary Bowman of Beaverton, Ore., uses this crackerjack method to shell stubborn, barely open pistachios. Holding the nut in one hand, insert the tip of a pistachio-shell half into the opening. Twist the shell half 90 degrees in either direction, or until the closed nut pops open.

Caramelized Onions at the Ready

Martha Cunningham of San Francisco, Calif., often uses caramelized onions to lend a complex, earthy sweetness to many dishes, including burgers, focaccia, and mashed potatoes. But since they can take upwards of an hour to make, she came up with a way to ensure that there's always a stash on hand.

1. Make a large batch and portion the onions into zipper-lock freezer bags, rolling them from the bottom up to expel as much air as possible.

2. Seal the bags and store them in the freezer, where they will keep for up to 3 months.

Shoo-In Solution for Spice Storage

In a small kitchen, it can be hard to find enough room for an extensive collection of spices and herbs. For quick and easy access that frees up counter, cabinet, and drawer space, Laura Major of Paonia, Colo., keeps her stash in the pockets of an over-the-door organizer designed for shoes.

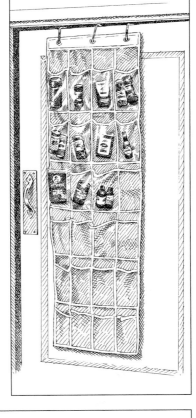

No-Slip Dish Towel

The oven door handle is a convenient place to hang kitchen towels, but the smooth bar offers little traction and the cloth often slips off and falls to the floor. Ed Bindon of Fairfax, Va., devised this simple fix:

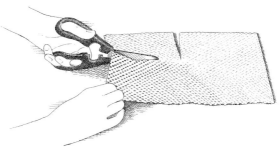

1. Cut a sheet of nonslip shelf liner about 5 inches wide and long enough to wrap around the handle of your oven.

2. Wrap the liner around the oven handle and secure it with double-sided tape; hang the towel over the liner.

Quick-Measure Salad Dressing

Rather than dirty her measuring cups, spoons, and whisk every time she wants to make her favorite vinaigrette, Elizabeth Zeller Montgomery of Brooklyn, N.Y., came up with this practical solution. Separately measure out the oil and vinegar (we like a 3:1 ratio) and then pour them into a clear plastic bottle, using a permanent-ink pen to mark the level of the mixture after you've added each ingredient. As long as you keep the bottle, you'll never again have to dirty a measuring cup or spoon for these components. Add any solid ingredients (such as garlic, herbs, or mustard), close the bottle, and shake it until the dressing is thoroughly mixed. The bottle can be washed and reused for easier mixing next time.

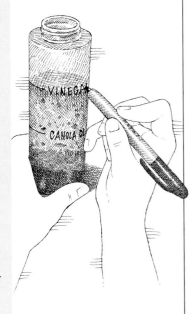

Six-Pack Chillin'

Since he doesn't have enough space in his refrigerator to store bottled beverages upright, Matt Jaffe of Providence, R.I., has found a clever way to store them horizontally, without them rolling around: He fastens a large binder clip around two wires of one of the shelves (from below) and stacks the drinks next to it in a pyramid. The clip holds everything in place, and it can easily be moved right or left to support more or fewer bottles.

Spice-Rubbed Steak on the Grill

Done wrong, this dish resembles a dusty old boot. But apply some science with your rub and it's a bold way to dress up a less expensive cut.

> BY ANDREA GEARY

As a dedicated practitioner of the silk-purse-out-of-a-sow's-ear approach to cooking, I enjoy the challenge of transforming inexpensive ingredients into a memorable meal. But I've always conceded that when it comes to grilled steaks, there's no way around it: You get what you pay for.

With their tender texture and big-time beef flavor, pricey cuts from the middle of the steer (like rib eyes and T-bones) need little more than salt, pepper, and a few minutes over a hot fire to render them impressive. Try that minimalist technique on cheaper steaks from farther down the animal (the sirloin and the round) and you get meat that's chewy and dry, with flavors that veer toward liver-y and gamy. It's probably these flavor and texture challenges that inspire cooks to take a page from the barbecue manual and apply spice rubs to less expensive steaks. Unfortunately, in my experience that approach doesn't really work. Because cheap steaks exude little fat to bond with the spices, the rub tends to fall off in chunks. If by some stroke of luck the rub remains intact, it usually tastes dry and dusty, plus nuances of flavor can vaporize over the fire.

Still, my skinflint tendencies aren't easily subdued. Surely there was a way to create a recipe for inexpensive grilled steak that was also tender and juicy, with a flavorful, crunchy crust that stayed in place.

Calling All Glutamates

First I had to find a steak that provided the best taste and texture for the money, so I looked to the sirloin and the round, settling on what we here in New England call the shell sirloin steak (for alternate names see the recipe headnote). Tasters described the shell steak as having a relatively beefy taste, unlike cuts from the round, which were liver-y.

Salting the shell steaks before cooking was a given. Salt sprinkled liberally on the surface of the meat draws moisture from inside, which over time is then reabsorbed as the meat sits, seasoning it and changing

Crosshatch scoring helps the crisp spice crust stay on the meat.

the structure of the muscle fibers so that they hold on to more juices. But I'd have to do more than that to close the gap between a $6 steak and a $12 steak. Some recipes suggest that allowing a spice rub to sit on the meat for a period of time enables its flavors to be absorbed for more complex-tasting results. Science, however, refutes this: Most flavor compounds in spices are fat-soluble rather than water-soluble, so they can't penetrate below the surface of the steak. Furthermore, in tests of marinades, we've found that other than salt, the only water-soluble flavor compounds that can travel deep into the meat are glutamates.

So, what about glutamates? Scanning my pantry, I singled out two of the most potent sources of these compounds: tomato paste and—odd as it may sound—fish sauce, a condiment that we've called upon in other unlikely applications to amp up savory taste. I applied a rub made with kosher salt and a couple of teaspoons each of these two ingredients (to compensate for their extra sodium I cut back a little on the salt) and applied it to a set of steaks an hour before grilling. The difference in these steaks was remarkable: They boasted a much deeper flavor without any trace of my secret enhancements. Spurred by this success, I decided to add ½ teaspoon

each of garlic powder and onion powder to the rub. Though neither substance contains significant levels of glutamates, their water-soluble flavors are potent enough (especially in concentrated powdered form) that even if they penetrated only ¼ inch into the meat, they might make a difference in the overall flavor. Tasters confirmed that my hunch was correct: The steaks treated with the powdered alliums along with salt, tomato paste, and fish sauce had noticeably richer flavor. On to the spice rub.

Spicing Things Up

My plan was to treat the steak with the salt-and-glutamate-packed paste first, wait an hour, and then apply a second, more conventional dry rub right before grilling. I tried a variety of rubs, but I found that those made mostly with dried herbs lost their flavor, while those based on spices fared better. It turns out that the flavors in herbs like rosemary, sage, and thyme fade in the intense heat of the grill, but the compounds in certain spices do much better, particularly those containing capsaicin—namely, peppers, chiles, and paprika. Thus, rubs made predominantly from chile or pepper were clearly the way to go.

First I tried rubs made with preground spices, but these formed a coating that was more pasty than crunchy. Since I had some time to spare between applying the salty glutamate rub and firing up the grill, I tried toasting some whole spices (cumin, coriander, red pepper flakes, and black peppercorns) in a skillet along with some earthy-tasting dried New Mexican chiles, and then I ground them coarsely in a coffee grinder. To round out the flavors, I also incorporated sugar, paprika, and ground cloves before pressing the rub onto the surface of the steak.

Tasters pronounced these steaks juicy, tender, and flavorful, and they greatly preferred the more robust texture of this home-ground rub. Still, there were two problems to be solved. First, despite the toasting step, the spices retained a slightly raw taste, the result of being cooked with very little fat, so the flavors couldn't "bloom." Second, tasters requested a more substantial crust. I sheepishly informed them that there had been more rub when I started grilling, but half of it had been left on the cooking grate. Clearly, I needed to find a way to help the spices stick to the steak and not to the grate.

PHOTOGRAPHY: CARL TREMBLAY

I remembered when a coworker who was developing a recipe for pan-fried pork chops had difficulty persuading the breading to adhere to the meat. He eventually came up with the clever solution of making shallow cuts into the meat to give the breading more purchase. Doing the same with my steaks before adding the first rub seemed likely to be doubly advantageous: It would increase the surface area, which could give that first rub more opportunity to really get into the meat, plus it could help the spice rub stick to the meat.

As I liberally greased the cooking grate in preparation for grilling my newly crosshatched steaks, I wished that there were some way to put a layer of oil on the steaks themselves without disturbing their spice crust (which—I was pleased to see—was sticking quite nicely). The easy solution: A light spritz of vegetable oil spray or oil from a mister helped the steaks keep their rub intact through the grilling process.

These steaks were crusty and crunchy on the outside, with just enough heat and spice to complement the meat's rich flavor, and that little bit of added fat imparted by the spray gave the spices that fully developed "bloomed" flavor that tasters were after. The tender and juicy meat belied its $5.99-per-pound price tag. My inner cheapskate quietly rejoiced.

STEP BY STEP | A STAY-PUT SPICE RUB THAT TURNS CHEAPER STEAK INTO "CHOICE"

SCORE MEAT
Shallow slits cut into the steak help the salt paste and spice rub adhere to the meat and penetrate more deeply.

APPLY PASTE
A paste of onion and garlic powders, salt, tomato paste, and fish sauce boosts beefy flavor and tenderizes the meat.

APPLY SPICE RUB
Toasting then grinding dried chiles and spices leads to a more substantial crust with complex flavor.

SPRAY WITH OIL
A light misting of oil blooms the spices on the grill and helps the rub cling to the meat.

GRILLED STEAK WITH NEW MEXICAN CHILE RUB
SERVES 6 TO 8

Shell sirloin steak is also known as top butt, butt steak, top sirloin butt, top sirloin steak, and center-cut roast. Spraying the rubbed steaks with oil helps the spices bloom, preventing a raw flavor.

Steak
- 2 teaspoons tomato paste
- 2 teaspoons fish sauce
- 1½ teaspoons kosher salt
- ½ teaspoon onion powder
- ½ teaspoon garlic powder
- 2 (1½- to 1¾-pound) boneless shell sirloin steaks, 1 to 1¼ inches thick

Spice Rub
- 2 dried New Mexican chiles, stemmed, seeded, and flesh torn into ½-inch pieces
- 4 teaspoons cumin seeds
- 4 teaspoons coriander seeds
- ½ teaspoon red pepper flakes
- ½ teaspoon black peppercorns
- 1 tablespoon sugar
- 1 tablespoon paprika
- ¼ teaspoon ground cloves
  Vegetable oil spray

1. FOR THE STEAK: Combine tomato paste, fish sauce, salt, onion powder, and garlic powder in bowl. Pat steaks dry with paper towels. With sharp knife, cut ¹⁄₁₆-inch-deep slits on both sides of steaks, spaced ½ inch apart, in crosshatch pattern. Rub salt mixture evenly on both sides of steaks. Place steaks on wire rack set in rimmed baking sheet; let stand at room temperature for at least 1 hour. After 30 minutes, prepare grill.

2. FOR THE SPICE RUB: Toast chiles, cumin, coriander, pepper flakes, and peppercorns in 10-inch skillet over medium-low heat, stirring frequently, until just beginning to smoke, 3 to 4 minutes. Transfer to plate to cool, about 5 minutes. Grind spices in spice grinder or in mortar with pestle until coarsely ground. Transfer spices to bowl and stir in sugar, paprika, and cloves.

3A. FOR A CHARCOAL GRILL: Open bottom vent completely. Light large chimney starter mounded with charcoal briquettes (7 quarts). When top coals are partially covered with ash, pour two-thirds evenly over grill, then pour remaining coals over half of grill. Set cooking grate in place, cover, and open lid vent completely. Heat grill until hot, about 5 minutes.

3B. FOR A GAS GRILL: Turn all burners to high, cover, and heat grill until hot, about 15 minutes. Leave primary burner on high and turn other burner(s) to medium.

4. Clean and oil cooking grate. Sprinkle half of spice rub evenly over 1 side of steaks and press to adhere until spice rub is fully moistened. Lightly spray rubbed side of steak with vegetable oil spray, about 3 seconds. Flip steaks and repeat process of sprinkling with spice rub and coating with vegetable oil spray on second side.

5. Place steaks over hotter part of grill and cook until browned and charred on both sides and center registers 125 degrees for medium-rare or 130 degrees for medium, 3 to 4 minutes per side. If steaks have not reached desired temperature, move to cooler side of grill and continue to cook. Transfer steaks to clean wire rack set in rimmed baking sheet, tent loosely with aluminum foil, and let rest for 10 minutes. Slice meat thin against grain and serve.

GRILLED STEAK WITH ANCHO CHILE–COFFEE RUB

Substitute 1 dried ancho chile for New Mexican chiles, 2 teaspoons ground coffee for paprika, and 1 teaspoon cocoa powder for ground cloves.

GRILLED STEAK WITH SPICY CHIPOTLE CHILE RUB

Substitute 2 dried chipotle chiles for New Mexican chiles, 1 teaspoon dried oregano for paprika, and ½ teaspoon ground cinnamon for ground cloves.

Really Good Crab Cakes

Who says great crab cakes have to start with fresh-from-the-shell crabmeat? We wanted briny, sweet-tasting results—no matter what the starting point.

> BY LAN LAM <

It's a given that the best crab cakes are made with meat that's just been picked from the shell. But since fresh crabmeat is usually impossible to come by, I almost never make them at home. That's a shame, though, because crab cakes are relatively quick and easy to throw together: Most recipes call for simply mixing the shucked meat with aromatics, herbs, spices, and a binder like mayo or beaten egg; forming cakes and dredging them in bread crumbs; and quickly pan-frying them until they're golden brown and crisp.

But is fresh-shucked meat really the only acceptable option? As we discovered in a recent crabmeat tasting (see "Crabmeat"), a couple of brands of pasteurized crabmeat (available either canned or in the refrigerated section of most supermarkets) are surprisingly good alternatives to the fresh stuff. I decided to make it my goal to come up with the best possible crab cakes—sweet, plump meat delicately seasoned and seamlessly held together with a binder that didn't detract from the seafood flavor—regardless of whether I was starting with fresh crabmeat.

An unusual binder holds the crab cake together—and lets the clean crabmeat flavor shine through.

Milking It

The obvious first step: figuring out what type of packaged crabmeat to use. Species aside, all crabmeat is graded both by size and by the part of the crab from which it's taken. Most crab cake recipes call for plump, pricey jumbo lump or lump, while some suggest finer, flakier backfin crabmeat.

I was pretty sure my colleagues would prefer the meatier texture of jumbo lump or lump, but I made crab cakes with all three grades just to double-check. I put together a bare-bones recipe, mixing 1 pound of meat with mayonnaise and eggs, forming the mixture into eight cakes, rolling them in panko (super-crisp Japanese bread crumbs), and pan-frying them. No contest: Tasters overwhelmingly preferred the cakes made with jumbo lump or lump crabmeat. Flavor was

another matter. Not only were the binders dulling the sweet crabmeat flavor, but all three batches tasted and smelled inescapably fishy. When I mentioned the result to our science editor, he suggested soaking the meat in milk to rid it of its unpleasant fishiness. It was a great quick trick. When I submerged the crabmeat in 1 cup of milk, the fishiness washed away after just a 20-minute soak. (For more information, see "Fix for 'Fishy' Seafood," page 31.)

In a Bind

Figuring I'd solved the toughest problem, I moved on to consider more conventional crab cake decisions like flavors and binders. Celery and onion (both briefly sautéed before joining the crabmeat) plus Old Bay seasoning were classic additions that nicely rounded out the rich flavor of the crabmeat. But the flavor-muting binders were a trickier issue. Reducing and/or leaving out the mayo or egg allowed the clean crabmeat flavor to come through. However, the unfortunate (if predictable) consequence was that the binder-free batches fell apart during cooking.

Putting aside the mayo and eggs for the moment, I tried the first two out-of-the-box ideas that

came to mind: a béchamel and a panade. Unfortunately, both tests flopped. The former, a combination of milk, flour, and butter, rendered the crab mixture mushy. The latter, a thick paste made from milk and bread that's often used in meatballs, was sticky and difficult to incorporate without breaking apart the crabmeat. Even worse, the starches and dairy in both binders deadened the crab flavor just as much as the mayonnaise and eggs had.

I was feeling short on ideas when I remembered a product I had used when I worked in high-end restaurants: "Meat glue," as it's commonly referred to, is a powdered protein that some chefs use to help bind foods together. Buying this stuff was out of the question here, but what about cobbling together a hack version? I couldn't turn protein into powder, but I could puree it. More specifically, I could call on another idea from my restaurant days: a mousseline. This delicate, savory mousse is composed mainly of pureed meat or fish and just a little cream. To enhance the briny sweetness and plump bite of the crabmeat, I figured I'd use shrimp. I wouldn't need much of it, and since the shrimp would be pureed, I could use whatever size was cheapest.

To that end, I blitzed 6 ounces of shrimp in the food processor with 6 tablespoons of cream, plus the Old Bay, a little Dijon mustard, hot sauce, and fresh lemon juice for punchy flavor. As I'd hoped, the resulting mousse was a great stand-in; in fact, our science editor noted that this was a true meat glue. Pureeing the shrimp released fragments of sticky muscle proteins that delicately held the clumpy pieces of crabmeat together through the breading and cooking process. When tasters raved about the clean crab flavor that I had achieved, I knew this idea was a keeper. Their only quibble: The inside texture of the cakes was a bit too springy and bouncy, and a few stray clumps of crabmeat were falling off during cooking. Scaling back the mousse mixture by a third took care of the bounce, but pieces were still breaking off as I flipped the cakes.

Give It a Rest

I had one other, more subtle idea in mind to help make the crab cakes a bit more sturdy: briefly chilling them before cooking, which allows them to firm up,

Crab Cake Clarity

Most recipes resort to flavor-dulling binders like mayonnaise and eggs. Instead, we employ a two-step approach that enhances the meat's delicate flavor while providing just as much structure.

BIND WITH SHRIMP
A puree of shrimp and cream holds the cakes together without dulling the meat's delicate flavor.

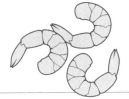

FIRM UP IN FRIDGE 40°
Resting the cakes in the refrigerator for 30 minutes helps them set.

forming a less fragile cake. I ran a side-by-side test, refrigerating one batch for a half-hour before pan-frying, while immediately cooking the other. The chill paid off: These cakes not only felt noticeably sturdier than the unrested batch but also held up considerably better during cooking.

My tasters' one lingering request concerned the breading. The panko was definitely crispier than traditional bread crumbs, but the flakes soaked up moisture from the cakes, losing some of their crunch and falling off the sides. Color was also a problem, as the only surfaces that browned nicely were those that came in contact with the pan. My two quick fixes: crushing half of the panko to make smaller pieces that would adhere better to the cakes and toasting all of the crumbs before coating to deepen and even out their color and beef up their crunch.

By starting with readily available pasteurized crabmeat and devising a few easy tricks to clean up its flavor and keep the meat neatly bound, I'd created a recipe for crab cakes that I could make even without fresh crabmeat.

BEST CRAB CAKES
SERVES 4

Fresh crabmeat will make these crab cakes taste even better. With packaged crab, if the meat smells clean and fresh when you first open the package, skip steps 1 and 4 and simply blot away any excess liquid. Serve the crab cakes with lemon wedges and our recipe for Remoulade Sauce, available free at www.CooksIllustrated.com/jun12.

- 1 pound lump crabmeat, picked over for shells
- 1 cup milk
- 1½ cups panko bread crumbs
  Salt and pepper
- 2 celery ribs, chopped
- ½ cup chopped onion
- 1 garlic clove, peeled and smashed
- 1 tablespoon unsalted butter
- 4 ounces shrimp, peeled, deveined, and tails removed
- ¼ cup heavy cream
- 2 teaspoons Dijon mustard
- ½ teaspoon hot pepper sauce
- 1 teaspoon lemon juice
- ½ teaspoon Old Bay seasoning
- 4 tablespoons vegetable oil

1. Place crabmeat and milk in bowl, making sure crab is totally submerged. Cover and refrigerate for at least 20 minutes.

2. Meanwhile, place ¾ cup panko in small zipper-lock bag and finely crush with rolling pin. Transfer crushed panko to 10-inch nonstick skillet and add remaining ¾ cup panko. Toast over medium-high heat, stirring constantly, until golden brown, about 5 minutes. Transfer panko to shallow dish and stir in ¼ teaspoon salt and pepper to taste. Wipe out skillet.

3. Pulse celery, onion, and garlic in food processor until finely chopped, 5 to 8 pulses, scraping down bowl as needed. Transfer vegetables to large bowl. Rinse processor bowl and blade and reserve. Melt butter in now-empty skillet over medium heat. Add chopped vegetables, ½ teaspoon salt, and ⅛ teaspoon pepper; cook, stirring frequently, until vegetables are softened and all moisture has evaporated, 4 to 6 minutes. Return vegetables to large bowl and let cool to room temperature. Rinse out pan and wipe clean.

4. Strain crabmeat through fine-mesh strainer, pressing firmly to remove milk but being careful not to break up lumps of crabmeat.

5. Pulse shrimp in now-empty food processor until finely ground, 12 to 15 pulses, scraping down bowl as needed. Add cream and pulse to combine, 2 to 4 pulses, scraping down bowl as needed. Transfer shrimp puree to bowl with cooled vegetables. Add mustard, hot pepper sauce, lemon juice, and Old Bay seasoning; stir until well combined. Add crabmeat and fold gently with rubber spatula, being careful not to overmix and break up lumps of crabmeat. Divide mixture into 8 balls and firmly press into ½-inch-thick patties. Place cakes on rimmed baking sheet lined with parchment paper, cover tightly with plastic wrap, and refrigerate for 30 minutes.

6. Coat each cake in panko, firmly pressing to adhere crumbs to exterior. Heat 1 tablespoon oil in now-empty skillet over medium heat until shimmering. Place 4 cakes in skillet and cook without moving them until golden brown, 3 to 4 minutes. Using 2 spatulas, carefully flip cakes, add 1 tablespoon oil, reduce heat to medium-low, and continue to cook until second side is golden brown, 4 to 6 minutes. Transfer cakes to platter. Wipe out skillet and repeat with remaining 4 cakes and remaining 2 tablespoons oil. Serve immediately.

ILLUSTRATION: JAY LAYMAN

Chinese Chicken Lettuce Wraps

Stringy, tasteless meat can mar this easy stir-fry served in lettuce cups. A classic Chinese technique came to the rescue.

≥ BY KEITH DRESSER ≤

There aren't many chain restaurant dishes that are worth making at home, but Chinese chicken lettuce wraps is one exception. Originally part of Cantonese banquet spreads, this dish (known as *sung choy bao*) was popularized in this country by places like P.F. Chang's and the Cheesecake Factory. At its best it offers tender morsels of chicken and crunchy vegetables stir-fried in a salty-sweet sauce and served in crisp lettuce cups—ideal either as an appetizer or as a light meal.

The recipes I found shared more or less the same technique: Stir-fry the chicken over high heat, add chopped vegetables, pour in the sauce and toss to coat, and spoon the mixture into Bibb lettuce leaves. I didn't bother trying recipes that called for ground chicken, since commercial ground meat is often processed so fine that it cooks up stringy and chalky. But even when I painstakingly diced the chicken breast by hand, the meat cooked up dry and bland; plus, all the sauces I tried needed a little punching up, too.

To introduce more flavor and juiciness, I soaked the chopped chicken in soy sauce and rice wine. When this step didn't do enough, I switched to chicken thighs, which boast more intramuscular fat, making them less prone to drying out when stir-fried and giving them richer, meatier flavor.

I also wondered if instead of finely (and fussily) dicing the meat by hand I could use the test kitchen's food processor method for grinding meat. This involved briefly freezing the thighs to firm them up and then pulsing them until coarsely chopped. The results? Not bad—and way faster than hand chopping. But the machine invited a new problem: Even after I froze the meat, a small amount of the chicken inevitably became overprocessed, releasing sticky meat proteins that glued the larger pieces together into chewy clumps during cooking. Tossing the chopped pieces with oil before cooking helped but also turned the dish greasy.

The idea of coating the pieces wasn't a bad one, though, and reminded me that a handful of the more traditional recipes I'd come across called for "velveting" the chicken. In this common Chinese technique, the meat is dipped into a cornstarch slurry that forms a barrier against clumping and also helps it retain moisture. I gave it a whirl, whisking a couple of teaspoons of cornstarch and a little sesame oil into the soy-wine mixture and tossing it with the processor-chopped chicken before stir-frying. This was the breakthrough I'd been hoping for. My tasters raved

about these tender, juicy, distinct bits of chicken.

The other major components—the vegetables and the aromatics—were much simpler to nail down. Most recipes include either water chestnuts or celery for crunch, but tasters agreed that using both was ideal. I also added a handful of sliced shiitake mushrooms for earthy depth and chew, along with garlic and scallions.

As for the sauce, I built complexity into the traditional oyster sauce, soy sauce, and rice wine mixture by adding toasted sesame oil, sugar, and red pepper flakes. (Per tradition, I'd also be passing salty-sweet hoisin sauce as a tableside condiment.) Spooned into the tender Bibb cups, this stir-fry was as bold and complex as it was light, and it came together in less than an hour.

CHINESE CHICKEN LETTUCE WRAPS
SERVES 4 AS A MAIN DISH OR 6 AS AN APPETIZER

To make an entrée, serve this dish with steamed white rice.

Chicken
- 1 pound boneless, skinless chicken thighs, trimmed and cut into 1-inch pieces
- 2 teaspoons Chinese rice wine or dry sherry
- 2 teaspoons soy sauce
- 2 teaspoons toasted sesame oil
- 2 teaspoons cornstarch

Sauce
- 3 tablespoons oyster sauce
- 1 tablespoon Chinese rice wine or dry sherry
- 2 teaspoons soy sauce
- 2 teaspoons toasted sesame oil
- ½ teaspoon sugar
- ¼ teaspoon red pepper flakes

Stir-Fry
- 2 tablespoons vegetable oil
- 2 celery ribs, cut into ¼-inch pieces
- 6 ounces shiitake mushrooms, stemmed and sliced thin
- ½ cup water chestnuts, cut into ¼-inch pieces
- 2 scallions, white parts minced, green parts sliced thin
- 2 garlic cloves, minced
- 1 head Bibb lettuce (8 ounces), washed and dried, leaves separated and left whole
  Hoisin sauce

A last-minute addition of scallion greens and hoisin sauce gives the stir-fry a fresh burst of flavor.

1. FOR THE CHICKEN: Place chicken pieces on large plate in single layer. Freeze meat until firm and starting to harden around edges, about 20 minutes.

2. Whisk rice wine, soy sauce, oil, and cornstarch together in bowl. Pulse half of meat in food processor until coarsely chopped into ¼- to ⅛-inch pieces, about 10 pulses. Transfer meat to bowl with rice wine mixture and repeat with remaining chunks. Toss chicken to coat and refrigerate for 15 minutes.

3. FOR THE SAUCE: Whisk all ingredients together in bowl; set aside.

4. FOR THE STIR-FRY: Heat 1 tablespoon oil in 12-inch nonstick skillet over high heat until smoking. Add chicken and cook, stirring constantly, until opaque, 3 to 4 minutes. Transfer to bowl and wipe out skillet.

5. Heat remaining 1 tablespoon oil in now-empty skillet over high heat until smoking. Add celery and mushrooms; cook, stirring constantly, until mushrooms have reduced in size by half and celery is crisp-tender, 3 to 4 minutes. Add water chestnuts, scallion whites, and garlic; cook, stirring constantly, until fragrant, about 1 minute. Whisk sauce to recombine. Return chicken to skillet; add sauce and toss to combine. Spoon into lettuce leaves and sprinkle with scallion greens. Serve, passing hoisin sauce separately.

PHOTOGRAPHY: CARL TREMBLAY

Fresh Pasta Without a Machine

Pasta made from scratch delivers eggy-rich ribbons with springy yet delicate chew.
But what if, instead of a pasta roller, you have only a rolling pin?

⋟ BY DAN SOUZA ⋞

One challenge I've always wanted to set for myself is figuring out how to make pasta with nothing more than the dough, a rolling pin, and some elbow grease. While mechanical pasta rollers aren't all that expensive, many home cooks don't own them. But as anyone who has ever attempted to roll out a block of hard pasta dough by hand knows, it's no easy task. The dough has a tendency to spring back—and if it isn't rolled out gossamer thin, the pasta will never achieve the right al dente texture when cooked. So how do Italian cooks manage to pull off this feat? One answer: years of perseverance.

In her *Essentials of Classic Italian Cooking* (1992), Marcella Hazan devotes no fewer than six pages to the classic hand-rolling technique perfected in the Emilia-Romagna region of Italy. Employing extra-thin, super-long rolling pins measuring 1½ inches in diameter and 32 inches in length, Italians in this part of the country have developed a series of stretching movements that can transform a lump of firm dough into a thin, delicate sheet. Besides the obvious drawback of needing a generous work surface to accommodate the pin, Hazan is the first to admit that this traditional technique must be exhaustively practiced "until the motions are performed through intuition rather than deliberation."

While I'm typically game for a hard-won lesson in authenticity, even I have limits. I wanted a dough that any cook could roll out with ease on the first try and that would cook up to that incomparably tender, silky yet slightly toothsome texture that makes fresh pasta so worth making.

Zero Luck

In addition to centuries of experience, Italians have another hand-rolling advantage—the best kind of flour for the job: *doppio zero*, or 00. The name denotes the fine talcum-like grind that gives pasta and baked goods made with the flour an almost creamy mouthfeel. Also important is its protein content; the brand that we used had around 9 percent. To see what I was missing, I mail-ordered some and mixed up a batch of dough following a typical approach: I put the usual ratio of 2 cups of flour to

Our carefully formulated dough and rolling technique not only make fresh pasta easy to pull off but also produce the best noodles we've ever had.

three whole eggs in a food processor and processed until they formed a cohesive ball. I then turned the dough out on the counter, kneaded it for several minutes, and set it aside to relax for about 20 minutes. Sure enough, the 00 produced a malleable dough that was far easier to work with than dough made from all-purpose flour.

To achieve similarly soft dough, my first inclination was to dilute the protein content of all-purpose flour (which boasts 10 to 12 percent protein) by cutting it with cake flour (which has 6 to 8 percent protein). I substituted increasing amounts of cake flour for all-purpose and noted that swapping even a quarter of the all-purpose flour for cake flour had a dramatic impact on both the raw dough and the cooked noodles. With 25 percent cake flour in the mix, my dough was much softer, less elastic, and easier to roll out. Unfortunately, what I had gained in convenience I lost in the texture of the cooked strands, which released a lot of starch into the cooking water and emerged with a pitted, pebbly surface. Our science editor explained why:

For noodles to remain intact and leach only a little starch into the cooking water, the starch granules in the flour need to be fully surrounded by a strong network of proteins. But the bleach in cake flour not only weakens the proteins but also makes the starch more absorbent and prone to bursting—a good thing when you want a tender cake but not when you're making pasta. Clearly, I needed a different strategy for producing softer, more malleable dough, so I turned my attention to the amount of liquid in the recipe.

Is Wetter Better?

Traditional pasta dough is about 30 percent water (compared with around 55 percent hydration for a basic sandwich loaf), all of which comes from the eggs. I figured that simply upping the hydration level would create a softer dough that would be easier to roll out, so I experimented with adding plain water to a batch of dough and an extra egg white (the white accounts for 80 percent of an egg's moisture) to another. Just as I'd hoped, these more hydrated doughs were more extensible—at least initially. But they had their downsides: First, the wetter surface of the dough caused considerable sticking, which required the heavy use of bench flour during rolling and led to cooked pasta with a starchy, gummy surface. Second, by adding more water, I'd allowed for too much gluten development, creating dough that, although easier to roll out at first, developed a greater tendency to snap back to its original shape once stretched out; this also meant pasta that cooked up tough and chewy. Still, I felt I was on to something by increasing the liquid in my recipe. Olive oil is a common addition to many fresh pasta recipes. What if I introduced it instead of water?

I mixed up a few more batches of dough, adding increasing amounts of olive oil. As the oil amount increased, the dough became more supple and easier to roll out. But because fat coats the proteins, inhibiting gluten formation, too much oil once again weakened the dough's structure, leading to excess starch loss in the water and a compromised texture. I found my upper limit at 2 tablespoons of oil.

I was finally getting somewhere, but this dough was still far from user-friendly.

That's All, Yolks

Up to this point I had tried adding water, protein (from egg whites), and fat to my dough, but I hadn't experimented with the one ingredient that contains all three: yolks. Many pasta doughs substitute yolks for some of the whole eggs, and for good reason. While yolks still contain about 50 percent water, they are also loaded with fat and emulsifiers, both of which limit gluten development. However, unlike doughs made with cake flour or excessive amounts of oil, dough made with extra yolks still has plenty of structure thanks to the coagulation of the egg proteins. To 2 cups of flour, two whole eggs (I ditched one whole egg from the traditional formula), and 2 tablespoons of olive oil, I kept adding yolks until I had a truly soft, easy-to-work dough that also boiled up nice and tender. The magic number proved to be six extra yolks.

This dough took on a beautiful yellow hue, yielded to gentle pressure with a rolling pin, and cooked up into delicate ribbons with a springy bite. While tasters had been concerned that the pasta would taste too eggy, they needn't have feared. The sulfurous compounds responsible for the flavor we associate with eggs reside primarily in the whites, not the yolks.

I had cleared some big hurdles, but I wasn't finished. I turned my attention to finding the best way to rest, roll, and cut the pasta.

A Little R&R

After being mixed, pasta dough is often rested for 20 to 30 minutes to allow the flour to fully hydrate and the newly formed gluten to cross-link into a network and then relax. Given that 30 minutes makes for a friendlier dough, would longer be even better? To find out, I made a batch and let the dough sit at room temperature for an extended period of time, cutting and rolling out pieces every 30 minutes. As I suspected, after an hour, my dough was significantly more malleable—and it continued to soften over the next three hours (I found four hours of resting time to be ideal though not critical for success). All I had to do now was divide the dough into manageable pieces and grab a heavy rolling pin—right?

Well, almost. This dough was worlds away from the dense blocks I'd struggled with in the past, but it still required a bit of technique. I knew I needed to avoid using too much bench flour: A little cling is a good thing, as it prevents the dough from springing back too easily. Plus, as I'd already learned, excess flour doesn't get incorporated into the dough and turns the surface of the pasta coarse and gummy.

With that in mind, I first cut the dough into six manageable pieces. Working with one at a time, I dusted each piece lightly with flour and used my fingers to flatten it into a 3-inch square. From there I switched to a rolling pin and doubled it to a 6-inch square. After another light dusting of flour, I began working the dough. I started with the pin in the middle of the dough and first rolled away, returned to the middle, and then rolled toward me. When the dough reached 6 by 12 inches, I gave it another dusting of flour and then repeated the

SCIENCE ## Formula for Soft Dough

The biggest hurdle to rolling out dough without a pasta roller is that it takes muscle to stretch it gossamer thin. Our solution? Create a super-malleable dough that doesn't snap back when you roll it. We did this by adding a generous splash of olive oil, which coats the flour proteins, limiting their ability to form gluten so the dough stays more elastic. We also mixed in six extra egg yolks. Yolks are loaded with fat and emulsifiers that also limit gluten development—but because their proteins coagulate when heated, adding structure, they ensure that the pasta is strong enough to stay intact when boiled.

LOTS OF OIL AND MORE YOLKS

rolling process until the dough measured roughly 6 by 20 inches.

From here, the possibilities were limitless. Lasagna was a given. For ribbon-style pasta, I allowed the sheets to dry on kitchen towels until firm around the edges (a step that enabled me to avoid dusting with more flour) before folding them up in 2-inch intervals and slicing crosswise to the desired thickness.

With dough that's this easy to roll out and that cooks up into wonderfully springy, delicate noodles, I'd wager that even cooks with pasta machines might be tempted to leave them in the cabinet.

FOOLPROOF APPROACH TO ROLLING AND CUTTING PASTA DOUGH BY HAND

What's the trick to turning a lump of pasta dough into long, silky strands—without a pasta roller? Starting with a soft, malleable dough is half the battle. The other half: dividing the dough into small, manageable pieces and working with them one at a time.

2. START SQUARE
Working with reserved piece, dust both sides with flour, then press cut side down into 3-inch square. With rolling pin, roll into 6-inch square, then dust both sides again with flour.

1. WORK WITH SMALL PIECES
Shape dough into 6-inch cylinder; wrap in plastic wrap and let rest for at least 1 hour. Divide into 6 equal pieces. Reserve 1 piece; rewrap remaining 5.

3. ROLL FROM CENTER, ONE WAY AT A TIME
Roll dough to 6 by 12 inches, rolling from center of dough one way at a time, then dust with flour. Continue rolling to 6 by 20 inches, lifting frequently to release from counter. Transfer dough to kitchen towel and air-dry for about 15 minutes.

4. FOLD INTO FLAT ROLL
Starting with short end, gently fold dried sheet at 2-inch intervals to create flat, rectangular roll.

5. CUT INTO STRIPS
With sharp knife, cut into 3/16-inch-thick noodles.

6. UNFURL
Use fingers to unfurl pasta; transfer to baking sheet.

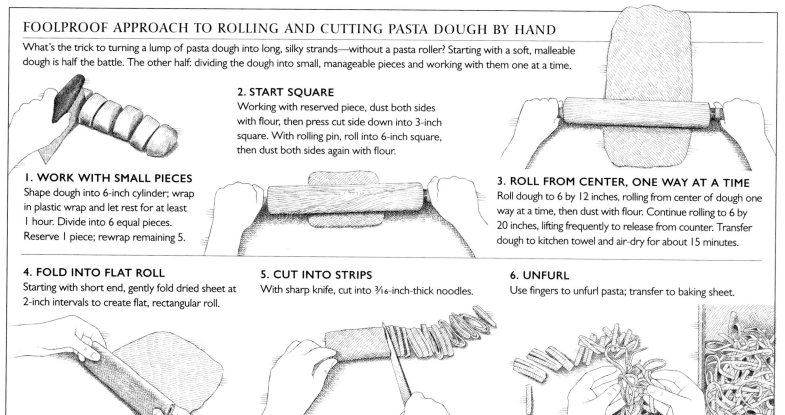

ILLUSTRATION: JOHN BURGOYNE, JAY LAYMAN

FRESH PASTA WITHOUT A MACHINE
MAKES 1 POUND; SERVES 4 TO 6

If using a high-protein all-purpose flour like King Arthur brand, increase the amount of egg yolks to seven. The longer the dough rests in step 2 the easier it will be to roll out. When rolling out the dough, avoid adding too much flour, which may result in excessive snapback. For our free recipe for Tomato–Brown Butter Sauce and directions for shaping this dough into farfalle, garganelli, and maltagliati, go to www.CooksIllustrated.com/jun12.

- 2   cups (10 ounces) all-purpose flour
- 2   large eggs plus 6 large yolks
- 2   tablespoons olive oil
- 1   tablespoon salt
- 1   recipe sauce (recipes follow)

1. Process flour, eggs and yolks, and oil in food processor until mixture forms cohesive dough that feels soft and is barely tacky to touch, about 45 seconds. (If dough sticks to fingers, add up to ¼ cup flour, 1 tablespoon at a time, until barely tacky. If dough doesn't become cohesive, add up to 1 tablespoon water, 1 teaspoon at a time, until it just comes together; process 30 seconds longer.)

2. Turn dough ball onto dry surface and knead until smooth, 1 to 2 minutes. Shape dough into 6-inch-long cylinder. Wrap with plastic wrap and set aside at room temperature to rest for at least 1 hour and up to 4 hours.

3. Cut cylinder crosswise into 6 equal pieces. Working with 1 piece of dough (rewrap remaining dough), dust both sides with flour, place cut side down on clean work surface, and press into 3-inch square. Using heavy rolling pin, roll into 6-inch square. Dust both sides of dough lightly with flour. Starting at center of square, roll dough away from you in 1 motion. Return rolling pin to center of dough and roll toward you in 1 motion. Repeat steps of rolling until dough sticks to counter and measures roughly 12 inches long. Lightly dust both sides of dough with flour and continue rolling dough until it measures roughly 20 inches long and 6 inches wide, frequently lifting dough to release it from counter. (You should be able to easily see outline of your fingers through dough.) If dough firmly sticks to counter and wrinkles when rolled out, dust dough lightly with flour.

4. Transfer pasta sheet to kitchen towel and let stand, uncovered, until firm around edges, about 15 minutes; meanwhile, roll out remaining dough. Starting with 1 short end, gently fold pasta sheet at 2-inch intervals until sheet has been folded into flat, rectangular roll. With sharp chef's knife, slice crosswise into 3⁄16-inch-thick noodles. Use fingers to unfurl pasta and transfer to baking sheet. Repeat folding and cutting remaining sheets of dough. Cook noodles within 1 hour.

5. Bring 4 quarts water to boil in large Dutch oven. Add salt and pasta and cook until tender but still al dente, about 3 minutes. Reserve 1 cup pasta cooking water. Drain pasta and toss with sauce; serve immediately.

TO MAKE AHEAD: Follow recipe through step 4, transfer baking sheet of pasta to freezer, and freeze until pasta is firm. Transfer to zipper-lock bag and store for up to 2 weeks. Cook frozen pasta straight from freezer as directed in step 5.

OLIVE OIL SAUCE WITH ANCHOVIES AND PARSLEY
MAKES 1 CUP; ENOUGH FOR 1 POUND PASTA

Mincing the anchovies ensures that their flavor gets evenly distributed. Use a high-quality extra-virgin olive oil in this recipe; our preferred brand is Columela.

- ⅓   cup extra-virgin olive oil
- 2   garlic cloves, minced
- 2   anchovy fillets, rinsed, patted dry, and minced
     Salt and pepper
- 4   teaspoons lemon juice
- 2   tablespoons chopped fresh parsley

1. Heat oil in 12-inch skillet over medium-low heat until shimmering. Add garlic, anchovies, ⅛ teaspoon salt, and ½ teaspoon pepper; cook until fragrant, about 30 seconds. Remove pan from heat and cover to keep warm.

2. To serve, return pan to medium heat. Add pasta, ½ cup reserved cooking water, lemon juice, and parsley; toss to combine, adding remaining cooking water as needed to adjust consistency. Season with salt and pepper to taste; serve immediately.

WALNUT CREAM SAUCE
MAKES 2 CUPS; ENOUGH FOR 1 POUND PASTA

- 1½   cups (6 ounces) walnuts
- ¾   cup dry white wine
- ½   cup heavy cream
- 1   ounce Parmesan cheese, grated (½ cup)
     Salt and pepper
- ¼   cup minced fresh chives

1. Toast walnuts in 12-inch skillet over medium heat until golden and fragrant, 2 to 4 minutes. Process 1 cup walnuts in food processor until finely ground, about 10 seconds. Transfer to small bowl. Pulse remaining ½ cup walnuts in food processor until coarsely chopped, 3 to 5 pulses. Bring wine to simmer in now-empty skillet over medium-high heat; cook until reduced to ¼ cup, about 3 minutes. Whisk in cream, walnuts, Parmesan, ¼ teaspoon salt, and ½ teaspoon pepper. Remove pan from heat and cover to keep warm.

2. To serve, return pan to medium heat. Add pasta, ½ cup reserved cooking water, and chives; toss to combine, adding remaining cooking water as needed to adjust consistency. Season with salt and pepper to taste; serve immediately.

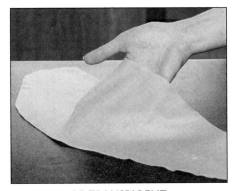

Italy's Ratatouille

Like its French sibling, *ciambotta* starts out with a slew of watery vegetables.
But the right steps create a stew that's hearty, more concentrated, and deeply satisfying.

⇒ BY CELESTE ROGERS ⇐

Southern Italy's *ciambotta* is a ratatouille-like stew that peasant farmers have been feasting on for centuries, and it's easy to understand why. When mopped up with a piece of crusty bread, this chock-full-of-veggies stew makes a substantial, stick-to-your-ribs meal—with nary a trace of meat. The key components—chunks of potatoes, bell peppers, onions, zucchini, eggplant, and tomatoes—cook with plenty of fruity olive oil until the vegetables soften and thicken the tomatoey broth.

To bring ciambotta into my kitchen, I combed through Italian cookbooks and earmarked a range of recipes. Each one called on a Dutch oven or other high-sided pot, and many instructed to simply throw in the vegetables all at once and let the mixture simmer until the flavors had melded. While I appreciated the ease of the walk-away method, when I gave these recipes a try, the universal result was a muddy-tasting, mushy stew that lacked depth. What I'd had in mind was tender-firm vegetables sunken into a thick, luxurious sauce. Most of all, I wanted both elements to boast rich, complex flavor.

Chunks of potatoes saturated with the flavors of the stew help distinguish *ciambotta* from ratatouille.

Thinking Outside the Pot

The first task: Concentrate the flavor of each vegetable. My instinct was to roast them, reasoning that the dry heat of the oven would drive off excess moisture and develop flavorful browning, so I oiled and lightly salted red bell pepper, eggplant, zucchini, and potato (Yukon Gold for now) pieces; placed them on separate baking sheets; and got the oven going. A long, slow roast yielded slightly dehydrated, wonderfully caramelized results, but since I could roast only two sheets at a time, the process was taking 50 minutes per batch—and that was before I'd even gotten to making the broth.

So I took a 180-degree turn, limiting myself to the stovetop and my Dutch oven. I sautéed the veggies in individual batches over high heat before adding a can of whole tomatoes that I'd roughly chopped and a couple of cups of water that would form the base of the broth. But while cooking each vegetable separately helped them develop better color and flavor, the vessel's high sides still trapped steam and prevented them from burning off enough moisture—particularly the waterlogged eggplant, peppers, and zucchini. But this was only the beginning of my problems: The eggplant had soaked up a good bit of the cooking oil and tasted greasy, the potatoes were a tad underdone and weren't absorbing enough flavor from the stew, the zucchini and peppers were too mushy, and the broth was woefully thin.

I decided to tackle the eggplant first, calling on our favorite pretreatment to help curb its tendency to soak up oil: salting and microwaving the eggplant before sautéing it, which collapses its spongy flesh and limits its capacity to absorb oil. But

while those steps kept the greasiness issue at bay, they also created another glitch: The parcooked eggplant started to disintegrate as it simmered in the stew, and the mushy result was unacceptable.

Or was it? It dawned on me that the eggplant's finicky texture might be a perfect solution to my too-thin broth. Deciding to embrace its mushiness, I made another batch in which I treated the eggplant, sautéed it, and allowed it to simmer in the broth until it had broken down completely. The results were a revelation: My previously thin broth had transformed into a full-bodied, silky sauce. I also incorporated one more step to build up the stew's flavor: After batch-sautéing the vegetables and bringing them back together in the Dutch oven, I pushed them to the edges of the pan to form a clearing and browned a healthy spoonful of tomato paste. This left a precious fond (flavorful browned bits) on the bottom of the pot, which I then deglazed with the canned tomatoes and water. Flavorful, full-bodied sauce? Check. Now I was getting somewhere.

However, I still had the mushy peppers and zucchini to deal with. If I wanted to preserve their crisp-tender bite, I'd have to limit how long they cooked. I also wanted to increase their flavor. The solution: Get them out of the high-sided Dutch oven and sauté them on their own in a skillet, whose shallow sides would allow the vegetables' exuded water to quickly evaporate. I gave it a try while the rest of the stew simmered, browning the peppers and zucchini together for about 10 minutes and then adding them to the Dutch oven, off heat, once the eggplant had broken down completely. After letting the stew sit for 20 minutes

What's a Pestata?

A relative of pesto, *pistou*, *picada*, and gremolata, *pestata* is a potent garlic, herb, and olive oil puree. When stirred into the *ciambotta* toward the end of cooking, its grassy bite freshens the rich, earthy flavors of the stew.

FRESHENING UP
A *pestata* made with olive oil, fresh oregano and basil, garlic, and red pepper flakes brightens the stew.

PHOTOGRAPHY: CARL TREMBLAY

COAXING BIG FLAVOR OUT OF WATERY PRODUCE

Eggplant, potatoes, zucchini, peppers, and onions have plenty of flavor to offer—provided you cook off their excess water. Then, to develop the stew's savory depth, build a concentrated fond with tomato paste.

BUILD STEW BASE
To deepen their flavors, cook the potatoes, onion, and eggplant (parcooked so it breaks down to thicken the stew) in a Dutch oven.

ENHANCE FOND
Sautéing tomato paste builds up a savory crust, which we deglaze with water and canned tomatoes to boost the stew's flavor.

SAUTÉ WATERY VEGGIES IN SKILLET Browning the peppers and zucchini separately in a shallow pan cooks off moisture and deepens their flavor.

ADD PESTATA
Clear the center of the pan, add the *pestata*, and briefly sauté. The herb-garlic mixture will add a fresh burst of flavor.

COMBINE AND WAIT
After marrying the two batches of vegetables, let the stew stand for 20 minutes to allow the flavors to meld.

---

to meld the flavors, I called my colleagues for a tasting. When they applauded the firm-tender bite of the skillet-sautéed vegetables, I knew that adding another pan to the recipe had been well worth it.

Trading Wax for Starch

The last item on my to-do list was the potatoes. I'd assumed that the Yukon Golds' moderately waxy, moderately starchy flesh would resist breaking down in my stew, and it did—to a fault. In fact, the potatoes were not only too firm but also strangely bland. When I did a little research, I learned that acid from the tomato broth was actually retarding the breakdown of the potatoes' cell walls, preventing their flesh from softening and soaking up flavor from the broth. The obvious solution: Start with the least waxy (read: most delicate) potato available— the russet. Sure enough, the texture of the potatoes in the next batch was markedly better. Though these floury spuds typically crumble apart when cooked, the acid from the tomato broth ensured that they held their shape just enough but still absorbed some of the savory broth.

Pump Up the Pestata

Though the flavor of my ciambotta was rich and round, I still felt that it could benefit from an additional burst of flavor and immediately thought of a *pestata*. While not a traditional player in ciambotta recipes, this pesto-like garnish features a pulverized mixture of garlic, olive oil, hot pepper flakes, and fresh herbs that's often incorporated into soups and stews to add brightness. For my version, I processed heady oregano and basil, six cloves of garlic, a couple of tablespoons of extra-virgin olive oil, and a touch of hot red pepper flakes in a food processor until the mixture was finely ground.

Cooking the pestata as a first step in the recipe (as is sometimes done in Italy) resulted in long exposure to heat that muted much of its punch. Instead, I preserved its potency by adding the paste to the zucchini and peppers during the final minutes

of cooking. Presto. As a finishing touch, I stirred loads of shredded fresh basil into the stew just before serving. The herb's fragrance intensified when it was incorporated into the hot stew, adding a powerful blast of summery flavor. At last, I had a ciambotta that was satisfying, rich, and complex.

ITALIAN VEGETABLE STEW (CIAMBOTTA)
SERVES 6 TO 8

Serve this hearty vegetable stew with crusty bread.

Pestata
- ⅓ cup chopped fresh basil
- ⅓ cup fresh oregano leaves
- 6 garlic cloves, minced
- 2 tablespoons extra-virgin olive oil
- ¼ teaspoon red pepper flakes

Stew
- 12 ounces eggplant, peeled and cut into ½-inch pieces
  Salt
- 4 tablespoons extra-virgin olive oil
- 1 large onion, chopped
- 1 pound russet potatoes, peeled and cut into ½-inch pieces
- 2 tablespoons tomato paste
- 2¼ cups water
- 1 (28-ounce) can whole peeled tomatoes, drained with juice reserved and chopped coarse
- 2 zucchini (8 ounces each), seeded and cut into ½-inch pieces
- 2 red or yellow bell peppers, stemmed, seeded, and cut into ½-inch pieces
- 1 cup shredded fresh basil

1. FOR THE PESTATA: Process all ingredients in food processor until finely ground, about 1 minute, scraping sides as necessary. Set aside.

2. FOR THE STEW: Toss eggplant with 1½

teaspoons salt in bowl. Line surface of large plate with double layer of coffee filters and lightly spray with vegetable oil spray. Spread eggplant in even layer over coffee filters. Microwave eggplant, uncovered, until dry to touch and slightly shriveled, 8 to 12 minutes, tossing once halfway through to ensure that eggplant cooks evenly.

3. Heat 2 tablespoons oil in Dutch oven over high heat until shimmering. Add eggplant, onion, and potatoes; cook, stirring frequently, until eggplant browns and surface of potatoes becomes translucent, about 2 minutes. Push vegetables to sides of pot; add 1 tablespoon oil and tomato paste to clearing. Cook paste, stirring frequently, until brown fond develops on bottom of pot, about 2 minutes. Add 2 cups water and chopped tomatoes and juice, scraping up any browned bits, and bring to boil. Reduce heat to medium, cover, and gently simmer until eggplant is completely broken down and potatoes are tender, about 20 to 25 minutes.

4. Meanwhile, heat remaining 1 tablespoon oil in 12-inch skillet over high heat until smoking. Add zucchini, bell peppers, and ½ teaspoon salt; cook, stirring occasionally, until vegetables are browned and tender, 10 to 12 minutes. Push vegetables to sides of skillet; add pestata and cook until fragrant, about 1 minute. Stir pestata into vegetables and transfer vegetables to bowl. Add remaining ¼ cup water to skillet off heat, scraping up browned bits.

5. Remove pot from heat and stir reserved vegetables and water from skillet into vegetables in Dutch oven. Cover pot and let stand for 20 minutes to allow flavors to meld. Stir in basil and season with salt to taste; serve.

Quick Tips Hall of Fame

Our readers are constantly showing us new ways to prep, cook, and problem-solve in the kitchen. Out of more than 1,000 published tips, here are a handful we use every day.

BY SHANNON FRIEDMANN HATCH & KEITH DRESSER

Reminder to Reserve Pasta Water

It's all too easy to forget to save a bit of pasta cooking water to thin a sauce when the recipe recommends it. Here's a surefire reminder: Before cooking the pasta, place a measuring cup inside the colander you'll use to drain it.

Tracking Dough Rise

Not every baker owns a dough-rising bucket with markings for tracking the rise of the dough, but any baker with a large, clear container can improvise one with this trick: After adding the dough to the container, mark its height by placing a rubber band around the container. This reference will make it easy to judge when the dough has doubled in volume.

Measuring Sticky Ingredients

Mist the inside of a measuring cup with vegetable oil spray before filling it with sticky ingredients such as honey and molasses. When emptied, the liquid will slip right out of the cup. Out of spray? Line the measuring cup with plastic wrap and discard after use.

Citrus Reamer Substitute

Kitchen tongs are a great tool to use when juicing a lemon, lime, or orange. Holding the tongs closed, stick the pincers into the halved fruit and use a twisting motion to extract juice.

Caring for Berries

Berries are prone to growing mold and rotting quickly. To keep mold at bay, rinse berries in a mild vinegar solution (1 part vinegar to 3 parts water) before drying them and storing them in a paper towel–lined airtight container.

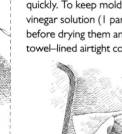

Keeping Fresh-Baked Bread Fresh

Without preservatives to keep it tasting fresh, artisanal loaves can quickly stale. We've found that storing the bread cut side down on a cutting board works better than wrapping the loaf in paper or plastic. The crust will stay dry, while contact with the board will keep moisture inside the crumb.

Peeling Ginger with a Spoon

Knotty ginger skin is nearly impossible to peel with a knife or vegetable peeler. Instead, use the edge of a spoon to scrape it off quickly and efficiently.

Egg Slicer for Fruit

Slicing individual pieces of fruit can be a tedious task. An egg slicer makes perfect slices of kiwi, strawberries (for shortcake), or banana in one quick motion.

Makeshift Bottle Opener

Bottle opener gone missing during a backyard barbecue? Try your grill tongs, which have an opening inside the handles just large enough to catch the edge of a bottle cap so you can gently pop the cap off.

Easy Pureed Garlic

In addition to grating nutmeg, citrus peel, and hard cheese, a rasp-style grater is an ideal tool for producing finely pureed garlic, shallot, or onion. For recipes such as Caesar salad or *aïoli*, peel a clove of garlic and grate it on the tool before adding it to the recipe.

Checking a Gas Grill's Fuel Tank

There's nothing worse than running out of fuel halfway through grilling. If your grill doesn't have a gas gauge, use this technique to estimate how much gas is left in the tank. Boil a cup of water and pour it over the side of the tank. Feel the metal with your hand. Where the water has succeeded in warming the tank it is empty; where the tank remains cool to the touch there is still propane inside.

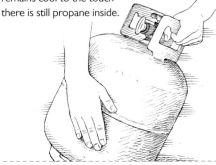

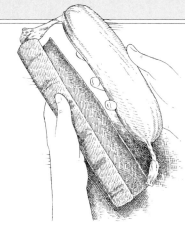

Keeping Cookie Dough Round

Using a cardboard paper towel roll to store refrigerator cookie dough helps the dough retain its shape. Once you've formed the dough into a log, roll it in plastic wrap and slide the dough inside the cardboard (slit lengthwise) to protect it in the fridge.

Freezing Cookie Dough

Keeping some frozen dough on hand means you can bake just as many, or as few, cookies as you like without first having to whip up a batch of dough. Form the dough into balls and arrange them on a sheet pan or cookie sheet to freeze. Once the individual balls of dough are frozen, simply place them in a zipper-lock freezer bag and stow in the freezer for up to two months.

No More "Mystery Meat"

When freezing raw meat for later use, wrap the meat in plastic wrap, place it in a zipper-lock freezer bag, and then cut off the grocery label and put it inside, facing out. At a glance, you'll know the exact cut, weight, and—most important—date of purchase, allowing you to gauge how long the meat has been lingering in the freezer.

Vinegar Fly Trap

Since so-called fruit flies are actually vinegar flies attracted to the odor of fermenting fruits and vegetables, use this simple solution to rid your kitchen of these annoying pests: Place a few drops of dish soap in a small bowl of vinegar on the counter and stir to combine. The vinegar lures the flies into the liquid, and the soap breaks the surface tension, preventing them from escaping.

Space-Saving Vegetable Prep

Many recipes call for adding ingredients at different points. Instead of a bowl for each prepped ingredient, layer them in a single large bowl, separated by sheets of waxed paper or plastic wrap. (The ingredients you'll need first should be on top.)

Organizing Pot Lids

Many cooks store their pans and lids in a single drawer. To keep the lids from sliding around and under the pans, install a slender expansion curtain rod at the front. Stand the lids up straight against the rod, so they are within sight and reach.

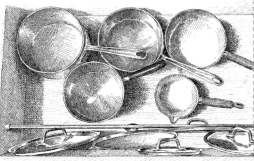

Salad to Go

Dressed salads prepared early and eaten later in the day are destined to turn limp. To transport a small amount of dressing, use one of the jars in which dry spices are packed. Their small size and tight seal are perfect for the job.

Grilled Spicy Pork Tacos (al Pastor)

This taqueria staple features juicy, spit-roasted marinated pork that's crispy at the edges and fork-tender within. Could we achieve that same trademark texture on the grill?

⇒ BY DAN SOUZA ⇐

Tacos al pastor, or "shepherd-style" tacos, are a Mexican taqueria classic made from thin slices of chile-marinated pork that's been tightly packed onto a vertical spit with layers of pork fat and then roasted. The cone-shaped stack is often topped with a whole pineapple whose tangy, sweet juices trickle down, encouraging the meat to caramelize as it turns. When the exterior is browned and crisp, thin shavings of the roasted pork and pineapple are carved off directly onto a warm tortilla and then topped with garnishes that contrast the rich meat: minced raw onion, cilantro, and a squeeze of fresh lime.

It's an adaptation of the lamb shawarmas (themselves inspired by Turkish doner kebabs) introduced to Mexico by Arab immigrants in the late 19th century, and it's my favorite kind of taco filling. I've often given thought to a homemade version to satisfy my frequent al pastor cravings but have always been deterred by the fact that my home kitchen lacks what you'd think would be an essential piece of equipment: a vertical spit. This time, however, my appetite got the better of me. I decided to see what it would take to make this super-flavorful meat at home.

Marinade Mishaps

I pored over the test kitchen's library of Mexican cookbooks and came away with a half-dozen recipes. All but one called for pork shoulder, which made sense; it's what the taquerias use because it's a flavorful, well-marbled cut.

Most of the marinade formulas I found looked relatively similar, too: Some assortment of whole dried guajillo, pasilla, and/or chipotle chiles (all readily available at most supermarkets) is toasted in a skillet and then combined with tomatoes or tomatillos, cumin, garlic, citrus juices, herbs and spices, and water. The mixture is simmered until the chiles are soft and is then pureed, strained, and married with the thin-cut strips of meat. But what

Our braise-then-grill method produces tender pork with burnished edges—plus, as a nod to the traditional garnish, grilled pineapple.

sounded like recipes for flavor-packed results turned out to be bland disappointments across the board. It wasn't that the marinades themselves weren't bold—the one I liked best (with fruity guajillos, tomatoes, lots of garlic, bay leaves, cumin, and cloves) was full-bodied and concentrated—but that no marinade travels more than a few millimeters beyond the surface of the meat. That meant it was crucial that the pork be sliced as thin as possible to allow the heady chile mixture to permeate every bite—a point, I soon realized, that would be one of the biggest challenges of pulling off tacos al pastor at home. Many taquerias have the benefit of a meat slicer to shave the roast paper-thin before coating it with the marinade. I'd have to make do with a sharp chef's knife. But since raw pork is squishy and hard to control with a knife, the thinnest uniform slices I could manage still measured a good half inch—too thick for the marinade to come through in each bite. Partially freezing the roast did make the meat sliceably firm but also tacked on an extra hour to the process, and I didn't want to wait that long. Stymied, I decided to turn my attention to the cooking method in hopes of finding an alternative solution.

Braising the Steaks

With the exception of one that opted for a skillet, all of the recipes I tried employed the broiler or a grill. The logic here seemed sound enough: Mimic the deep browning and crispy edges of authentic al pastor by exposing the marinated meat to the hottest possible heat source. According to tasters, there was no contest between the two methods; the grilled pork strips (for now, I'd stick with my ½-inch slabs) boasted better charring and crispier edges. The downside was that neither method produced the tender, juicy results you get at a taqueria, and the problem again boiled down to a matter of equipment. When spit-roasted, the pork turns out extra-succulent because it's continually basted by the layers of melting fat. But how could I get this result without a rotisserie?

It was time to seek professional help, and I turned to my favorite local source for tacos al pastor, Taqueria el Amigo in Waltham, Massachusetts. When I stepped into owner Jorge Calderón's kitchen, I made a surprising discovery: He doesn't own a vertical spit either. Instead, he makes tacos al pastor the way his grandmother did at her roadside stand in Mexico: First, he braises finely cubed pork butt in a tomato-based chile sauce until it's supremely tender and deeply infused with flavor, and then he scoops portions of the meat onto a griddle, where it sizzles to a browned patina.

His unusual approach sounded promising: Braising the pork in the chile sauce would simultaneously tenderize it and infuse it with flavor, putting to bed the problems associated with slicing the roast by hand. I hurried back to the test kitchen to try replicating his results. After whipping up a batch of my chile-tomato sauce, I nestled the ½-inch slabs of

Smoky Spice

This mild, fruity dried chile is easy to find in supermarkets and brings smoky flavor to the pork.

GUAJILLO CHILE

PHOTOGRAPHY: CARL TREMBLAY

pork (for now, I was hoping to avoid painstakingly cubing the meat) into the liquid; let it all simmer for a good two hours, by which time the meat was fall-apart tender; and then moved the pork slabs into a hot skillet to crisp.

It seemed my battle was half-won. The braised meat was incredibly tender, juicy, and infused with the complex chile sauce, which confirmed that there was no need to cube the pork butt. But tasters missed the charred crispness of the grilled versions. Easy fix, I figured; I'd simply brown the braised strips on the grill rather than in a skillet. Indeed, searing the meat for about five minutes per side over a single-level fire seemed to work well until I went to flip the pieces, which fell apart and slipped through the grill grate in shreds. Tender meat was one thing, but it had to be grillable, too, so I dialed back the braising time by 30 minutes. The result: meat that was plenty tender but still held its shape. (It was also a snap to grill some pineapple rounds right next to the pork; I coarsely chopped and transferred them to a bowl for garnishing each taco.)

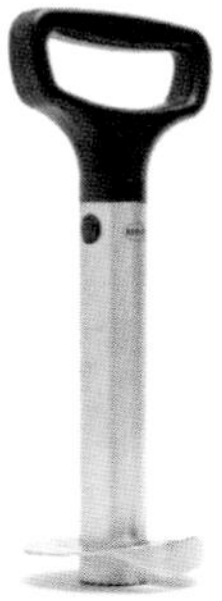

To replicate the appearance and texture of meat shaved from a spit, I sliced the crisped slabs crosswise into short ⅛-inch-thick strips. Now the meat was getting really good—full-flavored, crisp at the edges, and fork-tender—but I wished it were as succulent as the spit-roasted versions I'd had. That's when it dawned on me that a crucial part of the classic setup was missing: the melted fat that drips down, basting the meat as it cooks. I wasn't about to start grilling pieces of pork fat, but I did have a potful of braising liquid that was loaded with rendered drippings. I brushed the unctuous liquid over both sides of each pork slab before grilling and then, just before serving, tossed a little more of it, spiked with a bit of lime juice for brightness, with the grilled slices.

Now my tacos al pastor, imbued with all of the complexity and rich flavor of spit-roasted originals, brought the taste of a taqueria into my own kitchen.

SPICY PORK TACOS (AL PASTOR)
SERVES 6 TO 8

Boneless pork butt is often labeled Boston butt. If you can't find guajillo chiles, New Mexican chiles may be substituted, although the dish may be spicier. To warm tortillas, place them on a plate, cover with a damp kitchen towel, and microwave for 60 to 90 seconds. Keep tortillas covered and serve immediately.

10	large dried guajillo chiles, wiped clean
1½	cups water
1¼	pounds plum tomatoes, cored and quartered
8	garlic cloves, peeled
4	bay leaves
	Salt and pepper
¾	teaspoon sugar
½	teaspoon ground cumin
⅛	teaspoon ground cloves
3	pounds boneless pork butt roast
1	lime, cut into 8 wedges
½	pineapple, peeled, cored, and cut into ½-inch-thick rings
	Vegetable oil
18	(6-inch) corn tortillas, warmed
1	small onion, chopped fine
½	cup coarsely chopped fresh cilantro leaves

1. Toast guajillos in large Dutch oven over medium-high heat until softened and fragrant, 2 to 4 minutes. Transfer to large plate and, when cool enough to handle, remove stems.

2. Bring toasted guajillos, water, tomatoes, garlic, bay leaves, 2 teaspoons salt, ½ teaspoon pepper, sugar, cumin, and cloves to simmer in now-empty Dutch oven over medium-high heat. Cover, reduce heat, and simmer, stirring occasionally, until guajillos are softened and tomatoes mash easily, about 20 minutes.

3. While sauce simmers, trim excess fat from exterior of pork, leaving ¼-inch-thick fat cap. Slice pork against grain into ½-inch-thick slabs.

4. Transfer guajillo-tomato mixture to blender and process until smooth, about 1 minute. Strain puree through fine-mesh strainer, pressing on solids to extract as much liquid as possible. Return puree to pot, submerge pork slices in liquid, and bring to simmer over medium heat. Partially cover, reduce heat, and gently simmer until pork is tender but still holds together, 90 to 105 minutes, flipping and rearranging pork halfway through cooking. (Pork can be left in sauce, cooled to room temperature, and refrigerated, covered, for up to 2 days.)

5. Transfer pork to large plate, season both sides with salt, and cover tightly with aluminum foil. Whisk sauce to combine. Transfer ½ cup to bowl for grilling; pour off all but ½ cup remaining sauce from pot and reserve for another use. Squeeze 2 lime wedges into sauce in pot and add spent wedges; season with salt to taste.

6A. FOR A CHARCOAL GRILL: Open bottom vent halfway. Light large chimney starter filled with charcoal briquettes (6 quarts). When top coals are partially covered with ash, pour evenly over grill. Set cooking grate in place, cover, and open lid vent halfway. Heat grill until hot, about 5 minutes.

6B. FOR A GAS GRILL: Turn all burners to high, cover, and heat grill until hot, about 15 minutes. Turn all burners to medium.

7. Clean and oil cooking grate. Brush 1 side of pork with ¼ cup reserved sauce. Place pork on 1 side of grill, sauce side down, and cook until well browned and crisp, 5 to 7 minutes. Brush pork with remaining ¼ cup reserved sauce, flip, and continue to cook until second side is well browned and crisp, 5 to 7 minutes longer. Transfer to cutting board. Meanwhile, brush both sides of pineapple rings with vegetable oil and season with salt to taste. Place on other half of grill and cook until pineapple is softened and caramelized, 5 to 7 minutes per side; transfer pineapple to cutting board.

8. Coarsely chop grilled pineapple and transfer to serving bowl. Using tongs or carving fork to steady hot pork, slice each piece crosswise into ⅛-inch pieces. Bring remaining ½ cup sauce in pot to simmer, add sliced pork, remove pot from heat, and toss to coat pork well. Season with salt to taste.

9. Spoon small amount of pork into each warm tortilla and serve, passing chopped pineapple, remaining 6 lime wedges, onion, and cilantro separately.

STEP BY STEP | RE–CREATING TACOS AL PASTOR, MINUS THE ROTISSERIE

Our at-home approach achieves juicy meat with crisp edges—without specialized equipment.

BRAISE Gently simmering the pork roast (cut into ½-inch slabs) in a heady chile sauce tenderizes the meat and infuses it with rich flavor.

GRILL AND BASTE Searing the braised pork on the grill crisps up the edges; brushing it with the fatty braising liquid lends succulence.

COAT IN SAUCE Tossing the grilled pork (cut into ⅛-inch slices) with lime juice and braising liquid adds brightness and richness.

Sous Vide Chicken Salad?

Cooking chicken to precisely the right degree of doneness guarantees tender, juicy results. Poaching is one way—but we had a better, more foolproof idea.

≥ BY KEITH DRESSER ≤

Chicken salad can mean just about anything these days, from shredded meat dressed in vinaigrette to grilled strips tossed with leafy greens. But there's no beating the classic version: tender cubes lightly bound with mayonnaise and freshened up with celery and herbs. It's ideal sandwiched between bread slices, scooped into lettuce cups, or simply eaten by the forkful—provided that the chicken has been properly cooked. I've eaten enough disappointing versions to know that no amount of dressing or add-ins will camouflage dry, stringy meat. Chicken salad is only as good as the chicken itself.

I made it my goal to come up with a method for silky, juicy, delicately flavored chicken first and worry about finessing the accoutrements later. I paged through dozens of recipes, most of which specified the same cut of meat: bone-in, skin-on chicken breasts. (The bone, a poor conductor of heat, helps prevent the meat from overcooking.) As for the cooking method, the majority of recipes called for poaching.

My target doneness temperature for the white meat was 160 to 165 degrees, at which point the chicken is safely cooked through but still plenty juicy and tender. I stuck close to a conventional poaching method, bringing a pot of water to a subsimmer of 180 degrees and slipping in four breasts. Then things got fussy: Because the water temperature plunged as soon as I added the meat, I had to continually adjust the heat to maintain that below-simmer temperature. The results were succulent and tender, but having to constantly fiddle with the burner knob was definitely a pain. Cranking the heat higher from the start wasn't the answer: The outside of the meat dried out before the inside was done. There had to be a simpler, gentler way to prevent the meat from overcooking.

That's when my thoughts turned to *sous vide*, a restaurant technique in which vacuum-sealed foods are submerged in a water bath that's been preset to the food's ideal cooked temperature. The beauty of this method: It's impossible to overcook the food because the water temperature never exceeds the target doneness temperature. Sous vide ovens cost a fortune, but if I could approximate this technique

using ordinary kitchen equipment, I'd have a foolproof way to get perfectly cooked chicken.

Rather than heating the water before adding the chicken, I tried placing the breasts in a Dutch oven, covering them with cold water, and turning the burner to medium. When the water reached 165 degrees, I moved the pot off heat and let it sit, covered, so that the chicken could continue climbing toward 165 degrees with no risk of overshooting the mark.

Unfortunately, this first attempt was too gentle, as the water cooled before the chicken could fully cook through. I went through a dozen more tests in which I adjusted the cooking time, water temperature, and amount of water. It was a delicate balance: I needed enough water to fully submerge the chicken and hold the heat, but I didn't want to wait for several quarts of water to come up to temperature. At last, I hit on the ideal formula: four chicken breasts and 6 cups of water heated to 170 degrees and then removed from the heat, covered, and left to stand for about 15 minutes, by which time the meat was 165 degrees. The method was so foolproof that I was able to swap out bone-in meat for fuss-free boneless, skinless breasts and still get the same tender, juicy results. One final trick: Adding 2 tablespoons of salt to the water seasoned the meat nicely. I popped the meat onto a sheet tray and refrigerated it while I prepared the rest of the salad.

I knew that mayonnaise would be the dressing base, but I wanted to use as little of it as possible to keep the salad light and fresh tasting. After some experimentation, I found that just ½ cup was sufficient to bind the meat together, and I brightened its rich flavor with lemon juice and Dijon mustard. Minced celery, shallot, tarragon, and parsley added freshness and a cool, contrasting crunch.

With incomparably moist chicken and a light, fresh dressing, this salad was sure to be the star of my next picnic lunch.

CLASSIC CHICKEN SALAD
SERVES 4 TO 6

To ensure that the chicken cooks through, don't use breasts that weigh more than 8 ounces or are thicker than 1 inch. Make sure to start with cold water in step 1. This salad can be served in a sandwich or spooned over leafy greens. For our free recipes for Curried Chicken Salad with Cashews, Waldorf Chicken Salad, and Chicken Salad with Red Grapes and Smoked Almonds, go to www.CooksIllustrated.com/jun12.

   Salt and pepper
4 (6- to 8-ounce) boneless, skinless chicken breasts, no more than 1 inch thick, trimmed
½ cup mayonnaise
2 tablespoons lemon juice
1 teaspoon Dijon mustard
2 celery ribs, minced
1 shallot, minced
1 tablespoon minced fresh parsley
1 tablespoon minced fresh tarragon

1. Dissolve 2 tablespoons salt in 6 cups cold water in Dutch oven. Submerge chicken in water. Heat pot over medium heat until water registers 170 degrees. Turn off heat, cover pot, and let stand until chicken registers 165 degrees, 15 to 17 minutes.

2. Transfer chicken to paper towel–lined tray. Refrigerate until chicken is cool, about 30 minutes. While chicken cools, whisk mayonnaise, lemon juice, mustard, and ¼ teaspoon pepper together in large bowl.

3. Pat chicken dry with paper towels and cut into ½-inch pieces. Transfer chicken to bowl with mayonnaise mixture. Add celery, shallot, parsley, and tarragon; toss to combine. Season with salt and pepper to taste. Serve. (Salad can be refrigerated for up to 2 days.)

TECHNIQUE | THE GENTLEST WAY TO COOK CHICKEN

Our easy mock *sous vide* method guarantees supremely tender, juicy chicken.

START COLD   HEAT TO 170°   FINISH OFF HEAT

Rethinking Bean Dips

For creamy, complex-tasting bean dips, we began by removing some of the beans.

⇒ BY KEITH DRESSER ⇐

Although I love beans, I've rarely been impressed by bean dips. Most are dense and gluey, with any bean flavor buried under overzealous seasonings—the stuff you'd pass over at a party. To rescue this concept, my plan was twofold: highlight the beans' earthy-sweet flavors and build on their natural starchiness to create a smooth, creamy texture.

Rather than spend hours soaking and simmering dried beans, I decided to go with canned and started with meaty butter beans; their velvety texture and mellow flavor would pair well with other ingredients. I drained two 15-ounce cans—enough to make a party-size dip—rinsed the beans to remove excess starch, and pureed them with a few placeholder flavorings.

No surprise: The result was thick and sticky enough to use as brick mortar. Thinning the dip with water would fix the problem, but not without washing out flavor. Olive oil wasn't ideal either, as it overwhelmed the beans' delicate richness; plus, some tasters thought it rendered the dip greasy.

Realizing I needed something with body that wouldn't overpower the beans, I wondered if yogurt might do the trick. Indeed, ordinary yogurt worked fine, but thicker Greek-style yogurt was far better, enriching the dip without robbing it of flavor. In fact, this product was so concentrated that I could use just ¼ cup and still achieve the smoother, more velvety consistency that I was after.

And yet tasters complained that the dip was still slightly pasty and I realized that the culprit might be the beans themselves. Going for a more radical approach, I tried substituting half of the butter beans with 1 cup of green peas, which are lighter in texture. The results were encouraging. The peas' fresh sweetness brightened the butter beans and tinted the dip an attractive shade of pale green.

That left the seasoning to tend to. I figured bold ingredients were best avoided, lest they mask the beans' flavors. Instead, I focused on subtler additions such as herbs and citrus. After some testing, I settled on ¼ cup of fresh mint plus the white and light-green portions of a scallion, both processed with the beans and 2 tablespoons of lemon juice. Tasters told me that the flavor was close but remarked that they missed the bite of fresh garlic. I'd purposely omitted it until now, worried that its sharpness would dominate the flavor of the dip. I recalled a trick from our Caesar salad dressing, where we "cook" garlic in lemon juice, a step that hastens the conversion of its harsh-tasting compounds into the same, more mellow ones that form when garlic is heated. Happily, this was a perfect fix.

Once all the elements were blended, I let the dip rest for 30 minutes to allow the flavors to meld. The final flourish: a garnish to perk up the dip's rather homely facade. I thinly sliced the leftover dark-green portion of the scallion and sprinkled it over the top, along with 2 tablespoons of whole peas and a drizzle of extra-virgin olive oil.

This dip struck a perfect balance: creamy yet light, flavor-packed yet clean-tasting. In fact, the concept of pairing a starchy bean with a lighter legume or vegetable was so successful with my tasters that I devised four variations, all filled out with fresh herbs, citrus, and a dollop of creamy Greek yogurt.

BUTTER BEAN AND PEA DIP WITH MINT
MAKES ABOUT 2 CUPS

We prefer these dips when made with whole Greek yogurt, but 2 percent or 0 percent varieties can be substituted. Serve with chips, crackers, or vegetables. For our free recipe for Navy Bean and Artichoke Dip with Parsley, go to www.CooksIllustrated.com/jun12.

- 1 small garlic clove, minced
- ¼ teaspoon grated lemon zest plus 2 tablespoons juice
- 1 cup frozen baby peas, thawed and patted dry
- 1 (15-ounce) can butter beans, 2 tablespoons liquid reserved, beans rinsed
- 1 scallion, white and light-green parts cut into ½-inch pieces, green part sliced thin on bias
- ¼ cup fresh mint leaves
  Salt
- ¼ teaspoon ground coriander
  Pinch cayenne pepper
- ¼ cup plain Greek-style yogurt
  Extra-virgin olive oil, for drizzling

1. Combine garlic and lemon zest and juice in small bowl; set aside for at least 15 minutes. Set aside 2 tablespoons peas for garnish.

2. Pulse butter beans, reserved liquid, remaining peas, scallion whites and light greens, mint, ¾ teaspoon salt, coriander, cayenne, and lemon juice mixture in food processor until fully ground, 5 to 10 pulses. Scrape down bowl with rubber spatula. Continue to process until uniform paste forms, about 1 minute, scraping down bowl twice. Add yogurt and continue to process until smooth and homogeneous, about 15 seconds, scraping down bowl as needed. Transfer to serving bowl, cover, and let stand at room temperature for at least 30 minutes. (Dip can be refrigerated for up to 1 day.

Greek-style yogurt adds creamy body to the dips.

Let refrigerated dip stand at room temperature for 30 minutes before serving.)

3. Season with salt to taste. Sprinkle with reserved peas and scallion greens. Drizzle with oil and serve.

CANNELLINI BEAN AND EDAMAME DIP WITH TARRAGON

Increase lemon zest to ½ teaspoon. Substitute frozen edamame for peas, cannellini beans for butter beans, and tarragon for mint. Omit coriander and increase yogurt to ⅓ cup.

PINTO BEAN AND CORN DIP WITH CILANTRO

Substitute lime zest and juice for lemon, frozen corn for peas, pinto beans for butter beans, and cilantro for mint. Substitute ¼ teaspoon chipotle chile powder and ¼ teaspoon ground cumin for coriander.

PINK BEAN AND LIMA BEAN DIP WITH PARSLEY

Omit lemon zest. Substitute frozen lima beans for peas, pink beans for butter beans, and parsley for mint. Substitute ¼ teaspoon garam masala for coriander and increase yogurt to ⅓ cup.

PHOTOGRAPHY: CARL TREMBLAY

Indian Flatbread (Naan)

We set out to reproduce the charred exterior and tender interior of *naan* baked in a tandoor—but without the 1,000-degree heat.

⋟ BY ANDREW JANJIGIAN ⋞

I've re-created plenty of Indian curries, biryanis, and chutneys in my home kitchen, but *naan*, the cuisine's famous leavened flatbread, is something I had yet to tackle. That might be because it's considered "restaurant" bread, even in India. To create the ideal version featuring a light, airy interior and a pliant, chewy crust, the dough is baked in the traditional barrel-shaped, charcoal- or wood-fired clay oven known as a tandoor. These vessels weigh upwards of 600 pounds and often top 1,000 degrees, which explains how the crust gets so beautifully blistered—and also why few home cooks own tandoors. At the same time, I've often wondered if I really have to venture out for something as simple as flatbread. I decided it was time to give home-baked naan a shot.

I scoured the test kitchen's collection of Indian cookbooks and came away feeling optimistic. The ingredient list would be no problem. Most of the recipes I found called for some combination of flour, yeast, water, salt, yogurt, and sugar. And though I'd worried that getting good char on the bread without a tandoor would be tricky, most sources seemed to suggest that it could be done in a conventional oven on a preheated baking stone.

Rolling in the Dough

Aiming for a dough that was wet enough to stay moist during cooking but not so hydrated that it was too sticky or soupy to handle, I mixed together a few cups of all-purpose flour with a pinch of yeast, about ⅓ cup of low-fat yogurt, a little sugar, and some salt, along with enough water to make it pliable. I let the dough rise for a few hours, divided it into four balls, rolled them into thin disks, and slid them onto a baking stone that I'd preheated as hot as my oven would go (500 degrees).

Trouble started early, when I was rolling out the dough rounds and they snapped back like rubber

A hot cast-iron skillet is the best way to produce lightly charred and blistered, restaurant-quality naan at home.

bands. When I finally managed to get them flat, the loaves baked up dry and tough before they'd even had a chance to properly brown on the bottom, let alone develop any of those dark patchy blisters that, in my opinion, are the best part of naan. They also continued to rapidly lose more moisture as they cooled—a problem since, unlike in a restaurant, I couldn't exactly make each piece to order. Leaving the question on hold as to whether the oven was the best stand-in for a tandoor, I decided the first order of business was to create a dough that was softer but still pleasantly chewy.

One change to make right off the bat: switching from low-fat yogurt to the whole-milk kind. The extra fat would coat the flour proteins, weakening gluten formation by preventing them from binding to each other too tightly, as well as hold in more moisture for a more tender bread. With this change, my next batch of dough was easier to roll out, but it baked up too soft; the inside was like sandwich bread. I wondered if the higher protein (as much

as 14 percent) in bread flour might be a better bet. But bread flour created so much chew that the resulting bread was leathery. High-protein all-purpose flour, such as King Arthur brand, was a better choice, producing naan that boasted a near-ideal texture. As I pulled apart an oven-fresh piece, I couldn't help but admire its tender chew. But then the inevitable happened: The thin rounds cooled almost instantly and were tough by the time I pulled the next batch off the baking stone a few minutes later. To buy each piece some time, I needed to figure out a way to keep the dough from drying out.

The solution wasn't more water; that would just make the dough loose and sticky. More fat was a better idea, since besides impeding gluten formation it limits water evaporation from the starches during baking, minimizing moisture loss. To that end, I tried adding vegetable oil to the dough, 1 teaspoon at a time, discovering that the more I added the more tender and capable of staying soft the breads became. The dough maxed out at 5 teaspoons per cup of flour; any more and the bread was greasy. But I had one more fat source in mind to boost moisture retention: an egg yolk. While unusual in naan recipes, egg yolks often turn up in other types of bread for just this reason. (I stayed away from whole eggs, knowing that the white's structure-enhancing proteins would toughen the dough.)

The last tweak I made before moving on to the cooking method was refrigerating the dough for several hours to keep it from snapping back during stretching. It was a holdover from my Thin-Crust Pizza recipe (January/February 2011), from which I learned that cold fermentation encourages the relaxation of gluten strands so that the dough is more flexible. An added bonus: Preparing the dough the day before freed up time the next day for cooking the rest of the meal.

With the dough formula nailed down, I moved on to face the real challenge of making naan at home: getting good color and char without a tandoor.

Naan Sense

Since the oven wasn't browning the bread fast enough, I figured my best alternative was the hottest, most powerful heat source I had: a grill. I fired up

PHOTOGRAPHY: CARL TREMBLAY

some charcoal, expecting to come away with beautifully grill-marked breads. To say my first attempt was a disaster would be an understatement. Like a poorly cooked piece of meat, the bottom blackened while the top remained practically raw. I thought the fire was just too hot so I downsized it on my next test, but even a smaller fire produced the same charred result. Flipping the dough midway through cooking also wasn't the answer—it merely dried out the bread.

I took a step back to consider what really happens when naan cooks in a tandoor. The shaped dough is slapped directly onto the tandoor's inside wall, where it sticks and cooks in minutes, without ever being flipped. While heat radiating from the coals at the bottom of the oven helps cook the bread's exposed side, more important is the heat conducted through its walls, which also trap moisture to keep the bread soft. I could see now that a grill wasn't the best substitute for a tandoor. But neither was a pizza stone in the oven, since that method also exposed the bread to drying air currents. My choice became clear: a skillet on the stovetop.

So for my next test, I slipped my stretched and shaped dough onto a preheated cast-iron skillet. It puffed up quickly, and after a few minutes the bottom had browned a bit; I flipped it to finish cooking the top side. The result was a dramatic improvement on anything I'd made so far—lightly browned and bubbled in spots and tender inside. It wasn't perfect, though. The bread ballooned as it baked, which made it cook unevenly when I flipped it; the crust was a bit floury; and the loaves still dried out too quickly as they sat.

None of these issues were hard to fix. I poked the dough with a fork before putting it in the pan to let steam escape and prevent puffing. Improving the crust and prolonging the optimal tender texture of the bread required a two-tiered approach. First, I misted the dough with water before cooking it to moisten the flour that coated it. I also covered the

INDIAN ORIGINAL

Traditionally, naan cooks against the superheated clay wall of a cylindrical tandoor. Heat radiating from the coals below also chars the exposed side, so the bread never needs to be flipped.

Finding the Right Heat to Replicate a Tandoor

We initially thought that a grill or preheated pizza stone would best approximate the intense heat of a tandoor, which cooks naan mainly by heat conducted through its walls. We were wrong. The best alternative? A trusty cast-iron skillet.

GRILL? NO

A grill's searing heat gets close to that of a tandoor. The problem: It only chars the bottom of the bread, while the top remains barely cooked. (Flipping only dries out the bread.)

PIZZA STONE IN OVEN? NO

Baked on a pizza stone in the oven, the bread encounters the conductive heat of the stone, which we wanted, and the drying heat of the oven's air currents, which we didn't.

COVERED SKILLET? YES

A covered skillet delivers heat to the bottom and top of the bread, producing loaves that are nicely charred but still moist. To ensure a tender interior, we mist the dough with water.

pan to trap steam around the bread as it baked.

My simple approach created naan as good as any from a restaurant. Brushed with a little melted butter after cooking, it makes for a delicious edible utensil, perfect for tearing into bite-size pieces to dip into curries, chutneys, or even stew.

INDIAN FLATBREAD (NAAN)
MAKES 4 PIECES

This recipe worked best with a high-protein all-purpose flour such as King Arthur brand. Do not use nonfat yogurt in this recipe. A 12-inch nonstick skillet may be used in place of the cast-iron skillet. For efficiency, stretch the next ball of dough while each naan is cooking.

- ½ cup ice water
- ⅓ cup plain whole-milk yogurt
- 3 tablespoons plus 1 teaspoon vegetable oil
- 1 large egg yolk
- 2 cups (10 ounces) all-purpose flour
- 1¼ teaspoons sugar
- ½ teaspoon instant or rapid-rise yeast
- 1¼ teaspoons salt
- 1½ tablespoons unsalted butter, melted

1. In measuring cup or small bowl, combine water, yogurt, 3 tablespoons oil, and egg yolk. Process flour, sugar, and yeast in food processor until combined, about 2 seconds. With processor running, slowly add water mixture; process until dough is just combined and no dry flour remains, about 10 seconds. Let dough stand for 10 minutes.

2. Add salt to dough and process until dough forms satiny, sticky ball that clears sides of workbowl, 30 to 60 seconds. Transfer dough to lightly floured work surface and knead until smooth, about 1 minute. Shape dough into tight ball and place in large, lightly oiled bowl. Cover tightly with plastic wrap and refrigerate for 16 to 24 hours.

3. Adjust oven rack to middle position and heat oven to 200 degrees. Place heatproof plate on rack.

Transfer dough to lightly floured work surface and divide into 4 equal pieces. Shape each piece into smooth, tight ball. Place dough balls on lightly oiled baking sheet, at least 2 inches apart; cover loosely with plastic coated with vegetable oil spray. Let stand for 15 to 20 minutes.

4. Transfer 1 ball to lightly floured work surface and sprinkle with flour. Using hands and rolling pin, press and roll piece of dough into 9-inch round of even thickness, sprinkling dough and work surface with flour as needed to prevent sticking. Using fork, poke entire surface of round 20 to 25 times. Heat remaining 1 teaspoon oil in 12-inch cast-iron skillet over medium heat until shimmering. Wipe oil out of skillet completely with paper towels. Mist top of dough lightly with water. Place dough in pan, moistened side down; mist top surface of dough with water; and cover. Cook until bottom is browned in spots across surface, 2 to 4 minutes. Flip naan, cover, and continue to cook on second side until lightly browned, 2 to 3 minutes. (If naan puffs up, gently poke with fork to deflate.) Flip naan, brush top with about 1 teaspoon melted butter, transfer to plate in oven, and cover plate tightly with aluminum foil. Repeat rolling and cooking remaining 3 dough balls. Once last naan is baked, serve immediately.

QUICKER INDIAN FLATBREAD (NAAN)

This variation, which can be prepared in about two hours, forgoes the overnight rest, but the dough may be a little harder to roll out.

After shaping dough in step 2, let dough rise at room temperature for 30 minutes. After 30 minutes, fold partially risen dough over itself 8 times by gently lifting and folding edge of dough toward middle, turning bowl 90 degrees after each fold. Cover with plastic wrap and let rise for 30 minutes. Repeat folding, turning, and rising one more time, for total of three 30-minute rises. After last rise, proceed with recipe from step 3.

Dressing Up Carrot Cake

This American classic has a lot going for it: moist cake, delicate spice, tangy cream cheese frosting. If only it were handsome enough to serve to company, too.

⇒ BY ANDREA GEARY ⇐

As showstopper desserts go, carrot cake is often overlooked, and that's a shame. That's not because it's difficult or fussy to make; on the contrary, carrot cake is a relatively easy option since the typical "dump and stir" method means there's no need to haul out the stand mixer. It's also not passed over for lack of flavor; between its moist, fragrantly spiced crumb that's chock-full of plump raisins and crunchy nuts and its luxurious cream cheese frosting, it brings more to the table than many desserts. The problem really boils down to aesthetics. Traditional carrot cake is a rather homely confection—a snack cake typically baked in a serviceable 13 by 9-inch pan and topped with frumpy-looking frosting. That's fine for an informal family dinner but not as the finale for a fancier occasion.

Building a layer cake would be the obvious way to dress it up, but stacking delicately slim slabs into a lofty tower comes with plenty of obstacles. For starters, the carrots that moisten and sweeten the cake also make it sticky and prone to breaking—and a real nightmare to slice horizontally. Additionally, no more than two layers (baked in separate pans) of that moist, heavy cake can be stacked without risk of toppling. I've seen bakeries pull off tall, stately carrot cakes but not without compromising the frosting. To make it thick enough to keep the cake structurally sound, they load it up with powdered sugar, dulling the characteristic tang of the cream cheese.

My challenges were several: For layers that were both slender and sturdy, I'd have to lighten the crumb without sacrificing moisture. I'd also have to rework the frosting to support a taller profile, but I was determined to avoid a sickly sweet concoction.

Thinking Inside the Box

Putting aside the frosting for the moment, I made a first attempt at the cake by following a conventional formula: Flour, baking powder, salt, cinnamon, clove, and nutmeg were whisked together in one bowl, and eggs, brown sugar, vanilla extract, and vegetable oil (oil, not butter, is almost always used) in another. I folded shredded carrots, raisins, and chopped pecans into the wet ingredients; added the dry; divided the batter between two 9-inch round cake pans; and pushed them into a 350-degree oven to bake for 45 minutes. (Because the vegetable adds moisture to the batter, carrot cakes bake longer than other types.)

After allowing the layers to cool for a full 90 minutes (warm cakes are more likely to break when

Pressing toasted nuts into the frosting (rather than incorporating them into the batter) helps the cake cut cleanly.

handled and will melt the frosting), I tried to neatly trim and halve the cakes. For a seemingly straightforward job, it was a disaster. The tacky crumbs stuck to my knife as I tried to shave off the domed top of each layer, and the blade seemed to snag every nut it hit as I sliced the cakes horizontally. Moving the sliced layers without breaking them also proved nearly impossible.

I was starting to reconsider the homely charms of a sheet cake when, on a visit to a wholesale club, I spotted a rectangular layer cake that stood four tiers high. The layers had been baked in shallow jelly roll pans and then stacked with frosting. Quantity-wise, it was more cake than I wanted, but the slender, uniform layers were intriguing: Could I bake my cake in a rimmed baking sheet, divide it into four equal pieces, and stack them into a tall, rectangular cake?

As it turned out, this concept had a lot going for it: In a standard 18 by 13-inch rimmed baking sheet, the cake baked in a mere 16 minutes and took only 30 minutes to cool. Another bonus: Because the middle set almost as quickly as the edges, the cake didn't dome, rendering the trimming step unnecessary. Feeling smug, I summoned tasters—but they weren't more than a bite into my four-tier confection before they identified a major flaw that brought me down to earth: The carrots were crunchy. Thanks to the drastically reduced baking time, the coarse shreds hadn't had a chance to soften.

Baking Soda pH-ix

As a knee-jerk reaction, I tried cooking and pureeing the carrots before incorporating them into the batter, but then their texture was completely lost. I didn't want crunch, but I did want the star of the dessert to be identifiable. I tried grinding raw carrots in the food processor and finely grating them, but the resulting bits also disappeared into the crumb.

Then a light bulb went on: When developing my recipe for Home Fries (January/February 2012), I added baking soda—an alkali—to the cooking water to soften the exteriors of the boiled potato chunks, which raised the pH of the liquid and caused the pectin in the potato cell walls to break down. Would baking soda have the same effect on carrots?

I added a teaspoon of baking soda (the cake already contained 2 teaspoons of baking powder) to another batch of batter and crossed my fingers. Any worry I had that the cake would fall (a common consequence of overleavening) or that it would have a metallic, chemical taste was for naught. Thanks to

Structural Solution

For a cream cheese frosting that's stiff enough to hold several layers of cake in place, we used tangy buttermilk powder—along with confectioners' sugar—to add body.

POWDERED BUTTERMILK

the baking soda's pH-boosting effect, the carrots were visible but tender, and the crumb was incredibly light yet moist, with no off-flavors. I had just two more changes to make before moving on to the frosting: Since the nuts that caught on my knife during slicing caused the cake to tear, I eliminated them for now. And because the raisins looked clunky in these slim, lighter-than-ever layers, I swapped in daintier currants.

STEP BY STEP | BUILDING A BEAUTIFUL LAYER CAKE

1. MAKE A THIN CAKE
Bake batter on baking sheet to create thin, level cake that doesn't need to be split horizontally.

2. CUT INTO RECTANGLES
Slice cooled sheet cake into four equal rectangles.

3. STACK 'EM
Spread frosting over rectangular layer placed on cardboard; repeat with remaining layers.

4. NUTS ON THE SIDES
Press chopped pecans onto sides of cake to hide any imperfections and add crunch.

Frosted Over

The next step: a tangy frosting. Most recipes are basic mixtures of butter, cream cheese, and confectioners' sugar, but ratios vary. Go heavy on the cream cheese and you get a rich, bright frosting, but one that is perilously soft and likely to trickle down the sides of the cake or—even worse—cause the layers to slip and slide. Adding sugar solves the structural issues but masks the cream cheese flavor.

The standard recipe I tried (12 ounces of cream cheese, 8 ounces of butter, 2 cups of confectioners' sugar, and 2 teaspoons of vanilla extract) fell victim to both of these faults: It was too soft and too sweet. Adding acidic lemon juice, sour cream, and yogurt punched up the tang but also introduced more liquid, thereby necessitating more sugar for thickening—a vicious circle. I even tried stirring in some melted white chocolate, but tasters found the cocoa butter flavor distracting in even the smallest concentration. Finally, a cream cheese "miracle frosting" (thickened with roux) was rejected because its airy consistency didn't contrast with my newly lightened cake.

It wasn't until I started rummaging through the test kitchen pantry for ideas that I came across a potential fix: buttermilk powder. I wondered if its pleasantly cheesy tang would do the trick in my frosting. I added 2 tablespoons to my frosting and was delighted to find that the mixture was not only flavorful but also markedly tangy. In fact, adding ⅓ cup of powder made the frosting so potent that I could increase the sugar by 1 cup, for a consistency that was structurally sound but still not overly sweet.

I was getting close, but my cake was not yet special-occasion ready. Specifically, the delicate cut surfaces released crumbs as I assembled the layers, meaning that while the frosting on top of the cake looked pristine, the sides were a wreck. That's where the nuts came back into the equation. To camouflage the imperfections—and satisfy tasters who missed the crunch of the pecans in the cake—I pressed toasted nuts onto the crumb-speckled sides.

I'd had my doubts that a carrot layer cake was feasible but gladly proved myself wrong. With nothing but a sheet pan and the surprise help of a few pantry ingredients, I'd managed to reengineer humble carrot cake as a four-tier, nut-crusted confection that could claim its place among the most glamorous desserts.

CARROT LAYER CAKE
SERVES 10 TO 12

Shred the carrots on the large holes of a box grater or in a food processor fitted with the shredding disk. Do not substitute liquid buttermilk for the buttermilk powder. To ensure the proper spreading consistency for the frosting, use cold cream cheese. If your baked cake is of an uneven thickness, adjust the orientation of the layers as they are stacked to produce a level cake. Assembling this cake on a cardboard cake round trimmed to a 6 by 8-inch rectangle makes it easy to press the pecans onto the sides of the frosted cake.

Cake

- 1¾ cups (8¾ ounces) all-purpose flour
- 2 teaspoons baking powder
- 1 teaspoon baking soda
- 1½ teaspoons ground cinnamon
- ¾ teaspoon ground nutmeg
- ½ teaspoon salt
- ¼ teaspoon ground cloves
- 1¼ cups packed (8¾ ounces) light brown sugar
- ¾ cup vegetable oil
- 3 large eggs
- 1 teaspoon vanilla extract
- 2⅔ cups shredded carrots (4 carrots)
- ⅔ cup dried currants

Frosting

- 16 tablespoons unsalted butter, softened
- 3 cups (12 ounces) confectioners' sugar
- ⅓ cup buttermilk powder
- 2 teaspoons vanilla extract
- ¼ teaspoon salt
- 12 ounces cream cheese, chilled and cut into 12 equal pieces
- 2 cups (8 ounces) pecans, toasted and chopped coarse

1. FOR THE CAKE: Adjust oven rack to middle position and heat oven to 350 degrees. Grease 18 by 13-inch rimmed baking sheet, line with parchment paper, and grease parchment. Whisk flour, baking powder, baking soda, cinnamon, nutmeg, salt, and cloves together in large bowl.

2. Whisk sugar, oil, eggs, and vanilla together until mixture is smooth. Stir in carrots and currants. Add flour mixture and fold with rubber spatula until mixture is just combined.

3. Transfer batter to prepared baking sheet and smooth surface with offset spatula. Bake until center of cake is firm to touch, 15 to 18 minutes. Cool in pan on wire rack for 5 minutes. Invert cake onto wire rack (do not remove parchment) and then reinvert onto second wire rack. Cool cake completely, about 30 minutes.

4. FOR THE FROSTING: Using stand mixer fitted with paddle, beat butter, sugar, buttermilk powder, vanilla, and salt on low speed until smooth, about 2 minutes, scraping down bowl as needed. Increase speed to medium-low; add cream cheese, 1 piece at a time; and mix until smooth, about 2 minutes.

5. Transfer cooled cake to cutting board, parchment side down. Using sharp chef's knife, cut cake and parchment in half crosswise and then lengthwise to make 4 equal rectangles, about 6 by 8 inches each.

6. Place 6 by 8-inch cardboard rectangle on cake turntable or plate. Place 1 cake rectangle, parchment side up, on cardboard and carefully remove parchment. Using offset spatula, spread ⅔ cup frosting evenly over cake layer. Repeat with two more layers of cake, frosting each layer with ⅔ cup frosting and pressing gently on each layer to level. Place last rectangle of cake on top and frost top of cake with 1 cup frosting. Use remaining frosting to coat sides of cake. (It's fine if some crumbs show through frosting on sides, but if you go back to smooth top of cake, be sure that spatula is free of crumbs.)

7. Hold cake with 1 hand and gently press chopped pecans onto sides with other hand. Chill for at least 1 hour before serving.

TO MAKE AHEAD: The cake may be refrigerated for up to 24 hours before serving.

See How It Stacks Up
Video available FREE for 4 months at www.CooksIllustrated.com/jun12

Perfectly Popped Corn

Stovetop popcorn can be tricky: Most of the time you wind up burning some kernels, while others never pop at all. The best method that we've found for avoiding both problems calls for first placing a few kernels in high-smoke-point oil (such as canola or peanut) and then removing the pan from the heat as soon as they pop. Add the rest of the kernels, cover the pan, and wait 30 seconds before returning it to the stove to finish popping the corn. When we tested this method, we got great results each time: no scorching and only one or two unpopped "old maids." Why does it work? Preheating the oil with "test" kernels indicates when the oil has reached the optimal popping temperature (around 380 degrees), and the 30-second off-burner wait allows all of the kernels to gradually heat to the same temperature—so they pop almost simultaneously.

1. Heat 3 tablespoons oil and 3 popcorn kernels over medium heat in covered 4-quart pan.

2. When test kernels burst, remove pot from heat and add ⅓ cup popcorn.

3. Cover pot and wait 30 seconds before returning pan to heat.

4. When kernels start to pop, shake pan (with lid slightly ajar) until popping slows to 1 to 2 seconds between pops.

Keeping Salad Dressing Together with Garlic

In our Foolproof Vinaigrette recipe (September/October 2009), we use ½ teaspoon of mayonnaise to keep normally incompatible oil and vinegar combined after whisking. Mayonnaise works well in this role because it contains egg yolks, which are rich in a phospholipid called lecithin, a superb emulsifier. Lecithin coats the surface of water droplets, preventing them from merging with one another and helping them remain suspended in oil.

Mustard contains a carbohydrate called mucilage that acts as an effective emulsifier. That's why mustard powder often shows up in dressings. But there's another common vinaigrette ingredient with untapped emulsifying potential: garlic. We found that ¼ teaspoon of garlic paste (made by mashing minced garlic and coarse salt with the side of a chef's knife or by rubbing a clove on a rasp-style grater) per ¼ cup of vinaigrette worked nearly as well as mayonnaise to stabilize dressing. Chopped or finely minced garlic, on the other hand, showed little emulsifying ability, since the emulsifiers remained bound within its cell walls.

The Best Way to Revive Leftover Pizza

Reheated leftover pizza always pales in comparison with a freshly baked pie. The microwave turns it soggy, while throwing it into a hot oven can dry it out. We recently discovered a reheating method that really works: Place the cold slices on a rimmed baking sheet, cover the sheet tightly with aluminum foil, and place it on the lowest rack of a cold oven. Then set the oven temperature to 275 degrees and let the pizza warm for 25 to 30 minutes. This approach leaves the interior of the crust soft, the cheese melty, and the toppings and bottom hot and crisp but not dehydrated.

Why does this method work? Like other breads stored for a day, pizza crust initially hardens not through moisture loss but because its starches undergo a process called retrogradation, whereby the starch molecules crystallize and absorb moisture, making the pizza crust appear stiff and dry. As long as the pizza has been stored well wrapped, however, retrogradation can be temporarily reversed by reheating the pizza to at least 140 degrees—the temperature at which the starch crystals break down

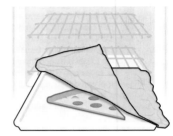

WINNING WARMUP
Place pizza (on a baking sheet wrapped in foil) on the bottom rack of a cold oven. Set temperature to 275 degrees and heat for 25 minutes.

and release the trapped moisture, softening the crust. Placing the slices in a cold oven lets them warm up gradually, with ample time to release moisture and soften, while sealing the pan helps keep them from drying out as they reheat. Finally, placing the pan as low as possible in the oven means the slices are heated from the bottom up, so the underside of the crust crisps but the toppings don't shrivel.

Frothier Foam

A reader Quick Tip in our May/June 2011 issue described a way to froth milk by microwaving it in the glass beaker of a French press and then pumping the hot milk into a thick foam with the press's plunger. Since then, we've found that reversing the process and frothing while the milk is still cold produces a creamier, longer-lasting, and more billowy foam.

Here's why: Agitating milk when it's cold lets you pump more air bubbles into it. As you pack in more air, the bubbles become smaller and the foam becomes denser. Frothing hot milk produces bigger, weaker bubbles because the proteins have already bound to one another and are less able to coat and stabilize the air bubbles. When milk is heated after frothing, however, the proteins coat the air bubbles before cross-linking and are able to reinforce the structure of the foam that's already been created.

Here's the updated technique: Fill a French press's glass beaker no more than one-third full with cold milk. Froth vigorously with the plunger until the milk doubles in volume (about 20 seconds). Remove the plunger and microwave the beaker on full power for 30 to 45 seconds or until the foam rises nearly to the top. You can also use a sealable glass jar: Shake cold milk forcefully in the tightly sealed jar for about 20 seconds, remove the lid, and microwave the jar. (This method produces a slightly coarser foam.)

FROTHED COLD   **FROTHED HOT**
For a creamier, longer-lasting foam for your espresso, froth milk before you heat it.

ILLUSTRATION: JOHN BURGOYNE, JAY LAYMAN

INDEX
May & June 2012

NEW RECIPES ON THE WEB
Available free for 4 months at
www.CooksIllustrated.com/jun12

Chicken Salad with Red Grapes and Smoked Almonds
Curried Chicken Salad with Cashews
Fresh Farfalle Without a Machine
Fresh Garganelli Without a Machine
Fresh Maltagliati Without a Machine
Navy Bean and Artichoke Dip with Parsley
Remoulade Sauce
Tomato–Brown Butter Sauce
Waldorf Chicken Salad

COOK'S LIVE VIDEOS
Available free for 4 months at
www.CooksIllustrated.com/jun12

Best Crab Cakes
Butter Bean and Pea Dip with Mint
Carrot Layer Cake
Chinese Chicken Lettuce Wraps
Classic Chicken Salad
Fresh Pasta Without a Machine
Grilled Steak with New Mexican Chile Rub
Indian Flatbread (Naan)
Italian Vegetable Stew (Ciambotta)
Spicy Pork Tacos (al Pastor)
Testing Graters

Best Crab Cakes, 9

Chinese Chicken Lettuce Wraps, 10

Grilled Steak with New Mexican Chile Rub, 7

Classic Chicken Salad, 20

Butter Bean and Pea Dip with Mint, 21

Indian Flatbread (Naan), 23

Carrot Layer Cake, 25

Spicy Pork Tacos (al Pastor), 19

Italian Vegetable Stew (Ciambotta), 15

Fresh Pasta Without a Machine, 13

AMERICA'S TEST KITCHEN
Public television's most popular cooking show

Join the millions of home cooks who watch our show, *America's Test Kitchen*, on public television every week. For more information, including recipes and program times, visit www.AmericasTestKitchenTV.com.

AMERICA'S TEST KITCHEN RADIO

Tune in to our new radio program featuring answers to listener call-in questions, ingredient taste test and equipment review segments, and in-depth reporting on a variety of topics. To listen to episodes, visit www.AmericasTestKitchen.com/Radio.

NEW! ONLINE COOKING SCHOOL

Learn how to think—and cook—like a pro from real test cooks who work here at America's Test Kitchen. We combine personalized instruction with leading-edge technology to offer an unparalleled learning experience. Try it free at www.TestKitchenSchool.com.

DOWNLOAD OUR FREE
COOK'S ILLUSTRATED iPHONE APP

Features a collection of our top recipes, along with tastings, videos, and useful timer and shopping list features. CooksIllustrated.com members can access 19 years of recipes, videos, tastings, and more. Go to www.CooksIllustrated.com/iPhone.

Follow us on Twitter: twitter.com/TestKitchen
Find us on Facebook: facebook.com/CooksIllustrated

Red

Manzano

Thai

Baby

Burro

Plantain

Cavendish

BANANAS

COOK'S
ILLUSTRATED

Real Jerk Chicken
We Get the Smoke Right

Grilled Beef Short Ribs
Indoor/Outdoor Method

Best Raspberry Sorbet
The Science of Smooth

Grill-Smoked Salmon
Can We Keep It Moist?

Juicy Turkey Burgers
It's in the Grind

Tasting American Cheddars

Quick Corn Salsas
Fresh Flavor, Perfect Texture

Testing Vegetable Peelers
Chilled Fresh Tomato Soup
Spanish Pasta with Shrimp
Homemade Hamburger Buns

www.CooksIllustrated.com
$5.95 U.S./$6.95 CANADA

0 8>

0 74470 62805 7

CONTENTS

July & August 2012

HEIRLOOM LETTUCES Butterhead lettuces form tender, loose, rounded leaves. Some varieties, like rust-dappled, lime-green Speckles, are sweet and rich; others, like Pirat, are spicy and herbaceous. Baseball-size Tom Thumb is a miniature butterhead, ideal for individual salads. Cos lettuces, like Red Rose and Sweet Romaine, are long and sturdy, with a firm center rib and savory flavor. Looseleaf varieties, which include ruffled, bracingly bitter Lolla Rossa and frilly Red Tango, branch from a single stalk instead of forming a compact head. Hardy summer crisp lettuces, such as mild Red Wine Batavian, have tall, wavy-edged leaves and a crunchy texture. Winter Density, a butterhead-romaine cross, boasts broad, dark green leaves with good chew. Tiny petite crystal lettuces, prized for their delicate, suede-like leaves, succulent texture, and complex flavors, are often used as garnishes.

COVER (Watermelon): Robert Papp; BACK COVER (Heirloom Lettuces): John Burgoyne

America's TEST KITCHEN

RECIPES THAT WORK®

America's Test Kitchen is a very real 2,500-square-foot kitchen located just outside of Boston. It is the home of *Cook's Illustrated* and *Cook's Country* magazines and is the workday destination of more than three dozen test cooks, editors, and cookware specialists. Our mission is to test recipes over and over again until we understand how and why they work and until we arrive at the best version. We also test kitchen equipment and supermarket ingredients in search of brands that offer the best value and performance. You can watch us work by tuning in to *America's Test Kitchen* (www.AmericasTestKitchenTV.com) on public television.

COOK'S
ILLUSTRATED

Founder and Editor — Christopher Kimball
Editorial Director — Jack Bishop
Editorial Director, Magazines — John Willoughby
Executive Editor — Amanda Agee
Test Kitchen Director — Erin McMurrer
Managing Editor — Rebecca Hays
Senior Editors — Keith Dresser
Lisa McManus
Associate Features Editors — Elizabeth Bomze
Danette St. Onge
Copy Editors — Nell Beram
Megan Chromik
Associate Editors — Andrea Geary
Amy Graves
Andrew Janjigian
Chris O'Connor
Dan Souza
Test Cook — Lan Lam
Assistant Editors — Hannah Crowley
Shannon Friedmann Hatch
Taizeth Sierra
Assistant Test Cooks — Dan Cellucci
Sara Mayer
Celeste Rogers
Executive Assistant — Christine Gordon
Assistant Test Kitchen Director — Gina Nistico
Test Kitchen Manager — Leah Rovner
Senior Kitchen Assistant — Meryl MacCormack
Kitchen Assistants — Maria Elena Delgado
Ena Gudiel
Andrew Straaberg Finfrock
Executive Producer — Melissa Baldino
Associate Producer — Stephanie Stender
Production Assistant — Kaitlin Hammond
Contributing Editors — Matthew Card
Dawn Yanagihara
Consulting Editor — Scott Brueggeman
Science Editor — Guy Crosby, Ph.D.
Managing Editor, Web — Christine Liu
Online Associate Editors — Eric Grzymkowski
Mari Levine
Roger Metcalf
Senior Video Editor — Nick Dakoulas

Design Director — Amy Klee
Art Director — Julie Cote
Deputy Art Director — Susan Levin
Associate Art Director — Lindsey Timko
Deputy Art Director, Marketing/Web — Erica Lee
Designers, Marketing/Web — Elaina Natario
Mariah Tarvainen
Staff Photographer — Daniel J. van Ackere
Photo Editor — Steve Klise

Vice President, Marketing — David Mack
Circulation Director — Doug Wicinski
Circulation & Fulfillment Manager — Carrie Fethe
Partnership Marketing Manager — Pamela Putprush
Marketing Assistant — Lauren Perkins
Customer Service Manager — Jacqueline Valerio
Customer Service Representatives — Jessica Amato
Morgan Ryan

Chief Operations Officer — David Dinnage
Production Director — Guy Rochford
Senior Project Manager — Alice Carpenter
Workflow & Digital Asset Manager — Andrew Mannone
Production & Imaging Specialists — Judy Blomquist
Heather Dube
Lauren Pettapiece
Systems Administrator — Marcus Walser
Development Manager — Robert Martinez
Software Project Manager — Michelle Rushin
Business Analyst — Wendy Tseng
Web Developers — Chris Candelora
Cameron MacKensie
Human Resources Director — Adele Shapiro

VP New Media Product Development — Barry Kelly
Social Media Manager — Steph Yiu

Chief Financial Officer — Sharyn Chabot
Director of Sponsorship Sales — Anne Traficante
Retail Sales & Marketing Director — Emily Logan
Client Service Associate — Kate May
Publicity — Deborah Broide

PRINTED IN THE USA

THE SEARCHERS

Two years ago, I set out with two of my kids, Caroline and Emily, on horseback over Egg Mountain to find our way up through winding trails to the next town, about eight miles north as the crow flies. I was riding my twitchy paint, Concho; Caroline was on her half-blind Appaloosa, Dakota; Emily was on her 18-year-old pony; and Rhoda, a neighbor, was astride her great moose of a horse, Gypsy. (It's like riding an overstuffed sofa.) The route is a series of twists and turns and requires a sharp memory. The problem was, as soon as we got high up, we found that loggers had clear-cut the mountaintop and the landscape appeared ragged and unfamiliar. After leading our horses through a large field of felled trees and swamp, I set out searching for the way forward. At one point, I got within a few yards of the trail but turned back, thinking it was a dead end. Eventually, we trotted home, disappointed and bone tired.

One of my favorite Westerns, *The Searchers*, was directed by John Ford and starred John Wayne. The story is bittersweet. Two sisters are kidnapped, one is found murdered, and rescuing the younger sister becomes the driving narrative. The screenplay is a tangle of conflicting morals and motives. At one point, Wayne even tries to shoot the abducted girl rather than let her live among the Comanches. Finally, Wayne reunites the girl with her family and he walks away alone, still an unhappy searcher. (The movie was loosely based on the true story of Cynthia Ann Parker, who was abducted at age 9; lived among the Comanches for 24 years; was the mother of the last free Comanche chief, Quanah Parker; and, once "rescued," spent the remaining 10 years of her life trying to get back to her family. She died of heartbreak.)

This country was founded on searching for religious or economic freedom; take your pick. Then we headed west in search of better farmland, a pass through the Rocky Mountains, gold, and the Pacific Ocean. And my generation has been on an eternal quest for $40 vodka, bungee jumping, unpronounceable fruits from the Amazon basin, and colon cleansing, and it has a religious fascination with chakras. This week, my 14-year-old is stuck on Juicy Couture; last month it was architectural Legos. I can't wait until she turns 15.

Searching is usually about the search itself, not the destination. If one listens to Buddhists, such as Pema Chödrön, one starts to think that life is nothing more than the struggle. She says, "The truth is that things don't really get solved." So one might start to think that *The Searchers* was some sort of Buddhist production—a training video, perhaps. Wayne moves through the narrative, mostly angry, often violent, and resolves nothing. He rides in at the beginning of the movie and rides out at the end. So what exactly does one do when one reaches the shores of the Pacific? Well, like Lewis and Clark, you turn around and walk back.

Lots of teenagers are anxious to leave small towns. Even the Amish provide Rumspringa, a period of experimentation when a teenager reaches 16. Eventually, one chooses baptism in the church or one leaves the life forever. But in our small town, we are not searchers. We do seek deer and rabbits, trout and turkeys, but many old-timers have never left the state, much less the town itself. I was in a Shaw's supermarket recently—two towns over—and was recognized by a local. She asked where I lived, and when I told her, she looked gobsmacked and blurted out, "Where?"

The problem is that once you're bitten with the search bug, it's hard to kick the habit. Many sign up for yoga teacher training, Chinese lessons, bodywork, or early retirement with a heavy schedule of writing workshops and flying instruction. This whole menu of self-improvement is appealing, and as a searcher myself, I speak from experience. But

Christopher Kimball

when I step through the screen door of Sherman's Country Store and I see the same crowd, seated at the same wooden table and drinking the same Green Mountain coffee every time I go in, it makes me wonder if life is indeed about evolution. It would be comforting to exist happily as a distant relative of Lucy, walking mostly upright, dragging my knuckles. All I would have to search for is food; survival was pretty much the only truth 3 million years ago.

In *Lonesome Dove*, Larry McMurtry's Pulitzer Prize–winning epic, Gus McCrae is the ultimate searcher. He convinces his business partner, Woodrow Call, to ride a herd north. It wasn't a business proposition; it was a search for adventure and romance—he was in pursuit of his old sweetheart, Clara. He found her in Ogallala, Nebraska, but he quickly turned away from the settled life. Gus died a few months later, ending up stuck with an arrow after recklessly galloping across an open prairie just for the joy of it.

Unlike John Wayne, Gus McCrae had it all. He was a searcher who also enjoyed the simple pleasures. He once said to Lorena, an unhappy working girl who was desperate to get to San Francisco, "If you want any one thing too badly, it's likely to turn out to be a disappointment. The only healthy way to live life is to learn to like all the little everyday things, like a sip of good whiskey in the evening, a soft bed, a glass of buttermilk, or a feisty gentleman like myself."

Gus could have survived as a cripple but decided instead to die of his wounds.

He chose death over life, explaining his decision to Woodrow by saying, "It's not dying I'm talking about; it's living." As he slipped away, his last words were, "By God, Woodrow; it's been one hell of a party." At least Gus was clever enough to enjoy the ride.

FOR INQUIRIES, ORDERS, OR MORE INFORMATION

www.CooksIllustrated.com
At www.CooksIllustrated.com, you can order books and subscriptions, sign up for our free e-newsletter, or renew your magazine subscription. Join the website and gain access to 19 years of *Cook's Illustrated* recipes, equipment tests, and ingredient tastings, as well as companion videos for every recipe in this issue.

COOKBOOKS
We sell more than 50 cookbooks by the editors of *Cook's Illustrated*.
To order, visit our bookstore at www.CooksIllustrated.com.

COOK'S ILLUSTRATED MAGAZINE
Cook's Illustrated magazine (ISSN 1068-2821), number 117, is published bimonthly by Boston Common Press Limited partnership, 17 Station St., Brookline, MA 02445. Copyright 2012 Boston Common Press Limited Partnership. Periodicals postage paid at Boston, Massachusetts, and additional mailing offices, USPS #012487. Publications Mail Agreement No. 40020778. Return undeliverable Canadian addresses to P.O. Box 875, Station A, Windsor, ON N9A 6P2. POSTMASTER: Send address changes to *Cook's Illustrated*, P.O. Box 6018, Harlan, IA 51593-1518. For subscription and gift subscription orders, subscription inquiries, or change-of-address notices, visit us at www.AmericasTestKitchen.com/customerservice, call us at 800-526-8442, or write us at *Cook's Illustrated*, P.O. 6018, Harlan, IA 51593-1518.

FOR LIST RENTAL INFORMATION Contact Specialists Marketing Services, Inc., 777 Terrace Ave., 4th Floor, Hasbrouck Heights, NJ 07604; 201-865-5800.

EDITORIAL OFFICE 17 Station St., Brookline, MA 02445; 617-232-1000; fax 617-232-1572. Subscription inquiries, visit www.AmericasTestKitchen.com/customerservice or call 800-526-8442.

POSTMASTER Send all new orders, subscription inquiries, and change-of-address notices to *Cook's Illustrated*, P.O. Box 6018, Harlan, IA 51593-1518.

BY ANDREA GEARY & DAN SOUZA

Round or Oval Dutch Oven?

Does an oval cast-iron Dutch oven cook as well as a round one?

EMILY HOOD
WEST LEBANON, N.H.

➤Since our favorite Dutch oven in the test kitchen has long been a round model, we've never put this question to the test. To answer it, we bought a 6¾-quart Le Creuset oval enameled cast-iron Dutch oven, the closest equivalent to our favorite 7¼-quart round oven. (A quick refresher in geometry assured us that despite their difference in capacity, the surface areas of the two Dutch ovens were very similar.) So would the two long ends of the oval pot, which are never directly over the burner, make for uneven cooking and browning?

To our surprise, we found that beef chunks browned equally well in the two vessels, and long pork roasts were also evenly colored. The key, it turns out, is the cast-iron material of the ovens: Because it's not an especially efficient conductor of energy, cast iron takes longer to heat up than less substantial materials, but once thoroughly heated, it retains heat very well, making those end areas not in direct contact with the burner just as capable of browning meat as the center.

The bottom line: As long as you adequately preheat it, an oval cast-iron Dutch oven should cook as well as a round model, without any adjustments to cooking times or procedures.

IN GOOD SHAPE
Round and oval Dutch ovens work equally well.

Baking Pies in Disposable Pie Plates

I usually bake pies in glass, but for an upcoming bake sale, I'll need to use disposable aluminum pie plates. Do you have any tips for success?

TAMMY LAMOREAUX
BOSTON, MASS.

➤We prefer baking pies in Pyrex plates because the glass evenly distributes heat (for great browning) while providing a clear view (so we can easily judge when the crust is done). We place our glass pie plates on a preheated baking sheet for an extra-crisp, golden bottom crust that doesn't get soggy when filled.

Initially, we assumed that disposable aluminum pie plates would absorb and conduct heat too quickly, leading to burnt crusts, so we omitted the baking sheet. But after blind-baking a few pie shells in them, we found just the opposite to be true—the bottoms were still pale and damp long after the fluted edges had crisped and browned. Placing them on a preheated baking sheet helped, but the sides were still undercooked and tended to slump after we removed the pie weights to let the insides of the shells brown.

It turns out that due to their thin walls, aluminum plates can't hold or transfer a significant amount of heat from the oven to the crust. The upshot is that crusts bake more slowly in aluminum, so they need to spend more time in the oven. For prebaking empty crusts, you'll need to increase the time that the crust bakes with weights by up to 10 minutes or until you see any visual doneness cues indicated by the recipe. For filled double-crust pies, increase the baking time by up to 10 minutes and cover the top of the pie with aluminum foil if it starts to get too dark. Place aluminum pie plates on a preheated baking sheet for a well-browned bottom crust and for added stability when moving pies out of the oven.

Cooking with Coconut Oil

I've read that coconut oil may be good for you. But how does it perform in recipes?

CASSIE KANZ
PECONIC, N.Y.

➤Once demonized, coconut oil is experiencing a comeback. As long as the oil isn't hydrogenated (which creates the dreaded trans fats that clog arteries), some scientists say that it isn't as bad as once thought. In fact, coconut oil may even have health benefits such as boosting metabolism and strengthening the immune system. It's also gaining popularity with vegans as a nondairy butter substitute. Coconut oil is sold in two forms, both solid at room temperature: refined, which has virtually no taste or aroma, and virgin, which retains a strong coconut flavor. Since we have limited use for an oil that makes food smell and taste like a piña colada, we tested only the refined product.

We tried the melted oil in chocolate chip cookies and found that it performed just as well as melted butter, though we missed butter's sweet dairy flavor. Ditto when we creamed the oil for cake and used it to sauté carrots. (Because of its steep price—about $8 for 16 ounces—coconut oil is impractical for deep frying.) In an all-butter pie crust, subbing coconut oil for butter required an adjustment. Most pie dough needs to be chilled before rolling, but coconut oil becomes hard and brittle when refrigerated, leading to dough that is too firm to roll out without cracking. The simple fix: Rest the dough on the counter instead of in the fridge.

BUTTER SUB
Flavorless refined coconut oil makes a good stand-in for butter.

In short: If you're avoiding dairy, refined coconut oil makes a perfectly good substitute for butter (or oil, for that matter) in baking and sautéing.

Pantry Panade

I don't always keep white sandwich bread on hand. Can I substitute dry panko bread crumbs for fresh when I'm making a panade?

MIMI STEARNS
JUNO BEACH, FLA.

➤A panade is a milk-and-bread paste that's folded into ground meat before shaping it into meatloaf and meatballs or even burgers; the bread starches absorb milk to form a gel that coats and lubricates the meat, keeping it moist and tender.

We found that when we kept the milk at 2 tablespoons and did a straight swap of ½ cup of panko for ½ cup of fresh bread crumbs in a panade that we mixed into burgers, the panko crumbs swelled to twice their volume and resembled fresh crumbs. They didn't form a paste, though, so we increased the amount of milk to help the panko break down and disperse evenly in our patties. Bottom line? Panko can be thought of as a sort of fresh bread-crumb concentrate. Here's the substitution formula: For every slice of bread (or ½ cup of fresh crumbs) and 2 tablespoons of milk called for, use ¼ cup of panko and 3 tablespoons of milk.

½ CUP FRESH CRUMBS + 2 TBS MILK
Our standard panade formula.

¼ CUP PANKO + 3 TBS MILK
To substitute, use less panko and more milk.

Porcini versus Shiitake

In your May/June 2012 issue, you featured a chart showing that dried shiitake mushrooms have 15 times more flavor-building nucleotides than dried porcini. Should I switch to dried shiitakes from now on when I want to boost meaty flavor?

RICHARD BRANDON
BOSTON, MASS.

➤To find out how well dried shiitake mushrooms stand in for porcini, we used each type of mushroom in a vegetable soup that calls for ⅛ ounce of dried mushrooms and a mushroom sauce that uses ½ ounce of dried mushrooms. The results? The soup made with shiitakes was deemed meatier, with less pronounced mushroomy flavor, than its porcini counterpart—a plus for a majority of our tasters. The shiitake sauce, on the other hand, lost out to the porcini version for its relatively mild mushroom flavor.

In the future, we'll consider substituting shiitakes for porcini mushrooms in dishes in which we value meaty, *umami*-boosting qualities, and we'll save pricier dried porcini (they often cost twice as much as shiitakes) for times when we really want to feature their distinctive mushroom taste.

FLAVOR-BOOSTING FUNGI
The dried shiitake mushroom (left) offers meatier flavor than porcini—at half the price.

Alcohol in Baking

I'm curious to try your Foolproof Pie Dough (September/October 2010) recipe, which uses vodka. Will some be left in the baked crust, or does it completely burn off in the oven?

MICHAEL SCHIAPARELLI
MASON, OHIO

➤Because alcohol binds with water during cooking, trace amounts will remain in food as long as there's still moisture. This includes our Foolproof Pie Dough, which we partially moisten with vodka since alcohol—unlike water—does not contribute to gluten development, so you can use more liquid, which in turn leads to a tender, easy-to-roll dough. When we sent a filled, double-crust pie made with the dough to a lab for analysis, it found that 5 percent of the vodka's alcohol (or about ¼ teaspoon) remained—far too little for any of its flavor to be detected. In a single crust that was "blind-baked" without filling, the trace amount of alcohol left was too tiny to be measured.

In sum, the alcohol that remains in our Foolproof Pie Dough after baking is minuscule, even if it's baked with a filling, which gets in the way of alcohol vaporizing.

WHAT IS IT?

I found this odd-looking thing on my grandfather's farm. Can you tell me what it is?

JULIA DOOHER
BALTIMORE, MD.

HERE'S THE SCOOP
The first utensil expressly designed for dispensing ice cream.

You've found a Clad's Disher, the very first mechanical ice cream server, which was invented in 1876 by William Clewell, owner of a confectionery shop in Reading, Pennsylvania. The disher allowed soda fountain operators to measure out consistent portions of ice cream and deposit them "on a plate or saucer in a molded and attractive condition." Clewell's patented design was manufactured by Mr. Valentine Clad, a Philadelphia tinsmith.

The server spooned ice cream into the bell-like mold and then inverted it over a dish. A few turns of the heart-shaped key on top rotated two scraper blades around the inside, releasing the frozen dessert. When we tried out this quaint dipper, we were struck by the novelty of the cone-shaped scoops that it produced—but its two-handed operation was clunky and awkward compared with modern-day scoops.

Tony Tonic

I recently noticed a new brand of tonic water at the supermarket called Fever-Tree and was shocked to see that the price was many times what I usually pay. Isn't all tonic water the same?

IDA SUTTON
SAN PEDRO, CALIF.

➤Tonic water began as an antimalarial treatment made from bitter quinine extracted from the bark of the cinchona, or "fever," tree. The addition of sugar (and gin) made it more palatable. Today most commercial brands are made with synthetic quinine and high-fructose corn syrup.

Fever-Tree, a British company, has gone back to the drink's roots, using cinchona-derived quinine and cane sugar in its Premium Indian Tonic Water, which makes for an expensive mixer—$6.99 for a four-pack of 7-ounce bottles, or about 25 cents an ounce. When we compared Fever-Tree with Schweppes tonic water (about 6 cents per ounce) in gin and tonics, some tasters really enjoyed its more restrained bitterness. But most of us preferred the familiar bracing (albeit synthetic) kick of Schweppes. Bottom line? Purists may prefer Fever-Tree, but we're sticking with the supermarket stuff.

TOP-SHELF TONIC
Fever-Tree Tonic Water offers mellower flavor at a steep price.

Seasoning a Mortar and Pestle

The granite mortar and pestle I gave my daughter leaves small, gritty particles in the food when she uses it. Is there something she can do to prevent this?

MARTY SCHMIERER
ALAMEDA, CALIF.

➤Grit can be an issue with any new mortar and pestle, but seasoning solves the problem. It's done by repeatedly grinding grains of raw rice in the mortar until the resulting powder is white and grit-free.

To determine exactly how much grinding is necessary, we ground 3 tablespoons of raw white rice in a brand-new granite mortar until it was reduced to a fine powder (about eight minutes). We repeated this process two more times, until the powder was nearly as white as a control batch ground in an electric spice grinder. We then tasted guacamole that we pulverized with the tool, and its smooth consistency was further proof that the mortar was grit-free.

Errata

➤ A photograph comparing canned tomatoes with fresh in our March/April 2012 issue featured Muir Glen Whole Plum Tomatoes instead of the brand's whole round tomatoes, which won our tasting.

➤ In the same issue, we reported that the American Kitchen by Regal Ware Tri-Ply Stainless Steel Covered 12-Inch Sauté Pan was 1.78 millimeters thick; it is 2.3 millimeters thick.

SEND US YOUR QUESTIONS We will provide a complimentary one-year subscription for each letter we print. Send your inquiry, name, address, and daytime telephone number to Notes from Readers, *Cook's Illustrated*, P.O. Box 470589, Brookline, MA 02447, or to NotesFromReaders@ AmericasTestKitchen.com.

ILLUSTRATION: JOHN BURGOYNE

Quick Tips

⇒ COMPILED BY SHANNON FRIEDMANN HATCH ⇐

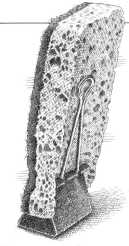

Spring Cleaning
Kitchen and household spray cleaners can take up valuable cabinet space under your kitchen sink. Rachel Paris-Lambert of East Seattle, Wash., takes her organization to the next level by installing a spring-tension curtain rod near the top of her cabinet. Spray bottles can then hang by their trigger levers, leaving plenty of room underneath for other supplies.

Homemade Sponge Holder
Letting air circulate around wet kitchen sponges—instead of laying them flat on the counter—helps them dry faster and stay mildew-free. Rather than purchasing a caddy or a tray, Ravi Singh of Glen Ellyn, Ill., fashioned a stand with a large binder clip. Attach the clip to the short end of a sponge and then press the "arms" of the clip flat against the sponge.

A More Appealing Can Opener
A lot of electric can openers boast a handy built-in magnet that holds the can lid after removal, preventing it from falling into your food. Most manual can openers lack that feature, but Leonard Corazza of East Islip, N.Y., found that he could upgrade his by simply gluing a strong magnet (or two) to the end of the opener's handle.

Steadying Stuffed Peppers
It can be tricky to stuff bell peppers since their uneven, bulbous ends make unsteady bases. Nancy Sullivan of Milwaukee, Wis., prevents topples with this method.

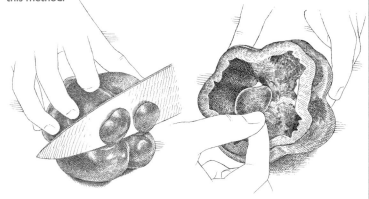

1. Trim the lobes on the bottom of the pepper to create a flat surface so the pepper stands upright, reserving the trimmed pieces.

2. Drop the trimmings into the pepper cavity to plug up any holes created by cutting and then fill the pepper with stuffing.

Reducing the Footprint of Canned Goods
Canned foods can quickly occupy most of your pantry, even when stacked. Realizing that these staples would take up much less real estate if stored on their sides, Riley Neill of San Antonio, Texas, corralled them in a magazine file (at least 5 inches wide). Its sides prevent the cans from rolling, and its slim profile frees up shelf space.

A Better Way to Freeze Leftovers
In the test kitchen, we routinely freeze extra homemade stock and pesto in metal muffin tins or plastic ice cube trays, but Allen Field of Portland, Ore., has found an even better way: He uses silicone molds instead. The flexible material releases frozen blocks with ease, eliminating the hassle of banging, twisting, or warming traditional tins and trays.

SEND US YOUR TIPS We will provide a complimentary one-year subscription for each tip we print. Send your tip, name, and address to Quick Tips, *Cook's Illustrated*, P.O. Box 470589, Brookline, MA 02447, or to QuickTips@AmericasTestKitchen.com.

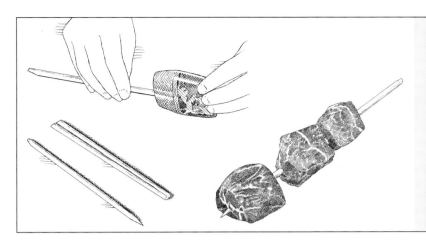

Make Your Own Skewers

Having run out of metal skewers while making large batches of kebabs, Francis Hodgins of Philadelphia, Pa., discovered a new use for the collection of wooden takeout chopsticks lingering in her kitchen drawer: She transformed them into sturdy skewers for meat chunks by honing one end with a pencil sharpener.

ID-ing Beverages

To help their guests keep track of their drinks at backyard gatherings, Momi and David Subiono of Captain Cook, Hawaii, collect rubber bands in various colors and sizes. They stretch around bottles, cans, and cups, tagging drinks at a glance. Wider bands even offer space to write a name.

Shelling Fresh Coconut

Opening the hard shell of a fresh, whole coconut is only half the battle: You then need a sharp knife and steady hand to pry the meat away from the shell. Rose-Marie de Rensis of West Hartford, Conn., found that freezing the whole coconut makes the shell pop away from the flesh as soon as you crack it open.

1. Freeze the coconut overnight.
2. Whack the frozen fruit around its equator with the dull side of a cleaver and then peel the shell off of the meat. An additional benefit: The coconut water inside will be frozen, making it easy to remove without any spillage or waste.

Cleaning Grill Tools on the Go

Chuck Sheffield of Dallas, Texas, has a new way to tote soiled grilling tools home from picnics and campsites: He puts them in a large plastic sealable container filled with water and a few drops of dishwashing soap. The grungy tools get a presoak on the road, which makes for easy cleaning at home.

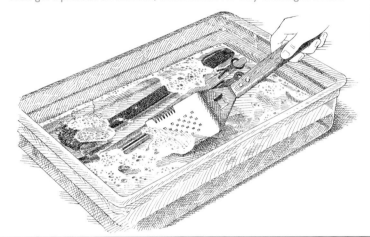

Quicker Chilling

When you need to quickly chill a liquid—whether it's an ice cream base or a soup—recipes often instruct you to pour it into a metal bowl set in a larger bowl filled with ice water. Jennifer Hadley of Madison, Wis., has found a way to speed up the process: She pours the liquid into a metal Bundt pan and then places the Bundt pan in an ice bath. More of the liquid comes in contact with cold metal in a Bundt pan than in a bowl, so the temperature nose-dives faster.

No More Sooty Hands

Filling a chimney starter with a precise amount of charcoal can be a messy enterprise, but David Detlef of Alexandria, Va., has a handy solution: He repurposes the long plastic bags in which his newspapers are delivered, using them as mitts. The bags keep his hands clean as he reaches into the sack to grab handfuls of coal.

Grill-Roasted Beef Short Ribs

With all their flavorful, well-marbled meat, short ribs seem perfect for the grill.
The problem? Getting the texture just right—without having to constantly fiddle with the fire.

⋟ BY LAN LAM ⋞

I usually reserve buying short ribs for the frosty winter months. It's a great time of year to let the moist heat and long, slow cooking of a braise do what it does best: convert this cut's abundant collagen into gelatin, which coats the protein fibers and makes the ribs meltingly tender. But while casting around at the meat counter this summer for something new and different to grill, my eyes landed on short ribs. I wondered why I shouldn't take this supremely flavorful cut (which also happens to have more meat on it than almost any other rib around) to the grill instead of the same old steak or burger. I was envisioning ribs with tender meat with a little bit of chew and a nicely browned, crusty exterior. And to distinguish them a bit from your typical slab of barbecue ribs, I'd skip the barbecue sauce in favor of a bold spice rub and a sweet-tart glaze that would balance their richness.

Watch the Fat Melt Away

The first decision: bone-in or boneless ribs? Leaving aside the glaze for the moment, I purchased some of each type and then mixed up a fragrant spice rub of salt, pepper, cayenne, ground cumin, and ground fennel. For good measure, I also threw in two commonly used pork-rib rub ingredients: garlic powder and brown sugar.

To ensure that the ribs' collagen had sufficient time to melt, I built a low-temperature indirect fire, placing some unlit briquettes on the grill grid and covering them with hot coals to generate a fire that would burn steadily for several hours. I sprinkled both batches of ribs with my rub and arranged them on the cooler side of the grates to grill-roast, occasionally rotating and flipping them until both were tender, about four hours later. But when I brought in both platters of ribs for tasting, my colleagues frowned. Instead of being beautifully marbled slabs, the boneless ribs had shrunk and blackened so much that my colleagues dubbed them "meat brownies."

Basting the ribs with a sweet and tangy mustard glaze during grill roasting develops a rich, lacquered crust.

What had happened? Well, without a bone to insulate the meat from the heat of the grill—low as it was—the boneless samples simply shriveled up and dried out. (If I'd pulled the ribs off the grill any sooner, the collagen wouldn't have broken down enough and they'd have been tough.) Though far from perfect, the bone-in ribs at least had a fighting chance of developing a tender interior by the time a crisp crust had formed.

Into the Oven and Out Again

Now I just needed to figure out how to optimize the texture of the bone-in ribs, which, among other problems, weren't cooking evenly. Although I'd flipped them every 30 minutes or so during cooking, there were still small pockets of unrendered fat, and some ribs were definitely more tender than others. The problem was this: In order to render fat and become tender, meat needs to reach a temperature hot enough for the tough collagen to start to melt (140 to 165 degrees). But if the meat gets too hot, so much moisture burns off that it becomes dry and jerky-like. To make matters worse, even a carefully monitored grill inevitably produces hot and cold spots, so the results within a single batch of ribs can be dramatically

different. This was not a problem that was going to go away, either. Maintaining a steady, perfectly consistent grill temperature is a near impossible feat, and let's face it: Even die-hard grillers don't want to fuss for hours on end, rearranging meat, opening and closing vents, and adding hot coals. It was clear that to make this work, I was going to need a more controlled environment. I would have to bring the ribs indoors to cook partway in the oven, where even heating is effortless and temperature adjustment is as easy as turning a dial. I hoped that by finishing the ribs on the grill I'd give them the substantial, smoky crust I wanted.

I sprinkled each of three batches of spice-rubbed meat with a little red wine vinegar to help cut richness, covered them with foil (to create a steamy cooking environment so the ribs would cook more quickly and evenly), and slid the pans into 300-degree ovens until the ribs hit 140, 165, and 175 degrees, respectively (80, 105, and 120 minutes later). Then I moved the operation outside to slowly finish each batch on the grill. When the ribs were dark and crusty an hour and a half later, I called my tasters for lunch.

The results were clear: The ribs pulled from the oven at 140 degrees were rubbery—obviously still packed with collagen. At the other end of the spectrum, so much collagen had broken down in the 175-degree batch that the meat had a disagreeable, shredded pot roast–like texture. The 165-degree ribs, on the other hand, boasted tender meat that sliced neatly.

For a foolproof indicator of final doneness, I made another batch of ribs, standing grillside after

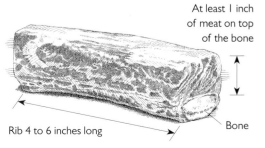

PHOTOGRAPHY: CARL TREMBLAY; ILLUSTRATION: JOHN BURGOYNE

they had been on the fire for an hour, evaluating the meat's texture and taking its temperature at regular intervals. One-hundred ninety-five degrees turned out to be the magic number for the finished meat: Intramuscular fat had completely melted and most of the collagen had broken down, turning the meat tender—but not so much so that it disintegrated at the touch of a fork.

Glazed Over

With the meat of the matter sorted out, I moved on to create a few glazes. The red wine vinegar that I had added to the ribs before baking tempered their fattiness somewhat, but they could still stand up to more tangy flavors. I started with a classic Dijon mustard and brown sugar mixture and then came up with a fruity blackberry and bourbon variation. Finally, hoisin and tamarind took center stage in an Asian-inspired version.

To achieve a substantial lacquered crust, I brushed the ribs every time I rotated them on the grill. This allowed each layer of glaze to dry out and give the subsequent layer a base to which it could adhere. It was a bit of work, but any doubt I had that frequent glazing was worth the trouble was erased when tasters devoured the latest batch before I could even get my hands on one rib.

With meaty, finger-licking results like these, I'd no longer need to wait for the dead of winter to make short ribs. In fact, they are now at the top of the list for my next summer cookout.

GRILL-ROASTED BEEF SHORT RIBS
SERVES 4 TO 6

Make sure to choose ribs that are 4 to 6 inches in length and have at least 1 inch of meat on top of the bone (see "The Perfect Short Rib for Grill Roasting").

Spice Rub
- 2 tablespoons kosher salt
- 1 tablespoon packed brown sugar
- 2 teaspoons pepper
- 2 teaspoons ground cumin
- 2 teaspoons garlic powder
- 1¼ teaspoons paprika
- ¾ teaspoon ground fennel
- ⅛ teaspoon cayenne pepper

Short Ribs
- 5 pounds bone-in English-style beef short ribs, trimmed
- 2 tablespoons red wine vinegar
- 1 recipe glaze (recipes follow)

1. FOR THE SPICE RUB: Combine all ingredients in bowl. Measure out 1 teaspoon rub and set aside for glaze.

2. FOR THE SHORT RIBS: Adjust oven rack to middle position and heat oven to 300 degrees. Sprinkle ribs with spice rub, pressing into all sides of ribs. Arrange ribs, bone side down, in 13 by 9-inch baking dish, placing thicker ribs around perimeter of baking dish and thinner ribs in center. Sprinkle vinegar evenly over ribs. Cover baking dish tightly with aluminum foil. Bake until thickest ribs register 165 to 170 degrees, 1½ to 2 hours.

3A. FOR A CHARCOAL GRILL: Open bottom vent halfway. Arrange 2 quarts unlit charcoal into steeply banked pile against 1 side of grill. Light large chimney starter half filled with charcoal (3 quarts). When top coals are partially covered with ash, pour on top of unlit charcoal to cover one-third

---

KEY STEP | START IN THE OVEN

This atypical start guarantees perfectly cooked ribs.

Bake the ribs until they reach 165 degrees, 1½ to 2 hours. At this temperature, the conversion from collagen into gelatin is well under way and the ribs can be transferred to the grill.

---

of grill with coals steeply banked against side of grill. Set cooking grate in place, cover, and open lid vent halfway. Heat grill until hot, about 5 minutes.

3B. FOR A GAS GRILL: Turn all burners to high, cover, and heat grill until hot, about 15 minutes. Leave primary burner on medium and turn off other burner(s). Adjust primary burner as needed to maintain grill temperature of 275 to 300 degrees.

4. Clean and oil cooking grate. Place short ribs, bone side down, on cooler side of grill about 2 inches from flames. Brush with ¼ cup glaze. Cover and cook until ribs register 195 degrees, 1¾ to 2¼ hours, rotating and brushing ribs with ¼ cup glaze every 30 minutes. Transfer ribs to large platter, tent loosely with foil, and let rest for 5 to 10 minutes before serving.

MUSTARD GLAZE
MAKES ABOUT 1 CUP

- ½ cup Dijon mustard
- ½ cup red wine vinegar
- ¼ cup packed brown sugar
- 1 teaspoon reserved spice rub
- ⅛ teaspoon cayenne pepper

Whisk all ingredients together in bowl.

BLACKBERRY GLAZE
MAKES ABOUT 1 CUP

- 10 ounces (2 cups) fresh or frozen blackberries
- ½ cup ketchup
- ¼ cup bourbon
- 2 tablespoons packed brown sugar
- 1½ tablespoons soy sauce
- 1 teaspoon reserved spice rub
- ⅛ teaspoon cayenne pepper

Bring all ingredients to simmer in small saucepan over medium-high heat. Simmer, stirring frequently to break up blackberries, until reduced to 1¼ cups, about 10 minutes. Strain through fine-mesh strainer, pressing on solids to extract as much liquid as possible. Discard solids.

HOISIN-TAMARIND GLAZE
MAKES ABOUT 1 CUP

- 1 cup water
- ⅓ cup hoisin sauce
- ¼ cup tamarind paste
- 1 (2-inch) piece ginger, peeled and sliced into ½-inch-thick rounds
- 1 teaspoon reserved spice rub
- ⅛ teaspoon cayenne pepper

Bring all ingredients to simmer in small saucepan over medium-high heat. Simmer, stirring frequently, until reduced to 1¼ cups, about 10 minutes. Strain through fine-mesh strainer, pressing on solids to extract as much liquid as possible. Discard solids.

Jamaican Jerk Chicken

We came up with a great recipe for this classic Caribbean marinade. But to replicate the elusive smoke flavor, we had to take a chemistry lesson.

⇒ BY CELESTE ROGERS ⇐

I never would have guessed that the reading list for my Jamaican jerk chicken recipe would include articles in *Chemosphere* and *Journal of Sensory Studies*. After all, the roots of this approach to marinating and cooking meat date back more than 300 years, when Taino Indians inhabited the island's forests along with escaped African slaves brought over by the British when they colonized the country. There the refugees used salt, pepper, and the fragrant berries of the pimento (aka allspice) trees to flavor and preserve strips of wild boar, and they employed the tree's leaves and branches to slowly smoke the meat.

The primitive technique has come a long way since then, but the flavors still reflect the Jamaican original. Rather than boar meat smoked in fire pits, most modern-day jerk recipes call for marinating the meat—chicken, pork, and goat are all common—with an intensely flavorful liquid paste of allspice berries, fiery Scotch bonnet chiles, thyme, and a dozen or so other herbs and spices and then smoking it over pimento wood. When this is done well, the meat emerges aromatic, woodsy, spicy, and sweet (the marinade often includes a little sugar), with a clean, lingering burn from the fresh chiles—an appealing flavor profile that inspired me to come up with a recipe of my own. Chicken was my meat of choice, and for the sake of even cooking, I'd stick with individual parts rather than a whole bird.

Little did I know that jerk recipes are rife with pitfalls. Dense, thick spice pastes were tricky to spread evenly over the meat and tended to stick to the hot grill grates and burn. Thinner, more liquid-y concoctions ran right off the chicken pieces and into the fire—but not before they saturated the skin and prevented it from rendering and browning. Drier, rublike mixtures tasted dull and dusty. Beyond that, none of the marinades hit on the ideal aromatic-sweet-spicy balance I was hoping for, and since pimento wood isn't easy to come by here in

Our thick, heady marinade seasons the chicken in just 30 minutes and stays put on the skin during grilling.

the Northeast, I was stuck with a widely available option: hickory. Needless to say, I had a lot of work ahead of me.

A Real Jerk

Nailing down the flavor and consistency of the marinade seemed like the obvious first step, so I lined up a slew of potential ingredients, set up a basic indirect fire to cook the chicken (I'd revisit the grilling method later), and got busy. Allspice, thyme, and chiles (I'd use habaneros in place of hard-to-find Scotch bonnets) were definites, as were scallions for their grassy freshness, plenty of garlic, and salt (which we've discovered is the most important element of any marinade). From there, I went about adding—and subtracting—herbs, spices, and condiments until I'd come up with a formula that got me close to the complex balance I was after: the aforementioned core elements, plus coriander seeds and peppercorns (coarsely ground in a spice grinder with the allspice berries) and a mixture of dried thyme, basil, and rosemary for woodsy depth; ground nutmeg and ginger, plus a touch of brown sugar for warmth and sweetness, respectively; a good

amount of grated lime zest and yellow mustard for brightness; and soy sauce for a savory boost.

At this point, the marinade's flavor was relatively full-bodied, but the consistency was a little too thick. So I scoured my pantry for liquid helpers and spotted vegetable oil. Sure enough, a few spoonfuls of that loosened things up just enough for the marinade to thoroughly coat and cling to the chicken pieces. Even better, between the salt and the soy sauce, the chicken tasted well seasoned after just 30 minutes of marinating. (Later on I tested the outer limits of marinating times—up to 24 hours—and happily discovered that the longer the chicken sat, the more flavorful the meat became, thanks to the water-soluble flavor compounds in the marinade ingredients penetrating even further. It's just a matter of how much time you have.)

Trickle-Down Theory

Back to the grilling method. Cooking the chicken over the cool side of an indirect fire (where all the coals are banked to one side of the grill) was a close imitation of the traditional low-fire method, and it ensured that the chicken stayed juicy. But while gentle heat made for succulent meat, it didn't do much for the skin, which was pale and rubbery. I modified my coal setup and made use of the hotter half of the grill as well, spreading the briquettes evenly over one side, which gave me the space I needed to sear the marinated chicken pieces in one batch before finishing them on the cooler half of the grill.

Unfortunately, there was a major (albeit predictable) snag in my plans to brown and render the skin: the marinade, most of which had soldered to the metal grates by the time the skin dehydrated enough to get any color. I thought that simply switching the order of operations—from searing first to searing last—might solve the problem by allowing the marinade to dry out and set on the skin before I put it face-to-face with the hot grates, but at that point the fire had died down considerably and didn't offer enough heat for searing. My frustration was building, but my colleagues reminded me that I had one more trick to try: a barbecue technique that we had devised for prolonging a grill's heat output. I placed a batch of unlit coals in the kettle, followed by a batch that I'd ignited as usual in a chimney starter, the idea being that the lit briquettes would slowly ignite the unlit batch. I gave it a whirl and was relieved to find that did it: The delayed fire setup accommodated both the meat and the skin.

PHOTOGRAPHY: CARL TREMBLAY

Sending New Smoke Signals

I liked to think I was making progress, but the truth was that I'd been putting off the most challenging part of my jerk recipe—the elusive pimento wood smoke flavor—until the very end. There was no way I was shelling out for mail-order wood every time I wanted some Jamaican barbecue, but one purchase for the sake of comparing the real deal with hickory wood seemed reasonable. So I ordered some pimento chips and prepared a double batch of my recipe, one cooked over hickory and the other over my costly pimento.

The difference was clear: While the hickory wood infused the meat with an assertive smokiness, the pimento wood lent the chicken a fresher, sweeter, and more herbal smoke flavor that tasters preferred. How could I make hickory taste like pimento?

That's where the science journals came in. To get a better understanding of smoke flavor, I decided to sift through some articles about wood and the types of flavor compounds they release when they smolder. The research made sense: Depending on the type of wood, some of these compounds (known as phenols and terpenes) can be robust and meaty (like hickory) or cleaner and more delicate (like pimento). That much I'd inferred from my taste test. What was enlightening, however, was an article that I came across in *Flavour & Fragrance Journal* detailing the flavor compounds of edible spices and herbs. It had never occurred to me that I could "smoke" herbs and spices, but the idea sounded promising. Allspice berries were an obvious source of pimento wood flavor compounds, so I added a couple of tablespoons to the packet with my hickory chips, whipped up another batch of the jerk marinade, and got grilling. This test was a real breakthrough: I hadn't quite nailed the complexity of the pimento wood flavor just yet, but the warm fragrance of the allspice berries had made a noticeable difference. This got me wondering what else my spice cabinet might have to offer. Two bottles jumped out at me: dried rosemary and dried thyme; both happen to contain many of the flavor compounds in the leaves of the pimento tree. Two tablespoons of each helped even out the smoke flavor, save for one familiar problem: Smoked dry, the herbs and spices were smoldering too quickly, resulting in the same carbonized off-flavors you get when wood burns too hot. I tried soaking and draining the spice mixture, but that simply washed out their flavor. So I opted for the halfway point: moistening the spices with just enough water (2 tablespoons) to dampen the smolder and still preserve their delicate flavor.

I was in Massachusetts when I took a bite of that final batch of jerk chicken, but thanks to the marinade's complexity and the delicate warmth of my faux pimento wood packet, I could just as easily have been standing in Jamaica's Boston Bay.

JERK CHICKEN
SERVES 4

For a milder dish, use one seeded chile. If you prefer your food very hot, use up to all three chiles including their seeds and ribs. Scotch bonnet chiles can be used in place of the habaneros. Wear gloves when working with the chiles.

Jerk Marinade

- 1½ tablespoons whole coriander seeds
- 1 tablespoon whole allspice berries
- 1 tablespoon whole peppercorns
- 1–3 habanero chiles, stemmed, quartered, and seeds and ribs reserved, if using
- 8 scallions, chopped
- 6 garlic cloves, peeled
- 3 tablespoons vegetable oil
- 2 tablespoons soy sauce
- 2 tablespoons finely grated lime zest (3 limes), plus lime wedges for serving
- 2 tablespoons yellow mustard
- 1 tablespoon dried thyme
- 1 tablespoon ground ginger
- 1 tablespoon packed brown sugar
- 2¼ teaspoons salt
- 2 teaspoons dried basil
- ½ teaspoon dried rosemary
- ½ teaspoon ground nutmeg

Chicken

- 3 pounds bone-in chicken pieces (split breasts cut in half, drumsticks, and/or thighs)
- 2 tablespoons whole allspice berries
- 2 tablespoons dried thyme
- 2 tablespoons dried rosemary
- 2 tablespoons water
- 1 cup wood chips, soaked in water for 15 minutes and drained

1. FOR THE JERK MARINADE: Grind coriander seeds, allspice berries, and peppercorns in spice grinder or mortar and pestle until coarsely ground. Transfer spices to blender jar. Add habanero(s), scallions, garlic, oil, soy sauce, lime zest, mustard, thyme, ginger, brown sugar, salt, basil, rosemary, and nutmeg and process until smooth paste forms, 1 to 3 minutes, scraping down sides as necessary. Transfer marinade to gallon-size zipper-lock bag.

2. FOR THE CHICKEN: Place chicken pieces in bag with marinade and toss to coat; press out as much air as possible and seal bag. Let stand at room temperature for 30 minutes while preparing grill, flipping bag after 15 minutes. (Marinated chicken can be refrigerated for up to 24 hours.)

3. Combine allspice berries, thyme, rosemary, and water in bowl and set aside to moisten for 15 minutes. Using large piece of heavy-duty aluminum foil, wrap soaked chips and moistened allspice mixture in foil packet and cut several vent holes in top.

4A. FOR A CHARCOAL GRILL: Open bottom vent halfway. Arrange 1 quart unlit charcoal briquettes in single layer over half of grill. Light large chimney starter one-third filled with charcoal briquettes (2 quarts). When top coals are partially covered with ash, pour evenly over unlit briquettes, keeping coals arranged over half of grill. Place wood chip packet on coals. Set cooking grate in place, cover, and open lid vent halfway. Heat grill until hot and wood chips are smoking, about 5 minutes.

4B. FOR A GAS GRILL: Place wood chip packet over primary burner. Turn all burners to high, cover, and heat grill until hot and wood chips begin to smoke, 15 to 25 minutes. Turn primary burner to medium and turn off other burner(s).

5. Clean and oil cooking grate. Place chicken, with marinade clinging and skin side up, as far away from fire as possible, with thighs closest to fire and breasts furthest away. Cover (positioning lid vent over chicken if using charcoal) and cook for 30 minutes.

6. Move chicken, skin side down, to hotter side of grill; cook until browned and skin renders, 3 to 6 minutes. Using tongs, flip chicken pieces and cook until browned on second side and breasts register 160 degrees and thighs/drumsticks register 175 degrees, 5 to 12 minutes longer.

7. Transfer chicken to serving platter, tent loosely with foil, and let rest for 5 to 10 minutes. Serve warm or at room temperature with lime wedges.

Wood Chip Packet with a Jamaican Accent

The delicately fragrant, herby smoke of pimento wood is a fundamental element of jerk flavor. We weren't about to mail-order the hard-to-find timber every time we got a craving, but with a little help from our spice cabinet, we came up with a pretty close imitation.

AUTHENTIC SOURCE
In Jamaica, the wood and leaves of the pimento (aka allspice) tree produce a distinctly sweet, fresh, herbal smoke.

HOMEGROWN APPROACH
To replicate that profile, we add allspice berries, dried thyme, and rosemary to hickory chips.

Introducing Grill-Smoked Salmon

There's more to smoked salmon than the thin, glossy slices stacked on bagels.
With a little time—and a sweet touch—we produced silky, smoky dinnertime fillets.

⇒ BY ANDREW JANJIGIAN ⇐

The process of smoking fish over hardwood to preserve its delicate flesh has a long tradition, and rich, fatty salmon is well suited to the technique. But smoked salmon's unique taste and texture don't come easy: The translucent, mildly smoky slices piled on bagels are produced by ever-so-slowly smoking (but not fully cooking) salt-cured fillets at roughly 60 to 90 degrees, a project that requires specialized equipment and loads of time (at least 24 hours and as long as five days). Then there is hot smoking, a procedure in which cured fillets are fully cooked at higher temperatures (100 to 250 degrees) for one to eight hours. The higher heat results in a drier texture and a more potent smokiness, so the fish is often flaked and mixed into dips and spreads.

Both approaches deliver terrific results—but are impractical (if not impossible) for a home cook to pull off. Sure, you can impart a touch of smokiness by tossing wood chips onto hot charcoal and quickly grilling fish, but I had also heard of a lesser-known, more intriguing option that captures both the intense, smoky flavor of hot-smoked fish and the firm but silky texture of the cold-smoked type. It's easy because the fish is cooked via indirect heat on a grill—a familiar and uncomplicated technique. And although the resulting fillets have a distinctive taste, they are not overpoweringly salty or smoky, so they're suitable as an entrée either warm from the grill or at room temperature.

To try out these smoky, succulent fillets, I scoured cookbooks for recipes. The typical first step in smoking fish is to cure the flesh with salt; some authors recommended brining, others directly salting the fillet. To keep the preparation time in check, I steered away from recommendations for curing the fish for longer than an hour or two.

The other criteria, smoking temperature and length of exposure—both crucial to the final result—

Portioning a whole fillet into pieces and placing them on a foil rectangle makes this silky, delicate fish easy to get off the grill.

were all over the map. One recipe called for smoking the fish at 350 degrees for a modest 20 minutes; another let it go twice as long at only 275 degrees.

In Treatment

With so many factors at play, I decided to try a simple brine first, soaking a center-cut, skin-on fillet (retaining the skin would make it easier to remove the fillet from the grill) in the test kitchen's usual 9 percent solution of salt and water for two hours. For the time being, I used a moderate amount of coals, dumping 4 quarts of lit charcoal on one side of the grill, along with a few soaked wood chunks to provide the smoke. I placed the fish on the cooking grate opposite the coals, popped the cover on the grill, and smoked the fish until it was still a little translucent at the center, about 25 minutes.

The result was illuminating if not exactly spectacular. The brine had the unfortunate effect of making the salmon terribly bloated, plus it seemed to highlight the fish's natural oiliness in an unpleasant way—a far cry from the supple but firm texture I was

after. When I thought about it, it made sense: Unlike lean, dry proteins such as turkey breast and pork tenderloin, salmon contains so much fat and moisture that a brine only makes it seem waterlogged.

For my next try, I covered the salmon in a generous blanket of kosher salt—its coarse texture makes it cling to food better than table salt—and refrigerated it uncovered on a wire rack on a baking sheet. After an hour, a considerable amount of liquid had been drawn to the surface of the flesh. I knew that if I waited any longer, the fluid would start to migrate back into the salmon through the process of osmosis, once again leading to a bloated texture, so I promptly removed it from the refrigerator, blotted the moisture with a paper towel, and took it out to the grill for smoking. This sample was considerably better than the brined fish: incredibly moist yet still firm—and not at all soggy. It wasn't perfect, though, since most tasters found it too salty to be enjoyed as a main dish. I tried dialing down the amount of salt as well as salting for a shorter amount of time, but alas, the fish didn't achieve the proper texture.

Back at my desk, I looked for a solution in the recipes that I'd collected and came across a few that called for adding sugar to the cure. I knew that, like salt, sugar is hygroscopic, meaning it attracts water. Could sugar pull moisture from the salmon as effectively as salt? Not quite: Because individual molecules of sucrose are much larger than sodium and chloride ions, sugar is, pound for pound, about 12 times less effective than salt at attracting moisture. Still, it was a workable option; I just had to do some tinkering. Eventually, I determined that a ratio of 2 parts sugar to 1 part salt produced well-balanced taste and texture in the finished salmon. Using these proportions, the fish firmed up nicely; plus, it was far less salty and the sugar counterbalanced its richness.

Smoldering Issues

With a reliable curing method in hand, I could finally fine-tune my smoking technique. My current setup was far from ideal: By the time the fish was sufficiently smoky, it was dry and flaky. Conversely, when it was cooked perfectly—still silky and slightly pink in the interior, or about 125 degrees—the smoke flavor

PHOTOGRAPHY: CARL TREMBLAY

was faint. Adding more wood chunks only gave the fillet a sooty flavor. Instead, I tried to cool down the temperature of the grill by reducing the amount of charcoal from 4 quarts to 3. This helped somewhat, since the fish cooked more slowly (a full 30 to 40 minutes) and had more time to absorb smoke.

But the smoke flavor still wasn't as bold as I wanted. Rather than manipulating the cooking time any further, I turned to the salmon itself, cutting the large fillet into individual serving-size portions. This seemingly minor tweak resulted in big payoffs: First, it ensured more thorough smoke exposure (in the same amount of time) by creating more surface area. Second, the delicate pieces were far easier to get off the grill in one piece than a single bulky fillet. (To that end, I also started placing the fillets on a piece of foil coated with vegetable oil spray.) Finally, I found that I could now use an even cooler fire (produced with a mere 2 quarts of charcoal): The smaller fillets still reached their ideal serving temperature in the same amount of time that the single, larger fillet had taken. Plus, the gentler fire rendered the fillets incomparably tender.

With a smoky, rich taste and a silky, supple texture, my quickie smoked salmon recipe was complete. To provide some contrasting flavors, I devised a homemade mayonnaise that incorporates many of the garnishes that are commonly served on a smoked salmon platter—hard-cooked egg, capers, and dill. With these sauces and a reliable method, I had a recipe that was, to put it plainly, smoking hot.

GRILL-SMOKED SALMON
SERVES 6

Use center-cut salmon fillets of similar thickness so that they cook at the same rate. The best way to ensure uniformity is to buy a 2½- to 3-pound whole center-cut fillet and cut it into 6 pieces. Avoid mesquite wood chunks for this recipe. Serve the salmon with lemon wedges or with our "Smoked Salmon Platter" Sauce, or for our free recipe for Apple-Mustard Sauce, go to www.CooksIllustrated.com/aug12.

- 2 tablespoons sugar
- 1 tablespoon kosher salt
- 6 (6- to 8-ounce) center-cut skin-on salmon fillets
- 2 wood chunks soaked in water for 30 minutes and drained (if using charcoal) or 2 cups wood chips, half of chips soaked in water for 15 minutes and drained (if using gas)

1. Combine sugar and salt in bowl. Set salmon on wire rack set in rimmed baking sheet and sprinkle flesh side evenly with sugar mixture. Refrigerate, uncovered, for 1 hour. With paper towels, brush any excess salt and sugar from salmon and blot dry. Return fish on wire rack to refrigerator, uncovered, while preparing grill.

2A. FOR A CHARCOAL GRILL: Open bottom vent halfway. Light large chimney starter one-third filled with charcoal briquettes (2 quarts). When top coals are partially covered with ash, pour into steeply banked pile against side of grill. Place wood chunks on top of coals. Set cooking grate in place, cover, and open lid vent halfway. Heat grill until hot and wood chunks begin to smoke, about 5 minutes.

2B. FOR A GAS GRILL: Combine soaked and unsoaked chips. Use large piece of heavy-duty aluminum foil to wrap chips into foil packet and cut several vent holes in top. Place wood chip packet directly on primary burner. Turn primary burner to high (leave other burners off), cover, and heat grill until hot and wood chips begin to smoke, 15 to 25 minutes. Turn primary burner to medium. (Adjust primary burner as needed to maintain grill temperature of 275 to 300 degrees.)

3. Clean and oil cooking grate. Fold piece of heavy-duty foil into 18 by 6-inch rectangle. Place foil rectangle over cool side of grill and place salmon pieces on foil, spaced at least ½ inch apart. Cover grill (positioning lid vent over fish if using charcoal) and cook until center of thickest part of fillet registers 125 degrees and is still translucent when cut into with paring knife, 30 to 40 minutes. Transfer to platter and serve, or allow to cool to room temperature.

"SMOKED SALMON PLATTER" SAUCE
MAKES 1½ CUPS

- 1 large egg yolk
- 2 teaspoons Dijon mustard
- 2 teaspoons sherry vinegar
- ½ cup vegetable oil
- 2 tablespoons capers, rinsed, plus 1 teaspoon caper brine
- 1 large hard-cooked egg, chopped fine
- 2 tablespoons minced shallot
- 2 tablespoons minced fresh dill

Whisk egg yolk, mustard, and vinegar together in medium bowl. Whisking constantly, slowly drizzle in oil until emulsified, about 1 minute. Gently fold in capers, brine, hard-cooked egg, shallot, and dill.

Now We're Smokin'

The two most common methods for smoking fish are cold and hot smoking. Both approaches require special equipment and a serious time investment and result in a product that is more of an ingredient than a main dish. Our unique hybrid recipe produces an entrée that captures the uniquely smooth and lush texture of cold-smoked salmon and the forward smokiness of hot-smoked salmon. The best part? It cooks in only 30 to 40 minutes on a regular charcoal or gas grill.

COLD-SMOKED
Slick and silky; mild smoke.

HOT-SMOKED
Dry and firm; potent smoke.

HYBRID GRILL-SMOKED
Ultra-moist; rich, balanced smoke.

The Best Grilled Turkey Burgers

Most turkey burgers are dry, bland, or loaded up with flavor-blunting fillers. We made more than 200 burgers to figure out a better way.

> BY DAN SOUZA

I figured I was licked before I even got started. The assignment was to create turkey burgers that tasted every bit as meaty, tender, and juicy as the beef kind—and the judges would be my colleagues, all of them hard-core hamburger devotees. It was a tall order for a couple of reasons: For one thing, the test kitchen brings all poultry to a much higher temperature (160 degrees) than beef (which we often cook medium-rare, or 125 degrees), which means that far more moisture will be squeezed out of the meat during cooking. What's more, turkey lacks beef's high percentage of lubricating fat. That accounts for its appeal as a healthier alternative to beef in a burger, but it also explains why these lean patties usually cook up dry, chalky, and bland.

Plenty of recipes try to compensate for those shortcomings by packing ground turkey with a slew of spices and binders that provide flavor and lock in moisture, respectively, but my tasters deemed every version that I tried a failure—and I tried many. Most burgers were still dry, and those that did offer some flavor tasted more like overdressed turkey meatloaf than burgers. I can't say I was surprised; loading up the meat with additives is a Band-Aid approach that ignores the real problem at heart: the meat itself.

The meat sounded like the right starting point to me, so I shelved my cynicism for the time being and decided to work toward a turkey burger that delivered everything I look for in a beef version—that is, tender, juicy, and flavorful meat without the distraction of my spice cabinet or other superficial fixes. And if I could throw it over a hot grill to give the meat some smoky char, all the better.

Ground to a Fault

We've been pretty clear about our stance on supermarket ground meat for burgers. It may be a timesaver, but when we want to make the meatiest,

For juicy, tender, and flavorful turkey burgers, we start by ditching commercially ground meat.

juiciest, most tender burgers we can, we grind our own—and if my test recipes were any indication, avoiding the preground stuff would be even more important when it came to turkey burgers. The vast majority of commercial ground meat is processed so fine that it turns pasty and dense, and poultry tends to be the worst offender. What's more, supermarket ground turkey is typically ultra lean—an immediate setback when you're going for flavor and juiciness. Grinding my own meat would allow me to control both the cut of meat and the size of the grind.

The obvious starting point was thigh meat, as this cut boasts a decent amount of fat and flavor. I bought a large thigh (about 2 pounds), removed the skin and bone, trimmed it of excess sinew, and then followed our grinding procedure: Cut the meat into ½-inch pieces, freeze them for about 40 minutes to firm them up, and then process the meat in three batches in a food processor.

About 20 pulses gave me coarsely chopped meat that produced tender, nicely loose-textured burgers, and the flavor of these dark-meat patties was significantly richer than any turkey burger I'd had

to date. But I still had plenty of work to do before I got to the juiciness and rich meatiness of a beef burger. Thanks to the requisite 160-degree doneness temperature, my all-thigh patties were still parched.

Juicing Up

Mixing the turkey with a panade (a liquid-and-bread-crumb paste that traps moisture and prevents the meat proteins from binding together too tightly) was the most common moisture-enhancing solution I came across. But it was also universally unsuccessful. While the paste did add juiciness, it also dulled the already mild flavor of the turkey and made the patties meatloaf-like—precisely the consistency I was trying to get away from by grinding my own meat. Other recipes took a more drastic approach, "fattening up" the ground turkey with butter and bacon fat. One even mixed in turkey sausage—and, not surprisingly, the result tasted like a sausage burger. I'll admit, adding fat to the burgers did make them taste juicier (and richer), but it also felt like cheating; at that point, why not just make a beef burger?

Thinking about those two goals, however, triggered an important reminder. While developing a recent stir-fry recipe, we discovered an unlikely technique for improving tenderness and juiciness in lean pork: lightly coating it with baking soda before cooking. When applied to meat, this alkali raises the meat's pH, which tenderizes its muscle fibers and gives it a looser structure that's more capable of retaining water. The quick pretreatment had made all the difference with the pork loin; no reason it shouldn't work for turkey, too, right?

I gave it a shot, mixing up one batch of burgers with a pinch of baking soda and leaving another untreated, and then quickly seared the burgers over a hot fire. When my tasters gave me approving nods as they munched on these noticeably juicier, more tender patties, I knew I was getting somewhere. But I wasn't done yet.

One of our other favorite pantry staples for improving dry meat is gelatin, which absorbs up to 10 times its weight in water. I tried hydrating varying amounts of the unflavored powder in chicken broth and adding the mixture to the turkey when grinding it. Another good move. Just 1 tablespoon of gelatin in 3 tablespoons of broth further compensated for some of the moisture lost during cooking.

Spurred on by these successes, I challenged myself to push the moisture factor a little further and was reminded of the recipe I'd tried with turkey sausage. It had failed for tasting too sausage-y, but it was remarkably juicy, thanks to the finely processed meat, which causes the proteins to stretch out and link up into a stronger network that traps fat and moisture. I got to thinking: If I was already grinding the turkey in the food processor, why not try making my own sausage-like mixture by grinding a portion of the meat even further? I added ½ cup of coarsely ground meat back to the processor along with salt (which activates the meat's sticky proteins), the baking soda, and softened gelatin; let it rip until the mixture turned sticky and smooth; and then, with the processor running, drizzled in 2 tablespoons of vegetable oil until incorporated.

It worked like gangbusters. When mixed into the remaining ground turkey, this emulsion trapped copious amounts of moisture and fat, resulting in the juiciest turkey burger I'd ever had. There was just one caveat, and it was predictable: My homemade turkey sausage was binding the meat together too firmly.

Staying Loose

In the same way that a teacher might place a balloon between two overzealous middle school dancers, I needed to add something to the ground turkey to keep its sticky proteins from embracing too tightly. I experimented with various cooked grains and starches—even beans. But while most of them did produce more tender patties, none left me with the loose burger texture I was after, and most of them muted the turkey's flavor.

That's when I switched to mixing vegetables—both raw and cooked—into the meat and hit upon the winner: raw white mushrooms. Chopped in the food processor and then mixed into my turkey emulsion, the mushrooms actually provided three unique benefits: They interrupted some protein binding to increase tenderness; provided extra moisture as their water-filled cells broke down during cooking; and, thanks to their high level of glutamates, helped boost meatiness. The mushrooms also inspired me to swap in soy sauce for the salt, bumping up savoriness even more. Just five minutes per side over a hot fire was enough to char and cook my mouthwatering turkey burgers—now every bit as enticing as their beefy brothers.

JUICY GRILLED TURKEY BURGERS
SERVES 6

If you are able to purchase boneless, skinless turkey thighs, substitute 1½ pounds for the bone-in thigh. To ensure the best texture, don't let the burgers stand for more than an hour before cooking. Serve the burgers with Malt Vinegar–Molasses Burger Sauce or your favorite toppings, or go to www.CooksIllustrated.com/aug12 for our free recipes for Classic Burger Sauce, Chile-Lime Burger Sauce, and Apricot-Mustard Burger Sauce.

- 1 (2-pound) bone-in turkey thigh, skinned, boned, trimmed, and cut into ½-inch pieces
- 1 tablespoon unflavored gelatin
- 3 tablespoons low-sodium chicken broth
- 6 ounces white mushrooms, trimmed
- 1 tablespoon soy sauce
   Pinch baking soda
- 2 tablespoons vegetable oil, plus extra for brushing
   Kosher salt and pepper
- 6 large hamburger buns

1. Place turkey pieces on large plate in single layer. Freeze meat until very firm and hardened around edges, 35 to 45 minutes. Meanwhile, sprinkle gelatin over chicken broth in small bowl and let sit until gelatin softens, about 5 minutes. Pulse mushrooms in food processor until coarsely chopped, about 7 pulses, stopping and redistributing mushrooms around bowl as needed to ensure even grinding. Set mushrooms aside; do not wash food processor.

2. Pulse one-third of turkey in food processor until coarsely chopped into ⅛-inch pieces, 18 to 22 pulses, stopping and redistributing turkey around bowl as needed to ensure even grinding. Transfer meat to large bowl and repeat two more times with remaining turkey.

3. Return ½ cup (about 3 ounces) ground turkey to bowl of food processor along with softened gelatin, soy sauce, and baking soda. Process until smooth, about 2 minutes, scraping down bowl as needed. With processor running, slowly drizzle in oil, about 10 seconds; leave paste in food processor. Return mushrooms to food processor with paste and pulse to combine, 3 to 5 pulses, stopping and redistributing mixture as needed to ensure even mixing. Transfer mushroom mixture to bowl with ground turkey and use hands to evenly combine.

4. With lightly greased hands, divide meat mixture into 6 balls. Flatten into ¾-inch-thick patties about 4 inches in diameter; press shallow indentation into center of each burger to ensure even cooking. (Shaped patties can be frozen for up to 1 month. Frozen patties can be cooked straight from freezer.)

5A. FOR A CHARCOAL GRILL: Open bottom vent completely. Light large chimney starter filled with charcoal briquettes (6 quarts). When top coals are partially covered with ash, pour evenly over half of grill. Set cooking grate in place, cover, and open lid vent completely. Heat grill until hot, about 5 minutes.

5B. FOR A GAS GRILL: Turn all burners to high, cover, and heat grill until hot, about 15 minutes. Leave primary burner on high and turn off other burner(s).

6. Clean and oil cooking grate. Brush 1 side of patties with oil and season with salt and pepper. Using spatula, flip patties, brush with oil, and season second side. Place burgers over hot part of grill and cook until burgers are well browned on both sides and register 160 degrees, 4 to 7 minutes per side. (If cooking frozen burgers: After burgers are browned on both sides, transfer to cool side of grill, cover, and continue to cook until burgers register 160 degrees.)

7. Transfer burgers to plate and let rest for 5 minutes. While burgers rest, grill buns over hot side of grill. Transfer burgers to buns, add desired toppings, and serve.

MALT VINEGAR–MOLASSES BURGER SAUCE
MAKES ABOUT 1 CUP

- ¾ cup mayonnaise
- 4 teaspoons malt vinegar
- ½ teaspoon molasses
- ¼ teaspoon Worcestershire sauce
- ¼ teaspoon salt
- ¼ teaspoon pepper

Whisk all ingredients together in bowl.

How We Built a Better Burger

Swapping out lean, bland commercial ground turkey for freshly ground turkey thighs (we use a food processor) was only our first step toward a juicier, more meaty-tasting burger.

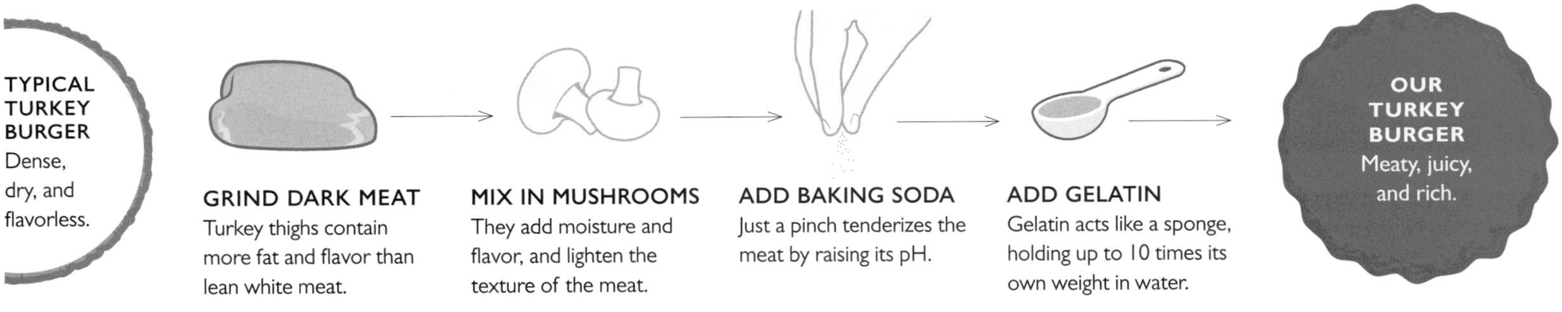

TYPICAL TURKEY BURGER Dense, dry, and flavorless.

GRIND DARK MEAT Turkey thighs contain more fat and flavor than lean white meat.

MIX IN MUSHROOMS They add moisture and flavor, and lighten the texture of the meat.

ADD BAKING SODA Just a pinch tenderizes the meat by raising its pH.

ADD GELATIN Gelatin acts like a sponge, holding up to 10 times its own weight in water.

OUR TURKEY BURGER Meaty, juicy, and rich.

ILLUSTRATION: JAY LAYMAN

Bringing Back Potato Rolls

Could the old-fashioned trick of adding stodgy mashed potatoes to bread really create rolls with the lightest, most tender texture?

⇒ BY ANDREA GEARY ⇐

These days baking bread almost always seems to mean creating a crusty loaf with a big, irregular crumb and a sourdough tang. Maybe it's shamefully retro, but sometimes I long for a homemade bread with a soft, moist, light crumb and a delicate crust. I'm not talking about the decadently buttery rolls associated with holiday dinners (though I do love those) but something a bit leaner as well as more versatile—a bread that could either be shaped into sandwich buns or formed into small dinner rolls. My hankering, I realized, was for good old-fashioned potato rolls. This bread delivers the same soft tenderness of a classic American dinner roll but without its richness. What's more, the dough would work equally well for burger buns—something I've always wanted a great recipe for.

In the past I assumed that potato bread must boast only a little mashed potato—how else could it be so light and airy? But a roundup of recipes showed that the bread could include virtually any amount of potato, from 2 tablespoons to 2 cups. There was also no consensus on what form the potatoes should take. Some called for freshly mashed spuds (and often a bit of the cooking water), others for cold leftovers, still others for the instant kind. I even found a few recipes simply requiring the addition of dried potato starch. Almost none of the recipes specified what type of potato to use, and even peeling them wasn't a given.

To my surprise, all of the recipes I tried produced loaves that were remarkably tender and moist—even the ones made with instant potatoes and potato starch. But I did notice a few trends. First, the more potato in the mix the softer and more airy the bread—but only up to a point. Too much potato and the bread began to be weighed down by the load. Second, doughs made with warm, freshly mashed spuds seemed to rise more quickly than those that employed cold potatoes or the packaged products, and doughs that included the cooking water from the potatoes rose fastest of all.

Thanks to the magical properties of potatoes, these rolls will be just as good on day two as they are when fresh.

A Stodgy Explanation

Before I went any further, it seemed time to get at the fundamental question: How is it that mashed potato, a food that is almost synonymous with stodge, has the ability (in the right amount) to bestow such a light, soft character on bread in the first place? Our science editor enlightened me: When potatoes are boiled, their starch granules swell with water. When those swollen starches are mixed into bread dough, they physically interfere with the flour proteins' ability to link together and form gluten, thus weakening the dough's structure so that it bakes up softer and more tender. What's more, potato starch granules are four to five times larger than wheat starch granules and can thus hold much more water than the wheat starches can, making potato bread moister than straight wheat bread and contributing to our perception of the crumb as soft and light.

Armed with these facts, I was ready to figure out how much potato was optimal and what form it should take to achieve just the fluffy texture I wanted. Though the instant spuds and potato starch had actually produced decent results, I don't normally keep either product in my cabinet. I also vetoed cold leftover mash, since that's not something I could count on having on hand either. I would start with freshly boiled peeled potatoes (tasters found that the skins contributed an earthiness that they didn't want in dough destined for sandwich rolls) and keep the amount on the lower end of the spectrum, with just ¼ cup (2 ounces) replacing 2 ounces of all-purpose flour. I also opted for russet potatoes, thinking that their floury texture would serve me best. After mashing the potatoes with butter, I kneaded them in a stand mixer with the flour, whole egg, milk (which some recipes added for a subtle dairy sweetness), salt, sugar, and yeast and then left the dough to rise for an hour before shaping it into sandwich rolls. After another rise—45 minutes this time—I baked the batch in a 425-degree oven.

I was on the right track: These rolls had a tenderness approaching that of richer breads, even though they contained just 2 tablespoons of butter. Excited by this effect, I wondered just how far I could push

Potato-Roll Highs (and Lows)

The more mashed potato we added to our dough the better the results—until we hit 1 full cup, at which point the rolls started to collapse under the weight of the spuds. But switching from all-purpose flour to higher-protein bread flour gave the dough the strength it needed to support the mash, so the rolls baked up tall, light, and fluffy.

LOW RISE
Avoid all-purpose flour.

HIGH RISE
Use high-protein bread flour.

PHOTOGRAPHY: CARL TREMBLAY

the potato's magical properties. I increased the mash by another ¼ cup, decreasing the flour by the same 2 ounces, and the rolls got even lighter and fluffier. I ended up with the same results whether I created a feathery mash using a ricer or pounded the potatoes into glueyness with a potato masher.

Light—and Lightning Fast
The more I upped the potato, the less time the dough needed to rise. I chalked that up to the dispersal of more warm potato throughout the dough, since yeast thrives in a warm environment. But when I did a little research, I learned that there was a more potato-specific reason behind the faster rise: The potassium in potatoes activates yeast, and the more of it there is the quicker and more vigorous the rise. Furthermore, when potatoes are boiled, they leach almost half of their potassium into the cooking water—helping to explain why so many recipes added it to the dough. I found that when I switched from using 5 tablespoons of milk to the same amount of potato water, the proofing times dropped still more.

Emboldened by these successes, I increased the potatoes from ½ cup to a full packed cup, reducing the flour by a corresponding 4 ounces. However, this time the dough fell flat, making coarse-crumbed rolls with a compromised rise. Could it be that a full cup of potato was just too much to cram into my bread? Before failing so dramatically, this batch had risen in record time, and I was reluctant to give that up. But maybe the problem was not with the potatoes; maybe I had chosen the wrong flour for the job.

Clearly, the protein in the two-odd cups of all-purpose flour in my recipe wasn't providing enough muscle to support ½ pound of freeloading potato starch. But what if I switched to higher-protein bread flour? This simple swap did the trick: The increased protein provided just enough stable yet tender structure to support the potatoes, yielding rolls that were not only perfectly risen but also the lightest, airiest yet. And I could use the same dough for sandwich rolls or dinner rolls, depending on how large I made the pieces.

Now that I know how and why adding potatoes to bread improves its texture (not to mention how potatoes speed up bread preparation), I'm ready to start a potato bread renaissance.

POTATO BURGER BUNS
MAKES 9 ROLLS

These rolls are ideal for both burgers and sandwiches. Don't salt the cooking water for the potatoes. A pound of russet potatoes should yield just over 1 very firmly packed cup (½ pound) of mash. To ensure optimum rise, your dough should be warm; if your potatoes or potato water is too hot to touch, let cool before proceeding with the recipe. This dough looks very dry when mixing begins but will soften as mixing progresses. If you prefer, you may portion the rolls by weight in step 5 (2.75 ounces of dough per roll).

    1   pound russet potatoes, peeled and cut into
        1-inch pieces
    2   tablespoons unsalted butter, cut into 4 pieces
    2¼ cups (12⅓ ounces) bread flour
    1   tablespoon sugar
    2   teaspoons instant or rapid-rise yeast
    1   teaspoon salt
    2   large eggs, 1 lightly beaten with 1 teaspoon
        water and pinch salt
    1   tablespoon sesame seeds (optional)

1. Place potatoes in medium saucepan and add water to just cover. Bring to boil over high heat; reduce heat to medium-low and simmer until potatoes are cooked through, 8 to 10 minutes.

2. Transfer 5 tablespoons potato water to bowl to cool; drain potatoes. Return potatoes to saucepan and place over low heat. Cook, shaking pot occasionally, until any surface moisture has evaporated, about 1 minute. Remove from heat. Process potatoes through ricer or food mill or mash well with potato masher. Measure 1 very firmly packed cup potatoes and transfer to bowl. Reserve any remaining potatoes for another use. Stir in butter until melted.

3. Combine flour, sugar, yeast, and salt in bowl of stand mixer. Add warm potato mixture to flour mixture and mix with hands until combined (some large lumps are OK). Add 1 egg and reserved potato water; mix with dough hook on low speed until dough is soft and slightly sticky, 8 to 10 minutes.

4. Shape dough into ball and place in lightly greased container. Cover tightly with plastic wrap and allow to rise at room temperature until almost doubled in volume, 30 to 40 minutes.

5. Turn out dough onto counter, dusting with flour only if dough is too sticky to handle comfortably. Pat gently into 8-inch square of even thickness. Using bench knife or chef's knife, cut dough into 9 pieces (3 rows by 3 rows). Separate pieces and cover loosely with plastic.

6. Working with 1 piece of dough at a time and keeping remaining pieces covered, form dough pieces into smooth, taut rounds. (To round, set piece of dough on unfloured work surface. Loosely cup hand around dough and, without applying pressure to dough, move hand in small circular motions. Tackiness of dough against work surface and circular motion should work dough into smooth, even ball, but if dough sticks to hands, lightly dust fingers with flour.) Cover rounds with plastic and allow to rest for 15 minutes.

7. Line 2 rimmed baking sheets with parchment paper. On lightly floured surface, firmly press each dough round into 3½-inch disk of even thickness, expelling large pockets of air. Arrange on prepared baking sheets. Cover loosely with plastic and let rise at room temperature until almost doubled in size, 30 to 40 minutes. While rolls rise, adjust oven racks to middle and upper-middle positions and heat oven to 425 degrees.

8. Brush rolls gently with egg wash and sprinkle with sesame seeds, if using. Bake rolls until deep golden brown, 15 to 18 minutes, rotating and switching baking sheets halfway through baking. Transfer baking sheets to wire racks and let cool for 5 minutes. Transfer rolls from baking sheets to wire racks. Serve warm or at room temperature.

POTATO DINNER ROLLS
MAKES 12 ROLLS

For our free Potato Dinner Rolls flavor variations (Potato Dinner Rolls with Roasted Garlic and Chives, Potato Dinner Rolls with Parmesan and Black Pepper, and Potato Dinner Rolls with Cheddar and Mustard), go to www.CooksIllustrated.com/aug12.

Line rimmed baking sheet with parchment paper. In step 5, divide dough square into 12 pieces (3 rows by 4 rows). Shape pieces into smooth, taut rounds as directed in step 6. Transfer rounds to prepared baking sheet and let rise at room temperature until almost doubled in size, 30 to 40 minutes. Bake on upper-middle rack until rolls are deep golden brown, 12 to 14 minutes, rotating baking sheet halfway through baking.

All About Tomatoes

Here's our guide to making the most of those luscious in-season tomatoes, as well as what the supermarket has to offer the rest of the year. BY DANETTE ST. ONGE

BUYING THE BEST

Even buying tomatoes at the height of summer won't guarantee that you're getting juicy, flavorful fruit, but keeping these guidelines in mind will help.

Choose Locally Grown

The most important way to help ensure a flavorful tomato is to buy a locally grown one. Why? First, the less distance the tomato has to travel the riper it can be when it's picked. Second, commercial high-yield production can strain the tomato plant, resulting in tomatoes without enough sugars and other flavor compounds to make them tasty. Third, to withstand the rigors of machine harvesting and long-distance transport, commercial varieties are engineered to be sturdier with thicker walls and less of the jelly and seeds that give a tomato most of its flavor.

Try an Heirloom

Grown for decades from naturally pollinated plants and seeds that haven't been hybridized (unlike commercial varieties), heirlooms are some of the best local tomatoes you'll find.

Looks Aren't Everything

Oddly shaped tomatoes are fine (only commercial tomatoes have been bred to be perfectly symmetrical). Even cracked skin is OK, but avoid tomatoes that are overly soft or leaking juice. Choose tomatoes that smell fruity and feel heavy.

STORAGE SMARTS

Don't Refrigerate

Cold damages enzymes that produce flavor compounds and ruins texture by rupturing tomato cells, turning the flesh mealy. Even cut tomatoes should be kept at room temperature, tightly wrapped in plastic wrap, and used within a few days.

Freeze for the Off-Season

If you have a glut of end-of-summer tomatoes, core them and freeze them whole in freezer storage bags for later use in sauces. Freezing preserves tomato flavor better than canning. (That method's high temperature destroys tomato flavor even more than cold does.)

Store Stem End Down

Place unwashed tomatoes stem end down at room temperature. We've found that this prevents moisture from escaping and bacteria from entering through the scar, prolonging shelf life. If the vine is still attached, though, leave it on and store tomatoes stem end up.

Anatomy of a Flavorful Tomato

The best-tasting tomatoes tend to have thin walls, which leaves more room for the most flavorful part of the tomato: the jelly that surrounds the seeds, which is three times richer in savory glutamates than the flesh is. Some sources recommend removing the seeds to avoid their bitter taste, but we haven't found that they negatively affect flavor. If you do choose to remove the seeds for aesthetic reasons, strain them and reserve the jelly.

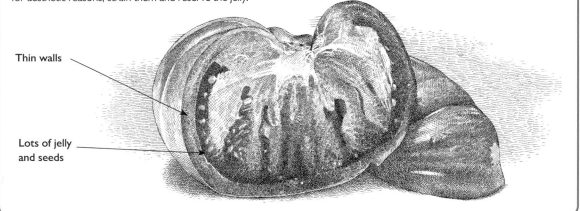

Thin walls

Lots of jelly and seeds

Supermarket Standouts

When we can't get tomatoes at our local farm market, we look for the following varieties at the grocery store.

➤ **Kumato:** These startlingly green-brown European imports have more fructose than conventional tomatoes, which makes them taste sweeter. Tasters also found their texture meatier.

➤ **UglyRipe:** These knobby-looking fruits are left on the living vine longer than most other commercial varieties, which explains why our tasters found them sweeter and juicier. Because of their delicateness, each fruit is individually packed in protective foam netting.

In the Can

Canned tomatoes are better stand-ins than bland off-season fresh options. When you want a chunkier texture in your finished dish, choose diced tomatoes—they contain more calcium chloride (added by manufacturers to maintain firmness) than whole tomatoes. Whole and crushed give a smoother, more broken-down texture when cooked.

Test Kitchen Favorites

Whole:	Muir Glen Organic
Crushed:	Tuttorosso
Diced:	Hunt's
Puree:	Muir Glen Organic
Juice:	Campbell's
Paste:	Goya

Bag 'em with a Banana

If you find yourself with hard, under-ripe tomatoes, store them in a paper bag with a banana or an apple, both of which naturally emit the ethylene gas that hastens ripening.

Don't Be Fooled by "Vine Ripened"

This term indicates only that the tomatoes were picked when 10 percent of the skin started to "break," or turn from green to red. Since most of their maturation happens off the vine, they'll never taste as good as naturally ripened fruit. That said, we prefer them to regular supermarket tomatoes, which are picked when fully green and blasted with ethylene gas to develop texture and color.

PREPPING TECHNIQUES

Coring

Inserting the tip of a sharp paring knife at an angle about 1 inch into the tomato just outside of the core allows you to free the tough stem and minimize the flesh that's cut away.

Chopping

Place round tomatoes cored side down to create a stable surface. (For a plum tomato, first slice off one long side to make a stable surface.) Slice, stack slices in pairs, and cut into strips. Turn stack and slice crosswise.

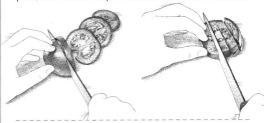

Grating

When you need to crush only a couple of tomatoes, grate halved, unpeeled tomatoes on the large holes of a grater rather than opening a whole can.

Blanching and Peeling

If you don't own a serrated peeler, blanching is the easiest way to remove tomato skins. Scoring an X into the bottom of the tomato (core it first) causes the skin to curl back in the boiling water, giving you an easy place to begin peeling after blanching.

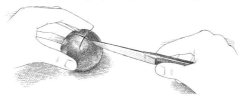

1. Using paring knife, score X in bottom of tomato.

2. Blanch in boiling water for 15 to 30 seconds (riper tomatoes need less time). Transfer tomatoes to ice-water bath.

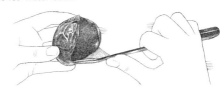

3. Grab curled skin from bottom and strip off.

> **Easy Peeling**
> We found that the Messermeister Pro-Touch Serrated Peeler ($10) cleanly pulls skin off tomatoes, with no need for blanching.

COOKING TIPS

➤ Choose Plums

Meaty plum (or Roma) tomatoes contain less moisture than other varieties, making them best suited for sauces, stews, and canning.

➤ Salt Tomatoes for Uncooked Recipes

For raw-tomato applications like salsa, it's best to salt the chopped tomatoes, let them stand for 30 to 60 minutes, and pat them dry before using. The salt not only forces flavor compounds to separate from proteins, making them accessible to our tastebuds for a fuller and more complex flavor, but also rids the fruit of excess moisture.

➤ Don't Cook Tomatoes in Reactive Metal

Tomato acid will not only react with cast iron or uncoated copper or aluminum and leave food tasting harsh and metallic but also damage the surface of the cookware.

➤ Don't Add Tomatoes Too Early

The acid that tomatoes release during cooking can prevent other foods from breaking down. To ensure that all the elements achieve the proper texture, ingredients like onions and beans should be fully softened before the tomatoes are introduced.

➤ Tame Tartness with Sugar

Tomatoes vary in sweetness, so it's important to taste dishes during cooking and adjust the seasoning as necessary. Adding a pinch or two of sugar can tone down acidity and enhance flavor from proteins.

QUICK FRESH TOMATO SAUCE
MAKES 2 CUPS; ENOUGH FOR 1 POUND PASTA

In-season, locally grown tomatoes are essential for this recipe and the one that follows. To keep the garlic from burning, start the olive oil and garlic in a cold pan.

- 3 tablespoons extra-virgin olive oil
- 4 garlic cloves, minced
- 2 pounds tomatoes, cored, peeled, and cut into ¾-inch chunks
  Salt and pepper
- ¼ cup chopped fresh basil

Stir oil and garlic together in large skillet. Turn heat to medium and cook until garlic is sizzling and fragrant, about 2 minutes. Stir in tomatoes and ½ teaspoon salt. Bring to rapid simmer and cook, stirring occasionally, reducing heat if sauce begins to stick to bottom of pan, until thickened and chunky, 15 to 20 minutes. Remove from heat. Stir in basil and season with salt and pepper to taste.

SLOW-ROASTED TOMATOES
SERVES 4

These tomatoes can be served as a side dish or used in salads and sandwiches. When finished with the recipe, don't discard the cooking oil, which will have a slight tomato flavor. Instead, refrigerate it in an airtight container for up to one week to use in salad dressing or as a dipping sauce for bread.

- ½ cup extra-virgin olive oil
- 4 garlic cloves, sliced thin
- 2 pounds tomatoes, cored and cut crosswise into ½-inch-thick slices
  Salt and pepper

1. Adjust oven rack to middle position and heat oven to 325 degrees.

2. Grease bottom of 13 by 9-inch baking dish with 2 tablespoons oil and sprinkle half of garlic across bottom of dish. Arrange tomato slices in pan, overlapping edges as needed to fit. Pour remaining 6 tablespoons oil over tomatoes and sprinkle with salt and remaining garlic. Roast tomatoes until they are slightly shriveled and most of their juice has been replaced with oil, 1½ to 2 hours.

3. Remove dish from oven and let tomatoes cool in oil for at least 15 minutes, or up to 4 hours. To serve, remove tomatoes from oil with slotted spoon (reserving oil if desired) and season with salt and pepper to taste. (Cooled tomatoes and oil can be refrigerated together in airtight container for up to 1 week; return to room temperature before serving.)

Perfecting Chilled Tomato Soup

Throw tomatoes into a blender and puree? Not so fast. For a full-flavored soup, even top-notch tomatoes have to be treated just right.

> BY DAWN YANAGIHARA <

On a sweltering day, an icy bowl of chilled soup is one of summer's great pleasures. Vegetable-filled gazpacho has its place, but ripe, peak-season tomatoes deserve a soup in which they don't have to share the spotlight. An ideal cold tomato soup would capture the essence of the fruit in silky-smooth liquid form: light yet satisfying, savory yet sweet, and deeply flavorful yet simple. But my many failed attempts at attaining tomato soup perfection last August proved that exemplary fruit alone doesn't guarantee success. My results ranged from the thin, mealy mess that I got from blending raw tomatoes with a couple of ice cubes to an over-thickened, ketchuplike sludge that was the upshot of simmering tomatoes with tomato juice for half an hour before chilling. Determined to get it right this season, I loaded up on tomatoes at a farmers' market and headed into the kitchen.

But before I started cooking, I studied my past recipe flops. It occurred to me that in order to get the best of both worlds—fresh yet potent flavor—a hybrid half-raw, half-cooked approach might be in order. I knew that oven roasting is an effective way to concentrate flavor, so I halved the fruit crosswise (to help excess moisture escape) and experimented until I determined that roasting the tomatoes for about 25 minutes at 375 degrees was enough to intensify their taste. I pureed the roasted tomatoes with an equal amount of uncooked fruit and strained out the skins and seeds, happily finding that this approach produced both deep, sweet flavor and bright, tangy freshness.

But pureed tomatoes alone do not a soup make, so next I looked for ways to round out the flavor. Red bell pepper (a common addition) overwhelmed the tomatoes, as did fresh herbs, even when used in tiny amounts. Garlic and mild shallot seemed like natural additions but only if I tamed their raw pungency. I roasted two garlic cloves and one sliced shallot together with the tomatoes for the first 15 minutes, removing them from the oven as soon as they had softened. When I pureed the raw and roasted tomatoes with the gently roasted aromatics, the soup's flavor improved, but it was still missing some tomatoey backbone.

Using equal parts fresh and roasted tomatoes yields complex flavor.

It made sense to turn to a test kitchen secret weapon in tomato-based recipes: tomato paste. I blended some into my next batch, and sure enough, a small dose of the sweet paste dramatically upped the flavor quotient. Finally, smoked paprika and cayenne pepper added even more layers of complexity.

With the flavor profile complete, I now had to focus on texture. As it stood, my soup was dismally thin and runny. Cream added body but also dulled the fresh tomato flavor, and even worse, the acidic tomatoes made it curdle. Blending some bread along with the tomatoes thickened the mixture, but its starchiness seemed out of place in the cool, fresh soup.

Inspiration struck one evening as I was making a batch of mayonnaise. I watched the slow drizzle of oil into eggs transform into creamy billows as the ingredients formed an emulsion. Lo and behold, 6 tablespoons of olive oil added gradually to the blender as I pureed the tomatoes took them from a thin liquid to a rich, spoon-coating consistency. The olive oil also added a satisfying richness, and its fruity, peppery notes were an ideal accent to the savory-sweet tomatoes. Strained and chilled for at least two hours to let the flavors blend, the soup was velvety and delicious. Finally, as is the case with many soups, this one benefited greatly from a touch of acid. Just a teaspoon of sherry vinegar perked up all of the flavors.

Served with crostini or *frico* (thin, crisp cheese wafers) for textural contrast, the chilled tomato soup was summertime perfection in a bowl.

CHILLED FRESH TOMATO SOUP
SERVES 4

In-season, locally grown tomatoes and good-quality extra-virgin olive oil are ideal for this recipe. Serve the soup with Garlic and Burrata Crostini or Frico; for our free recipes, go to www.CooksIllustrated.com/aug12.

- 2 pounds tomatoes, cored
- 1 shallot, sliced thin
- 2 garlic cloves, unpeeled
- 2 teaspoons tomato paste
- 1/8 teaspoon smoked paprika (optional)
  Pinch cayenne pepper
  Salt
- 6 tablespoons extra-virgin olive oil, plus extra for drizzling
- 1 teaspoon sherry vinegar, plus extra as needed
  Pepper (optional)

1. Adjust oven rack to middle position and heat oven to 375 degrees. Line rimmed baking sheet with aluminum foil and lightly spray with vegetable oil spray.

2. Cut 1 pound tomatoes in half horizontally and arrange cut side up on prepared baking sheet. Arrange shallot and garlic cloves in single layer over 1 area of baking sheet. Roast for 15 minutes, then remove shallot and garlic cloves. Return baking sheet to oven and continue to roast tomatoes until softened but not browned, 10 to 15 minutes longer. Let cool to room temperature, about 30 minutes.

3. Peel garlic cloves and place in blender with roasted shallot and roasted tomatoes. Cut remaining 1 pound tomatoes into eighths and add to blender along with tomato paste; paprika, if using; cayenne; and 1/2 teaspoon salt. Puree until smooth, about 30 seconds. With motor running, drizzle in olive oil in slow, steady stream; puree will turn orange in color.

4. Pour puree through fine-mesh strainer into nonreactive bowl, pressing on solids in strainer to extract as much liquid as possible. Discard solids. Stir in vinegar. Cover and refrigerate until well chilled and flavors have blended, at least 2 hours or up to 24 hours.

5. To serve, stir soup to recombine (liquid separates on standing). Taste and adjust seasoning with salt and vinegar, as needed. Ladle soup into chilled bowls, drizzle sparingly with extra oil, and grind pepper over each, if using. Serve immediately.

PHOTOGRAPHY: CARL TREMBLAY

Rescuing Tabbouleh

To fix this sadly degraded dish, we stopped pouring a key ingredient down the drain.

⇒ BY SUSAN LIGHT ⇐

Tabbouleh has long been a meze staple in the Middle East, but these days it can be found in the refrigerator case of virtually every American supermarket. Its brief (and healthful) ingredient list explains its popularity: Chopped fresh parsley and mint, tomatoes, onion, and bits of nutty bulgur are tossed with lemon and olive oil for a refreshing appetizer or side dish. It all sounds easy enough, but following a recipe or picking up a pint at the market reveals that most versions are hopelessly soggy, with flavor that is either too bold or too bland.

Another problem is that there's no agreement on the correct proportions for tabbouleh. Middle Eastern cooks favor loads of parsley (75 to 90 percent of the salad), only employing a sprinkle of bulgur as a texturally interesting garnish. Most American recipes, on the other hand, invert the proportions, transforming the green salad into an insipid pilaf smattered with herbs. I decided to take a middle-of-the-road approach for a dish that would feature a hefty amount of parsley as well as a decent amount of bulgur.

Bulgur is made by boiling, drying, and grinding wheat kernels, so it only needs to be reconstituted in cool water. But specific advice on how to prepare the grains is all over the map. Rehydration times range from a cursory five minutes all the way up to several hours. And then there's the amount of liquid: Some recipes call for just enough to plump the grains; others employ the "pasta method," soaking the bulgur in lots of water and then squeezing out the excess.

Working with ½ cup of medium-grind bulgur (the easiest size to find) and first rinsing the grains to remove any detritus, I experimented with innumerable permutations of time and amount of water. My initial finding: The grains required at least 90 minutes to tenderize fully. Second: The less liquid I used the better the texture. Soaking the bulgur in excess water only made it heavy, damp, and bland. In the end, a mere ¼ cup of liquid was enough for ½ cup of dried bulgur. The grains absorbed the liquid almost instantly and then slowly swelled into 1 cup of tender, fluffy grains as they rested.

With my method settled, I switched to soaking the bulgur in lemon juice instead of water, as some cookbooks recommend. This was a no-brainer—eliminating water from the recipe only made sense for a salad that can taste washed out.

Next up: parsley. To my 1 cup of reconstituted bulgur, I added 1½ cups of chopped parsley and ½ cup of chopped mint. These quantities still put the emphasis on the bright, peppery parsley but didn't discount the lemony bulgur and refreshing mint.

Our frugal, flavorful trick: soaking the bulgur in the drained tomato juice.

As for the rest of the salad, 6 tablespoons of extra-virgin olive oil tempered the tart lemon juice, and three chopped ripe tomatoes and two sliced scallions (preferred over red or white onion) rounded out the mix. A smidge of cayenne pepper along with the usual salt and pepper added zing. Finally, I considered garlic and cucumbers. Tasters soundly rejected these additions, complaining that they detracted from the salad's clean flavor (in the case of the former) and overall texture (in the case of the latter).

I set out pita bread wedges and romaine lettuce leaves (traditional accompaniments) and summoned tasters for feedback. They were happy enough with the texture, but the flavors of the salad, they lamented, weren't cohesive—tabbouleh features bold ingredients and my method wasn't giving them time to blend. This was easy to resolve: I simply reworked my method to give the bulgur a chance to absorb any of the liquids—namely, olive oil and juices from the tomatoes—in the salad. Soaking the bulgur for 30 to 40 minutes, until it began to soften, and then combining it with the remaining ingredients and letting it sit for an hour until fully tender gave everything time to mingle, resulting in a perfectly well-balanced dish.

I had just one final issue to deal with. Over the course of testing, I had noticed that depending on variety, the tomatoes contributed different amounts of liquid to the tabbouleh, sometimes diluting its flavor and making it soupy. The solution? Salting. Tossing the tomatoes in salt and letting them drain in a colander drew out their moisture, precluding sogginess. I was about to pat myself on the back when

a light bulb went on: By discarding the tomato juice, I was literally pouring flavor down the drain. What if I reserved this savory liquid and used it to soak the bulgur? For my next try, I put a bowl under the colander to catch the juices and prepared a salad using 2 tablespoons of the tomato liquid (along with an equal amount of lemon juice) to soak the bulgur, whisking the remaining 2 tablespoons of lemon juice with oil for the dressing. At last, here was tabbouleh with fresh, penetrating flavor and a light texture that would make cooks—from anywhere around the globe—proud.

TABBOULEH
SERVES 4

For tips on buying bulgur, see page 30. Serve the salad with the crisp inner leaves of romaine lettuce and wedges of pita bread. For our free recipe for Spiced Tabbouleh, go to www.CooksIllustrated.com/aug12.

3	medium round tomatoes, cored and cut into ½-inch pieces
	Salt and pepper
½	cup medium-grind bulgur
¼	cup lemon juice (2 lemons)
6	tablespoons extra-virgin olive oil
⅛	teaspoon cayenne pepper
1½	cups chopped fresh parsley
½	cup chopped fresh mint
2	scallions, sliced thin

1. Toss tomatoes and ¼ teaspoon salt in large bowl. Transfer to fine-mesh strainer, set strainer in bowl, and let stand for 30 minutes, tossing occasionally.

2. Rinse bulgur in fine-mesh strainer under cold running water. Drain well and transfer to second bowl. Stir in 2 tablespoons lemon juice and 2 tablespoons juice from draining tomatoes. Let stand until grains are beginning to soften, 30 to 40 minutes.

3. Whisk remaining 2 tablespoons lemon juice, oil, cayenne, and ¼ teaspoon salt together in large bowl. Add drained tomatoes, soaked bulgur, parsley, mint, and scallions; toss gently to combine. Cover and let stand at room temperature until flavors have blended and bulgur is tender, about 1 hour. Toss to recombine, season with salt and pepper to taste, and serve immediately.

PHOTOGRAPHY: CARL TREMBLAY

Spanish-Style Pasta with Shrimp

Fideuà, a rich seafood paella made with toasted noodles instead of rice, would be a tempting one-pot meal—if only it didn't take hours to make.

⇒ BY THE *COOK'S ILLUSTRATED* TEST KITCHEN ⇐

The biggest star of traditional Spanish cooking is arguably paella, but there's another closely related dish equally deserving of raves: *fideuà*. This richly flavored dish swaps the rice for thin noodles that are typically toasted until nut-brown before being cooked in a garlicky, tomatoey stock loaded with seafood and sometimes chorizo sausage. As with the rice in paella, the noodles (called *fideos*) should be tender but not mushy. But whereas paella tends to be moist but not soupy, fideuà is often a little brothy.

One thing that paella and fideuà have in common: a lengthy and involved cooking process. Almost all of the recipes we tried called for the same series of steps: Simmer fish and shellfish scraps to create stock. Toast the fideos and put together a flavorful base (the *sofrito*) by slowly reducing fresh tomatoes with aromatics and seasonings. Combine the sofrito with the stock and then simmer the toasted noodles and seafood in this rich-tasting liquid until cooked. Finally, put the whole thing in the oven to create a crunchy layer of pasta on top.

Our crash course in the genre taught us that the results were often well worth the effort. But just as with paella, tinkering with fideuà is part of the art. We decided that our tweaks would be aimed at streamlining a recipe but leaving it every bit as deeply flavorful as the more time-consuming versions.

Breaking Pasta (Rules)

Our first decision was to keep things simple in the seafood department and go with shrimp alone. Our next step was to make a stock without even dirtying a pot. We knew that shrimp shells can build a surprisingly flavorful broth without much help, so we combined the shells from 1½ pounds of shrimp in a bowl with some water and a bay leaf and microwaved until the shells turned pink and the water was hot. The resulting broth wasn't bad for something that took such little effort, but its taste improved when we replaced

Briny shrimp, toasted pasta, garlic, and two kinds of paprika create a flavor-packed one-dish meal that takes just an hour to make.

a portion of the water with chicken broth and added a small measure of white wine for brightness.

Fideos come in varying thicknesses and shapes, including short, straight strands and coiled nests of thin, vermicelli-like noodles. We found that snapping spaghettini (more widely available than fideos) into pieces gave us a fine approximation of the first type of fideos. Not all fideuà recipes call for toasting the pasta, but skipping that step led to a dish that tasted weak and washed out. So what was the best way to toast? The oven provided controlled heat but required repeatedly moving a baking sheet in and out in order to stir the noodles—which added another item to the dirty-dish pile. Toasting on the stovetop in a skillet—the same skillet in which the dish would be cooked and served—also required stirring, but this was much easier to monitor.

Next we examined the sofrito. This flavor base shows up in a variety of forms in Spanish dishes but always features some combination of aromatics—onion, garlic, celery, and bell pepper are common—slow-cooked in oil to soften and concentrate their flavors. In fideuà, onion and garlic are

typical, along with tomato. In the interest of efficiency, we ruled out preparing the sofrito separately, in another skillet. We also finely chopped our onion so that it would cook quickly and added ¼ teaspoon of salt to help draw out moisture so that the onion softened and browned even faster in the oil.

Fresh tomatoes would take time to cook down, so we opted for canned diced tomatoes that we drained well and chopped fine. Added to the skillet with the softened onion, they reduced to a thick paste in a matter of minutes. Then we introduced minced garlic and cooked the mixture for a minute to bloom the flavors. When we pitted fideuà made with our abbreviated sofrito against a traditional slow-cooked version, tasters were hard pressed to taste any difference.

Our next task: getting the right proportion of liquid to pasta. For 8 ounces of pasta, 3¾ cups of liquid was the perfect amount. It allowed the pasta to soak up enough liquid to become tender while leaving just a little behind in the skillet.

Building Flavor

It was time to fine-tune the flavors. A mixture of sweet and Spanish smoked paprikas won praise for its balance of smokiness and earthy sweetness, and while we liked the distinctly Spanish flavor of saffron, it wasn't worth the exorbitant cost, so we left it out. Half a teaspoon of anchovy paste, a go-to flavor booster in the test kitchen, added to the sofrito along with the garlic and paprika offered depth, and its flavor blended seamlessly with the shrimp.

Speaking of the shrimp, we found that simmering them in the stock with the pasta rendered them rubbery. Adding them during the last five minutes of cooking and covering the skillet improved their texture but not their wan flavor. A quick soak in olive oil, garlic, salt, and pepper took care of that problem.

Some recipes finish fideuà in the oven, turning the surface of the pasta crisp and brown—a nice contrast with the tender noodles and seafood underneath. The broiler seemed ideal for achieving such a crust, but when its intense heat toughened up the shrimp, we decided to make a small change: After scattering the raw shrimp over the surface of the pasta, we gently stirred them into the noodles to partially submerge them and protect them from the heat.

PHOTOGRAPHY: CARL TREMBLAY

WEEKNIGHT SPANISH–STYLE PASTA WITH SHRIMP

A series of shortcuts allowed us to create this traditionally labor-intensive, paella-like dish in a single skillet in just an hour.

SEASON SHRIMP
Marinating shrimp in olive oil, garlic, salt, and pepper infuses them with flavor as we prepare other ingredients.

MAKE INSTANT STOCK
Microwaving shrimp shells with diluted chicken broth and a bay leaf creates quick, surprisingly rich-tasting stock.

TOAST NOODLES
Cooking pasta (broken into pieces) in a skillet with olive oil until well browned develops deep, nutty flavor.

COOK IN BROTH
Simmering the noodles in stock and a quick *sofrito* of sautéed onion, garlic, and tomatoes lets them soak up lots of flavor.

ADD SHRIMP; BROIL
Partially submerging the shrimp under the pasta and then transferring the skillet to the broiler creates a crisp, browned crust.

Finally, we accompanied our fideuà with two traditional condiments: lemon wedges and a spoonful of *aïoli*, a garlic mayonnaise that adds richness.

What had our tweaks accomplished? A recipe for Spanish-style fideuà that delivered terrific flavor, in far less time and with far less effort.

SPANISH-STYLE TOASTED PASTA WITH SHRIMP
SERVES 4

In step 5, if your skillet is not broiler-safe, once the pasta is tender transfer the mixture to a broiler-safe 13 by 9-inch baking dish lightly coated with olive oil; scatter the shrimp over the pasta and stir them in to partially submerge. Broil and serve as directed. Serve this dish with lemon wedges and Aïoli (recipe follows), stirring it into individual portions at the table.

- 3 tablespoons plus 2 teaspoons extra-virgin olive oil
- 3 garlic cloves, minced (1 tablespoon)
  Salt and pepper
- 1½ pounds extra-large shrimp (21 to 25 per pound), peeled and deveined, shells reserved
- 2¾ cups water
- 1 cup low-sodium chicken broth
- 1 bay leaf
- 8 ounces spaghettini or thin spaghetti, broken into 1- to 2-inch lengths
- 1 onion, chopped fine
- 1 (14.5-ounce) can diced tomatoes, drained and chopped fine
- 1 teaspoon paprika
- 1 teaspoon smoked paprika
- ½ teaspoon anchovy paste
- ¼ cup dry white wine
- 1 tablespoon chopped fresh parsley
  Lemon wedges
- 1 recipe Aïoli (optional) (recipe follows)

1. Combine 1 tablespoon oil, 1 teaspoon garlic, ¼ teaspoon salt, and ⅛ teaspoon pepper in medium bowl. Add shrimp, toss to coat, and refrigerate until ready to use.

2. Place reserved shrimp shells, water, chicken broth, and bay leaf in medium bowl. Cover and microwave until liquid is hot and shells have turned pink, about 6 minutes. Set aside until ready to use.

3. Toss spaghettini and 2 teaspoons oil in broiler-safe 12-inch skillet until spaghettini is evenly coated. Toast spaghettini over medium-high heat, stirring frequently, until browned and nutty in aroma (spaghettini should be color of peanut butter), 6 to 10 minutes. Transfer spaghettini to bowl. Wipe out skillet with paper towel.

4. Heat remaining 2 tablespoons oil in now-empty skillet over medium-high heat until shimmering. Add onion and ¼ teaspoon salt; cook, stirring frequently, until onion is softened and beginning to brown around edges, 4 to 6 minutes. Add tomatoes and cook, stirring occasionally, until mixture is thick, dry, and slightly darkened in color, 4 to 6 minutes. Reduce heat to medium and add remaining garlic, paprika, smoked paprika, and anchovy paste. Cook

TECHNIQUE | IT'S A SNAP

Since traditional short *fideos* noodles are hard to find, we came up with an easy way to break long strands into even lengths.

Loosely fold 4 ounces of spaghettini in kitchen towel, keeping pasta flat, not bunched. Position so that 1 to 2 inches of pasta rests on counter and remainder of pasta hangs off edge. Pressing bundle against counter, press down on long end of towel to break strands into pieces, sliding bundle back over edge after each break.

until fragrant, about 1½ minutes. Add spaghettini and stir to combine. Adjust oven rack 5 to 6 inches from broiler element and heat broiler.

5. Pour broth through fine-mesh strainer into skillet. Add wine, ¼ teaspoon salt, and ½ teaspoon pepper and stir well. Increase heat to medium-high and bring to simmer. Cook uncovered, stirring occasionally, until liquid is slightly thickened and spaghettini is just tender, 8 to 10 minutes. Scatter shrimp over spaghettini and stir shrimp into spaghettini to partially submerge. Transfer skillet to oven and broil until shrimp are opaque and surface of spaghettini is dry with crisped, browned spots, 5 to 7 minutes. Remove from oven and let stand, uncovered, for 5 minutes. Sprinkle with parsley and serve immediately, passing lemon wedges and, if using, Aïoli separately.

SPANISH-STYLE TOASTED PASTA WITH SHRIMP AND CLAMS

Reduce amount of shrimp to 1 pound and water to 2½ cups. In step 5, cook pasta until almost tender, about 6 minutes. Scatter 1½ pounds scrubbed littleneck or cherrystone clams over pasta, cover skillet, and cook until clams begin to open, about 3 minutes. Scatter shrimp over pasta, stir to partially submerge shrimp and clams, and proceed with recipe as directed.

AÏOLI
MAKES ¾ CUP

- 1 garlic clove, finely grated
- 2 large egg yolks
- 4 teaspoons lemon juice
- ¼ teaspoon salt
- ⅛ teaspoon sugar
  Ground white pepper
- ¾ cup olive oil

In large bowl, combine garlic, egg yolks, lemon juice, salt, sugar, and pepper to taste until combined. Whisking constantly, very slowly drizzle oil into egg mixture until thick and creamy. Season with salt and pepper to taste.

Fresh Corn Salsa

In search of a corn salsa with fresh, sweet flavor and crisp texture, we turned to a 3,000-year-old cooking technique.

≥ BY KEITH DRESSER ≤

I love the ease, flavor, and brightness of fresh salsas. And of all of summer's produce, corn just might be my favorite as a central ingredient for these vibrant dishes: Its juicy, crisp texture lights up simply prepared chicken or fish and is equally terrific with chips. Plus, corn's natural sweetness makes it an exemplary foil for salsa's signature spicy chiles and tart citrus juice.

Many salsa recipes call for grilling the corn, but that approach isn't always convenient. It makes sense when I have additional foods to throw on the fire, but it would also be nice to have a less complicated version that I could whip up without striking a match. And without char from the grill, the sweet flavor and crisp texture of fresh-picked corn could really shine.

My first thought was to simply use raw corn, since I wanted fresh, clean flavor. But I quickly learned that although uncooked kernels taste perfectly sweet, their interiors can be somewhat starchy and their hulls slightly chewy. I tried using the microwave to barely cook the corn, but the results were inconsistent. Even with frequent stirring, the delicate kernels cooked unevenly: Some boasted the plump tenderness I wanted, while others emerged still raw and chewy.

I traded the microwave for pots of salted water and cooked both whole cobs and stripped kernels for times ranging from two to seven minutes. These samples were indeed more consistently cooked—but they were also *too* cooked. Even just two minutes of boiling destroyed the freshness that I was trying to retain. For a more gentle approach, I tried pouring some boiling water onto a bowlful of kernels, but this corn remained virtually unchanged because the water cooled too quickly. To hold on to a little more heat, I reversed the process, putting the kernels directly into the pot of boiling water, removing the pan from the stove, and letting the corn steep for 10 minutes. This was closer to what I was looking for: The inside of the kernel had lost any trace of starchiness. The hull, though, was still chewy.

Softening the hull without overcooking the center seemed impossible until I considered salsa's natural partner: the tortilla chip. Corn tortillas are formed out of masa, a dough made with ground hominy,

which is dried corn that has been soaked in alkaline limewater. This ancient process, called nixtamalization, was first used by Mesoamerican cultures thousands of years ago to soften corn and loosen the hulls. Could I get a similar effect by introducing an alkali to the cooking water for my corn? A quarter teaspoon of baking soda added to the boiling water worked like magic: As the corn steeped, its hulls softened just enough that they weren't leathery, but the kernels still burst with crisp sweetness.

With the corn texture just where I wanted it, I turned to the other ingredients. Unlike grilled corn salsa, which boasts complex smokiness, my salsa made with simply cooked corn plus some accents was relatively one-dimensional. I tried a host of fruit and vegetable add-ins but soon learned that it was all too easy to overwhelm corn's delicate flavor and texture. Fruits that were sweet but with a hint of acidity (like tomato, pineapple, mango, and peach) worked best, while more potent, primarily sweet choices like red bell peppers were overwhelming. As for texture, extra-crunchy ingredients like fennel masked the delicate crispness of the corn; elements that were either softer (like avocado) or of a similar crisp-tender nature (like cucumber) did not. Herbs and chiles were essential additions, as was finely minced shallot.

Now I just needed to tie everything together. To bolster the slightly acidic fruit with even more tartness, I tried a variety of vinegars and citrus juices. Tasters found lemon juice and all types of vinegar too brassy and harsh; their preference was mildly acidic lime juice. On its own, though, lime juice pooled at the bottom of the bowl. A tablespoon of vegetable oil and a tiny bit of honey whisked into the lime juice helped give the dressing body so that it could cling to the solids. Fresh-tasting and a cinch to prepare, these corn salsas will be making regular appearances on my warm-weather menus.

FRESH CORN SALSA
WITH TOMATO
MAKES 3 CUPS

Do not substitute frozen corn for fresh. For a tip on shucking corn, see page 30. For a spicier salsa, add some or all of the jalapeño seeds and ribs. This salsa can be served atop chicken or fish or with corn chips.

- 3 ears corn, kernels cut from cobs (2¼ cups)
- ¼ teaspoon baking soda

Salt and pepper
- 2 tablespoons lime juice
- 1 tablespoon vegetable oil
- ½ teaspoon honey
- 1 tomato, cored, seeded, and cut into ¼-inch pieces
- 1 shallot, minced
- 1 jalapeño chile, stemmed, seeded, and minced
- ¼ cup chopped fresh cilantro

1. Bring 2 cups water to boil in small saucepan over high heat. Stir in corn, baking soda, and ¼ teaspoon salt; remove pan from heat and let stand for 10 minutes. Drain corn and let cool slightly, about 10 minutes.

2. Whisk lime juice, oil, honey, and ⅛ teaspoon salt together in bowl. Add corn, tomato, shallot, jalapeño, and cilantro to lime juice mixture and toss to combine. Let stand for 10 minutes. Season with salt and pepper to taste; serve.

FRESH CORN SALSA
WITH AVOCADO AND TOASTED CUMIN

Add ½ teaspoon toasted cumin seeds and ⅛ teaspoon cayenne pepper to lime juice mixture in step 2. Substitute 1 avocado cut into ¼-inch pieces and 3 thinly sliced scallions for tomato.

FRESH CORN SALSA
WITH JÍCAMA AND PINEAPPLE

Substitute ¾ cup pineapple (cut into ¼-inch pieces) and ½ cup jícama (cut into ¼-inch pieces) for tomato. Substitute 1 minced serrano chile for jalapeño.

FRESH CORN SALSA
WITH MANGO AND CUCUMBER

Add ¼ teaspoon chipotle chile powder to lime juice mixture in step 2. Substitute half of peeled mango cut into ¼-inch pieces and 1 small peeled and seeded cucumber cut into ¼-inch pieces for tomato. Omit jalapeño and substitute mint for cilantro.

FRESH CORN SALSA
WITH PEACH AND RADISHES

Substitute 1 peeled peach cut into ¼-inch pieces and 4 thinly sliced radishes for tomato. Substitute 1 minced habanero chile for jalapeño, and basil for cilantro.

Perfect Raspberry Sorbet

The most important ingredient in raspberry sorbet isn't the raspberries. It's the water.

≥ BY ANDREW JANJIGIAN ≤

Sorbet has always been the neglected stepchild of homemade frozen desserts. This is a shame, because good sorbet can hold its own against ice cream any day. A well-made batch is almost as creamy and smooth as its dairy-based relative, but rather than finishing with mouth-coating richness, it should be delicately icy and dissolve on the tongue, leaving behind an echo of clean, concentrated fruit flavor.

But delicacy is where most recipes get hung up. The majority of homemade sorbets don't have superfine ice crystals—they have big, jagged crystals that raze the tongue—and are so hard they're impossible to get out of the carton. I've also scooped plenty of versions that are crumbly, coarse, and dull and have watched seemingly stable sorbets melt into syrupy puddles within minutes of leaving the freezer.

Despite this long list of hazards, I was determined to figure out a way to pull off the perfect batch. For flavor, I was set on raspberry—not only is it a quintessential summer fruit but the berries also freeze well, meaning I could make this summertime flavor any time of year.

The right ratio of water to sugar is key to a velvety-smooth sorbet that's easy to scoop.

Icebreakers

Before I got to churning, I reviewed what I knew about sorbet. Regardless of how ripe, sweet, and juicy the fruit, freezing a puree of straight berries doesn't work. The relatively small amount of moisture in the fruit will freeze completely and its crystals will be separated only by the berries' fibers. The result—a solid, impenetrable block—wouldn't be pretty.

To get sorbet with the ideal consistency—delicately icy, velvety smooth, and easily scoopable—adding both water and sugar is crucial. The two work in tandem. Some of the water freezes, which creates ice crystals. But because sugar depresses the freezing point of water, some of it will also remain liquid. This so-called "free" water lubricates the ice crystals, producing a smooth, scoopable texture. My challenge, then, would be to achieve just the right balance of water and sugar in the base.

With that in mind, I mixed up my first batch of the base in a blender using 4 cups of berries, ½ cup of water, and ¾ cup of sugar—which I hoped could sweeten the mixture just enough and provide exactly the right ratio of sugar to water. Once the mixture was smooth, I strained it and poured it into my ice cream machine; churned it for 30 minutes, until it froze to a soft-serve consistency; transferred it to a

container; and put it in the freezer overnight.

The next morning I summoned my colleagues for a taste. I wasn't expecting perfection on the first go-round, but from their frowns I could tell I was far from my goal. It wasn't the flavor that needed help. It was the texture that was in all sorts of trouble. Though not rock hard, the sorbet was still too solid to scoop (even when thawed at room temperature for a while). Worse, it was as grainy as a granita.

At this point I understood sorbet well enough to know that adding more water to the mixture would solve the hardness problem by creating more free water, and by the time I'd doubled the liquid the sorbet was perfectly scoopable. But by solving the first problem I'd exaggerated the second, as the ice crystals were now larger and coarser than ever. Apparently, increasing the amount of free water in the base came at a cost.

Fortunately, I had an idea about how to keep the water at 1 cup while still enhancing scoopability and minimizing the size of the crystals: separating out a small amount of the base and freezing it separately, then adding it back into the rest. Our science editor had explained to me that, because the small portion would freeze much more rapidly than if I tried to freeze the whole batch, there wouldn't be enough

time for large ice crystals to grow, and instead very small ice crystals would be formed. Then, when I added this frozen mix back to the rest of the base (which would have been chilled in the meantime), the tiny crystals would act as a catalyst, triggering a chain reaction that very rapidly forms equally small crystals in the bigger mix. (In technical terms, the seed crystals provide "nucleation sites" for new crystals to form.) I gave this a whirl here, freezing a small amount of the base before churning it together with the rest of the base. It was certainly a worthwhile move; everyone agreed that this latest batch was noticeably smoother. But it still hadn't achieved the velvety texture of professionally made sorbet.

One thing I hadn't yet tried was playing with the amount of sugar. At the same time that it depresses the freezing point of water so that some of the water never freezes, it also reduces the tendency of ice crystals to grow large, thus contributing to smoother texture.

See Science in Action

Video available FREE for 4 months at www.CooksIllustrated.com/aug12

We had to solve four problems before we arrived at a scoopable, smooth, dense, and stable sorbet.

PROBLEM 1: TOO HARD TO SCOOP | THE TESTS: VARY WATER AND SUGAR AMOUNTS

For sorbet that's soft enough to scoop, some water should freeze but some should remain liquid and "free" to flow between the ice crystals, providing the sensation of creaminess. Added water and sugar are critical. Water ensures that there's enough of it in the mix to remain free. Sugar aids the process by getting in the way of the water freezing.

ROCK SOLID
Straight fruit puree with no added water or sugar freezes into an impenetrable mass.

GETTING SOFTER
A half cup of water plus ¾ cup of sugar creates some free water, and the sorbet starts to soften.

★ **JUST RIGHT**
One cup of water and nearly 1 cup of sugar and corn syrup produce a creamy, scoopable texture.

PROBLEM 2: ICY, GRAINY TEXTURE | THE TEST: SPEED UP FREEZE TIME

Big ice crystals turn sorbet grainy. Freezing the base as fast as possible is the antidote. First, it doesn't give the base time to form large crystals. Second, once small "seed" crystals get started, they trigger a chain reaction, continuously turning more unfrozen water into equally tiny crystals.

TRADITIONAL SLOW FREEZE
When the whole base is transferred directly to the ice cream maker, it freezes slowly, giving large, grainy ice crystals time to form.

★ **FAST FREEZE**
Freezing 1 cup of the base allows it to freeze rapidly, forming small "seed" crystals. When it is combined with the refrigerated remainder, it initiates a chain reaction, causing more small crystals to form immediately.

PROBLEM 3: CRUMBLY TEXTURE, DULL TASTE | THE TESTS: CALIBRATE CHURN TIMES

Too much churning has a negative effect on the final texture of sorbet: Because the dessert has no fat or protein to stabilize the air bubbles incorporated during churning, longer churning times produce sorbets that are loose, crumbly, and dull-tasting.

40 MINUTES
Overchurned sorbet looks promisingly thick but freezes up crumbly and dull-tasting.

30 MINUTES
As the churning time is reduced, less air is incorporated, improving the texture of the final product.

★ **20 MINUTES**
Churning just long enough for the mixture to reach the consistency of a thick milkshake produces dense, flavorful sorbet.

PROBLEM 4: RAPID MELTING | THE TESTS: TRY STABILIZERS

Sorbet is prone to rapid melting once it is scooped and served. Commercial manufacturers stave off melting by incorporating ingredients like guar gum and locust bean gum that trap some of the free water so it won't readily leak out at room temperature. Instead of those additives, we tried gelatin and pectin.

NO STABILIZER
Once out of the freezer, stabilizer-free sorbet quickly melts into a watery mess.

1 TSP GELATIN
While it greatly improves stability, gelatin creates a sorbet that is strangely rubbery.

★ **1 TSP PECTIN**
Pectin, which is also found naturally in berries, slows melting and produces a likable texture.

The only problem was that, flavor-wise, I had the sugar right where I wanted it. When I tried increasing it to 1 cup, it smoothed out the sorbet's texture but created an achingly sweet dessert. That got me thinking of another trick we used in our ice cream recipe: swapping some of the sugar for corn syrup. Like sugar, this sweetener interrupts the flow of water molecules, preventing the formation of large crystals. But because corn syrup tastes a lot less sweet than sugar, I could use a fair bit of it without oversweetening the sorbet.

I moved forward with that idea in my next several batches, swapping in varying amounts of corn syrup for sugar. The more sugar I replaced with syrup the softer and smoother the texture became. The winning batch contained ½ cup plus 2 tablespoons of sugar and ¼ cup of corn syrup, the combination of which offered an ideal balance of sweetness, smoothness, and scoopability.

Bound to Work

At last, the texture of the sorbet was ideal when eaten straight out of the freezer. But once it sat for even a few minutes at room temperature, it began to liquefy into a soupy mess. This is the potential downfall to depressing the freezing point of a frozen dessert: The unfrozen water is literally free to move about and quickly leaks from the mixture, leaving the ice surrounded by syrupy puddles.

Professional sorbet manufacturers get around this problem with stabilizers like guar gum and locust bean gum. These additives act like sponges, corralling the free water within a loose matrix so that it can remain unfrozen while still not flowing freely. I couldn't get my hands on either of those products, but I did have access to two other possibilities: gelatin and pectin, both of which I tried in subsequent batches.

When it came to curbing melting, both products got the job done, but the gelatin had a downside: It left the sorbet with an unpalatable plastic-like firmness, even when used sparingly. No deal, said my tasters. Pectin, on the other hand, was an all-around success. After testing with varying amounts of the powder, I learned that a mere teaspoon (bloomed first in the water) was enough to keep the sorbet from immediately puddling without overdoing the firmness as the gelatin had. Besides, raspberries (like most fruits) naturally contain pectin in their cell walls. I was just adding more of a good thing.

Churn Accordingly

My sorbet was finally starting to come together, save for one nagging problem: The quality of the churned base was inconsistent. Every few batches, the mixture came out of the canister not with a soft-serve consistency but with a crumbly, fluffy texture and a noticeably duller berry flavor that more closely resembled a raspberry snow cone. Since some batches were coming out perfectly smooth and brightly flavored, I suspected that the problem was the result of my churning method and not the base itself. Was I under- or overchurning the sorbet?

Admittedly, I hadn't paid much attention to the churning time before that point. In fact, I'd never given much thought to how long any frozen dessert should be churned because most ice cream and sorbet recipes I've made end with the same directive: "Churn according to manufacturer instructions." But the more I thought about it, the more I realized that this vague set of instructions made no sense. Just as mixing times will vary for different types of cake batter, so, too, should the churning times be specific for different types of frozen desserts. I also thought some visual cues would be helpful.

With a timer and a thermometer at the ready, I poured several identical batches of my sorbet base into canisters and let the mixtures churn for increasing lengths of time, noting their temperatures and how their consistencies varied based on churning time. Then I proceeded as usual, transferring each batch to a container that I stuck in the freezer.

The results were surprising: The longest-churned batch was the thickest coming out of the canister but also the most granular and snowlike after freezing. I'd assumed that, just as with ice cream, the longest possible stay in the machine would result in a smoother sorbet because the constant agitation would help prevent large ice crystals from forming after the move to the freezer, but this test proved me wrong. Instead, longer churning times seemed to give the free-water and ice crystal mixture more time to grow ever-larger ice crystals. In fact, the best batch came from a base that I stopped churning almost as soon as the mixture started to thicken up, right around 18 degrees and the 20-minute mark.

To look at this batch, you wouldn't have expected it to turn into a nicely dense, stable sorbet; at the point at which I stopped the machine, it had a loose, pourable consistency, like a milkshake, because less water was frozen. But after an overnight stint in the freezer, it set up perfectly. A little research explained the difference between the two frozen desserts: During churning, air gets incorporated in the mixture. However, unlike with ice cream, in which a certain amount of incorporated air—known as "overrun"—contributes a pleasing lightness to the custard, that air renders sorbets loose and crumbly and dulls their flavor. This is because ice cream contains fat and protein, both of which act to stabilize the air bubbles. Sorbet, on the other hand, contains no cream. The only thing it has available to surround and stabilize the air bubbles is ice crystals, and they are not very good at the job, particularly as they grow larger in the freezer overnight (or with longer churning). The added air also dilutes the concentration of flavor in every bite. The upshot: a loose and crumbly, duller-tasting dessert that easily falls apart after overnight freezing.

To guarantee good results, I came away with a visual cue, which ensured that the sorbet would turn out dense and smooth no matter what ice cream machine was used: The color of the mixture began to lighten up considerably soon after it started to

thicken, a sure sign that it was beginning to take on air and was in need of a transfer to the freezer.

With my sorbet finally smooth and stable every time, the only remaining tasks were to punch up the berries' intensity—a pinch of salt did the trick—and dream up a few flavor variations. Fruity ruby port made for a natural pairing, as did bracing ginger and mint, not to mention the healthy shot of lime juice I added to make a "rickey" version. With four recipes on file, I knew this sorbet formula would get me through a summer's worth of entertaining—and that this frozen dessert would no longer play second fiddle to a quart of ice cream.

RASPBERRY SORBET
MAKES 1 QUART

Super-chilling part of the sorbet base before transferring it to the ice cream machine will keep ice crystals to a minimum. If using a canister-style ice cream machine, be sure to freeze the empty canister for at least 24 hours and preferably 48 hours before churning. For self-refrigerating machines, prechill the canister by running the machine for five to 10 minutes before pouring in the sorbet mixture. Allow the sorbet to sit at room temperature for five minutes to soften before serving. Fresh or frozen berries may be used. If using frozen berries, thaw them before proceeding. Make certain that you use Sure-Jell engineered for low- or no-sugar recipes (packaged in a pink box) and not regular Sure-Jell (in a yellow box).

- 1 cup water
- 1 teaspoon Sure-Jell for Less or No Sugar Needed Recipes
- ⅛ teaspoon salt
- 1¼ pounds (4 cups) raspberries
- ½ cup (3½ ounces) plus 2 tablespoons sugar
- ¼ cup light corn syrup

1. Combine water, Sure-Jell, and salt in medium saucepan. Heat over medium-high heat, stirring occasionally, until Sure-Jell is fully dissolved, about 5 minutes. Remove saucepan from heat and allow mixture to cool slightly, about 10 minutes.

2. Process raspberries, sugar, corn syrup, and water mixture in blender or food processor until smooth, about 30 seconds. Strain mixture through fine-mesh strainer, pressing on solids to extract as much liquid as possible. Transfer 1 cup mixture to small bowl and place remaining mixture in large bowl. Cover both bowls with plastic wrap. Place large bowl in refrigerator and small bowl in freezer and cool completely, at least 4 hours or up to 24 hours. (Small bowl of base will freeze solid.)

3. Remove mixtures from refrigerator and freezer. Scrape frozen base from small bowl into large bowl of base. Stir occasionally until frozen base has fully dissolved. Transfer mixture to ice cream machine and churn until mixture has consistency of thick milkshake and color lightens, 15 to 25 minutes.

4. Transfer sorbet to airtight container, pressing

firmly to remove any air pockets, and freeze until firm, at least 2 hours. Serve. (Sorbet can be frozen for up to 5 days.)

RASPBERRY–LIME RICKEY SORBET

Reduce water to ¾ cup. Add 2 teaspoons grated lime zest and ¼ cup lime juice to blender with raspberries.

RASPBERRY–PORT SORBET

Substitute ruby port for water in step 1.

RASPBERRY SORBET
WITH GINGER AND MINT

Substitute ginger beer for water in step 1. Add 2-inch piece of peeled and thinly sliced ginger and ¼ cup mint leaves to blender with raspberries. Decrease amount of sugar to ½ cup.

Picking the Best Vegetable Peeler

Why do some peelers skin produce with ease while others barely make the cut?

> BY LISA McMANUS <

Maybe the wartime cartoonists who depicted military KP duty weren't directly commenting on how punishing it can be to peel vegetables with a lousy tool, but the images of grimacing soldiers surrounded by piles of potatoes suggest the same point: that dull, inefficient peelers make a mountain of tiresome work out of a simple task.

A good peeler should be fast and smooth, shaving off just enough of the skin to avoid the need for repeat trips over the same section but not so much that the blade digs deeply into the flesh and wastes food. Whatever the task, the peeler should handle bumps and curves with ease and without clogging or losing its edge. And when the work is done, your hand shouldn't feel worse for the wear.

Those were the standards I kept in mind as I rounded up vegetable peelers to test: 10 models (whittled down from an original roster of 16 after preliminary tests) of various shapes, materials, and prices ($3.50 all the way up to $18). My goal was to see if anything could best our old favorite, the Messermeister Pro-Touch Fine Edge Swivel Peeler. One by one, I put each peeler through produce boot camp, subjecting the tools to lightweight tasks like potatoes, carrots, and apples, as well as more challenging terrain like gnarly celery root, tough-skinned butternut squash, delicate ripe tomatoes, and knobby ginger. I also ran a precision test by pulling each blade across pieces of Parmesan cheese and chocolate, noting whether the peelers chipped at and stumbled along the blocks or if they pulled off long, elegant curls.

By the end of testing, all but three of the peelers had passed muster. Even better, we found two models that tackled every task effortlessly, including a dark horse that narrowly eked out the win.

Mind the Gap

Peelers are simple tools—basically evolved paring knives with double blades—and with the exception of a few innovative designs, most models can be classified in one of two categories based on the orientation of the blade to the handle. On "straight" peelers, the blade extends directly out from the handle; "Y" peelers look like wishbones,

with a blade running perpendicular to the handle. In practice, they function similarly: You can both whittle away from yourself and pare toward yourself.

Right off the bat, I discovered that, with one exception, the type of material used to make the blade wasn't a tipping point for how a peeler performed. While the lone ceramic blade had dulled and discolored by the end of testing, the other nine stainless or carbon steel blades came away more or less unscathed. So what accounted for why some models removed peels with ease while others struggled? After closer scrutiny, I realized that it boiled down to a handful of subtle design distinctions.

First: the distance between the peeler's blade and the bridge that arches across it, holding it at each end. Ideally, this gap measured about an inch at its highest point; any narrower and the peels got stuck in the opening, forcing testers to tediously stop and off-load the waste by hand. The OXO was a good example of this, as its ½-inch opening clogged frequently. Worse, the space on the Chef'n peeler was so tight that chocolate curls shattered and vegetable peels didn't lift away. Conversely, models with wider apertures discarded peels easily but lacked leverage and control.

Cutting Edge Design

Another significant design detail lies in how the blade of a vegetable peeler is constructed. The reason peelers have two parallel blades is that the leading half of the blade—the one that travels first as you pull or push the peeler over the food—acts as a guide for the cutting edge that follows.

This "guide" blade doesn't cut: It just holds the cutting blade at a fixed angle and depth, so it skims along taking off the peel, rather than bouncing off the top of the food or digging too deeply and sticking. The entire peeler blade rotates to follow the curves of the food, so the guide and blade stay in the same relationship to the surface of the food, peeling consistently.

However, depending on the relative positions of the guide and blade, some peelers, such as the Calphalon model, dug in too deeply, taking off too much food with each stroke, while others (the OXO and Rachael Ray models) skimmed too shallowly or bounced off, requiring many extra strokes to skin a vegetable.

Then there was the ride itself: how fluidly—or, in several cases, jerkily—the peeler moved across the surface. Not surprisingly, potatoes and carrots were smooth sailing for most models. It was the gnarly, tendril-wreathed celery root and curvy fresh

What Makes a Winner

The most effective peelers don't just have the sharpest blades. Two other design details are what separate the winning Kuhn Rikon peeler from the rest of the pack.

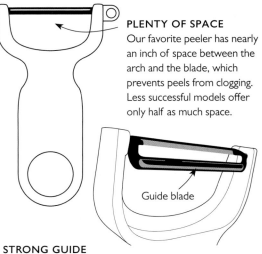

PLENTY OF SPACE
Our favorite peeler has nearly an inch of space between the arch and the blade, which prevents peels from clogging. Less successful models offer only half as much space.

Guide blade

STRONG GUIDE
Only one of the two blades on a vegetable peeler does the cutting. The other blade acts as a guide. It travels first over the surface of the food and keeps the cutting edge that follows it at a fixed angle. A tiny ridge on the guide of our winner ensures smooth, steady peeling by stiffening this blade and minimizing surface drag.

ginger that weeded out the weaker peelers, but we didn't understand why until we consulted Dr. Daniel Braunstein, a senior lecturer in mechanical engineering from the Massachusetts Institute of Technology. He explained that a good guide should reduce friction and, in turn, surface drag. But the most important distinction he pointed out was that two of our top three peelers sported a raised ridge running along the front of the guide. This ridge has two purposes: It reinforces the guide's stiffness, and because it protrudes, it means that less of the guide's surface will be in contact with the food, allowing the peeler to glide like butter.

One of those two ridged models, the Original Swiss Peeler by Kuhn Rikon, was our all-around winner. The Y-shaped peeler is a featherweight (³⁄₈ of an ounce), but it's surprisingly sturdy, and its razor-sharp blade effortlessly skinned anything we threw at it—and at $3.50, it's a steal. Alternatively, for those who prefer a straight peeler, our former favorite, the Messermeister Pro-Touch Fine Edge Swivel Peeler ($10), followed close behind.

ILLUSTRATION: JAY LAYMAN

TESTING VEGETABLE PEELERS

We tested 16 vegetable peelers. Six (Microplane Easy Prep Straight Peeler, Rösle Crosswise Swivel Peeler, Zyliss Smoothglide Peeler, Zyliss Y Peeler, CIA Masters Collection Vegetable Peeler, and OXO Good Grips Y Peeler) were eliminated, yielding a final lineup of 10. Peelers are listed below in order of preference. All were purchased online. Sources for top models appear on page 32.

PERFORMANCE

We measured time and average peel thickness as we pared potatoes and carrots. We also peeled bumpy celery root, tough butternut squash, ripe tomatoes, and knobby ginger root and made Parmesan shavings and chocolate curls. Peelers rated highest if they were smooth and efficient in all tests, with minimal food waste.

EASE OF USE

We rated each peeler on how easy and comfortable it was to use on a variety of foods, averaging the impressions of testers with varying hand sizes.

DESIGN

We considered weight, shape, material, and other factors that contributed to comfort, efficiency, and durability. As a final test, we compared the peelers we'd used in the testings with new versions of each tool while peeling apples, assessing whether they had lost sharpness over the course of testing.

HIGHLY RECOMMENDED

KUHN RIKON Original Swiss Peeler
Model: 2212 Price: $3.50
Blade: Carbon steel
Weight: ⅜ oz
Avg. Peel Thickness: 0.90 mm

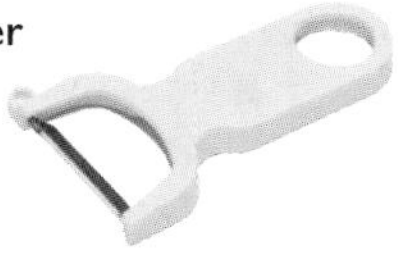

	PERFORMANCE	
Performance	★★★
Ease of Use	★★★
Design	★★★

TESTERS' COMMENTS: Don't be fooled by its featherweight design and cheap price tag. This Y-shaped peeler easily tackled every task, thanks to a razor-sharp blade and a ridged guide, which ensured a smooth ride with minimal surface drag.

MESSERMEISTER Pro-Touch Fine Edge Swivel Peeler
Model: 800-58 Price: $10
Blade: Stainless steel
Weight: 1½ oz
Avg. Peel Thickness: 0.82 mm

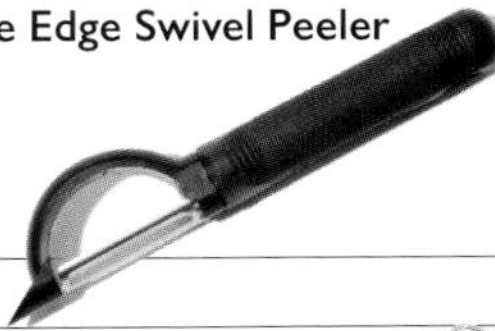

Performance	★★★
Ease of Use	★★★
Design	★★★

A stellar choice for those who prefer a straight peeler. Lightweight, sharp, and comfortable, this model rivaled the winner, gliding over fruits and vegetables and producing almost transparent peels. Its high arch meant no clogging.

RECOMMENDED

WMF Profi Plus Horizontal Vegetable Peeler
Model: 1872616030 Price: $18
Blade: Stainless steel
Weight: 3¼ oz
Avg. Peel Thickness: 1.08 mm

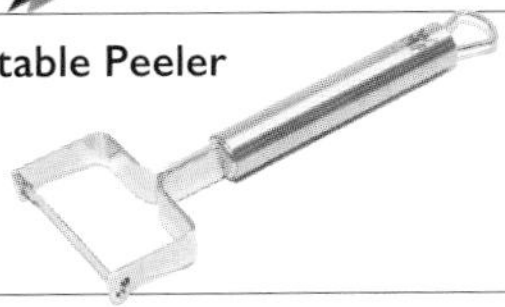

Performance	★★½
Ease of Use	★★★
Design	★★★

The other model with a ridged guide, this sturdy, sharp—and most expensive—peeler glided over everything from carrots to rough-textured celery root, though its peels were thicker than some.

MESSERMEISTER Culinary Instruments Swivel Peeler, Y Shape
Model: 900-189 Price: $7.50
Blade: Stainless steel
Weight: 1 oz
Avg. Peel Thickness: 1.11 mm

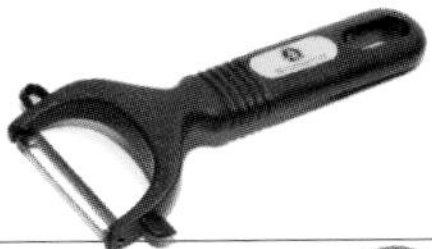

Performance	★★½
Ease of Use	★★
Design	★★

Though it quickly removed wide swaths of peel and off-loaded waste easily, this Y peeler was outshone by its sibling when it skinned a little too deep. Its broad blade was a bit tricky to maneuver around smaller potatoes and curvy, bumpy celery root.

SWISSMAR Swiss Classic Peeler, Scalpel Blade
Model: 00447 Price: $10.17
Blade: Stainless steel
Weight: ⅝ oz
Avg. Peel Thickness: 1.05 mm

Performance	★★½
Ease of Use	★★
Design	★★

Sharp and maneuverable, this lightweight peeler bit through the toughest peels with ease but also stripped away a good bit of flesh. A closer look revealed why: Its blade has a curved belly that bites deeply, creating more waste.

RECOMMENDED WITH RESERVATIONS

RACHAEL RAY TOOLS 3-in-1 Veg-A-Peel Vegetable Peeler/Brush
Model: 55250 Price: $9.06
Blade: Stainless steel
Weight: 1⅜ oz
Avg. Peel Thickness: 1.05 mm

Performance	★★½
Ease of Use	★★
Design	★½

Peels were thin and waste was minimal; in fact, this model often required a few extra strokes. We might have liked this peeler's attached vegetable brush if it didn't mean that our thumb was prone to gripping the blade on the other side as we scrubbed—ouch.

OXO Good Grips Swivel Peeler
Model: 20081 Price: $7.99
Blade: Stainless steel
Weight: 2⅜ oz
Avg. Peel Thickness: 0.71 mm

Performance	★★
Ease of Use	★½
Design	★★

This model produced the thinnest peels and the least amount of waste, but we often needed to go over patches again to finish the job. Many testers found the thick handle fatiguing and clunky. Its low bridge clogged frequently.

NOT RECOMMENDED

KYOCERA Ceramic Y Peeler
Model: CP-10N Price: $8.12
Blade: Ceramic
Weight: 1 oz
Avg. Peel Thickness: 1.05 mm

Performance	★½
Ease of Use	★
Design	★★

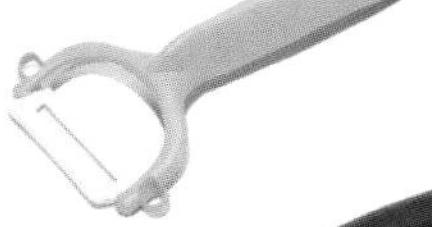

Potatoes and carrots were no problem, but the high bridge provided less leverage and control. This peeler struggled with celery root and utterly failed to skin butternut squash. Its ceramic blade was noticeably duller after testing.

CALPHALON Vegetable Peeler
Model: GT101 Price: $7.95
Blade: Stainless steel
Weight: 1⅞ oz
Avg. Peel Thickness: 1.22 mm

Performance	★½
Ease of Use	★½
Design	★½

This blade skinned most vegetables but not without stripping away a good bit of flesh, too. This tool's roadblock was butternut squash, on which the blade jammed and quit, and it was the only stainless steel model to lose some of its edge.

CHEF'N PalmPeeler
Model: 102-040-005 Price: $5.99
Blade: Stainless steel
Weight: ⅝ oz
Avg. Peel Thickness: 0.94 mm

Performance	★½
Ease of Use	★
Design	★

Wearing this peeler like a ring means you can't see what you're doing—an unnerving idea when working with a blade. The low bridge prevented peels from falling away, so we had to tediously brush them off; the tool also shattered every chocolate shaving.

The New World of Cheddar

Plain, rubbery American cheddars never measured up to the British stuff. But by merging Old and New World techniques, some domestic creameries are waging a revolution.

⇛ BY AMY GRAVES ⇚

Your average block of American cheddar doesn't resemble the complex-tasting farmhouse-style wheels that have been produced in England for centuries, but that hasn't stopped shoppers from snatching it up. In 2010, cheddar accounted for more than 30 percent of the cheese produced in this country, with supermarket shelves stocking more than 3 billion pounds of the shrink-wrapped, smooth-textured blocks—all of which helps explain why it's the variety you're most likely to see melted on a burger or oozing from a grilled cheese. Whether cheddar boasts distinct, nuanced flavors has never mattered much; most people seem to think cheddar is supposed to be a plain-Jane cheese.

But American cheddar is poised to climb out of this rut. Many well-stocked supermarkets, gourmet cheese shops, and online sources now offer "artisanal" domestic cheddars that claim to rival the English stuff and fetch prices just as high—which in many cases means more than double the cost of supermarket cheddar. And it's not just grassroots dairy farms that are shaking things up: A couple of the biggest names in domestic cheddar production have debuted higher-end lines intended not as burger toppings but as candidates for fine cheese plates.

We were intrigued but skeptical: Other than gourmet-sounding names like "reserve" and "vintage," what exactly might distinguish these fancy cheeses from the supermarket stuff—and would they really be worth the significant uptick in cost? There was only one way to find out: We held a tasting, sampling nine artisanal cheddars from both small and large producers straight from the package. (Fine cheeses like these aren't intended for cooking.) We also set up benchmarks on either end of the spectrum, adding our supermarket favorite, Cabot Private Stock, to the mix, and later pitting the domestic winners against Keen's Cheddar, long considered one of the gold standards of English farmhouse cheddars.

The first thing we noticed was that all of the cheddars tasted remarkably different. In fact, the spectrum of flavors was so broad—everything from mellow and buttery to pungent and sulfurous—that we were surprised that all of these cheeses could be labeled cheddar. Texture also varied hugely. Some cheddars were so dry that they crumbled in our hands, while others were as moist and creamy as Monterey Jack. One thing was clear, though: Our top cheddars were worth every penny. Several didn't just edge out our supermarket favorite, Cabot Private

Stock (which still placed respectably in the contest): They wowed us with "intensely nutty," "buttery" tang and creamy-textured crumbliness. So just what was going on in the cheese-making process that produced such varied results?

It's a Wrap

As with most cheeses, cheddar begins with adding a mix of starter cultures to milk. The cultures (each creamery uses a proprietary blend) cause the milk to separate, at which point the liquid whey is pressed out and the remaining curds are shaped into blocks or wheels, vacuum-sealed in plastic or bandaged in cloth (more on wrapping methods later), and aged anywhere from two months to two or more years. The particular methods used to press and shape the cheese, known as "cheddaring," are responsible for this varietal's firm, close-knit texture.

Creameries that employ traditional methods stack, turn, and press the curds by hand to achieve the desired moisture level (which must not exceed 39 percent, according to the U.S. Food and Drug Administration's definition of cheddar). Larger-scale manufacturers automate the process by pouring the inoculated milk into closed vats that regulate temperature and moisture and use centrifugal force to press the curds and extract whey.

If we'd had to guess, we'd have predicted that the handmade cheddars would be the runaway favorites—for no good reason other than that we associate "artisanal" with "better." But as it turned out, two of our three favorite cheeses were actually machine-made.

We moved on to look at other variables that might explain our preferences and homed in on how the cheese was wrapped. "Clothbound" isn't just another gourmet-sounding label. It refers to cheeses

cloaked in lard- or butter-laminated cheesecloth or linen. Wrapped in these porous fabrics, the cheddars lose moisture, form a rind, and in our lineup developed what tasters described as "fruity," "buttery" depth and a pleasantly "crystalline," "Parmesan-like" structure. All of the clothbound cheeses, in fact, were well liked. These characteristics came at a cost: Because making clothbound cheese is a labor-intensive process that produces less yield than wrapping cheese in plastic (moisture loss means the cheese shrinks during aging), these were among the most expensive cheddars in our lineup.

But once again, tradition wasn't everything. Our winning cheddar turned out to be a plastic-wrapped specimen, whose "buttery," caramel-like flavor with hints of "fruity" sweetness had tasters raving. Like all the plastic-wrapped cheeses, this one boasted an underlying "creaminess," thanks to the airtight packaging that locks in moisture. That we could be so taken by a shrink-wrapped cheese didn't surprise Dean Sommer, a cheese and food technologist at the Wisconsin Center for Dairy Research. "Any notion that plastic film–wrapped cheese is somehow inferior is, in my opinion, dead wrong," he told us. It's simply a "different animal" from the bandage-wrapped cheeses, with a more "lactic" versus "earthy" flavor that can range from sweet, like our winner's profile, to sharp, depending in part on how long the cheese is aged. Our top-ranked cheese, aged for just nine to 12 months, was one of the youngest in the lineup. Longer aging of the other plastic-wrapped cheeses, however, proved to be a mixed bag. Aging gives the enzymes in the bacterial cultures more time to convert the milk sugar (lactose) into lactic acid, and in one two-year-old cheese aging produced what tasters praised as "appropriately" sharp flavors. But

British versus American: It's a Tie

Our tasting convinced us that American creameries are producing some top-notch cheddars, but the competitor in us still wondered how domestic cheeses stack up to the stuff from the old country. In an Olympic-style competition, we tasted our favorite American cheddars, Milton Creamery's Prairie Breeze and Cabot's Clothbound, against one of Britain's most famous cheddars, a 12-month-old bandaged wheel from Keen's.

The contest ended in a draw. Fans of the "barnyard-y," "musty" flavors that are typical of traditional English cheddars leaned toward Keen's, while those who favor more "butterscotch-y" cheddars preferred the American cheeses. The only factor that tipped the balance in favor of the domestic cheddars was price. At $31.96 per pound—twice as much as Prairie Breeze—Keen's might be best saved for your next trip to England. –A.G.

OLD ENGLISH
If you like your cheddar funky and musty-tasting, Keen's Cheddar, made in Somerset since 1899, may be for you.

TASTING ARTISANAL CHEDDAR

Twenty-one Cook's *Illustrated* staff members sampled 10 cheddars at room temperature, rating them on flavor, texture, and sharpness. Brands were selected from among top sellers at cheese markets and recent winners of American Cheese Society awards. A second blind tasting compared winners in the first round with our favorite British cheddar (see "British versus American: It's a Tie").

HIGHLY RECOMMENDED

MILTON CREAMERY Prairie Breeze
Price: $15.98 per lb **Aged:** 9 to 12 months
Cheddaring: Traditional **Aging Material:** Plastic
Comments: This cheese was one of the youngest in the lineup, but thanks to an extra cocktail of bacterial cultures, it wowed tasters with "deeply rich," "buttery" flavors and a "sweet" finish that reminded some of "pineapple." It boasted a "crumbly" yet "creamy" texture reminiscent of "young Parmesan."

CABOT Cellars at Jasper Hill Clothbound Cheddar
Price: $23.98 per lb **Aged:** 10 to 14 months
Cheddaring: Modern **Aging Material:** Cloth
Comments: Cabot's high-end line—the priciest American cheese we tasted—is also inoculated twice and won raves from tasters for its "mature sharpness" and "rich dairy flavor" that they likened to Gruyère. But the bigger draw: its "craggy" texture that broke into addictively "jagged," "crystalline" shards.

RECOMMENDED

BEST BUY

TILLAMOOK
Vintage White Extra Sharp Cheddar Cheese
Price: $9.50 per lb **Aged:** At least 2 years
Cheddaring: Modern **Aging Material:** Plastic
Comments: Compared with the company's other cheddars, this two-plus-year-old cheese is "vintage," but unlike some other long-aged samples, its sharpness was "appropriately bold" and "balanced." Fans of smoother cheddars will appreciate its "extremely creamy" texture—not to mention its affordable price tag.

BEECHER'S Flagship Reserve Handmade Cheese
Price: $25 per lb **Aged:** 12 months
Cheddaring: Traditional **Aging Material:** Cloth
Comments: Besides conventional cheddar descriptors like "nutty" and "sharp," this "firm," "grainy" clothbound cheese earned compliments for more complex flavors like "buttery walnuts" and a "gamy," "Parmesan-like" tang. No wonder: Like our two favorites, it received a second shot of nontraditional cultures.

GRAFTON VILLAGE
Vermont Clothbound Cheddar
Price: $15.99 per lb **Aged:** At least 6 months
Cheddaring: Traditional **Aging Material:** Cloth
Comments: A classic example of clothbound cheddar, this sample was wrapped in a butter-dipped cloth and soaked up a "fruity and nutty" flavor hinting of "caramel." It breaks into "firm" shards, which makes it a bit tricky to slice but a pleasure to eat out of hand.

RECOMMENDED, CONTINUED

FISCALINI FARMSTEAD
Bandage-Wrapped Raw Milk Cheddar
Price: $24 per lb **Aged:** 18 months
Cheddaring: Traditional **Aging Material:** Cloth
Comments: As artisanal cheddars go, this cheese was well liked but unremarkable. Its "complex," "fruity" aroma prompted the same pineapple analogy as our winner, but its texture was softer and creamier—even "waxy" and "squeezable," according to some.

CABOT Private Stock
Classic Vermont Cheddar Cheese
Price: $8.49 per lb **Aged:** Up to 16 months
Cheddaring: Modern **Aging Material:** Plastic
Comments: The flavor of this "no-frills" crowd-pleaser—also our favorite supermarket cheddar—was "straight-up sharp" but "not distinctive," with a "firm and creamy" texture that reminded us of "what you'd find on the end of a toothpick at a cocktail party."

SHELBURNE FARMS 2-Year-Old Farmhouse Cheddar Cheese
Price: $19 per lb **Aged:** 2 years
Cheddaring: Traditional **Aging Material:** Plastic
Comments: After two years of aging in plastic, this cheddar tasted like "wet wool" and "barnyard funk"—a trait that some thought made it a "serious cheddar," while others weren't convinced. But all were agreed: The plastic's moisture-locking seal ensured a "moist, creamy," "mouth-coating" texture.

RECOMMENDED WITH RESERVATIONS

WIDMER'S CHEESE CELLARS
Two Year Old Cheddar Cheese
Price: $7.90 per lb **Aged:** 2 years
Cheddaring: Traditional **Aging Material:** Plastic
Comments: Neon orange and shrink-wrapped, this cheddar looked the most like a supermarket block and tasted like it, too. Though deemed an "all-around good snacking cheddar," its "mild" profile was "lackluster" in comparison with others in the lineup, and we're not sure we'd go out of our way to mail-order it.

GRAFTON VILLAGE
Classic Reserve 2-Year Aged Vermont Raw Milk Cheddar Cheese
Price: $17.99 per lb **Aged:** 2 years
Cheddaring: Traditional **Aging Material:** Plastic
Comments: Thanks to a combination of aging, moisture content, and bacteria cultures, this cheddar was so "sulfurous" that it elicited comparisons to "rotten eggs." Only those who wanted a really "funky" cheddar found this one palatable, though many appreciated its "rich and creamy texture."

---

another plastic-sealed cheese, also aged for two years, blew right past sharp all the way to "rotten eggs," a profile that some tasters found barely tolerable.

Culture Shock

So how could two cheeses aged for the same amount of time and packaged the same way embody such different flavors? According to Sommer, the moisture level of the cheeses could play a role, but so could each maker's specific blend of bacteria. In fact, the bacterial culture in our favorite cheddar, Prairie Breeze from

Iowa's Milton Creamery, likely had a big influence on its flavor. This cheese maker takes the culturing process to another level by adding a second round of bacterial cultures to its cheese. We learned from Sommer that it's not just a repeat of the first culture cocktail; these secondary bacteria are strains more typically found in Parmesan and Emmentaler than in cheddar, lending the cheese the subtle "butterscotch-y" and "gamy" undertones that earned tasters' highest praise.

Naturally, that information prompted us to check the culturing details of the other cheddars

we'd tasted, and as it turned out, the particularly "toasty," "earthy," "complex" flavors of two other cheddars, including our close runner-up, Cabot Clothbound, are also the result of that second dose of alternative bacteria.

So much for plain-Jane American cheddar. By the end of testing, we were convinced not only that the hybridization of traditional and modern cheddar-making methods leads to a top-notch product but also that these new-school American cheeses more than hold their own with the stalwarts across the Atlantic.

A New Spin on Sorbet

Ice cream and sorbet, even when kept tightly sealed, eventually turn icy and exhibit freezer burn due to the temperature swings created when the freezer door is opened and closed, which cause them to continuously melt and refreeze. We wondered if melting down these iced-over frozen desserts and giving them a spin in an ice cream maker could restore their smooth, creamy texture.

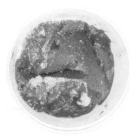

CAN THIS BE SAVED?
Yes. Freezer-burnt sorbet can be restored by churning.

To find out, we let batches of our vanilla ice cream and raspberry sorbet thaw completely, churned them in our favorite Whynter SNÖ ice cream machine, and then refroze them according to the recipes. The ice cream came out airy and crumbly, but the sorbet emerged from its return trip as good as new. Here's why: The fats and proteins in custard-based ice creams tenaciously hold on to air that's incorporated during the churning process even after being melted, making the ice cream more brittle and overaerated with a subsequent round of churning and freezing. Sorbet, which contains very little protein and little or no fat, gives up the incorporated air easily, making a respun base as good as a fresh one. The bottom line? There's no point in respinning ice cream, but sorbet (either homemade or store-bought) that has turned hard and icy can easily be revitalized via a repeat trip through an ice cream maker.

TECHNIQUE | EASIEST–EVER WAY TO SHUCK CORN

Removing the husk and silk from an ear of corn is a chore, and a "corn de-silker" gadget that we tested proved to be a bust. But now we've found a better way: A short stint in the microwave and a quick shake are all it takes to cleanly slide off the corn husk and silk. The cob will heat up a bit, but the kernels won't be cooked.

1. With sharp chef's knife, cut off stalk end of cob just above first row of kernels. Place 3 or 4 ears at a time on microwave-safe plate and microwave on full power for 30 to 60 seconds.

2. Hold each ear by uncut end in 1 hand. Shake ear up and down until cob slips free, leaving behind husk and silk.

Each Clam in Its Own Time

When cooking hard-shell clams in the test kitchen, we've noticed that there can be as much as a five-minute difference between when the first clam opens and the last clam opens (indicating doneness). Clams can easily overcook once opened, leaving them chewy and shriveled. To ensure perfectly cooked clams, remove each clam as it opens and hold them in a plate-covered bowl, where they'll stay warm while the rest of the clams finish cooking. This method becomes unwieldy when cooking loads of clams, but if it's just a dozen or two, we've found that it's well worth the extra effort to guarantee the best texture.

SCIENCE EXPERIMENT Staving Off Staling in Bread

While developing our recipe for Potato Burger Buns (page 15), we noticed that not only were the rolls incredibly soft and moist right out of the oven but, unlike other breads, they were as soft and fresh a day later. Could the potatoes be playing a role?

EXPERIMENT

We baked one batch of our potato rolls according to the recipe; in a second batch we replaced the mashed potatoes with the same weight of all-purpose flour (8 ounces), adding extra water to compensate for the moisture contributed by the mash. We stored both batches of rolls at room temperature for two days.

RESULTS

After one day, the potato rolls were almost as moist as when they came out of the oven, while the all-wheat rolls were noticeably firm and dry. After two days, the wheat rolls were inedible, but the potato rolls remained soft and remarkably fresh-tasting.

EXPLANATION

As baked bread cools, its starches begin to crystallize, trapping water inside the hardened crystal structures. This process of "retrogradation" (more commonly known as staling) explains why bread becomes firm and appears to dry out as it sits on the counter. When bread contains potato, however, this reaction is tempered. The starch molecules in potatoes contain negatively charged phosphates that deter them from recombining, and diluting flour with potato makes it harder for the wheat starches to crystallize as well. The net effect? Potato breads stay soft much longer.

SHOPPING Bulgur Primer

Bulgur is made from parboiled or steamed wheat kernels/berries that are then dried, partially stripped of their outer bran layer, and coarsely ground. Don't confuse it with cracked wheat, which is not parcooked. Most recipes using bulgur call for medium grind, which we rinse to remove any detritus and simply soak in water or another liquid until tender.

A HAPPY MEDIUM
Most recipes call for medium-grind grains.

Bulgur is sold in four numbered grind sizes, but bulk bins and many U.S. brands often don't identify the grind by number or provide a description of the size—and when they do, they're inconsistent. This guide should help. For our Tabbouleh recipe on page 19, use medium or coarse bulgur.

FIND THE RIGHT GRIND

#1	FINE	The smallest grind, similar to couscous in appearance.
#2	MEDIUM	The most widely available size in bulk bins and supermarket brands, with grains about the size of sesame seeds or kosher salt.
#3	COARSE	Slightly coarser than medium grind but interchangeable with it in recipes.
#4	EXTRA-COARSE	Nearly whole kernels that closely resemble steel-cut oats. Used in pilaf and stuffing.

INDEX

July & August 2012

Raspberry Sorbet, 25

Juicy Grilled Turkey Burgers, 13

Jerk Chicken, 9

Grill-Smoked Salmon, 11

Tabbouleh, 19

Grill-Roasted Beef Short Ribs, 7

Potato Burger Buns, 15

Spanish-Style Toasted Pasta with Shrimp, 21

Fresh Corn Salsa with Tomato, 22

AMERICA'S TEST KITCHEN
Public television's most popular cooking show

Join the millions of home cooks who watch our show, America's Test Kitchen, on public television every week. For more information, including recipes and program times, visit www.AmericasTestKitchenTV.com.

AMERICA'S TEST KITCHEN RADIO

Tune in to our new radio program featuring answers to listener call-in questions, ingredient taste test and equipment review segments, and in-depth reporting on a variety of topics. To listen to episodes, visit www.AmericasTestKitchen.com/Radio.

NEW! ONLINE COOKING SCHOOL

Learn how to think—and cook—like a pro from real test cooks who work here at America's Test Kitchen. We combine personalized instruction with leading-edge technology to offer an unparalleled learning experience. Try it free at www.TestKitchenSchool.com.

DOWNLOAD OUR FREE *COOK'S ILLUSTRATED* iPHONE APP

Features a collection of our top recipes, along with tastings, videos, and useful timer and shopping list features. CooksIllustrated.com members can access 19 years of recipes, videos, tastings, and more. Go to www.CooksIllustrated.com/iPhone.

Follow us on Twitter: twitter.com/TestKitchen
Find us on Facebook: facebook.com/CooksIllustrated

Chilled Fresh Tomato Soup, 18

PHOTOGRAPHY: CARL TREMBLAY; STYLING: MARIE PIRAINO

Petite
Emerald
Crystal

Lolla
Rossa

Petite
Ruby
Crystal

Sweet
Romaine

Red Rose
Romaine

Tom Thumb

Speckles

Pirat

Winter
Density

Red
Tango

Petite
Verde
Crystal

Red Wine
Batavian

HEIRLOOM
LETTUCES

NUMBER 118

SEPTEMBER & OCTOBER 2012

COOK'S
ILLUSTRATED

Grilled Pork Chops
Solving the "Too Thin" Problem

Better Chicken Fajitas

Meatier Meatloaf
Say Goodbye to Fillers

Which Chicken Should You Buy?
Air-Chilled Birds Win Tasting

All-New Guide to Grill Roasting

French Apple Cake
Custard, Cake, and Crunch

Testing Blenders
How Much Does Durability Cost?

Mediterranean Green Beans
Perfect Oatmeal in 10 Minutes
Thai Chicken and Noodle Stir-Fry
Better Pumpkin Bread

www.CooksIllustrated.com
$5.95 U.S./$6.95 CANADA

CONTENTS
September & October 2012

COOK'S ILLUSTRATED

Founder and Editor	Christopher Kimball
Editorial Director	Jack Bishop
Editorial Director, Magazines	John Willoughby
Executive Editor	Amanda Agee
Test Kitchen Director	Erin McMurrer
Managing Editor	Rebecca Hays
Senior Editors	Keith Dresser
	Lisa McManus
Associate Features Editors	Elizabeth Bomze
	Danette St. Onge
Copy Editors	Nell Beram
	Megan Chromik
Associate Editors	Andrea Geary
	Amy Graves
	Andrew Janjigian
	Chris O'Connor
	Dan Souza
Test Cook	Lan Lam
Assistant Editors	Hannah Crowley
	Shannon Friedmann Hatch
	Taizeth Sierra
Assistant Test Cooks	Dan Cellucci
	Sara Mayer
	Celeste Rogers
Executive Assistant	Christine Gordon
Assistant Test Kitchen Director	Gina Nistico
Test Kitchen Manager	Leah Rovner
Senior Kitchen Assistant	Meryl MacCormack
Kitchen Assistants	Maria Elena Delgado
	Ena Gudiel
	Andrew Straaberg Finfrock
Executive Producer	Melissa Baldino
Associate Producer	Stephanie Stender
Production Assistant	Kaitlin Hammond
Contributing Editors	Matthew Card
	Dawn Yanagihara
Consulting Editor	Scott Brueggeman
Science Editor	Guy Crosby, Ph.D.
Managing Editor, Web	Christine Liu
Online Associate Editors	Eric Grzymkowski
	Mari Levine
	Roger Metcalf
Senior Video Editor	Nick Dakoulas
Design Director	Amy Klee
Art Director	Julie Cote
Deputy Art Director	Susan Levin
Associate Art Director	Lindsey Timko
Designers, Marketing/Web	Mariah Tarvainen
Staff Photographer	Daniel J. van Ackere
Photo Editor	Steve Klise
Vice President, Marketing	David Mack
Circulation Director	Doug Wicinski
Circulation & Fulfillment Manager	Carrie Fethe
Partnership Marketing Manager	Pamela Putprush
Marketing Assistant	Joyce Liao
Customer Service Manager	Jacqueline Valerio
Customer Service Representatives	Jessica Amato
	Morgan Ryan
Chief Operations Officer	David Dinnage
Production Director	Guy Rochford
Senior Project Manager	Alice Carpenter
Production and Traffic Coordinator	Brittany Allen
Asset & Workflow Manager	Andrew Mannone
Production & Imaging Specialists	Judy Blomquist
	Heather Dube
	Lauren Pettapiece
Systems Administrator	Marcus Walser
Business Analyst	Wendy Tseng
Web Developers	Chris Candelora
	Cameron MacKensie
Human Resources Director	Adele Shapiro
VP New Media Product Development	Barry Kelly
Social Media Manager	Steph Yiu
Chief Financial Officer	Sharyn Chabot
Director of Sponsorship Sales	Anne Traficante
Retail Sales & Marketing Director	Emily Logan
Client Service Associate	Kate May
Publicity	Deborah Broide

PRINTED IN THE USA

HEIRLOOM BEANS Heirloom beans are centuries old, and many were cultivated by early Americans. The BROWN TEPARY has a meaty, dense texture. MIDNIGHT BLACK beans are popular in regional dishes like Cuba's *Moros y Cristianos*. The pea-size PINQUITO is commonly served alongside barbecue. SANGRE DE TORO beans are distinguished by their "bull's blood" hue and sweet, earthy flavor. AYOCOTE MORADO beans are slightly starchy, with subtle roasted undertones. MORTGAGE LIFTER beans are reminiscent of russets and butter. BLACK CALYPSO beans also have a distinct potato flavor under their Dalmatian coats. Large SNOWCAPS' boiled-peanut taste pairs well with pork. OJO DE CABRA (goat's eye) and striped RIO ZAPE beans are both similar to pinto beans. ZUNI GOLDS are nutty, with a velvety texture. CHRISTMAS LIMAS taste of chestnuts. Tuscan ZOLFINI beans are often served on toasted bread with olive oil and coarse salt. **COVER** *(Tomatoes)*: Robert Papp; **BACK COVER** *(Heirloom Beans)*: John Burgoyne

America's
TEST KITCHEN

RECIPES THAT WORK®

America's Test Kitchen is a very real 2,500-square-foot kitchen located just outside Boston. It is the home of *Cook's Illustrated* and *Cook's Country* magazines and is the workday destination of more than three dozen test cooks, editors, and cookware specialists. Our mission is to test recipes over and over again until we understand how and why they work and until we arrive at the best version. We also test kitchen equipment and supermarket ingredients in search of brands that offer the best value and performance. You can watch us work by tuning in to *America's Test Kitchen* (www.AmericasTestKitchenTV.com) on public television.

SOUNDS OF SILENCE

The Calvin Coolidge homestead sits just south of Route 4 in Plymouth Notch, Vermont. It is a collection of buildings—a general store, the Union Christian Church, the white clapboard Coolidge home with an attached barn, and an assortment of smaller homes and outbuildings—located in a small salad bowl valley that, to this day, feels remote and unattached to the modern world. This is where Coolidge grew up, where he took the oath of office (in a modest front parlor after Warren Harding's sudden death), and where his father ran the general store. On the second floor of that store is the "Summer White House," a modest, and probably exceedingly hot, office where the affairs of nations were discussed while one could hear the clicking of horse-drawn mowers in the fields below.

America's heroes used to be the strong, silent type. Shane. Gregory Peck. Chuck Yeager. Lincoln. (The Gettysburg Address lasted all of three minutes.) Coolidge was born out of the Vermont tradition of holding one's tongue, reserving one's opinion until asked. As Coolidge often said, "I have noticed that nothing I never said ever did me any harm." As president, he was even more guarded: "The words of a president have an enormous weight," wrote Coolidge, "and ought not to be used indiscriminately."

We live in the midst of change. This makes us hungry for the promise of action, for the proposition that we need a new vision of the future. I recently had lunch with Peter Workman, a well-known book publisher, and his response to my query about how he was dealing with the digital revolution was, "Well, we are going to publish the best books we can." Coolidge would agree; "Four-fifths of all our troubles would disappear, if we would only sit down and keep still."

Walking in the woods is my meditation, my yoga. (For Vermonters, "downward dog" refers to a beagle hot on the trail of a brownie heading at full speed downhill.) During the past week, I was shadowed by a great horned owl who flew from branch to branch, swiveling its impassive head to get a better glimpse of the intruder. Minutes later, I saw a bear and her young cub walking through a lime-green clearing about 40 yards away, neither of them aware I was standing in plain view. Last weekend, I stumbled across a turkey hen and her brood and then met up with a good-size doe, feeding just a stone's throw away. The woods are indifferent to human affairs; that is why nature's conversation—birdsong and the helter-skelter scurrying of chipmunks—is restorative. The words in our heads float away, are absorbed by leaves, break apart into individual letters, and then disperse on the wind.

A recent midday hike brought me to the top of our mountain and an encounter with a summer storm. To the west, a bank of glowing cast-iron clouds was threatening. The wind picked up, the leaves turned silver, branches waved, and I headed smartly down toward my pickup. And then thunder crashed; rain came in sheets, spilling off the brim of my hat; and I stopped under a large oak and listened.

Silent Cal, as Coolidge was known, understood the sounds of silence, the power of words left unsaid. He was also quick-witted. Dorothy

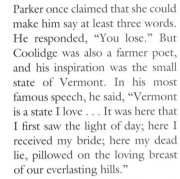

Christopher Kimball

Parker once claimed that she could make him say at least three words. He responded, "You lose." But Coolidge was also a farmer poet, and his inspiration was the small state of Vermont. In his most famous speech, he said, "Vermont is a state I love . . . It was here that I first saw the light of day; here I received my bride; here my dead lie, pillowed on the loving breast of our everlasting hills."

At the center of life in Vermont is stillness, a lifetime aversion to precipitate action, and a noble preference for listening over talking. Coolidge was never a popular president and, according to a recent Gallup poll, ranks just ahead of Rutherford B. Hayes and Richard Nixon. We are eager to follow leaders who construct a narrative about ourselves and our time and who, like Don Quixote, take action, tilting at windmills. The lesson of Coolidge has been lost: Be humble in the face of nature, work hard, and beware of riches. "Prosperity is only an instrument to be used, not a deity to be worshipped."

Standing just outside Coolidge's farmhouse, I considered that, just a century ago, a president was born to a shopkeeper and farmer; that his constant companion was the smell of freshly cut hay, molasses, and cider; and that he took inspiration from working the fields. At the store, I bought a bag of maple jelly beans for the kids and slowly turned back down the gravel path toward home. It may have been the postcard light or the circling of a red-tailed hawk, but I thought I heard "Step up," the sudden chatter of a sickle bar, and the heavy clang of a whippletree through the silence.

FOR INQUIRIES, ORDERS, OR MORE INFORMATION

www.CooksIllustrated.com
At www.CooksIllustrated.com, you can order books and subscriptions, sign up for our free e-newsletter, or renew your magazine subscription. Join the website and gain access to 19 years of *Cook's Illustrated* recipes, equipment tests, and ingredient tastings, as well as companion videos for every recipe in this issue.

COOKBOOKS
We sell more than 50 cookbooks by the editors of *Cook's Illustrated*.
To order, visit our bookstore at www.CooksIllustrated.com.

COOK'S ILLUSTRATED MAGAZINE

Cook's Illustrated magazine (ISSN 1068-2821), number 118, is published bimonthly by Boston Common Press Limited partnership, 17 Station St., Brookline, MA 02445. Copyright 2012 Boston Common Press Limited Partnership. Periodicals postage paid at Boston, Massachusetts., and additional mailing offices, USPS #012487. Publications Mail Agreement No. 40020778. Return undeliverable Canadian addresses to P.O. Box 875, Station A, Windsor, ON N9A 6P2. POSTMASTER: Send address changes to *Cook's Illustrated*, P.O. Box 6018, Harlan, IA 51593-1518. For subscription and gift subscription orders, subscription inquiries, or change-of-address notices, visit us at www.AmericasTestKitchen.com/customerservice, call us at 800-526-8442, or write us at *Cook's Illustrated*, P.O. 6018, Harlan, IA 51593-1518.

FOR LIST RENTAL INFORMATION Contact Specialists Marketing Services, Inc., 777 Terrace Ave., 4th Floor, Hasbrouck Heights, NJ 07604; 201-865-5800.
EDITORIAL OFFICE 17 Station St., Brookline, MA 02445; 617-232-1000; fax 617-232-1572. Subscription inquiries, visit www.AmericasTestKitchen.com/customerservice or call 800-526-8442.
POSTMASTER Send all new orders, subscription inquiries, and change-of-address notices to *Cook's Illustrated*, P.O. Box 6018, Harlan, IA 51593-1518.

NOTES FROM READERS

⇒ BY ANDREA GEARY, LAN LAM & DAN SOUZA ⇐

Jury-Rigging a Greens Saver

In your September/October 2011 issue, you tested exhaling into a bag of greens. It prolonged their shelf life, but you couldn't recommend it because of the "yuck" factor. But what if you built a mini generator from baking soda and vinegar, which produce carbon dioxide when combined?

TOM CLARK
NOBLESVILLE, IND.

➤Blowing into a bag of salad greens did extend their shelf life by introducing carbon dioxide, which slows spoilage, but as you said, we couldn't endorse such an unsanitary technique.

Intrigued by your idea, we came up with a "time-release" version of this method that would slightly delay gas production until we placed the "generator" in the bag of greens, preserving the maximum amount of CO2: Freeze 1 teaspoon of white vinegar in a 2- to 4-ounce container (such as a spice bottle) and then sprinkle 1 teaspoon of baking soda over the vinegar's surface. Next, cut a small, three-layer-thick square of paper towels and secure it over the container's opening with a rubber band. Place the container in a zipper-lock bag full of salad greens and seal it immediately. As the acidic vinegar melts, it combines with the alkaline baking soda to produce carbon dioxide. The paper towels let the gas seep into the bag while preventing any melting vinegar from leaking out. We admit that it's a little wacky, but this far more sanitary method works just as well as blowing into the bag, extending the life of the greens by up to five days (as long as the bag is kept sealed).

MAKE IT
Create a mini CO2 generator by freezing a little vinegar in a small container, sprinkling it with baking soda, and covering the container with paper towels.

USE IT
Seal the container in a zipper-lock bag with greens and refrigerate. As the vinegar melts, it will interact with the baking soda, providing up to five extra days of freshness.

Homemade Chocolate Ice Cream Shell

One of my favorite treats is a chocolate sauce that instantly hardens into a shell when poured over ice cream. Do you know of a homemade version?

BULLETS GILLESPIE
NASHVILLE, TENN.

➤When we sampled Smucker's Magic Shell over ice cream, we were impressed by the way it hardened upon contact but were less bowled over by its cloyingly sweet, mild chocolate taste. We set out to engineer a better-tasting homemade version that would please children and adults alike.

A quick review of the Magic Shell ingredients revealed that the "magic" was the third ingredient listed: coconut oil. Coconut oil is extremely high in saturated fat, which makes it solid at room temperature and brittle at cooler temperatures. Combining melted coconut oil in a 2:3 ratio with melted chocolate produced a satiny mixture that solidified into a perfect, shatteringly thin shell over ice cream. To make your own: Microwave 4 tablespoons of refined coconut oil, 3 ounces of chopped bittersweet chocolate, and a pinch of salt at 50 percent power until smooth (two to four minutes), stirring occasionally. Cool to room temperature and spoon or pour over ice cream.

"MAGICALLY" BRITTLE
Coconut oil is the key to a shatteringly thin chocolate coating.

Can Baked Goods Withstand a Slam?

I've always heard that slamming the oven door will cause a baking cake to fall. Is this true?

MICHAEL PENDLETON
ST. PAUL, MINN.

➤Cakes rise as tiny air bubbles in the batter expand in the heat of the oven. To find out if slamming the door shut would interrupt the process enough to spell disaster, we mixed batters for muffins, yellow cake, angel food cake, and cheese soufflé and loaded them into hot ovens. Just before each item reached its maximum height, we opened the oven door all the way and gave it a hard slam.

The sturdy muffins emerged unharmed, as did the yellow cake. Even the notoriously fragile angel food cake and the soufflé survived the vigorous slamming.

Why? A properly developed foam—whether powered by baking soda, baking powder, or beaten egg whites—is pretty resilient. While very rough handling (dropping a half-baked cake, for example) can make it collapse, there's no need to worry about slamming doors.

Brown Rice Syrup

I've seen brown rice syrup in natural foods stores. Can I use it in place of corn syrup?

SALLY MILLER
FRANKLIN, TENN.

➤Like corn syrup, brown rice syrup is made by treating the cooked grain with enzymes that convert starches into sugar; the resulting liquid is reduced until thick. To see if it makes a suitable substitute, we tasted Lundberg Organic Sweet Dreams Brown Rice Syrup plain and used it in two recipes in which we normally use corn syrup: chocolate frosting and glazed chicken.

Corn syrup is approximately 45 percent as sweet as sugar; Lundberg claims that its rice syrup is about 50 percent as sweet as sugar, and we found the sweetness levels comparable when we sampled the products plain. But the rice syrup's viscosity and pronounced cereal aroma made us skeptical about its feasibility as a stand-in for clear, neutral-tasting corn syrup.

To our surprise, tasters found the frosting and chicken samples very similar in taste, texture, and appearance—the complex flavors of the other ingredients masked the brown rice syrup's toasty notes. But since Karo corn syrup costs $3.50 per 16-ounce bottle while a 21-ounce jar of Lundberg rice syrup set us back $6, we'll stick with corn syrup.

Fixing Broken Custard

While I was cooking a custard sauce the other day, it overheated and turned lumpy, so I threw it out and started over. Could I have salvaged it?

CAITLIN MACDONALD
FRANKLIN, MASS.

➤When custards such as crème anglaise are heated, they turn thick and creamy as milk and egg proteins unfurl and bond with each other. However, if they are overheated, too many bonds form and the proteins clump.

To find a fix for lumps, we overcooked a simple custard to 205 degrees (the recommended temperature is 175 to 180 degrees), at which point it was full of large lumps. Rescuing the custard turned out to be a cinch with an immersion blender. A quick buzz effectively broke down the clumps, restoring a

ILLUSTRATION: JOHN BURGOYNE

perfectly creamy texture (which didn't break when we refrigerated the fixed custard).

If you notice lumps beginning to form in a custard, immediately pour it out of the hot pot into a bowl and pulse it with a handheld blender in five-second intervals until it is nearly smooth. This can take from 15 to 45 seconds, depending on how big the lumps are. Be careful not to overprocess or you can wind up with irreparably thin, watery custard. Don't use a blender or food processor; they incorporate too much air and will leave the mixture frothy, not creamy. After blending, pour the liquid through a fine-mesh strainer to remove any remaining lumps and continue with your recipe.

SMOOTHED OVER
Pulsing with an immersion blender restores smoothness to lumpy custard.

Cloudy Iced Tea

Why does my homemade iced tea turn cloudy when I refrigerate it? Is there any way to prevent this?

HELEN ROGERS
BRAINTREE, MASS.

➤The cloudiness is caused by caffeine and tannins bonding with each other when tea is refrigerated or iced. The hotter the original brewing water the more caffeine and tannins are extracted from the tea leaves, and the murkier the beverage will be. To determine the brewing temperature at which clouding first appears, we made several batches (each with five black tea bags and 1 quart of filtered water) at temperatures ranging from room temperature (68 degrees) to boiling (212 degrees) and refrigerated them overnight.

The next day, we saw signs of cloudiness in all of the samples that had been brewed above 100 degrees. The refrigerated room-temp brew, meanwhile, was still crystal clear but tasted weak compared with teas brewed with hot water. Increasing the number of tea bags and steeping at room temperature gave us a clear, smooth-tasting tea that wouldn't go murky when cold. To make it: Steep 10 tea bags in 1 quart of room-temperature water for eight hours and then refrigerate or serve over ice.

HOT BREWED: COLD BREWED:
CLOUDY TEA   CLEAR TEA

For crystal-clear, full-flavored iced tea, steep at room temperature, using 10 tea bags per quart instead of five.

Green versus Wax Beans

Can green and wax beans be used interchangeably?

DIANE SMITH
GRAND RAPIDS, MICH.

➤Green beans get their color from chlorophyll, and yellow wax beans are simply green beans that have been bred to have none of this pigment. So the questions are, does chlorophyll contribute to the flavor of green beans and will you miss it if it's not there?

We tasted green and wax beans steamed until crisp-tender and braised in our Mediterranean Braised Green Beans recipe (page 12). In both applications, tasters found very little difference in the flavors of the two beans, calling both sweet and "grassy." But wax beans did have one advantage over green: Because they have little color to lose during prolonged braising, their appearance changes less than that of green beans, which tend to turn a drab olive. So if you're making a long-cooked bean dish and are picky about aesthetics, go for the gold.

The Perils of Pyrex

I've heard that Pyrex glassware is susceptible to shattering. Is this true?

ALEX ROSENBERG
ARLINGTON, VA.

➤Shattering is relatively rare, but it can happen when glassware is exposed to sudden temperature changes (known as thermal shock), extremely high heat (over 425 degrees), or direct heat. In fact, in the past decade, we have experienced three such incidents in the test kitchen.

Precautions you can take to avoid shattering include fully preheating the oven before placing glassware inside (to avoid exposure to the very high temperatures that some ovens initially use to jump-start preheating); covering the bottom of the dish with a little liquid prior to cooking foods that may release juices (to keep the temperature of the dish even); placing hot glassware on a dry cloth (to avoid contact with a cool or wet surface); never placing glassware on a burner or under the broiler; never adding liquid to hot glassware; and never moving a glass dish directly from the freezer to the oven or vice versa. Both of the leading glassware brands in this country, Anchor-Hocking and World Kitchen (the U.S. manufacturer of Pyrex) offer more detailed instructions on all packaging and on their websites.

Clear glass cookware has many advantages: It's inexpensive, provides even browning, and makes it easy to monitor progress. But if you want to avoid glassware altogether when baking, we recommend Rose's Perfect Pie Plate by Rose Levy Beranbaum ($19.99) and the HIC 13 by 9-inch Porcelain Lasagna Baking Dish ($37.49). Both are ceramic and broiler-safe.

SEND US YOUR QUESTIONS We will provide a complimentary one-year subscription for each letter we print. Send your inquiry, name, address, and daytime telephone number to Notes from Readers, *Cook's Illustrated*, P.O. Box 470589, Brookline, MA 02447, or to NotesFromReaders@AmericasTestKitchen.com.

Quick Tips

⇒ COMPILED BY SHANNON FRIEDMANN HATCH ⇐

Making a Stand in the Digital Age

Judy DeStefano of New Port Richey, Fla., loves the convenience of following recipes on her e-reader, but it's sometimes difficult to read the screen when it's flat on the countertop. Her handy fix converts her knife block into a podium.

1. Use Velcro to attach a piece of wood that's a few inches longer than the e-reader horizontally on the slanted part of a knife block.

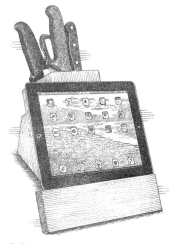

2. Rest the e-reader on top of the wood.

A Mouse (Pad) in the Kitchen

When Mike Meyers of Macclenny, Fla., is having a difficult time grasping a hard-to-open jar lid, he grabs his computer mouse pad. Its rubber bottom—engineered to anchor it to a desk—creates a good grip that helps budge stubborn lids.

Easier Stuffed Chiles

Poblano chiles are good for stuffing and baking, but filling their long, tubular shapes can be a challenge. Kris Lucius of Jamaica Plain, Mass., gets help from a drinking glass. After cutting off the poblano's top and removing its seeds, he sets it into the glass, which holds it upright and stable while it's stuffed.

Fridge Triage Box

Yuka Yoneda of Flushing, N.Y., hated throwing away expired food that had been pushed to the back of her refrigerator and forgotten. Her solution: Put anything in danger of going bad into a container on the top shelf. Now every time she opens the door, she's reminded of what should be consumed first.

Avoiding the Grind of French Press Cleaning

Katie Church of Denver, Colo., enjoys making coffee in her French press, but trying to remove the tiny grinds from between the plates and screen of the plunger after use disrupts her relaxing weekend ritual. To simplify the cleanup, she's developed this method: First, she fills the empty carafe halfway with soapy water. Then she inserts the plunger and rapidly moves it up and down a few times. The force of the water dislodges any stuck grounds—and scrubs the sides of the carafe.

Out, Damned Spot

Slicing pomegranates, beets, or cherries can leave bright pink or red stains on your cutting board that even endless scrubbing can't get out. Monica Riedel of Honaunau, Hawaii, makes the marks disappear with distilled white vinegar by blotting it on with a sponge. After a quick scrub and rinse, the surface is as good as new.

ILLUSTRATION: JOHN BURGOYNE

Creating Perfect Chocolate Curls

After producing nothing but a pile of broken shards when she tried to create perfectly spiraled chocolate curls, Joann Sherman of Garrison, N.Y., used to think that the decoration could only be created by pastry chefs. Then she learned the secret: warming the chocolate.

1. Wrap a chocolate bar in plastic wrap and then rub the palm of your hand against the edge of the bar until it is warm.

2. To make curls, remove the plastic and run a vegetable peeler along the chocolate bar toward you. Repeat the warming process as needed.

Preventing Oil Spills

Pouring olive oil often results not in a drizzle but a deluge. Derrick Manzlak of Braintree, Mass., remedied this situation by transferring the oil to a maple syrup dispenser. Its quick-closing spout gives him complete control over the pour. (Since the container is clear, be sure to store it in a dark cabinet to keep the oil from going rancid.)

Handling a Whole Roast Chicken

One of the most difficult parts of roasting a whole chicken is transferring the hot bird from the roasting pan to the carving board. Barbara Kram of Titusville, N.J., gets a better grip with this method.

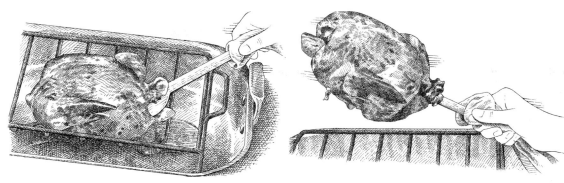

1. Insert the bowl of a long wooden spoon into the chicken's cavity.

2. Grasp the handle of the spoon with a towel, tilt the chicken slightly toward the handle, and lift it out of the pan.

Caring for Wooden Utensils and Cutting Boards

While most cooks know that butcher-block countertops or cutting boards should be treated with mineral oil to boost longevity, some forget that wooden utensils also benefit from an occasional dip. Anne Cowie of Cambridge, Mass., conveniently oils several tools at once.

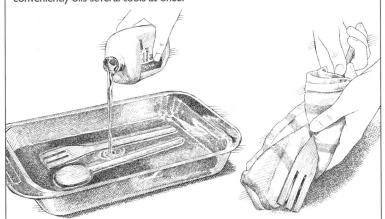

1. Pour food-grade mineral oil into a 13 by 9-inch baking dish to a ⅛-inch depth. (If your utensils are too long for the pan, use a rimmed baking sheet.) Lay clean utensils in the oil for 15 minutes; flip and let sit for 15 minutes longer.

2. Remove the utensils from the oil and wipe away the excess. Let them dry for 24 hours. Funnel any leftover oil into a container to reserve for future use.

Getting a Grip on Mini Muffin Tins

Miniature muffin tins are usually fitted with a rim that is too tiny to grasp with bulky oven mitts. Jennifer Chou of Berkeley, Calif., no longer struggles because she leaves one corner cup empty. Now she has a place to insert her thumb, allowing her to remove the tin without getting burned.

Baking Gear Hookup

Frequent baker Ellen Kunz of Neenah, Wis., had a designated space for her measuring utensils but still sometimes struggled with finding the exact cup or spoon she needed. To ensure that they were always in plain view, she attached adhesive hooks from an office supply store to the inside of her cabinet, ending the game of hide-and-seek once and for all.

Meatier Meatloaf

Meatloaf packed with bland, starchy fillers hardly deserves its name. Could we put the meatiness back in this American classic?

≥ BY CELESTE ROGERS ≤

Meatloaf made its debut in American cookbooks in the late 1800s, soon after the invention of the mechanical meat grinder. But the concept really took hold during the Great Depression, when tough times necessitated the use of cheap cuts like beef chuck and rump. Parsimonious cooks ground bits of bargain meat and stretched the number of portions by bulking it up with a moistened filler—bread crumbs, oatmeal, crackers, bulgur, rice, and even breakfast cereal were common. As the economy improved, the basic recipe (which included padding the meat with a filler) endured.

A primary reason for this continued popularity? Mixing moistened starch (the test kitchen typically uses a panade, or bread crumbs soaked in milk) into ground meat does a lot more than keep a cook within a budget. It also helps the loaf hold on to moisture, so it bakes up juicy and tender.

To demonstrate this, I mixed up two batches of a classic meatloaf recipe, omitting the panade from one. That left the usual trio of ground chuck, pork, and veal, into which I mixed sautéed onion, herbs and spices (parsley, thyme, and black pepper), Dijon mustard, and a couple of beaten eggs. Following the test kitchen's standard procedure, I baked the mixtures free-form by arranging a rectangle of aluminum foil on a wire rack set in a rimmed baking sheet and poking holes in it. This setup maximizes browning and allows fat to drip away during baking.

As I compared the loaves, I became a true believer in the hydrating power of a panade. The panade-free loaf was hopelessly dry, while the milk-and-bread-enhanced loaf was remarkably tender and juicy. But this test also shed light on a panade's undeniable flaw: Its bland starch dilutes meaty flavor. The panade-free loaf boasted a much beefier taste than the milk-and-bread-packed loaf. Wouldn't it be great to ensure juiciness in meatloaf without masking meaty flavor?

The sweet-tart flavors of a classic ketchup glaze balance this exceptionally meaty meatloaf.

Parting with Panade

As a first step toward that goal, I reviewed the properties of a panade, noting that it works in two ways: First, the paste physically interrupts the meat proteins from linking together into a tough matrix. Second, the paste absorbs and retains moisture that is squeezed out from the proteins as they shrink during cooking.

If I was going to get rid of the panade, adding some gelatin to the loaf only made sense. The unflavored powder is highly absorptive—it can hold up to 10 times its weight in water—and we have used it in the test kitchen to retain moisture in everything from meatballs to the ground meat in Bolognese sauce. A tablespoon of gelatin bloomed in ½ cup of chicken broth and the two beaten eggs turned out to be the right amount, helping the loaf stay juicy without creating a rubbery texture. With gelatin in the mix, I figured I could eliminate meekly flavored, gelatin-rich veal. This would get me one step closer to a meatier-tasting meatloaf by allowing me to increase the amounts of more richly flavored beef and pork.

Adding gelatin was a good start, but the loaf was still not juicy enough. My instinct was to incorporate pancetta, bacon, or salt pork, thinking that their fat would make up for the lack of moisture in the loaf. Unfortunately, no amount of lubricating fat could produce a sense of juiciness. While undeniably richer, the loaves were still parched. What's more, they had a predominant pork flavor that was unexpected (and unwelcome) in meatloaf.

Racking my brain for ideas, I thought about a store-bought frozen low-fat burger that I'd recently tasted that had been surprisingly moist. Hoping to get in on the secret, I took a trip to the supermarket and scanned several ingredient lists. Interestingly, prunes showed up on more than one label. It seemed like an odd addition, but our science editor explained that it made perfect sense: Fruit fiber is a natural sponge and readily absorbs moisture that is expelled by meat proteins during cooking. I went back to the kitchen and whipped up a prune-enriched meatloaf, happily finding that it baked up exceptionally juicy. Unhappily, the subtle but distinct sweetness of the loaf only detracted from my goal of maximizing meatiness.

Then it dawned on me: Why not use savory, water-rich mushrooms instead of sweet prunes? I ran the idea by our science editor and got an enthusiastic thumbs-up. Fungi, he explained, are made up of chitin, a polysaccharide that absorbs liquid and also firms up when cooked, holding on to the absorbed moisture even more tightly than the polysaccharides in fruit or vegetable fiber can.

I started another batch of meatloaf by sautéing sliced mushrooms in butter along with the onion until they browned and developed real depth of flavor, and then I stirred in minced garlic and a spoonful of tomato paste for complexity. When the mushrooms and aromatics were cooked down, I pulsed them in a food processor until they were finely chopped and then mixed them with the gelatin mixture and the ground beef and pork. Here was the breakthrough I'd been looking for—the most succulent loaf yet. Even better, the mushrooms contributed *umami* flavor that amplified meatiness.

The texture of my loaf was now much improved, and it boasted terrific meaty flavor. Nonetheless,

PHOTOGRAPHY: CARL TREMBLAY

when, as a final test, I sampled it alongside a traditional panade-enriched loaf, my newfangled loaf was still the drier of the two. I'd exhausted every option aside from adding back some panade, so when a colleague advised doing just that, I acquiesced. As it turned out, adding just half a slice (less than 20 percent of the amount of bread called for in a traditional recipe) satisfied all expectations for meatiness, producing a loaf that was just as moist as one loaded with panade. Instead of mixing the bread with milk, I combined it with the gelatin and egg mixture, adding 2 tablespoons of umami-rich soy sauce to keep a loose consistency.

A Classic Finish

I slid a final batch of meatloaf into a 350-degree oven and then set about creating a sweet and tangy glaze. I already knew that ketchup would be the central ingredient, and it only made sense to play up its sweet-tart flavor profile with brown sugar and fruity cider vinegar. For complexity, I also stirred in citrusy ground coriander and spicy hot sauce. I simmered the mixture over medium heat until it thickened to a syrupy consistency, about five minutes. When the meatloaf registered

SCIENCE Creating a Juicier, Meatier Meatloaf

Meatloaf typically contains a milk and bread panade that helps lock in moisture. But the textural enhancement comes at a cost: All of that starchy bread dulls flavor. Our recipe cuts way back on the panade but still produces a moist, meaty loaf.

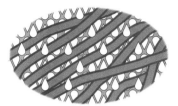

LOTS OF PANADE:
MOIST BUT NOT MEATY
A milk and bread paste creates a juicy loaf, but the starches from the typical three pieces of bread mask many of the flavor compounds in the meat.

NO PANADE:
MEATY BUT DRY
Without panade to trap liquid and lubricate the ground meat, the proteins will bind tightly together and squeeze out moisture.

A LITTLE PANADE:
MEATY AND MOIST
Adding sponge-like mushrooms and gelatin to the loaf traps moisture, allowing us to cut back the bread by more than 80 percent for an ultra-meaty loaf.

155 degrees (about 90 minutes later), I removed it from the oven and heated the broiler. I brushed the loaf with half of my ketchup concoction and slid it under the broiler for two minutes, then brushed on the remainder, and put it back under the heat until it started to brown. I let the loaf cool and then sliced it into thick slabs.

Success. With a few simple tricks, I'd managed to create a meatloaf for the 21st century that was both supremely meaty and ultra-moist.

MEATIER MEATLOAF
SERVES 6 TO 8

We recommend using ground chuck for this recipe.

Meatloaf

- 2 tablespoons unsalted butter
- 1 onion, chopped fine
- 6 ounces white mushrooms, trimmed and sliced thin
- 1 tablespoon tomato paste
- 3 tablespoons plus ½ cup low-sodium chicken broth
- 2 garlic cloves, minced
- 2 large eggs
- 2 tablespoons soy sauce
- 1 tablespoon unflavored gelatin
- ½ slice hearty white sandwich bread, torn into 1-inch pieces
- ⅓ cup minced fresh parsley
- 2 teaspoons Dijon mustard
- ¾ teaspoon pepper
- ½ teaspoon dried thyme
- 1 pound ground pork
- 1 pound 85 percent lean ground beef

Glaze

- ½ cup ketchup
- ¼ cup cider vinegar
- 3 tablespoons packed brown sugar
- 1 teaspoon hot sauce
- ½ teaspoon ground coriander

1. FOR THE MEATLOAF: Adjust oven rack to middle position and heat oven to 350 degrees. Fold heavy-duty aluminum foil to form 9 by 5-inch rectangle. Center foil on wire rack set in rimmed baking sheet. Poke holes in foil with skewer (about ½ inch apart). Spray foil with vegetable oil spray.

2. Melt butter in 12-inch skillet over medium heat. Add onion and mushrooms; cook, stirring occasionally, until beginning to brown, 10 to 12 minutes. Add tomato paste and cook, stirring constantly, until browned, about 3 minutes. Reduce heat to low; add 3 tablespoons broth and garlic; cook, scraping bottom of pan to loosen any browned bits, until thickened, about 1 minute. Transfer mushroom mixture to large bowl to cool.

3. Whisk eggs, remaining ½ cup broth, and soy sauce together in bowl. Sprinkle gelatin over egg mixture and let sit until gelatin softens, about 5 minutes.

4. Pulse bread in food processor until finely ground, 5 to 10 pulses. Add gelatin mixture, cooled mushroom mixture, parsley, mustard, pepper, and thyme to bread crumbs and pulse until mushrooms are finely ground, about 10 pulses, scraping down bowl as needed. Transfer bread-crumb mixture to large bowl. Add pork and beef and mix with hands to thoroughly combine.

5. Transfer meat mixture to foil rectangle and shape into 9 by 5-inch loaf using wet hands. Bake meatloaf until it registers 155 to 160 degrees, 75 to 90 minutes. Remove from oven and turn on broiler.

6. FOR THE GLAZE: While meatloaf cooks, bring all ingredients to simmer in small saucepan over medium heat. Cook, stirring occasionally, until thick and syrupy, about 5 minutes.

7. Spread half of glaze evenly over cooked meatloaf; place under broiler and cook until glaze bubbles and begins to brown at edges, about 2 minutes. Remove meatloaf from oven and spread evenly with remaining glaze; return to broiler and cook until glaze is again bubbling and beginning to brown, about 2 minutes longer. Let meatloaf cool for 20 minutes before slicing and serving.

The Long History of Enhancing Meat

Who knew meatloaf wasn't just the invention of thrifty housewives during the Great Depression? Turns out the idea of mixing meat with a tenderizing filler traces back to the fourth or fifth century AD, when the Roman cookbook *Apicius* presented a recipe for patties made of chopped meat, bread, and wine. But it wasn't until the late 1800s that American meatloaf was born, inspired by recipes offered by manufacturers of the newly invented meat grinder. The Depression only increased meatloaf's popularity, along with developments in food manufacturing that produced flavorful, inexpensive mix-ins like mustard and bouillon. In the 1940s, World War II rationing spawned meat-free loaves, whereas postwar creativity in the 1950s and '60s produced the likes of Bacon-Dill Meatloaf and Spicy Peach Loaf (*Good Housekeeping Cook Book*, 1955). In the 1970s and '80s, veal, pork, and beef "meatloaf mix" came into vogue, elevating the dish to dinner party–worthy status. In the 1990s, restaurateurs marketed upscale versions, and today, innovations continue as loaves are stuffed, wrapped, or laced with ethnic flavors.

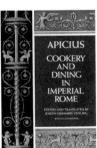

ORIGINAL HAMBURGER HELPER
These recipes from ancient Rome include one for meat patties enhanced by a bread and red wine panade.

Revamping Chicken Fajitas

Most fajitas are merely a bland, dry vehicle for the garnishes. We wanted chicken and vegetables that were truly worth eating.

⇒ BY DAN SOUZA ⇐

Fajitas originated in the 1930s when hungry ranch hands in the Rio Grande Valley of Texas gorged on grilled leftover beef trimmings wrapped in charred flour tortillas. In 1973, Houston restaurateur Ninfa Rodriguez Laurenzo picked up on the idea and started offering the dish (she called it "tacos al carbon") in her restaurant, Ninfa's, much to the delight of the locals. Fast-forward almost a decade to 1982, when enterprising chef George Weidmann of the Hyatt Regency's La Vista restaurant in Austin put "sizzling fajitas" on his menu. To say that his signature dish was a hit is putting it mildly: Surging sales made La Vista the most profitable restaurant in the Hyatt chain, and chefs across the country were quick to jump on the fajita bandwagon.

Today, fajitas are made with everything from steak to shrimp to chicken. But truth be told, it almost doesn't matter what the protein is, since it's usually buried under flavor-dulling gobs of sour cream and shredded cheese. I wanted to reinvigorate fajitas, using convenient boneless, skinless chicken breasts and finding a good way to cook them indoors for year-round appeal. My lighter, contemporary twist would abandon the stodgy Tex-Mex garnishes and put the spotlight where it belongs: on the chicken and obligatory peppers and onions.

Introducing a better plate of chicken fajitas: juicy, deeply seared meat, creamy roasted peppers and onions, and pickled radishes.

Strong (Flavor) Profile

Boneless, skinless chicken breasts may be convenient, but the downside is that they're also lean and somewhat bland. My first inclination was to pump them up with a brinerade—a concentrated liquid with the salt content of a brine plus the acid and seasonings of a marinade. The salt seasons the meat and helps keep it moist during cooking while the herbs, spices, and acid begin to penetrate the surface of the flesh with robust flavor.

I gave it a shot, mixing up a punchy concoction of salt, lime juice, garlic, cumin, and cayenne pepper—some of the key flavors of Mexican cuisine. I also added oil—important because the flavor compounds in cayenne and cumin are largely fat soluble. I pounded the breasts to a ½-inch thickness so they would fit tidily into tortillas and then slipped them into the brinerade. After 30 minutes, I removed the chicken, wiped off the excess moisture, and seared it in a hot skillet. Unfortunately, by the time the meat was adequately charred, it was also dry as a bone.

I needed a way to get the chicken to brown faster, and even blacken slightly in spots. Would adding sugar to the brinerade do the trick? Since it caramelizes much more quickly (and at lower temperatures) than meat browns, I had high hopes. Sure enough, 1 teaspoon of sugar was just right, rapidly charring without contributing a noticeable sweetness. To further allude to the smoky heat of the grill, I stirred heady smoked paprika into the brinerade.

I now had some seriously flavorful chicken, but in spite of the brinerade it was difficult to keep it moist in the blazing-hot skillet. What if I compromised by searing just one side of the chicken over high heat and finishing the other side over low heat?

I gave it a shot, and lo and behold, the chicken that I'd charred on only one side was indeed juicier. I had to wonder, though: If the low heat of a stove was good, would the indirect heat of the oven be even better? To find out, I seared a batch on one side over high heat and then flipped the breasts and transferred the skillet to a 200-degree oven for 10 minutes. After letting it rest, I sliced up my moistest chicken yet and then tossed it back into the skillet to soak up the flavorful pan juices. Next up: vegetables.

Strip Search

Fajitas' ubiquitous peppers and onions have a firm footing in Mexican cuisine, where they are known as *rajas*, or strips. While most rajas we eat stateside seem like an afterthought, they frequently take center stage in Mexico. In fact, *rajas con crema*—strips of roasted pepper and onion cooked down with tangy Mexican cultured cream—are often served alone in a tortilla. Providing a rich counterpoint to the lean chicken seemed an ideal way to breathe new life into my fajitas.

I threw a final batch of chicken into its brinerade and then followed a promising-looking rajas recipe using poblano chiles (they have a fruitier flavor than the usual bell peppers), which I broiled to blister the skins. After letting the broiled chiles steam in a covered bowl for about 10 minutes, most of the skins slipped right off (though I did leave some charred bits behind for flavor). I sliced the chiles and sautéed them along with onion strips and then stirred in sour cream (my substitute for hard-to-find crema). That's where things started to fall apart—literally. First, the sour cream curdled as it made contact with the hot pan. Then, as I stubbornly persevered, the roasted poblanos overcooked into green mush.

My first move was to swap heavy cream for the sour cream. The latter's high level of acidity and relatively low fat content make it a prime candidate for curdling, whereas fattier heavy cream is remarkably stable. To make up for the cream's lack of tang, I added a splash of lime juice toward the end of cooking. And to preserve my perfectly roasted poblanos,

Pepping Up Fajitas with Poblanos

Forget the ho-hum grilled bell peppers and onions typically served with fajitas. Here, we take a cue from Mexican cuisine, charbroiling strips of fruity, complex-tasting poblano chiles and then simmering them with onions, cream, and lime juice. The tangy concoction, called *rajas con crema*, provides a rich counterpoint to the lean chicken.

THE PEPPER TO PICK

We like the convenience of boneless, skinless chicken breasts, but their lack of fat and flavor is a hazard. Here's how we achieve meat that is well charred, juicy, and meaty-tasting.

SEAR ON ONE SIDE
Cook marinated breasts over high heat without moving until thoroughly charred.

TRANSFER TO OVEN
Flip breasts and finish in a gentle 200-degree oven, which ensures the breasts won't overcook.

TOSS IN PAN JUICES
After resting chicken, slice and return to skillet. Toss in flavorful juices before serving.

I added them at the last minute to rewarm with the onions and cream. Final touches of garlic, thyme, and oregano tied everything together.

After searing the chicken, finishing it in the oven, and charring some flour tortillas, I proudly laid out my modern fajita feast, offering crumbled *queso fresco*, chopped cilantro, lime wedges, and spicy pickled radishes for garnishing. These skillet fajitas provide all of the easy-to-love flavor of their grilled forebears—no shredded cheddar or salsa required.

SKILLET CHICKEN FAJITAS
SERVES 4

We like to serve these fajitas with crumbled *queso fresco* or feta in addition to the other garnishes listed.

Chicken

- ¼ cup vegetable oil
- 2 tablespoons lime juice
- 4 garlic cloves, peeled and smashed
- 1½ teaspoons smoked paprika
- 1 teaspoon sugar
- 1 teaspoon salt
- ½ teaspoon ground cumin
- ½ teaspoon pepper
- ¼ teaspoon cayenne pepper
- 1½ pounds boneless, skinless chicken breasts, trimmed and pounded to ½-inch thickness

Rajas con Crema

- 1 pound (3 to 4) poblano chiles, stemmed, halved, and seeded
- 1 tablespoon vegetable oil
- 1 onion, halved and sliced ¼ inch thick
- 2 garlic cloves, minced
- ¼ teaspoon dried thyme
- ¼ teaspoon dried oregano
- ½ cup heavy cream
- 1 tablespoon lime juice
- ½ teaspoon salt
- ¼ teaspoon pepper

8–12 (6-inch) flour tortillas, warmed

- ¼ cup minced fresh cilantro
  Spicy Pickled Radishes (recipe follows)
  Lime wedges

1. FOR THE CHICKEN: Whisk 3 tablespoons oil, lime juice, garlic, paprika, sugar, salt, cumin, pepper, and cayenne together in bowl. Add chicken and toss to coat. Cover and let stand at room temperature for at least 30 minutes or up to 60 minutes.

2. FOR THE RAJAS CON CREMA: Meanwhile, adjust oven rack to highest position and heat broiler. Arrange poblanos, skin side up, on aluminum foil–lined rimmed baking sheet and press to flatten. Broil until skin is charred and puffed, 4 to 10 minutes, rotating baking sheet halfway through cooking. Transfer poblanos to bowl, cover, and let steam for 10 minutes. Rub majority of skin from poblanos and discard (preserve some skin for flavor); slice into ¼-inch-thick strips. Adjust oven racks to middle and lowest positions and heat oven to 200 degrees.

3. Heat oil in 12-inch nonstick skillet over high heat until just smoking. Add onion and cook until charred and just softened, about 3 minutes. Add garlic, thyme, and oregano and cook until fragrant, about 15 seconds. Add cream and cook, stirring frequently, until reduced and cream lightly coats onion, 1 to 2 minutes. Add poblano strips, lime juice, salt, and pepper and toss to coat. Transfer vegetables to bowl, cover, and place on middle oven rack. Wipe out skillet with paper towels.

4. Remove chicken from marinade and wipe off excess. Heat remaining 1 tablespoon oil in now-empty skillet over high heat until just smoking. Add chicken and cook without moving it until bottom side is well charred, about 4 minutes. Flip chicken; transfer skillet to lower oven rack. Bake until chicken registers 160 degrees, 7 to 10 minutes. Transfer to cutting board and let rest for 5 minutes; do not wash out skillet.

5. Slice chicken crosswise into ¼-inch-thick strips. Return chicken strips to skillet and toss to coat with pan juices. To serve, spoon few pieces of chicken into center of warmed tortilla and top with spoonful of vegetable mixture, cilantro, and Spicy Pickled Radishes. Serve with lime wedges.

SPICY PICKLED RADISHES
MAKES ABOUT 1¾ CUPS

- 10 radishes, trimmed and sliced thin
- ½ cup lime juice (4 limes)
- ½ jalapeño chile, stemmed and sliced thin
- 1 teaspoon sugar
- ¼ teaspoon salt

Combine all ingredients in bowl. Cover and let stand at room temperature for 30 minutes (or refrigerate for up to 24 hours).

Watch Every Fajita Step
Video available FREE for 4 months at
www.CooksIllustrated.com/oct12

Mediterranean Braised Green Beans

Slow-cooking in a rich tomato sauce produces uniquely supple green beans infused with big flavor. Could we keep the ultra-tender texture but shortcut the process?

⇒ BY ANDREW JANJIGIAN ⇐

Quickly steamed or sautéed, lightly crisp green beans are commonplace. But there's a lesser-known approach that turns beans into something altogether different. Southern-style green beans are slowly braised in broth with ham hocks or bacon until they pick up smoky flavor. The time-honored Mediterranean take on the method, my personal favorite, calls for sautéing garlic and onions in olive oil, adding tomatoes and green beans along with water, and then simmering until the sauce is thickened and the beans are infused with tomato and garlic. The best part is the texture of the beans: The slow cooking renders them so meltingly tender that they're almost creamy.

There are just two problems: First, it takes at least two hours of cooking to turn the beans ultra-tender. (Some recipes call for shorter cooking times, but they don't produce the truly silky texture that makes this dish so special.) Second, I often find that by the time the skins have fully softened, the interiors have practically disintegrated. I wanted the beans to turn velvety-soft but remain intact. I also wanted a reasonable cook time—no more than an hour.

Before I started cooking, I brushed up on the makeup of green beans. Their pods are composed primarily of cellulose and pectin, polysaccharides that are the main building blocks of most plant cell walls. The tough fibers of cellulose are impossible to dissolve, but when pectin breaks down during cooking, water is able to enter the fibers, over time swelling and softening them. The key to speedier cooking, then, would be to focus on the pectin. Pectin is affected by pH and will break down more slowly in an acidic environment. It was therefore likely that one of the key components of my dish—tomatoes—was lengthening the cook time. To confirm my hunch, I made one batch of beans with tomatoes and another without. Sure enough, the tomato-free beans needed far less time to soften. (This also explains why tomatoless Southern braised beans cook more quickly than the Mediterranean kind.)

Tomatoes are integral to the dish, and ditching them wasn't an option. But fortunately, it's just as easy to speed up the breakdown of pectin as it

Starting the beans in an alkaline environment—and finishing them in an acidic one—produces ideal texture.

is to slow it down. As we learned while searching for a way to get the pectin in broccoli to rapidly disintegrate for our Broccoli-Cheese Soup (March/April 2011), all you need is an alkaline environment, which is as simple as adding baking soda to the pot.

For my next test, I sautéed onions and garlic (plus a smidge of cayenne); added the green beans, water, and ½ teaspoon of baking soda; and held off on incorporating the tomatoes. Just 10 minutes of simmering was enough to soften the beans significantly.

I could now use the acidity of the tomatoes to my advantage. Once added to the pot, they would slow any further breakdown of pectin while giving the cellulose time to swell with water and fully soften. I mixed in diced tomatoes and some tomato paste (for sweetness and depth) and continued simmering. When I lifted the lid about 45 minutes later, the beans were uniformly soft but not at all mushy.

One minor outstanding issue: The beans were a bit raggedy around the edges. So for the next batch, after incorporating the tomatoes, I moved the pot to a low oven where the beans could finish cooking in the more gentle heat. These beans were perfect, with tender skins, intact interiors, and rich flavor. To brighten things, I stirred in a little red wine vinegar, along with chopped parsley for freshness. I also threw together equally good variations with mint and feta and with potatoes and basil.

Crisp-tender green beans have their place, but it's nice to have the option to put an entirely different, satisfyingly rich side dish on the table.

MEDITERRANEAN BRAISED GREEN BEANS
SERVES 4 TO 6 AS A SIDE DISH

A dollop of yogurt spooned over the beans adds nice tang. To make a light entrée, serve the beans with rice or crusty bread. For our free recipe for Mediterranean Braised Green Beans with Potatoes and Basil, go to www.CooksIllustrated.com/oct12.

- 5 tablespoons extra-virgin olive oil
- 1 onion, chopped fine
- 4 garlic cloves, minced
  Pinch cayenne pepper
- 1½ cups water
- ½ teaspoon baking soda
- 1½ pounds green beans, trimmed and cut into 2- to 3-inch lengths
- 1 tablespoon tomato paste
- 1 (14.5-ounce) can diced tomatoes, drained with juice reserved, chopped coarse
- 1 teaspoon salt
- ¼ teaspoon pepper
- ¼ cup chopped fresh parsley
  Red wine vinegar

1. Adjust oven rack to lower-middle position and heat oven to 275 degrees. Heat 3 tablespoons oil in Dutch oven over medium heat until shimmering. Add onion and cook, stirring occasionally, until softened, 3 to 5 minutes. Add garlic and cayenne and cook until fragrant, about 30 seconds. Add water, baking soda, and green beans and bring to simmer. Reduce heat to medium-low and cook, stirring occasionally, for 10 minutes. Stir in tomato paste, tomatoes and their juice, salt, and pepper.

2. Cover pot, transfer to oven, and cook until sauce is slightly thickened and green beans can be easily cut with side of fork, 40 to 50 minutes. Stir in parsley and season with vinegar to taste. Drizzle with remaining 2 tablespoons oil and serve warm or at room temperature.

MEDITERRANEAN BRAISED GREEN BEANS WITH MINT AND FETA

Add ¾ teaspoon ground allspice with garlic and cayenne. Substitute 2 tablespoons chopped fresh mint for parsley. Omit 2 tablespoons oil in step 2. Sprinkle green beans with ½ cup crumbled feta cheese before serving.

PHOTOGRAPHY: CARL TREMBLAY

Upgrading Avocado Salads

Usually tossed into a pile of greens, mild-mannered avocado sinks to the bottom of the bowl like an afterthought. We wanted it in the limelight.

⇒ BY CELESTE ROGERS ⇐

Once exotic and rare, buttery avocado cut into chunks has become as ubiquitous a salad ingredient as croutons. Despite this trend, your standard leafy salad doesn't really do this fruit justice. Since greens and avocado both have mild flavor and delicate texture (not to mention similar color), the effect is often uninspiring. Worse, tossing ripe avocado with other salad ingredients tends to make it disintegrate, leading to a swampy mess.

But I'm a big avocado fan, and rather than banish it from my salad course altogether, I was determined to find a way to highlight its velvety smooth texture and subtle flavor. First, I turned my attention to a primary problem with salads that include avocados: the dressing, which never seems tailored for the job. Creamy dressings are too rich and often so flavorful that they overwhelm the avocado's mild taste. But I found that a standard vinaigrette of 3 parts olive oil to 1 part vinegar was also too rich: Tasters asked for more tartness to balance and brighten the buttery avocado. I tried dressing the salad with only vinegar—no oil—but surprisingly, tasters found that most bites were even less acidic. After some head-scratching, I realized that the vinegar, when not emulsified with oil, couldn't cling to the ingredients and was left pooling at the bottom of the bowl.

I needed an emulsified dressing made with minimal oil, so I took our Foolproof Vinaigrette recipe (September/October 2009), which uses ½ teaspoon of mayonnaise to stabilize the emulsion, and pushed it to its limits, decreasing the oil to 2 parts and finally 1 part. I found that the same amount of mayo was able to keep even a 1:1 mixture of oil to vinegar from separating. Tasters agreed that this uniquely acidic vinaigrette worked perfectly with the avocado.

With my dressing formulated, the flavor was there, and I was able to turn to assembling the complementary ingredients. Since avocados do very well in chunky salsas, I wondered if ditching the fluttery greens of a tossed salad and seeking out the bulkier ingredients of a chopped salad would be a better bet. Radishes were a definite: Their crisp, cool texture and sharp, peppery bite would be a good foil for the soft, rich avocado. Next, I singled out savory, aromatic shallot, which I would slice thinly. For balance, I needed something a little sweet and not very crunchy. The sweet-tart brightness of cherry tomatoes proved just the ticket. To round out their juiciness and to add complexity, I finished the salad with the bold, salty pop of some thinly shaved ricotta salata cheese

and the herbal notes of chopped fresh basil.

My job was almost done but not quite: I hadn't addressed presentation. When I tossed the salad, it didn't look very appealing: As expected, the avocado coated the other ingredients with an army-green film. But when I put avocado slices in the shape of a fan atop everything else already tossed in the dressing, it seemed like a garnish or an afterthought. Furthermore, each diner still faced the challenge of mixing the fruit into the rest of the salad in order to coat it with dressing but without it leaving its (visually off-putting) mark.

Then I had two brainstorms: Why not toss the avocado separately in dressing as well, and why not flip the usual arrangement by placing the avocado underneath the other ingredients instead of on top? This approach not only eliminated any chance of the avocado getting all over the other ingredients but also allowed the fruit to soak up any additional dressing dripping down from the rest of the salad's components. Now my salad didn't just have the perfect flavor combination: It looked great, too.

I came up with three variations on this winning formula. Each included a cool, crunchy element (fennel, endive, or jícama); a sweet-tart component (orange, apple, or mango); and a bold, savory touch (green olives, pungent blue cheese, or salty feta).

In all of these salads, avocado finally gets the treatment it deserves.

AVOCADO SALAD WITH TOMATO AND RADISH
SERVES 6

Crumbled feta cheese can be substituted for the ricotta salata.

1	large shallot, sliced thin
3	tablespoons red wine vinegar
1	garlic clove, minced
½	teaspoon mayonnaise
	Salt and pepper
3	tablespoons extra-virgin olive oil
3	avocados, halved, pitted, and cut into ¾-inch pieces
12	ounces cherry tomatoes, quartered
3	radishes, sliced thin
½	cup chopped fresh basil
3	ounces ricotta salata, shaved thin

1. Place shallot in 2 cups ice water and let stand for 30 minutes. Drain and pat dry with paper towels.
2. Whisk vinegar, garlic, mayonnaise, ¼ teaspoon

salt, and ¼ teaspoon pepper in nonreactive bowl until mixture appears milky and no lumps remain. Whisking constantly, slowly drizzle in oil. (Dressing should appear homogeneous, glossy, and slightly thickened, without pools of oil on surface.)
3. Gently toss avocados, 2 tablespoons dressing, and ½ teaspoon salt in bowl. Transfer avocados to large platter or individual plates.
4. Toss shallot, tomatoes, radishes, and basil with remaining dressing. Spoon tomato mixture over avocados and sprinkle with ricotta salata. Serve immediately.

AVOCADO SALAD WITH ORANGE AND FENNEL

Substitute sherry vinegar for red wine vinegar and ½ teaspoon hot paprika for garlic. Omit pepper. Starting with 3 oranges, remove 1 teaspoon finely grated zest from 1 orange and add to dressing in step 2. Peel, quarter, and cut oranges into ¼-inch pieces and add to vegetable mixture in step 4. Substitute 1 thinly sliced, cored fennel bulb for tomatoes; ⅓ cup toasted slivered almonds for radishes; ¼ cup chopped parsley for basil; and ¼ cup sliced green olives for ricotta salata.

AVOCADO SALAD WITH APPLE AND ENDIVE

Reduce shallot to 1 tablespoon minced and skip step 1. Substitute minced shallot and 1 teaspoon honey for garlic and substitute cider vinegar for red wine vinegar. Substitute 1 Fuji apple cut into 1-inch-long matchsticks for tomatoes, 1 thinly sliced head Belgian endive for radishes, ¼ cup minced chives for basil, and blue cheese for ricotta salata.

AVOCADO SALAD WITH MANGO AND JÍCAMA

Reduce shallot to 1 tablespoon minced and skip step 1. Substitute shallot and pinch cayenne for garlic and substitute ½ teaspoon lemon zest and 3 tablespoons lemon juice for red wine vinegar. Substitute 2 peeled mangos cut into ½-inch pieces for tomatoes, 2 cups peeled jícama cut into 2-inch-long matchsticks for radishes, and feta cheese for ricotta salata. Reduce basil to ¼ cup and add ¼ cup chopped mint to salad.

Complete Guide to Grill Roasting

The oven isn't your only option for roasting meat. For cuts that cook over moderate heat, the grill works just as well—if not better. Here's how to do it right. BY SHANNON FRIEDMANN HATCH

TURN YOUR GRILL INTO AN OVEN

Building a moderate, indirect fire and covering the grill turns it into an outdoor oven for cuts like prime rib, whole chicken, and pork loin.

Venting Helps
Adjusting the vents on the lid and bottom of a charcoal grill helps regulate the heat. We prefer to leave the vents on the lid and grill bottom partially closed, which prevents the coals from burning too fast and helps the grill retain heat.

Catchall for Drips
When grill-roasting fatty cuts, we place a disposable aluminum roasting pan beneath the meat to catch drippings.

Briquettes Do It Better
We like natural hardwood charcoal for grilling, but it's not the best choice for grill roasting. Though both hardwood charcoal and briquettes burn fast and hot for the first 30 minutes, we've found that hardwood then abruptly turns to ash while the briquettes keep going, taking hours to fall below 250 degrees.

Smoking Permitted—and Encouraged
If you'd like, add a couple of soaked wood chunks or a packet of aluminum foil–wrapped chips to the fire to infuse the meat with smoke flavor.

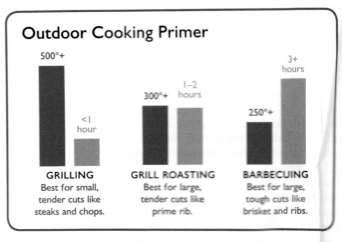

Outdoor Cooking Primer

GRILLING	GRILL ROASTING	BARBECUING
500°+ / <1 hour	300°+ / 1–2 hours	250°+ / 3+ hours
Best for small, tender cuts like steaks and chops.	Best for large, tender cuts like prime rib.	Best for large, tough cuts like brisket and ribs.

BUILDING THE FIRE

To create indirect heat on a charcoal or gas grill, we use one of two fire setups: banked or split. Both setups create a hot zone and a cool zone.

BANKED CHARCOAL FIRE
All of the coals are piled on one side of the grill, creating a long-lasting fire with a hotter side and a cooler side. Cuts with more intramuscular fat (like prime rib) or those that benefit from a deeply browned crust (like beef tenderloin) can be quickly seared over the heat to create flavorful browning and then transferred to the cooler side to finish cooking.

GAS GRILL SETUP
Preheat the grill and then leave the primary burner on high, or as directed in the recipe; turn off other burners and place the food on the cooler side of the grill.
➤ TIP: Rotate the food during cooking so the side that starts out closest to the fire doesn't cook too quickly.

SPLIT CHARCOAL FIRE
Coals are piled on either side of the kettle, creating a cool, evenly heated area in the middle; there's no need for rotating the food. Since the two hot areas have fewer coals that burn out faster than coals banked to one side, the setup is ideal for quicker-cooking items, such as whole chickens, that don't need to be seared.
➤ TIP: The coals should be piled high against the side of the grill to form tall but narrow piles; with wider piles, the cool spot in the middle won't be large enough to protect the food from direct heat.

GAS GRILL SETUP
A split fire only works on gas grills with at least three burners, so we typically don't call for this setup in recipes tailored for gas. If your grill does have the requisite burners and configuration, after preheating, turn the center burner off and leave the end burners on. Cook the food over the turned-off burner.

Upgrading Avocado Salads

Usually tossed into a pile of greens, mild-mannered avocado sinks to the bottom of the bowl like an afterthought. We wanted it in the limelight.

⇒ BY CELESTE ROGERS ⇐

Once exotic and rare, buttery avocado cut into chunks has become as ubiquitous a salad ingredient as croutons. Despite this trend, your standard leafy salad doesn't really do this fruit justice. Since greens and avocado both have mild flavor and delicate texture (not to mention similar color), the effect is often uninspiring. Worse, tossing ripe avocado with other salad ingredients tends to make it disintegrate, leading to a swampy mess.

But I'm a big avocado fan, and rather than banish it from my salad course altogether, I was determined to find a way to highlight its velvety smooth texture and subtle flavor. First, I turned my attention to a primary problem with salads that include avocados: the dressing, which never seems tailored for the job. Creamy dressings are too rich and often so flavorful that they overwhelm the avocado's mild taste. But I found that a standard vinaigrette of 3 parts olive oil to 1 part vinegar was also too rich: Tasters asked for more tartness to balance and brighten the buttery avocado. I tried dressing the salad with only vinegar—no oil—but surprisingly, tasters found that most bites were even less acidic. After some head-scratching, I realized that the vinegar, when not emulsified with oil, couldn't cling to the ingredients and was left pooling at the bottom of the bowl.

I needed an emulsified dressing made with minimal oil, so I took our Foolproof Vinaigrette recipe (September/October 2009), which uses ½ teaspoon of mayonnaise to stabilize the emulsion, and pushed it to its limits, decreasing the oil to 2 parts and finally 1 part. I found that the same amount of mayo was able to keep even a 1:1 mixture of oil to vinegar from separating. Tasters agreed that this uniquely acidic vinaigrette worked perfectly with the avocado.

With my dressing formulated, the flavor was there, and I was able to turn to assembling the complementary ingredients. Since avocados do very well in chunky salsas, I wondered if ditching the fluttery greens of a tossed salad and seeking out the bulkier ingredients of a chopped salad would be a better bet. Radishes were a definite: Their crisp, cool texture and sharp, peppery bite would be a good foil for the soft, rich avocado. Next, I singled out savory, aromatic shallot, which I would slice thinly. For balance, I needed something a little sweet and not very crunchy. The sweet-tart brightness of cherry tomatoes proved just the ticket. To round out their juiciness and to add complexity, I finished the salad with the bold, salty pop of some thinly shaved ricotta salata cheese

and the herbal notes of chopped fresh basil.

My job was almost done but not quite: I hadn't addressed presentation. When I tossed the salad, it didn't look very appealing: As expected, the avocado coated the other ingredients with an army-green film. But when I put avocado slices in the shape of a fan atop everything else already tossed in the dressing, it seemed like a garnish or an afterthought. Furthermore, each diner still faced the challenge of mixing the fruit into the rest of the salad in order to coat it with dressing but without it leaving its (visually off-putting) mark.

Then I had two brainstorms: Why not toss the avocado separately in dressing as well, and why not flip the usual arrangement by placing the avocado underneath the other ingredients instead of on top? This approach not only eliminated any chance of the avocado getting all over the other ingredients but also allowed the fruit to soak up any additional dressing dripping down from the rest of the salad's components. Now my salad didn't just have the perfect flavor combination: It looked great, too.

I came up with three variations on this winning formula. Each included a cool, crunchy element (fennel, endive, or jícama); a sweet-tart component (orange, apple, or mango); and a bold, savory touch (green olives, pungent blue cheese, or salty feta).

In all of these salads, avocado finally gets the treatment it deserves.

AVOCADO SALAD WITH TOMATO AND RADISH
SERVES 6

Crumbled feta cheese can be substituted for the ricotta salata.

- 1   large shallot, sliced thin
- 3   tablespoons red wine vinegar
- 1   garlic clove, minced
- ½   teaspoon mayonnaise
-    Salt and pepper
- 3   tablespoons extra-virgin olive oil
- 3   avocados, halved, pitted, and cut into ¾-inch pieces
- 12   ounces cherry tomatoes, quartered
- 3   radishes, sliced thin
- ½   cup chopped fresh basil
- 3   ounces ricotta salata, shaved thin

1. Place shallot in 2 cups ice water and let stand for 30 minutes. Drain and pat dry with paper towels.
2. Whisk vinegar, garlic, mayonnaise, ¼ teaspoon

salt, and ¼ teaspoon pepper in nonreactive bowl until mixture appears milky and no lumps remain. Whisking constantly, slowly drizzle in oil. (Dressing should appear homogeneous, glossy, and slightly thickened, without pools of oil on surface.)
3. Gently toss avocados, 2 tablespoons dressing, and ½ teaspoon salt in bowl. Transfer avocados to large platter or individual plates.
4. Toss shallot, tomatoes, radishes, and basil with remaining dressing. Spoon tomato mixture over avocados and sprinkle with ricotta salata. Serve immediately.

AVOCADO SALAD WITH ORANGE AND FENNEL

Substitute sherry vinegar for red wine vinegar and ½ teaspoon hot paprika for garlic. Omit pepper. Starting with 3 oranges, remove 1 teaspoon finely grated zest from 1 orange and add to dressing in step 2. Peel, quarter, and cut oranges into ¼-inch pieces and add to vegetable mixture in step 4. Substitute 1 thinly sliced, cored fennel bulb for tomatoes; ⅓ cup toasted slivered almonds for radishes; ¼ cup chopped parsley for basil; and ¼ cup sliced green olives for ricotta salata.

AVOCADO SALAD WITH APPLE AND ENDIVE

Reduce shallot to 1 tablespoon minced and skip step 1. Substitute minced shallot and 1 teaspoon honey for garlic and substitute cider vinegar for red wine vinegar. Substitute 1 Fuji apple cut into 1-inch-long matchsticks for tomatoes, 1 thinly sliced head Belgian endive for radishes, ¼ cup minced chives for basil, and blue cheese for ricotta salata.

AVOCADO SALAD WITH MANGO AND JÍCAMA

Reduce shallot to 1 tablespoon minced and skip step 1. Substitute shallot and pinch cayenne for garlic and substitute ½ teaspoon lemon zest and 3 tablespoons lemon juice for red wine vinegar. Substitute 2 peeled mangos cut into ½-inch pieces for tomatoes, 2 cups peeled jícama cut into 2-inch-long matchsticks for radishes, and feta cheese for ricotta salata. Reduce basil to ¼ cup and add ¼ cup chopped mint to salad.

Watch the Salads Take Shape
Video available FREE for 4 months at
www.CooksIllustrated.com/oct12

Complete Guide to Grill Roasting

The oven isn't your only option for roasting meat. For cuts that cook over moderate heat, the grill works just as well—if not better. Here's how to do it right. BY SHANNON FRIEDMANN HATCH

TURN YOUR GRILL INTO AN OVEN

Building a moderate, indirect fire and covering the grill turns it into an outdoor oven for cuts like prime rib, whole chicken, and pork loin.

Venting Helps

Adjusting the vents on the lid and bottom of a charcoal grill helps regulate the heat. We prefer to leave the vents on the lid and grill bottom partially closed, which prevents the coals from burning too fast and helps the grill retain heat.

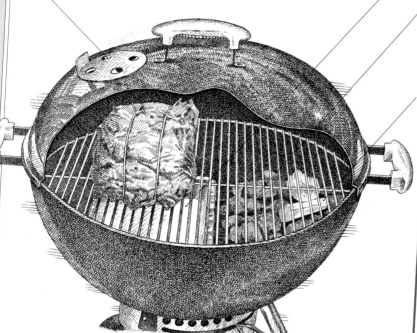

Catchall for Drips

When grill-roasting fatty cuts, we place a disposable aluminum roasting pan beneath the meat to catch drippings.

Briquettes Do It Better

We like natural hardwood charcoal for grilling, but it's not the best choice for grill roasting. Though both hardwood charcoal and briquettes burn fast and hot for the first 30 minutes, we've found that hardwood then abruptly turns to ash while the briquettes keep going, taking hours to fall below 250 degrees.

Smoking Permitted—and Encouraged

If you'd like, add a couple of soaked wood chunks or a packet of aluminum foil–wrapped chips to the fire to infuse the meat with smoke flavor.

Outdoor Cooking Primer

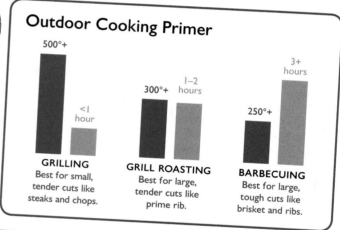

GRILLING	GRILL ROASTING	BARBECUING
Best for small, tender cuts like steaks and chops.	Best for large, tender cuts like prime rib.	Best for large, tough cuts like brisket and ribs.

500°+ <1 hour
300°+ 1–2 hours
250°+ 3+ hours

BUILDING THE FIRE

To create indirect heat on a charcoal or gas grill, we use one of two fire setups: banked or split. Both setups create a hot zone and a cool zone.

BANKED CHARCOAL FIRE

All of the coals are piled on one side of the grill, creating a long-lasting fire with a hotter side and a cooler side. Cuts with more intramuscular fat (like prime rib) or those that benefit from a deeply browned crust (like beef tenderloin) can be quickly seared over the heat to create flavorful browning and then transferred to the cooler side to finish cooking.

SPLIT CHARCOAL FIRE

Coals are piled on either side of the kettle, creating a cool, evenly heated area in the middle; there's no need for rotating the food. Since the two hot areas have fewer coals that burn out faster than coals banked to one side, the setup is ideal for quicker-cooking items, such as whole chickens, that don't need to be seared.

➤ TIP: The coals should be piled high against the side of the grill to form tall but narrow piles; with wider piles, the cool spot in the middle won't be large enough to protect the food from direct heat.

GAS GRILL SETUP

Preheat the grill and then leave the primary burner on high, or as directed in the recipe; turn off other burners and place the food on the cooler side of the grill.

➤ TIP: Rotate the food during cooking so the side that starts out closest to the fire doesn't cook too quickly.

GAS GRILL SETUP

A split fire only works on gas grills with at least three burners, so we typically don't call for this setup in recipes tailored for gas. If your grill does have the requisite burners and configuration, after preheating, turn the center burner off and leave the end burners on. Cook the food over the turned-off burner.

FAVORITE CUTS AND HOW TO HANDLE THEM

For the most well-seasoned, juicy results, we recommend salting or brining these grill-roasting go-tos. Salting is best for cuts that are already relatively moist and well marbled; because it introduces moisture to the meat, brining provides added insurance against drying out for leaner cuts. When salting, use 1 teaspoon of kosher salt per pound of meat; for brining, use ¼ cup of table salt per 2 quarts of water (for a chicken, use ½ cup table salt).

CUT	BRINE/SALT TIME	TYPICAL FIRE	COMMENTS
Top Sirloin Roast (3 to 4 pounds)	Salt 6 to 24 hours	Banked	A lengthy exposure to salt helps tenderize this inexpensive, exceptionally beefy roast.
Beef Tenderloin (6 pounds)	Salt 6 to 24 hours	Banked	Adding a little smoke to the fire will give this mild-tasting roast a flavor boost.
Prime Rib (7 pounds)	Salt 6 to 24 hours	Banked	When trimming, leave about ¼-inch-thick layer of fat to baste the meat and prevent it from drying out.
Whole Chicken (3½ to 4 pounds)	Salt 6 to 24 hours or brine 1 hour	Split	Start the bird breast side down to allow the grill marks to fade and the skin to brown more evenly.
Whole Turkey (12 to 14 pounds)	Salt 24 to 48 hours or brine 6 to 12 hours	Split	Birds larger than 14 pounds risk burning before the interior is cooked through. Propping up the bird on a V-rack helps prevent scorching.
Turkey Breast (5 to 7 pounds)	Salt 6 to 24 hours or brine 3 to 6 hours	Banked	Look for breasts smaller than 7 pounds, which will cook through by the time the fire burns out—no coal replenishing necessary.
Boneless Pork Loin (2½ to 3 pounds)	Salt 6 to 24 hours or brine 1½ to 2 hours	Split	To prevent drying out, look for roasts with at least ⅛-inch-thick layer of fat on one side.
Bone-In Pork Roast (4 to 5 pounds)	Salt 6 to 24 hours	Banked	Ask your butcher to remove the tip of the chine bone and cut the remainder of the bone between the ribs for easy carving.

THREE KEYS TO THE BEST RESULTS

Use a Thermometer
Since the type of grill and even the weather can affect cooking times, the only way to ensure proper doneness is to take the meat's temperature. We highly recommend the instant-read Thermoworks Splash-Proof Super-Fast Thermapen ($89) and the Taylor Instruments Wireless Remote Thermometer ($21.95).

Rack It Up
To protect the bottom crust from turning soggy as the meat rests, set the roast on a wire rack as it cools.

Don't Rush the Rest
Resting meat for at least 20 minutes (or as long as 40 minutes for very large roasts) after cooking helps it hold on to precious juices. Want proof? Four-pound pork roasts cooked at 400 degrees that we sliced immediately after cooking shed an average of 10 tablespoons of liquid, while meat rested for 40 minutes lost an average of just 2 teaspoons.

If You Want Smoke

While charcoal will infuse a little smokiness into grill-roasted meat (gas adds none), adding wood chunks or chips to the fire is the only way to get a real boost of smoke.

CHIPS OR CHUNKS? Chips work on charcoal and gas grills, but use chunks only on a charcoal grill. They must sit on a pile of lit coals to smoke.

WRAP CHIPS IN FOIL Sealing chips in a foil packet with slits prevents them from igniting while allowing smoke to escape. On a gas grill, place the packet directly on top of the primary burner; on a kettle, put it directly on the lit charcoal.

PICK A GOOD WOOD Widely available hickory is our standard. For food that isn't heavily spiced, we also like apple and cherry wood. Avoid mesquite, which can impart an acrid flavor. (See "Wood Smoke Taste Test," page 30.)

GOOD SOAK = MORE SMOKE Soaking chunks in cold water for one hour before use prevents them from igniting over the coals and allows them to smolder slowly. (Wood chips are sometimes soaked, sometimes not, depending on how quickly they're meant to ignite.)

➤**TIP: Instant Soaked Chunks:** Soak wood chunks ahead of time for one hour, drain, seal in a zipper-lock bag, and freeze. When ready to cook, place the frozen chunks on the grill, where they'll defrost quickly.

GRILL-ROASTING RECIPES
Available free for 4 months at www.CooksIllustrated.com/oct12.
Grill-Roasted Pork Loin
Grill-Roasted Prime Rib
Grill-Roasted Turkey Breast
Grill-Roasted Whole Chicken
Inexpensive Grill-Roasted Beef
  with Garlic and Rosemary

ILLUSTRATION: JOHN BURGOYNE

French Apple Cake

This French classic is neither a cake, nor a custard, nor a clafouti. But with a bit of culinary magic, it could be all three.

> ⇒ BY ANDREW JANJIGIAN ⇐

How the heck did they make this?" That's what I asked myself as I sat in a tiny Parisian bistro marveling over a slice of apple cake. I'd tasted plenty of apple cakes before, but none that came anywhere close to this. The custardy base that surrounded the apples was rich, creamy, and dense but not in the least bit heavy. The butter-soft apple slices, simultaneously tart and sweet, were perfectly intact despite their tender texture. And above the rich custard sat a double layer of real cake—light and airy on the inside, with a beautifully golden-brown, crisp top. Together, the contrasting layers made for one amazing dessert.

I appealed to the restaurant owner for a recipe, or at least an explanation of how the cake had been prepared, but she declined. So I returned to the States with nothing more than a memory—and a desire to sort out the secrets of that cake.

The apple cake recipes I unearthed in my research yielded some useful clues. They all followed a simple approach: Stir eggs, milk, vanilla, and melted butter or oil together; whisk in flour, sugar, salt, and leavening until smooth; add cut-up apples; pour the batter into a springform pan; and bake until the fruit has softened and the cake has set. But the results varied widely: Some produced a crumb that was dry, airy, and cakelike, while others were moist and puddinglike. The consistency of the apples varied as well: Some held on to their shape tenaciously, even to a leathery fault, while others practically dissolved into the cake, leaving it a sodden mess. None of the cakes were particularly attractive when sliced; either they were so soft that the slices sagged or the apples dragged beneath the knife, leaving a ragged edge. But most important, not one of these cakes displayed the stratified layers that my Parisian cake did. To get that, I assumed that I'd have to create two separate batters. But for the time being, it made the most sense to focus on one layer at a time.

Observe: Amazing Apple Cake

Video available FREE for 4 months at
www.CooksIllustrated.com/oct12

This rich-tasting cake doesn't contain a speck of butter. Its only fat is oil, which allows more of the apples' tart fruitiness to stand out.

From the Bottom Up

I started with the bottom layer—which meant I actually ended up starting with the apples. When I went back and remade the most promising of the cakes I had tested, a problem became immediately apparent. This particular cake got much of its flavor from using a variety of apples, and they cooked quite differently. Some were so soft as to be mushy, while others were dry and leathery. In addition, the different varieties released moisture into the surrounding cake to varying degrees, creating sodden patches here and there. So my first order of business would be to get the apples to cook more consistently.

The simplest way to do that, of course, would be to limit myself to just one type of apple. Since I wanted the apples to hold their shape entirely, I opted for Granny Smiths; among the firmer apples, their tartness stood out most clearly against the sweet, dense background of the cake. To add back some of the complexity lost by using just one kind of apple, I tossed the apples with a tablespoon of Calvados, a French apple brandy, along with a

teaspoon of lemon juice, and I substituted neutral-flavored vegetable oil for the butter used in the original batter, since the butter flavor tended to obscure that of the apples.

As for texture, the Granny Smiths held their shape nicely after baking, but they were susceptible to leatheriness, which made the cake difficult to slice cleanly. I tried macerating the slices in sugar to soften them, but that only made them drier and therefore tougher when baked. In the end, precooking them in the microwave for a few minutes—just to the point that they were pliable—was all the head start they needed. (See "Ensuring Tender Apples.") In the finished cake, the apples were tender and easily sliced but still retained their structure.

I could now focus on the texture of the custardy cake layer itself. Even with apples that released less water, the cake remained somewhat soupy at the center. I assumed that the batter itself contained too much liquid, so I tried reducing the amount of milk or increasing the amount of flour it contained, but both adjustments only served to make the cake pasty and grainy. Adding another egg did firm it up a bit, but it also left it a bit tough because of the extra white. I then tried adding just another egg yolk. This was a step in the right direction, as it gave the cake more cohesiveness while also enhancing its custardlike qualities. Adding a third yolk improved things even further.

But my cake was still wet at the center. After some thought, I wondered whether the problem was not too much moisture in the batter but rather that it wasn't cooking long and low enough. This cake wasn't merely custardlike; it was a real custard, especially with two extra egg yolks in the mix. I'd been cooking it at 375 degrees, but maybe it could stand to be cooked more gently, allowing the eggs to set up before so much moisture was wrung from the apples. So for my next test, I lowered the temperature to 325 degrees and dropped the cake one rack lower in the oven, so that it would cook from the bottom up and brown more slowly on top. After nearly an hour, a toothpick inserted into the center of the cake came out clean, and after it cooled, the cake had the perfect texture: The apples were tender and moist, fully embedded in a custardy matrix that was silky and smooth from center to edge.

Batter Up: It's a Two-for-One

To produce this cake's distinct layers, we started with a simple base batter and, with key additions, made it work in two ways.

CAKE
Adding extra flour to 1 cup of the base batter created a tender, airy top.

CUSTARD
Adding two extra yolks to the rest of the base batter created a creamy, dense bottom.

Divide and Conquer

At this point I had a perfect custardy base layer and could focus on creating a cakelike topping for it. I wasn't that happy about having to make two separate batters, but I saw no other option if I wanted distinct layers. Rather than start from scratch completely, though, I returned to my tasting notes from those first trial recipes to find one with a batter that had a more cakelike consistency.

But when I looked more closely at the batter recipes, I noticed something interesting: Minor variations aside, they really only differed in the ratio among a few key ingredients. The drier, more cakelike ones contained more flour and fewer eggs, while the more custardy ones had a far higher ratio of eggs to flour. Was it possible that I didn't need two separate batters after all? Maybe I just needed to get my one batter to behave differently, depending on where it was in the cake.

To test this theory, I began by simply doubling the overall amount of batter and dividing it into two portions. I added the apples to one half, poured this mixture into the pan and then poured the remaining batter over it, and baked the cake as before. The results were promising: Though the batter was identical in both layers, the top half—since it lacked moisture-contributing apples—was already much more open and cakelike. It wasn't perfect yet, though. It was a bit too moist and dense, and it didn't form much of a crisp crust on its top surface.

But what if I just increased the flour and lost the extra egg yolks in the top batter? The simplest way to do that, I figured, would be to make the batter in two stages: First, combine all of the ingredients except for the extra egg yolks. Then divide the batter in two and add the yolks to one half and a few tablespoons of flour to the other half.

This time around, the cake was near perfection: creamy and custardy below and airy above. True, it wasn't quite crisp enough on top, but fortunately sprinkling it with granulated sugar just before it went into the oven solved that, giving my cake its own crisp top layer. Finally I had equaled that Paris cake of my memory. But here's the best part: When I served the cake to a baker friend one night, do you know what he said? "How the heck did you do that?"

FRENCH APPLE CAKE
SERVES 8 TO 10

The microwaved apples should be pliable but not completely soft when cooked. To test for doneness, take one apple slice and try to bend it. If it snaps in half, it's too firm; microwave it for an additional 30 seconds and test again. If Calvados is unavailable, 1 tablespoon of apple brandy or white rum can be substituted.

- 1½ pounds Granny Smith apples, peeled, cored, cut into 8 wedges, and sliced ⅛ inch thick crosswise
- 1 tablespoon Calvados
- 1 teaspoon lemon juice
- 1 cup (5 ounces) plus 2 tablespoons all-purpose flour
- 1 cup (7 ounces) plus 1 tablespoon granulated sugar
- 2 teaspoons baking powder
- ½ teaspoon salt
- 1 large egg plus 2 large yolks
- 1 cup vegetable oil
- 1 cup whole milk
- 1 teaspoon vanilla extract
- Confectioners' sugar

1. Adjust oven rack to lower-middle position and heat oven to 325 degrees. Spray 9-inch springform pan with vegetable oil spray. Place prepared pan on rimmed baking sheet lined with aluminum foil. Place apple slices into microwave-safe pie plate, cover, and microwave until apples are pliable and slightly translucent, about 3 minutes. Toss apple slices with Calvados and lemon juice and let cool for 15 minutes.

2. Whisk 1 cup flour, 1 cup granulated sugar, baking powder, and salt together in bowl. Whisk egg, oil, milk, and vanilla together in second bowl until smooth. Add dry ingredients to wet ingredients and whisk until just combined. Transfer 1 cup batter to separate bowl and set aside.

3. Add egg yolks to remaining batter and whisk to combine. Using spatula, gently fold in cooled apples. Transfer batter to prepared pan; using offset spatula, spread batter evenly to pan edges, gently pressing on apples to create even, compact layer, and smooth surface.

4. Whisk remaining 2 tablespoons flour into reserved batter. Pour over batter in pan and spread batter evenly to pan edges and smooth surface. Sprinkle remaining 1 tablespoon granulated sugar evenly over cake.

5. Bake until center of cake is set, toothpick inserted in center comes out clean, and top is golden brown, about 1¼ hours. Transfer pan to wire rack; let cool for 5 minutes. Run paring knife around sides of pan and let cool completely, 2 to 3 hours. Dust lightly with confectioners' sugar, cut into wedges, and serve.

ILLUSTRATION: JOHN BURGOYNE

Ten-Minute Steel-Cut Oatmeal

We wanted creamy, thick oatmeal without the usual 30 minutes of cooking— and we were prepared to challenge centuries of Scottish tradition to get it.

> BY ANDREA GEARY <

"Nemo me impune lacessit" was the motto of the kings of ancient Scotland. It means "No one attacks me with impunity" or, more plainly, "Don't mess with me." I resided in Scotland for several years, and I can confirm that, though the kings are long gone, that fiercely proud and sometimes downright pugnacious spirit lives on. It takes a brave (or perhaps foolish) person to criticize any aspect of Scottish identity, but as it happens I have a serious problem with one of the country's most iconic dishes: oatmeal.

I would eat traditional Scottish oat porridge every day if I could. It's delicious and sustaining, and preparing it couldn't be simpler: Steel-cut oats, which are dried oat kernels cut crosswise into coarse bits, are gently simmered in lightly salted water until the hard oats swell and soften and release some of their starch molecules into the surrounding liquid. Those freed starches bond with the liquid, thickening it until the oatmeal forms a substantial yet fluid mass of plump, tender grains. So, what's the problem? That transformation from gravelly oats to creamy, thick porridge takes 30 minutes minimum; closer to 40 minutes is preferable. There's just no way I can squeeze that into a busy weekday morning.

To reduce the prebreakfast rush, some cooks allow steel-cut oats to just barely bubble in a slow cooker overnight, but I've never had luck with that approach. After eight hours the oats are mushy and blown out and lack the subtle chew of traditionally prepared oatmeal. If I was going to work my favorite kind of oatmeal into my regular breakfast rotation, I'd have to find a quicker way to cook it. My goal: perfect porridge that required fewer than 10 minutes of active engagement.

Don't Be Gruel

Oat cookery has changed very little over the centuries, which explains why I had so few leads on alternative timesaving methods. In fact, the only Scot-sanctioned shortcut I knew was one I'd learned while working as a breakfast cook at a small hotel in Scotland: soaking the steel-cut oats in tap water overnight to initiate the hydration of the grain. Thinking that I'd give this approach some further scrutiny, I prepared two batches of oatmeal using a

After an overnight soak in just-boiled water, it takes only 10 morning minutes to turn steel-cut oats into creamy porridge.

fairly standard ratio of 1 cup oats to 4 cups water. I soaked one measure of the grains overnight in room-temperature water and cooked the other straight from the package and then compared their respective cook times. As it turned out, presoaking saved some time, but not enough. Almost 25 minutes passed before the soaked oats morphed into the loose yet viscous result I was after—only about 15 minutes faster than the unsoaked batch. I wasn't quite convinced that some sort of presoak treatment wouldn't

help, but for now I went back to the drawing board.

As a matter of fact, I had a trick in mind. We'd had the same timesaving goal when developing our Creamy Parmesan Polenta (March/April 2010), and we'd discovered an unlikely addition that sped things up considerably: baking soda. Introducing just a pinch of the alkali to the pot raised the pH of the cooking liquid, causing the corn's cell walls to break down more quickly, thereby allowing water to enter and gelatinize its starch molecules in half the time. I thought that the baking soda might have a similarly expediting effect with my steel-cut oats, so I dropped a pinch into the pot and waited. And waited. Twenty minutes later, I had the creamy porridge I was after, but a mere five-minute savings wasn't going to do it. I decided to ditch the baking soda idea.

I hadn't abandoned the notion of jump-starting the hydration process with a presoak, but I obviously needed a more aggressive method than simply resting the oats in a bowl of room-temperature water. That's when my thoughts turned from presoaking to parcooking. Surely boiling water would hasten the softening of the oats faster than room-temperature water, right? To find out, I brought the oats and the water to a boil together, cut the heat, covered the pot, and left it to sit overnight. When I uncovered the pot the next morning, I knew I was getting somewhere. Thanks to this head start, the coarse, gravelly oats I'd started with had swelled and fully softened. I was encouraged and flipped on the burner to medium to see how long it would take before the cereal turned creamy and thickened. About 10 minutes of simmering later, the porridge was heated through and viscous—but was also mushy and pasty like the slow-cooker oats. Simmering the oats for less time wasn't the answer: It left the liquid in the pot thin and watery. As surprising as it seemed, I could only conclude that parcooking

---

KNOW YOUR OATS

The cereal aisle stocks a variety of oat products—but not all of them make for a good bowl of oatmeal.

GROATS
Whole oats that have been hulled and cleaned. They are the least processed oat product, but we find them too coarse for oatmeal.

STEEL-CUT OATS
Groats cut crosswise into coarse bits. We strongly prefer them in oatmeal; they cook up creamy yet chewy with rich, nutty flavor.

ROLLED OATS
Groats steamed and pressed into flat flakes. They cook faster than steel-cut but make for a gummy, lackluster bowl of oatmeal.

by bringing the oats up to a boil with the water was too aggressive, causing too many starch molecules to burst, which turned the oats to mush and caused the surrounding liquid to become pasty.

Still, things were looking up. A 10-minute cook time was a major step in the right direction. In my next test, I decided to split the difference between the Scottish room-temperature soak and the mushy boiled-water method. Instead of bringing the oats to a boil with the water, I boiled the water by itself, poured in the oats, covered the pot, and then left them to hydrate overnight. The next morning I got the pot going again. With this slightly more gentle method, 10 minutes later the oatmeal was perfectly creamy and not at all blown out or sticky.

I had just one other problem to solve—this one a classic oatmeal quandary. Though the finished oatmeal looked appropriately creamy in the pot, the mixture continued to thicken after I poured it into the bowl as the starches continued to absorb the water. By the time I dug in, the result was so thick and pasty that I could stand my spoon in it.

That's when I seized on my last adjustment: I would cut the heat before the oatmeal had achieved its ideal thickness and then let it sit for a few minutes, until it thickened up just enough. I gave it a whirl, simmering the oatmeal for a mere five minutes and then moving the pot off the heat to rest. Five minutes later my tasters and I dug into a bowl of perfect porridge: creamy and viscous and not the least bit pasty. Goal achieved.

Oat Cuisine

My tasters' only critical comment: Though a bowl of unadulterated oatmeal might be traditional in Scotland, on this side of the Atlantic we like ours loaded up with toppings. Of course I could easily serve my cereal with the usual fixings (brown sugar, maple syrup, dried fruit, etc.), but I wondered if I could change the flavor of the porridge more fundamentally by swapping out some of the water for more flavorful liquids and by adding some punchier ingredients.

Our science editor and I agreed that letting milk or juice sit out overnight might be pushing food-safety limits (water was fine, he assured me), so I looked over my recipe and came up with an alternative approach that worked brilliantly: rehydrating the oats in just 3 cups of boiling water and withholding the last cup of liquid until the following morning, when it could be replaced with milk, juice, or something else right before simmering. This way, I could adjust the ingredients to make enough varieties of oatmeal to please even the most jaded palate. I came up with apple-cinnamon made with cider, a tropical take made with bananas and coconut milk, a carrot cake spin made with carrot juice, a cardamom-scented cranberry-orange variation made with orange juice, and a peanut-honey-banana version made with milk and creamy peanut butter.

As much as the Scots are known for being proud and stubborn, they are also known for their inventiveness and imagination. It is, after all, Scots whom we have to thank for penicillin, Sherlock Holmes, and television. I'm confident that my 10-minute steel-cut oatmeal will appeal to the innovative side of the national character.

TEN-MINUTE STEEL-CUT OATMEAL
SERVES 4

The oatmeal will continue to thicken as it cools. If you prefer a looser consistency, thin the oatmeal with boiling water. Customize your oatmeal with toppings such as brown sugar, toasted nuts, maple syrup, or dried fruit. For our free recipes for Banana-Coconut Steel-Cut Oatmeal and Peanut, Honey, and Banana Steel-Cut Oatmeal, go to www.CooksIllustrated.com/oct12.

4 cups water
1 cup steel-cut oats
¼ teaspoon salt

1. Bring 3 cups water to boil in large saucepan over high heat. Remove pan from heat; stir in oats and salt. Cover pan and let stand overnight.

2. Stir remaining 1 cup water into oats and bring to boil over medium-high heat. Reduce heat to medium and cook, stirring occasionally, until oats are softened but still retain some chew and mixture thickens and resembles warm pudding, 4 to 6 minutes. Remove pan from heat and let stand for 5 minutes. Stir and serve, passing desired toppings separately.

APPLE-CINNAMON STEEL-CUT OATMEAL

Increase salt to ½ teaspoon. Substitute ½ cup apple cider and ½ cup whole milk for water in step 2. Stir ½ cup peeled, grated sweet apple, 2 tablespoons packed dark brown sugar, and ½ teaspoon ground cinnamon into oatmeal with cider and milk. Sprinkle each serving with 2 tablespoons coarsely chopped toasted walnuts.

CARROT SPICE STEEL-CUT OATMEAL

Increase salt to ¾ teaspoon. Substitute ½ cup carrot juice and ½ cup whole milk for water in step 2. Stir ½ cup finely grated carrot, ¼ cup packed dark brown sugar, ⅓ cup dried currants, and ½ teaspoon ground cinnamon into oatmeal with carrot juice and milk. Sprinkle each serving with 2 tablespoons coarsely chopped toasted pecans.

CRANBERRY-ORANGE STEEL-CUT OATMEAL

Increase salt to ½ teaspoon. Substitute ½ cup orange juice and ½ cup whole milk for water in step 2. Stir ½ cup dried cranberries, 3 tablespoons packed dark brown sugar, and ⅛ teaspoon ground cardamom into oatmeal with orange juice and milk. Sprinkle each serving with 2 tablespoons toasted sliced almonds.

Watch the Oatmeal Happen
Video available FREE for 4 months at
www.CooksIllustrated.com/oct12

Really Good Pumpkin Bread

To rescue this bread from mediocrity, start by taking the canned flavor out of the pumpkin.

≥ BY LAN LAM ≤

After testing a half-dozen different recipes for pumpkin bread, I found myself thinking of it as the John Doe of quick breads: No loaf was remarkably bad—and none was remarkably good. They were all just fine.

But if I'm going to make something, even a quick bread, I want it to be more than OK: I want it to be great, something to make guests exclaim rather than yawn. For that, I knew I'd need a bread that had just the right texture—neither too dense nor too cakey—and a rich pumpkin flavor that was properly tempered with sweetness and gently enhanced rather than obscured by spices.

I reasoned that the best pumpkin bread needed to begin with the best pumpkin puree, which, of course, would mean made from scratch rather than canned. Unfortunately, after spending two hours seeding, roasting, scraping, and pureeing (and then washing all the dishes) I'd changed my recipe from "quick bread" to "what-a-pain bread." And after all that, the loaf made with the from-scratch puree was only marginally better than the one made with canned. Forget that idea.

But I was definitely going to have to do something to improve the canned puree, since it had noticeable off-flavors, described by tasters as "metallic" and "raw." After I failed in my attempts to mask that canned flavor by using more spices or adding molasses or prune puree (the spices overwhelmed the pumpkin flavor, while the other two just tasted slightly odd), I wondered if I was overthinking the problem: The puree tasted raw, so why not just cook it? I dumped a can of the puree into a saucepan and stirred it over medium heat until it just barely began to caramelize. I then cooled it down and quickly stirred together another batch of bread using this cooked-down puree. When I pulled the loaves from the oven and sliced them, tasters marveled at the way the bread had changed: The pumpkin flavor was full and rich, no longer raw-tasting or metallic.

Unfortunately, though, the texture of these loaves was a little dense and dry. By cooking down the pumpkin I had driven off some of the moisture, a problem that was easily solved by adding a bit of buttermilk. But caramelizing the puree had also increased its sweetness, throwing off the balance of flavors. I needed to add a bit of tanginess to the mix. It occurred to me that, since gently tangy cream cheese is often slathered onto slices of pumpkin bread, I might try directly incorporating it into the batter. The only downside was that doing so would require dirtying a stand mixer that I would then have to wash. But as I was cooking off my pumpkin puree, I realized that I might be able to just chuck the cream cheese into the pan of hot puree, achieving the dual goals of melting the cream cheese and cooling the puree. I cut a block of cream cheese into small chunks, tossed them into the pan with the hot puree, and stirred—the lumps became streaks that melted away with a few swirls of the spatula.

Now that I'd gone this far, I decided maybe I could put the mixing bowl away and just stir everything together in the saucepan. I cracked my eggs into the measuring cup with the buttermilk, gave them a quick whisk and then stirred them into the puree. Next came the dry ingredients, which were easy to mix in. I flew through the process of dividing up the batter into the prepared pans and put them into the oven. After an anxious wait, I took out loaves that had perfectly balanced flavor plus just the texture I was after: moist but not greasy, with a crumb that was neither cakey nor dense and rubbery.

The only thing left to tackle was adding some textural contrast to my bread. I liked toasted walnuts added to the batter, but I still wanted something more crunchy and flavorful to complement the bread's crumb and flavor. Well, I thought, why not add something to the top? Sprinkled on just before baking, a simple streusel gave the perfect amount of sweet crunch to each slice. As a bonus, the topping prevented the surface of the loaf from getting soggy when stored overnight, so my bread was just as delicious the next day. John Doe no longer, this was a pumpkin bread to make you sit up and take notice.

PUMPKIN BREAD
MAKES 2 LOAVES

The test kitchen's preferred loaf pan measures 8½ by 4½ inches; if using a 9 by 5-inch loaf pan, start checking for doneness five minutes early.

Topping
- 5 tablespoons packed (2¼ ounces) light brown sugar
- 1 tablespoon all-purpose flour
- 1 tablespoon unsalted butter, softened
- 1 teaspoon ground cinnamon
- ⅛ teaspoon salt

Bread
- 2 cups (10 ounces) all-purpose flour
- 1½ teaspoons baking powder
- ½ teaspoon baking soda
- 1 (15-ounce) can unsweetened pumpkin puree
- 1 teaspoon salt
- 1½ teaspoons ground cinnamon
- ¼ teaspoon ground nutmeg
- ⅛ teaspoon ground cloves
- 1 cup (7 ounces) granulated sugar
- 1 cup packed (7 ounces) light brown sugar
- ½ cup vegetable oil
- 4 ounces cream cheese, cut into 12 pieces
- 4 large eggs
- ¼ cup buttermilk
- 1 cup walnuts, toasted and chopped fine

1. FOR THE TOPPING: Using fingers, mix all ingredients together in bowl until well combined and topping resembles wet sand; set aside.

2. FOR THE BREAD: Adjust oven rack to middle position and heat oven to 350 degrees. Grease two 8½ by 4½-inch loaf pans. Whisk flour, baking powder, and baking soda together in bowl.

3. Combine pumpkin puree, salt, cinnamon, nutmeg, and cloves in large saucepan over medium heat. Cook mixture, stirring constantly, until reduced to 1½ cups, 6 to 8 minutes. Remove pot from heat; stir in granulated sugar, brown sugar, oil, and cream cheese until combined. Let mixture stand for 5 minutes. Whisk until no visible pieces of cream cheese remain and mixture is homogeneous.

4. Whisk together eggs and buttermilk. Add egg mixture to pumpkin mixture and whisk to combine. Fold flour mixture into pumpkin mixture until combined (some small lumps of flour are OK). Fold walnuts into batter. Scrape batter into prepared pans. Sprinkle topping evenly over top of each loaf. Bake until skewer inserted in center of loaf comes out clean, 45 to 50 minutes. Let breads cool in pans on wire rack for 20 minutes. Remove breads from pans and let cool for at least 1½ hours. Serve warm or at room temperature.

PUMPKIN BREAD WITH CANDIED GINGER

Substitute ½ teaspoon ground ginger for cinnamon in topping. Fold ⅓ cup minced crystallized ginger into batter after flour mixture has been added in step 4.

Watch Lan Make the Bread
Video available FREE for 4 months at
www.CooksIllustrated.com/oct12

The Whole Chicken Story

Buying a chicken to roast is simple, right? Well, given the myriad brands, confusing labels, and alarming news reports, choosing the best bird has never been more complicated.

> BY LISA McMANUS <

We've seen some pretty staggering statistics about meat consumption in this country, but this one really takes the cake: The U.S. poultry industry, the largest in the world, processes upwards of 8 billion chickens destined for the dinner table each year. Today, Americans consume about 84 pounds of chicken per person annually. These birds, once a protein so luxurious that the 1928 campaign promise to put one in "every pot" seemed unreachable, have become a cheap supermarket staple.

But the ability to pick up a chicken at any local market doesn't make shopping easy. On the contrary, there's a multitude of brands and a wide range of prices—not to mention alarming news reports that raise concerns about health, conscience, and politics. Beyond that, you need a degree in agribusiness to decode most of the packaging lingo: What's the difference between "all natural," "free range," and "organic"? What does "vegetarian fed" mean—and if other birds are not being fed vegetarian meal, just what are they eating? And most important, what tastes best when you strip away the sales pitches?

Those were the questions we started with as we rounded up eight national and large regional brands of whole fresh supermarket chicken, which we seasoned minimally, roasted, and carved into piles of white and dark meat for tasting. (Later, we'd decode the real meaning of all those terms on the labels and see if any of them led us to the best chicken.) What we were looking for: meat that was rich, clean-tasting, tender, and moist. What we got: an astonishing range of flavors and textures. Some birds boasted "chicken-y" meat that was pleasantly moist; others tasted utterly bland or, worse, faintly metallic, bitter, or liver-y. Chalky, dry meat was a common, predictable complaint, but surprisingly, so was too much moisture.

Puzzled by the dramatic differences among the brands, we compared product labels and processing

No More Chicken Little

Today's commercial chickens grow to twice the size in about half the time as chickens raised 60 years ago. These days, most producers use the Cornish Cross, a breed genetically engineered to have more breast meat.

1950
Typical broiler live weight at 10 weeks: 3 pounds.

1980
Typical broiler live weight at 7 weeks: 4 pounds.

2011
Typical broiler live weight at 6 weeks: 6 pounds.

claims; talked to experts; and sent the chickens to an independent laboratory for analysis of their protein, fat, sodium, moisture, and other characteristics to help us figure out what might have shaped our preferences.

Factory Fowl

One characteristic we could rule out immediately: breed. Almost all supermarket chickens are white-feathered Cornish Crosses, a variety that has been engineered to grow to full weight in a mere five to eight weeks, on the smallest possible amount of chicken feed, as well as to feature large breasts and stumpy legs to yield more white meat. "They're breast-meat machines," said Doug Smith, associate professor of poultry science at North Carolina State University. Most of the big poultry companies are "vertically integrated," meaning they control everything from breeding and feeding the birds, to medical care, to slaughter and processing, to transportation, to sales and marketing. This keeps costs down and production up—hence the 8 billion served.

Along the way, intensive farming has led to trade-offs. Typically, birds get doses of antibiotics from their earliest days not only to help prevent and treat diseases rampant in their crowded conditions but also to help them grow faster. Some producers even inject antibiotics into eggs, and most routinely add them to the chicken's feed, a soy and corn mix often bulked up with feather meal (ground-up chicken feathers) and other animal byproducts left over from slaughter, as well as scraps like commercial bakery leftovers. (This may sound bad enough, but it gets worse. In a recent study analyzing feather meal, Johns

Hopkins researchers found residue of arsenic; they also found traces of caffeine and the active ingredients in Benadryl, Tylenol, and Prozac, which had been fed to chickens to alter their moods.) Raised indoors, the birds move little and feed constantly until they're rounded up for the processing plant. Once there, the chickens are hung by their feet and dipped headfirst into an electrically charged bath that stuns them. Next, a machine cuts their throats, and they are bled, plunged into hot water and plucked, eviscerated by machines, and then chilled together in a cold bath (where bacterial contamination can spread).

It is in this water chilling system that chickens plump up, absorbing up to 14 percent of their body weight in water, which is chlorinated to help kill bacteria. (Since chicken is priced by the pound, of course you're paying for that water.) Labeling law says that this water gain must be shown on the product label, and in fact, six of the eight chickens in our lineup were processed this way. Of those six, one was also "enhanced" (read: injected) with a solution of chicken broth, salt, and flavorings, further plumping up its weight.

This water chilling process (and/or enhancing) helped explain why tasters found the meat in several of these birds to be unnaturally spongy, with washed-out flavor.

Up in the Air

That left just two birds that weren't water-chilled. Instead, they were air-chilled, a method in which each bird is hung from a conveyor belt that circulates them along the ceiling of a cold room. According

ILLUSTRATION: JAY LAYMAN

to Theo Weening, the global meat buyer for Whole Foods Markets, this popular European chilling method is just catching on in the United States, and it produces a superior bird. Why? "First, you don't add water, so you don't dilute the flavor," Weening said. He also noted that "air chilling breaks down the muscle tissue and gives a better texture."

Our tasters concurred, noting that these two chickens, Mary's Free Range Air Chilled Chicken ($1.99 per pound), a California-based bird sold out west, and Bell & Evans Air Chilled Premium Fresh Chicken ($3.29 per pound), based in Pennsylvania and sold east of the Rockies, took top marks for flavor and texture. They were juicy without being soggy. What's more, the lab tests showed that these two air-chilled birds also contained more fat, giving them an inherent flavor advantage. (A higher percentage of fat in these birds makes sense, since less water is taking up a percentage of their total composition.)

Chicken Choices

Flavor and texture aside, there's another major factor to consider: your conscience. Consumer concern about poultry factory processing methods has motivated some companies to do a little better by us—and by the birds. This includes limiting or eliminating antibiotic use because of concerns about bacteria becoming drug-resistant and affecting human health;

allowing chickens some (usually limited) access to the outdoors, the only legal definition of "free range"; and using "vegetarian" (free of animal byproducts) feed and swearing off "junk" food like low-quality bakery leftovers and other scraps used to fatten birds. Some brands seek organic certification. Translation: The birds are not given antibiotics; eat organic, vegetarian feed that's free of pesticides and animal byproducts; and have some access to the outdoors (although how much is not regulated—and may, in fact, be extremely limited). (Our top two brands have organic lines, but we chose to taste their more widely available conventional birds.) A few even adopt more "humane" killing processes, including a new method of administering anesthesia developed by animal rights activist and scientist Temple Grandin.

After we tallied the results, we were glad to learn that both of our winning brands, Mary's and Bell & Evans, follow these more responsible production methods (including the use of anesthesia), though neither yet indicates it on the label. (Labeling claims on poultry, however, come with lots of caveats. See "Decoding Chicken Labels.") Other than air chilling, these alternative growing and processing methods may not directly affect the flavor of the chickens, but they may keep the birds, and us, healthier down the road, which makes us feel better about buying them.

Decoding Chicken Labels

Many claims cited on poultry packaging have no government regulation, while those that do are often poorly enforced. Here's how to evaluate which claims are meaningful—and which are full of loopholes or empty hype.

NOT JUST HYPE

➤ **Air Chilled** means that chickens were not water-chilled en masse in a chlorinated bath and the meat did not absorb any water during processing. (Water-chilled birds can retain up to 14 percent water—which must be printed on the label—diluting flavor and inflating cost.) Instead, individual chickens hang from a conveyor belt and circulate around a cold room.

➤ **USDA Organic** is considered the gold standard seal for organic labeling. Poultry must eat organic feed that doesn't contain animal byproducts, be raised without antibiotics, and have access to the outdoors (how much, however, isn't regulated).

BUYER BEWARE

➤ **American Humane Certified** is a program that verifies the use of standards that promote animal health and reduce stress, but these practices are widespread industry norms like ensuring that chickens are stunned before their throats are cut. Some standards aren't humane: Beak cutting of egg-laying hens is allowed.

➤ **Raised Without Antibiotics** and other claims regarding antibiotic use are important; too bad they're not strictly enforced. (The only rigorous enforcement is when the claim is subject to the USDA Organic seal.) Loopholes seem rife, like injecting the eggs—not the chickens—with antibiotics or feeding them feather meal laced with residual antibiotics from treated birds.

➤ **Natural** and **All Natural** are ubiquitous on food labels. In actuality, the USDA has defined the term just for fresh meat, stipulating only that no synthetic substances have been added to the cut. Producers may thus raise their chickens under the most unnatural circumstances on the most unnatural diets, inject birds with broth during processing, and still put the claim on their packaging.

➤ **Hormone-Free** is empty reassurance, since the USDA does not allow the use of hormones or steroids in poultry production.

➤ **Vegetarian Fed** and **Vegetarian Diet** sound healthy, but are they? Since such terms aren't regulated by the government, you're relying on the producer's notion of the claim, which may mean feeding chickens cheap "vegetarian" bakery leftovers. The winners of our whole chicken tasting, Mary's and Bell & Evans, assured us that their definitions mean a diet consisting of corn and soy. –L.M.

TASTING Boneless, Skinless Breasts

Americans roast plenty of whole chickens, but they cook even more chicken breasts. The lean white meat portions account for 60 percent of the chicken sold in stores, and the vast majority of those are the boneless, skinless variety. For that reason, we decided to follow up our whole chicken tasting with an evaluation of the most popular cut.

As it happened, we recommended only one of the eight breasts we sampled without reservations, and it was the only brand to track closely with its whole chicken counterpart. What's more, tasters' comments made clear that while flavor is paramount in whole birds, chicken breasts (which we tasted lightly salted and baked to 165 degrees) are all about texture. In fact, tasters deemed the flavor of this blandest part of the bird more or less the same across the board.

Our investigation homed in on processing. And it was only when we asked the manufacturer of our winner, Bell & Evans, to walk us through its methods that we uncovered a good, albeit peculiar, lead for our findings: Once a Bell & Evans whole chicken is broken down into parts, the breasts are "aged" on the bone in chilled containers for as long as 12 hours before the bones (and skin) are removed. This aging period, it turns out, actually improves tenderness.

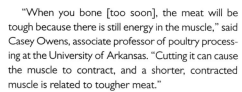

BELL & EVANS
Aged on the bone for up to 12 hours.

"When you bone [too soon], the meat will be tough because there is still energy in the muscle," said Casey Owens, associate professor of poultry processing at the University of Arkansas. "Cutting it can cause the muscle to contract, and a shorter, contracted muscle is related to tougher meat."

Owens also explained that while four to six hours of chilling before boning is effective—and 12 hours is ideal—many companies skip the aging process altogether. Why? Building time into the process costs money. Instead, some opt for shortcut tenderizing methods like electrical stimulation of the carcass, which forces the breast muscle to contract and relax, releasing its energy.

Tasters noticed the difference, lauding Bell & Evans breasts for being "mega-juicy and tender" (not to mention praising their "clean, chicken-y" flavor) and deeming the texture of breasts that came from an electrically stimulated carcass "unremarkable." Its $6.99 per pound price tag makes Bell & Evans the second priciest brand in our lineup, but we think the premium results more than justify the premium expense. For complete tasting results, go to www.CooksIllustrated.com/oct12.

–Amy Graves

TASTING WHOLE CHICKENS

Twenty-one America's Test Kitchen staffers sampled eight brands of whole chickens (seasoned lightly and roasted, in our preferred size of 4 pounds). In blind tastings, tasters evaluated the light and dark meat on flavor, texture, moistness, and overall appeal. Sodium per serving is from product labels; fat percentage is of the whole bird and was determined by an independent laboratory. Information about antibiotics, feed, and chilling method were obtained from packaging labels and/or directly from manufacturers. Scores were averaged and brands appear below in order of preference.

HIGHLY RECOMMENDED

MARY'S Free Range Air Chilled Chicken (also sold as Pitman's)
Price: $1.99 per lb
Distribution: California, Oregon, Washington, Hawaii, Arizona, and Nevada
Antibiotic Use: "No antibiotics ever"
Vegetarian Feed: Yes
Chilling Method: Air
Fat: 14.2%
Sodium: 85 mg per 4 oz serving
Comments: Air chilling plus a higher percentage of fat (compared with the more diluted water-chilled chicken) added up to a bird that tasters raved was "clean," "sweet," "buttery," "savory," "chicken-y," and "juicy," with "richly flavored" dark meat that was "so moist" and "tender." In sum: "Really perfect."

BELL & EVANS Air Chilled Premium Fresh Chicken
Price: $3.29 per lb
Distribution: East of the Rockies
Antibiotic Use: "No antibiotics ever"
Vegetarian Feed: Yes
Chilling Method: Air
Fat: 15.6%
Sodium: 75 mg per 4 oz serving
Comments: Thanks to almost three hours of air chilling, this bird's white meat was "perfectly moist," "rich and nutty," and "concentrated and chicken-y," and its dark meat "silky-tender" yet "firm." Several tasters remarked that it seemed "really fresh" and "clean-tasting." Also helpful to flavor: It had the highest fat percentage of any bird in the tasting.

RECOMMENDED

SPRINGER MOUNTAIN FARMS Fresh Chicken
Price: $1.89 per lb
Distribution: National, with concentration east of Mississippi
Antibiotic Use: "No antibiotics ever"
Vegetarian Feed: Yes
Chilling Method: Water, "may contain up to 5% retained water"
Fat: 6.3%
Sodium: 80 mg per 4 oz serving
Comments: Compared with that of our air-chilled winners, this water-chilled bird's meat was "extremely mild-tasting." It also contained the least amount of fat. Even so, tasters thought both the white and dark meat boasted "nice chew." It bears the seal "American Humane Certified"—which mainly guarantees standard industry practices (see "Decoding Chicken Labels").

COLEMAN ORGANIC Whole Chicken (also sold as Rosie Organic Whole Chicken)
Price: $2.29 per lb
Distribution: National
Antibiotic Use: "No antibiotics"
Vegetarian Feed: Yes
Chilling Method: Water, "may contain up to 5% retained water" (some birds are air-chilled; package will specify)
Fat: 12%
Sodium: 80 mg per 4 oz serving
Comments: Its "super-moist meat" came across as "tender" but "not mushy" in both white and dark samples. However, tasters ranked its flavor as "middle-of-the-road," only "moderately chicken-y," or "a bit bland."

RECOMMENDED, CONTINUED

EMPIRE KOSHER Broiler Chicken
Price: $3.89 per lb
Distribution: National
Antibiotic Use: "Never ever administered antibiotics"
Vegetarian Feed: Yes
Chilling Method: Water, koshered (salted, soaked, and rinsed)
Fat: 9.2%
Sodium: 290 mg per 4 oz serving
Comments: Reactions to this kosher chicken's high sodium level were mixed: Some tasters found its white meat "rich" and "brothy"; others found it a bit too "salty." Fans of its dark meat dubbed it "roasty" and "intense," though a few found it "funky" and "gamy."

RECOMMENDED WITH RESERVATIONS

PERDUE Fresh Whole Chicken
Price: $1.99 per lb
Distribution: National
Antibiotic Use: "Perdue does not use antibiotics for growth promotion"
Vegetarian Feed: Yes
Chilling Method: Water, "may contain up to 4% retained water"
Fat: 9.8%
Sodium: 80 mg per 4 oz serving
Comments: Your "basic," "bland" chicken that some found "super-tender" but others deemed "dry," with meat that "sticks to your teeth." Perdue uses antibiotics "only when necessary" but boasts of being "USDA Process Verified." In this case, it simply means the birds are vegetarian fed (which can mean a diet of bakery scraps) and are not kept caged within the chicken houses—which is standard practice.

GOLD KIST FARMS Young 'n Tender All Natural Chicken (also sold as Pilgrim's)
Price: $1.99 per lb
Distribution: Florida to Arizona, in the South (half of chickens produced are sold as store brands across the U.S.)
Antibiotic Use: Yes
Vegetarian Feed: No
Chilling Method: Water, "may contain up to 5% retained water"
Fat: 14.42%
Sodium: 65 mg per 4 oz serving
Comments: This somewhat "bland" bird had "soft-textured meat that kind of melted in [the] mouth." Others called it "mushy" and "spongy." In sum: "Pretty average chicken, not great."

TYSON Young Chicken
Price: $1.69 per lb
Distribution: National
Ingredients: Contains up to 12 percent chicken broth, sea salt, natural flavorings
Antibiotic Use: Yes
Vegetarian Feed: No
Chilling Method: Water
Fat: 9.4%
Sodium: 150 mg per 4 oz serving
Comments: You know something's fishy when your chicken has an ingredient list. Though most judged it "OK," some found this broth-injected bird "spongy," "wet," and "bland beyond description."

A Better Blender—or Bust

When our affordable favorite went kaput after less than a year, we had to wonder: How much would we need to spend for durability and a little peace of mind?

> BY TAIZETH SIERRA

In 2009, we spent weeks test-driving 10 blenders and eventually found two machines that could easily do it all: crush ice, make frozen drinks, and blend lump-free smoothies, milkshakes, and hummus—and without damaging our eardrums. Those were the Vitamix 5200 and the KitchenAid 5-Speed Blender. We'd already been fans of the Vitamix. This Ferrari of blenders ($449), the darling of restaurant chefs, has gone unmatched in the test kitchen for years. The KitchenAid didn't quite rival the Vitamix, but it proved itself a worthy, far more affordable ($150) alternative, so we ranked it number one.

But since that time, some readers and test kitchen staffers who purchased the KitchenAid reported that their machines leaked or that the jar cracked after less than a year of use. Though many of these folks were die-hard smoothie makers who used their blenders daily, this was hardly the level of durability that we thought we were signing on for. So we circled back to square one with a simple question: Is the Vitamix really the only blender that can stand up to constant, hard-core use, or might there be another, less expensive contender that can also stay the course?

To find out, we corralled nine models—everything from an affordable $40 appliance to our luxe benchmark, the Vitamix, as well as a new copy of the KitchenAid. And you can be sure that we raised the bar since the last round of testing. Hummus, crushed ice, margarita, and milkshake tests were givens, but to separate the workhorses from the wimps, every day for a month we also made smoothies in each one with fibrous frozen pineapple and stringy raw kale.

Nuts and Bolts

The losers—and there were many—were easy to pick out. Some blenders flat-out failed at ice crushing. Others sputtered their way through milkshakes and fruit smoothies. The task of demolishing kale proved the downfall of a number of machines. The best that some could do was chop the leaves into small pieces, while one lesser model completely broke down during the challenge. Only two models plowed through this and every other task without flinching.

To make sense of why these two machines did so much better than the others, we consulted Dr. Daniel J. Braunstein, senior lecturer in mechanical engineering at MIT, who explained that there are three key factors that make or break a blender's performance: jar shape, the number and position of the blades, and motor strength. The motor spins the blades to create a vortex, which pulls the food toward the blades, then to the bottom of the jar, and back up the sides to start all over again.

That's why flat-bottomed jars generally slowed the blending process. Their 90-degree angles impeded flow (think of the speed you can reach taking a curve, as opposed to going around a corner), whereas curvy models, like one by Breville, kept the food moving at a steady clip. Gentle tapering also helped move food to the blades.

The length of the blades and how they were configured also altered a blender's performance; this actually mattered more than whether a jar was fitted with four or six spikes. To maximize the chance that they'd whack the food, it was crucial not only that the blades be fixed at different positions and angles but also that the gap between the blade and the jar be minimal. (This way the food couldn't fall and get trapped at the bottom or pass by at the edges without being chopped.) This "wingspan" helped

Successor to the King?

Proven, exceptional durability and an überpowerful motor helped make legendary but pricey Vitamix a champ. But we have a promising, far less expensive co-winner in the Breville Hemisphere Control. Its smart design features six blades of varying length set at different angles, ensuring that nothing will escape getting whacked (critical to smooth results), as well as a rounded jar bottom that facilitates movement. Like the Vitamix, the Breville is made from crack-resistant Eastman Tritan™ copolyester.

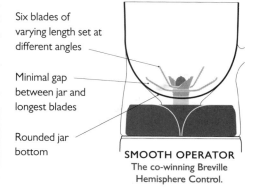

Six blades of varying length set at different angles

Minimal gap between jar and longest blades

Rounded jar bottom

SMOOTH OPERATOR
The co-winning Breville Hemisphere Control.

explain the velvety-smooth drinks made by the better machines, particularly the Vitamix and the Breville (whose blades left a gap of less than ¼ inch from the jar walls), and the lumpy output of lower-ranking models like the Hamilton Beach Wave, whose blades left gaps as wide as ¾ inch from the wall.

The final piece of the puzzle: motor strength. More power behind the blades increases their contact with food and literally gives the blender the energy to face down the toughest jobs, so we weren't altogether surprised when blenders with three of the highest wattages performed best. The top two machines also had automatic shutoffs that allowed their motors to take a breather when faced with particularly strenuous tasks instead of shifting into overdrive and potentially burning out.

Long-Term Commitment

Those factors helped us figure out what makes a blender work well out of the box, but we hadn't yet addressed the KitchenAid's Achilles' heel: durability. Our new copy of this blender did, in fact, show signs of breaking down by the end of testing (the blade apparatus loosened and a rubber gasket popped out), so we removed it from our final rankings. We also took a closer look at the materials used to create blender jars and made an important discovery: KitchenAid manufactures its pitchers from commercial-grade polycarbonate, whereas our top two performers use Eastman Tritan™ copolyester, considered more durable and resistant to impact and the harsh combination of heat, water pressure, and dishwasher chemicals.

Not unexpectedly, one of those two blenders was the Vitamix. Just as it has for years, this test kitchen stalwart proved that there's virtually nothing it can't handle, thanks to its long-armed, well-configured blades and souped-up (1,380-watt) motor. Its performance comes at a steep price, but its exceptional durability (not to mention seven-year warranty) makes it cheaper in the long run than a less expensive blender that needs continual replacing.

But we have a co-winner: the Hemisphere Control by Breville. It sports all three key blender features: long blades, each set at a different position and angle; a bowl-shaped jar; and a relatively powerful (750-watt) motor. As a result, it sailed through every test. At $200, it's less than half the price of the Vitamix. If it proves as durable as that machine—and during the coming months we will continue to test its powers by making multiple kale smoothies in it every day—we may award it the sole top spot. We'll keep you posted.

TESTING BLENDERS

We tested nine blenders, heavily weighting the durability test when we tallied the score. Our former winner, the KitchenAid 5-Speed Blender, is not included in the final lineup. Its blade apparatus loosened during testing and it lost a rubber gasket—problems that we think indicate a high risk of eventual leaking (for details, visit www.CooksIllustrated.com/oct12).

DURABILITY
We evaluated whether performance declined during overall testing, administering a test in which we made kale and frozen fruit smoothies in each model every day for a month. (One brand broke down before we finished testing.)

SPEED
We added yellow and blue food coloring to plain yogurt, timing how long it took to turn green with the blender on low.

NOISE
We recorded decibel levels during each test and noted whether models whined or rattled. Quiet models got 3 stars.

HUMMUS
We processed chickpeas, olive oil, and tahini on high, preferring models that made an evenly emulsified, smooth spread.

FRUIT SMOOTHIE
We pureed frozen fruit with juice and yogurt on high (or the "puree" or "liquefy" settings), assigning high marks for smooth purees.

KALE SMOOTHIE
We blended kale and frozen fruit chunks with juice on high (or the "puree" or "liquefy" settings), assigning high marks for purees with little or no pulp.

MILKSHAKE
We made extra-thick chocolate milkshakes on high, giving highest marks to blenders that left no unprocessed streaks.

MARGARITA
We blended alcohol, juice, ice cubes, and sugar on high (or the "frozen drink" setting). The best blenders produced a uniform slush.

ICE CRUSHING
We pulsed small and large ice cubes (adding liquid only if the blender's manual recommended it). We rated highest the models that produced uniform "snow."

HIGHLY RECOMMENDED · PERFORMANCE · TESTERS' COMMENTS

VITAMIX 5200
Model: 5200
Price: $449

Durability	★★★	Hummus	★★½
Speed	★★½	Fruit Smoothie	★★★
Noise	★★½	Kale Smoothie	★★★
		Milkshake	★★½
		Margarita	★★★
		Ice Crushing	★★★

Years of hard-core test kitchen use have not compromised this blender's superior performance. Its hummus and milkshakes weren't as silky-smooth as others, but its 1,380-watt motor propelled it through most tasks with ease.

CO-WINNER

BREVILLE The Hemisphere Control
Model: BBL605XL
Price: $199.99

Durability	★★★	Hummus	★★★
Speed	★★½	Fruit Smoothie	★★★
Noise	★★★	Kale Smoothie	★★½
		Milkshake	★★
		Margarita	★★★
		Ice Crushing	★★★

With a curved jar, six well-configured blades, and a relatively powerful (750-watt) motor, this blender excelled at almost every task—and at less than half the cost of our co-winner. If it stands the test of time, we may eventually make it our sole winner.

RECOMMENDED WITH RESERVATIONS

NINJA Professional Blender
Model: NJ600
Price: $99.99

Durability	★★	Hummus	★★★
Speed	★★★	Fruit Smoothie	★★½
Noise	★½	Kale Smoothie	★
		Milkshake	★★½
		Margarita	★★
		Ice Crushing	★★★

This 1,000-watt blender, with a central shaft bearing three sets of food processor–like blades, crushed ice in seven seconds. Unfortunately, it left margaritas crunchy and couldn't fully break down tough, fibrous kale.

HAMILTON BEACH Rio Commercial Bar Blender
Model: HBB250R
Price: $109.99

Durability	★★★	Hummus	★★★
Speed	★★	Fruit Smoothie	★★★
Noise	★	Kale Smoothie	★★
		Milkshake	★
		Margarita	★★½
		Ice Crushing	★

This low-cost, moderately powered (480-watt) blender was a whiz with hummus and fruit smoothies. But its fluted jar trapped ice cubes, and its four short, poorly positioned blades couldn't reach kale without a good spatula push.

NOT RECOMMENDED

CUISINART Blend and Cook Soup Maker
Model: SBC-1000
Price: $199

Durability	★★	Hummus	★★★
Speed	★½	Fruit Smoothie	★★
Noise	★★	Kale Smoothie	★★
		Milkshake	★
		Margarita	★★
		Ice Crushing	★★

While it had six blades and plenty of power (900 watts), the large, flat bottom of the jar didn't do this machine any favors. It made excellent hummus but failed to blend a shake, emitting a burning smell as it tried.

HAMILTON BEACH Wave Maker 2-Speed Blender
Model: 53205
Price: $39.99

Durability	★★	Hummus	★★
Speed	★½	Fruit Smoothie	★★
Noise	★★★	Kale Smoothie	★
		Milkshake	★
		Margarita	★½
		Ice Crushing	★

Thanks to its flat-bottomed jar and four very short blades that were not only symmetrical but also set directly atop one another, this 360-watt blender either struggled or flat-out failed to perform most tasks.

OSTER 7-SPEED Reversing Motor Blender
Model: BVCB07-Z
Price: $59.99

Durability	★	Hummus	★
Speed	★	Fruit Smoothie	★★★
Noise	★	Kale Smoothie	★½
		Milkshake	★
		Margarita	★★★
		Ice Crushing	★½

This model had six blades and a pretty strong motor (600 watts), but the jar tapered so dramatically that large chunks and thick food couldn't reach the blades. Its performance declined during testing.

WARING PRO Professional Food and Beverage Blender
Model: PBB201
Price: $99.95

Durability	★	Hummus	★
Speed	★	Fruit Smoothie	★
Noise	★	Kale Smoothie	★
		Milkshake	★
		Margarita	★½
		Ice Crushing	★

Given its four short blades, a cramped jar with a flat bottom, and a weak motor, it was no surprise that this 360-watt blender failed at most tasks. Furthermore, it began emitting a noxious odor and making an awful rattling noise almost immediately.

KITCHEN NOTES

⇒ BY ANDREW JANJIGIAN & DAN SOUZA ⇐

Reheating Steak—Without Overcooking It

The best method we have found for cooking steaks is to slowly warm them in the oven and then sear them in a hot skillet. This produces medium-rare meat from edge to edge, with a well-browned crust. Could this same method work for leftovers?

The answer is yes. When we rewarmed leftover cooked steaks in a low oven and then briefly seared them, the results were remarkably good. The reheated steaks were only slightly less juicy than freshly cooked ones, and their crusts were actually more crisp.

Here's the method: Place leftover steaks on a wire rack set in a rimmed baking sheet and warm them on the middle rack of a 250-degree oven until the steaks register 110 degrees (roughly 30 minutes for 1½-inch-thick steaks, but timing will vary according to thickness and size). Pat the steaks dry with a paper towel and heat 1 tablespoon of vegetable oil in a 12-inch skillet over high heat until smoking. Sear the steaks on both sides until crisp, 60 to 90 seconds per side. Let the steaks rest for five minutes before serving. After resting, the centers should be at medium-rare temperature (125 to 130 degrees).

REWARMED—BUT NOT RUINED
Our method for reheating steak leaves it so juicy and pink that it's hard to distinguish it from freshly cooked meat.

Wood Smoke Taste Test

Hickory and mesquite are the most readily available types of smoking wood, but some grilling pros swear by more exotic woods. To see for ourselves how much difference the choice of wood really makes, we used eight types to smoke chicken, salmon, baby back ribs, and pork chops.

Our old standby, hickory, though acceptable across the board, was deemed "generic." Mesquite's distinctive "barbecue potato chip" flavor was universally disliked, while "sweet," "subtle" apple and cherry wood were big hits in every application.

WOOD	CHICKEN	FISH	BEEF AND PORK	COMMENTS
Apple	✓+	✓+	✓+	An all-around hit, with "sweet," "fruity," "subtly complex" flavor.
Cherry	✓+	✓+	✓+	Well liked for "mild," "fruity" sweetness.
Hickory	✓	✓	✓	Overall, "generic but good," with "balanced" flavor.
Oak	✓	✓	✓	"Mild," "nutty," and "herbal," with hints of "vanilla."
Maple	✓	✗	✓	Evoked pleasant memories of "bacon" for some but was "resin-y" on salmon.
Alder	✗	✓	✓	"Delicate" flavor with notes of "coriander" and "juniper," though some found it "bitter" with chicken.
Pecan	✗	✗	✓	"Intense" and "spicy" with pork but brought "cigarette-like" off-flavors to chicken and fish.
Mesquite	✗	✗	✗	In general, "harsh" and "acrid," reminding some of "burnt rubber."

TECHNIQUE

THE BEST WAY TO SIFT POWDERED SUGAR

For attractive, evenly coated results, the lightest possible touch is a must when dusting desserts with confectioners' sugar.

Hold a fine-mesh strainer in one hand and gently tap its side with a finger from the opposite hand. (Do not shake the strainer itself; this will produce heavy spots.) Move the sieve over the next area to be covered and repeat.

Baking with Rye Flour for Longer-Lasting Bread

Traditional German and Scandinavian breads made with 100 percent rye flour are known for staying fresh for weeks after baking. This is because rye flour is rich in water-absorbent carbohydrates called pentosans that allow it to hold ten or more times its weight in water. (Wheat flour is only able to absorb twice its weight.) What's more, pentosans don't retrograde (stale) and harden into a crystalline structure after baking and cooling, as the starches in other flours do.

We wondered if we could use rye's anti-staling properties to preserve bread, so we made three loaves of our whole-wheat sandwich bread: one according to the original recipe (which calls for 2 cups of bread flour and 3 cups of whole-wheat flour), one in which we replaced ¾ cup (25 percent) of the whole-wheat flour with rye flour, and one in which we subbed 1½ cups (50 percent) of rye flour for the whole-wheat flour. (Rye flour can't be directly substituted for all-purpose or bread flour because it has different gluten-forming properties.)

After storing the bread for five days unwrapped and at room temperature, we compared the loaves. Unsurprisingly, the all-wheat loaf was stale, tough, and dry. The 25 percent–rye loaf had fared only slightly better, but the loaf made with half rye and half whole wheat was remarkably soft and moist—and stayed that way for two more days. The rye did add its characteristic flavor to the loaf but didn't appreciably alter its texture. The bottom line: If you don't mind the distinctive flavor of rye, swapping half of the whole-wheat flour in a bread recipe with rye flour will make it shelf-stable for up to a week.

The Benefits of a Good Rest

Recipes for scones sometimes provide a make-ahead option that involves refrigerating the dough overnight so it can simply be shaped and then popped into the oven the next day. But now we've found that resting the dough overnight has another benefit: It makes for more symmetrical and attractive pastries. Rested dough is far easier to shape cleanly than unrefrigerated dough is, and it bakes up noticeably taller, smoother, and with crispier edges. The explanation is simple: As with other doughs, including pizza dough, resting lets scone dough's gluten relax completely, so that it doesn't snap back during shaping or baking. Does this mean that from now on we'll always rest our scone dough? Not necessarily. But it's nice to know that when we do, our scones will only improve.

NOT RESTED
Squat and not as professional-looking.

RESTED
Taller, with well-defined edges.

Avoiding a Collapsing Weber

The Weber One-Touch Gold 22.5-Inch Charcoal Grill is our favorite kettle grill, but it has a flaw: If you don't install the three-leg assembly supporting the kettle correctly the first time, there's no going back. Removing and reassembling certain parts will cause them to loosen, and sooner or later when you try to move the grill around your backyard, it will start to fall apart or even collapse. With its illustration-only manual, Weber doesn't make this critical assembly easy—nor does it warn you of the consequences if you don't get it right the first time. Here are some tips to help properly assemble the grill.

1. ATTACH 2 LEGS TO TRIANGLE
Following manual, slide 2 legs that get wheels onto long rod of triangle "shelf."

2. PUT HUBCAPS ON STRAIGHT
Slide wheels onto rod next to legs, then gently tap hubcaps on with hammer, taking special care to put on straight. If hubcaps go on at angle, DO NOT REMOVE. Their interior is made of soft aluminum that will mold itself around rod. Removing and reattaching will loosen fit, making hubcaps—and wheels—more prone to falling off.

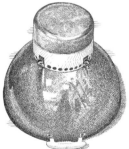

3. IDENTIFY WHERE WHEELED LEGS GO
Turn kettle upside down and identify 2 short tubes directly opposite 1 handle. This is where you will insert legs with wheels. If you insert wheeled legs in wrong tubes, rolling grill will stress contact points, loosening legs and causing grill to become unstable.

4. INSERT WHEELED LEGS; DON'T TWIST!
Insert legs straight into tubes without twisting or rocking. DO NOT REMOVE. Small buttons inside tubes create indentations in soft aluminum of legs as you insert them, ensuring tight fit. Twisting, rocking, or removing and reinserting can lead to too-wide grooves and loose legs.

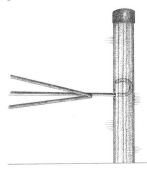

5. ATTACH TRIANGLE TO THIRD LEG
Insert hooked point of triangle into third leg, making sure it goes into hole pointing UP, so it will point DOWN when kettle is turned upright, helping to hold legs together.

6. INSERT THIRD LEG INTO KETTLE
Insert third leg into remaining short tube without twisting or rocking.

Deep Frying 101: Treating Your Oil Right

For fried food that's light, crisp, and not greasy, the proper oil temperature is critical. Most deep frying starts with oil between 325 and 375 degrees, but the temperature drops when food is added. Once the oil recovers some heat, it should remain somewhere between 250 and 325 degrees (depending on your recipe) for the duration of cooking. To maintain the proper oil temperature, use a clip-on deep-fry thermometer and keep close watch.

If the oil starts lightly smoking, that's a sign that it's overheated and starting to break down; remove the pot from the heat until the oil cools to the correct temperature. If the oil has given off a significant amount of smoke, it will impart an off-flavor to foods and should be discarded. (Make sure to thoroughly pat food dry before frying because water can cause oil to decompose, lowering its smoke point by as much as 30 degrees.)

On the other hand, food fried in oil that's too cool will retain too much moisture and emerge soggy. If the temperature drops too low, bring the oil back up to your target range before frying the next batch.

Smoke-Free Roasting

It takes high heat to get roast chicken with crackling-crisp skin, but rendered fat dripping into the bottom of a blazing-hot roasting pan often burns, filling the kitchen with smoke. The usual preventive measure is to add water or broth to the pan to limit the temperature to 212 degrees (too low for fat to burn), but this produces steam that thwarts any skin crisping. Could we have a smoke-free kitchen *and* crispy skin?

Theorizing that a fat-absorbent barrier might help, we filled one disposable aluminum pie plate with rice, one with kosher salt, and one with sliced bread and then placed each plate in a roasting pan underneath a chicken in a V-rack. The results? Remarkably, each fix worked just as well as the next at eliminating nearly all of the smoke. That seemed odd to us, since those three ingredients have rather different absorption capabilities, and it got us thinking that maybe it was the pie plate, not what we put in it, that was helping. We tested an empty pie plate alone and it worked nearly as well as each of the filled pie plates had—but a stack of two disposable pie plates set underneath the V-rack was perfect and didn't require wasting any food.

It turns out that the thin pie plates, and the small air gap between them, absorb and transfer far less heat than the thick-bottomed roasting pan, so the fat drippings never reach smoking temperatures.

NO SMOKING ALLOWED
To prevent a smoke-filled kitchen, stack two aluminum pie plates beneath the roasting rack.

Wet into Dry or Dry into Wet?

Most recipes for bread dough or batter call for combining the dry ingredients separately from the liquid ingredients and then stirring the wet stuff into the dry, rather than the other way around. But does the order really matter? We mixed different types of dough and batter both ways to find out.

With thick pancake batter, we got perfectly acceptable results either way. But for baked goods made from drier doughs, like yeast breads, biscuits, scones, quick breads, and muffins, the order was crucial. When we added the wet ingredients to the dry ones, we got pockets of flour and a messy, crusted mixing bowl. Mixing the dry ingredients into the wet was far more successful. Following this order made for a more supple dough that was easier to combine thoroughly without overmixing (which can overdevelop gluten), so it turned out more delicate, finely textured results. It also made cleanup easier.

BY AMY GRAVES, LISA McMANUS & TAIZETH SIERRA

NEW PRODUCT Individual Steak Thermometers

With an instant-read thermometer, we can find out in a jiffy if steaks are ready. But to see if mini thermometers inserted individually into steaks for the duration of cooking would save a little on poking and checking, we tested sets from CDN, Redi-Check, Rösle, and Outset (priced from $10.95 to $34.95 for four) on grilled steaks. The first issue: All the sets use the doneness temperatures close to those deemed safe by the FDA, which, in our view, leads to overcooked food. While some of the thermometers merely indicated the words "Rare," "Medium," and "Well," those that showed temperature started at 140 degrees—a problem when our rule is that a steak reaches rare at 120 degrees. Second, their miniature faces were barely larger than a nickel, with tiny, hard-to-read type. Third, sticking them into the steaks wasn't easy; if we pushed them in too deep, they gave inaccurate readings. The final blow? Only one set (from CDN; $18.20) had four accurate thermometers. We're sticking with our favorite instant-read thermometer, the Thermoworks Splash-Proof Super-Fast Thermapen ($89), with its large, clear display and fast, accurate readings.

NOT WELL DONE
Like all the sets we tested, these individual steak thermometers from CDN were hard to read, and temperature readings began at 140 degrees, our definition of "medium."

EQUIPMENT UPDATE Pineapple Slicer

Earlier this year we chose the Rösle Pineapple Slicer as our favorite tool for slicing and coring a whole pineapple. The only problem? Its $30 price. Now another manufacturer has come along with a similar corkscrew design costing a third less. For $19.99, the

A CUT ABOVE
The OXO Ratcheting Pineapple Slicer lets us core a whole pineapple quickly and with more confidence than our previous favorite.

OXO Ratcheting Pineapple Slicer let us cut into the pineapple without having to remove and reposition our hands with each twist, making the task go a little faster. The measurement markings on the shaft of the OXO slicer also let us gauge how deeply to cut into the fruit without punching through the bottom. This feature allowed us to remove a good ½ inch more fruit than the Rösle, which had us relying solely on our intuition to know when to stop slicing. Another boon: The OXO's narrower slicing base let us lay it flat in a drawer—not so with the wider Rösle base.

EQUIPMENT UPDATE Immersion Blenders

In 2010 we tested immersion blenders and chose the inexpensive and efficient Kalorik Sunny Morning Stick Mixer as our favorite for the way it effortlessly produced velvety soup and airy whipped cream. Unfortunately, many readers who purchased it found that it wasn't very durable. In some cases, the machine stopped working after the first use. So we bought two fresh copies and returned to the kitchen for daily tests for more than a month. One of the machines blended more than 360 chocolate milkshakes perfectly (including pulverizing malted milk balls and cookie bits) and pureed 30 batches of chickpeas and tahini into hummus before giving up the ghost. But at the other end of the spectrum, another copy of the same blender stopped working during the first 30 seconds of use (far short of the manufacturer's recommended limit of not more than a minute of use at a time). Our new winner is the former runner-up, the KitchenAid 3-Speed Hand Blender ($59.99). Recently, KitchenAid updated this model and it performed beautifully and consistently in all of our tests. Even better, it has no time restrictions on use.

STICKING POWER
The reliable KitchenAid 3-Speed Hand Blender aced our toughest blending tests.

EQUIPMENT UPDATE
Pyrex Liquid Measuring Cup

The tempered-glass Pyrex Liquid Measuring Cup is an American classic; Julia Child's own Pyrex 1- and 2-cup measures are in the Smithsonian's National Museum of American History. For straightforward simplicity and durability, it's hard to beat—years of use in the test kitchen have demonstrated that it is nearly unbreakable, with minimalistic, red-painted markings that resist fading. Last year, Pyrex came out with a new cup that was oversize and cone-shaped, with busy, hard-to-decipher markings that can only be read from the inside. When we tested it against competitors (May/June 2011), it came in last place. What was worse, Pyrex planned to stop making the old cup. Fortunately, since that time, World Kitchen, the U.S. manufacturer of Pyrex, has decided to keep producing the old version.

THE CLASSIC CUP
The unbeatable traditional version of the Pyrex Liquid Measuring Cup is back on the market.

The Pyrex 2-Cup Measuring Cup ($5.99) is our "new" favorite liquid measuring cup.

NEW PRODUCT Bread Warmer

The Bear Bun Warmer ($7.95) was created to make sure everyone gets a warm roll, whether he or she is served first or last. To test how well it works, we soaked the bear-shaped terra-cotta disk in water and then heated it in the microwave for two minutes before wrapping it in a cloth napkin with cinnamon rolls. We tucked the same number of oven-fresh cinnamon rolls in a separate napkin, with no bun warmer. Then we charted their cooling from an oven-warm 148 degrees. After 15 minutes, the rolls with the bun warmer were still piping hot at 143 degrees; rolls wrapped up alone had cooled to 118 degrees. Ten minutes later, rolls with the bun warmer were 120 degrees, and those without had dropped to a cool 98 degrees. The Bear Bun Warmer extends that just-from-the-oven pleasure a bit longer—making it worth the small effort of soaking and preheating.

TOASTY TEDDY
The Bear Bun Warmer keeps rolls and buns oven-warm for 15 minutes.

For complete testing results, go to www.CooksIllustrated.com/oct12.

Sources

Prices were current at press time and do not include shipping. Contact companies to confirm information or visit www.CooksIllustrated.com for updates.

PAGE 23: ELECTRIC JUICER
• Breville Juice Fountain Plus: $149.99, item #HWJE98XL, Harvest Essentials (877-759-3758, www.harvestessentials.com).

PAGE 29: BLENDERS
• Vitamix 5200: $449, item #5200, Vitamix (800-848-2649, www.vitamix.com).
• Breville Hemisphere Control: $199.99, item #BBL605XL, Breville USA (866-273-8455, www.brevilleusa.com).

PAGE 32: PINEAPPLE SLICER
• OXO Ratcheting Pineapple Slicer: $19.99, item #1127580, OXO (800-545-4411, www.oxo.com).

PAGE 32: IMMERSION BLENDER
• KitchenAid 3-Speed Hand Blender: $59.99, item #KHB2351, KitchenAid (800-541-6390, www.shopkitchenaid.com).

PAGE 32: LIQUID MEASURING CUP
• Pyrex 2-Cup Measuring Cup: $5.99, item #6001075, World Kitchen (800-999-3436, www.shopworldkitchen.com).

PAGE 32: BREAD WARMER
• Bear Bun Warmer: $7.95, item #4225, Bay Village Store (440-871-5150, www.bayvillagestore.com).

INDEX
September & October 2012

AMERICA'S TEST KITCHEN
Public television's most popular cooking show

Join the millions of home cooks who watch our show, *America's Test Kitchen*, on public television every week. For more information, including recipes and program times, visit www.AmericasTestKitchenTV.com.

AMERICA'S TEST KITCHEN RADIO

Tune in to our new radio program featuring answers to listener call-in questions, ingredient taste test and equipment review segments, and in-depth reporting on a variety of topics. To listen to episodes, visit www.AmericasTestKitchen.com/Radio.

NEW! ONLINE COOKING SCHOOL

Learn how to think—and cook—like a pro from real test cooks who work here at America's Test Kitchen. We combine personalized instruction with leading-edge technology to offer an unparalleled learning experience. Try it free at www.OnlineCookingSchool.com.

DOWNLOAD OUR FREE
COOK'S ILLUSTRATED iPHONE APP

Features a collection of our top recipes, along with tastings, videos, and useful timer and shopping list features. CooksIllustrated.com members can access 19 years of recipes, videos, tastings, and more. Go to www.CooksIllustrated.com/iPhone.

Follow us on Twitter: twitter.com/TestKitchen
Find us on Facebook: facebook.com/CooksIllustrated

Pumpkin Bread, 24

Mediterranean Braised Green Beans, 12

Skillet Chicken Fajitas, 9

Ten-Minute Steel-Cut Oatmeal, 23

Meatier Meatloaf, 7

Avocado Salad with Tomato and Radish, 13

Thai-Style Stir-Fried Noodles with Chicken, 15

Easy Grilled Boneless Pork Chops, 11

French Apple Cake, 21

Indian-Style Spinach with Fresh Cheese, 19

PHOTOGRAPHY: CARL TREMBLAY; STYLING: MARIE PIRAINO

Brown Tepary

Zuni
Gold

Pinquito

Black Calypso

Ayocote
Morado

Zolfini

Snowcap

Midnight
Black

Ojo
de Cabra

Mortgage Lifter

Sangre
de Toro

Christmas Lima

Rio Zape

HEIRLOOM BEANS

NUMBER 119

NOVEMBER & DECEMBER 2012

COOK'S
ILLUSTRATED

Pepper-Crusted
Beef Tenderloin
The Science of Peppercorns

Turkey on the Grill

Updating
Shepherd's Pie
Less Work, Better Pie

Top 20 Ways to Save
Time in the Kitchen

Testing Pepper Mills
Does $100 Buy a Better One?

Best Vegetarian Chili
Finding Meaty Flavor

Tasting Cocoa Powders
Supermarket Standby Wins

Better Baked Eggs
Roasted Root Vegetables
Rethinking Biscotti

www.CooksIllustrated.com
$5.95 U.S./$6.95 CANADA

0 74470 62805 7

1 2>

CONTENTS

November & December 2012

COOK'S ILLUSTRATED

Founder and Editor **Christopher Kimball**
Editorial Director **Jack Bishop**
Editorial Director, Magazines **John Willoughby**
Executive Editor **Amanda Agee**
Test Kitchen Director **Erin McMurrer**
Managing Editor **Rebecca Hays**
Senior Editors **Keith Dresser**
Lisa McManus
Senior Editor, Features **Elizabeth Bomze**
Associate Editors, Features **Molly Birnbaum**
Danette St. Onge
Copy Editors **Nell Beram**
Megan Chromik
Associate Editors **Andrea Geary**
Amy Graves
Andrew Janjigian
Chris O'Connor
Dan Souza
Test Cook **Lan Lam**
Assistant Editors **Hannah Crowley**
Shannon Friedmann Hatch
Taizeth Sierra
Assistant Test Cooks **Dan Cellucci**
Sara Mayer
Celeste Rogers
Executive Assistant **Christine Gordon**
Assistant Test Kitchen Director **Gina Nistico**
Test Kitchen Manager **Leah Rovner**
Senior Kitchen Assistant **Meryl MacCormack**
Kitchen Assistants **Maria Elena Delgado**
Ena Gudiel
Andrew Straaberg Finfrock
Executive Producer **Melissa Baldino**
Associate Producer **Stephanie Stender**
Production Assistant **Kaitlin Hammond**
Contributing Editors **Matthew Card**
Dawn Yanagihara
Consulting Editor **Scott Brueggeman**
Science Editor **Guy Crosby, Ph.D.**
Managing Editor, Web **Christine Liu**
Associate Editors, Web **Eric Grzymkowski**
Mari Levine
Roger Metcalf
Senior Video Editor **Nick Dakoulas**

Design Director **Amy Klee**
Art Director **Julie Cote**
Deputy Art Director **Susan Levin**
Associate Art Director **Lindsey Timko**
Designer, Marketing/Web **Mariah Tarvainen**
Staff Photographer **Daniel J. van Ackere**
Photo Editor **Steve Klise**

Vice President, Marketing **David Mack**
Circulation Director **Doug Wicinski**
Circulation & Fulfillment Manager **Carrie Fethe**
Partnership Marketing Manager **Pamela Putprush**
Marketing Assistant **Joyce Liao**
Customer Service Manager **Jacqueline Valerio**
Customer Service Representative **Jessica Haskin**

Chief Operations Officer **David Dinnage**
Production Director **Guy Rochford**
Senior Project Manager **Alice Carpenter**
Production & Traffic Coordinator **Brittany Allen**
Asset & Workflow Manager **Andrew Mannone**
Production & Imaging Specialists **Judy Blomquist**
Heather Dube
Lauren Pettapiece
Systems Administrator **Marcus Walser**
Business Analyst **Wendy Tseng**
Web Developers **Chris Candelora**
Cameron MacKensie
Human Resources Director **Adele Shapiro**

VP New Media Product Development **Barry Kelly**
Social Media Manager **Steph Yiu**

Chief Financial Officer **Sharyn Chabot**
Director of Sponsorship Sales **Anne Traficante**
Retail Sales & Marketing Director **Emily Logan**
Client Service Associate **Kate May**
Sales Associate **Morgan Ryan**
Publicity **Deborah Broide**

PRINTED IN THE USA

FRUIT CONFECTIONS Popular in Asia, tart HAW FLAKES are based on the bright-red hawthorne berry. Chewy COCADAS, sold throughout Latin America, are a combination of shredded coconut, sugar syrup or sweetened condensed milk, and almond or vanilla extract. In Lebanese MALBAN, apricot paste surrounds a pistachio-studded jelly or nougat center. Dusted with confectioners' sugar, TURKISH DELIGHT or *lokum* is made with fresh fruit juice, like lemon. Intensely flavored PÂTES DE FRUITS, made by cooking down fruit with sugar, are coated with coarse sugar. TAMARIND CANDY is a sour, spicy, and salty treat popular in Thailand and Mexico. Bittersweet ORANGETTES are made by simmering orange peels in sugar syrup before dipping them in chocolate. DRIED FIGS and CORDIAL CHERRIES get a shot of liquor filling and a chocolate dunk. In DATE NUT ROLLS, the sweet fruit is enhanced with a coconut coating and a blanched almond crown. COVER *(Persimmons)*: Robert Papp; BACK COVER *(Fruit Confections)*: John Burgoyne

America's Test Kitchen is a very real 2,500-square-foot kitchen located just outside Boston. It is the home of *Cook's Illustrated* and *Cook's Country* magazines and is the workday destination of more than three dozen test cooks, editors, and cookware specialists. Our mission is to test recipes over and over again until we understand how and why they work and until we arrive at the best version. We also test kitchen equipment and supermarket ingredients in search of brands that offer the best value and performance. You can watch us work by tuning in to *America's Test Kitchen* (AmericasTestKitchenTV.com) on public television.

RECIPES THAT WORK®

WHAT YOU NEED (AND NO MORE)

I was recently given a book titled *Vermont Is Where You Find It*. Full-page black-and-white photos face off against simple snippets of conversation on the opposite page. One of my favorites is, "Did you ever find the horse that everybody's been looking for?" The answer: "I thought if I was a horse where would I go and I went and he had!" I also liked, "Hey, you, how do I get to the Plattsburg Ferry?" The reply was, "If I was going to the Plattsburg Ferry, I wouldn't start from here." The last conversation was, "How far is it to Fairfax?" "Dunno." "Does this road go to Fairfax?" "Dunno." "Say, you don't know much, do you?" "Nope . . . but I ain't lost!"

I found myself picking up the book over and over again, looking at the photos, and rereading the bits of humor. Did I describe the book? Well, it's 7 by 9 inches; it's thin, just 120 pages; and it's hardbound with a faded barn-red cloth cover. Like Vermont, it's unassuming.

I soon realized that the book had captured the essence of Vermont: Make a life from just what you need. The clothes are sensible, the farm equipment is old and just good enough to get the job done, and the houses are white clapboard, with higgledy-piggledy additions added only when a family has grown beyond the four walls. A Vermont landscape slowly develops into a perfectly natural state, groomed by cows and horses, tilled, seeded, and harvested to produce winter fodder, and houses are placed in practical spots, near a road and not high up on a mountainside since Vermonters never look out a window to admire the view. (That's because they are outside all day in the middle of the view.) Barns, sheds, henhouses, and sugar shacks are all located near the back porch so it's easy to do chores. Large maples line up next to stone walls since the meadows in between are meant for grazing. Every bit of landscape is there for a purpose, because it's useful, or has finally outlived its purpose, at which point the tractor or harrow is left to rust at the exact spot where it broke down.

The same can be said for conversation in Vermont; why use 10 words when five will do? Calvin Coolidge was once introduced with a long oratory regarding the virtues of a sturdy oak walking stick that was to be presented to the president as he came to the podium. When the speech was over, he rose, accepted the gift, looked at it for a few seconds, and said firmly, "Ash." One word was sufficient. Economy of words is a lost virtue.

The images come one after another: a bearded old-timer whittling a stick, his cap tilted back and off to one side; another wearing a banded fedora in a rocker, reading the Burpee catalog. Kids and dogs around the water pump, in the backs of wagons, and on the front porch of the country store. A Gloucestershire Old Spot sow with a litter of piglets. Farmer Johns, work jackets frayed at the cuffs, hats with earflaps, and tall rubber boots half-laced. An older man in a wool three-piece suit with a weathered, contemplative face. Flatbed wagons pulled by teams with towering mounds of loose hay. A bend in the dirt road, skirting around a 200-year-old maple; a road twisting down out of the hills toward a town in a distant valley; a dust cloud on a dry, dirt road from a horse pulling a dogcart; and a hot, summer

Christopher Kimball

road ending in a covered bridge. Dumpling women with flower-print dresses and wire-rimmed spectacles sewing patchwork comforters. White churches and white marble tombstones. Snow-dusted yards, dented sap buckets, piles of rough kindling, and axes held in midair. Barns attached to houses, carriage barns, horse barns, and three-story barns. Corn being shucked, cows being milked, and logs being sawn with two-man crosscut saws.

The book asks, "What's he talkin' about?" The answer is, "He don't say." And one about sheep: "Nice lot of sheep up there on the hill . . . 'bout ready for shearin', too." The response: "Appears so . . . from this side."

Then, all of a sudden, I realized my mistake. Old-time Vermonters didn't own anything. Things were borrowed to make a living: a maple tree, a horse team, a wagon, or a water pump. The objects in those landscapes owned themselves: the trees, the dogs, the cows, the pastures, and the winding roads. What old-time Vermonters needed to live happily was to live without needing.

I end with a story that is no stranger to this column. A city kid was visiting Vermont for the summer and was seen poking a toad with a stick. A local boy came up and said, "Stop poking that toad." The city kid said, "Well, it's my toad, and I guess I can do what I like," at which point the Vermont boy looked at him hard and then said slowly, "Here in Vermont, he's his own toad." Just so.

FOR INQUIRIES, ORDERS, OR MORE INFORMATION

CooksIllustrated.com
At CooksIllustrated.com, you can order books and subscriptions, sign up for our free e-newsletter, or renew your magazine subscription. Join the website and gain access to 20 years of *Cook's Illustrated* recipes, equipment tests, and ingredient tastings, as well as companion videos for every recipe in this issue.

COOKBOOKS
We sell more than 50 cookbooks by the editors of *Cook's Illustrated*.
To order, visit our bookstore at CooksIllustrated.com.

COOK'S ILLUSTRATED MAGAZINE

Cook's Illustrated magazine (ISSN 1068-2821), number 119, is published bimonthly by Boston Common Press Limited partnership, 17 Station St., Brookline, MA 02445. Copyright 2012 Boston Common Press Limited Partnership. Periodicals postage paid at Boston, Mass., and additional mailing offices, USPS #012487. Publications Mail Agreement No. 40020778. Return undeliverable Canadian addresses to P.O. Box 875, Station A, Windsor, ON N9A 6P2. POSTMASTER: Send address changes to *Cook's Illustrated*, P.O. Box 6018, Harlan, IA 51593-1518. For subscription and gift subscription orders, subscription inquiries, or change-of-address notices, visit us at AmericasTestKitchen.com/customerservice, call us at 800-526-8442, or write us at *Cook's Illustrated*, P.O. 6018, Harlan, IA 51593-1518.

FOR LIST RENTAL INFORMATION Contact Specialists Marketing Services, Inc., 777 Terrace Ave., 4th Floor, Hasbrouck Heights, NJ 07604; 201-865-5800.

EDITORIAL OFFICE 17 Station St., Brookline, MA 02445; 617-232-1000; fax 617-232-1572. Subscription inquiries, visit AmericasTestKitchen.com/customerservice or call 800-526-8442.

POSTMASTER Send all new orders, subscription inquiries, and change-of-address notices to *Cook's Illustrated*, P.O. Box 6018, Harlan, IA 51593-1518.

NOTES FROM READERS

⇒ BY ANDREA GEARY, LAN LAM & CELESTE ROGERS ⇐

Miracle Scallions

A friend told me that if you store cut scallions in a glass of water, they'll grow back. Is that true?

JEAN GORDON
BEAVERCREEK, ORE.

➤ Intrigued, we trimmed three bunches of scallions to about 3 inches above the white bulbs and set each bunch in a glass with 2 inches of tap water. We placed the glasses on a sunny windowsill, changed the water daily, and watched for developments.

We were happily surprised to find that the scallion tops grew back quickly—about an inch per day. After a week, we cut off the new green tops and tasted them. They were pleasantly pungent and actually more crisp and fresh-tasting than many store-bought scallions. Encouraged, we repeated the process with the same scallions; this time the tops grew half as fast, came back skinnier, and tasted a bit milder.

The nutrients stored in the scallion's white bulb are sufficient to regrow the tops once or twice, but the plants eventually run out of fuel. If you use scallion greens more often than whites, though, this is a clever way to ensure that you'll always have a supply on hand. One shopping note: Select scallions with roots longer than ½ inch, as they'll grow faster.

DAY 1   DAY 3

Hot or Cold Water for Stock?

Why do some recipes for chicken stock start with cold water and others with boiling water? Does the temperature really matter?

WHITNEY HOLLAND
HINGHAM, MASS.

➤ To find out, we prepared a recipe for simple chicken stock both ways, adding 4 quarts of either cold tap water or boiling water to raw chicken pieces in two pots and then gently simmering both stocks for 3 hours.

Tasters noted that the cold-water-start sample was more transparent, while the stock made with boiling water was slightly cloudy. As for flavor, tasters couldn't detect any significant differences. Our science editor explained that the higher initial temperature of the boiling water extracts more insoluble proteins from the meat and bones, making the stock appear cloudy as it cools back down to a simmer. (The other broth was simply brought to a gentle simmer and never reached a full boil.) These insoluble proteins, however, don't contribute any taste.

In our book, that's good news: With no need to boil water separately, there's one less thing to worry about when making stock.

"Real" Buttermilk?

I recently spotted "real" buttermilk at my supermarket. How is it different from the buttermilk that I usually see?

ROGER ROBINSON
NEW YORK, N.Y.

➤ In the old days, buttermilk was simply the liquid left behind after cream was churned into butter. As unpasteurized cream sat "ripening" for a few days before churning, naturally occurring bacteria caused it to ferment by converting milk sugars into lactic acid, which made the resulting buttermilk mildly sour and slightly thickened.

But since virtually all milk and cream is now pasteurized at high temperatures, a process that kills off those bacteria, most buttermilk sold today is cultured buttermilk, made by reintroducing lactic-acid bacteria to pasteurized skim or low-fat milk. Often, it's also reinforced with salt and thickeners like carrageenan and starch. Few commercial manufacturers today sell buttermilk that's truly a byproduct of the butter-making process, and the only one we found locally was Kate's Real Buttermilk. (Even Kate's, though, is made by adding bacterial cultures, since its butter is churned from pasteurized cream.)

We tested Garelick Farms Cultured Lowfat Butter Milk against Kate's. Though Garelick Farms, unlike Kate's, contains additives, we noticed little difference in flavor or consistency when we tasted the two straight. (Some tasters noted that Kate's was a bit "brighter.") We then used both in our buttermilk drop biscuits and in creamy coleslaw. Again, most tasters found them identical. Since conventional buttermilk is easier to find and costs about 65 cents less per quart, we're happy to continue using it for baking and cooking.

Prepping Apples in Advance

Will it affect the quality of the filling if I cut apples the day before I assemble apple desserts?

PETER JENKINS
ATLANTA, GA.

➤ Cutting damages the cells of apples, allowing enzymes and compounds stored separately within each cell to mix with one another and with the oxygen in the air, creating brown-colored pigments. To see if this brown color does anything more than mar the fresh look of the fruit, we compared an apple crumble made with just-cut fruit with crumbles made with apples that we had cut and peeled (and refrigerated in zipper-lock bags) one and two days earlier. The brown apples and the fresh apples baked up equally tender and juicy and were similar in flavor, and—surprisingly—all had pretty much the same light golden color. It turns out that as the apples' cell walls rupture during baking, acids are released that partially break down the brown pigments, resulting in a lighter color.

BEFORE BAKING

The bottom line: If you're going to cook apples, it's fine to prep them a day or two in advance.

AFTER BAKING

Aerating White Wine

I know that it's common to aerate red wine before serving, but now I'm seeing white-wine aerators for sale. Is there any point in aerating white wine?

KATE LANCASTER
CAMBRIDGE, MASS.

➤ Typically, wine is aerated by letting it rest in a wide, shallow vessel for anywhere from a few minutes to several hours. Though this is most commonly done with young red wines, some connoisseurs advocate it for young whites as well. To see for ourselves if aerating white wines is beneficial, we tested the technique on 11 bottles representing a range of ages, varietals, qualities, and styles. We used the "flash" aerating technique that we recommended for reds in our January/February 2012 issue, when we found that pouring wine back and forth 15 times softened tannins, brought out complex aromas, and balanced flavors.

We quickly learned that 15 pours was far too many for delicate whites, making them taste watery, so for subsequent tastings, we poured each wine between pitchers only five times before comparing them with unaerated samples. Most tasters found the aerated samples "less fruity" and "less acidic," not to mention "dull," "flat," and "characterless."

Our conclusion? Without the harsh tannins that make some young reds hard to drink, white wines don't benefit from aeration, and "white-wine aerators" are nothing more than a gimmick.

Strange-Looking Scallops

I recently cooked some scallops and one of them was a pinkish color, not white like the others. I threw it out since I was afraid that there was something wrong with it—but was there?

EILEEN HANNA
SAN JOSE, CALIF.

➤ The part of the scallop that's sold at the fish counter is the large adductor muscle that opens and closes its shell. This muscle takes its color from the reproductive gland that lies next to it inside the shell. In male scallops, the gland is grayish white and hence the muscle remains white. Female scallops turn pink only when they're spawning; during this period, their glands fill with orange roe and turn bright coral, giving the adductor muscle a rosy hue.

To see if there were any differences besides color, we pan-seared and tasted white male scallops alongside peachy female scallops. They cooked in the same amount of time and had identical textures, although tasters did note that the pink scallops—which retained their tint even after cooking—had a somewhat sweeter, richer flavor. Both colors, however, are absolutely normal and do not indicate anything about the freshness, doneness, or edibility of a scallop.

FEMALE   **MALE**
Coral-colored female scallops taste slightly sweeter and richer than white male scallops.

Resting Citrus Juice for Cooking

In your March/April 2012 issue, you recommended resting lemon and lime juices before using them in drinks to improve flavor. Does this also make a difference in cooking?

COURTNEY ANDERSON
CAMBRIDGE, MASS.

➤ With juices destined for citrus ades and cocktails, we found that a 4-hour rest allowed aromatic compounds in the lemon and lime oils to oxidize, for a mellower yet more complex flavor. To address your question, we made lime bars and *spaghetti al limone* with both fresh-squeezed and rested juices.

Many tasters asserted that the cookies made with

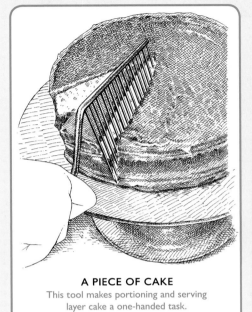

A PIECE OF CAKE
This tool makes portioning and serving layer cake a one-handed task.

Your tool is a cake breaker from the 1930s or '40s. According to the 1931 patent, C.J. Schneider's invention promised to break cake into "even, beautiful portions, free from crumbs, leaving the most delicate cake, frosting, or filling intact."

We purchased a vintage breaker and tried it out, pressing the 3½-inch, chrome-plated prongs straight down through a frosted two-layer cake and then turning the Bakelite handle to the right to release the slice onto a plate. The gadget formed neat wedges without pushing crumbs into the filling the way a chef's knife did. The prong marks were barely noticeable, and as each slice was separated, it was easy to plate it with just a twist of the wrist

With a delicate angel food cake, the tool was less successful: The prongs seriously squashed our airy cake and left deep grooves in the sides of each slice, whereas a sharp serrated knife sliced cleanly through the crumb without crushing it.

rested lime juice were more "lime-y." But when it came to the lemon-dressed spaghetti, the results were less clear-cut. A few tasters found the pasta made with rested lemon juice more flavorful, while others felt that the batches tasted the same.

Even with relatively simple recipes like these, the many variables that affect citrus flavor during cooking (including the length of cooking time, the amount of heat and stirring, and even the serving temperature) make it nearly impossible to predict when resting juice will be worthwhile—but it certainly can't hurt.

Strong Coffee Made Drinkable

I saw a recipe for coffee that called for adding eggshells to the ground coffee before brewing. What is the purpose of this addition?

KATELYN WARDEN
WALTHAM, MASS.

➤ The tradition of adding eggshells to brew is linked with so-called cowboy (or campfire) coffee, which is made by boiling ground coffee in water. Since the resulting drink can taste acidic, bitter, or too strong due to the high heat (which releases tannic acids) and extended contact between the coffee and the water, some campfire cooks add a crumbled eggshell to the mix in hopes of tempering sharp flavors. The finished drink is then strained or ladled off, leaving the grinds and shell behind.

The practice makes a lot of sense: Eggshells are composed mostly of calcium carbonate, a fairly alkaline material that has the ability to absorb some of the acid in the coffee. In fact, when we made traditional and campfire brews with and without eggshell added to the ground coffee, the eggshell samples boasted a significantly mellower (but less complex) taste than the shell-less ones.

We wondered if eggshells could also be used to extract bitter compounds from coffee that accidentally turns out too strong, so we purposely brewed a batch for too long, lightly crushed an eggshell (rinsed in vinegar and then water to kill any bacteria), stirred it into the potent coffee, and strained out the shell. Indeed, this quick treatment produced a milder cup.

IT ACTUALLY WORKS
Adding a crumbled eggshell to coffee mellows its flavor.

Erratum

In our September/October 2012 issue, we incorrectly used the phrase "genetically engineered" to describe the poultry industry's use of selective crossbreeding to develop specific traits in chickens raised for meat. This phrase was not meant to give the impression that the chicken's genome was altered artificially through genetic modification.

SEND US YOUR QUESTIONS We will provide a complimentary one-year subscription for each letter we print. Send your inquiry, name, address, and daytime telephone number to Notes from Readers, *Cook's Illustrated*, P.O. Box 470589, Brookline, MA 02447, or to NotesFromReaders@AmericasTestKitchen.com.

Quick Tips

⇒ COMPILED BY SHANNON FRIEDMANN HATCH ⇐

Pick Up (Chop)Sticks

While cracking eggs into a hot skillet, Abby Oelker of Cambridge, Mass., accidentally dropped a piece of shell into the pan. Thinking quickly, she removed the pan from the heat, grabbed a pair of chopsticks, and carefully extracted the shell without burning her fingers or disrupting the sizzling eggs.

Thinking Outside the (Wine) Box

Instead of discarding her box of wine after finishing the last glass, Barbara Ann Pentrack of Lancaster, Ohio, saved it for stowing and dispensing reusable plastic grocery bags. She removed the wine bag and spout and then filled the empty box with plastic bags. When she needs one, she pulls it through the hole in the front of the box.

Make Your Own Cake-Decorating Comb

Eliza Lawrence of Otisfield, Maine, has found a use for the unsolicited credit cards that she receives in the mail.

1. Trim the long side of a clean credit card with a pair of pinking shears or other decorative scissors.

2. After frosting a cake, use the serrated edge of the card to create a ridged design along the sides. (The flat edge of the card can be used to smooth the frosting.)

A Hot Potato Trick

Many potato recipes call for processing hot peeled potatoes through a ricer. Veronica Parsons of Mountain View, Calif., and Sandra Brown of Mississauga, Ontario, realized that they could save a step—and their fingers—by ricing the spuds skin on. (Note: The discarded skins need to be cleaned from the hopper after each press.)

Thumbs-Up Cookie Shaping

While thumbprint cookies get their name from the digit that's used to make the jam-filled indentation, Linda George of Twain Harte, Calif., prefers to use a clean rubber wine cork. It creates a perfect circle every time and keeps her hands clean.

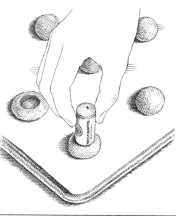

A Slick New Use for Olive Oil Tins

Rather than purchase a caddy to keep her cooking utensils within reach on the countertop, Therese McRae of Bellevue, Wash., repurposed an empty gallon-size olive oil tin by removing its top with a can opener. An added bonus: Its metal front holds a magnetized kitchen timer.

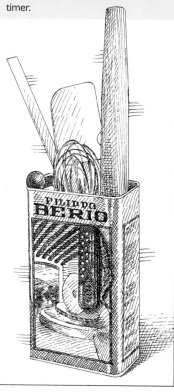

SEND US YOUR TIPS We will provide a complimentary one-year subscription for each tip we print. Send your tip, name, and address to Quick Tips, *Cook's Illustrated*, P.O. Box 470589, Brookline, MA 02447, or to QuickTips@AmericasTestKitchen.com.

ILLUSTRATION: JOHN BURGOYNE

Stopping Hot Splashes

An immersion blender creates a one-pot solution for pureeing ingredients into smooth soups. However, unlike a traditional blender with an airtight top, the handy tool is little more than a stick with a blade and the hot contents can splatter out when it's in use. Ruth TerBush-Nelle of Petoskey, Mich., cuts a hole in a disposable aluminum pan, inverts it on top of the pot, and inserts the immersion blender in the hole to prevent any mess.

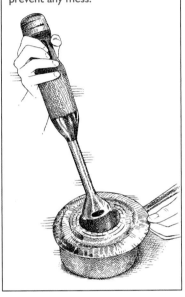

Easy Minced Ginger

Mincing large quantities of fibrous ginger can be a chore. Freezing the peeled root before mincing helps, but Jeffrey Weiss of Dallas, Texas, has found that slicing the frozen ginger and giving the pieces a spin in his rotary grater completes the task in no time.

Pop Secret Seasoning

Sprinkling popcorn with table salt usually results in a pile of salt at the bottom of the bowl—and a bland snack. Clingy superfine popcorn salt is available for purchase, but Pam Sansbury of Midwest City, Okla., has found that it's easy to make your own.

1. Pulse salt in a spice grinder for about 30 seconds (its texture should be very fine). Pour the pulsed salt into an empty spice jar fitted with a perforated shaker lid.

2. Season the popcorn in a very large bowl, carefully stirring to evenly distribute the salt.

A Pie-Measuring Method

For Iva Palacios Konieczka of Charlestown, Mass., the holidays mean lots of pie making. Rather than pulling out a ruler every time she rolls out a crust, she uses masking tape to create a 12-inch square on her countertop to use as a guide for rolling out a 12-inch crust.

Creating Under-the-Cabinet Storage

Looking to conserve cabinet space, Dawn McCarthy of Raleigh, N.C., attached two wooden napkin holders, spaced as far apart as her longest cutting board, to the underside of an upper cabinet. The napkin holders act as brackets, holding multiple stacked cutting boards.

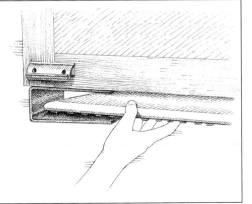

Flattening Out Parchment Paper

Parchment paper is a kitchen workhorse, but it comes with one drawback: It curls into a scroll the second it is cut from the roll. Lloyd Lehn of Annadale, Va., has a simple solution.

1. Lightly crumple the sheet of parchment paper.

2. Unfold the parchment and smooth it flat. The folds will help keep it from curling.

Containing Lids

Kathleen Sayce of Nahcotta, Wash., borrowed from her office to organize the disarray of plastic lids in her kitchen cabinet. A magazine box keeps reusable container lids in one place for easily retrieval. (Depending on the height of your cabinet, you may have to lay the box flat on its long side.)

Classic Roast Turkey on the Grill

Cooking your bird on the grill frees up the oven for all those other holiday dishes— but does it have to mean giving up clean, oven-roasted flavor?

> BY LAN LAM

Every Thanksgiving I find myself in the same predicament. At the 11th hour, while the turkey roasts away in the oven, countless foil-wrapped side dishes wait (and wait) for their turn to cook or reheat. All I can do is hope that my family won't notice that the holiday dinner is late . . . again.

Moving the turkey out to the grill would be a great solution, and the test kitchen has developed recipes for grill-roasted turkey with deep, smoky flavor. But I come from a family of staunch traditionalists, who insist on classic, clean-tasting turkey. I'd have to find a way to grill-roast the bird so it emerged tasting pretty much as if it had been roasted in the oven—meaning no smoky or sooty flavors. If it worked, I'd be well on my way to a low-stress holiday.

I wanted a recipe that would work on both gas and charcoal grills, and since it would be more of a challenge to get pure, smoke-free flavor on a charcoal grill, I tackled that scenario first.

As I formulated a plan, I realized that the grill is potentially even better than the oven for roasting a turkey since it could eliminate a perennial turkey-roasting problem: The lean white meat cooks faster than the fattier legs and thighs. In an oven, heat hits the bird from all angles, so to prevent the breast from drying out while the dark meat finishes cooking, we have always taken extra steps: flipping the turkey during roasting, icing the breast before cooking, or shielding it with aluminum foil. But on a grill, most of the heat comes from below the bird, plus there is no roasting pan in the way. As long as the bird is placed breast side up on the grill grate, the fatty leg quarters are guaranteed more exposure to heat, ensuring that all parts of the bird emerge evenly cooked.

With its pure, classic flavor, this turkey will satisfy traditionalists while leaving your oven free.

A Burning Ring of Fire

Inspired by the prospect of a super-simple approach, I perused recipes and found three recommended grill setups: banked, split, or "ring." Banked fires call for piling lit coals on one side of the grill and then placing the bird on the grate opposite the coals, while a split fire divides the coals into two piles, one on either side of the bird. The unusual ring-shaped setup involves inverting a disposable aluminum roasting pan in the center of the kettle and encircling it with coals; this supposedly cooks the bird evenly from all sides. On paper, the ring setup sounded promising. In reality, the fat dripping from the turkey ran down the sloped sides of the pan and straight into the hot coals, where it ignited, engulfing the bird in a ring of flames. Next.

Of the two remaining options, a banked fire would require rotating the bird since only one side could be exposed to the hot coals at a time. A split fire requires no rotating—the better choice.

To ensure moistness and seasoning, I could either salt or brine. Salting made more sense since

it eliminates the hassle of finding space in a fridge for a container large enough to hold both the brine and the bird. It was also easier to crisp the skin if it didn't start out waterlogged.

With my decision made, I loosened the skin on a turkey, applied kosher salt directly on the meat and in the cavity, wrapped the turkey in plastic wrap, and put it in the refrigerator. The next day, I lightly coated the skin with oil to help it brown, lit a full chimney of charcoal, and dumped half on each side of the kettle. After positioning the turkey breast side up on the grate between the coals, I set my timer since I knew I'd have to add briquettes at specific intervals to maintain the fire. Two hours later, I'd gone through 2 additional quarts of charcoal and was trying to figure out how much more I'd need to light before the bird was cooked through. I was losing my patience: Repeatedly replenishing a fire is OK on a lazy summer day, but I certainly wouldn't want to have to babysit the grill on one of the busiest cooking days of the year. To add insult to injury, when the bird was finally cooked, a few colleagues asked how I'd managed to impart a smoky taste without using wood chips. What was going on?

According to our science editor, the smoky flavor that we associate with grilling comes mostly from soot particles that are stirred up and land on the food when the lid is lifted. Even more of that grilled taste is imparted when flare-ups occur, creating additional soot particles. This information led me to two new goals: first, finding a way to leave the lid on the grill for the entire cooking time, and second, roasting the bird more gently, so there would be fewer smoke-generating flare-ups.

If I wasn't going to open the lid during grilling, I'd have to build a longer-lasting fire. It only made sense to use a technique we've used when grill-roasting other meats: Simply arrange some unlit coals in the kettle with hot coals piled on top. The unlit coals slowly ignite and start to produce some real heat just as the top layer of coals disintegrates into ash.

To lower the overall temperature of the grill (and thus prevent flare-ups), I took a cue from our Memphis-Style Barbecued Spareribs recipe (July/August 2010) and experimented with placing a disposable pan partially filled with water between the

PHOTOGRAPHY: CARL TREMBLAY

two piles of coals. It was intended to absorb heat, decreasing the overall temperature of the grill, and it did just that. With my new setup, the temperature dropped from 400 degrees down to a moderate 325 degrees.

It was time to try my new approach. I prepped a bird; placed a disposable pan filled with 3 cups of water in the center of the kettle; arranged 1½ quarts of unlit coals topped with 2 quarts of lit coals on each side; added the bird; replaced the lid; and let it go for about 3 hours. I let the turkey rest for 45 minutes and then carved samples for my colleagues. Bingo. The grill flavor was no longer detectable.

Crisp-Skin Secrets

Having achieved juicy, clean-tasting meat, I was ready to address the skin, which wasn't crisping enough. No problem. I simply pulled out the test kitchen's arsenal of crisp-skin techniques: placing slits along the backbone to speed up the rendering of excess fat, patting the skin dry with paper towels, and rubbing the skin with baking powder to help break down its proteins. Sure enough, these tricks worked like a charm and I now had a beautifully bronzed, crisp-skinned turkey that looked and tasted every bit as though I'd pulled it from the oven.

The only thing left to do was adapt my recipe for a gas grill, which required a couple of modifications. Since many models have only two burners, it was impossible to mimic the split fire setup by placing the turkey on a cooler area between two lit burners. Instead, I would have to leave one burner on medium as my main heat source and grill-roast the turkey alongside it. This meant that I had no choice but to rotate the turkey halfway through grill-roasting. And since a large disposable roasting pan wouldn't fit on all gas grills, I put the water in two disposable pie plates placed directly on the burners.

Now that my oven is freed up and roasting a bird is as simple as striking a match, my next Thanksgiving is sure to be less stressful. And because my grill-roasted turkey is a dead ringer for an oven-roasted bird, just how I pulled it off will be my little secret.

SIMPLE GRILL-ROASTED TURKEY
SERVES 10 TO 12

Don't use table salt for this recipe; it is too fine. If using a self-basting turkey (such as a frozen Butterball) or a kosher turkey, don't salt in step 1, but do season with salt in step 2. Check the wings halfway through roasting; if they are getting too dark, slide a small piece of foil between the wing and the cooking grate to shield the wings from the flame. As an accompaniment, try our Gravy for Simple Grill-Roasted Turkey, available free at CooksIllustrated.com/dec12.

- 1 (12- to 14-pound) turkey, neck and giblets removed and reserved for gravy
  Kosher salt and pepper
- 1 teaspoon baking powder
- 1 tablespoon vegetable oil
  Large disposable aluminum roasting pan (if using charcoal) or 2 disposable aluminum pie plates (if using gas)

1. Place turkey, breast side down, on work surface. Make two 2-inch incisions below each thigh and breast along back of turkey (4 incisions total). Using fingers or handle of wooden spoon, carefully separate skin from thighs and breast. Rub 4 teaspoons salt evenly inside cavity of turkey, 1 tablespoon salt under skin of each breast, and 1 teaspoon salt under skin of each leg.

2. Combine 1 teaspoon salt, 1 teaspoon pepper, and baking powder in small bowl. Pat turkey dry with paper towels and evenly sprinkle baking powder mixture all over. Rub in mixture with hands, coating entire surface evenly. Wrap turkey tightly with plastic wrap; refrigerate for 24 to 48 hours.

3. Remove turkey from refrigerator and discard plastic. Tuck wings underneath turkey. Using hands, rub oil evenly over entire surface.

4A. FOR A CHARCOAL GRILL: Open bottom vent halfway and place disposable pan filled with 3 cups water in center of grill. Arrange 1½ quarts unlit charcoal briquettes on either side of pan

---

(3 quarts total) in even layer. Light large chimney starter two-thirds filled with charcoal briquettes (4 quarts). When top coals are partially covered with ash, pour 2 quarts of lit coals on top of each pile of unlit coals. Set cooking grate in place, cover, and open lid vent halfway. Heat grill until hot, about 5 minutes.

4B. FOR A GAS GRILL: Place 2 disposable pie plates with 2 cups water in each directly on 1 burner over which turkey will be cooked. Turn all burners to high, cover, and heat grill until hot, about 15 minutes. Turn primary burner (burner opposite pie plates) to medium and turn off other burner(s). Adjust primary burner as needed to maintain grill temperature of 325 degrees.

5. Clean and oil cooking grate. Place turkey, breast side up, in center of charcoal grill or on cooler side of gas grill, making sure bird is over disposable pans and not over flame. Cover (placing vents over turkey on charcoal grill) and cook until breasts register 160 degrees and thighs/drumsticks register 175 degrees, 2½ to 3 hours, rotating turkey after 1¼ hours if using gas grill.

6. Transfer turkey to carving board and let rest, uncovered, for 45 minutes. Carve turkey and serve.

Cleaning a Grimy Grill Lid

We're fanatics about making sure that we thoroughly clean our grill grates before grilling, but we often forget to give the same attention to the grill lid. Over time, grease and smoke oxidize and turn into carbon that builds up under the lid and eventually becomes patchy flakes that look like peeling paint. To see if this carbon buildup imparts any ashy off-flavors to food, we took the filthiest lid we could find in the test kitchen and used it to grill-roast turkey and fish, comparing the results after following the same recipes on a new grill with a shiny clean lid. Most of us didn't detect any off-flavors, but we do recommend cleaning the inside of the grill lid on a regular basis to prevent the strips from flaking off and landing on your food. The peeling carbon comes off easily with light scrubbing with steel wool and water. (Don't waste your time trying to clean off any buildup that isn't already flaking. When we attempted to remove every speck of the shiny carbon layer, none of the methods we tried—lemon juice and salt; vinegar and baking soda; S.O.S pads; or even spraying the surface with Easy-Off, sealing the lid in a plastic garbage bag, and letting it sit in the sun for several hours—made much of a dent.)

NEEDS A SCRUB
That's not peeling paint: It's carbon buildup.

Watch It Become Beautiful
Video available FREE for 4 months at CooksIllustrated.com/dec12

Pepper-Crusted Beef Tenderloin

Tenderloin with a crunchy peppercorn crust sounds ideal—but not when it cracks off the roast or has a flavor so spicy that it overpowers the beef.

> BY CELESTE ROGERS <

When it comes to special-occasion entrées, it's hard to beat beef tenderloin. It's easy to make—just oven-roast it until it's done—and, as the absolute tenderest cut of beef, it's luxurious to eat.

But that tenderness comes at a cost—and I'm not just talking about the very high price it fetches at the butcher's counter. In addition to buttery texture, these roasts are renowned for the meekness of their beef flavor. To counter this, they are often dressed up with flavor-packed flourishes. One such enhancement is a pepper crust. Though I've always put this particular embellishment on individual filets mignons, pepper is such a great complement to beef that I was eager to give it a try on a whole roast.

I knew that the idea had merit as soon as I started digging for recipes: There were dozens. But when I prepared the most promising of the bunch, a number of problems revealed themselves that hadn't when I'd put peppercorns on steaks. First, I had to tie the roast with kitchen twine to ensure that it cooked evenly from end to end, but when I removed the string, the surrounding peppercorns came with it. More cracked pepper rained down on the carving board as I sliced the roast—even when I used my sharpest carving knife and the gentlest strokes. Worst of all, the peppercorns' crunch was wimpy, while their heat was pungent and lingering. The only good part: the meat itself, which had been gently cooked and, as a result, was juicy and uniformly rosy.

My goal was clear: Create a crunchy crust that stayed put but was not punishingly spicy.

Sticking It to the Meat
Initially, I drew on prior test kitchen solutions for crusting meat, coating the surface with various sticky substances before packing on the peppercorns. My edible "glues" included a mixture of mayonnaise and gelatin, another of finely grated Parmesan cheese and olive oil, and one that's named for a painter's trick: I "primed" the roast with a dusting of cornstarch before brushing it with foamed egg white.

I immediately dismissed the mayo-gelatin and cornstarch–egg white combinations due to their leaving unattractive white residue on the meat. The

Gutsy peppercorns perfectly complement a juicy beef tenderloin roast.

Parmesan-oil paste fixed the crust beautifully and lent a rich, flavorful punch, but the cheesiness obscured the pepper and beef flavors that I wanted to highlight.

I turned to the beef itself, wondering if I might be able to transform its surface into a pepper magnet through mechanical or chemical means. A colleague suggested that I try roughing up its surface with a sandpaper-like mixture of gritty kosher salt enhanced with some baking soda. The latter would raise the beef's pH, in turn triggering enzymes in the meat to dissolve some of the surface proteins, which would hopefully create a tacky exterior. Not wanting to turn the roast's exterior to mush, I kept the volume of baking soda small—only ¼ teaspoon—and skipped any resting time. Sure enough, the surface became sticky after a brief rubdown. I pressed on ½ cup of cracked peppercorns that I mixed with a few tablespoons of oil. I then sprayed the twine I would use to tie the roast with vegetable oil—that way, it wouldn't stick to the meat when I removed it—and transferred the roast to a 300-degree oven.

This time, the peppercorns held tight to the tenderloin even after slicing, and my tasters applauded the gorgeously crusted roast I served for lunch that day. Until they dug in. Then they winced and reached for water, complaining that the heat was too aggressive now that every bite was loaded with peppercorns.

SCIENCE
Manipulating Pepper's Heat and Flavor

For a crust that was satisfyingly crunchy, we needed to use so much cracked pepper that its spiciness overwhelmed the mild flavor of the meat. Simmering the peppercorns in oil before applying them to the roast tamed their heat by pulling out an oil-soluble compound known as piperine. Unfortunately, this treatment also dulled the pepper's flavor by drawing out three other oil-soluble compounds—limonene, sabinene, and pinene—that together are largely responsible for creating the citrusy, piney notes that give pepper its depth.

To restore complexity to our lackluster pepper, we scanned databases used by perfumists and flavorists to identify aromatic ingredients that might share those dominant flavor compounds. We zeroed in on two: orange zest (95 percent limonene) and nutmeg (58 percent pinene and sabinene). By adding these ingredients to the oil-simmered peppercorns, we created a crust that was not too spicy, but still full of distinct pepper flavor. –C.R.

SUBTRACT PIPERINE
To tame the peppercorns' heat, we simmered them in oil, but along with the heat, we lost flavor.

ADD BACK LIMONENE, PINENE, AND SABINENE
By adding nutmeg and orange zest to the crust, we replaced three key flavor compounds lost during simmering.

Taming the Fire

It was time to bring down the heat level to the point at which it was enhancing rather than overpowering the meat's flavor. To do so, I took a cue from a study funded by the National Institutes of Health that demonstrated that both sucrose (table sugar) and citric acid can effectively temper the spiciness of black pepper. I tried mixing a little sugar into the salt rub, and I found that it not only lessened tasters' perception of heat but also enhanced the pepper's more subtle flavors, thus lending more complexity. I tabled the addition of citric acid until later, imagining tart fruit juices as a good base for an accompanying sauce.

The sugar hadn't tamed the heat enough, though, so I abandoned all further attempts to dampen the pepper's heat with other ingredients and turned to an approach that the test kitchen has used in other such situations: simmering the cracked pepper in oil. We've found this an effective way to mellow piperine, the flavor compound responsible for peppercorns' pungency. But as I did some further reading, I learned that piperine is also soluble in alcohol and acid, which inspired my next test. I simmered a batch of peppercorns in each of the three liquids (using neutral-flavored vodka for the alcohol test and white vinegar for the acid test), drained away the spicy liquids, and then mixed the tamed pepper with fresh oil (to help the crust stick).

Tasters' universal verdict: All three methods were highly successful at mellowing the heat, but vodka and vinegar were nonstarters because the former gave the meat a boozy taste while the latter turned it gray. The oil-simmered peppercorns, on the other hand, lent a pleasant spiciness without generating any off-flavors or negatively affecting appearance.

Flavor Finessing

That said, less heat came at a cost. Simmering the peppercorns in oil had drawn out not only their spiciness but also the nuanced piney and floral flavors that contributed much to making this dish so good. Essentially, I'd been pitching the best part of the peppercorns into the trash.

Looking for a way to restore these flavors, I did more digging and discovered some interesting information. It turns out that three of the main flavor compounds in peppercorns—sabinene, pinene, and limonene—are also found in high concentrations in the oil in orange zest (95 percent limonene) and nutmeg (58 percent pinene and sabinene). Intrigued, I tried adding both to the rub. Sure enough, mixing a tablespoon of zest and ½ teaspoon of ground nutmeg with the simmered and drained peppercorns hit the mark, restoring a balance of flavors that made the crust taste more like, well, pepper. (See "Manipulating Pepper's Heat and Flavor.")

I was ready for the final flourish: those tangy fruit juice–based sauces. I'd already stripped the orange's zest, so I figured I'd squeeze out the juice and combine it with some red wine, beef broth, and other pantry staples for a complex-tasting finish.

KEY STEPS | PREPARING—AND PACKING ON—A PEPPERCORN CRUST

Most peppercorn crusts either bring big crunch or grip the meat—but rarely both. Here's how we got it right.

CRACK For a crunchy crust that also sticks, coarsely crack—don't pulverize—the peppercorns.

SIFT To remove the dusty bits of ground pepper, sift the cracked peppercorns in a strainer.

"GLUE" Rub the meat with salt, sugar, and baking soda to make the surface tacky.

Liking those results, I also mixed up a version with pomegranate juice and port. Both sauces were hits, their fruity tang slightly tempering the peppercorns' aromatic, toasty heat, not to mention gussying up this luxe cut to qualify as holiday dinner-party fare.

PEPPER-CRUSTED BEEF TENDERLOIN ROAST
SERVES 10 TO 12

Not all pepper mills produce a coarse enough grind for this recipe. For alternative methods for cracking peppercorns, see "Cracking Down on Peppercorns," page 30. Serve with Red Wine–Orange Sauce (recipe follows), if desired. For our free recipes for Pepper-Crusted Center-Cut Beef Tenderloin Roast (this 2-pound roast comes trimmed and serves six) and Pomegranate-Port Sauce, go to CooksIllustrated.com/dec12.

4½	teaspoons kosher salt
1½	teaspoons sugar
¼	teaspoon baking soda
9	tablespoons olive oil
½	cup coarsely cracked black peppercorns
1	tablespoon finely grated orange zest
½	teaspoon ground nutmeg
1	(6-pound) whole beef tenderloin, trimmed

1. Adjust oven rack to middle position and heat oven to 300 degrees. Combine salt, sugar, and baking soda in bowl; set aside. Heat 6 tablespoons oil and peppercorns in small saucepan over low heat until faint bubbles appear. Continue to cook at bare simmer, swirling pan occasionally, until pepper is fragrant, 7 to 10 minutes. Using fine-mesh strainer, drain cooking oil from peppercorns. Discard cooking oil and mix peppercorns with remaining 3 tablespoons oil, orange zest, and nutmeg.

2. Set tenderloin on sheet of plastic wrap. Sprinkle salt mixture evenly over surface of tenderloin and rub into tenderloin until surface is tacky. Tuck tail end of tenderloin under about 6 inches to create more even shape. Rub top and side of tenderloin with peppercorn mixture, pressing to make sure peppercorns adhere. Spray three 12-inch lengths kitchen twine with vegetable oil spray; tie head of tenderloin to

maintain even shape, spacing twine at 2-inch intervals.

3. Transfer prepared tenderloin to wire rack set in rimmed baking sheet, keeping tail end tucked under. Roast until thickest part of meat registers about 120 degrees for rare and about 125 degrees for medium-rare (thinner parts of tenderloin will be slightly more done), 60 to 70 minutes. Transfer to carving board and let rest for 30 minutes.

4. Remove twine and slice meat into ½-inch-thick slices. Serve.

RED WINE–ORANGE SAUCE
MAKES 1 CUP

2	tablespoons unsalted butter, plus 4 tablespoons cut into 4 pieces and chilled
2	shallots, minced
1	tablespoon tomato paste
2	teaspoons sugar
3	garlic cloves, minced
2	cups beef broth
1	cup red wine
¼	cup orange juice
2	tablespoons balsamic vinegar
1	tablespoon Worcestershire sauce
1	sprig fresh thyme
	Salt and pepper

1. Melt 2 tablespoons butter in medium saucepan over medium-high heat. Add shallots, tomato paste, and sugar; cook, stirring frequently, until deep brown, about 5 minutes. Add garlic and cook until fragrant, about 1 minute. Add broth, wine, orange juice, vinegar, Worcestershire, and thyme, scraping up any browned bits. Bring to simmer and cook until reduced to 1 cup, 35 to 40 minutes.

2. Strain sauce through fine-mesh strainer and return to saucepan. Return saucepan to medium heat and whisk in remaining 4 tablespoons butter, 1 piece at a time. Season with salt and pepper to taste.

See the Crunch Created
Video available FREE for 4 months at CooksIllustrated.com/dec12

Updating Shepherd's Pie

Think this classic of tender meat and rich gravy topped with mashed potatoes is the ultimate comfort food? The cook who has spent 5 hours preparing it might disagree.

> BY ANDREA GEARY

I once made a fabulous shepherd's pie. It was the very antithesis of those watery, gray, flavorless pies pushed by frozen food companies and school cafeterias. But this story is not about that shepherd's pie, because I will never make that particular recipe again.

The reason is simple: It took most of a day to produce. After boning, trimming, and cutting up lamb shoulder, I seared the meat in batches (making a greasy mess of the stovetop in the process) and braised it with vegetables and homemade stock for a couple of hours. From there, I reduced the cooking liquid to make a sauce, chopped the cooked meat, replaced the spent vegetables with fresh, and transferred the filling to a baking dish. Finally, I prepared the mashed potatoes (boiling, mashing, mixing) and piped them over the filling. While the top crisped in the oven, I cleaned up the kitchen—no small feat because I had used almost every piece of cooking equipment I owned. I loved that pie—but only a blissfully uninformed diner would call that dish comfort food; an honest cook would likely describe it as marathon food.

Another thing: Though it made a very satisfying meal, the pie was heavy. Shepherd's pie may be a holdover from a time when physical laborers needed robust sustenance, but as someone who enjoys a 21st-century urban lifestyle, I can't really justify eating like a preindustrial farmer. But I admit: The classic combination of meat, gravy, and potatoes is undeniably attractive on chilly winter nights. Maybe I could make a place in my life for modernized shepherd's pie—a bit lighter, much less messy, and a lot quicker to prepare. Now *that* would be comforting indeed.

Make It Ground, Please

I'm not the first to think shepherd's pie needs an overhaul, and the most common shortcut is to use ground meat. Ground lamb seemed the obvious choice until I learned in *Irish Traditional Cooking*

You'd never guess from its rich, savory depth that we make this dish with lean ground beef.

by Darina Allen, godmother of the cuisine, that modern-day shepherd's pie in Ireland is almost always made with beef. Since beef is more popular in the United States, ground beef it would be.

But it took me only one test to realize that I couldn't simply swap out chunks of meat for the ground kind; the two don't cook the same way. Searing chunks produces tender meat with a lovely brown crust. Ground beef, on the other hand, presents so much surface area to the pan that it gives up considerably more moisture as it cooks. The result: nubbly, dry crumbles that don't brown well. No thanks.

So, my meat left unbrowned, I nonetheless persevered. I added onions and carrots and let them soften a bit, and then I introduced some flour to thicken the eventual sauce. I stirred in herbs along with some beef broth and let the whole thing simmer and reduce while I cooked and mashed the potatoes. I transferred the filling to a baking dish and—thinking I was simplifying things—ditched my piping bag and spread the potatoes on top with a rubber spatula,

which turned out to be messy and difficult because the soupy filling conspired against me. Finally, I placed the pie in the oven to crisp the top.

Had my aim been to re-create the shepherd's pie served on budget airlines and in hospitals, I could have called this a success. The meat, even unbrowned, was chewy; the carrots were cooked to mush; and the "gravy" tasted pretty much like what it was: thickened canned beef broth.

Fond of Flavor

Fortunately, I had a good lead on how to improve the meat's texture. We recently discovered that treating pork with baking soda tenderizes the meat by raising its pH. Hoping to achieve the same effect here, I stirred ½ teaspoon of baking soda and 2 tablespoons of water (to ensure that it would distribute evenly) into the raw ground meat and let the mixture rest while I prepared the mashed potatoes. That did the trick, rendering the meat soft and tender, even after several minutes of simmering. On to beefing up the filling's lackluster flavor.

Since my gravy would not be based on browned meat flavors, I looked to other options. An approach to vegetarian gravy looked promising: Cook onions and mushrooms in a skillet with a little bit of fat over fairly high heat until they're deep brown and a fond starts to form in the pan; then stir in tomato paste and garlic and allow the fond to get quite dark. I went ahead with this method, deglazing the pan with some fortified wine (ordinary red wine required me to use so much it left the sauce boozy) after a good layer of fond had developed. Then I added flour and, when the mixture was very deeply browned, fresh thyme and bay leaves, followed by beef broth and Worcestershire sauce to liberate that valuable crust from the bottom of the skillet. I was rewarded with a sauce that boasted rich color and savory depth.

With my sauce bubbling and thick, I added 1½ pounds of ground beef broken into chunks and covered the skillet for roughly 10 minutes, lifting the lid once during cooking to stir. That's when I noticed the small pools of grease exuded by the meat. One downside of not browning the meat was that I had no opportunity to pour off its fat. I wondered if switching from 85 percent lean ground beef (the test kitchen's

PHOTOGRAPHY: CARL TREMBLAY

usual choice) to 93 percent lean beef would help. Happily, the leaner beef stayed moist and tender, thanks to the baking soda treatment, and only a few tiny pools of fat remained. To get rid of these, I first tried adding more flour, but mixed in so late in the process, it tasted raw and starchy. Instead, I turned to the Asian trick of stirring in a slurry of cornstarch and water, which took care of the problem very nicely.

As for the spuds, the recipe I'd been using calls for a full stick of butter and 1 cup of half-and-half—not exactly the lighter approach I was going for. I cut the amount of butter in half and subbed milk for the half-and-half. Because soft, moist mashed potatoes would merge with the gravy rather than form a crust, I also decreased the dairy by 50 percent and added an egg yolk for extra structure.

For convenience's sake, I elected to leave the cooked filling in the skillet—except that I still had to resolve the issue of spreading the solid potatoes over the soupy mixture. I decided to give piping another go, but this time, I eschewed my fancy pastry bag and star tip for a zipper-lock bag with a corner cut off. Depositing the potatoes onto the filling from above was far easier than trying to spread them over a wet base. Once they were in place, I smoothed them with the back of a spoon and traced ridges in them with a fork; that way they'd get really crusty under the broiler.

One problem remained: The browned, crispy potato topping certainly looked appealing, but its flavor paled in comparison with the robust filling. Looking to add some pizzazz, I reviewed the British Isles' various regional potato dishes, and a recipe for champ, Ireland's simple mixture of mashed potatoes and chopped scallions, caught my attention. Stirring a handful of chopped scallion greens into my own mash freshened the whole dish without adding heft.

With its simmered lean ground beef, rich but not heavy gravy, and lighter, fresher mash, my updated shepherd's pie was not just faster to make than the traditional version but also less guilt-inducing—and still every bit as delicious. At last, comfort food that even the cook could enjoy.

Shepherd's Pie Makeover

Between trimming, searing, and braising chunks of stew meat and then mashing and piping the potato topping, traditional shepherd's pie is an all-afternoon project. Plus, it's hefty fare. Here's how we freshened up the concept and got dinner on the table in about an hour.

SWAP GROUND BEEF FOR STEW MEAT
Ground meat cooks in less than half the time required by bigger chunks and needs no butchering.

BROWN VEGETABLES, NOT MEAT
Browning ground beef turns it pebbly. Instead, we brown vegetables and tomato paste to create a rich fond.

LIGHTEN UP THE MASHED POTATOES
Less butter, milk instead of half-and-half, and sliced scallions lighten up the spuds.

SHEPHERD'S PIE
SERVES 4 TO 6

Don't use ground beef that's fattier than 93 percent or the dish will be greasy.

1½	pounds 93 percent lean ground beef
2	tablespoons plus 2 teaspoons water
	Salt and pepper
½	teaspoon baking soda
2½	pounds russet potatoes, peeled and cut into 1-inch chunks
4	tablespoons unsalted butter, melted
½	cup milk
1	large egg yolk
8	scallions, green parts only, sliced thin
2	teaspoons vegetable oil
1	onion, chopped
4	ounces white mushrooms, trimmed and chopped
1	tablespoon tomato paste
2	garlic cloves, minced
2	tablespoons Madeira or ruby port
2	tablespoons all-purpose flour
1¼	cups beef broth
2	teaspoons Worcestershire sauce
2	sprigs fresh thyme
1	bay leaf
2	carrots, peeled and chopped
2	teaspoons cornstarch

1. Toss beef with 2 tablespoons water, 1 teaspoon salt, ¼ teaspoon pepper, and baking soda in bowl until thoroughly combined. Set aside for 20 minutes.

2. Meanwhile, place potatoes in medium saucepan; add water to just cover and 1 tablespoon salt. Bring to boil over high heat. Reduce heat to medium-low and simmer until potatoes are soft and tip of paring knife inserted into potato meets no resistance, 8 to 10 minutes. Drain potatoes and return to saucepan. Return saucepan to low heat and cook, shaking pot occasionally, until any surface moisture on potatoes has evaporated, about 1 minute. Remove pan from heat and mash potatoes well. Stir in melted butter. Whisk together milk and egg yolk in small bowl, then stir into potatoes. Stir in scallion greens and season with salt and pepper to taste. Cover and set aside.

3. Heat oil in broiler-safe 10-inch skillet over medium heat until shimmering. Add onion, mushrooms, ½ teaspoon salt, and ¼ teaspoon pepper; cook, stirring occasionally, until vegetables are just starting to soften and dark bits form on bottom of skillet, 4 to 6 minutes. Stir in tomato paste and garlic; cook until bottom of skillet is dark brown, about 2 minutes. Add Madeira and cook, scraping up any browned bits, until evaporated, about 1 minute. Stir in flour and cook for 1 minute. Add broth, Worcestershire, thyme, bay leaf, and carrots; bring to boil, scraping up any browned bits. Reduce heat to medium-low, add beef in 2-inch chunks to broth, and bring to gentle simmer. Cover and cook until beef is cooked through, 10 to 12 minutes, stirring and breaking up meat chunks with 2 forks halfway through. Stir cornstarch and remaining 2 teaspoons water together in bowl. Stir cornstarch mixture into filling and continue to simmer for 30 seconds. Remove thyme and bay leaf. Season with salt and pepper to taste.

4. Adjust oven rack 5 inches from broiler element and heat broiler. Place mashed potatoes in large zipper-lock bag and snip off 1 corner to create 1-inch opening. Pipe potatoes in even layer over filling, making sure to cover entire surface. Smooth potatoes with back of spoon, then use tines of fork to make ridges over surface. Place skillet on rimmed baking sheet and broil until potatoes are golden brown and crusty and filling is bubbly, 10 to 15 minutes. Let cool for 10 minutes before serving.

ILLUSTRATION: JAY LAYMAN

Roasted Root Vegetables

How do you get five different vegetables to cook simultaneously in the same pan and all come out perfectly? The solution starts with the right cuts.

⋛ BY LAN LAM ⋚

Want to transform humble root vegetables into a side dish that's the star of the dinner? Stick them in the oven.

Well, OK, it's not quite that easy. But it's pretty close. Few techniques are more effective at transforming a root vegetable into something richly flavored and complex than roasting, and it takes almost no effort. The key to success is cutting whatever root you are cooking into equal-size pieces so they all cook evenly. After that, you just toss them with some oil and pop them into a hot oven to cook until they become tender inside and their exteriors brown and caramelize.

Of course, that's if you're cooking just one vegetable. I wanted to roast an assortment, a dish that's become very popular during the past couple of years for its rich variety of textures and flavors. Easy enough, it seemed. Since the technique for roasting one type of vegetable worked so well, I didn't question the advice of recipes that directed me to do the same when I diversified. I put together a complementary combination—sweet carrots, parsnips, and shallots; earthy celery root; and peppery turnips—and then cut everything except the shallots into uniform chunks.

It took only one test to convince me that this was not a good idea. After roasting the lot in a 400-degree oven for 1½ hours, I found myself with a medley of every possible bad result, from raw and crunchy to charred and desiccated. Only the shallots, which I'd simply peeled and left whole, came out tender with crisp, caramelized exteriors.

Roasting each vegetable separately would surely get me better results, but that much effort was out of the question for this side dish. I wanted to find an approach that would reliably produce an assortment of perfectly roasted root vegetables, all on the same sheet pan. And if I could somehow shorten the usual lengthy cooking time, all the better.

Lan Roasts the Roots
Video available FREE for 4 months at CooksIllustrated.com/dec12

Roasting the vegetables on a preheated baking sheet results in deep caramelization, which means plenty of rich flavor.

Making the Cut
Instead of trying to cut the veggies into equal pieces, I decided to let the density and texture of each vegetable determine its particular shape. I started with the carrots. Since cutting them into chunks had left them undercooked, this time I cut them into sticks about 2½ inches long, halving or quartering pieces so the diameter of each was no more than an inch. My thought was that the greater surface area of this shape would allow the interior to cook faster. After the same 90 minutes in a 400-degree oven, I was pleased to find that these roots were now tender and nicely browned.

Parsnips were up next. Since both are cylindrical, I cut them into the same shape as the carrots. But parsnips are more fibrous than carrots, and they came out a little stringy and chewy. It occurred to me that a trick we use to make tough cuts of meat seem more tender—cutting them across the grain to shorten their fibers—might help here. I sliced the parsnips on the bias into 1-inch-wide oblong disks, and roasted them at 400 degrees with the carrot sticks. After 90

minutes, the cross-cut parsnips were nearly as soft and tender as the roasted carrots.

Clearly I'd found the secret to this dish. I peeled and cut celery root, which I now knew to be the slowest-cooking veggie in the bunch, into ¾-inch-thick slices, which I then cut into planks, creating the optimal amount of direct contact with the baking sheet. Sure enough, when added to the next test with the carrots and parsnips, the celery root was as tender and well browned as its two compatriots.

Finally, I considered the turnips. Since they had charred while the other roots remained too hard in my initial tests, it made sense to take the opposite approach with them and minimize surface area. After trying several different methods of cutting the turnips into eighths, I found that the most effective was to cut them horizontally and then slice each half into four wedges. With their relatively small surface area, these pieces cooked through at just the right slow tempo.

Speed It Up
With each vegetable cut to the right shape, all were cooking at the same rate, but I wanted to see if I could bring them in at less than 90 minutes. I had noticed that during the first hour of cooking, the veggies were merely warming up and not actually browning or even softening. I tried covering them with foil when they first went into the oven to see if that would speed up cooking. With the foil trapping moisture and creating steam, the veggies were piping hot after just 20 minutes, but they still took nearly an hour more to brown once I took off the foil. Not good enough.

But I also noticed that after I removed the foil, the vegetables sat in a pool of juices that took at least 15 minutes to evaporate. So for my next test, instead of covering the raw vegetables with foil, I put all except the quick-cooking turnips in the microwave. A 10-minute zap in a bowl softened them enough so they released liquid, which I then drained off. After incorporating the uncooked turnips and giving them all a quick toss in oil, I spread them over a baking sheet that I'd preheated while the roots were in the microwave, for even faster cooking and better browning. Just 25 minutes later, the bottoms of the vegetables were golden brown. I stirred them so the unbrowned sides faced down and rotated the pan for even cooking. After 15 minutes more, I removed the pan from the oven. To my delight, all the veggies were moist on the inside and sported crisp, golden-brown crusts—and I'd done it in less than an hour.

A simple garnish of chopped parsley was all that these richly flavored vegetables really needed, but I couldn't resist the urge to dress them up further. For deep savory flavor, I created a topping made from crispy bacon, minced shallot, sherry vinegar, and chives. A bright salsa made of orange, parsley, almonds, and cumin highlighted their sweet caramelized notes. Finally, a Turkish spice blend brought thyme, sesame seeds, and orange and lemon zests to the mix.

ROASTED ROOT VEGETABLES
SERVES 6

Use turnips that are roughly 2 to 3 inches in diameter. Instead of sprinkling the roasted vegetables with chopped parsley (tarragon or chives may also be substituted), try garnishing them with one of the toppings that follow.

- 1 celery root (14 ounces), peeled
- 4 carrots, peeled and cut into 2½-inch lengths, halved or quartered lengthwise if necessary to create pieces ½ to 1 inch in diameter
- 12 ounces parsnips, peeled and sliced 1 inch thick on bias
- 5 ounces small shallots, peeled
     Kosher salt and pepper
- 12 ounces turnips, peeled, halved horizontally, and each half quartered
- 3 tablespoons vegetable oil
- 2 tablespoons chopped fresh parsley

1. Adjust oven rack to middle position, place rimmed baking sheet on rack, and heat oven to 425 degrees. Cut celery root into ¾-inch-thick rounds. Cut each round into ¾-inch-thick planks about 2½ inches in length.

Eliminating Moisture for Speedier Cooking
Before root vegetables can fully caramelize, any moisture they release must be driven off. To speed up the process, we microwaved all but the turnips (which cook relatively quickly without any help) before putting them in the oven. Ten minutes softened them enough that they released some of their liquid, which we simply drained off. Now the veggies browned in just 40 minutes—instead of the 90 minutes required for the oven-only approach.

2. Toss celery root, carrots, parsnips, and shallots with 1 teaspoon salt and with pepper to taste in large microwave-safe bowl. Cover bowl and microwave until small pieces of carrot are just pliable enough to bend, 8 to 10 minutes, stirring once halfway through microwaving. Drain vegetables well. Return vegetables to bowl, add turnips and oil, and toss to coat.

3. Working quickly, remove baking sheet from oven and carefully transfer vegetables to baking sheet; spread into even layer. Roast for 25 minutes.

4. Using thin metal spatula, stir vegetables and spread into even layer. Rotate pan and continue to roast until vegetables are golden brown and celery root is tender when pierced with tip of paring knife, 15 to 25 minutes longer. Transfer to platter, sprinkle with parsley, and serve.

BACON-SHALLOT TOPPING
MAKES ABOUT ⅓ CUP

- 4 slices bacon, cut into ¼-inch pieces
- ¼ cup water
- 2 tablespoons minced shallot
- 1 tablespoon sherry vinegar
- 2 tablespoons minced fresh chives

Bring bacon and water to boil in 8-inch skillet over high heat. Reduce heat to medium and cook until water has evaporated and bacon is crisp, about 10 minutes. Transfer bacon to paper towel–lined plate and pour off all but ½ teaspoon fat from skillet. Add shallot and cook, stirring frequently, until softened, 2 to 4 minutes. Remove pan from heat and add vinegar. Transfer shallot mixture to bowl and stir in bacon and chives. Sprinkle over vegetables before serving.

ORANGE-PARSLEY SALSA
MAKES ABOUT ½ CUP

- ¼ cup slivered almonds
- ¼ teaspoon ground cumin
- ¼ teaspoon ground coriander
- 1 orange
- ½ cup fresh parsley leaves, minced
- 2 garlic cloves, minced
- 2 teaspoons extra-virgin olive oil
- 1 teaspoon cider vinegar
- ¼ teaspoon kosher salt

1. Toast almonds in 10-inch skillet over medium-high heat until fragrant and golden brown, 5 to 6 minutes. Add cumin and coriander; continue to toast, stirring constantly, until fragrant, about 45 seconds. Immediately transfer to bowl.

2. Cut away peel and pith from orange. Use paring knife to slice between membranes to release segments. Cut segments into ¼-inch pieces. Stir orange pieces, parsley, garlic, oil, vinegar, and salt into almond mixture. Let stand for 30 minutes. Spoon over vegetables before serving.

TURKISH SPICE BLEND
MAKES ABOUT ¼ CUP

- 2 tablespoons sesame seeds, toasted
- 4 teaspoons minced fresh thyme
- ¼ teaspoon kosher salt
- ¼ teaspoon finely grated orange zest
- ¼ teaspoon finely grated lemon zest

Combine all ingredients in bowl. Sprinkle over vegetables before serving.

SHAPING ROOTS FOR ROASTING

The trouble with roasting a medley of vegetables is that each type cooks at a different rate. For uniformly tender, caramelized results, cut each one into a specific shape and size.

CELERY ROOT PLANKS
A wide, flat shape accelerates the cooking and browning of this dense vegetable.

CARROT STICKS
Long, slender sticks have a large surface area that browns quickly.

PARSNIP DISKS
Cutting on the bias across the fibrous cores to create oblong disks makes each bite tender.

WHOLE SHALLOTS
Left whole, small shallots cook at the same rate as the other vegetables.

TURNIP CHUNKS
Cutting turnips into eighths minimizes the surface area of the quick-cooking, watery vegetable.

The Best Vegetarian Chili

The key to a great vegetarian chili is not finding a substitute for the meat. It's finding substitutes for what the meat brings to the chili.

⇒ BY LAN LAM ⇐

I love chili, but I admit that vegetarian versions are usually the last kind I'd think to make. Most lack depth and complexity, so while they may taste lively and bright initially, their flavor fades. They rely on beans and chunky veggies for heartiness—but in truth that heartiness is just an illusion. Neither ingredient offers any real replacement for the flavor, texture, and unctuous richness that meat provides. It doesn't help matters that such chilis are typically made with canned beans and lackluster commercial chili powder.

But do vegetarian chilis really have to be this way? I set out to build a version as rich, savory, and deeply satisfying as any meat chili out there—one that even meat lovers would make on its own merits, not just to serve to vegetarian friends.

Heat and Beans

The first ingredient to tackle was the seasoning that gives the dish its name. Though we've found premade chili powders to recommend, even the best can't compete with a powder that you grind yourself from dried chiles. Plus, the commercial products tend to have a gritty, dusty texture that comes from grinding chiles whole—including the stems and seeds, which never fully break down. For my homemade blend, I opted for two widely available dried chiles: mild, sweet ancho and earthy New Mexican. I toasted them to bring out their flavor and then, after removing the stems and seeds, pulverized the peppers to a fine powder in a spice grinder with some dried oregano.

Next up: beans. For greater complexity, I wanted to use a mix of beans with different characteristics, singling out sweet, nutty cannellinis and meaty, earthy pintos. Canned beans are certainly convenient, but they also tend to be bland and mushy, so I opted for dried, calling on our quick-brining method. This entails bringing the beans to a boil in a pot of salted water and then letting them sit, covered, for an hour. The brine ensures soft, creamy beans (sodium ions from salt weaken the pectin in the bean skins, for a softer texture) that are well seasoned and evenly cooked.

Meanwhile, the beans' hour-long rest gave me plenty of time to prep the remaining ingredients.

For the best flavor and texture, use at least two types of dried beans.

I started out with my dried chile and oregano powder, cumin for earthy depth, and finely chopped onions for sweetness. I sautéed the onions just until they began to brown and then added the spices to bloom in the hot oil. In went my brined, rinsed beans and water; then I covered the pot and placed it in a 300-degree oven. (If they were on the stovetop, I'd have to stir the beans to prevent scorching, but in the more even, gentle heat of the oven they could simmer unattended.) I checked the beans periodically as they cooked. After 45 minutes, they were just tender. This was a great time to introduce a can of diced tomatoes, which I whizzed up in a food processor with lots of garlic and some fresh jalapeños to kick up the heat. The tomatoes would keep the beans from falling apart during the remainder of cooking, since the basic building blocks of legumes—polysaccharides—do not readily dissolve in acidic conditions. Another 2 hours and the beans were perfectly cooked: creamy and tender but not blown out.

But I still had just a pot of flavored beans. Now to turn it into a real chili . . .

"Beefing" It Up

Besides the beans, most vegetarian chilis replace the bulk that meat contributes with some combination of diced vegetables. But these recipes miss a major point: In addition to adding volume and flavor, meat gives chili its distinctive texture. Properly made meat chili is a homogeneous mixture of ground or diced meat napped in a thick, spicy sauce. No matter how you slice or dice them, cut vegetables can't deliver that same sturdy texture. They also tend to water down the dish.

In my research I'd come across vegetarian chilis that called for nuts, seeds, or grains, and with nothing to lose I decided to try a few of these more unusual add-ins. Chopped pumpkin seeds were a failure: They didn't break down during cooking, leaving sharp, crunchy bits that tasters found distracting. Long-grain rice, meanwhile, turned to mush by the time the beans were cooked through, and large, round grains of pearl barley were too chewy and gummy. Finally, I hit the jackpot: I stirred in some nutty little granules of bulgur when I added the tomatoes to the pot. Even after the long simmer, these precooked wheat kernels (which are normally plumped up by a quick soak in water) retained their shape, giving the chili the textural dimension that it had been missing.

My recipe was progressing nicely, but it still didn't have the rich depth of flavor that could help turn what was a good chili into something great. I knew that the canned tomatoes were introducing some savory flavor, but I needed a more potent source, so I added a few dollops of *umami*-packed tomato paste as well as a few tablespoons of soy sauce.

But the flavor was still too one-dimensional. While developing a vegetable soup recently, I'd learned that umami boosters fall into two categories—glutamates and nucleotides—and that they have a synergistic effect when used together. Dried mushrooms are rich in nucleotides and could amplify the effect of the glutamate-rich soy sauce and tomatoes. Since I was already grinding my chile peppers, I simply tossed in some chopped, dried shiitake mushrooms at the same time, in order to take advantage of their flavor-boosting qualities without adding distinct chunks of mushroom.

Sure enough, this batch was the meatiest yet. But could I take things even further? I reviewed a list of umami-rich foods and was surprised to see that walnuts contain more than twice as many glutamates as do tomatoes. From the failed pumpkin seed test I knew that I didn't want to add crunch, so for my next batch I toasted some walnuts, ground them in a food processor, and then stirred them into the chili along with the tomatoes and bulgur. In terms of savory depth, tasters unanimously deemed this batch the winner to date, and there were added bonuses: The fat from the nuts offered some richness, and the tannins in the skins contributed a slightly bitter note that balanced the other flavors.

Now my chili had complexity, but it still didn't have the lingering depth of a meat chili. I took a step back and thought about what meat really brings to chili. Its fat not only contributes flavor but also boosts that of the other ingredients and affects how you taste them. The flavor compounds in spices (chile peppers and cumin, in particular) are far more soluble in fat than in water, so a watery sauce dulls their flavor, whereas oils and fats allow them to bloom. What's more, fat coats the surface of your mouth, giving flavors staying power on the palate. I began slowly increasing the amount of vegetable oil that I was using to sauté the aromatics and found that ¼ cup brought the flavors into focus and allowed them to linger pleasantly instead of disappearing after a few seconds.

Everything was perfect but for one issue: When I took the chili out of the oven, I found that some of the fat had separated out, leaving a slick on top. A quick stir helped, but at the suggestion of our science editor, I tried a more vigorous stir followed by a 20-minute rest. This led to a thick, velvety chili that you could stand a spoon in. Here's why: Stirring released starches from the beans and bulgur, which absorbed the water in the sauce, allowing the sauce to stabilize around the fat droplets and prevent the oil from separating out again—in a sense creating a kind of emulsion.

There was nothing left to do but stir in some cilantro for a touch of freshness and then let my tasters loose on the topping bar. Whether garnished with a little of everything or just a dollop of sour cream, each bite of chili was hearty and full-flavored—and no one missed the meat.

BEST VEGETARIAN CHILI
SERVES 6 TO 8

We prefer to make this chili with whole dried chiles, but it can be prepared with jarred chili powder (our favorite brand is Spice Islands). If using chili powder, grind the shiitakes and oregano and add them to the pot with ¼ cup of chili powder in step 4. We also recommend a mix of at least two types of beans, one creamy (such as cannellini or navy) and one earthy (such as pinto, black, or red kidney). For a spicier chili, use both jalapeños. Serve the chili with lime wedges, sour cream, diced avocado, chopped red onion, and shredded Monterey Jack or cheddar cheese, if desired.

Salt
1 pound (2½ cups) dried beans, picked over and rinsed
2 dried ancho chiles
2 dried New Mexican chiles
½ ounce dried shiitake mushrooms, chopped coarse
4 teaspoons dried oregano
½ cup walnuts, toasted
1 (28-ounce) can diced tomatoes, drained with juice reserved
3 tablespoons tomato paste
1–2 jalapeño chiles, stemmed and coarsely chopped
6 garlic cloves, minced
3 tablespoons soy sauce
¼ cup vegetable oil
2 pounds onions, chopped fine
1 tablespoon ground cumin
7 cups water
⅔ cup medium-grind bulgur
¼ cup chopped fresh cilantro

1. Bring 4 quarts water, 3 tablespoons salt, and beans to boil in large Dutch oven over high heat.

Remove pot from heat, cover, and let stand for 1 hour. Drain beans and rinse well. Wipe out pot.

2. Adjust oven rack to middle position and heat oven to 300 degrees. Arrange anchos and New Mexican chiles on rimmed baking sheet and toast until fragrant and puffed, about 8 minutes. Transfer to plate and let cool, about 5 minutes. Stem and seed anchos and New Mexican chiles. Working in batches, grind toasted chiles, mushrooms, and oregano in spice grinder or with mortar and pestle until finely ground.

3. Process walnuts in food processor until finely ground, about 30 seconds. Transfer to bowl. Process drained tomatoes, tomato paste, jalapeño(s), garlic, and soy sauce in food processor until tomatoes are finely chopped, about 45 seconds, scraping down bowl as needed.

4. Heat oil in now-empty Dutch oven over medium-high heat until shimmering. Add onions and 1¼ teaspoons salt; cook, stirring occasionally, until onions begin to brown, 8 to 10 minutes. Lower heat to medium and add ground chile mixture and cumin; cook, stirring constantly, until fragrant, about 1 minute. Add rinsed beans and water and bring to boil. Cover pot, transfer to oven, and cook for 45 minutes.

5. Remove pot from oven. Stir in bulgur, ground walnuts, tomato mixture, and reserved tomato juice. Cover pot and return to oven. Cook until beans are fully tender, about 2 hours.

6. Remove pot from oven, stir chili well, and let stand, uncovered, for 20 minutes. Stir in cilantro and serve. (Chili can be made up to 3 days in advance.)

Meet the Meaty Alternatives

Classic chili relies on meat for texture, savory flavor, and richness. We got all of that in our meatless chili with the help of some surprising add-ins.

BULGUR
Small grains of tender, chewy wheat add a hearty textural element.

WALNUTS
Ground toasted walnuts add richness and body as well as tons of flavor-boosting glutamates.

SHIITAKES
These nucleotide-rich dried mushrooms have a synergistic effect when combined with glutamates, cranking up savory *umami* flavor even more.

The Smart Kitchen

Having a few specialized techniques up your sleeve will make you a better, more efficient cook. Here are the tricks we turn to every day to make our kitchen work faster and easier.

BY SHANNON FRIEDMANN HATCH

TIPS TO SAVE MINUTES, HOURS, OR EVEN DAYS

Proofing Bread Dough

Jury-rigging a proofing box in your oven is faster than waiting for dough to rise at room temperature. Adjust an oven rack to the middle position and place a loaf or cake pan in the bottom of the oven. Place the dough on the middle rack and pour 3 cups of boiling water into the pan. Close the oven door and allow the dough to rise as instructed. If you limit the time that the oven door is open, the proof box can be used for both the first and second rise without need to refresh the water.

Chilling White Wine

Wrap the bottle in a wet kitchen towel and place it in the freezer. Since cooling occurs when heat is transferred away from an item, the water in the towel—a much more efficient conductor of heat than air—will quickly freeze, dropping the temperature of the wine to 50 degrees in only 30 minutes. (Note: The towel will be frozen solid. To release it, place it briefly under warm running water.)

Softening Butter

Cutting butter into cubes is one way to hasten softening, but this trick is even faster: Place the cold butter in a plastic bag and use a rolling pin to pound it to the desired consistency in a matter of seconds.

Boiling Water

Speed the tedious process of boiling water by dividing the water into two pots, one large enough to hold the total amount of water. When both vessels are boiling, carefully pour the water from the smaller pot into the larger and proceed as directed.

Ripening Rock-Hard Fruit

Climacteric fruits (including apples, apricots, avocados, bananas, mangos, nectarines, peaches, pears, plums, and tomatoes) ripen off the plant once their ethylene—a colorless, odorless gas—content reaches a certain level. Hasten ripening by storing unripe fruit in a brown paper bag with ripe fruit already producing copious amounts of ethylene, such as bananas.

Aerating Red Wine

Decanting a wine for several hours exposes much of its surface area to oxygen, which breaks down tannins and sulfur compounds, softening harsh flavors. Pouring the wine from one pitcher to another 15 times achieves the same effect in seconds.

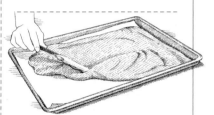

Cooling Pastry Creams and Puddings

To speed the cooling process, spread out the pastry cream or pudding across a rimmed, parchment paper–covered baking pan, and then cover it with another piece of parchment to prevent a skin from forming. Snip a number of holes in the top layer of parchment to allow steam to escape.

Cooking Brown Rice

Presoaking brown rice will trim cooking time—if you can plan ahead. Place the rice and premeasured room temperature water (1½ cups of water per cup of rice) directly into a pot or rice cooker and let it soak for 6 to 24 hours. Cook for 30 minutes as directed, adding salt if desired.

A Quick Dip to Warm Up

Thawing frozen meat and taking the chill off of refrigerator-cold food can require hours—even days. Here's how a water bath can help.

FOOD	METHOD	TIME
Eggs	Place whole eggs in 125-degree water to cover.	5 minutes
Cream cheese	Submerge foil-wrapped package in 80-degree water to cover.	10 minutes
Soft, creamy cheeses (such as Brie and Camembert)	Place cheese in a zipper-lock bag in 4 quarts of 80-degree water.	About 1 hour, or until cheese reaches 72 degrees
Thin cuts of frozen meat (such as chicken breasts, steaks, and chops)	Seal frozen meat in a zipper-lock bag and submerge it in very hot (140-degree) water.	Chicken thaws in less than 8 minutes, other cuts in roughly 12 minutes
Frozen turkey	Place turkey in a bucket of cold water, changing the water every 30 minutes.	30 minutes per pound

Cleaning a Spice Grinder
Add several tablespoons of raw white rice to the grinder and pulverize to a fine powder. This will absorb residue and oils.

Chopping Celery
Rather than breaking off one or more ribs for a small amount of chopped celery, chop the entire stalk across the top. It is easier to get just the amount you need, and storing the celery is more convenient, since the whole stalk gets shorter as you use it.

Scrubbing a Blender
Fill the dirty blender bowl halfway with hot water and add a couple of drops of liquid dish soap. With the top firmly in place, turn the blender on high for 30 seconds. Most of the debris pours right out with the soapy water, and the blender jar need only be rinsed or washed lightly by hand.

Prepping for Cake Baking
While measuring the dry ingredients for the cake you're baking at the moment, also measure ingredients for future cakes into two or three zipper-lock bags. Label each with the date, the name of the cake, and the location of the recipe and pop them into the freezer for future use.

Seeding Tomatoes
When seeding tomatoes, your salad spinner is a speedy alternative to scooping the guts out by hand. Core and cut the tomatoes into small pieces and spin them until most of the seeds are released. Repeat the spinning process as necessary to remove excess seeds.

Wiping Down a Microwave
Fill a microwave-safe bowl with water and microwave for 10 minutes. The steam loosens dried food particles so they can be wiped off with ease.

Mincing Garlic
Not even professional chefs can match the speedy, precise work of a good garlic press. Our favorite from Kuhn Rikon ($20) breaks down cloves more finely and evenly than a knife can, which means better distribution of garlic flavor throughout a dish.

Zap Time from Recipes
The microwave isn't just for reheating leftovers. For some applications, it's the most efficient appliance in the kitchen.

INSTANT DRIED HERBS Why wait days for herbs to air-dry when the microwave can dehydrate them in minutes? Place hearty herbs (such as sage, rosemary, thyme, oregano, mint, and marjoram) in a single layer between two paper towels and microwave for 1 to 3 minutes.

HANDS-OFF CARAMEL Boiling sugar to make caramel on the stove without burning it can be tricky, but it's a snap in the microwave. Place 1 cup of sugar, 2 tablespoons of corn syrup, 2 tablespoons of water, and ⅛ teaspoon of lemon juice in a microwave-safe measuring cup or glass bowl. Microwave until the mixture is just beginning to brown, 5 to 8 minutes. Remove the caramel from the microwave and let it sit on a dry surface for 5 minutes or until it darkens to a rich honey brown.

EASY-PEEL GARLIC Rather than tediously stripping away their papery exterior, microwave skin-on garlic cloves for 15 seconds. Their skin will peel right off.

BAKED POTATOES IN A HURRY The microwave can cut a russet potato's hour-long baking time in half. Poke a few holes in each potato with a fork and microwave them for 6 to 12 minutes, turning halfway through cooking (the potatoes should be slightly soft to the touch). Transfer the potatoes to the middle rack of a preheated 450-degree oven and bake until a skewer easily glides through the flesh, about 20 minutes.

Ready-to-Use Parchment Paper
Streamline your cooking/baking prep by cutting multiple pieces of parchment paper into lengths to fit a baking sheet. Then, to prevent them from curling, store the cut pieces in the baking sheet weighed down with a second baking sheet.

Peeling Hard-Cooked Eggs
After draining the hot water from the pot used to cook the eggs, shake the pot back and forth to crack the shells. Add enough ice water to cover the eggs and let cool. The water seeps under the broken shells, allowing them to be slipped off without a struggle.

Making a Cheat Sheet
Rather than flip through a cookbook every time you need to know the doneness temperature of bread, meats, and fish, write the information on an index card, laminate it, and attach it to your thermometer's protective case.

Brewing Morning Coffee
Pre-measure ground coffee into individual coffee filters and then stack the coffee-filled filters back into an empty coffee can or another airtight container and store it in the freezer until it's time to brew the next pot.

Perfect Baked Eggs

Ideally, this dish should feature tender whites and runny yolks—but it almost never does.
We baked hundreds of eggs trying to crack the code.

⋟ BY CELESTE ROGERS ⋞

Scrambled, hard-boiled, or over-easy are fine for everyday breakfast, but when I'm hosting brunch, I want an egg dish with a little more substance and style. On those occasions, I'm tempted to turn to baked eggs. The preparation might be a bit old-school, but when done well, it's undeniably elegant: individual ramekins (often lined with a dairy-enriched base or enhanced with savory add-ins), each filled with a gently set white surrounding a rich, runny yolk. It's a great dish for entertaining since there's no *à la minute* cooking at the stove.

But the reality is that most recipes fail in one of two predictable ways. I've enjoyed perfectly runny, creamy yolks and firm yet tender whites but rarely both in the same ramekin. It turns out that there's concrete egg science behind the problem: For the yolks to stay liquid, their temperature needs to hover around 150 degrees—and no higher. But maddeningly, the whites are just starting to turn opaque at that temperature and need to reach about 165 degrees to be properly cooked. That means that in order to achieve the set-white, runny-yolk ideal, the cook must work some magic, manipulating the cooking process so that the white firms up before the yolk, not the other way around. It was a tall order, so I stockpiled eggs, rounded up all the ramekins in the test kitchen, and got crackin'.

Highs and Lows

Most of the methods I came across fell into one of two categories: low and slow or high and fast. The gentlest cooked the eggs (often set in a water bath to temper the heat transfer) for 40 minutes in a 200-degree oven. The speediest called for less than 10 minutes of baking with the oven cranked to its maximum temperature. I even came across a more direct (and rather drastic) solution to the white-yolk differential in legendary French chef Auguste Escoffier's *Larousse Gastronomique*, in which he suggested separating the

Baked eggs won't be flawless without help from a second element: a savory spinach "liner" that provides a buffer against the heat of the dish.

eggs, baking the whites alone until they begin to set, and then adding the yolks to the ramekins. I decided not to go there, though; separating eggs and returning the yolks to the whites midway through cooking was hardly the fuss-free approach I was looking for.

Instead, I played it safe and decided to start by experimenting with gentle-heat methods. In addition to trying a water bath, I even tested nestling the ramekins in salt (a weaker heat conductor and therefore a better insulator than water). These approaches proved highly effective at preventing overcooked extremes—tough, rubbery whites and dry, chalky yolks—but the yolk still invariably thickened and turned pasty before the white was fully set.

Maybe, I thought, increasing the heat would help establish the large temperature difference I needed between the edge of the ramekin (where the whites were) and the center (the yolks). For that I turned to the broiler, loading the ramekins into an empty pan for easy transport. But my first attempt was a disaster. Just a few minutes under the blazing heat was too much: At the surface, the whites were

blistered and the yolks dry, and digging a spoon underneath revealed a loose, watery mess. I knocked the temperature down to 500 degrees and tried preheating the empty ramekins for a couple of minutes in hopes of giving the whites a head start. When the ramekins were hot, I slid an egg into each one and then returned them to the oven to finish. The results? Overkill. The yolks were fine, but direct contact with the scorching ramekin walls browned the edges of the whites and turned them rubbery.

Putting Down Roux

I took a step back and reviewed my results thus far. Maybe I just needed a buffer between the ramekin and the egg. With that in mind, I borrowed the idea of lining the ramekin with a rich base and decided to experiment with a solid, fixing on one of my omelet favorites: spinach. I simply defrosted frozen spinach, wrung it dry, briefly sautéed it, and mixed in some heavy cream to make a more cohesive cushion for the eggs.

The result wasn't disastrous, but it wasn't perfect either, mostly because the creamed spinach was still loose enough that the egg white could swim under and around it, coming into direct contact with the bottom and sides of the hot ramekin, where it seized up and browned. Plus the straight-up spinach–heavy cream mixture tasted a bit too rich and dull. My next order of business: Thicken up the spinach barrier so that the egg could no longer leak through and, while I was at it, work some supporting flavors into the mix.

I decided on a roux to tighten things up, so I melted some butter, added a minced shallot for depth, and then whisked in some flour. Instead of heavy cream, I poured in half-and-half, along with grated Parmesan cheese. I stirred the thawed and squeezed spinach into the cheesy sauce with pinches of ground nutmeg, dry mustard, salt, and pepper. The creamy, well-seasoned mixture tasted good enough to eat on its own, so I spooned about ¼ cup into each ramekin. I pushed some halfway up the sides and left an indented mound in the middle (this would help keep the yolk in the center of the dish), loaded the ramekins into a baking dish, and popped the whole thing into the hot oven to preheat for a few minutes before adding an egg to each cup. When I pulled the baking dish out of the oven

PHOTOGRAPHY: CARL TREMBLAY

The inherent challenge in achieving a perfectly cooked baked egg is that the yolk needs to stay liquid (with a temperature hovering around 150 degrees) while the white needs to solidify (with a temperature of 165 degrees). Here are some of the wrong turns we took before getting both components to cook just right.

BAKED IN WATER BATH
THEORY: Water slows the heat transfer, giving the whites time to solidify without overcooking the yolks.
OUTCOME: Perfect whites; pasty yolks.

BAKED IN SALT BED
THEORY: Salt is an even better insulator than water, providing the yolks with more protection.
OUTCOME: Perfect whites; slightly less pasty yolks.

BAKED IN BLAZING HOT RAMEKINS
THEORY: The walls of preheated ramekins should give the whites a head start without harming the yolks.
OUTCOME: Perfect yolks; blistered whites.

---

10 minutes after adding the eggs, I knew I was on the right track. The surfaces of the eggs looked a bit scathed from the blast of heat (nothing a spritz of vegetable oil before baking couldn't fix), but the hot creamed spinach barrier had effectively cradled the whites so that they were tender throughout and the yolks were still jiggly. But as I waited a few minutes for the piping hot eggs to cool down enough to taste, I noticed the yolks firming up. And by the time I could comfortably eat a spoonful, carryover cooking had ruined my breakfast, leaving me with rubbery whites and chalky yolks.

Because of residual heat, I would have to remove the eggs from the oven shy of their ideal final temperature (165 degrees) and allow them to finish cooking on the counter. After baking several more batches, I found that the eggs had to be pulled out when they looked quite underdone—roughly at the 7-minute mark, when the whites registered only 145 to 150 degrees, were just barely opaque, and trembled like Jell-O. But what a difference a 10-minute rest made. When I nicked the rested eggs with my fork, the whites were fully set (having climbed to the

approximate target of 165 degrees), and the yolks gushed out their rich, golden sauce. Since taking the individual temperature of six eggs was a hassle, I was happy to find during subsequent tests that I could abandon the thermometer—the jiggly appearance of the whites was a consistent indicator of when to remove the eggs from the oven.

Knowing that I had solved the great baked egg conundrum tasted almost as good as that first bite of tender egg coated in Parmesan-laced creamed spinach. The only thing missing was some toast—and perhaps a mimosa.

BAKED EGGS FLORENTINE
SERVES 6

In order for the eggs to cook properly, it is critical to add them to the hot filling–lined ramekins quickly. Use 6-ounce ramekins with 3¼-inch diameters, measured from the inner lip. It is imperative to remove the eggs from the oven just after the whites have turned opaque but are still jiggly—carryover cooking will finish the job. We developed this recipe using a glass baking dish; if using a metal baking pan, reduce the oven temperature to 425 degrees. This recipe can be doubled. If doubling, bake the ramekins in two 13 by 9-inch dishes and increase the baking times in steps 3 and 4 by 1 minute. For our free recipe for Baked Eggs Lorraine, go to CooksIllustrated.com/dec12.

- 2 tablespoons unsalted butter
- 1 large shallot, minced
- 1 tablespoon all-purpose flour
- ¾ cup half-and-half
- 10 ounces frozen spinach, thawed and squeezed dry
- 2 ounces Parmesan cheese, grated (1 cup)
  Salt and pepper
- ⅛ teaspoon dry mustard
- ⅛ teaspoon ground nutmeg
  Pinch cayenne pepper
  Vegetable oil spray
- 6 large eggs

1. Adjust oven rack to middle position and heat oven to 500 degrees.

2. Melt butter in medium saucepan over medium heat. Add shallot and cook, stirring occasionally, until softened, about 3 minutes. Stir in flour and cook, stirring constantly, for 1 minute. Gradually whisk in half-and-half; bring mixture to boil, whisking constantly. Simmer, whisking frequently, until thickened, 2 to 3 minutes. Remove pan from heat and stir in spinach, Parmesan, ¾ teaspoon salt, ½ teaspoon pepper, mustard, nutmeg, and cayenne.

3. Lightly spray six 6-ounce ramekins with oil spray. Evenly divide spinach filling among ramekins. Using back of spoon, push filling 1 inch up sides of ramekins to create ⅛-inch-thick layer. Shape remaining filling in bottom of ramekin into 1½-inch diameter mound, making shallow indentation in center of mound large enough to hold yolk. Place filled ramekins in 13 by 9-inch glass baking dish. Bake until filling just starts to brown, about 7 minutes, rotating dish halfway through baking.

4. While filling is heating, crack eggs (taking care not to break yolks) into individual cups or bowls. Remove baking dish with ramekins from oven and place on wire rack. Gently pour eggs from cups into hot ramekins, centering yolk in filling. Lightly spray surface of each egg with oil spray and sprinkle each evenly with pinch salt. Return baking dish to oven and bake until whites are just opaque but still tremble (carryover heat will cook whites through), 6 to 8 minutes, rotating dish halfway through baking.

5. Remove dish from oven and, using tongs, transfer ramekins to wire rack. Let stand until whites are firm and set (yolks should still be runny), about 10 minutes. Serve immediately.

TO MAKE AHEAD: Follow recipe through step 3, skipping baking of lined ramekins. Wrap ramekins with plastic wrap and refrigerate for up to 3 days. To serve, remove plastic and heat lined ramekins, directly from refrigerator, for additional 3 to 4 minutes (10 to 11 minutes total) before proceeding with recipe.

A Cradle for Your Egg

Our key to perfect baked eggs: cradling them in preheated ramekins lined with a filling. The hot filling gives the whites just the right jump start on cooking, allowing them to set while the yolks remain runny.

To ensure that the yolk stays centered (and away from the heat of the ramekin walls), we mound some of the filling in the middle of the ramekin and create a cavity that holds the yolk in place.

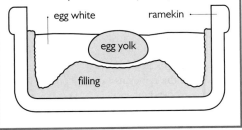

egg white   ramekin

egg yolk

filling

Crispy Potato Latkes

For truly crisp latkes, we had to eliminate the one thing potatoes are loaded with.

⇒ BY ANDREW JANJIGIAN ⇐

Latkes come in all shapes and sizes. But the aim for best texture is always the same: delicate and light throughout, with a creamy, buttery-soft interior surrounded by a shatteringly crisp outer shell. Unfortunately, many recipes produce latkes that soak up oil like a sponge, leaving them greasy and soft inside and out. Others are crisp outside but gluey and starchy within. Still others are simply undercooked and tough, with the texture and flavor of raw potato. Determined to produce a crispy specimen with real contrast between the crust and the center, I stockpiled potatoes and got to work.

Most latke recipes consist of the same core elements and a simple formula: Combine raw potatoes and onions and toss them with beaten egg, starch, salt, and pepper. Shallow-fry mounds of the thick batter until the disks are crisp and golden brown.

Trouble is, raw potatoes exude tons of moisture when their cells are broken, and excess water is the enemy of crispiness; more moisture leads to a wetter interior, and water that seeps out of the pancake during frying drags down the temperature of the oil, leading to a soggier, greasier result. That meant both the variety of potato and how I processed it would greatly affect the latkes' texture.

One quick test settled the spud question: Russets, with their high concentration of moisture-absorbing starch, produced the driest and crispiest pancakes. As for the cutting method, shredded (versus ground or chopped) potatoes yielded superior texture, the fine threads forming a lacy, weblike matrix.

That said, even floury russets gave up a tremendous amount of water, so I defaulted to the test kitchen's favorite potato-drying method: wringing out the shreds in a dry dish towel. After a few good squeezes, I mixed the dried shreds with grated onion (a fine pulp gave the latkes good flavor without adding any noticeable texture of its own), a couple of eggs, and potato starch that I'd drained from the exuded potato liquid and added back to the batter. Then I fried up another batch. Without all that water, these pancakes were on the right track—crispier for sure but also a bit raw-tasting and still oily.

The tricky thing was that these two problems presented something of a Catch-22: If I fried the latkes long enough to ensure a fully cooked interior,

the crust became too dark. But if I lowered the oil temperature so that they cooked more slowly, they absorbed too much of the oil.

Precooking the potatoes seemed like a good way to deal with this, but when I quickly blanched the spuds, they turned mushy and bland, the water literally washing away their potato flavor. Forget that.

Could the microwave do a better job? I placed the shredded, squeezed potatoes in a covered bowl and zapped them for a couple of minutes before mixing them with the other ingredients. Sure enough, the batch of latkes they produced was the best yet: tender inside and shatteringly crisp outside. And the greasiness? Nowhere to be found.

Wondering if there was more to the microwave than I'd thought, I did some research and uncovered an interesting explanation. A potato's starch granules begin to absorb water at temperatures as low as 137 degrees. Briefly heating the shreds in the microwave causes the starches to corral the water they contain into a gel, preventing it from leaching into the batter and lowering the oil temperature. In other words, the microwave had solved the greasiness problem, too. Latke mission accomplished.

CRISPY POTATO LATKES
SERVES 4 TO 6 AS A SIDE DISH

We prefer shredding the potatoes on the large holes of a box grater, but you can also use the large shredding disk of a food processor; cut the potatoes into 2-inch lengths first so you are left with short shreds. Serve with applesauce and sour cream.

- 2 pounds russet potatoes, unpeeled, scrubbed, and shredded
- ½ cup grated onion
-   Salt and pepper
- 2 large eggs, lightly beaten
- 2 teaspoons minced fresh parsley
-   Vegetable oil

1. Adjust oven rack to middle position, place rimmed baking sheet on rack, and heat oven to 200 degrees. Toss potatoes, onion, and 1 teaspoon salt in bowl. Place half of potato mixture in center of dish towel. Gather ends together and twist tightly to drain as much liquid as possible, reserving liquid in liquid measuring cup. Transfer drained potato mixture to second bowl and repeat process with remaining potato mixture. Set potato liquid aside and let stand so starch settles to bottom, at least 5 minutes.

2. Cover potato mixture and microwave until just

Zapping the potato shreds in the microwave before frying is key to the latkes' super-crisp crust.

warmed through but not hot, 1 to 2 minutes, stirring mixture with fork every 30 seconds. Spread potato mixture evenly over second rimmed baking sheet and let cool for 10 minutes. Don't wash out bowl.

3. Pour off water from reserved potato liquid, leaving potato starch in measuring cup. Add eggs and stir until smooth. Return cooled potato mixture to bowl. Add parsley, ¼ teaspoon pepper, and potato starch mixture and toss until evenly combined.

4. Set wire rack in clean rimmed baking sheet and line with triple layer of paper towels. Heat ¼-inch depth of oil in 12-inch skillet over medium-high heat until shimmering but not smoking (350 degrees). Place ¼-cup mound of potato mixture in oil and press with nonstick spatula into ⅓-inch-thick disk. Repeat until 5 latkes are in pan. Cook, adjusting heat so fat bubbles around latke edges, until golden brown on bottom, about 3 minutes. Turn and continue cooking until golden brown on second side, about 3 minutes longer. Drain on paper towels and transfer to baking sheet in oven. Repeat with remaining potato mixture, adding oil to maintain ¼-inch depth and returning oil to 350 degrees between batches. Season with salt and pepper to taste, and serve immediately.

TO MAKE AHEAD: Cooled latkes can be covered loosely with plastic wrap and held at room temperature for up to 4 hours. Alternatively, they can be frozen on baking sheet until firm, transferred to zipper-lock bag, and frozen for up to 1 month. Reheat latkes in 375-degree oven until crisp and hot, 3 minutes per side for room-temperature latkes and 6 minutes per side for frozen latkes.

Introducing Dacquoise

This multilayered showpiece of meringue and buttercream coated in ganache might just be the best dessert you'll ever make—plus you can prepare it the day before.

⟩ BY ANDREA GEARY ⟨

There could be no more stunning finale to a holiday celebration than a chocolate dacquoise. Named for Dax, a town in southwestern France where the dessert was first made, the confection is all sleek planes and clean right angles, elegantly enrobed in glossy dark chocolate studded with toasted nuts. Slicing it reveals a layered interior of light, nutty meringue sandwiched with silky buttercream. But you rarely see dacquoise anywhere but fancy patisseries or high-end restaurants—and with good reason: Making one is a project to rival all projects. The good news? Not only can you make this impressive showpiece at home but you can have it ready long before your guests arrive. In fact, this dessert improves when it's assembled a day or two before serving, as the flavors meld and the buttercream softens the meringue.

Here's how a pastry chef makes a dacquoise: She whips egg whites with sugar to make a meringue, into which she folds finely chopped nuts. Then she pipes the meringue into several flat layers, bakes them for up to 3 hours at a very low temperature, and then leaves them in the oven for an extended time to dry out completely. When the meringues are crisp, she layers them with buttercream (made from more egg whites, a screaming-hot sugar syrup, and a generous amount of butter). Finally, she coats the whole construction in a shiny ganache made with chocolate and warm cream.

All that is no big deal in a professional pastry shop, where there's no shortage of skilled workers, specialized equipment, big ovens, and egg whites. But for the process to be manageable at home, I would have to eliminate some of its more bothersome features: namely the fussy piping, the long baking and drying times, and that tricky sugar syrup. If possible, I would do something with all those orphaned egg yolks, too. And after all the time and effort I'd be putting in, I didn't want my dacquoise to just satisfy my guests; I wanted it to render them speechless.

Do the Meringue

Meringue is typically made by whipping egg whites (and perhaps an acid such as cream of tartar, which provides greater stability by preventing excess

Layers of almond-hazelnut meringue, rich espresso buttercream, and dark chocolate ganache make for a stunning holiday dessert.

bonding and coagulation) until they begin to retain air and form soft mounds in the bowl. The sugar is then slowly added while the whipping continues, until it dissolves and the mixture thickens, forming stiff, glossy peaks when the beaters are pulled from the surface. For dacquoise, finely ground nuts are folded in at this point, and then the meringue pieces are piped and baked. Meringue made this way, though, is a bit crunchy, leading to a dacquoise that can be hard to slice (and eat) even when left to sit for a while. My research revealed an intriguing alternative: an "automatic meringue," in which the whites and sugar were combined at the start. Not only did it sound easier than a traditional meringue but it might also produce a better texture, so I gave it a try.

The automatic meringue was indeed easy—I just dumped egg whites, cream of tartar, and sugar into the bowl of a stand mixer and let it rip. However, it took twice as long as the traditional method to reach stiff peaks, plus it baked up as dense and firm as Styrofoam. Sugar, it turns out, interferes with the unfolding and bonding of egg white proteins,

so adding it too early made for a slower process and denser meringue.

Obviously that was the wrong direction. But it gave me an idea: What if I went back to the traditional method of adding sugar once soft peaks formed but withheld some of it until the end? Would that lighten up the texture? I gave it another go, this time adding just half of the sugar between the soft- and stiff-peak stages and folding in the remainder at the end with the ground nuts. Now the egg white proteins were freer to expand, forming a light, airy foam in just 4 minutes. Once baked, this meringue had a crisp, delicate texture that was the perfect foil for buttercream—and was easier to slice and eat.

With the meringue's texture nailed down, I considered its shape. I wanted a rectangular dacquoise because it would be easier to slice neatly than a round one. Reluctant to use a pastry bag to pipe the meringue, I spooned it into four piles on two baking sheets and tried using an offset spatula to coax the piles into uniform rectangles. But despite my best efforts, they were all different sizes, with rounded blobs for corners.

Then I had a brainstorm: Why not bake the meringue in one big piece? That way, I could use just one sheet (eliminating the need to bake in batches) and trim the baked meringue into even pieces with squared-off edges. I drew a 13 by 10½-inch rectangle on a piece of parchment that I then placed on a rimless baking sheet. Using the lines as a guide, I spread meringue over it in an even layer.

Essential Tools

With an offset spatula, spreading and smoothing ganache and buttercream is a snap. Our favorite for this recipe is the **Ateco 7.75-Inch Offset Spatula ($8.60).**

The only tool that can cut the meringue without shattering it is a long, sharp, serrated knife. Our favorite is the **Wüsthof Classic 10-Inch Bread Knife ($89.95).**

Water Rescue

Most dacquoise recipes call for baking the meringue at about 200 degrees for anywhere from 1 to 3 hours and then letting it dry in the oven for several hours more. I found that even 2 hours of baking, followed by a full 3-hour rest, left my oversize meringue still chewy and impossible to cut neatly. With the temperature that low, I'd have to bake the meringue for a full 3 hours and rest it for at least as long in order to get it nice and crisp. While it was all hands-off waiting, I wanted to trim any time I could from the process.

What if I upped the heat? Although in this application I didn't need the meringue to be bright white (since it would be covered up by the buttercream), meringue baked at 300 degrees was too brown and tasted slightly burnt. With the oven at 250 degrees, I found my sweet spot: The meringue had a creamy taupe color and a firm, crisp texture after only 90 minutes of baking and the same amount of time drying.

The higher temperature sped things up, but it also caused a new problem: The surface of the meringue was now drying out faster than the bottom, forming a brittle crust that ballooned out and crumbled as soon as I took a knife to it. Though meringue and moisture are normally bitter enemies, I wondered if lightly spritzing water on the top before baking would help. This counterintuitive solution worked: Since water can't go above 212 degrees (the temperature at which it evaporates), it delayed the setting of the surface until most of the moisture had evaporated from the bottom layer, forming a

DIY Deluxe
Our dacquoise is not just easier than a professional-bakery version—it's better.

MORE GANACHE
We spread ganache on the exterior as well as between the layers for rich chocolate in every bite.

EASIER BUTTERCREAM
Most buttercreams call for egg whites and a fussy hot sugar syrup. Ours skips the syrup and uses up yolks left over from making the meringue.

LIGHTER MERINGUE
This meringue is ready in half the time that most recipes take. It's also lighter and easier to slice and eat.

meringue that remained intact and cooked evenly.

I now had what looked like a plank of acoustical tile. It took some trial and error before I found the right tools and technique for dividing it into four strips. A serrated bread knife, a gentle scoring motion, and a ruler ensured that each piece was trimmed to a perfect rectangle. I had the building blocks—now for the mortar to hold it together.

Wanted: The Right Buttercream
In its simplest (and most achingly sweet) form, buttercream is just creamed butter and powdered sugar. Not wanting cloying sweetness, I ruled out that type. The trouble is, most other buttercreams rely on egg whites, which would leave me with more leftover yolks. I also wanted to avoid using a hot sugar syrup (which requires a candy thermometer to bring the syrup to precisely 240 degrees), further narrowing the options. My salvation came in the form of a confection I'd never made before: a German buttercream, which is whipped together from butter and pastry cream, a simple custard made with egg yolks that doesn't need a thermometer.

I whisked the yolks with cornstarch, milk, and sugar over medium heat for a few minutes, until thickened. After cooling the pastry cream, I whipped it with an equal amount of softened butter until the mixture came together to form a velvety-smooth buttercream. It seemed a winner until I took a taste. Disappointingly, its flavor was flat and stodgy.

Dacquoise often includes a coffee-flavored element, and a few teaspoons of espresso powder mixed into the buttercream definitely improved matters. But something was still lacking. I found the missing element on the liquor shelf in the form of almond liqueur. Just an ounce gave the buttercream the sophistication it deserved and complemented the nutty meringue. I stacked the strips of meringue, spreading buttercream between each layer; thinly coated the exterior with it as well; and then let my dacquoise firm up in the fridge while I prepared its crowning glory—the shiny chocolate ganache.

Ganache Adds Panache
To make the ganache, I poured warm cream over finely chopped bittersweet chocolate and stirred the mixture until it was smooth, adding a couple teaspoons of corn syrup for enhanced shine. After it had cooled a bit, I poured the ganache over the chilled dacquoise and smoothed it over each side with an offset spatula. For the final touch, I decorated the top of the dacquoise with toasted hazelnuts and patted some sliced almonds onto its sides.

It looked spectacular, but when I ate a slice, I knew that something was still missing. Only the outer edges of my dacquoise boasted chocolate flavor and that just wasn't enough. Next time around, I made twice as much ganache and spread some on each layer of meringue, alternating with the buttercream. Now there was crisp, nutty meringue; rich buttercream; and silky ganache in every bite.

Tasters greeted this last dacquoise with a near

silence that made me nervous. Had I gotten it horribly wrong? Was it too sweet? Too crunchy? Had the meringue glued their jaws together? No. The dessert had merely rendered them speechless.

CHOCOLATE-ESPRESSO DACQUOISE
SERVES 10 TO 12

The components in this recipe can easily be prepared in advance. Use a rimless baking sheet or an overturned rimmed baking sheet to bake the meringue. Instant coffee may be substituted for the espresso powder. To skin the hazelnuts, simply place the warm toasted nuts in a clean dish towel and rub gently. We recommend Ghirardelli Bittersweet Chocolate Baking Bar with 60% cacao for this recipe.

Meringue
- ¾ cup blanched sliced almonds, toasted
- ½ cup hazelnuts, toasted and skinned
- 1 tablespoon cornstarch
- ⅛ teaspoon salt
- 1 cup (7 ounces) sugar
- 4 large egg whites, room temperature
- ¼ teaspoon cream of tartar

Buttercream
- ¾ cup whole milk
- 4 large egg yolks
- ⅓ cup (2⅓ ounces) sugar
- 1½ teaspoons cornstarch
- ¼ teaspoon salt
- 2 tablespoons amaretto or water
- 1½ tablespoons instant espresso powder
- 16 tablespoons unsalted butter, softened

Ganache
- 6 ounces bittersweet chocolate, chopped fine
- ¾ cup heavy cream
- 2 teaspoons corn syrup

- 12 whole hazelnuts, toasted and skinned
- 1 cup blanched sliced almonds, toasted

1. FOR THE MERINGUE: Adjust oven rack to middle position and heat oven to 250 degrees. Using ruler and pencil, draw 13 by 10½-inch rectangle on piece of parchment paper. Grease baking sheet and place parchment on it, ink side down.

2. Process almonds, hazelnuts, cornstarch, and salt in food processor until nuts are finely ground, 15 to 20 seconds. Add ½ cup sugar and pulse to combine, 1 to 2 pulses.

3. Using stand mixer fitted with whisk, whip egg whites and cream of tartar on medium-low speed until foamy, about 1 minute. Increase speed to medium-high and whip whites to soft, billowy mounds, about 1 minute. With mixer running at medium-high speed, slowly add remaining ½ cup sugar and continue to whip until glossy, stiff peaks form, 2 to 3 minutes. Fold nut mixture into egg whites in 2 batches. With offset spatula, spread meringue evenly into 13 by

DACQUOISE MADE DOABLE

Here's how to assemble the three different components of dacquoise—cooled, baked meringue; buttercream; and ganache—into a dessert that looks as though it was made in a professional bakery.

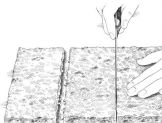

1. TRIM MERINGUE EDGES
Using serrated knife and gentle, repeated scoring motion, trim edges of cooled meringue to form 12 by 10-inch rectangle.

2. MEASURE AND MARK
With long side of rectangle parallel to counter, mark both long edges at 3-inch intervals.

3. CUT INTO 4 STRIPS
Repeatedly score surface by gently drawing knife from top mark to bottom mark until cut through. Repeat to make 4 strips.

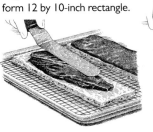

4. TOP 3 STRIPS WITH GANACHE
Place 3 strips on wire rack and spread ¼ cup ganache evenly over each. Refrigerate for 15 minutes.

5. TOP 1 STRIP WITH BUTTERCREAM
Spread remaining strip with ½ cup buttercream.

6. STACK STRIPS
Invert 1 ganache-coated strip on top of buttercream-coated strip. Spread with buttercream. Repeat. Invert final ganache-coated strip on top.

7. COAT WITH BUTTERCREAM
Coat sides of cake with half of remaining buttercream; coat top with remainder. Smooth and refrigerate until firm.

8. TOP WITH GANACHE
Pour warm ganache over cake and spread in thin, even layer, letting excess flow down sides. Spread thinly across sides.

9. GARNISH WITH NUTS
Use spatula to lift cake off rack. Arrange whole hazelnuts on top of cake and, holding cake with 1 hand, gently press almonds onto sides.

10½-inch rectangle on parchment, using lines on parchment as guide. Using spray bottle, evenly mist surface of meringue with water until glistening. Bake for 1½ hours. Turn off oven and allow meringue to cool in oven for 1½ hours. (Do not open oven during baking and cooling.) Remove from oven and let cool to room temperature, about 10 minutes. (Cooled meringue can be kept at room temperature, tightly wrapped in plastic wrap, for up to 2 days.)

4. FOR THE BUTTERCREAM: Heat milk in small saucepan over medium heat until just simmering. Meanwhile, whisk yolks, sugar, cornstarch, and salt in bowl until smooth. Remove milk from heat and, whisking constantly, add half of milk to yolk mixture to temper. Whisking constantly, return tempered yolk mixture to remaining milk in saucepan. Return saucepan to medium heat and cook, whisking constantly, until mixture is bubbling and thickens to consistency of warm pudding, 3 to 5 minutes. Transfer pastry cream to bowl. Cover and refrigerate until set, at least 2 hours or up to 24 hours. Before using, warm gently to room temperature in microwave at 50 percent power, stirring every 10 seconds.

5. Stir together amaretto and espresso powder; set aside. Using stand mixer fitted with paddle, beat butter at medium speed until smooth and light, 3 to 4 minutes. Add pastry cream in 3 batches, beating for 30 seconds after each addition. Add amaretto mixture and continue to beat until light and fluffy, about 5 minutes longer, scraping down bowl thoroughly halfway through mixing.

6. FOR THE GANACHE: Place chocolate in heatproof bowl. Bring cream and corn syrup to simmer in small saucepan over medium heat. Pour cream mixture over chocolate and let stand for 1 minute. Stir mixture until smooth. Set aside to cool until chocolate mounds slightly when dripped from spoon, about 5 minutes.

7. Carefully invert meringue and peel off parchment. Reinvert meringue and place on cutting board. Using serrated knife and gentle, repeated scoring motion, trim edges of meringue to form 12 by 10-inch rectangle. Discard trimmings. With long side of rectangle parallel to counter, use ruler to mark both long edges of meringue at 3-inch intervals. Using serrated knife, score surface of meringue by drawing knife toward you from mark on top edge to corresponding mark on bottom edge. Repeat scoring until meringue is fully cut through. Repeat until you have four 10 by 3-inch rectangles. (If any meringues break during cutting, use them as middle layers.)

8. Place 3 rectangles on wire rack set in rimmed baking sheet. Using offset spatula, spread ¼ cup ganache evenly over surface of each meringue. Refrigerate until ganache is firm, about 15 minutes. Set aside remaining ganache.

9. Using offset spatula, spread top of remaining rectangle with ½ cup buttercream; place on wire rack with ganache-coated meringues. Invert 1 ganache-coated meringue, place on top of buttercream, and press gently to level. Repeat, spreading meringue with ½ cup buttercream and topping with inverted ganache-coated meringue. Spread top with buttercream. Invert final ganache-coated strip on top of cake. Use 1 hand to steady top of cake and spread half of remaining buttercream to lightly coat sides of cake, then use remaining buttercream to coat top of cake. Smooth until cake resembles box. Refrigerate until buttercream is firm, about 2 hours. (Once buttercream is firm, assembled cake may be wrapped tightly in plastic and refrigerated for up to 2 days.)

10. Warm remaining ganache in heatproof bowl set over barely simmering water, stirring occasionally, until mixture is very fluid but not hot. Keeping assembled cake on wire rack, pour ganache over top of cake. Using offset spatula, spread ganache in thin, even layer over top of cake, letting excess flow down sides. Spread ganache over sides in thin layer (top must be completely covered, but some small gaps on sides are OK).

11. Garnish top of cake with hazelnuts. Holding bottom of cake with 1 hand, gently press almonds onto sides with other hand. Chill on wire rack, uncovered, for at least 3 hours or up to 12 hours. Transfer to platter. Cut into slices with sharp knife that has been dipped in hot water and wiped dry before each slice. Serve.

ILLUSTRATION: JOHN BURGOYNE

Rethinking Biscotti

Italians like these cookies dry and hard, while American versions are buttery and more tender. We wanted something in between—that is, crisp but not tooth shattering.

≥ BY ANDREW JANJIGIAN ≤

Biscotti literally means "twice-baked." These classic Italian cookies are baked once as a single, oblong loaf. The loaf is then sliced into thin planks, which are returned to the oven to fully dry. The result: crunchy, nutty (almond is a popular flavor), finger-shaped cookies that are perfect alongside a cup of coffee—or, as in Italy, a glass of sweet *vin santo*.

What separates one style from another mostly boils down to texture—specifically, just how crunchy or soft the cookies are. The most traditional biscotti, known as *cantuccini*, or *biscotti di Prato*, are extremely hard; they are meant to be dunked into a liquid to soften them before taking a bite (that's where the vin santo comes in). Then there are American biscotti—the big, buttery, much softer kind sold in coffeehouse chains, which are more like sugar cookies masquerading as biscotti. Both styles have their supporters, but for my own recipe, I wanted a hybrid: a cookie with big flavor and even bigger crunch but nothing so hard that it would jeopardize my dental work—a cookie that could be dipped into coffee but didn't need to be.

Use a serrated knife to slice the parbaked loaves into individual cookies before returning them to the oven for their second bake.

Whipped into Shape

A quick scan of several recipes suggested—and a subsequent biscotti bake-off confirmed—that the cookies' crunch or lack thereof corresponded with the amount of butter in the dough. Not surprisingly, batches made with little (or even no) fat were rock-hard, while doughs enriched with a full stick (8 tablespoons) of butter baked up much softer, thanks to the fat's tenderizing effect. Keeping that in mind, I began experimenting with a basic creaming formula—beat the butter and sugar; alternately fold in the dry ingredients (flour, baking powder, coarsely chopped almonds, salt, and spices) with the wet (eggs and vanilla or almond extract)—and varying the amount of butter in each batch.

Half a stick turned out to be the ideal compromise;

the dough was neither too hard nor too lean. The only problem was that a mere 4 tablespoons of butter (plus 1 cup of sugar) didn't give the stand mixer enough to work with. Instead of beating air into the butter to lighten it, all the mixer could do was soften the fat, and the resulting biscotti were dense and squat. My other idea for giving the dough some lift was to up the baking powder, but this was only effective to a point; any more than 2 teaspoons and the biscotti baked up crumbly. (The carbon dioxide produced by baking powder is more effective at expanding existing air bubbles than it is at creating its own.)

It was time to brainstorm: What other elements of the dough could be aerated in the stand mixer? I scanned my ingredient list and landed on an ingredient so obvious I was surprised I hadn't thought of it sooner: eggs. Reversing the order of operations, I whipped two eggs until they were light in color and then added the sugar and continued to beat the mixture. Finally, I folded in the butter (melted and cooled), followed by the dry ingredients. When it came time to shape the dough, I deliberately

portioned it into two relatively short, wide logs; that way, the cut cookies would span 4 inches from end to end—perfect for repeat dunking. To give the finished cookies a nice sheen, I brushed the logs with a beaten egg white. I then baked the logs for about a half-hour, sliced them on the bias into ½-inch-thick cookies, and returned those to the oven for round two.

The good news was that my unorthodox dough-mixing technique was a major breakthrough: The whipped eggs gave the dough the lightness and lift it had been lacking. But despite their lighter, more open crumb, the biscotti were still making my teeth work too hard for a bite. Also, I'd added a judicious amount of almond extract to bring out the nuts' flavor, but its distinct taste was surprisingly faint.

Hard Case

Too little fat had been partially responsible for the overly hard cookies I'd made, but apparently it wasn't the only factor. That's when the bread baker in me began to wonder if the dough had developed too much gluten (the network of proteins that gives baked goods their structure). In the moist environment of a bread dough, lots of gluten produces chewiness, as the gluten strands resist being pulled apart; in a dry cookie, the result is hardness, as the gluten resists breaking.

My first thought was to try using lower-protein cake flour in place of the all-purpose, since its reduced gluten content would result in weaker gluten structure. The swap did make the biscotti easier to eat but not in a good way: To the extent that the cake flour made the biscotti less hard, it also made them more fragile. Even mixing all-purpose and cake flours was a bust.

I was starting to realize that less gluten was not the answer. What I really needed was a way to modify the texture of the biscotti so that the gluten it contained had less impact on the overall hardness of the cookie, while still providing the crumb itself with plenty of structure.

That's when I remembered one of the early recipes I tried that called for finely ground (rather than coarsely chopped) almonds. The nuts had gotten lost in the biscotti, but they'd also made the cookies much more crumbly—and a little bit of crumbliness might be just what these cookies needed. Moving ahead with this idea, I swapped out ½ cup of flour for an equal amount of almonds that I had ground to a fine powder in the food processor. (Since I was now using the processor to grind the nuts, I also used it to whip the eggs, which worked just as well as the stand mixer.) One bite and I knew I was onto something. These biscotti were still plenty hard, but the almond meal made them far easier to bite into. In fact, they were breaking apart too easily, so I tried again, scaling back the almond meal to ¼ cup. This time I hit the nail on the head. The cookies' texture was perfect: crunchy but easy to bite.

What was it about the nut meal that produced a more breakable cookie? According to our science editor, the ground nuts broke up the gluten structure so that there were smaller pockets of gluten networks rather than one large one. As a result, the cookies gave way more easily when bitten, but the crumb itself didn't lose its hard crunch. (See "Why Nuts Take Some Bite out of Biscotti.") And to appease those who missed the bursts of nuttiness from whole pieces, I added back 1 cup of coarsely chopped almonds when it came time to fold in the dry ingredients.

Flavor Boost

All that remained was to beef up my working recipe's still-weak almond flavor. The curious thing was that the almond extract aroma was strong during the first baking but had all but vanished by the time the cookies had baked twice. A little research explained: As it turns out, benzaldehyde, the main compound responsible for the flavor and aroma of almonds, is highly volatile and had evaporated during the twice-baked cookies' long exposure to heat. To compensate, I figured I needed to start with a higher-than-average dose and experimented until I found that 1½ teaspoons—triple the amount that I had started with—did the trick. Similarly, I found that I had to load up on other ingredients with volatile compounds like aromatic herbs, spices, and zest when I developed my anise, hazelnut-orange, hazelnut-lavender, and pistachio-spice variations. (Since vanilla extract was only providing background notes to the biscotti flavor, I found that I could keep its amount at just ½ to 1 teaspoon.)

At last, I had a set of biscotti recipes I could be proud of: Boldly flavored and crunchy, these biscotti were hard, yes, but far from hard to eat, given the hordes of tasters who kept asking for more.

ALMOND BISCOTTI
MAKES 30 COOKIES

The almonds will continue to toast while the biscotti bake, so toast the nuts only until they are just fragrant. See page 31 for tips on coating in chocolate. For our free recipe for Hazelnut-Lavender Biscotti, go to CooksIllustrated.com/dec12.

1¼ cups (6¼ ounces) whole almonds, lightly toasted
1¾ cups (8¾ ounces) all-purpose flour
2 teaspoons baking powder
¼ teaspoon salt
2 large eggs, plus 1 large white beaten with pinch salt
1 cup (7 ounces) sugar
4 tablespoons unsalted butter, melted and cooled
1½ teaspoons almond extract
½ teaspoon vanilla extract
Vegetable oil spray

1. Adjust oven rack to middle position and heat oven to 325 degrees. Using ruler and pencil, draw two 8 by 3-inch rectangles, spaced 4 inches apart, on piece of parchment paper. Grease baking sheet and place parchment on it, ink side down.

2. Pulse 1 cup almonds in food processor until coarsely chopped, 8 to 10 pulses; transfer to bowl and set aside. Process remaining ¼ cup almonds in food processor until finely ground, about 45 seconds. Add flour, baking powder, and salt; process to combine, about 15 seconds. Transfer flour mixture to second bowl. Process 2 eggs in now-empty food processor until lightened in color and almost doubled in volume, about 3 minutes. With processor running, slowly add sugar until thoroughly combined, about 15 seconds. Add melted butter, almond extract, and vanilla and process until combined, about 10 seconds. Transfer egg mixture to medium bowl. Sprinkle half of flour mixture over egg mixture and, using spatula, gently fold until just combined. Add remaining flour mixture and chopped almonds and gently fold until just combined.

3. Divide batter in half. Using floured hands, form each half into 8 by 3-inch rectangle, using lines on parchment as guide. Spray each loaf lightly with oil spray. Using rubber spatula lightly coated with oil spray, smooth tops and sides of rectangles. Gently

For Double-Baked Cookies, Double—or Triple—the Spice
While turning out batch after batch of biscotti, we noticed that many of the flavors we added to the dough—almond extract and aromatic herbs and spices—started off strong and fragrant but faded once the cookies had baked twice, since the successive exposure to heat kills off many of their volatile flavor compounds. To compensate, we loaded up on them, in some cases tripling the amount we started with.

brush tops of loaves with egg white wash. Bake until loaves are golden and just beginning to crack on top, 25 to 30 minutes, rotating pan halfway through baking.

4. Let loaves cool on baking sheet for 30 minutes. Transfer loaves to cutting board. Using serrated knife, slice each loaf on slight bias into ½-inch-thick slices. Lay slices, cut side down, about ¼ inch apart on wire rack set in rimmed baking sheet. Bake until crisp and golden brown on both sides, about 35 minutes, flipping slices halfway through baking. Let cool completely before serving. Biscotti can be stored in airtight container for up to 1 month.

ANISE BISCOTTI

Add 1½ teaspoons anise seeds to flour mixture in step 2. Substitute anise-flavored liqueur for almond extract.

HAZELNUT-ORANGE BISCOTTI

Substitute lightly toasted and skinned hazelnuts for almonds. Add 2 tablespoons minced fresh rosemary to flour mixture in step 2. Substitute orange-flavored liqueur for almond extract and add 1 tablespoon grated orange zest to egg mixture with butter.

PISTACHIO-SPICE BISCOTTI

Substitute shelled pistachios for almonds. Add 1 teaspoon ground cardamom, ½ teaspoon ground cloves, ½ teaspoon pepper, ¼ teaspoon ground cinnamon, and ¼ teaspoon ground ginger to flour mixture in step 2. Substitute 1 teaspoon water for almond extract and increase vanilla extract to 1 teaspoon.

SCIENCE Why Nuts Take Some Bite out of Biscotti

We wanted our biscotti to pack just as much crunch as the traditional Italian kind but also to break apart easily when you take a bite. Adding extra butter to the dough helped, but our ultimate solution was cutting the flour with finely ground nuts. While butter merely made the cookie more tender, ground nuts actually weakened its structure.

Both ingredients influence the texture because of their effect on gluten, the web of flour proteins that gives baked goods structure. The fat in butter "shortens" the gluten strands by surrounding individual strands and preventing them from linking up into larger networks. Ground nuts interfere with gluten formation in a slightly different way, getting in between pockets of gluten to create microscopic "fault lines" in the biscotti, which allow the hard cookie to break apart easily under the tooth. –A.J.

CRUNCHY—BUT NOT A JAWBREAKER

In Search of the Perfect Pepper Mill

This everyday gadget has been designed and redesigned a thousand times. But does a fancier mill mean the perfect grind?

> BY AMY GRAVES <

What is it with the pepper mill these days? Sleek, battery-driven models and one-handed ratchet designs compete with traditional hand-crank mills—and most look as though they've fallen prey to decorative whims. For our money, a pepper mill has one purpose: to swiftly crank out the desired size and amount of fresh ground pepper, without any guesswork in grind selection or extra strain on our wrists. Simple criteria, and yet many models fail to measure up.

We tested pepper mills in 1996 and 2007, and both times we chose the Unicorn Magnum Plus ($45) as our winner for quickly producing an abundance of uniformly ground pepper with minimal effort. But some of us have always had our quibbles with this mill. Its grind adjuster lacks fixed settings, requiring trial and error to get the target-size grind. While the mill holds a lot of peppercorns, the ring covering the loading chamber can slide open during grinding, allowing the peppercorns to spill right back out. And although it churns out coarse and medium pepper easily, the mill fails to produce truly fine pepper no matter how tightly we crank the grind adjuster.

To see if any new mills could outdo the Unicorn Magnum Plus, we rounded up nine contenders, both manual and battery-powered, priced from $27 to nearly $100, and got grinding.

Adjusting to the Grind

To get a handle on grind speed and ease of operation, we first tested each mill by fine-grinding peppercorns over a digital scale and timing how long it took for each model to produce the equivalent of 2 tablespoons, or 15.3 grams. Speeds ranged from just longer than 1½ minutes to a whopping 14 minutes. The surprise here was that the bigger mills, with the capacity to grind more peppercorns at one time, were not always the fastest. The stubby Trudeau Easy Grind and Peugeot Saint Malo proved just as speedy as (or even speedier than) the much bigger Unicorn Magnum Plus. We realized that part of their success was due to their handles. Instead of twisting at the top, these mills use crank handles that rotate in a wide arc, grinding continuously as well as offering

greater leverage with each turn for faster grinding.

Crank handles may be the most efficient, but comfort is important, too. Heavy, awkward models slowed testers down; models that took extra work to grasp, like one "key-top" design mill, had testers constantly repositioning their hands. Mills with smooth, padded handles or rounded tops that fit users' hands aided, rather than hampered, grinding.

What about mills that require no elbow grease at all? They sound enticing, but battery-driven mills turned out to be nonstarters. One, which cost an astounding $99.95, had us prying apart a complicated mechanism at the base to insert six AAA batteries. The other was the same mill that took a painful 14 minutes to grind 2 tablespoons of pepper.

Finer Points

If quick output were everything, it would be easy to sort winners from losers. But we often want a different-size grind of pepper depending on the dish, and changing the grind size on many of the mills caused trouble. Some relied on a small adjustable screw at the bottom of the grinder that frequently had us resorting to pliers to loosen it. Mills with a finial at the top controlling adjustment meant that every time we filled the hopper with peppercorns we had to recalibrate the grind size as well. Our favorite mills removed the trial and error of grind selection with clear markings that shifted neatly into place.

The final consideration for a pepper mill is grind quality. Getting a mix of fine powder and coarse chunks doesn't help in recipes when you want one or the other. Only two out of the 10 models in our lineup consistently produced just the right grind size in every setting, while the rest (like our former winner) spat out a mix of dust and cracked peppercorns. When we took the mills apart to look at their inner workings, we began to understand why.

All pepper mills work more or less the same way: A

grooved and serrated rotating nut, which is attached to a metal shaft, fits into a stationary, serrated ring. As the nut rotates, its grooved channels lead peppercorns toward the serrations on both the ring and the nut, first cracking then slicing the peppercorns between them. When you turn the adjustment knob, a spring at the center presses the nut and the ring together to change the grind size: tighter for fine, looser for coarse. But in some mills, like the Unicorn Magnum Plus, the spring lacked the ability to fully compress its ring and nut, impeding their ability to deliver a truly fine grind. In other models, the ring and nut were set so far apart in the coarse grind setting that they frequently spat out whole, uncracked peppercorns. The successful models, like our winner, had well-proportioned springs that allowed the ring and nut to be cranked to just the right distance apart.

Looking inside also provided a clue as to why two mills in particular lagged far behind the others in speed: the material of their nuts and rings. While the most efficient models in our lineup used steel mechanisms, the nuts and rings of these poky models were made of ceramic. Because ceramic is more brittle than steel—and more prone to breaking—their grooves and serrations weren't as deep or sharp. As a result, these mills took far longer to grind.

At the end of testing, we finally found a winner to best the Unicorn Magnum Plus. The carbon steel grind mechanism of the Derwent from Cole & Mason ($40) features seven large grooves on the nut (most have only five) that taper into finer grooves at the base. These allow it to swiftly channel peppercorns toward the deep, sharp serrations on its ring, for fast, efficient grinding. Its spring provides just the right tension to bring the nut and the ring the appropriate distance together (or apart) to create a uniform grind in each of its six fixed, clearly marked grind sizes. We also appreciated its clear acrylic body, which allows you to track when you need a refill.

A Great Set of Gears

All pepper mills operate the same way: A nut revolves inside a stationary ring, crushing peppercorns between them. But fine differences in the design of our winning mill, the Derwent from Cole & Mason, made a big difference in its performance.

Carbon steel construction allows for deep, sharp serrations in both the nut and the ring that swiftly slice and shear the peppercorns.

Lots of grooves in the **nut** quickly guide peppercorns toward the **ring**.

A well-proportioned spring brings the nut and the ring just the right distance apart to create the target grind size.

ILLUSTRATION: JOHN LAYMAN

RATING PEPPER MILLS

We rated 10 pepper mills with steel or ceramic grind mechanisms, both manual and battery-driven, and evaluated them on the criteria below. The mills are listed in order of preference. All were purchased online, and the source for our top model appears on page 32.

GRIND QUALITY

We ground 1 tablespoon of fine pepper with each mill and shook it through a fine-mesh sieve for 30 seconds; then we weighed what was too coarse to pass through the sieve. For coarse-grind consistency, we ground 1 tablespoon of coarse pepper with each mill, shook it through a fine-mesh sieve for 30 seconds, and weighed what was too fine to remain in the sieve. For the grinds in between, we visually assessed the ground pepper, comparing it with both coarse and fine.

EASE OF USE

We rated each mill on how easy it was to fill with peppercorns, adjust to different grind settings, and hold and operate for right- and left-handed users with different hand sizes.

FINE-GRIND SPEED

We timed how long it took for each mill to grind 15.3 grams (2 tablespoons) of fine pepper.

	CRITERIA	TESTERS' COMMENTS

HIGHLY RECOMMENDED

COLE & MASON Derwent Gourmet Precision Pepper Mill
Model: H59401G PM **Price:** $40
Grind Mechanism: Carbon steel
Capacity: Scant ½ cup

Grind Quality ★★★
Ease of Use ★★★
Fine-Grind Speed ★★ (3 min)

When it comes to grind quality, this mill is tops. It made grind selection a snap, with clear markings corresponding to grind size, and every one of its six fixed settings performed well. Its transparent acrylic body proved easy to load and grasp.

RECOMMENDED

PEUGEOT DAMAN u'Select Shaftless Pepper Mill
Model: PM25441 **Price:** $75
Grind Mechanism: Carbon steel
Capacity: ½ cup

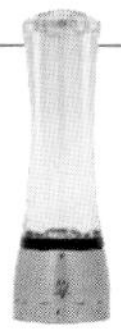

Grind Quality ★★½
Ease of Use ★★
Fine-Grind Speed ★★★ (2 min 15 sec)

This high-performing mill was fast and consistent, but if its peppercorn supply fell below 1 inch, output slowed. However, with no center shaft and a clever magnetized lid, this mill is a snap to refill. We would prefer that the grind-size adjuster click firmly into place: It can slip if you grab it during grinding.

TRUDEAU Easy Grind 6½-Inch Pepper Mill
Model: 0716027 **Price:** $33.99
Grind Mechanism: Carbon steel
Capacity: ⅔ cup

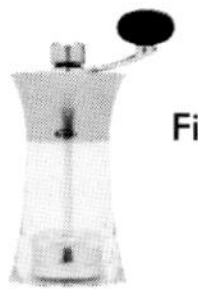

Grind Quality ★★½
Ease of Use ★★
Fine-Grind Speed ★★★ (1 min 40 sec)

This inexpensive crank-style mill lived up to its name with an easy-to-grip handle that had us cranking out pepper at a rapid clip. A downside: The grind adjustment dial has no fixed grind sizes, making it hard to get just the right pepper size.

UNICORN Magnum Plus Pepper Mill
Model: 61695 **Price:** $45
Grind Mechanism: Stainless steel
Capacity: 1⅛ cups

Grind Quality ★★
Ease of Use ★★
Fine-Grind Speed ★★★ (1 min 55 sec)

Our old favorite remains fast and efficient, with a generous capacity and a smooth operation, but its "fine" grind looked more like medium. There are no fixed grind settings, requiring trial and error to get the right grind size, and the loading ring twisted open during grinding, spilling out peppercorns.

RECOMMENDED WITH RESERVATIONS

VIC FIRTH 8-Inch Federal Pepper Mill
Model: FED08PM21 **Price:** $45.95
Grind Mechanism: Stainless steel
Capacity: ¼ cup

Grind Quality ★★★
Ease of Use ★★
Fine-Grind Speed ★½ (4 min 5 sec)

Comfortable to hold and twist, this wood mill produced uniform grinds in each setting. Its major flaws were a very small capacity to hold peppercorns, which were difficult to load, and poor output: It finely ground pepper at a very slow pace, even when we loosened the setting a few notches.

UNICORN KeyTop Professional Pepper Mill
Model: 91597 **Price:** $27
Grind Mechanism: Stainless steel
Capacity: Scant ½ cup

Grind Quality ★★½
Ease of Use ★★
Fine-Grind Speed ★★ (3 min)

The grind mechanism on this mill from Unicorn is smaller than that of its predecessor, and its key top was hard to grasp, slowing our efforts. It made a better fine grind than did the Magnum Plus but didn't produce uniformly coarse pepper.

NOT RECOMMENDED

WILLIAM BOUNDS Robo Steel Pepper Mill
Model: 30121 **Price:** $60
Grind Mechanism: Ceramic
Capacity: ¼ cup

Grind Quality ★★★
Ease of Use ★★
Fine-Grind Speed ★ (14 min)

Although it ground pepper to a uniform fine size, the coarse setting was troublesome, and this battery-powered mill took a lifetime to produce either one. Plus, the dial at the base, which controls the grind setting, got stuck, requiring pliers to loosen.

PEUGEOT Saint Malo 5.7 Inch Pepper Mill
Model: PM27483 **Price:** $49.95
Grind Mechanism: Carbon steel
Capacity: Scant ¼ cup

Grind Quality ★½
Ease of Use ★
Fine-Grind Speed ★★★ (1 min 55 sec)

This small crank-style mill ground pepper in a flash, but it was uncomfortable to hold and crank and fussy to load. Its fine grind produced too many large pieces—most likely because its crank handle loosened the finial that controls the grind setting.

PEUGEOT Elis Sense u'Select Stainless Pepper Mill
Model: PM27162 **Price:** $99.95
Grind Mechanism: Carbon steel
Capacity: ¼ cup

Grind Quality ★
Ease of Use ★★
Fine-Grind Speed ★★ (3 min 25 sec)

This battery-powered mill was frustrating to load—both batteries and peppercorns. On the model's coarsest setting, many whole peppercorns slipped past the grinder into the mix, and its "fine" pepper was not uniformly fine.

WILLIAM BOUNDS HM 11-Inch Proview Pepper Mill
Model: 04817 **Price:** $70
Grind Mechanism: Ceramic
Capacity: ⅔ cup

Grind Quality ★½
Ease of Use ★½
Fine-Grind Speed ★ (7 min)

This tall, heavy mill grinds pepper by twisting in both directions, but that didn't make it more efficient—its shallow-grooved, ceramic grinder took far longer than carbon steel to crack peppercorns.

Supermarket Cocoa Powder

These days cocoa powder fetches anywhere from $7 to nearly $24 per pound. But is price any indication of rich chocolate flavor?

> BY HANNAH CROWLEY <

Cocoa powder is a chocolate powerhouse, packing in more flavor ounce for ounce than any other form of chocolate. In the test kitchen, we reach for it constantly when making cookies, cake, pudding, hot chocolate—even chili—which is why we're picky about what brand we keep around. When we last tasted cocoa powders, in 2005, the supermarket cocoas produced such insipid results that we reluctantly resorted to sending away for the one brand that boasted real chocolate flavor and depth: Callebaut, which also rings in at a whopping $16 per pound (and that's without shipping).

But given that all chocolates (milk, bittersweet, unsweetened, etc.) have witnessed an upgrade in recent years, we wondered: Have supermarket cocoa options improved as well? Furthermore, several higher-end brands, such as Valrhona and Scharffen Berger, can now be found in many markets nationwide. That was all the convincing we needed to revisit the category. We didn't want to sacrifice quality for convenience, but if we could identify a brand that delivered the deep chocolate flavor we were after without the prohibitive cost or waiting for the postman, we'd happily make the switch.

Pretty soon we were baking up a storm, incorporating eight widely available brands of cocoa into chocolate butter cookies, chocolate cake, and hot cocoa. As they evaluated the samples on the intensity and complexity of the chocolate flavor, tasters reconfirmed that the brand of cocoa you use really does make or break a dessert or a drink. Lesser powders produced "wan" cakes and hot cocoa that tasted like "dust dissolved in water"; good versions delivered "profound" chocolate flavor and made cookies seem downright "luxurious."

At first we thought that differences might have to do with whether the cocoa was natural or Dutch-processed. Dutching, which was invented in the 19th century by Dutch chemist and chocolatier Coenraad Van Houten, raises the powder's pH, which neutralizes its acids and astringent notes and rounds out its flavor. (It also darkens the color.) But according to our numbers, whether a cocoa was Dutched didn't matter. Our winner was a natural powder, and there was no pattern to the rest of the rankings.

Fat content also seemed like a potential factor in the rankings. Cacao beans naturally contain 47 to 54 percent fat, and how much of that fat is retained after processing is a bragging point for many higher-end brands of cocoa. More fat suggests a richer-tasting product, and pricier brands often contain twice as much fat as do standard powders. But again, our preferences proved those assumptions wrong. Both our first- and last-place brands contained nearly the same low level of fat (about 11.5 percent), and in between those extremes the levels jumped up and down.

With pH and fat out of the running, we took a step back to remind ourselves of the main feature dividing the pack: bold, rich chocolate flavor. The top-ranking brands had it, the bottom-ranking didn't. To understand why this would be so, maybe we needed to answer a more fundamental question: Where does chocolate flavor come from, anyway?

The Whole (Bean) Story

It starts with the cacao pod—the football-shaped fruit of a stout tropical tree, Theobroma cacao, that grows below the jungle canopy in humid climates 20 degrees north and south of the equator, a swath of land sometimes referred to as the "Cocoa Belt." Each pod contains 20 to 50 beans, and inside each bean are the nibs—the dark, meaty flesh that is ground and later refined to make chocolate. When harvested, the pods and their contents neither smell nor taste like chocolate (in fact, the white flesh surrounding the beans is said to taste like a combination of watermelon, strawberries, and kiwi). After harvesting, the beans are left to ferment, a process that eats away at the fruity flesh surrounding the beans and initiates the development of flavors that are recognizably chocolaty. The beans are then dried, bagged, and sent to a processing facility to be roasted. (For more information, see "The Journey from Pod to Powder.")

This is the most exacting—and critical—phase of the process. Roasting triggers the Maillard reaction, in which proteins and sugars in food break down and develop more complex flavors. In cacao beans, this means the potential for nearly 500 new flavor compounds to be formed. To achieve this, manufacturers roast beans within the same relatively low temperature range following one of two methods: They either roast the beans whole and discard the shell after roasting (the traditional approach), or they remove the shell and roast just the nibs. To further develop flavor, chocolatiers often blend beans during roasting, mixing nibs and powder from various origins (manufacturers wouldn't reveal their bean sources to us) to achieve the exact specifications of color, texture, and flavor. During the final phases of roasting, some chocolatiers even carry out taste checks on the beans or nibs, scooping them from the roaster at 15-second intervals to nail down the exact point at which they believe flavors are optimized.

Figuring that the roasting phase of the process might shed some light on our cocoa preferences, we contacted all eight manufacturers to inquire about

The Journey from Pod to Powder

To deliver rich-tasting cocoa powder, producers must perfect every step of the process. But as we discovered, it's the roasting phase that affects flavor the most.

HARVEST PODS
Football-shaped pods are collected from tropical cacao trees. Each pod contains 20 to 50 beans surrounded by fruity flesh.

DRY BEANS
Beans are fermented for two to nine days and dried for up to several weeks before being bagged and sent to a processing facility.

ROAST NIBS
Beans are either roasted whole and then shelled or else shelled first, leaving just the meaty center—the nib—to roast. The latter approach produces richer-tasting cocoa.

GRIND POWDER
Roasted nibs are ground into a paste called chocolate liquor and then pressed to extract cocoa butter and ground again into small particles.

TASTING SUPERMARKET COCOA POWDER

Twenty-one *Cook's Illustrated* staff members tasted eight cocoa powders selected from a list of top-selling brands compiled by the Chicago-based market research firm SymphonyIRI Group, sampling them baked into chocolate cake and chocolate butter cookies and stirred into hot cocoa. An independent lab analyzed pH and fat content. Information on processing was provided by the respective cocoa companies. Prices were paid in Boston-area supermarkets and online, and brands appear below in order of preference.

RECOMMENDED

HERSHEY'S Natural Cocoa Unsweetened
Price: $3.49 for 8 oz (44 cents per oz)
Roasting Style: Nib **Fat:** 11.46%
Comments: Our winner is proof that you needn't look beyond the supermarket baking aisle for great cocoa. Hershey shells the nibs before roasting them and then grinds them very fine for cocoa boasting "assertive" chocolate flavor underlined by hints of "coffee," "orange," and "cinnamon."

DROSTE Cocoa
Price: $10.50 for 8.8 oz ($1.19 per oz)
Roasting Style: Nib **Fat:** 21.80%
Comments: This Dutch-processed import impressed tasters with "round," "bold" flavor and "lots of depth." If it didn't cost nearly three times as much as our winner, it would be an appealing alternative. We'll splurge on it for recipes calling for Dutched cocoa.

HERSHEY'S Special Dark Cocoa
Price: $3.49 for 8 oz (44 cents per oz)
Roasting Style: Nib **Fat:** 12.61%
Comments: A sibling of our winner, this blend of natural and Dutched cocoa tinted cakes and cookies such a deep color that one taster dubbed it "chocolate with a vengeance." But its "pleasant," "fruity" flavor didn't quite live up to the hue.

VALRHONA Cocoa Powder
Price: $11.99 for 8.82 oz ($1.36 per oz)
Roasting Style: Proprietary **Fat:** 21.94%
Comments: This "grown-up" Dutched powder was "dynamite" in cookies, in which lots of butter rounded its "smoky" notes into "pronounced" chocolate flavor. But its smokiness made leaner cake taste as though it was "cooked over wood chips."

RECOMMENDED WITH RESERVATIONS

GHIRARDELLI Natural Unsweetened Cocoa
Price: $5.59 for 10 oz (56 cents per oz)
Roasting Style: Nib **Fat:** 12.56%
Comments: Despite being nib-roasted, which gave other brands depth and richness, this "mild" powder tasted merely "respectable," with "smooth but undistinguished" flavor.

SCHARFFEN BERGER Unsweetened Natural Cocoa Powder
Price: $8.79 for 6 oz ($1.47 per oz)
Roasting Style: Whole bean **Fat:** 22.30%
Comments: Tasters who appreciated a lighter-bodied natural cocoa praised this brand for tasting "more milky than bittersweet." But for most of us, it was simply "lacking in rich flavor." Its sky-high price also knocked it down a notch.

NESTLÉ Toll House Cocoa
Price: $2.69 for 8 oz (34 cents per oz)
Roasting Style: Whole bean **Fat:** 12.31%
Comments: With "weak" chocolate flavor, this "kid-friendly" natural powder was described as "mild" and "one-dimensional."

EQUAL EXCHANGE Baking Cocoa
Price: $7.84 for 8 oz (98 cents per oz)
Roasting Style: Whole bean **Fat:** 11.54%
Comments: Some tasters picked up on "malty" and "caramel" notes in this Dutched cocoa, but most agreed that its chocolate flavor "lacked intensity" and was "almost an afterthought." Other tasters found it a little "sour" or even "acidic."

---

their methods and, sure enough, uncovered a pattern: The top brands in our lineup separate the nibs before roasting, while lower-ranking brands roast the whole bean, shelling afterward. According to Gregory Ziegler, a chocolate expert and professor of food science at Pennsylvania State University, roasting just the nibs offers a distinct advantage: The nibs roast more evenly outside the shell, making under- or over-roasting less probable. So why wouldn't all chocolatiers shell their beans first? Ziegler thinks it's probably just a bias toward tradition. Other experts we spoke with say money is the real issue. Roasters are extremely expensive, and since many manufacturers are equipped with traditional whole-bean roasters, they don't often upgrade.

On the Ground

After roasting, the nibs are ground into chocolate liquor (which contains both cocoa solids and cocoa butter); that liquor is then pressed to remove cocoa butter and ground into small particles. With this information in mind, we took a closer look at the cocoas and realized that some seemed to be ground finer than others—an observation that was confirmed when we put each powder under a microscope. Here again a pattern emerged: In general, our top brands had small, distinct particles, while weaker-tasting powders had much larger particles. Though manufacturers wouldn't disclose the aim of their grind size to us, our finding made sense: The smaller the particle the more surface area that's exposed, hence the more flavor that's released.

Our preferred brands, including our top pick, Hershey's Natural Cocoa Unsweetened, shared these two key features: They were roasted from nibs versus whole beans, and they boasted a smaller particle size. In cookies, cake, and hot cocoa, tasters repeatedly singled out Hershey's "intense," "bright" chocolate flavor and particularly deep complexity. Even better, this cocoa met our original goal: Not only is it one of the least expensive brands on the market but it's one of the most widely available, too.

We had just one more test before we were satisfied: To see how the Hershey's cocoa measured up to the Callebaut, we baked chocolate cakes with each brand and tasted them side by side. Just as it did in our previous tasting, the Callebaut wowed tasters, who swooned for its elegant "dark-chocolate" flavor. But the Hershey's didn't disappoint, earning high marks of its own.

The bottom line: We'll still stock Callebaut for special-occasion baking, but for everyday cocoa needs, Hershey's takes the cake.

Special-Occasion Cocoa

Our winning supermarket cocoa powder from Hershey's is a great everyday option. But we still love the exceptional depth and richness of our pricey, previous favorite from **Callebaut** ($16 per pound). We recommend mail-ordering a bag to keep on hand for holiday baking.

EQUIPMENT CORNER

⩾ BY HANNAH CROWLEY, AMY GRAVES, SACHA MADADIAN & TAIZETH SIERRA ⩽

NEW Parchment Cooking Bags

The traditional French cooking method *en papillote* uses parchment paper as a packet in which to bake—and serve—fish, chicken, meat, or vegetables. The enclosed cooking environment helps concentrate flavors while keeping delicate foods like fish moist and intact. In the past, we've found making packets from parchment paper cumbersome and substituted aluminum foil. A new product, PaperChef Culinary Parchment Cooking Bags ($3.79 for 10 bags), promises to eliminate the fuss: Simply slide food into these parchment bags and then fold the open end to seal. Chicken, fish, and vegetables cooked similarly in each wrapper, but the PaperChef bags were much more convenient and sped up preparation, taking 1½ minutes to fill and fold (compared with 2½ minutes for folding foil and 5½ minutes for crimping parchment). At 38 cents per bag, they are not as cheap as parchment sheets (19 cents) or foil (10 cents), but they do eliminate the need for scissors and a ruler and taming unruly sheets of curling parchment.

IT'S IN THE BAG
PaperChef Culinary Parchment Cooking Bags make a traditional French cooking method easy enough for a weeknight dinner.

Stovetop Smokers

Stovetop smokers, which smoke meat and other foods indoors, are metal vessels fitted with a wire rack set over a drip tray and covered with a lid. To see how they compare with outdoor smokers, we cooked salmon fillets and whole chickens on four models (priced from $40 to $100) and had varying success. Smoke flavor and cook times were more or less equal across the board; the difference mainly boiled down to ease of use. On the plus side, indoor smokers use special fine wood chips (sold separately) that don't require soaking. Size, though a manageable obstacle, is where they came up short. All four smokers fit just four fish fillets, and only those with domed (versus flat) lids could house a whole bird. For the others, we crimped aluminum foil over the chickens per the manufacturers' instructions, which worked fine. Ultimately, we preferred smokers with flat lids, such as the Camerons Stovetop Smoker ($54.95), whose promise of clean smoke flavor, moist meat, and easy storage made it our winner.

YES, SMOKING INDOORS
The Camerons smoker delivers results just as flavorful and moist as an outdoor model does, and it stores easily.

NEW Ultimate Turkey Rack

For perfectly roasted turkey, slower-cooking dark meat needs a head start, which is why we call for roasting poultry breast side down and flipping midway through. But flipping is a pain. The Ultimate Turkey Rack ($29.95), a metal stand that holds a handled spit, presents a viable alternative: Just slip the bird onto the spit, roast, and turn—no heavy lifting necessary. Its manufacturer claims it can handle any size bird, from 3-pound chickens to 30-pound turkeys. We used it to roast a 3½-pound chicken plus 14- and 24-pound turkeys. All of the birds fit and were easy to flip. However, once the turkeys were breast side up and ready to go back in the oven, we hit a snag: In this orientation, the birds protruded higher above the roasting pan and no longer fit in our smaller ovens. Luckily, we had larger ovens so the turkeys could finish roasting. In sum: The rack made flipping a snap. But before you buy, measure your oven: You need at least 15 inches between the ceiling (or top heating element) and the rack when set in the lowest position (where the roasting pan will sit).

SPITTING DISTANCE
The Ultimate Turkey Rack makes flipping roasted poultry easy. But measure your oven before buying it.

Boilover Devices

Leave a pan of milk or cream on the stove long enough, and it's sure to foam up and boil over. A lid won't stop overflows, but boilover devices purportedly prevent messes in a few different ways. Large silicone lids physically stop or slow boiling milk from escaping the pot. Small disks made of glass, ceramic, or stainless steel placed in the pot change the heat distribution of the contents or simply rattle to alert the cook. The disks were ineffective; glass and ceramic disks did audibly clatter as the milk began to boil, while a stainless steel disk barely made a sound, but none prevented a boilover. The only tool that prevented the milk from escaping the pot was the Kuhn Rikon Spill Stopper ($24.95). This bowl-shaped silicone lid (which doubles as a microwave splatter guard) has six central flaps that open just enough to let milk foam flow over its surface, where *it is contained by curved edges*. The tool

NO-MESS SUCCESS
The Kuhn Rikon Spill Stopper prevents overflows—but so does simply using a very large pot.

works, but unless you also need a splatter guard, we recommend using our equally effective method: Simply heat the milk in a pot much larger than necessary.

NEW Whiskey Stones

Although many experts claim that whiskey must be slightly diluted to be fully appreciated, whiskey stones offer an alternative for those who prefer to sip it neat—but not warm. Simply chill these rocks in the freezer and then plop them in a drink to maintain the optimal temperature (between 57 and 61 degrees, according to the connoisseurs we consulted). We tested three sets of stones in different materials, from granite to soapstone to glass, priced from $12 to $34, tracking the temperature of the whiskey in which they sat for 2 hours and comparing them with whiskey poured into a tumbler that had been chilled in the freezer. None successfully maintained our drink's temperature for a significant amount of time, but the American Château Art Glass Ice Cubes ($11.99) landed a stone's throw ahead of the rest, keeping our whiskey below 63 degrees for 30 minutes. We'd rather just prechill our glasses, which works just as well, if not better.

THE STONE COLD TRUTH
Whiskey stones may be fashionable, but they're not terribly functional.

For complete testing results for each item, go to CooksIllustrated.com/dec12.

Sources

Prices were current at press time and do not include shipping. Contact companies to confirm information or visit CooksIllustrated.com for updates.

PAGE 7: CARVING FORK
- Mercer Cutlery Genesis 6-Inch High-Carbon Carving Fork: $22.20, item #MER-M20806, InstaWares (877-514-6183, **instawares.com**).

PAGE 11: POTATO RICER
- RSVP International Potato Ricer: $13.95, item #127125, Cooking.com (800-663-8810, **cooking.com**).

PAGE 27: PEPPER MILL
- Cole & Mason Derwent Gourmet Precision Pepper Mill: $40, item #695221, Sur La Table (800-243-0852, **surlatable.com**).

PAGE 32: PARCHMENT COOKING BAGS
- PaperChef Culinary Parchment Cooking Bags: $3.79, Paper Chef (877-962-5423, **paperchef.com**).

PAGE 32: STOVETOP SMOKER
- Camerons Stovetop Smoker: $54.95, item #SMKW, Camerons (888-563-0227, **cameronsproducts.com**).

PAGE 32: TURKEY RACK
- Ultimate Turkey Rack: $29.95, *Ultimate Turkey Rack* (**ultimateturkeyrack.com**).

PAGE 32: BOILOVER DEVICE
- Kuhn Rikon Spill Stopper: $24.95, item #860007, Sur La Table.